The Bl

Albania

Austria Austria
Vienna

Belgium and Luxembourg
Bulgaria
China
Cyprus
Czech and Slovak
   Republics
Denmark
Egypt

France France
Paris and Versailles
Burgundy
Loire Valley
Midi-Pyrénées
Normandy
South West France
Corsica

Germany Berlin and eastern
   Germany

Greece Greece
Athens and environs
Crete
Rhodes and the
   Dodecanese

Hungary Hungary
Budapest

Southern India
Ireland

Italy Northern Italy
Southern Italy
Florence
Rome
Venice
Tuscany
Umbria
Sicily

Mexico
Morocco

Netherlands Netherlands
Amsterdam

Poland
Portugal

Spain Spain
Barcelona
Madrid

Sweden
Switzerland
Thailand
Tunisia

Turkey Turkey
Istanbul

UK England
Scotland
Wales
Channel Islands
London
Oxford and Cambridge
Country Houses of
   England

USA New York
Museums and Galleries of
   New York
Boston and Cambridge

Malaysia &
Singapore

Sean Sheehan & Patricia Levy

A&C Black • London
WW Norton • New York

BLUE GUIDE

First edition 1998

Published by A & C Black (Publishers) Limited
35 Bedford Row, London WC1R 4JH

A CIP catalogue record of this book is available from the British Library.

ISBN 0–7136–4157–6

Published in the United States of America by
WW Norton and Company, Inc
500 Fifth Avenue, New York, NY 10110

Published simultaneously in Canada by
Penguin Books Canada Limited
10 Alcorn Avenue, Toronto
Ontario M4V 3B2

ISBN 0–393–31641–6   USA

The author and the publishers have done their best to ensure the accuracy of all the information in Blue Guide in Malaysia and Singapore; however, they can accept no responsibility for any loss, injury or inconvenience sustained by any traveller as a result of information or advice contained in the guide.

Sean Sheehan and Patricia Levy lived in Singapore for six years and countless trips to Malaysia during that time helped prepare them for the writing of this guide. Their time is now divided between London and West Cork in Ireland.

Cover picture: detail of a monument in Penang, by Dave G. Houser/Corbis UK Ltd.
Title page illustration: Ubadiah Mosque, Kuala Kangsar.

Printed in Great Britain by Butler & Tanner Ltd, Frome and London.

Contents

How to use this Guide 8
Introduction 9

Practical Information
Planning your trip 11
Climate 13
Passports and formalities 14
Tour operators 16
Disabled travellers 17
Getting to Malaysia and
  Singapore 17
Currency regulations and
  money 18
Arriving in Malaysia and
  Singapore 19
Accommodation 19
Restaurants 20
Food and drink 21
Travelling around Malaysia 26
Women travellers 30
Travelling with children 31

Customs and manners 31
What to take 32
Health 32
Personal security and
  emergencies 33
Drugs 33
Opening hours 34
Tipping 34
Laundry 34
Time differences 34
Weights and measures 34
Telephone and postal services 34
Newspapers 35
Public toilets 35
Public holidays 35
National symbols 36
Festivals 36

Background Information
History 37
Geography 48
People 49
Religion 50
Architecture 52

Flora and Fauna 53
Language and Literature 55
Music and Dance 56
Further Reading 57
Glossary 61

The Guide
1 · **Kuala Lumpur** 63
Practical Information 66; Colonial Era Walk 79; Chinatown Walk 82;
Parliament Area Walk 83; Excursions from Kuala Lumpur 86

2 · **West coast: Kuala Lumpur to Perlis** 94
Fraser's Hill 94; Cameron Highlands 97
Perak 101 ~ Ipoh 103; Kuala Kangsar 109; Taiping 111;
    Bukit Larut (Maxwell Hill) 114; Teluk Intan 115; Pulau Pangkor 115
    Upper Perak 119
Penang 120 ~ Georgetown 125; Excursions from Georgetown 136;
    Batu Ferringhi 139
Kedah and Perlis 141 ~ Lembah Bujang 142; Gunung Jerai 143;
    Alor Setar 143; Langkawi 144
Perlis 150

3 · **Melaka** 151
Practical Information 153; Museum Tour 157; Chinatown Walk 164; Other places to see 167; Excursions from Melaka 169

4 · **East Coast: Kota Bharu to Johor Bahru** 171
Kelantan 171 ~ Kota Bharu 174
Terrengganu 183 ~ Kuala Besut 183; Pulau Perhentian 184; Merang 186; Pulau Redang 186; Kuala Terengganu 187; Marang 193; Pulau Kapas 194; Pulau Gemia 194; Rantau Abang 195; Dungan to Cherating 197
Pahang 199 ~ Kuantan 200; Teluk Chempedak 201;
Kuantan to Mersing 205; Pekan 205; Endau Rompin National Park 206
Johor 207 ~ Mersing 208; Pulau Tioman 209; Johor Bahru 215

5 · **Into the Interior** 223
Taman Negara National Park 223
From Kuala Lumpur to the northeast 233; Kuala Lipis 233
Kenong Rimba Park 234

6 · **Sabah** 236
Kotah Kinabalu 240; Practical Information 241; Excursions from Kota Kinabalu 251; Kinabalu Park 251
Sandakan 256; Excursions from Sandakan 260
Danum Valley Conservation Area 264
Semporna and Pulau Sipadan 265
Tawau 265

7 · **Sarawak** 266
Kuching 273; Practical Information 273; Excursions from Kuching 282
Bako National Park 282
Sri Aman 286
Sibu 287
Kapit 290
Belaga and Bintulu 293
Niah National Park 294
Miri 297
Gunung Mulu National Park 300
Kelabit Highlands 305

8 · **Singapore** 309
Practical Information 317; Orchard Road area 328; Colonial Walk 333; Little India Walk 340; Chinatown Walk 345; Singapore West 351; Singapore North 355; Singapore East 360; Excursions from Singapore 362

Index 365

Maps and plans

Country map   *inside front and back covers*

Regional maps
East Coast 173
Interior 225
Sabah 239
Sarawak 271
West Coast 95 .

Town plans
Georgetown 129
Ipoh 107
Johor Bahru 219
Khota Bharu 177
Kota Kinabalu 242–3
Kuala Lumpur 76–7
Kuala Lumpur STAR-LRT 68
Kuala Lumpur environs 87
Kuala Terengganu 190
Kuching 277
Melaka 158–9
Miri 299
Sandakan 258–9

Singapore
    Island map 310–1
    City map 330–1
    MRT network 319
    Chinatown Walk 347
    Colonial Walk 333
    Little India Walk 341
    Orchard Road 328–9

Parks
Bako National Park 283
Cameron Highlands 99
Gulung Mulu National Park 303
Mount Kinabalu 253
Taman Negara 229

Islands
Penang 124
Pulau Langkawi 147
Pulau Pangkor 119
Pulau Tioman 210

How to use this guide

The first section of this guidebook deals with the practicalities of visiting Malaysia and Singapore; then follows a brief history and background information on the land, people, religions, language, flora and fauna of both countries. Malaysia itself is divided into different regions, some of which are single destinations in themselves while others cover an area large enough to allow for a tour approach using different forms of transport.

We start in Kuala Lumpur, the capital city of Malaysia, then travel north up to Penang. After a look at Melaka, we journey down the east coast from Kota Bharu to Johor Bahru, followed by a visit to the interior of peninsular Malaysia. We then cross the South China Sea to Sarawak and Sabah, finally returning to the mainland to visit the island of Singapore.

Each chapter includes details on how to get around using the relevant forms of transport. Some regions, the east coast of peninsular Malaysia in particular, lend themselves to a tour by car or public buses; in other regions, like the states of Sabah and Sarawak in east Malaysia, private transport is neither necessary nor even useful.

Acknowledgements

Many thanks to all the people who helped with the research and writing of this book. We would like to thank the Singapore Tourist Board, the Malaysia Tourist Board, and Mohd Nasir Mohd Tahir of Pelangi Air. Thanks also to the countless people who patiently and kindly dealt with enquiries at tourist offices, bus and railway stations and assorted palces around the country. A special thanks to the editor, Gemma Davies, at A&C Black in London.

Our grateful thanks are also due to the following:
Christine Ong, Jo Lee, Paul Wong, Gary Tan and Lim Swee Yin in Penang.
Razali Ahmad in Pangkor.
Richard Hii in Miri.
Rosmala Mohd. Din in Sandakan.
Johari Hashim in Kuching.
Sherry Yau and Mohd Odzman b. Abd in Ipoh.
Chryss Chung and John Ting in Johor Bahru.
Poziah Abdul Kadir and Michelle Yeoh in Kota Kinabalu.
Billy Tang, John Brennan, Roger Jeganthan, and Elizabeth Soo in Kuala Lumpur.
Kuek Mei Ling, Christine Quek and Benny Ching in Singapore.
Mr Amran Abd Rahman, Deputy Director, Tourism Malaysia, London.
Sabah Tourism Promotion Corporation
Malaysia Tourism Promotion Board, Northern Region
Malaysia Tourism Promotion Board, Kuala Lumpur
Kable Public Relations

Introduction

Carried in the mental luggage of most travellers to Malaysia and Singapore are images of the countries they are visiting. It is not always possible to abandon those semi-historical evocations of a colonial frontier peopled by men in white pith helmets and languorous ladies buttering toast in the jungle, or fading literary images of lands of oriental mystery and exotic charm. Both Malaysia and Singapore have of course long-discarded their colonial past; they are self-confident states, assertively proud of their independence and modernity.

There are sound reasons for putting Malaysia and Singapore together in a guidebook; there are equally good arguments for keeping them apart. In terms of climate, ethnicity, history, culture, cuisine and politics, there are important similarities. Geographically, they are also very close—separated by a causeway that takes only ten minutes to walk across—but other geographical features point to some essential differences. Singapore is a tiny island city-state, 'invented one morning early in the 19th century by a man looking at map', as the novelist J.G. Farrell succinctly put it. The man was Stamford Raffles and an insignificant island, a mere 618 square kilometres in size, strategically placed between India and China was just the site that he was looking for for a new trading post. By comparison, peninsular Malaysia alone occupies an area of 329,749 square kilometres, the size of Florida or England. This does not include the eastern states of Sarawak and Sabah, part of the island of Borneo but also part of Malaysia and separated by 800km of water.

The differences in geography partly explain why visitors are attracted to the two countries for very different reasons. Singapore is conveniently compact—most places of interest can be reached on foot, bus or taxi from any of the hotels—and the island's appeal is suited to its small size. People come to Singapore to shop and shop, and then shop again. The country's phenomenal economic success (in Southeast Asia only Japan has a higher standard of living) is an essential part of its appeal. There are no great cathedrals but what seems to be their late twentieth century equivalent—magnificent hotels and visually stunning shopping plazas—are to be seen everywhere. While the cultural appeal of Singapore is not to be found in its indigenous art forms or its museums and galleries—the political regime has effectively marginalised art—there are undeniable attractions. The incredible variety of ethnic restaurants, for instance, does not merely serve consumer needs; it also allows for a fascinating and pleasurable introduction to Asian culture. Important colonial buildings have been carefully preserved, primarily for tourist dollars, but preserved nevertheless.

The small and manageable size of Singapore has also helped its authoritarian government to maintain power. The government of Malaysia, while essentially no different in its intentions or methods, has had to cope with a more volatile mix of races and cultures. This makes for a far more interesting country. Singapore is predominantly Chinese, and the minority Malays and Indians are kept strictly in their multi-cultural place (as indeed is everyone) but Malaysia is a fascinating mix of races and cultures that enthrals visitors. The east coast of peninsular Malaysia is Malay and Islamic; a west coast location like Penang is more Chinese than Singapore; Kuala Lumpur is a dynamic mix of Malay, Indian and Chinese; in Sarawak and Sabah the situation is very different: Malays and Chinese are hardly seen outside the towns and a bewildering array of races and cultures take their place.

Multi-cultural communities are not unique to Malaysia, but here the different races and cultures co-exist in a remarkably peaceful and tolerant way. Without denying the inevitable tensions that do exist, it remains a simple fact that there are no no-go areas in Malaysia, either for visitors or for Malaysian citizens.

Cultural diversity is only one of the many reasons why a visit to Malaysia is such a rewarding experience. The east coast of peninsular Malaysia, as well as being the heartland of Malay culture and its Islamic religion, has an unparalleled 400km of sandy beaches that are just waiting for the amateur snorkeller, swimmer, general water activist or beach layabout. There are 5-star resorts, putative eco-lodges, affordable hotels, budget chalets and wonderfully inexpensive Malay food that is far more satisfying than the run-of-the-mill European dishes served up for the sake of modernity. In towns like Kota Bharu there are opportunities to observe traditional arts and crafts like kite-making, silver and brass beating, dance and music.

There are notable places of historical interest in Malaysia and Singapore. While the town of Melaka (also spelt Malacca) is one of the few places with buildings that pre-date the colonisation of the peninsula by the British, evidence of the British imperial presence is scattered around in the most likely and unlikely places. In Kuala Kangsar, an obscure town in the state of Perak, it is still possible to see one of the original rubber trees that gave birth to an industry that kept the British in Malaya. More obvious reminders of the British Empire are to be found in Kuala Lumpur and Singapore, as well as a number of smaller towns, and colonial sightseeing is a part of the charm of both countries. Less charming are the reminders of the Second World War when Malaya, Singapore, Sarawak and what is now Sabah fell victim to a blistering Japanese invasion and occupation that lasted three years.

The ethnic mix and the cultural diversity, the beaches and water sports, the historical evocations of the past—never mind the increasingly more insistent reminders of the future (Kuala Lumpur currently has the tallest building on earth, and crass shopping malls are popping up everywhere in Malaysia, striving to emulate the rampant consumerism of Singapore)—are all runners-up for the visitor's attention compared to the possibilities that exist for appreciating wildlife and natural environments in Malaysia. Even in Singapore, where the ideology of capitalism is pursued with fervour, there is a precious pocket of rainforest at the Bukit Timah Nature Reserve which is best seen now before it is turned into a clinical theme park.

For tropical beauty, peninsular Malaysia's Taman Negara (National Park) is unsurpassed. It provides a unique opportunity to experience and explore primary, tropical rainforest uncompromised by a professionally managed tourist infrastructure.

If time is limited, a good case can be made for minimising one's time in Singapore and peninsular Malaysia and heading for Sarawak and Sabah. Despite the voracious chainsaw massacre of the rainforest that has taken place here, there are unparalleled possibilities for trekking in the jungle, river trips to observe proboscis monkeys, orang-utan rehabilitation centres, mountain climbing, pitcher plants and hornbills, and much more.

Practical Information

Planning your trip

Deciding where to go and what to see in Malaysia and Singapore is best under-taken in the context of your interests.

Wildlife and nature

Enthusiasts should head for **SABAH** where there are a number of prime attrac-tions. **Kinabalu National Park** has Southeast Asia's highest mountain which can be climbed in two days by anyone who is reasonably fit. There is also a **Rafflesia Forest Reserve** near the main town, Kota Kinabalu, where the world's largest flower may be seen. A short plane journey accesses the small town of Sandakan on the east coast of Borneo, an essential destination for anyone interested in wildlife. Offshore from Sandakan, the **Turtle Islands National Park** allows visitors to observe hawksbill turtles laying their eggs and a hatchery on the same island shows their eggs hatching and the baby turtles dashing for the sea. Also near Sandakan is a major **orang-utan rehabilitation centre** while a two-hour journey from the town brings you to the Kinabatangan river where the proboscis monkey, unique to Borneo, can be seen.

The neighbouring state of **SARAWAK** is also home to the proboscis monkey at the **Bako National Park**, which is also an excellent place to find pitcher plants. The **Semenggok Wildlife Rehabilitation Centre** also cares for orang-utans and like Bako can be reached from the small town of Kuching. Trekking in the jungle is possible as an independent activity, or through a number of tour agents in Miri and Kuching, and the **Bario Highlands** are particularly recom-mended because of their unusual location. The **Gunung Mulu National Park** is another worthwhile destination, boasting the largest limestone cave system in the world and a number of exhilarating treks and climbs. A minimum of one week would be needed to visit just some of Sabah and Sarawak's locations.

In **PENINSULAR MALAYSIA**, at least three days needs to be allowed for the major wildlife and nature attractions of **Taman Negara** (National Park). While in the capital, Kuala Lumpur, the **Selangor National Park** is well worth a day's excursion. The east coast has the appeal of turtle-watching at **Rantau Abang** in the state of Terengganu, while a number of small islands off the coast present superb opportunities for snorkelling and scuba diving.

SINGAPORE may seem to be all concrete and glass but the city has its own primary rainforest niche at Bukit Timah, highly recommended, and the offshore island of Pulau Ubin is surprisingly undeveloped.

History

The town of **Melaka**, on the west coast of peninsular **MALAYSIA**, is important to anyone interested in history. There are a number of buildings here that date back to the days of Portuguese and Dutch imperialism. Many of the places of historical interest in Malaysia are connected with British colonialism and **Kuala Lumpur** makes a convenient starting point. Apart from the historical architec-ture in the capital itself, the city provides easy road and rail access to the state of

Perak immediately to the north where the small towns of **Kuala Kangsar**, **Taiping** and **Ipoh** bear witness to the first arrival of the British in the early 19C.

The state of **Sarawak** bears the historical imprint of one unique family, the **Brookes**, who ruled the territory from the early 19C until the arrival of the Japanese in 1942. The town of **Kuching** was their capital and a couple of days could easily be spent there exploring the many reminders of the family's dynastic rule as the white raja.

SINGAPORE's colonial history has been well preserved and there are a number of important buildings and sites of interest. The Japanese invasion and occupation of Malaya and Singapore between 1942 and 1945 can be traced in a number of locations throughout Malaysia and Singapore.

Culture

The culture of **MALAYSIA** can be broadly divided into contemporary Malay, Chinese and Indian culture, and the indigenous, often endangered, cultures of Sarawak and Sabah. The east coast states of peninsular Malaysia, primarily **Terengganu** and **Kelantan**, are the bastions of traditional Malay culture and are worth visiting for this reason. **Penang**, on the other coast, has the liveliest and most vibrant Chinese culture to be found anywhere in this part of the world. Indian culture has small but fascinating pockets in the larger towns: **Kuala Lumpur**, **Penang**, and in **Singapore**.

A night or two spent in a longhouse is the best way to learn about and experience the cultures of the indigenous ethnic peoples of **Sarawak**. It is possible to do this independently but the better tour companies in Kuching and Miri have packages that include interpreters and offer a variety of destinations.

Visits to **Iban and Kelabit communities** are the most common but individual tours can be arranged to some of the smaller and more remote cultural groups. It is still possible to trek through the jungle looking for the few remaining forest-dwelling **Penans** that are on the brink of extinction due to the activities of the logging companies.

Sand and sun

These destinations are not the least among Malaysia's attractions. Almost the entire length of the east coast of the peninsula is one long beach strip and there is no shortage of resort-style accommodation centres to suit all budgets. The islands of Malaysia offer the most ideal beach locations where days can be spent indulging in water activities or just soaking up the guaranteed sunshine. The **Pherentian islands** off the coast of Terengganu are perhaps the least-known in this respect. Further south, the islands of **Tioman** and **Pangkor**, while more used to visitors, have not lost their attractions and it is still possible to find secluded spots away from the rest of the world.

Shopping

The ultimate destination for shoppers must be **SINGAPORE**. Here you will find a plethora of shopping plazas that sell just about every consumer item you can think of. 'Shop till you drop' is the unashamed slogan, but shop until your credit card starts ringing an alarm is probably more realistic. In the last few years, **Kuala Lumpur** in **MALAYSIA** has developed its own consumer paradise centred around a number of bustling shopping plazas in the heart of the capital.

The range of goods on sale cannot match Singapore but the prices are significantly lower.

Climate

The temperature in both Malaysia and Singapore is fairly constant all year at around 30°C and the humidity level is always very high. The temperature drops a little in highland areas, to about 22°C but humidity remains high. A significant factor that affects where and when to go to Malaysia is the monsoon season, sometimes just called the rainy season. During this period, between November and February, it is best to avoid the east coast of peninsular Malaysia and Taman Negara. Rainfall is heavy and frequent and it will not usually be

Average daily temperatures and monthly rainfall												
	Jan	Feb	Mar	April	May	June	July	Aug	Sept	Oct	Nov	Dec
Cameron Highlands												
max °C	21	22	23	23	23	23	22	22	22	22	22	21
min °C	14	14	14	15	15	15	14	15	15	15	15	15
rainfall mm	120	111	198	277	273	137	165	172	241	334	305	202
Kota Bharu												
max °C	29	30	31	32	33	32	32	32	32	31	29	29
min °C	22	23	23	24	24	24	23	23	23	23	23	23
rainfall mm	163	60	99	81	114	132	157	168	195	286	651	603
Kota Kinabalu												
max °C	30	30	31	32	32	31	31	31	31	31	31	31
min °C	23	23	23	24	24	24	24	24	23	23	23	23
rainfall mm	133	63	71	124	218	311	277	256	314	334	296	241
Kuala Lumpur												
max °C	32	33	33	33	33	32	32	32	32	32	31	31
min °C	22	22	23	23	23	23	23	23	23	23	23	23
rainfall mm	159	154	223	276	182	119	120	133	173	258	263	223
Kuching												
max °C	30	30	31	32	33	33	32	33	32	32	31	31
min °C	23	23	23	23	23	23	23	23	23	23	23	23
rainfall mm	683	522	339	286	253	199	199	211	271	326	343	465
Mersing												
max°C	28	29	30	31	32	31	31	31	31	31	29	28
min°C	23	23	23	23	23	23	22	22	22	23	23	23
rainfall	319	153	141	12	149	145	17	173	177	207	359	635
Penang												
max °C	32	32	32	32	31	31	31	31	31	31	31	31
min °C	23	23	24	24	24	24	23	23	23	23	23	23
rainfall mm	70	93	141	214	240	170	208	235	341	380	246	107
Tioman Island												
max °C	28	29	30	31	32	31	31	31	31	31	29	29
min °C	23	23	23	23	23	23	22	22	22	23	23	23
rainfall mm	319	153	141	12	149	145	17	173	177	207	359	635
Singapore												
max °C	31	32	32	32	32	32	31	31	31	31	31	30
min°C	21	22	23	23	23	23	22	22	22	22	22	22
rainfall mm	146	155	182	223	228	151	170	163	200	199	255	258

possible to visit the offshore islands. During these months there is also heavier rainfall along the west coast of peninsular Malaysia and Singapore, but it is rarely a problem and there is no reason not to travel to these areas during those months. In Singapore it is probably a little rainier than usual during the monsoon season but it has little effect on daily life. In both Malaysia and Singapore, even out of the rainy season, rain is frequent and by European standards quite violent, often occurring in the mid afternoon or very early morning and accompanied by great thunderclaps. These brief and noisy storms are known as 'Sumatras'. A folding umbrella is a vital piece of equipment and it is advisable to get out of the open and avoid trees during one of the frequent thunderstorms. Plastic macs are next to useless since they will generate more wetness from sweating than if you were exposed to the rain.

Acclimatising to the heat and humidity can be a problem especially for the frail or elderly. You will notice that local people instinctively seek out shade, airconditioning, and opportunities to take a break. Keeping up your fluid intake is very important so a bottle of water should always be carried. A first sign of dehydration is a headache and you should remember that far from relieving dehydration, alcohol makes it worse. It is a good idea to plan most of your activities for the early morning or evening when it is less hot and humid.

Towards the end of 1997, the burning of forests in Kalimantan (the part of the island of Borneo belonging to Indonesia) caused a health-threatening haze to spread across parts of Malaysia, and, to a lesser extent, Singapore. The fires, largely caused by oil-palm plantations seeking to clear forest areas, swept across hundreds of thousands of acres of land and the sun was obscured. The US-based air pollution index regards any reading above 500 to be significantly harmful, and in Kuching in Sarawak, where visibility was reduced to less than 100m, readings reached 650. In Kuala Lumpur, where air is trapped by a ring of hills, the problem was compounded by the growing problem of pollution caused by traffic, and asthmatics and the elderly were advised to stay indoors. Prime Minister Mahathir Mohamad donned a surgical mask and urged the public to follow his example. A state of emergency was declared in Sarawak in September and the airports were closed down.

Passports and Formalities

Malaysia. Citizens of the UK, the Republic of Ireland, Canada, Australia, New Zealand, Switzerland and the Netherlands do not require a visa to enter the country. Citizens of the United States and most other European countries do not require a visa for visits of less than three months. Nationals of other countries should contact their country's Malaysian embassy for details of visa applications. Your passport must be valid for three months after your date of arrival, six months in the case of Sarawak and Sabah.

On arrival in peninsular Malaysia your passport is normally stamped for one or two months and there should be no problem extending it for up to three months, sometimes longer. On arrival in Sarawak or Sabah your passport will be stamped again, usually for 30 days, regardless of whether or for how long you have been in the rest of Malaysia. It is difficult to obtain an extension for a longer stay in Sarawak. For visits to some parts of Sarawak and to all Malaysian National Parks it is necessary, in theory if not always in practice, to obtain a further special travel permit. Details are given in the text.

Malaysian Embassies abroad

Australia	7 Perth Avenue, Yarralumla, Canberra ACT 2600 (☎ 06-273 1543, fax 06-273 2496)
Canada	60 Boteler Street, Ottawa, Ontario KIN 8Y7 (☎ 613-241 5182, fax 613-241 5214)
Netherlands	Rustenburgweg 2, 2517 KE, The Hague (☎ 070-350 6506, fax 070-350 6536)
Singapore	301 Jervois Road, Singapore 1024 (☎ 02-235 0111, fax 65-7336135)
UK and Rep. of Ireland	45–46 Belgrave Square, London SW1X 8QT (☎ 0171-235 8033, fax 0171-235 5161)
United States	2401 Massachusetts Avenue NW, Washington DC 20008 (☎ 202-328 2700, fax 202-483 7661); 43rd Floor, Two Grand Central Tower, 140 East 45th Street, New York NY 10017 (☎ 212-490 2722, fax 212-490 8576); Suite 400, World Trade Center, 350 South Figueroa Street, Los Angeles, CA 90071 (☎ 213-621 2991, fax 213-671 1695)

Singapore. No visas are required by citizens of the UK, the Republic of Ireland, the United States, Canada, Australia or New Zealand. Most citizens of other European countries do not require a visa for stays of under three months. Passports of all visitors are normally stamped for 14 days and an extension for up to three months is normally available.

Singapore Embassies abroad

Australia	High Commission, 17, Forster Crescent, Yarralumla, ACT 2600, Canberra (☎ 6-273 3944; fax 6-273 3260)
Canada	Consulate. Suite 1305, 999 West Hastings Street, Vancouver, BC, V6C 2W2 (☎ 604-669 5115; fax 604-669 5153)
Malaysia	High Commission. 209 Jalan Tun Razak, Kuala Lumpur, 50400 (☎ 03-261 6277; fax 03-2616343)
UK and Republic of Ireland:	9 Wilton Crescent, London SW1X 8SA (☎ 0171-235 8315; fax 0171-235 4557)
United States	3501 International Place NW, Washington DC 20008 (☎ 202-537 3100; fax 202-537 0876); Consulate. 2424 SE Bristol, Suite 320, Newport Beach, CA 92660 (☎ 714-476 2330; 714-476 8301)

National Tourist Boards

Both countries have tourist boards in Britain and North America that can supply a good quantity of brochures, maps, lists of hotels, etc. Singapore is particularly well-organised in this respect and the *Singapore Official Guide*, updated monthly, is packed with useful information and maps. A useful web site for Sinagpore is: http://www.newasia/singapore.com. The Sabah Tourism Promotion Corporation has a web site at: http://www.jaring.my/sabah. The Sarawak web site is at: http://sarawak.gov.my/stb

Tourism Malaysia Offices abroad

Australia	65, York Street, Sydney, New South Wales, Australia 2000 (☎ 02-299 4441, fax 02-262 2026)

Canada   830 Burrard Street, Vancouver, Canada BC V6Z 2K4
                 (☎ 604-6898899, fax 604-6898804)
Singapore   10 Collyer Quay, #01-06 Ocean Building, Singapore 0104
                 (☎ 02-532 6321, fax 02-535 6650)
UK and Republic of Ireland 57 Trafalgar Square, London WC2N 5DU
                 (☎ 0171-930 7932, fax 0171-930 9015)
United States of America 595 Madison Avenue, Suite 1800, New York, NY
                 10022 (☎ 212-754 1113, fax 212-754 116)
                 Suite 804, 818 West 7th St, Los Angeles, CA 90017 (☎ 213-
                 689 9702, fax 213-689 1530)
Singapore Tourist Promotion Board (STPB) Offices abroad
Australia   Level 11, AWA Building, 47 York Street, Sydney NSW 2000
                 (☎ 02-9290 2888; fax 02-9290 2555
Canada   121 King Street West, Suite 1000, Toronto, Ontario, M5H 3T9
                 (☎ 416-363 8898; fax 416-363 5752)
UK   1st Floor, Carrington House, 126–130 Regent Street, London,
                 W1R 5FE (☎ 0171-437 0033; fax 0171-734 2191)
United States 12th Floor, 509 Fifth Avenue, New York, NY 10036
                 (☎ 212-3024861; fax 212-302 4801); 180N Stetson Ave,
                 Suite 1450 Chicago, IL 60601 (☎ 312-938 1888; fax 312-938
                 0086); 8484 Wilshire Boulevard, Suite 510, Beverly Hills, CA
                 90211 (☎ 213-8521901; fax 213-852 0129)

Tour operators

Details are given below of tour companies in the UK and the USA that offer pack-
aged holidays to Malaysia and/or Singapore. Pre-arranged holidays are well
worth considering because they can offer good combined flight and accommodation deals. A number of specialist nature and wildlife tours are available. They
tend to be fairly expensive and it is worth checking their prices with the local
tour operators mentioned in the text under Kuala Lumpur, Kuching and Miri.
Trips can be arranged in advance through these Malaysia-based companies;
some of the tour operators listed below also work with these agencies.

Tour operators in the UK
Abercrombie & Kent, Sloane Square House, Holbein Place, London SW1W
8NS (☎ 0171-730 9600).
British Airways Holidays, Pacific House, Hazelwick Avenue, Crawley, West
Sussex RH10 1NP (☎ 01293 723170).
Eastern & Oriental Express, Sea Containers House, 20 Upper Ground,
London SE1 9PF (☎ 0171-928 6000).
Magic of the Orient, 2 Kingsland Court, Three Bridges Road, Crawley, West
Sussex RH10 1HL (☎ 01293 537700). Adventure tours in Sarawak and Sabah.
Malaysia Experience, 42–44 Station Road, North Harrow, Middlesex, HA2
7SE (☎ 0181-424 9548. Tailormade trips for all interests to peninsular
Malaysia, Sabah and Sarawak, islands.
MAS, 247–249 Cromwell Road, London SW5 9GA (☎ 0171-341 2000). The
Malaysian national airline has a number of fly-drive and trekking packages.

Tour operators in the United States
Abercrombie & Kent, 1520 Kensington Road, Oak Brook, IL 60521
(☎ 1-800-3237308).
Cox & Kings, 511 Lexington Avenue, Suite 355, New York, NY 10017
(☎ 1-800-9991758).
Nature Expeditions International, 474 Wilamette Street, Eugene, OR97440
(☎ 503-4846529).
Vacationland, 150 Post Street, Suite 680, San Francisco, CA 94108
(☎ 1-800-2450050).

Disabled travellers

Neither country is particularly accessible for disabled travellers although
Singapore, being compact and modern, is better in this respect than Malaysia.
The **Singapore Council of Social Services**, 11 Penang Lane, Singapore,
issues a helpful booklet detailing the help available in shopping centres, banks
and hotels. In the UK, help and information is available from **RADAR**, 25
Mortimer Street, London W1N 8AB (☎ 0171-250 3222). In North America,
contact the **Society for the Advancement of Travel for the Handicapped**,
347 Fifth Avenue, New York, NY 10016 (☎ 212-4477284) or Keroul, 4545
Avenue, Pierre de Coubertin, CP 1000, Station M., Montreal, Quebec HIV 3R2
(☎ 512-2523104).

Getting to Malaysia and Singapore by air

From the UK

There are daily regular flights to Kuala Lumpur and Singapore, and from Kuala
Lumpur connections can be made to every other corner of the country,
including Sarawak and Sabah. Non-stop flights to both Kuala Lumpur and
Singapore are available through the national airlines—Malaysia Airlines (MAS)
and Singapore Airlines (SIA)—as well as British Airways and Qantas. The
journey takes about 13 hours. Less expensive flights involve one, two or three
stops along the way and are available with a number of airlines. According to
the number of stopovers, this journey could take as long as 22 hours.

For current prices check the advertisements in the Sunday newspapers, magazines such as *Time Out* in London, and discount agents such as Trailfinders at
42–48 Earls Court Rd, London W8 6FT (☎ 0171-938 3366), Travel Bug at 597
Cheetham Hill Road, Manchester M8 5EJ (☎ 0161-721 4000). Students and
young people should contact STA Travel at 86 Old Brompton Road, London SW7
3LQ (☎ 0171-361 6262) or in Bristol at 25 Queens Road BS8 1QE (☎ 0117-
929 4399), Manchester 75 Deansgate M3 2BW(☎ 0161-834 0668).

The airlines below all have direct or indirect flights to Kuala Lumpur and/or
Singapore. See also the information on tour companies above.

Airlines in the UK
Air India, 17 New Bond Street, London W1 (☎ reservations: 01753 684828)
British Airways, 156 Regent Street, London W1 (☎ 0171-434 4700)
Finnair, 14 Clifford Street, London W1X 1RD (☎ 0171-408 1222)
KLM, 8 Hanover Street, London W1 (☎ 0181-750 9200)
Malaysian Airlines, 247–249 Cromwell Road SW5 9GA (☎ 0171-341 2000)

Pakistan International Airlines, 45–46 Piccadilly, London W1 (☎ 0171-287 2585)
Qantas, 182 Strand, London W1 (☎ 0345 747767)
Singapore Airlines, 143–147 Regent Street, London W1 (☎ 0181-747 0007)

From the USA
The most direct route is from the west coast of the United States, taking about 19–21 hours. Flights from the east coast will involve at least one stopover to Kuala Lumpur, or direct to Singapore. Check for current prices in newspapers such as the *LA Times, San Francisco Examiner, New York Times* and *Chicago Tribune*.

The airlines below all have direct or indirect flights to Kuala Lumpur and/or Singapore. See also the information on tour companies above.

Airlines in the USA
Air Canada ☎ 1-800-555 1212
Air India ☎ 1-800-223 7776
British Airways ☎ 1-800-247297
Canadian Airlines ☎ 1-800-5551212
Cathay Pacific ☎ 1-800-233 2742
Finnair ☎ 1-800-950 5000
KLM ☎ 1-800-374 7747. In Canada 1-800-361 5073

Lufthansa ☎ 1-800-645 3880
Malaysia Airlines ☎ 1-800-421 8641
Northwest Airlines ☎ 1-800-225 2525
Pakistan International Airlines (PIA) ☎ 1-800-221 2552
Singapore Airlines ☎ 1-800-742 3333
United Airlines ☎ 1-800-538 2929

Getting to Malaysia and Singapore by train
There is a train route from Bangkok to Kuala Lumpur (24 hours, US$85) and Singapore (28 hours, US$100), via Hat Yai in southern Thailand, crossing the border at the Malaysian town of Padang Besar before going on to Butterworth. From Yat Hai, it is also possible to take a different train to the Thai border town of Sungai Golok from where it is a short walk across the border to Rantau Panjang in Malaysia. Buses travel from here to Kota Bharu just 30km away. The whole journey, including the bus, takes at least 20 hours and will cost about US$80. Tickets for either rail routes from Thailand can be purchased from travel agents in Bangkok.

In Malaysia, tickets are purchased through KTM (see Kuala Lumpur), the Malaysian rail system. In Singapore, tickets are purchased at the railway station.

The upmarket version of the rail route between Bangkok, Singapore and Kuala Lumpur is the luxurious **Orient Express**. Further information is available from Orient Express Ltd, Sea Containers House, 20 Upper Ground, London SE1 9PF (☎ 0171-928 6000; fax 0171-620 1210).

Currency regulations and money
There are no current restrictions on the amount of currency you can take in or out of both Malaysia and Singapore.

Travellers' cheques are recommended for safety and convenience. They can be cashed at banks, most moneychangers and hotels, as well as some shops geared to the tourist trade. **Credit cards** are widely accepted in both countries but sometimes it is necessary to check that no illegal surcharge is being made. If you have a personal identification number (PIN) for your American Express, Mastercard or Visa card it is possible to withdraw cash from automatic teller machines (ATMs); these are everywhere in Singapore and in some of the larger towns in Malaysia. However, when bargaining for the price of something, it is usually assumed that cash is being used and not a credit card.

When travelling in Sabah and Sarawak, it is advisable to carry sufficient *ringgit* in cash. There are no banks or ATMs in the jungle.

When first arriving in Kuala Lumpur or Singapore, you will require a small amount of local currency for the taxi into town. Airports will have an exchange office open but it is a good idea to arrive with about M$100 or S$100 in cash.

Malaysia. The unit of currency is the **ringgit** (**RM**), divided into 100 **sen**. Notes come in M$1, M$5, M$10, M$20, M$50, M$100, M$500 and M$1000 denominations. 1 sen, 5 sen, 10 sen, 20 sen and 50 sen coins are used.

The major **banks** in Malaysia will usually have an exchange facility: the United Malayan Banking Corporation (UMBC), Maybank, Bank Bumiputra and the Hong Kong and Shanghai Bank. Moneychangers stay open later, until around 20.00, and the rates are usually very similar.

Singapore. The unit of currency is the **Singapore dollar**, divided into 100 **cents**, written in this book as S$. Notes come in S$1, S$2, S$5, S$10, S$20, S$50, S$100, S$500, S$1000 and S$10,000 denominations. 1 cent, 5 cent, 10 cent, 20 cent, 50 cent and S$1 coins are used.

The major **banks** in Singapore will usually have an exchange facility: the Development Bank of Singapore (DBS), Hong Kong and Shanghai Bank, Standard Chartered and Overseas Union Bank. Moneychangers stay open later, until around 20.00, and the rates are usually very similar.

Arriving in Malaysia and Singapore

Malaysia's tourist information organisation is the **Malaysian Tourist Promotion Board** (MTPB) which also calls itself simply **Tourism Malaysia**. It has offices at the larger airports and in all the main towns, and details are given in the text. There will always be someone who speaks English. As well as general brochures on the state's places of interest, there will sometimes be accommodation lists available. The level of knowledge and the amount of help that will be given tends to vary according to the personnel but usually there is a friendly willingness to assist visitors.

Singapore's tourist information organisation is the **Singapore Tourist Promotion Board** (STPB) and details of its offices are given in the text. It has a huge range of information on virtually every aspect of Singapore that might be of interest to visitors. Good maps covering the transport system are also available.

Accommodation

In both Malaysia and Singapore **hotel** rooms can be reserved on the phone, or by fax from overseas. Many of the major international hotel chains, or their agencies, have their own internet pages which provide information (including e-mail addresses) on individual hotels in both Malaysia and Singapore. At particularly busy times, especially the Chinese New Year period, which is usually around late January/early February, there might be difficulty securing a room so booking ahead is advisable. When first arriving in either Kuala Lumpur or

Singapore, it is advisable to have your first few nights' accommodation booked in advance.

Most hotels will have a range of rooms to suit different budgets and usually the quoted rate is for the room: a single person or a family with two young children pay the same. The prices quoted in this book apply to a standard double with its own bathroom and air conditioning (unless stated otherwise). As many hotels will have a range of rooms, it is often a good idea to ask to see some of the different rooms. Sometimes it is possible to negotiate the rate, especially if staying two or more nights. It is not necessary to leave your passport with reception and you should not be asked to do so. Cheaper hotels will ask for payment when you book in, though the more usual practice is to settle the bill when booking out.

In Malaysia there is a 5 per cent government tax that applies to all hotel rooms. Less expensive hotels will include this in their quoted rates, but if not the quoted room rate will often appear as, e.g. M$100+ (meaning plus 5 per cent) or M$100++ (meaning plus 5 per cent and plus 10 per cent service charge).

Another, cheaper option in Malaysia is a **guest house** (*rumah tumpangan*) which will offer very basic facilities and may be slightly sleazy. The better ones are often full, so you could try phoning in advance. The **Government Rest Houses** offer excellent value for money and are often in old colonial buildings with huge rooms and a very laid-back atmosphere. They, too, are very much in demand and booking ahead is recommended. **Hostels** usually offer dormitory accommodation and can be noisy, with flimsy walls and little privacy. But they are great places for networking and finding out about other people's travel experiences. They usually have noticeboards where useful up-to-the-minute information can be found as well as notebooks for visitors to record details of their travels. In Malaysia it may be possible to stay in a **longhouse**. Many now have arrangements with tour companies and have become a bit commercialised, but in a genuine one, where you will have to negotiate your own price, you will probably find very primitive plumbing. Although you may be given a room of your own, if the family give theirs up for you, it is more likely that you will be offered a mat on the floor with everyone else so that you can watch the inhabitants going about their daily business.

Restaurants

One of the great pleasures in visiting Singapore and Malaysia is trying out the infinite variety of tastes and textures in the thousands of eating places you will encounter there. Restaurants range from the highly elaborate and formal (and only relatively expensive) to a stall at the kerbside, with the vast majority being small, pleasantly furnished places serving inexpensive and very tasty food. In Singapore you can sample cuisines from virtually all over the world, given that added pep of a dash or so of chilli, necessary to please the Singaporean palate. In Malaysia the predominant cuisine is Malay with Western fast food adapted to Muslim values, although in the bigger cities 'Western' restaurants range from bland steak-and-chip joints to those specialising in French provincial or Italian food. Indian food is well represented in Malaysia as well and there are many Chinese cuisines, especially Cantonese.

For the most part in **Malaysia** it is more fun—and much cheaper—to eat in local food places than in hotel restaurants which cater to foreigners with watered-down versions of local specialities or with a mixture of continental dishes on offer. If you want to eat Malay food, it is quite difficult to find a high-class Malay restaurant since Malay cooking is traditionally home cooking and entertaining is done at home. Look for **night markets**, especially during Ramadan, when local specialities are prepared for those breaking the day's fast. Chinese restaurants are easier to find than Malay ones and can get exorbitantly expensive if you go for seafood or shark's fin. On some menus the prices are not marked because the rate for certain food items changes daily. Make sure you ask before ordering.

Occurring at the rate of about five per street all over Malaysia are **kedai kopi**, or **coffee shops**, which serve snacks and a deliciously thick coffee made with condensed milk and sugar, about two thousand calories per sip.

In **Singapore** the food situation becomes even more Bacchanalian. Singaporeans dedicate much of their leisure time to food and have long conversations about the best place to eat chicken rice or chilli crab. When a restaurant comes into vogue, there are queues down the street to get in. Its kudos lasts only until the next place gets a good write-up in the *Straits Times* or another good place opens up. The same goes for areas of restaurants. A few years ago, Gluttons Corner was the place to go, followed by Newton Circus. More recently the reconstituted Bugis Street had a brief moment of fame followed by the renovated Lau Pa Sat and then Boat Quay and Collier Quay which are still probably the trendiest places, for a while at least. Holland Village has a certain permanent status, especially with local expatriates, while every **hawker centre** bursts at the seams day and night. Hawker centres are well worth a try.

The tables are common to all stalls and you can order dishes from as many different stalls as you like. A good hawker centre will have five or six Chinese stalls selling different specialities, one or two Malay food stalls, an Indian place and some interesting hybrids, as well as a Singaporean version of Western café type food, dessert stalls, beer stalls, and, if you are lucky, a fresh fruit drink stall selling fresh coconut milk and sugar cane juice.

The classiest restaurants in Singapore are generally to be found in the many 5-star hotels where the quality of food, atmosphere and service is excellent, while being less expensive than their counterparts in Europe.

Food and drink

Chinese food in Singapore and to a lesser extent in Malaysia is infinite in its style of cooking, price range, ambience and location. The regions of China are well represented here, the most common type being Cantonese which originates from southeast China.

Cantonese

Cantonese cuisine—the Chinese food most familiar to Westerners—uses very fresh vegetables, fish and meat, which are stir-fried and often coated in one of many different varieties of piquant sauce. A Cantonese meal should ideally be eaten by at least ten people so that several dishes can be shared. The meal usually starts with some cold cuts: slices of barbecued pork or chicken perhaps served with jelly fish as a contrast. If it is to be an elaborate meal, soup might be the next dish; often it is shark's fin. A hot meat dish served with vegetables might then be followed by a fish dish.

Finally rice and/or noodles are served followed by a rather perfunctory sweet dish and slices of fresh fruit. Chinese tea is served throughout the meal. When the pot is empty, you should lift the lid and leave it perched on the side of the pot for the waitress to refill. A Cantonese meal lasts at least an hour and a half.

The squeamish should be prepared for a deep fried chicken head to be served with a chicken dish. Fish heads are also generally left in place. If you happen to be eating with fishermen, do not flip the fish over on its plate as they believe that this will cause their boat to sink the next time they go out.

An alternative for lunch is **dim sum** (sometimes called Dian Xing), which consists of lots of little steamed or deep-fried pastries which are served from trolleys—as the waitress passes, point to the dish you want and she will note it down on your bill. Some trolleys contain vats of boiling soup in which you can have cabbage and other greens cooked at your table. The pastries contain anything and everything and one interesting dish you might like to try is deep-fried chicken feet dipped in mustard! In smarter places all you get is a menu with some set meals, or you can order the *dim sum* à la carte.

Teochew (Chiu Chow)
Teochew food is having a renaissance in Singapore and is well worth sampling. Its origins are south Chinese from an area around Swatow. The food is typically steamed in its own juices and served plain without the spicy sauces of Cantonese cooking. As in all Chinese cuisines, seafood features largely on a Teochew menu.

Beijing
Beijing-style food is usually offered in most restaurants although there are few dedicated solely to this cuisine from the northwest of China. It is typically served with steamed buns or noodles rather than rice. The signature dish of this region is of course **Peking Duck**, which usually has to be ordered in advance. The dish consists of the duck skin only, roasted on a spit and coated in a sweet sauce and then rolled up in a crêpe and served with plum sauce. You can have the duck meat later in another dish if you choose. An entire Beijing meal would probably work out more expensive than a Cantonese one, because more expensive ingredients are used and because the Beijing restaurants are generally located in the big hotels where the prices are higher.

Sezuan
Many visitors' favourite is Sezuan food, which is dominated by quick stir-fried dishes which are characteristically dry and strongly flavoured with chilli and garlic. Historically, this intense flavouring is accounted for by the region's distance from the sea. Chilli, garlic and other preservatives were used to keep the food fresh and to pep up the taste of the many dried items going into the food. Sesame oil and paste are used liberally and tastes and textures are contrasted so that a dish may, for example, combine soft meat with crunchy toasted nuts.

Vegetarian
China also has a long tradition of vegetarianism. Many Chinese still practise Buddhism and so spend part of their life on a vegetarian diet, usually on the first and fifteenth day of the lunar month. There are many restaurants, in Singapore especially, which serve only vegetarian food. For non-vegetarians, the wonderful

thing about it is that you would never know that you are not eating meat. Gluten and tofu are manipulated into the shape and taste of meat and the dishes are called after the meat-filled originals; sweet and sour pork is actually fried gluten balls in sweet and sour sauce, while paper chicken looks and tastes exactly like its animal counterpart. In addition there are many hawker stalls and restaurants serving a variety of dishes called yong tau fu, which is a little like steamboat (see below) except that you choose your items and they are cooked for you at the stall. The dishes can either be served in a plain stock or in a tasty coconut and chilli sauce. The ingredients are usually vegetarian with a few vegetables stuffed with fish ball.

Singaporean-style

There are many other regional cuisines represented in Singapore which I am going to group together under the generic heading Singaporean-style food. These cuisines are typified by the little dishes of chilli paste and dried chillis which sit on every Singaporean restaurant table or are laid out along the counter at hawker stalls. **Steamboat** food, originally from Hainan, is enjoyable. Restaurants compete madly for the best value steamboat buffet. When you choose your restaurant (and open air is best) you pay first and are given an odd-shaped sauce boat with charcoal (or an electric plate) burning inside. The boat is filled with a thick or thin sauce, as you prefer, and then you go to the buffet table and load up with diced seafood, fish balls, strips of raw pork, beef and chicken and a startling array of vegetables, tofu and condiments. You then take it back to your table and dip it in the sauce until it is cooked.

Also worth trying are the **seafood restaurants** along the east coast where some peculiarly Singaporean dishes are available. Chilli or pepper crab are likely to be on offer—you choose your own live crab from a vat and receive it later served with a hammer and tongs. Seafood restaurants are the noisiest places I have ever been to and can be quite dangerous as pieces of crab shell fly about. Another favourite at these restaurants is **drunken prawns**, where the unfortunate crustaceans meet their doom by drowning in a glass of brandy. They are served to you whole and the delicacy is said to be the head which becomes full of brandy as the unfortunate creature drowns.

Hawker stalls

Hawker stalls serve a whole variety of quickly cooked and tasty dishes which cannot be bettered by an expensive restaurant. Many of them are based on mee—thick yellow egg noodles boiled and then fried with an amazing variety of additions. **Mee Rebus**, served in coconut sauce topped with egg, shrimp and vegetables, is particularly good. Its constituents vary according to region, becoming meatier in Malaysia. **Char Kway Teow** is another very popular dish, consisting of flat noodles served with clams and boiled egg and topped with chilli and black bean sauce. **Mee Goreng**, another standard lunch dish, is egg noodles fried in soy sauce with added bits and pieces of beef, pork and seafood. These are all very spicy but most Singaporeans add some extra chilli. No account of Singaporean food is complete without a description of chicken rice. It is served everywhere in both Malaysia and Singapore, and the value of one stall over another is in the quality of the thin watery soup poured over this dish of rice, cold sliced chicken and spring onions. The customer adds condiments to taste.

Malay

Malay food is not widely represented except in food centres. There are a few restaurants serving high Malay cuisine and these are well worth visiting if you are in Singapore or Kuala Lumpur or Johor Bahru. Usually their prices range around the middle to high bracket but they are often accompanied by cultural dances and really constitute an evening out. In the **hawker centres** Malay food is often a coconut-based curry of seafood, beef or chicken served with chilli-drenched vegetables such as bittergourd, or cooked cucumber which is cooling as well as spicy. Most dishes are served with a coconut and lemon grass sauce as well as **sambal** (a fiery paste made from dried chillis), **ikan bilis** (anchovy) and vinegar. Other specialities are **spicy fish baked in banana leaf**. Names are always in Malay but you can see the food laid out in front of you. Less fashionable nowadays are **Nasi Padang** restaurants where all the dishes are displayed in heated containers. The accompaniments to all of this are plain boiled rice, fried rice or *nasi lemak* (rice cooked in coconut sauce with sambal), peanuts and *ikan bilis*.

Roti jon (also spelt as roti John), which is French bread dipped in egg and chilli and ground beef and fried and served with cucumber and *sambal*, may be Malay in origin because it appears most frequently on Malay stalls. Also served on Malay food stalls is **tahu goreng**, deep-fried tofu cakes served with sweet peanut sauce, *sambal* and cucumber. Malay or Singaporean **satay** is wonderful and should be tasted at every opportunity. This dish consists of ground beef or chicken marinated in a sweet sauce, barbecued and served with peanut sauce.

It is important to note that Malay food is traditionally eaten with the right hand. You may seriously offend people if you use both hands (see Customs and manners, p 31). If you cannot manage one-handed, ask for cutlery.

Indian food

Indian food in Singapore and Malaysia is possibly better than in India. North and south Indian food are well represented here. North Indian food is drier, often using a '*tandoor*' or clay oven to cook the food. Sauces are thick and rich, nut-based or using cream or yoghurt. Meat, fish and vegetable dishes are served with *naan* (oven baked bread in various styles), yoghurt or *raita* (yoghurt mixed with chilli and raw vegetables), and *dahl* (a soup made from lentils). Desserts are milk-based, either vermicelli cooked in evaporated milk and highly flavoured with cardamom and other spices, or thick, fudge-like creations. South Indian cuisine favours vegetarian cooking but can include meat dishes as well. Worth sampling is a **thali**, which arrives on a steel plate or a banana leaf laid out with five or six curried dishes, rice and a piece of bread, either deep-fried (*poori* or *paratha*) or cooked on a griddle (*chapatti*). For breakfast, do not leave without trying **masala dosa**, a rice flour pancake filled with curried potato and served with coconut sauce.

There are also many **kedai kopi**, which are usually run by Muslim Indians and serve wonderful curries as well as **roti canai**, or **murtabak** (pancakes made with leavened dough, filled with lamb, beef, egg, chicken or vegetables, or a mixture of these), served with fiery curry sauce. Another classic dish is **chicken biryani**, which is served from a vast pot where layers of rice, dyed yellow with turmeric, are mixed with very tender chicken pieces and steamed for hours on end. This is often served with a thin watery lentil soup. Fresh lime juice is sometimes available and is a wonderful accompaniment to Indian food. Try to eat only with your right hand or ask for cutlery. Sinks are stationed around the restaurant and customers wash their hands before and after eating.

Fruit

Malaysia and Singapore provide an excellent opportunity to taste some of the strangest fruits in the world. They are cheap, abundant and safe to eat.

The **durian** looks like an armour-plated melon and smells like a gas leak. The flesh inside is the strangest mixture of sweet and sour you ever tasted—a cross between garlic and vanilla custard. Durians are available from July to August and from November to February. The Singaporeans love them but, because of their smell, you will see signs forbidding their presence in many places.

Another locally available fruit is the **rambutan**, a sort of large lychee encased in a red hairy skin. It is very sweet and juicy and has a stone inside. Rambutans are usually in season from May to September.

Mangosteens have a crusty-looking purple skin and contain two or three segments of fruit which taste like a cross between a strawberry and a grape. They are around from June to September.

Jackfruit is available all year round but is best bought in segments. It is a long, green, armoured-looking fruit tasting a little rubbery but sweet with a strong smell. The seeds can be eaten when cooked. This fruit grows easily in Singapore and can often be seen growing in people's gardens, wrapped up in paper bags to keep the birds away.

Custard apples are small green fruits whose thin skin easily splits away exposing soft white flesh. They are also known as 'soursops'. They taste something like a lemon. A soursop is ripe when it is beginning to blacken on the outside.

Persimmons are available in Singapore. They are like mangoes but slightly tarter and are best eaten when the fruit is quite hard.

Pomelos are like huge, sweet grapefruits and are usually opened for you by the seller with a machete. They are very thirst-quenching on a hot day but at least three people are needed to eat one.

You will recognise **starfruits** from their appearance, usually green or yellow and shaped like a five-pointed star. They make a refreshing juice drink, tasting something like fresh garden peas.

Also available are pineapples, bananas, oranges and apples, as well as coconuts, sea coconuts, guava, water apples, lychees, vast watermelons, imported rock melon, mangoes, limes and so on. You can buy them by the slice which is a fairly safe activity, in Singapore at least, or get them juiced into a refreshing inexpensive drink.

Drink

Drinking is a very important activity in Malaysia and Singapore with a vast array on offer. Water is safe to drink in Singapore and most big towns in Malaysia. In smaller places, hotels often provide boiled water as well as hot water and a variety of tea bags. Mineral water is readily available. All the canned drinks familiar in the West are readily available including flavoured mineral water, isotonic drinks, the big names and some local copies. Very sweet drinks tend to make you more thirsty though. There are also some interesting drinks in packets, such as chrysanthemum tea, which is nice but sweet. Lemon tea, soya milk and flavoured soya milk are also available in packets. Try soya milk with mango or rock melon.

Fruit is wonderfully cheap in Singapore and Malaysia and fresh juice stalls are everywhere. Sugar cane juice is refreshing but calorific, or try young coconut milk straight from the coconut, once it has been sliced open. Afterwards you can scoop out the flesh and eat it.

Hot drinks are quite interesting too. Milo and Horlicks are very popular if you like that kind of thing, and coffee has some interesting manifestations too. In Malay coffeeshops it is served very strong with a great dollop of sweetened condensed milk in the bottom and sugar. You might also try it flavoured with cinnamon. If you don't like sugar, ask for one without. Cendol is an Indonesian drink-cum-dessert often found in Singapore and Malaysia and has kidney beans and aduki beans as well as pandan jellies floating about in a mix of coconut and *gula melaka*, a kind of brown sugary stuff.

Alcohol is expensive in both Singapore and Malaysia. Local beers are Tiger and Anchor while most of the other big names are available. Guinness is popular in Malaysia and a special non-alcoholic variety can be bought! A local version of Guinness is ABC stout. Chinese people seem to like brandy and most supermarkets carry an enormous range.

Travelling around Malaysia

By air

Malaysian Airlines (MAS) have an extensive network of domestic routes that connect all the main towns in peninsular Malaysia, as well as large and small towns in Sarawak and Sabah.

There are some special fares. **Night tourist fares** are available between Kuala Lumpur and some other towns: Kota Bharu, Penang, Alor Setar, Kota Kinabalu and Kuching. There is a special one-way and return trip excursion fare between Kuala Lumpur and most towns in Sarawak and Sabah. There is a **family fare** that applies to a return journey made within 30 days: if one family member pays the full fare, the spouse and/or children receive a 25 per cent discount. Blind or disabled passengers receive a 50 per cent discount. There are no student discounts for non-Malaysians.

Travelling by air is well worth considering for journeys in Sarawak and Sabah. Flights save a lot of time and are not very expensive. Full details are given in the relevant sections of the guide.

By train

Travelling by train in peninsular Malaysia can be a delight because the rail system is safe, comfortable and affordable. However, it is also slow (for example, it takes six hours from Kuala Lumpur to Butterworth), the toilet facilities are basic and the food is atrocious. There are two lines. One runs between Thailand and Singapore via Butterworth and Kuala Lumpur. The second line branches off this line at Gemas, between Singapore and Kuala Lumpur, and runs up to the northeast of the country to near Kota Bharu.

North-bound train schedule
Singapore—Gemas—Kuala Lumpur

Train No.		ER/2	ES/66	XSP/6	ES/68	EM/60	SM/12
Singapore	Dep.	07.50	10.00	14.15	17.35	21.25	22.30
Johor Bahru		08.13	10.31	14.38	18.06	21.50	22.54
Kluang		09.19	12.04	15.41	20.23	23.25	00.33
Gemas		10.56	14.12	17.06	22.40	01.28	02.30
K. Lumpur	Arr.	13.32		19.44		05.30	05.50

Kuala Lumpur—Ipoh—Butterworth—Arau—Haadyi

Train No.		XSP/4	ER/2	EL/8	EM/54
K. Lumpur	Dep.	08.15	13.45	20.45	22.15
Ipoh		11.15	16.44	00.08	02.20
K. Kangsar		12.09	17.42	01.36	03.37
Taiping		12.42	18.19	02.20	04.26
Butterworth		14.18	19.57		06.37
Alor Setah				05.58	
Haaydi	Arr.			09.00	

South-bound train schedule
Haaydi—Arau—Butterworth—Ipoh—Kuala Lumpur

Train No.		ER/1	XSP/3	EL/7	EM/53	SM/9
Haaydi	Dep.			15.50 (Thai time)		
Alor Setar				20.02		
Butterworth		08.00	13.55		22.00	22.00
Taiping		09.25	15.29	23.13	23.59	23.59
K. Kangsar		10.01	16.03	23.51	00.48	00.48
Ipoh		10.49	16.52	00.49	01.51	01.51
K. Lumpur	Arr.	14.10	20.00	05.10	06.15	06.15

Kuala Lumpur—Gemas—Singapore

Train No.		ES/65	XSP/5	ER/1	ES/67	EM/59	SM/11
K. Lumpur	Dep.		07.35	14.15		21.05	22.15
Gemas		06.00	09.54	16.39	17.15	00.37	01.32
Segamat		06.29	10.16	17.15	17.42	01.36	02.37
Kluang		08.14	11.22	18.22	19.09	03.14	04.03
Johor Bahru		10.21	12.27	19.25	20.34	04.53	05.42
Singapore	Arr.	11.10	13.15	20.13	21.20	06.00	06.40

East Coast Schedule
Kuala Lumpur—Tumpat—Kuala Lumpur

Train No.		XW/16		XW/17
K. Lumpur	Dep.	20.20	Arr.	06.10
Gemas		22.46		02.53
Jerantut		01.51		23.55
Kuala Lipis		02.45		23.03
Krai		06.04		19.48
Wakaf Bahru		07.13		18.30
Tumpat	Arr.	07.35	Dep.	18.30

Singapore—Tumpat—Singapore

Train No.		XST/14		XST/15
Tumpat	Arr.	08.54	Dep.	19.30
Kuala Lipis		03.53		23.59
Gemas		23.45		04.05
Johor Bahru		20.45		06.43
Singapore	Dep.	20.20	Arr.	07.35

International Express
Butterworth—Bangkok—Butterworth

Train No.		1E/48		IE/49
Bangkok	Arr.	09.50 (Thai time) Dep.		15.15 (Thai time)
Haadyai		18.10 (Thai time)		07.02 (Thai time)
Alor Satar		15.59		10.54
Sungei Petani		15.09		11.44
Bukit Mertajam		14.35		12.18
Butterworth	Dep.	14.25	Arr.	12.44

There are **express** trains and less expensive **ordinary** trains. For long journeys always use the express trains unless you want to stop at every station along the route. Melaka and Taman Negara are the two most important destinations in peninsular Malaysia that cannot be reached directly by train.

There is only one short rail line in East Malaysia, a 55km route between Kota Kinabalu and Tenom in Sabah. The service is very slow but the journey between Tenom and Beaufort is worth travelling for its scenic views (further details can be found in the relevant section of the guide).

A **Visit Malaysia Railpass** allows for ten or 30 days' unlimited travel on any route, including travel to and from Singapore. The cost is US$55 for ten days (US$28 for children between four and 12); US$120 (US$60) for 30 days. These rates do not include the cost of a sleeper—another RM30 for each journey—but will cover first-class seats subject to availability. The railpass can be purchased in Kuala Lumpur and Singapore and some of the other main stations in Malaysia.

Tickets may be booked in advance through **Keretapi Tanah Melayu** (KTM): Passenger Services Division, KTM Berhad, Jalan Sultan Hishamuddin, 50621, Kuala Lumpur (☎ 03-2738000; fax 03-2736527; e-mail: passenger@ktmb. com.my). In the UK, Explorers Tours, 223 Coppermill Road, Wraysbury, TW19 5NW (fax 01753 682660) acts as an agent for KTM and tickets may also be booked through them.

By bus

It is possible to travel just about anywhere in **peninsular Malaysia** by bus. There is a state system, **Ekspress Nasional**, as well as numerous private companies that offer a comparable service. Long-distance buses are modern, air-conditioned, clean and comfortable. Seats can be booked in advance at the bus station where the booths of the different companies clearly display their schedules and prices. At holiday times, such as the Chinese New Year and Hari Raya, booking ahead is essential, but normally tickets are best purchased a couple of hours before departure or perhaps a day earlier. There is no significant difference in the fares between the state buses and the various private companies. Tickets are not normally refundable. A recommended private bus company is *Nice* and though a little more expensive than Ekspress Nasional, it does use new coaches, serves a meal on the journey and is faster than travelling by train. Details are provided under the main towns and cities covered by its routes. In **Sarawak** buses are only worth considering for journeys between Kuching and Miri via Bintulu and Sibu. In **Sabah** there is a good system of modern buses and mini-buses plying all the main routes. The mini-buses only leave when full. Turn up early in the morning for a popular route, for example, Kota Kinabalu to Sandakan.

By car
There is an extensive system of modern roads throughout peninsular Malaysia, making car hire a viable option. Expect to pay about RM110 a day for a 1.3 Malaysian-built Proton Saga. In Sarawak and Sabah the road system is less extensive than in the rest of the country and is less likely to be used by visitors. Most roads are now paved but a four-wheel drive is still advisable in East Malaysia.

In peninsular Malaysia the **North–South Highway** runs for 900km from Singapore to the border with Thailand, with a system of tolls (about RM1 for every 6km) along the way. There are no tolls in Singapore. In Malaysia, **Route 1** follows more or less the same route as the North–South Highway, but without tolls. **Route 2** runs from Kuala Lumpur to Kuantan on the east coast. **Route 4** crosses Malaysia from Kota Bharu to Butterworth. **Route 8** runs down the east coast from Kota Bharu to Johor Bahru.

Only the North–South Highway and Route 1 get crowded with traffic, especially around Kuala Lumpur. The other main roads are wonderfully free of traffic jams. The main towns are another matter, especially Kuala Lumpur which is a horror to drive in and is best avoided by car.

Driving is on the left, a legacy of British rule, and road signs are usually graphic and international in character. It is common practice for Malaysians, and Singaporeans to a lesser extent, to flash their headlights when claiming a right of way or a wish to overtake. Giving way to other traffic is not a common practice. On highways the speed limit is 100km an hour; on other main roads it is 80km an hour. In built up areas the speed limit is 50km an hour.

Garages for fuel are usually located on main roads near towns. Petrol costs a little over a dollar a litre in Malaysia and more in Singapore, so much so that there is a gas tank check at the Singapore side of the border. Drivers must have a three-quarters full tank of petrol on leaving Singapore. This is to deter locals from driving over the causeway to fill their tanks. Failure to have the required amount in your tank results in a fine! If you are renting a car the agency will have it registered with a motoring organisation and will give you emergency phone numbers.

Car hire
Cars can be hired from any of the main airports or through the larger hotels in all major towns. Details are given in the relevant sections of the guide. Fly-drive holidays are an option offered by some of the tour operators in the UK and the USA (see p 16).

By taxi

There are two types of taxi in Malaysia: local taxis and long-distance taxis. **Local taxis** are usually unmetered outside of Kuala Lumpur and it is always advisable to confirm the fare before setting off on any journey. Details are given in the guide of local rates and it is always a good idea to ask at the hotel reception desk for these. Foreign visitors can expect often to be charged a little more than locals but this is often such a small amount, a couple of *ringgit*, that it is rarely worth arguing about. Taxis can be hailed anywhere but are usually readily available outside hotels and train and bus stations.

Towns in Malaysia will have a **long-distance taxi station**, often adjoining the bus station, and usually covering routes to all the neigbouring or most obvious destinations. The fare is usually about 50–75 per cent more than the bus fare. Two people hiring a taxi will pay twice the rate if they do not wish to wait until another two passengers turn up.

Hitchhiking

It is unlikely that you would do any hitchhiking in Singapore or that, if you did, anyone would understand what you were doing. Lifts are easier to come by in Malaysia, especially if you look tidy and carry a backpack. Malaysians love to chat and particularly with a foreigner. In remote areas cars are scarce but drivers will give you a ride if they can. Asking for lifts at roadside stopping places is a good idea. You should try to hitch in pairs, especially if you are a woman. There is always a risk with this kind of travel. Also be careful what you wave at as passing taxis will stop even if they have two or three other passengers and then you will have to pay.

Women travellers

Malaysia and Singapore must be two of the safest places in the world for women travellers. Having said that, you should be aware of the fact that Malaysia is a Muslim country and people are offended by the sight of exposed flesh. In most of Malaysia it is possible to wear shorts and a T-shirt without experiencing problems, but in the northeast you should respect people's views and keep shoulders, chests and thighs covered. Both countries seem to have more than their fair share of flashers but that is about the worst thing that may happen to you and then only if you wander alone into dark streets or the parks at night. Topless sunbathing is **not** acceptable, although in very touristy places like Tioman women seem to get away with it. To advise on whether or not you should be friendly with strangers is problematic because nine times out of ten it is a genuinely friendly person who wishes to chat or even take you home to his family. You must decide whether the risk is worth it.

Women should pay particular attention to the effects of the climate. Vaginal thrush is a common problem but is easily cured with antibiotic cream available over the counter. In deepest Malaysia you might find that some toilets are primitive hole and bucket arrangements, so be prepared with your own store of tissue paper and soap.

Travelling with children

One of the best things about a holiday in Singapore and Malaysia is that they are both such great places for children. The variety of wildlife, transport, food, activities and the incredible friendliness of people towards children makes it a pleasure both for you and for them. People love children in Malaysia, especially blonde haired ones. Chinese people will try a surreptitious stroke of golden hair in the hope that it will bring them money! On the beach and on long train journeys your children will find adults happy to spend their time entertaining them and they will often be asked to pose for photographs. The usual caution with strangers has of course to be applied but as long as they are in sight and happy there should be no problem. The problem might be teaching them not to be so trusting when they get home! Food is no problem for small children. Fast food is available everywhere in Singapore and even in quite small towns in Malaysia, and hawker stalls are bound to have something that they will eat.

As even a few minutes in the sun can cause sunburn, it is important to keep children covered with sunscreen. In the sea there are a few nasties to watch out for. A common accident is stepping on a sea urchin which can be very painful. On beaches there can be sandflies and mosquitoes so repellent is a good idea. Macaques might look cute but they can be vicious and so can dogs. Rabies is a possibility with all mammals. Children are also prone to headlice and threadworms which can be contracted through eggs in the soil carried to the mouth.

Disposable nappies are available everywhere although it is probably a good idea to carry a supply to some of the more remote places.

Customs and manners

Singapore is a cosmopolitan place. No-one minds much what you do as long as you pay for it. In Malaysia, however, you may well inadvertently cause offence so there are a few things to remember. Dress is important and has already been discussed (see p 30). Malays believe that the left side of the body is bad so they avoid using the left hand for eating, greetings or for handing things to you. Chinese people on the other hand (no pun intended) may offer you things with both hands and make a little bow. You should do the same and take the offering with both hands. In Malay restaurants your food may not come with a fork and spoon (never with a knife) so you must eat with your right hand only, breaking off each piece of food and scooping it up with your fingers. The same applies to eating in Indian restaurants. In Singapore you will get a spoon and fork and no-one will pay any attention to what hand you use. In Chinese restaurants you can eat how you like except that if you are sharing a big dish between lots of people it is not good form to put your chopsticks into your mouth and then back into the shared dish of food. You drop the food in your mouth without making contact and take pieces of food from the dish carefully making sure that you touch only your own piece of food and don't chase it around the plate.

Malay men and women usually do not touch, even to shake hands, so watch to see if someone of the opposite sex offers his/her hand before you make physical contact. The soles of the feet are taboo, so do not put your feet up in front of anyone. You must take off your shoes before you enter anyone's home whatever their ethnic background.

Pointing and putting your hands on your hips are rude and you will notice that both Malays and Singaporeans beckon with their hand upside down rather than held up and with one finger wiggling as in the West. Singaporeans will attract your attention with a peculiar squeaky noise made with their lips (the noise which in England rude young men make at girls they are attracted to). A Malay will greet you with 'Where are you going?' and a Chinese will ask you 'Have you eaten yet?' Neither are prying into your private life—these are standard greetings among the two communities. If you visit a family at home it is customary to bring a gift of sweets.

What to take with you

You should pack a basic **medical kit** containing the following: painkillers; an anti-diarrhoea medicine such as Lomotil; rehydration powders, although this is just salt and sugar and you can mix it yourself if need be; antibiotics if you are going a long way off the beaten track; a dry antiseptic powder (easier to carry and better in the damp climate); and water sterilising tablets.

You should take a minimum of **clothing**. Once you get there, you may want to buy batik, T-shirts, shoes and other items of clothing, all available at much lower prices than you would pay at home. What you do take should be informal and made of cotton or some other natural fibre. You might want a sweatshirt or cardigan for air-conditioned buses or shopping malls and especially the cinema and restaurants. A bumbag is convenient if you don't mind the inelegant shape it gives you. Plastic bags, especially zip lock type ones, are very useful for packing. Soap flakes or travel wash is a good idea. Other things you will need, such as torches, mosquito repellent, suntan lotion, shampoo, etc., can all be bought there, even in small towns. A universal adapter is a good idea if you are carrying electrical things. If you are travelling on a low budget a little travel kettle can be a godsend, although even quite cheap hotels provide hot water.

Health

There are no required inoculations for visiting Malaysia or Singapore unless you are coming from an area infected with cholera or yellow fever (in which case you will need an immunisation certificate). Vaccinations that could be considered are those for tetanus and diphtheria, typhoid and hepatitis A.

Mosquitoes can be a problem, causing outbreaks of the potentially fatal dengue fever in some years. The precautions are to cover up as much as possible and to wear repellent in the two hours after sunrise and after sunset, when mosquitoes are most active.

The most likely health problem is an attack of diarrhoea due to infections caused by bacteria and viruses. About 40 per cent of cases are due to one bacterium, *enterotoxigenic Escherichia coli*, which unlucky travellers ingest in food or drink or when swimming. Sea water contaminated by sewage is a common cause. Bacteria and viruses survive in ice cubes and are not always killed by alcohol. They thrive on buffet-style food, unwashed fruit and salads. Anti-microbial drugs (sulphonamides) give about 50 per cent protection and newer antibiotics, such as cotrimoxazole or ciprofloxacin, are even better. The problem with taking these drugs, especially as a precaution, is that they have side-effects so you should consult your doctor before travelling. The simplest treatment for diarrhoea is to drink lots of fluids, if necessary adding sachets of salt and glucose.

Health insurance is essential. Medical fees are nowhere near as high as those prevailing in the USA but some form of protection is still necessary. If you are planning to go trekking in the jungle in East Malaysia check that the policy does not exclude a claim arising from this under 'dangerous activities'.

A useful **medical kit** would include an elementary pain-killer such as Panadol, some form of antihistamine, something for stomach upsets and diarrhoea (consider a prescription for an antibiotic), an antiseptic and insect repellent.

Visitors not used to the tropical heat and humidity of Malaysia and Singapore should be aware of the risk of sunburn and dehydration. A high-factor sun lotion is essential if any sunbathing is planned. It is also essential to drink plenty of fluids. An attack of prickly heat or a fungal infection is quite likely so use prickly heat talcum powder which is readily available in shops and pharmacies across Malaysia and Singapore.

Travellers can use government hospitals in both Malaysia and Singapore. For minor medical problems it is often more convenient to use a private doctor. A charge for one visit is usually around RM30 and the fee often includes the medication. Ask your hotel for the address of a local private clinic. Doctors in both countries should be able to speak and understand English.

Personal security and emergencies

Malaysia and Singapore are both very safe places to travel in. Theft is a problem anywhere and you should take care of personal belongings here just as you would elsewhere, especially on long-distance bus journeys. Keep passports and money in a secure place and always keep the numbers of travellers' cheques separate from the cheques themselves. Many hotels will have a safe deposit in the room or at least a safety deposit box at reception.

Pickpocketing is a real danger in Orchard Road in Singapore and in Johor Bahru. But the rules you may have ingrained in you about speaking to strangers just do not apply, especially in Malaysia. If you get into difficulties you will find any number of people going out of their way to help.

In both Malaysia and Singapore report a crime to the nearest police station. For insurance claims it will usually be necessary to have some official document from the police verifying what has been reported.

Emergency numbers

Malaysia	**Singapore**
Police and/or ambulance ☎ 999	Police and/or ambulance ☎ 999
Fire brigade ☎ 994	Fire brigade ☎ 995

Drugs

Do not even think about illicit drugs in Malaysia or Singapore. Both countries have mandatory death penalties for very small amounts of drugs and both countries have executed Westerners for such offences. The distinction between soft drugs like marijuana and hard drugs like heroin and cocaine is **NOT** one made by the judges who have no choice but to impose a death penalty when someone is found guilty.

Opening hours

In Malaysia and Singapore banks are usually open from 10.00 to 15.00 and on Saturday from 09.30 to 11.30. Post office hours in both countries are usually 08.00 to 17.00, Monday to Friday, and 08.00 to 12.00 on Saturday.

In the more Islamic states of Kelantan, Terengganu, Kedah and Perlis, Sunday is a normal working day, Thursday is the equivalent of a Saturday, and Friday is a holiday. This applies to banks, post offices and all government offices.

Tipping

Most restaurants and hotels in Singapore include a service charge in the bill and tipping is not expected anywhere and is positively frowned on. In Malaysia tipping is more common in hotels and upmarket restaurants but not taxis or less expensive places.

Laundry

Most hotels have a laundry service which charges per item and can be expensive. The cheaper hotels charge less or you can find a public service. Laundry takes about 24 hours. In Singapore there are launderettes where you can do your own washing.

Time differences

Standard time in Malaysia and Singapore is eight hours ahead of Greenwich Mean Time (seven hours ahead of British Summer Time).

When it is 12.00 in Malaysia or Singapore it is the following times elsewhere:

London: 04.00　　　　　　　　San Francisco: 20.00 (previous night)
Paris/Rome: 05.00　　　　　　New York: 23.00 (previous night)
Sydney: 14.00

Weights and measures

Malaysia and Singapore use the metric system of weights and measures.

Telephone and postal services

Malaysia. Every Malaysian town has a **General Post Office** where stamps can be purchased and mail sent. **Telephones** using coins are becoming less common than ones requiring a phone card. There are two systems—Telekom and Uniphone—each with their own telephone boxes and telephone cards, and it makes sense to carry a card for each system. Both cards can be used to make international calls and are available in the following values: RM10, RM20 or RM50; a RM5 Uniphone card is also available.

To make an overseas call dial 001, then the country code, then the area code minus the first 0, and then the subscriber's number. To ring Malaysia from Britain dial 0060 before the area code minus the first zero and then the subscriber's number. From the United States ☎ 011-60, then the area code minus the first zero and then the subscriber's number.

Singapore. Stamps can be purchased at the General Post Office in Exeter Road or any other post office. **Telephones** using coins are becoming less common than ones requiring a phone card. Telephone cards, costing from S$2 upwards, are available from post offices, small shops and all 7-Eleven stores. International calls can be made and faxes can be sent in comfort from Comcentre at 31 Exeter Road or the General Post Office. There are also a number of public phones labelled 'Worldphone' for making international calls using coins.

To make an overseas call dial 005, then the country code, then the area code minus the first 0, and then the subscriber's number. To ring Singapore from the UK dial 0065 and then the subscriber's number. From the United States dial 011-65, then the subscriber's number.

Singapore has no area code.

Newspapers

Both Malaysia and Singapore have English-language newspapers, the most important of which are *The New Straits Times* and the *Singapore Straits Times* respectively. Both are government controlled and reflect government views. International English-language newspapers and magazines are readily available in Singapore and Kuala Lumpur as well as in other large Malaysian towns. Magazines such as *Newsweek* and the *Economist* are readily available throughout the region.

Public toilets

The general standard of hygiene in public toilets is high in both countries, far higher than in most other Asian countries. In Singapore, standards are as high—if not higher—than in Europe or North America. The more remote the area, the less exacting are the standards of cleanliness. In towns all hotels and restaurants will have toilets that are well maintained.

Public holidays

In both Malaysia and Singapore a number of public holidays change their dates each year, being based on a lunar calendar.

Malaysia

1 January	New Year's Day
Late January/February	Chinese New Year
February	Thaipusam
March/April	Hari Raya Puasa
May	Pesta Kaamatan (Sabah only)
1 May	Labour Day
May/July	Hari Raya Haji
June	Gawai Dayak (Sarawak only)
4 June	Yang di-Pertuan Agong's birthday
June/July	Maal Hijrah (Mohammed's journey to Medina from Mecca)
August	Birthday of the Prophet Mohammed
31 August	National Day
November	Deepavali
25 December	Christmas Day

Singapore

1 January	New Year's Day
Late January/February	Chinese New Year

March/April	Hari Raya Puasa
March/April	Good Friday
1 May	Labour Day
May	Vesak Day
May/July	Hari Raya Haji
9 August	National Day
November	Deepvali
25 December	Christmas Day

National symbols

The national symbol of Singapore (apart from the intensely ugly merlion) is the Vanda Miss Joaquim orchid. Other things to show respect to are the flag, the national anthem and Lee Kwan Yew. Other national figures can be poked fun at but only a little. In Malaysia the national symbol is the kite that you see on Malaysian Airlines' planes. Proton cars are not an official symbol but everyone is very proud of them.

Festivals

Chinese New Year is the major holiday period across Malaysia and Singapore, except for the east coast of peninsular Malaysia and East Malaysia. It is one time of year when the whole country seems to be on the move and all forms of transport are oversubscribed. Colourful parades and dragon dances take place along Orchard Road in Singapore and in places such as Penang, Melaka and Kuala Lumpur dragon dances pop up everywhere.

Thaipusam is an important Hindu festival celebrating Lord Subramaniam. The best places to view this astonishing spectacle is in Singapore and the Batu Caves outside Kuala Lumpur (see p 91).

Ramadan is the ninth month of the Islamic calendar and is marked by fasting between dawn and dusk. It usually occurs between February and March but it can finish as late as April. Along the east coast of peninsular Malaysia this means that any Malay restaurant will be closed during the day. This can sometimes be inconvenient but it does not affect the larger hotels and it is usually possible to find a non-Muslim Indian restaurant or a Chinese place open. Ramadan should not deter anyone from visiting this part of the country.

Hari Raya Puasa marks the end of Ramadan. It is the only day in the year when Malay royal palaces are open to the public.

Vesak Day is a Buddhist holiday and Buddhist temples are filled with celebrants marking the birth of Buddha.

Pesta Kaamatan is a harvest festival of the Kadazan people.

Gawai Dayak is an equivalent harvest festival for the Iban and Bidayuh peoples of Sarawak. It is the best possible time of the year for visiting a longhouse.

Dragon Boat Festival is marked in Penang, Melaka, Singapore and Kota Kinabalu with colourful boat races where boats are made up to look like dragons. The festival celebrates a Chinese scholar who protested against government corruption by throwing himself into a river where he drowned.

Deepavali is a Hindu festival celebrating the triumph of Light over Dark. Special services take place at all Hindu temples.

Background Information

History

(For the history of Sabah and Sarawak see pp 236 and 266 respectively.)

Early History
There are few sources for the history of what is now called Malaysia before about 1400 that yield definite and reliable information. Human remains found in Sarawak date back some 40,000 years while on the peninsula the remains go back only about 10,000 years. Next to nothing is known for sure about the nature and course of migration into the region but the consensus is that various waves of people from south China drifted into what is now Malaysia over different periods of time. Just when the process began and how long it lasted is likely to remain speculative. **Orang Asli** ('original people') is the name given to the first people who arrived on the peninsula, and their descendants can still be found in small groups in peninsular Malaysia.

Historians are far more confident about explaining and understanding the significance of the Malay archipelago and the way this shaped many centuries of the region's history. The cyclical monsoon wind systems dictated the emergence of the Malay world as the natural link between the great civilisations of India and China. Monsoon winds from the northwest carried vessels from India during the summer, and towards the end of the year they could return on northeast winds.

The Malay world also had an intrinsic worth that made the region more than a convenient staging post. The jungle interior was a treasure house of valuable resins and rattans, as well as of precious aromatic woods like camphor, while the land yielded valuable metals like gold and tin. The epithet **Golden Chersonese** was bestowed by early Greek geographers, a pointer presumably to the region's reputation as a source of precious gold. Cowrie shells—a form of currency before coins—probably left the east coast of peninsular Malaysia from 2000 BC onwards and the first Indian traders may have arrived around AD 300. Their exact intentions cannot be confirmed but there is little doubt about the extent of **Indian influence** on the Malay archipelago. The introduction of **Islam** is the most obvious legacy but the rituals and concepts of Malay court life can also be traced back to India.

Some time around the 7C, the **maritime empire of Srivijaya** rose to prominence. Based in Sumatra in modern Indonesia, its realm of power most likely included the lower half of the peninsula's west coast, roughly from Melaka down to and including Johor. Very little is known for certain but by the end of the 14C this Sumatran-based network was in serious decline. From its decline, however, a new maritime entrepôt emerged, this time centred on Melaka, and its growing prosperity ensured its illustrious place in the Malay world.

Melaka

The development of Melaka's prosperity, beginning in the early 15C, was not accidental. Melaka was strategically located on the all-important India–China trade route and the Melaka river provided convenient access to the jungle interior and the gold-mining areas upriver. Merchants, moreover, were quick to appreciate the security provided by the first ruler, **Parameswara** (see p 151), and their endorsement of Melaka ensured its success. Parameswara was connected to the old Srivijayan Empire, although the nature of this connection remains obscure, and it seems likely that early Melaka was able to build on the experience of the earlier Srivijayan Empire.

Trade and Spice

Traders from countries in north and western Europe found themselves passing up and down the Straits of Melaka to reach the **Moluccas**—a group of islands in east Indonesia—because of the wealth of spices to be found there. Nutmeg, pepper, cinnamon and ginger were highly valued for their preservative value and practical use in disguising the taste of meat that had to be stored over the long winter months. The use of hay had not been developed in Europe and most farm animals were slaughtered in late autumn and the meat salted and dried. Everyone quickly tired of the monotonous taste of salt and pickles and the meat became staler as the winter went on. Merchants stood to make handsome profits because the spices, weighing little and small in volume, could be transported in bulk.

At first the spices reached Europe by way of a torturous overland route by camel through Syria and then by sea to Venice. The route joined part of the **Silk Road**—the way of all trade from China and India to Europe—that had functioned for some 200 years before **Vasco da Gama** (1469–1525) changed everything.

> Early Portuguese voyages of discovery were spearheaded by Prince Henry the Navigator (1394–1460) who was able to bring together mercantile interest in the spice trade and gold with anti-Muslim sentiment and a propagandistic quest for the mythical Prester John, a kingly priest rumoured to be living somewhere in the East.
>
> When Vasco da Gama reached India, Dom João III, who had been ruling Portugal for 17 years, was determined to circumvent the dependence on Muslim traders. The individual most clearly responsible for this venture was Afonso de Albuquerque. He took Goa (southern India) in 1510 and the following year seized the town and port of Melaka. The primary depot for the spices of the Moluccas was captured within a month.

When da Gama's expedition sailed to India via southern Africa in 1497–99, the new sea route offered a chance to cut out the Arabian and Venetian middlemen and channel the profits to whoever could command the sailing route. The **Portuguese** were the first to monopolise the trade, taking Melaka in 1511 and establishing bases in India and China, only to be displaced by the Dutch who took over in the first half of the 17C.

The VOC (Vereenigde Oostindische Compagnie), the United Netherlands Chartered East India Company, was Holland's equivalent to Britain's East India Company. The VOC was formed in 1602; it was an amalgamation of a number of smaller Dutch trading houses which agreed to share profits rather than squabble over the pepper market that had begun in Java a decade earlier. The VOC, though officially independent, was in fact closely tied to the Dutch government and often acted as its foreign affairs department. In 1619 VOC headquarters were established in Jakarta, then known as Batavia, from where its commercial and intelligence-gathering network spread out across Asia.

As the **VOC** ventured into the Malay archipelago, it found an ally in the Johor court which badly needed an ally against both its traditional Sumatra-based enemies and the Portuguese empire. The VOC's agenda included the displacement of Portugal's sovereignty over the Straits of Melaka and so Johor contributed to the Dutch success—logistically, not militarily—in taking Melaka in 1641. After this, the state of affairs changed drastically. The VOC had no intention of shifting its headquarters from Batavia to Melaka; it was content to have secured control over the straits and henceforth Melaka was to be just another trading post in its vast Asian network rather than the international entrepôt it once was. Melaka's days of glory were over.

The space created by the demise of Melaka was soon filled by Johor, and by the end of the 17C **Johor** had no rivals in its maritime neighbourhood. The ruling family, the Laksamanas, seemed utterly secure and well on its way to establishing a dynasty that would stretch into the next century. Personal intrigue among the nobility, however, resulted in a coup and the assassination of the five-year-old heir to the Johor throne in 1699. The act of regicide proved divisive and Johor never fully recovered. It fragmented into a number of mini-kingdoms ruled by local leaders.

The eighteenth century

Beginning in the late 17C, various **Bugis** groups were on the move, fleeing from political dissension in Sulawesi and searching for a new home. The Dutch had broken their hold over the spice trade from the Moluccas. The Bugis people were famed for their skill as navigators, their prowess as warriors and their acumen as commercial networkers. At first they were accepted and even welcomed by Malay rulers who thought to exploit their usefulness. Over time though the growing confidence and ability of the Bugis came to pose a threat to the status quo. By the early 18C they had control of Riau, the capital of the Johor empire, and had begun to express an interest in the tin trade of Kedah and Perak. In 1756 they were able to lay siege to Melaka.

The **Chinese** were also reappearing on the scene. A prohibition that had prevented the Chinese from trading with southeast Asia was lifted by a new emperor and demand for traditional Malay products increased. In addition, European nations were keen to use the Malay world as a base for exchanging opium with China for tea.

Malaysia's monachy: the Sultans

Malaysia has a unique system for its rotating monarchy. The sultans, some of whom have family lines going back to the 16C and 17C, serve as titular heads of nine of the country's 13 states, and choose a king (*yang di-pertuan agong*) from among themselves to reign for five years. The nine states are Perlis, Perak, Kedah, Kelantan, Terengganu, Phang, Selangor, Negeri Sembilan and Johor.

There was no sense of an independent Malay country in the 18C. Instead there was a Malay world, concentrated in what is now peninsular Malaysia but including the islands of Borneo and Sumatra and numerous small islands in the vicinity and extending eastwards to islands east of Bali. This Malay world shared a political and social order based around a sultanate ruling a rivermouth society. The geography and available technology meant that inland territory was virtually inaccessible (though not to the stateless forest-dwelling communities that managed their own life in the jungle) and the rivers became the focus of social and political life. Chiefs had their 'capitals' at the mouth of the river, the logical place to control whatever came down it, where they sought to exert their hegemony over those living upriver.

The nine Malay hereditary sultanates developed as the various local groups vied for power in the peninsula. The sultan, before this Islamic Turkish term was introduced, had been known ceremonially as the *Yang di-Pertuan* ('he who is made the lord') or just *raja* (a generic term of Indian origin). The term was first used by the third ruler of Melaka (see p 152) who embraced Islam in 1430. In 1511 the second sultanate was created when Melaka was taken by the Portuguese and the ruler fled to Johor. This family split into factions and by the 18C various scions had set up the sultanates of Pahang and Perak. In the same period the sultanate of Selangor, near modern Kuala Lumpur, emerged when the Bugis, a seafaring tribe from South Sulawesi in modern Indonesia (see also p 86), set up a city state there. The modern state of Negeri Sembilan came into being under Minangkabu influence when nine smaller states created a defensive confederacy (these were later merged into one state when the British created the Federated Malay States). The two northern states, Kelantan and Terrengganu had existed since the 14C and went through various periods of vassalship to Melaka and Johor and, in the early 18C, Siam, when Siamese (Thai) ambitions accelerated. These states, and Kedah, were forced to accept Siam's overlordship and pay regular tribute and some sultans looked to Britain for assistance. In 1786 Penang was taken by **Captain Francis Light** in the name of the British monarch (see p 121), and during this period local leaders set themselves up as sultans. The ninth sultanship is Kedah whose sultans claim a royal line dating back several hundred years.

An air of sanctity and mysticism was cultivated around the sultan, similar to the notion of divine rule once attached to European monarchs and for basically the same reason—to inculcate respect and obedience and an unquestioning loyalty. A characteristic feature of this culture of kingship was an elaborate system of ceremonial procedures and practices and royal regalia in the form of costumes and ritual ornaments, vestiges of which are still very evident in contemporary Malaysian sultans.

In modern times the sultans have come into conflict with the modern state. They have considerable popularity in the rural areas and have the right of veto over state laws. Some of them have come under sharp criticism for their serious flouting of the law, extravagant expenditure of state funds and interference in national politics. In 1993 parliament introduced laws removing the sultans' immunity to the law, having already curtailed their huge stipends. The sultans of course vetoed the new law and the serious constitutional crisis was only resolved when parliament offered the compromise that prosecutions would only go ahead with the Attorney-General's consent. In 1994 a further law made it clear that the king could only act on the advice of government, effectively taking away the ability of the king to interfere in Malaysian affairs.

The nineteenth century

The 19C was a period of accelerated change for the Malay world. European nation states effected permanent changes and shaped the emergence of Malaysia and Indonesia as separate countries.

The 1824 **Anglo–Dutch Treaty** saw Britain and the Netherlands agree to demarcate their respective spheres of influence. The Straits of Melaka now divided the two empires, with the eastern side—what is now peninsular Malaysia—going to Britain, and the western side—Sumatra—to the Dutch. The islands to the south of Singapore also went to the Dutch.

British colonisation of the Malay world was never systematically planned by a government in London—quite the opposite in fact—because there was a strictly limited agenda on the British sphere of influence in southeast Asia. The need to exert some control over the bottleneck of water—the Straits of Melaka— that lay on the major India–China trade route was felt to have been achieved by the establishment of a naval base in Penang in 1786. The Malay peninsula itself was viewed as an uneconomic mass of impenetrable jungle and London turned a deaf ear to entreaties made by merchants in the area for a concerted British take-over. It was left to the dynamic individual, Thomas Stamford Raffles, to boldly go where no imperialist had gone before.

Sir Stamford Raffles (1781–1826)

Stamford Raffles was born at sea in the West Indies; aged 14 he joined the East India Company where he soon tired of 'the dry drudgery of the desk's dead wood'. When the Dutch were defeated by Napoleon the British gained temporary control of their eastern territories, which kept them free of the French enemy, and Raffles was sent to Java by the East India Company to oversee the administration; it was here that he first became convinced of the need for Britain to broaden its presence in the region. Eventually he obtained permission to establish a base on the island of Singapore, under the rule of the Sultan of Johor. Although it was not occupied by the Dutch, they did have a toehold on the island because of their support for the young Malay who claimed the Sultanate of Johor after his father had died without naming his successor. Raffles cleverly sought out the elder son and quickly signed a treaty with him which allowed the East India Company to establish a 'factory' (trading post) there in return for 5000 Spanish dollars. It was a gamble but his luck held: the Dutch refrained from attacking the island after Raffles left 300 soldiers and ten large guns there.

Chinese entrepreneurs flocked to Singapore after its establishment by Stamford Raffles in 1819. They came to engage in the buying and selling of the jungle products that had traditionally interested the Chinese in the Malay world, i.e. birds' nests, camphor and agar-agar (seaweed). European traders came to Singapore for other products like the antimony from Sarawak and gutta percha from Malay forests.

> Until the end of the 19C Europe depended on Sarawak for the supply of antinomy which was traded through Singapore. Gutta-percha, a resin from gutta-percha trees, had the quality of being mouldable while heated, turning rock-solid and waterproof after cooling down. As telegraphic cables were being laid under the Atlantic ocean and elsewhere, gutta-percha became a precious commodity.

After 1824 Penang, Melaka and Singapore were ruled by Britain, at first through the East India Company in Calcutta and later from London when they were formed into the Straits Settlements. That was as far as Britain wanted to go, but as Singapore prospered its business community pressed for expansion into the tin-mining areas opening up in the peninsula. But the expatriate businessmen balked at the prospect of having to negotiate with a myriad of small-scale Malay barons without military backup. London was not convinced of the investment potential and it was left to the more knowledgeable Governor of the Straits Settlements to move matters forward. The result was the 1874 Treaty of Pangkor when the Sultan of Perak was persuaded to accept a political adviser, officially entitled a Resident.

In the years that followed the Treaty of Pangkor, British rule gradually infiltrated the Malay states in the form of Residents, agents and governors. It would eventually lead to British Malaya.

Hugh Low (1819–1905)

The early history of British rule in Malaysia is closely associated with a small number of hardy individuals who joined the Civil Service and accepted overseas positions in the Far East. It is probably fair to say that most of them held racist views, at least when they first arrived, but those who chose to stay often grew to love the country and sometimes outgrew their prejudices. Reading their autobiographies and biographies it is difficult to imagine them ever fitting back into British society. Hugh Low (1819–1905) is one of the most interesting figures from this era, not least because of his extra-curricular interests. He spent 29 years as the British representative on the island of Labuan and was eventually rewarded for his patience by being appointed the Resident of Perak in 1877.

Whilst living on Labuan, he explored the Borneo neighbourhood and nurtured his interest in botany. He was the first known European to climb Mt Kinabalu. Shortly after his posting to Perak, he planted a dozen or so new plants that had come from South America via Kew Gardens and Ceylon (Sri Lanka). These were examples of *Hevea braziliensis* and within a couple of years they were over 4m high and bearing fruit. The plants needed five or six years' growth before useful amounts of latex could be drawn from them and when Low retired in 1889 he had no idea just how important his innovation was. It took Henry Ford and the motor car industry to bring the rubber tree onto the stockmarkets of the world, but by then Hugh Low had died.

British Malaya

In 1875 the first Resident of Perak, James Wheeler Birch, was murdered (see p 102). A general uprising was expected and troops from India and Hong Kong were brought in but there were never more than a couple of hundred Malays in arms and the whole event proved to be a minor upset. The British were now keen to extend their influence in the peninsula, partly out of fear of French expansion from Vietnam and a German presence in the Pacific. In 1877 a British agent was sent to Pahang, mainly because businessmen were convinced there was gold and tin in the area. This caused some Malay chiefs to rebel and in 1888 there were occasional outbreaks of disorder that became known as the **Pahang War**.

In 1896 the **Federated Malay States** came into being with the capital in Kuala Lumpur. In 1909 a treaty saw Siam's (Thailand) withdrawal from the northern states of Kedah, Terengganu and Kelantan and the assumption of British influence in what later became the Unfederated Malay States. In the process the modern border between Thailand (Siam became Thailand in 1939) and Malaysia was created.

By 1919 the whole Malay peninsula was within Britain's sphere of influence and European, mostly British, investment was swift to follow. In 1913 only a quarter of Malaya's tin mines were owned by Europeans; in 1937 the figure was two-thirds.

Second World War

The single, most costly, expenditure by the British government between the two world wars was on the Singapore dockyards; their completion added to the complacency that was so rudely shattered by the events following the Japanese attack on **Pearl Harbor** in December 1941 and their simultaneous landing on the northeast coast of Malaya at Kota Bharu. Two British warships—the newly built *Prince of Wales* and the *Repulse*—left Singapore to steam up the west coast. The plan was to locate the Japanese and halt their advance. Both ships were sunk on the same day.

On 15 February 1942, 50,000 Japanese found themselves in charge of 130,000 surrendering empire troops and 'the greatest disaster and worst capitulation in the history of the British Empire' (Winston Churchill). Four hundred years of empire-building by the British, Dutch and French were dismantled in some four months.

The Japanese were interested in Malaya for strategic reasons—cutting off US supplies which were sent to China through Burma—as well as economic ones—supplies of rubber and tin—and they set about creating a unitary Malay state that ignored the territorial barrier between Sumatra and Malaya that had been created by the Dutch and British over a century earlier. The atomic bomb put an end to their endeavours but for two weeks after the Japanese surrender in 1945 no British forces were in Malaya. The **Malayan Communist Party** (MCP) could have taken over the country but they too were taken by surprise and anyway were busy settling scores with Malay and Chinese collaborators. (Some of the communist Chinese who had fought as guerrillas alongside a small group of

British soldiers in the jungle duly received their British campaign medals.)

The tensions that erupted had been brewing long before the war. The Depression had forced the Malays and Chinese to compete where before they had warily tolerated one another. The first **Pan-Malayan Malay Congress** had been held in 1939.

End of Empire

A new world order beckoned after 1945 and Britain proposed a **Malayan Union** that offered equal citizenship to all inhabitants. It was rejected by Malays, and the consequent rise of Malay nationalism was closely tied to fears of Chinese domination in a country where, numerically and economically, the Malays could take little for granted. In March 1946 the United Malay National Organization (UMNO) was founded to fight the British proposal.

Malay nationalism had little in common with the clamour for independence that was rocking the rest of the British Empire. An UMNO resolution at the time spoke of 'the loss of faith and confidence of probably the only race in the world today who would voluntarily remain loyal to the British Empire'.

The British retreated before concerted Malay opposition and proposed instead a **Malayan Federation**; this would bring together the various federated and unfederated states and the Straits Settlements—but not Singapore—under a colonial-type rule and without automatic Chinese citizenship. While this was acceptable to the Malays it obviously upset the Chinese who now became more responsive to communist claims that the British Empire meant only exploitation. A period known as the **Emergency** began in 1948 when three European planters were murdered by communist guerrillas in Perak. The ensuing war for control of the country did not officially end until 1960.

> ### The Emergency
>
> The Emergency (1948–60)—so called because admission of a war would have invalidated insurance claims—began ominously for the British. Although the insurgents were heavily outnumbered, they possessed the same advantages that benefited guerrilla movements in other countries: a supply of weapons (from the Second World War), sympathy from the Chinese poor, and the element of surprise in attacking isolated, often unprotected, plantation managers before withdrawing back into the jungle. By 1950 over 100 civilians had fallen victim to the CTs ('communist terrorists' to the British) and the British army only compounded the problem by venting their frustration on villages, many of which were innocent of involvement. The worst incident occurred in December 1948 when 24 villagers were massacred by Scots Guards.
>
> The tide turned when General Sir Gerald Templer was put in charge of operations in 1952. By then the rubber plantations had developed their own defensive precautions and a scheme to 'resettle' squatter Chinese villages—that were providing food to the guerrillas—was well underway. In time some half a million villagers were forcibly moved from their settlements close to the jungle, housed behind barbed wire and subjected to daily searches. This draconian scheme was gradually tempered; money was spent on decent facilities and the inhabitants were allowed to purchase land around the villages. The nail in the coffin for the CTs was Britain's willing-

ness to move down the road of national independence—undermining the CTs' ideological thrust—and as more and more Malayans (i.e. Chinese, Malays and Indians) participated in various democratic structures, the defeat of the CTs was only a matter of time.

The Emergency ended in 1960 although a dwindling number of guerrillas stayed in the jungle, mounting fewer and fewer attacks, until in the mid 1980s the war came to a complete end.

Independence

In 1952 Sir Gerald Templer arrived in Malaya to oversee the formation of an independent Malaya (see p 92).

In 1961 the prime minister, **Tunku Abdul Rahman**, suggested the idea of an expanded Malaya that would include Singapore, north Borneo (Sabah), Brunei and Sarawak. There was fear of an independent Singapore controlled by communists and while the inclusion of Singapore in Malaya would increase the number of Chinese this would be counterbalanced by the non-Chinese populations of north Borneo and Sarawak.

In 1963 the **Federation of Malaysia** came into being. Despite an earlier agreement between Malaya, Indonesia and the Philippines, the latter two broke off relations with the new Federation. This began a period known as the **Confrontation**, with attacks into Sabah and Sarawak from Kalimantan. The Philippines conducted a more diplomatic campaign for their claim over Sabah and this was eventually settled amicably with the Philippines accepting Sabah as part of Malaysia. A more serious obstacle proved to be the **People's Action Party** (PAP) in Singapore.

On 9 August 1965, Singapore was forced to withdraw from the Federation. The PAP had been challenging the Malayan Alliance for votes and was attempting to capture the Chinese vote. Tensions rose and there were interethnic disorders in Singapore. The PAP spoke of a 'Malaysian Malaya' (with the implication that the Chinese could dominate), rather than a 'Malay Malaysia' which it attributed to the UNMO and the **Alliance Party**. The threat of communal violence was very real and helped convince Tunku Abdul Rahman of the need to expel Singapore.

But Singapore's expulsion did not solve Malaysia's problems. The fact remained that political power lay in the hands of the Malays while economic power was almost entirely in the hands of the Chinese. The government's policies of enforcing Malay as the national language and giving preferential treatment to Malays in employment hit Chinese and Indian communities hard and affected the educational opportunities of Chinese and Indian children. In the 1969 general election in Malaysia the ruling alliance failed to get a two thirds majority. Riots broke out and hundreds of people died in racial violence. The constitution was suspended, all discussion of Malay privileges was banned, and a new coalition was patched together from all the national parties except the DAP (Democratic Action party) which was Chinese dominated. This new coalition, the BN (Barisan National), won a landslide victory in 1974 and under the leadership of Tun Abdul Razak, Malaysia joined the non-aligned movement. But while diplomatic relations were renewed with the USSR and China, a simultaneous flushing out of all communist elements in society was taking place as both Malaysia and Thailand saw themselves as the next countries after Vietnam and Cambodia to fall into the communist bloc. By the 1978 general election the BN was well established in power, the internal communist threat was over and Malaysia's economy was very healthy indeed. In 1981 the party and the country was led by **Dr Mahathir Mohamed**, who still governs. Today, both Malaysia and Singapore are enjoying the fruits of economic prosperity. The citizens of Singapore, for instance, have an income second only to the Japanese. 80 per cent of the population own their own homes. Singapore has the world's busiest port, the third-largest oil refinery, and produces half the world's computer disk drives. No one in Singapore is homeless or desperately poor and there is virtually no crime. In the last decade, Malaysia's economic success has been equally spectacular.

In both countries a price has to be paid: the rights of the individual are to some extent circumscribed. In Singapore laws govern many aspects of Singaporean life. Examples include the Social Development Unit (see below), designed to produce a gene-pool of graduates for the future, and the 1988 law that imposed a fine of US$400 on those who did not flush public toilets after use. A squad of inspectors from the Ministry of the Environment toured toilets looking for non-flushers and photographs of offenders were duly published in the *Straits Times* newspaper.

> The **Social Development Unit** (SDU) is a government matchmaking organisation that was set up to counter the 'problem' of university-educated women failing to marry their intellectual equals. The SDU was set up in 1984 under the direction of the then prime minister Lee Kuan Yew who is reported to have expressed regret over the extension of equal educational opportunities to women. The SDU organises about 600 activities a year—parties, nature walks, sea tours and the like—to encourage women to find suitable graduate husbands. To help non-graduates meet and marry their intellectual equals, a Social Development Section (SDS) was set up in 1993. Both the SDU and the SDS have a nominal membership fee, the real criteria for membership is educational. There is also the Social Promotion Section (for those with GCSE-level grades). In the 1980s the government dropped its 'Breeding for Brilliance' campaign because its eugenic associations proved too strong.

More serious is the fact that a large number of offences carry a mandatory caning and the death penalty is frequently used for those found guilty of certain crimes. There are no juries in Singapore.

Control over Singapore's domestic newspapers is severe. The press is one of the most tightly controlled in the world, depending on an annual licence to print under the Newspaper Printing and Presses Act. Editors are thought by most observers to require official 'approval'; self-censorship is the name of the game.

In both Malaysia and Singapore, one party has managed to monopolise political power since the end of the Second World War. The political rulers of both countries constantly applaud the virtues of 'Asian values' to the detriment of putative decadent Western lifestyles. Obedience, filial piety and discipline are seen as inherently Asian values. Freedom of opinion, juries and some other aspects of Western-style democracy, are seen as alien to the Asian way of doing things.

What underpins the racial harmony and political stability of both Singapore and Malaysia is a sustained period of economic prosperity. Both countries have achieved a growth rate of over 8 per cent a year since the 1970s, with low inflation and full employment. In Malaysia this has resulted in a severe labour shortage and at least half a million illegal workers have entered the country. More than half of these come from Indonesia but thousands more pour in from China, Burma, Thailand, Bangladesh, the Philippines, India and Sri Lanka. In late 1997, when uncertainty over Malaysia's economic success led to massive losses on the country's stock exchange, Prime Minister Mahathir threatened to use the internal security laws to imprison currency speculators.

The ninth general election in Malaysia in 1995 saw another landslide victory for the **National Front Coalition** led by Datuk Seri Mahathir Mohamad. Only the mostly Christian Party Bersatu Sabah (PBS) in Sabah and the Pan Malaysian Islamic Party (known by its Malaysian acronym, PAS) in Kelantan have taken advantage of dissenting voices. Both these states, it has been claimed, continue to suffer from delays in central government investment. Mahathir's current term as Prime Minister will end in 1999 but he could well serve another term. Deputy Prime Minister Anwar Ibrahim appears to represent a more progressive and liberal image and seems destined to take over one day. As a radical student leader, Anwar Ibrahim spent two years in a detention camp.

In Singapore, being an opposition politician carries a heavier price: it is unlikely to be a profitable career move. In September 1997, the leader of the Workers' Party, J.B. Jegyaretnam, suffered yet again at the hands of the judiciary when he was successfully sued by Goh Chok Tong for making what was alleged to be defamatory remark. The International Commission of Jurists charged that the Singapore High Court was compliant to the political wish of the executive to silence their opponents by suing them for statements which would be taken as part of the political process elsewhere in the democratic world.

Forest Politics

Forest politics are a sensitive issue in Malaysia. Western environmentalists and the Malaysian government do not see eye to eye over the question of how best to manage the country's rainforests. Environmentalists feel justified in accusing the Malaysian government of inflicting irreversible ecological damage, wiping out precious flora and fauna and destroying the culture of indigenous forest-dwelling communities like the **Penans** in Sarawak. Malaysia responds by pointing out that it is pure hypocrisy for the West to take the moral high ground when it has destroyed its own forests. Malaysia argues that it is trying to conserve something and in doing so is making a better job of it than the West ever did. While this may be true, the question remains as to whether the long-term price, ecologically and culturally, is ever going to be worth the short-term profits that undoubtedly flow into the country, mostly via Japanese investment companies.

In recent years there have been attempts to reduce the impact of logging through various eco-friendly projects but despite these enough logging is going on to support a timber industry that earns US$3 billion from exports every year. (A single mature hardwood tropical tree is worth upwards of US$7000.) By 2005, it is estimated that all of Malaysia's primary rainforests—apart from the 14 per cent in national parks—will have been logged. The only good news is that in the areas where the eco-friendly selective logging has taken place perhaps some of the logged forests will return close to their original state.

Geography

Malaysia covers an area of 329,749 square kilometres, including the two states of East Malaysia—Sarawak (124,967 square kilometres) and Sabah (72,500 square kilometres). All of Malaysia shares a characteristic geography: a formidable mountainous interior fronted along the coastline by **alluvial plains**. In peninsular Malaysia a **range of mountains** runs down its central spine from the northern border with Thailand for about 500km. The average elevation is about 1000m with occasional peaks over 2000m. There are also a number of **limestone outcrops**, mainly in the Kuala Lumpur and Ipoh area. **Dense jungle** still covers much of the peninsula, especially in the north, and it is on the western side where a fertile plain runs down to the sea that the majority of the population lives. On the eastern side the mountains are closer to the sea and there is a long **400km-stretch of beach** from Kota Bharu in the northeast down to Kuantan.

East Malaysia is made up of a small northern part of the island of Borneo, most of which forms Kalimantan and is a part of Indonesia. The two states of Sarawak and Sabah are divided by the small, independent oil-rich state of Brunei. The same features—low lying coastal plains fronting mountains and jungles—are found in Sabah and Sarawak but there are fewer beaches. The highest mountain in Malaysia is **Mt Kinabalu** (4101m) in Sabah which rises up to dominate the surrounding countryside.

A defining feature of Malaysia's geography, one that has shaped the country's history as well as the land itself, is the presence of mighty rivers that flow down to the sea from the highlands. This is especially true of Sarawak. The **highlands** that form the interior and make up almost 75 per cent of the land are largely forested and form a **primary jungle ecology** that usually proves fascinating and unmissable for visitors to the country.

Less sensational than the jungle and hardly accessible, but nevertheless a characteristic feature of the country, are the **mangrove swamps** which are found along the west coast of peninsular Malaysia and along the Borneo coast.

Singapore is a small island—22.9km from north to south and 41.8km wide—which lies at the southern end of peninsular Malaysia and just 137km north of the equator. It is separated from Malaysia by the narrow Straits of Johor but with a 1.2km causeway linking the two countries (a second causeway is being planned). There are a number of small islands that belong to the republic of Singapore and two of the largest are of most interest to visitors. Sentosa island, to the south of Singapore island and connected by a causeway and cable car as well as a regular boat service, is largely devoted to tourism. Sleepy Pulau Ubin island, at the western end of Singapore, is largely undeveloped but inhabited and can be reached by a regular boat service.

The island's highest point is **Bukit Timah Hill** at 165m and it stands as part of a central granite hilly region which contains most of the island's water supply. The rest of the island is very low lying. In its past Singapore was mostly marsh and mangrove swamp, many of its hills being levelled for building and land reclamation. Reclamation projects have now created a new coastline along the south and west of the island.

The present size of Singapore, including all the islands, is 626 square kilometres but this figure will increase in the near future as further reclamation projects convert areas from the sea to land.

People

The people of Malaysia come from different ethnic backgrounds; not all are Malays. The proportion of Malays in Malaysia is somewhere just below 50 per cent but the ethnic make-up of the country is a highly charged topic, one that visitors should be diplomatic about in their conversations with Malaysians. Chinese make up about 35 per cent, Indians 9 per cent and indigenous tribes somewhere below 10 per cent.

> The **Orang Asli** arrived before the Malays and although their descendants may still be found in Orang Asli villages, practising their own animist religion, they are gradually being absorbed into mainstream of Malay life. There are three main Orang Asli groups: the Negritos, the Senoi and the Proto-Malays. The dwindling number of Negritos, presently around 2000, may be distantly related to tribes from India and the Andaman Islands. They live primarily in the forest interiors of Kelantan and Perak. The Senoi number over 40,000 and are mostly found in Perak, Pahang and Kelantan. Their language is related to the Mon-Khmer tribes of Cambodia and this may provide a clue to their origins. The Proto-Malays, also called the Aboriginal Malays, are thought to hail from Sumatra and other smaller islands at the western end of Indonesia. They live in the southern part of peninsular Malaysia and are most likely to be encountered around Tasek Chini.

Malaysia's **Malays** have an uncertain origin; they probably arrived in the peninsula from Sumatra but their earlier origins remain a matter for speculation. They first settled along the coasts of the peninsula where the climate made growing crops relatively easy. It has been said that this helps to account for the Malays' warm-hearted and friendly disposition. Malays do seem a remarkably placid people who like to take a relaxed approach to life. They are not impressed by people who raise their voices in anger or who display impatience in a crude or hostile manner.

Malays were traditionally farmers and the British colonial government saw little reason to change their way of life. The Chinese were seen to provide commercial skills and Indians were the manual labourers in the plantations. After independence, the Malays, having gained an appropriate degree of political control, wanted to redress an imbalance that left them on the periphery of economic power. The term *bumiputra* (literally 'sons of the soil') came to be associated with a system of positive discrimination designed to improve the economic status of Malays who saw themselves as unfairly disadvantaged. Prime Minister Mahathir's book, The Malay Dilemma, is still well worth reading for its candid insights into the Malay way of thinking on this sensitive subject.

The **Chinese** mostly arrived in the Malay peninsula and Singapore in the early 19C. They usually left behind a life of over-crowded poverty in southern China and were keen to work hard as tin miners and small shopkeepers. Their strong sense of cultural identity was preserved through a network of secret societies and clan associations (*kongsis*) that helped finance the building of elaborate temples. The Chinese continue to preserve their culture and the city of Penang is the most Chinese city in Malaysia. It has a stronger sense of traditional Chinese culture even than in Singapore where the Chinese make up 70 per cent of the population and hold both political and economic power. Both Malaysia and Singapore are acutely aware of the dangers of inter-ethnic tension, and religious and cultural freedom is scrupulously observed.

Clans and Secret Societies

Clan associations were family based organisations that restricted membership to those bearing the same surname. Such associations collected contributions from its members and built clan houses that contained their own temple as well as providing meeting rooms for clan members. A good clan association provided valuable assistance to its members in the form of various social welfare provisions, loans or grants; for example, to help with the expense of a funeral.

Secret societies provided similar social welfare facilities to its members but, unlike clan associations, were profit-making organisations. They usually restricted membership to speakers of a particular dialect group—Hokkien, for example—and for those Chinese immigrants who could not join a clan association, a secret society was the next best way of gaining security in return for a regular contribution. Some secret societies grew rich and powerful and there were conflicts with other societies as they competed for territorial rights. In Penang, especially, clan associations and secret societies overlapped when a strong leader would emerge with links to both types of organisation.

Most Malaysian **Indians** are descended from Tamil labourers who were brought to Malaya in the 19C by the British who wanted cheap labour for their plantations. Even today, the majority of south Indians continue to be among the poorest people in the country; many of the more successful Indians are from north India and came to Malaysia independently.

Religion

The comprehensive spread of Islam across what is now peninsular Malaysia can be traced back to the influence of Muslim traders from India, probably some time in the 13C. It was in 1258 that the Mongols captured Baghdad, hence the consequent closing of the spice route from the east to northern Europe through the Persian Gulf. The new route, through the Red Sea via India, was only open to Muslim ships and this greatly increased the power and influence of Muslim Indian merchants. It is likely that missionaries first came to the peninsula by way of Melaka, gradually extending their religion across the region. How exactly this was accomplished and how long it took is not known. The earliest reference is a 1303 inscription in Terengganu which sets out punishments for those failing to observe the Islamic moral code.

Islamic influence played a decisive role in the 19C in shaping a Malay consciousness in the northern states of Kedah, Kelantan and Terengganu. The religious divide was a barrier to Siamese overlordship and while Siam could control the states militarily and even politically, it could not impose the cultural hegemony, without which its ambitions were limited. This became accentuated after 1803 when the Wahabi sect—fundamentalists of their time—took Mecca and spread their evangelising word.

Virtually every Malay in Malaysia is a Muslim and there are also a number of Indian Muslims. The Muslim day of prayer is Friday and in every town across peninsular Malaysia the mosques will be full to overcrowding and there is usually an extended lunch hour which lasts from around 11.30 to 14.30. In the Islamic east coast states, Friday is the beginning of the weekend and banks and other offices will be closed for the day.

> Muslim fundamentalism is a social and political force to be reckoned with in the northern states on the east coast of peninsular Malaysia. It poses no threat whatsoever to tourists—unless they are looking for a ride in a roller-coaster, bumper car or a Ferris wheel. In late 1995 these were banned in the state of Kelantan because they allowed teenagers to have too much body contact. In another effort to curb moral decadence the state banned public singing and dancing. In 1996 the Kota Bharu Municipal Council ordered all supermarkets to set up separate payment counters for men and women.

Buddhism and Taois

Buddhism and Taoism are the two main religions of the Chinese in Malaysia. These two religions are mixed with a much older form of animism as well as Confucianism. Buddhism takes care of the Chinese person's spiritual life while Taoism pays regard to one's place in the physical world, and Confucianism refers to a social and moral code. Taoism includes a form of ancestor worship as well as the belief in feng shui—the basic harmony of all things on earth. Festivals such as the Hungry Ghost festival in August come from Taoism. At this time, unhappy ancestors are believed to walk the earth and offerings of food and hell money are left out for them. Chinese temples are dedicated to real people who have gained a kind of godhood and who can be appealed to for help in daily life. Many temples are dedicated to such gods as these but will have a side temple dedicated to Buddha. Those Chinese who are devout Buddhists avoid the Taoist elements of Chinese life and seek to attain *bodhisattvahood*, a state of enlightenment from which they can help others. For most Chinese people Buddhism boils down to a vegetarian diet twice each month and a kind of fatalistic belief in accepting what life brings.

Hinduism

The majority of Indians in Malaysia are Hindu. Hinduism has much in common with Buddhism including a belief in reincarnation. The ultimate aim of both religions is to achieve a state of grace and understanding and thus escape the endless cycle of birth and death. For Hindus *karma* is a belief that whatever you do in this life will have its consequences either now or in some future existence.

Dharma is the set of rules which must be obeyed in order to have a good life. Hindu temples always have a whole pantheon of gods in them. All of these are really only mythological manifestations of the one God who is represented in the triumvirate of Brahma, Vishnu and Shiva.

Architecture

Domestic Architecture

The traditional Malay house is built of timber and raised by stilts off the ground. The walls are also wooden or made from bamboo and the roof is constructed from atap, the leaves of the Nipah palm. The off-the-ground construction, the use of wood, windows that can open fully, and the roofing material, all contribute to a home that 'breathes', coping with the humidity and heat through a natural ventilation system that allows air to circulate within and through the rooms of the house.

Regional differences in domestic architecture are largely found in the shape of the roof. The basic design, known as *bumbung panjang* ('long roof'), has grilles at each end to facilitate air circulation, while the overhanging eaves allow heavy rain to sweep down away from the walls. The whole design of a traditional Malay house is highly functional but also very elegant, and some of the best examples are to be found in the northern states. Here, the Islamic influence may be seen in the use of highly ornamented woodwork, usually geometric in its style of patterning. Islam does not allow the representation of the human form in art and this not only accounts for the geometric designs but also for the delicate filigree work in the ornamented woodwork. A Thai influence may also be detected in the more frequent use of panelling and tiled roofs.

The traditional Malay house is rarely built nowadays but there are still plenty of examples of the indigenous form. Part of the pleasure in travelling through rural peninsular Malaysia is the occasional, and usually unexpected, discovery of a fine Malay house in its natural setting. The state of Melaka is particularly rich in this respect and the local style both here and in the neighbouring small state of Negri Sembilan is referred to as 'Minangkabau'.

Minangkabau

In the 16C and 17C people settled in what is now the small state of Negri Sembilan (west of Kuala Lumpur on the coast) from Minangkabau in Sumatra, on the other side of the Straits of Melaka. They were a farming people who used the buffalo in their paddy fields and the term Minangkabau loosely translates as 'the horns of the buffalo'. Their traditional farm houses had broad roofs that swept up from the centre into two peaks that resembles horns, and this style of roof building is now known as Minangkabau architecture. It has been borrowed by a number of Malaysian architects and incorporated into many large public buildings. The Putra World Trade Centre and the National Museum in Kuala Lumpur are two of the best examples.

Colonial architecture

Colonial architecture from the 16C to the 1930s can be found in most towns on the west coast of peninsular Malaysia. Most of it is British, although Melaka is more famous for its timbered high-gabled Dutch architecture. There are few examples of colonial architecture on the east coast, which was never as heavily colonised as the west. In east Malaysia most of the large towns were bombed to the ground during the Second World War but Kuching escaped and most of its glorious colonial buildings are still standing.

Kuala Lumpur has some truly splendid examples of British colonial architecture at its most whimsical and bizarre, largely due to the talents of two architects, A.C. Norman and A.B. Hubbock. Both men had spent time in India and felt that the style of Moghul palaces could be successfully transplanted to Muslim Malaya. In a number of smaller towns—Ipoh, Taiping and Kuala Kangsar (all in the state of Perak)—one may appreciate just how boldly and playfully the British set about making their visual mark on townscapes. Government offices, railway stations and police stations were often decked out with pediments and stately colonnades and other European architectural features. Neo-Palladianism may have found an unlikely and unique tropical context in Southeast Asia but the result is surprisingly pleasing. Functional features such as louvred windows, fans and verandahs were cleverly incorporated into the overall design to deal with the heat and humidity.

Penang is particularly rich in eclectic colonial architecture, some of it dating back to the closing decade of the 18C but most of it belonging to the 19C and early 20C. In most cases the architects were British, but often they were employed by wealthy Chinese merchants and the result is a unique combination of European symmetry as expressed in classical features such as pillars and pediments alongside a practical concern for functional features, such as large windows and doors to facilitate the circulation of air. The end result is often a Georgian-style home decorated in bright pastel colours to reflect the heat with louvred windows and saloon doors.

Flora and Fauna

The Malaysian jungle is both very old, about 120 million years, and very rich. There are over 200 mammal species, some 150,000 types of plant, 2500 different types of tree (a single acre of primary rainforest will have between 40 and 60 separate species), over 500 bird species and countless thousands upon thousands of different types of insect. **Alfred Russel Wallace** (1823–1913), who independently of Darwin propounded a theory of evolution by natural selection, was inspired to study nature by the diversity of life in Borneo.

Nowadays, the primary rainforests are being systematically logged; within a decade only the national parks will still have areas of primary rainforest. After logging, it does not take many years for secondary forest to fill the felled space but inevitably there is a serious decline in the flora and fauna. Exotic wonders of the jungle like an owl (*Glaucidium borneense*), the size of an adult's thumb or a small hawk (*Microhierax*), reputed to lay an egg almost the same size as itself, will soon be gone for ever.

Most of Malaysia's **larger mammals** are rarely seen by visitors and footprints of the Asian elephant are the most one can hope for. Even more elusive are the tiger, clouded leopard and the four species of wild cat that roam about in remote regions of the interior. It is possible, however, to catch glimpses of some other fascinating mammals like the tapir, the Malayan sun bear, the wild pig and the bearded pig, and the two species of deer on the peninsula: the *sambar* and the *kijang* (barking deer).

The tapir

The shy, harmless and nocturnal tapir, with it trunk-like snout, is one of Malaysia's strangest mammals. It has no form of defence other than its black coat broken by a central white area that covers more than half of its body. In the jungle night only this white strip appears—the black legs, head and shoulders camouflaged by the dark—thus fooling potential predators by its unlikely animal form. More germane to its survival, however, is the fact that man has left it alone. Unexplained taboos have protected it from indigenous hunters and it has never appealed to the trophy-hunting tourist.

Three species live in South America but the Malay tapir, *Tapirus bairdi*, is the only species to be found elsewhere. The head and body may reach a length of 1.95m and its height is about 1m.

With patience the tapir can be seen in **Taman Negara** (National Park), an essential destination for anyone visiting peninsular Malaysia with an interest in nature. The boat journey there, passing huge monitor lizards with dinosauric eyes and flashes of silky streaks of blue and orange from fast-disappearing kingfishers disturbed by the noise of the outboard engine, provides a suitable introduction to the attractions of the park. If a night spent in the jungle there, interrupted by pterodactyl croaks from the immense darkness all around, whets your appetite, then the place to head for is Sarawak and Sabah in East Malaysia.

In peninsular Malaysia there are five types of **monkey** to be found: the long-tailed macaque, pig-tailed macaque and three species of leaf monkey. In Sarawak and Sabah there are orang-utans (see pp 256, 285) and proboscis monkeys (see pp 261, 282). Two species of gibbon are more commonly heard than seen in the rainforest: the white-handed and the dark-handed gibbon.

Birds are a major attraction in Malaysia; on the peninsula the two best places to visit are the **Kuala Selangor Nature Park** near Kuala Lumpur, where migratory birds winter between September and May, and Taman Negara. In Taman Negara, as well as in the jungles of Sarawak and Sabah, there are beautiful kingfishers to be seen as well as the superb hornbills (see p 261, 282). In Singapore's **Bukit Timah Nature Reserve** there is a rich tropical birdlife, including the easily identified racquet-tailed drongos that fly overhead trailing their long tails. Other common birds to be seen in the region include the brahminy kite, bee-eaters, woodpeckers, bulbuls, orioles, the common tailorbird, flycatchers, myna birds, sunbirds and pittas.

Reptiles. Snakes come in 16 poisonous types in Malaysia, excluding the sea-snakes which are also poisonous; and there are two species of python: the reticulated python (*Python reticulatus*) and the shorter *Python curtus*.

In 1995 a man was crushed to death and partially swallowed by a giant 7m reticulated python in the state of Johor. The victim had left his home for a route through a forest, and when his brother went looking for him two hours later he came across the snake in the process of trying to swallow its victim. This bizarre incident was the first known case of its kind in Malaysia because the python is normally a meek creature. It is thought that the man stumbled upon the snake in the dark, treading on its body and sending it into a fury. It was estimated to be about 40 years old. Pythons can live to be a hundred and grow to over 10m in length.

The cobras, including the king cobra (*Naja hannah*) and pit-vipers, are the most common poisonous snakes.

Other reptiles include the leatherback turtle (see p 195), and hawksbill turtle (see p 261) and both the estuarine crocodile (*Crocoilus porosus*) and the freshwater crocodile (*Tomistoma schlegeli*). Lizards come in a variety of sizes and the small house version, known as the gecko (*Calotes cristatellus*), is commonly seen waiting patiently on a wall for a fly to move within its killing field. The largest of all lizards in Malaysia is the monitor lizard (*Varanus salvator*) which can grow to well over 2m in length and is often seen basking on the banks of a river.

There are at least a million known species of **insect** in the world and it is a fair bet that there are probably another million species waiting to be identified in Malaysia. The common ones that will be seen in the jungle are the giant ant (*Camponotus gigas*), the weaver ant (*Oecophylla smaragdina*), termites, stick insects, leaf insects and fireflies. Cicadas will certainly be heard, if not seen.

Malaysia's **flora** is equally as exciting and diverse as its fauna. Besides the areas of rainforest with their huge dipterocarp trees, lianas, epiphytes and shade tolerant undergrowth are areas of mangrove swamp where plants have developed salt tolerance and aerial roots. In mountainous regions a montane forest can be seen with dwarfed and stunted trees surviving alongside acid tolerant plants such as azaleas and the excellent carnivore pitcher plants. In areas of secondary growth where plant life is reclaiming logged areas the predominant plants are rattans and elephant grass, the typical jungle of the movies which has to be cut away with a parang, a long blade.

Language and Literature

Singapore has four national languages, English, Malay, Mandarin and Tamil, which is why the banknotes look so crowded. In schools the teaching medium is English while each ethnic group learns their 'own' language as well as Mandarin. Mandarin is an introduced language which no-one learns as their mother tongue: most Chinese start off by learning Hokkien or Teochew or Cantonese. The language learned by ethnic Indians in school is Tamil which, while being the language of the majority of Singaporean Indians, is not spoken by people from north India. Consequently, Singaporeans from north Indian families lose the opportunity to learn their mother tongue in school and have to consider taking private lessons instead. Thirty years ago the lingua franca in Singapore was Bazaar Malay, a kind of low Malay language. Now it is English.

In addition, there is a wonderful language called Singlish which is a glorious mix of all the tongues spoken in Singapore. Singlish keeps English grammar forms but introduces Malay and Hokkien vocabulary, so that going to lunch is *makanan ing*—a mixture of the Malay word for food and the English suffix -ing! Tenses and questions tend to disappear to be replaced by a series of suffixes which are pure innovation. *Lah* means a whole variety of things depending on how you say it, while *haw* means you disagree with or disapprove of what the other person says. The most famous piece of vocabulary from this new hybrid language is *kia su* which was once Hokkien but has now become a Singlish adjective meaning pushy, greedy and not wanting to be left out of anything that is going on. If you can do it, listen surreptitiously to some young Singaporeans talking—it's wonderful.

The situation is just as complex in **Malaysia**. The national language is Bahasa Malaysia, which is very close to the language spoken in Indonesia. It has two forms, a High Malay, used for formal occasions and when speaking to an important person and a low form, used within the family and in casual encounters. Malay is the language of instruction in schools, having replaced English after independence. The result is quite curious—older people, Indians and Chinese speak good English, while younger Malays have little or no English. In the last couple of years English has been reintroduced in schools as a second language. Indians and Chinese find English essential if they want to pursue a tertiary education, which they usually do abroad or in Singapore. As new words have become necessary they have been adopted from English, so, for example, a dress shop is called a *fesyen* (taken from fashion) shop. Many Malay words, but by no means all, are doubled to form a plural.

Of course there are also all the Chinese dialects still surviving within communities in Malaysia as well as Tamil and all the languages of Borneo.

The origins of **Malay literature** date back to the 15C. The most well-known early literary text is the 15C or 16C *Sejara Melayu* or *Malay Annals*, a kind of mythological history. In the 19C a writer called Munshi Abdullah, whose name you will recognise from street names, wrote the first modern novels which were not based on traditional legends or myths. His most well-known work is his autobiography, *Hikayat Abdullah*. In the early 20C a new school of novelists emerged which included Ahmad bin Mohammed. Today Malay literature flourishes. Writers to look out for are Lloyd Fernando whose novel *Scorpion Orchid* presents the multi-racial nature of Malaysian society in a realistic form, Lee Kok Liang who writes short stories, and K.S. Maniam whose novel *Mussafir* is about the problems of being both a Muslim and a Malay.

In **Singapore**, **literature** was dominated for a long time by English writers until Catherine Lim began to write, still in English but about Chinese culture. Philip Jeyaratnam is an excellent novelist, describing the difficulties of urban Singapore life. Lim Thean Soon is another good writer, while *A Candle or the Sun* by Gopal Baratham is about a group of Christians who fall foul of the government, mirroring the real events of the late 1980s.

Music and Dance

I suspect that traditional music and dance are to a great extent part of the tourist industry in 1990s Malaysia. Performances can be seen in the better cultural shows, especially those in the northeast of peninsular Malaysia. In

Kuala Lumpur the most authentic part of the cultural show will probably be a performance of *wayang kulit*—the shadow puppet theatre inherited from Indonesia. The puppet master sits with the orchestra of drums, violins, gongs and xylophone and narrates his story while manipulating the puppets behind a lit screen. The language is High Malay and he puts a great deal of melodrama into his stories of good and evil taken from the Indian epics. More common in cultural shows will be the various Kelantese court dances; look out for *silat*, a stylised martial art form, and *kuda kepang*, which is danced by men wearing wooden hobby horses.

During Chinese festivals, especially the Hungry Ghost festival in August, street theatres are set up and Chinese music and dance performed. The songs are usually sung in Hokkien and the singers, who wear highly stylised clothes and makeup, are accompanied by a Chinese orchestra.

Indian dance is also highly prized by its community, and in both Singapore and Kuala Lumpur there are schools of music and dance teaching the Bharata Natyam, the traditional dance forms which depend much on the careful movement of hands and eyes. Traditional instruments such as the *tabla* (a pair of small drums), *talam* (cymbals) and *vina* (single-stringed instrument) are also taught. In Singapore look out for cultural shows put on by *Annalakshmi*, an Indian restaurant with an associated dance school in the Excelsior shopping centre.

More modern music is loud and incomprehensible, as you will discover when you visit your first shopping centre in Malaysia. Chinese people tend to like Cantopop, a kind of Asian country and western while Malays go for heavy metal and a local variant sung by law in Bahasa Malaysia. Even newer is a Malay version of rap music, which has in some cases been banned because of the nature of the lyrics.

Further Reading

Literature

In 1887 **Joseph Conrad** made four round-trips between Singapore and Borneo's east coast as chief mate and these journeys gave him ideas and material for one short story, 'The End of the Tether' and four early novels: *Almayer's Folly, An Outcast of the Islands, Lord Jim* and *The Rescue*. Singapore is the 'great Eastern port' of Joseph Conrad's *Lord Jim, The Shadow-Line* and his short story 'The End of the Tether'; the descriptions in these stories are accurate portrayals of the area around the Padang and St Andrew's Cathedral. The setting for the second part of *Lord Jim* is based on Conrad's visits to the Berau river in Borneo, and the novel's account of Malay court life is partly based on Alfred Russel Wallace's *The Malay Archipelago* (1894), one of Conrad's favourite books and now available in the Oxford in Asia paperback series (Oxford University Press, 1989).

Somerset Maugham can be relied on for unsentimental observations of colonial Malaya and Singapore. In a British club in Singapore in 1960 he observed, 'I am no longer surprised that there is such a scarcity of domestic servants back home'. His short stories dealing with Southeast Asia are in his *Collected Short Stories Volume 3* (Heinemann, London, 1990) and various other editions by different publishers. His tales lay bare the passions stifled by the tedious routine and repressive decorum of British colonial life. 'The Letter' which has been filmed a number of times: the 1940 version starring Bette Davis is probably the best although the remake of 1947 with Ann Sheridan, renamed *The Unfaithful*, is also worth watching. Another Maugham short story is 'Upstation'—the best of them all—set in Borneo, it charts the deteriorating relationship between a government officer and his subordinate. In another story, 'Footprints in the Jungle'—based on a true story of a wife and her lover who plot the murder of the husband—Melaka is thinly disguised as Tanah Merah. In 'Neil MacAdam' it is equally obvious that Kuching is the town of Kuala Solar in the story.

King Rat by **James Clavell** (Hodder & Stoughton, London, 1962), also made into a film, is an intelligent and thoughtful novel about life in Singapore's Changi prison under the Japanese. The author was himself a prisoner in Changi.

Anthony Burgess wrote a trilogy of novels set in Malaya, *The Long Day Wanes* (Heinemann, London, 1956), written in the 1950s when Burgess was an education officer in the Colonial Service. He knew Malaya well, and there is no better account of that period in the country's history: the guerrilla war with the communists; the varied ethnic origin of the people; and the attitudes of the colonialists whose time to leave was rapidly approaching.

Paul Theroux was once a teacher in Singapore and it was here that he wrote his first novel. *Saint Jack* (Penguin, 1976) is set in Singapore while *The Consul's File* (Penguin, 1979) is a collection of short stories set in a small town in Malaysia. He also wrote a scathing essay on Singapore which is reprinted in his collection of autobiographical pieces, *Sunrise with Seamonsters* (Penguin, 1986).

The most interesting Singaporean novelist is **Philip Jeyaratnam**, the son of the most famous opposition politician in Singapore. Philip Jeyaratnam's stories, however, have their own artistic merit and are not narrowly political. *Abraham's Promise*, *Raffles Place* and a collection of short stories, *First Loves*, are recommended. They are all available in bookshops in Singapore.

History

General history. *The History of Malaysia*, Barbara Watson Andaya and Leonard Andaya (Macmillan) and *A History of Malaysia*, C. Mary Turnbull (Oxford University Press, 1989).

Colonial era. *Taming the Jungle*, Pat Barr (London, 1977) is a readable account of early British rule in Malaya—the 'Residency' system as it was then known—focusing on the lives of leading personalities like Frank Swettenham and Hugh Low. *Old Singapore*, Maya Jayapal (Oxford University Press, 1992), has a host of delightful colour plates and old photographs that evoke colonial Singapore more effectively than the text.

Second World War. *The Jungle is Neutral*, Spencer Chapman (Mayflower/Time-Life), is out of print but well worth trying to track down for its true tale of survival in the Malay jungle. *A Fearful Freedom*, Robert Hammond (Secker & Warburg, London, 1984), is the extraordinary story of Jim Wright's survival in the jungle for over three years after narrowly escaping capture by the Japanese in 1942 in southern Johor. Over 30 years passed before Jim Wright told the story of his appalling experiences. His strained but emotional relations with the Chinese communists who saved his life provide the focus of this fascinating glimpse into wartime Malaya. *The Price of Peace*, edited by Foong Choon Hon (Asiapac Books, Singapore, 1997), brings together various true accounts of the Japanese occupation of Singapore. *Women Beyond the Wire*, Lavinia Warner and John Sandilands (Arrow Books, London, 1997), is in a similar vein. *Singapore 1941–1942: The Japanese Version of the Malayan Campaign of World War II*, Masanobu Tsuji (Oxford University Press, 1988), offers a viewpoint on the war from the losing side. So, too, does *Syonan—My Story* by M. Shinozaki (Singapore, Times Books).

End of empire. In *End of Empire*, Brian Lapping (Granada, 1985), the book of a television series, Malaya forms one of the ten chapters charting the decline and fall of the British Empire. In just over 40 pages, with photographs, there is a very accessible account of Malaya's history. For a far lengthier treatment of the Emergency, 547 pages, the authoritative work is *The Communist Insurrection in Malaya, 1948–1960*, Anthony Short (Frederick Muller, 1975). Engaging, first-hand accounts of the war against the Chinese guerrillas by a Briton are to be found in *The Communist Menace in Malaya*, Harry Miller (Harrap, 1954), and *Jungle War in Malaya: the campaign against Communism 1948–1960* (Barker, 1972). *Rogue Trader*, Nick Leeson (Warner Books, London, 1996), delivers the story of the fall of the Barings financial world by the man who was responsible for the astonishing deed.

Contemporary politics. Francis Seow's *To Catch a Tiger* (Yale University Southeast Asian Studies, 1994) tells the inside story of a man who questioned the political status quo in Singapore. *No Man is an Island*, James Minchin (Allen & Unwin, North Sydney, 1986), is turgid reading despite its clever title but it does include informative accounts of how Lee Kuan Yew has ruled Singapore. The most readable and incisive book on Lee is still T.J.S. George's *Lee Kuan Yew* (London, 1973), once banned in Singapore. A more recent study is *Singapore: The pregnable fortress: A study in deception, discord and desertion* by Peter Elphick (Hodder & Stoughton, 1994). *Lee Kuan Yew*, Han Fook Kuang, Warren Fernandez and Sumiko Tan (Times Editions, Singapore, 1998) is a sycophantic account but with half the book devoted to verbatim speeches by Lee it provides a revealing, honest and up-to-date portrayal of his personal and political philosophy.

The Malay Dilemma, by Mahathir Mohamad, prime minister of Malaysia, was written in 1970 but is still well worth reading for its frank account of how the Malays came to be disadvantaged in their own country and the case for positive discrimination on their behalf. It is the sort of book you could never imagine your own prime minister or president writing.

Culture

A World Within, Tom Harrisson (Oxford University Press, 1984), provides a fascinating account of the Kelabits of Sarawak as well as being a true-life adventure story of organising resistance to the Japanese from his base in the Kelabit Highlands towards the end of the Second World War. *The Pagan Tribes of Borneo* (Oxford University Press, 1993), Charles Hose and William McDoughall, was first published in 1912 and remains a classic of Borneo ethnography. Two coffee table books, with A4 colour photography, are *The Ibans of Borneo*, D. Freeman, and *Penan*, A. & N. Rain. Both these books are best obtained in the huge MPH bookshop in Singapore. The *Peoples of Borneo*, Victor T. King (Blackwell, Oxford,

1993), is an academic but thoroughly accessible account of the lifestyles of the different ethnic groups.

Singapore Sketchbook, paintings by Graham Byfield and text by Gretchen Liu (Archipelago Press, Singapore, 1995), is full of delightful watercolours focusing on the near-extinct architectural legacy of old Singapore.

The Legacy of the Malay Letter, Annabel Teh Gallop (British Library, London, 1995), is a handsome volume whose central theme is that the finest Malay letters demonstrate in their calligraphy and decoration all that is best about Malay aesthetics.

For a humorous commentary on contemporary Malaysian culture, any of the collections of cartoons by **Lat** are recommended. Some of the best collections are *The Kampong Boy, Town Boy* and *Kampong Boy: Yesterday and Today* (Berita Publications, Kuala Lumpur). They are all readily available in bookshops in Kuala Lumpur and Penang.

The **Malay language** is a relatively easy language to learn. A very helpful guide is the Malay title in the *Colloquial* series from Routledge (London and New York, 1986), which includes cassettes or a CD.

Travel

The most interesting 19C travelogue covering peninsular Malaysia is Isabella Bird's *The Golden Chersonese: The Malayan Travels of a Victorian Lady* (Oxford University Press, 1980). Her writing reveals that she was a keen observer of the natural and colonial world she encountered. *My Life in Sarawak*, Margaret Brooke (Oxford University Press, 1986), is an equally engaging account by the wife of Sarawak's raja, Charles Brooke.

More recently, a number of writers have tried their hand at capturing the appeal of Borneo. James Barclay's *A Stroll Through Borneo* (Hodder & Stoughton, London, 1980) tells the tale of a five month trek in Sarawak and Kalimantan.

Into the Heart of Borneo, Redmond O'Hanlon (Penguin/Vintage, London, 1984), recounts the author's journey with the poet James Fenton up the Baleh river from Kapit to the Tiban mountains straddling the Sarawak/Kalimantan border. The dry humour is usually very engaging ('Oh yes', they're advised, 'take lots of postcards of the Queen, preferably on horseback, and showing all four legs, because they think she's all of a piece'), and there are plenty of informative anecdotes about the history and ecology of Sarawak; occasionally, however, insight and accuracy are sacrificed for flippancy and condescension.

Nature

Birds. *A Field Guide to the Birds of Borneo, Sumatra, Java & Bali*, by J. MacKinnon and K. Phillips (Oxford) is a useful and affordable guide book. So, too, is *A Field Guide to the Birds of South-East Asia* by B. King, M. Woodcock and M. Dickinson (Collins, London, 1976). Best of all though is the wonderful *The Birds of Borneo* by Bertram E. Smythies; a third edition was published in 1981 by the Sabah Society (PO Box 547, Kota Kinabalu, Sabah, Malaysia) and the Malayan Nature Society (PO Box 750, Kuala Lumpur, Malaysia).

Fruits. A very useful book to help identify the exotic fruits seen in the indoor and outdoor markets across Malaysia and Singapore is *Malaysian Fruits in Colour, Chin Hoong Fong and Yong Hoi-Sen* (Tropical Press, 29 Jalan Riang, 59100, Kuala Lumpur, Malaysia).

Wildlife. A volume in the Insight Guides series, *Southeast Wildlife Asia* edited by Hans-Ulrich Bernard *et al.* (Apa Publications, Singapore, 1994), has excellent colour photographs and a textual commentary on most of Malaysia's national parks and their associated flora and fauna. *Orang-Utan*, Barbara Harrison, (Oxford University Press, 1987) is a readable study.

Glossary

Baba and nonya: the men (*baba*) and women (*nonya*) of the Straits Chinese that arose as a result of intermarriage between different ethnic groups

Batu: the Malay word for rock, so, for example, Batu Ferringhi (the rock of the foreigner) in Penang

Bomoh: Malay traditional medicine man

Bugis: seafaring people who came to the Malay peninsula in the 15C, originally from Sulawesi (Celebes)

Bukit: the Malay word for hill; for example, Bukit Timah in Singapore

Bumiputra: literally 'sons of the soil', referring to Malays as the indigenous Malaysians

Casuarina: a tree native to Southeast Asia, distinguished by its leaves on slender branches, which resemble gigantic horsetails

Dato/Datuk: (Malay) the terms (literally 'grandfather') are general titles of distinction for males

Dyaks: a non-Muslim indigenous people of Borneo who mostly live along the banks of the larger rivers

Federated Malay States (FMS): the states of Perak, Selangor, Negri Sembilan and Pahang which were governed by a British Resident

Godown: a warehouse, usually by the riverside, in parts of Southeast Asia

Gopuram: (Malay) the richly decorated exterior façade of a Hindu temple

Gua: (Malay) cave

Gunung: (Malay) mountain

Haji: an honorific title, Arabic in origin, indicating one who has made the *haj* (pilgrimage) to Mecca

Halal: a general term used to describe food that has been prepared in accordance with Islamic beliefs

Hari Raya: the Muslim festival that marks the end of Ramadan

Istana: a word, probably Arabic in origin, that has entered the Malay language meaning palace. Sometimes it is also written as *astana*

Kampung: a Malay village (also spelt as kampong)

Kapitan China: a title, Portuguese in origin, indicating the head of a Chinese community

Kedai: the Malay word for shop

Kota: the Malay word for fort; for example, Kota Bharu

Kris: Malay wavy-bladed dagger

Kuala: the Malay word for river mouth; for example, Kuala Terengganu

Jalan: (Malay) road

Masjid: (Malay) mosque

Merdeka: the Malay word for freedom, and used to signify national independence

Minangkabau: a society that originated in Sumatra and settled along the west coast of peninsular Malaysia, mainly in the state of Negri Sembilan. Minangkabau buildings are characterised by a long sweeping roof and this feature was incorporated into Malay architecture

Orang Asli: the aboriginal tribes who are regarded as the earliest known inhabitants of the peninsula. *Orang* is the Malay word for people, *asli* means original

Padang: the Malay word for open land (originally the parade ground or playing field) now meaning any open grassy area but usually referring to the town square

Pantai: (Malay) beach

Pasar malam: (Malay) an open-air night market

Pulau: the Malay word for island; for example, Pulau Tioman

Ramadan: the Islamic month of fasting, usually occurring some time between late January and early April

Resident: the senior British administrator in the Federated Malay States

Ronggeng: a Malay dance that originated in Melaka

Roti: bread

Roti canai: flaky Indian bread that is usually eaten as a light meal with a curry sauce

Sampan: a small boat, derived from the Chinese san-pan (three boards)

Sarong: the Malay word for 'covering', meaning the wraparound skirt worn by both sexes

Selamat: the Arabic word for peace and used in Malay to mean greetings or welcome

Songkok: a fez-type cap, usually black in colour, worn by Malay men

Stengah: a corruption of the Malay sa'tenagh (one half) that became the familiar name for a half measure of whisky by the expatriate community during the colonial period

Straits Settlements: the colonial territories of Penang Island, Province Wellesley, Melaka and Singapore

Sungei (also spelt **sungai**): the Malay word for river

Tanjung: headland

Teluk: bay or fiord

Tuak: rice wine

Ulu: the Malay word for the headwaters of a river

Unfederated Malay States (UMS): the states of Kelantan, Terrenganu, Kedah, Perlis and Johor

Wayang: the Malay word for a stage drama. Wayang kulit is a shadow play using puppets

Yang di-pertuan agong: Malaysia's royal head of state

MALAYSIA

Kuala Lumpur

Kuala Lumpur, the capital of Malaysia and the country's largest city, is under-going rapid transformation. A city that not much more than a decade ago was still regarded as a rather sleepy capital now boasts the two tallest buildings in the world. The twin **Petronas Towers**—constructed at the rate of one floor every four days—peak at 450m (1475ft), which is 6.5m (21ft) higher than the Sears Tower in Chicago. (However, Malaysia may keep the world record for only a short while longer if the proposed 457m (1500ft) Chongging Tower in China is completed.) Petronas Towers is built of stainless steel clad in glass, with a linking bridge at the 44th floor. Inside, the floor plans are based on a motif of inter-linking squares and circles—representing harmony and strength—while the interiors are dressed in Malaysian timber and local stone. Designed by Cesar Pelli, the Argentine-born architect based in New York, the towers are seen as a fitting symbolic finale to an economic miracle that has transformed the cityscape of the capital. Malaysia's modernity is also being expressed by its plans to build the Multimedia Super Corridor, a 15km by 50km zone between the capital and the airport that will accommodate a newly planned city of Cyberjaya, the world's first IT (information technology) city designed from the ground up.

The downside to all this is that Kuala Lumpur has also inherited the woes of traffic and noise pollution. Six-lane highways and flyovers criss-cross the city with scant regard for the needs of pedestrians. Yet they cannot keep pace with the increasing number of made-in-Malaysia **Proton cars** that crawl bumper-to-bumper through the smaller streets of what was once one of Asia's sleepiest capitals. Fortunately, with a total population of only about two million, Kuala Lumpur's urban chaos is minuscule compared to Hong Kong or Bangkok. It is still possible to enjoy time here without feeling you are being slowly poisoned by exhaust fumes, and the city is a safe and friendly place to wander around.

Despite the concrete and glass structures that have turned one triangle of the city into a mini-Manhattan, Kuala Lumpur has not followed Singapore and cleansed itself to the point of sterility. There is life on the streets and plenty to see and explore. The old **colonial part** of the city has been wonderfully preserved. At night **Chinatown** is alive with colour and character. There are plenty of excellent hotels and restaurants to suit all budgets (see p 71) and a number of excursions use the city as a base. A stay of two or three days is the minimum required; five would enable the visitor to see and enjoy all that is available. A good place to begin might be a visit to the KL Tower (☎ 03-208 5448) where the RM8 entrance fee allows one to view the city landscape from near the top of this 421m (1381ft) structure.

History

Not many capital cities can trace their origin to an exact date but Kuala Lumpur was born in 1857 when a hardy but ultimately doomed group of Chinese tin-miners reached the confluence of the Klang and Gombak rivers. (See p 86, the History section to Excursions West below for more background information.) Their boats could not be poled any further upriver, so they left them and moved inland on foot, cutting their way through the jungle in the search for deposits of tin. Much wealth had already been generated by tin-mining in the state of Perak to the north. So though only 17 of the original party of 87 miners were alive after a month many more followed in their wake. Valuable deposits of tin were found just 6km from the confluence of the rivers and so the first wooden shacks were erected where boats could drop off the necessary supplies of food and equipment. Trading stores followed and Kuala Lumpur (Malay for 'muddy confluence') was born.

As tin-mining flourished so too did the Chinese secret societies that sought to control the profits. Groups of miners from different regions of China sought protection under their traditional secret societies while their bosses fought one another like gangsters. **Yap Ah Loy**, a gangster turned merchant, rose to prominence, becoming Kapitan (headman) of the lawless settlement until his death in 1885.

In 1880, **Frank Swettenham**, the British Resident of Selangor, made Kuala Lumpur the capital of Selangor state. By 1886, when a railway connected the city with the sea at Klang, Kuala Lumpur had become the capital of the Federated Malay States. By this time most of the original wooden dwellings had either been pulled down, or had been destroyed in a fire in 1881. The new shops and houses were built from brick and the population increased rapidly. People from all classes poured into the city: Chinese merchants with capital to invest; Chinese peasants with nothing but their labour to sell; Malay farmers; colonial civil servants and entrepreneurs; and, in the early years of the new century, tens of thousands of Tamils from southern India.

In the four decades between 1880 and 1920, nearly all the buildings that are of historical interest to today's visitor were built: the railway station, the colonial government buildings, the grandiose dwellings of the bourgeoisie along Jalan Ampang, and the temples that offered spiritual succour to the waves of dispossessed immigrants from China and India. For four decades after 1920, little of architectural or historical interest was built. Another burst of economic growth was needed to fuel the contemporary wave of modern Islamic-influenced skyscraper architecture, characterised by onion dome shaped outlines and lattice walls.

During the first half of the 20C, Kuala Lumpur played second fiddle to Singapore in terms of social sophistication and political prestige. The source of Malaysia's economic wealth—the tin mines and rubber plantations—was spread out across the country. Kuala Lumpur was always more of an administrative capital than a cultural and political centre. This partly explains why, when the Japanese invaded in December 1941, the city's British rulers did not believe that it was essential to defend it to the last. Japan's decisive victory at Slim River to the north of the capital on 7

January, sealed the fate of Kuala Lumpur. Four days later, the capital was captured.

It could be argued that both Malaya and Singapore were lost to the Japanese on 6 December 1941. On that fateful day, Lt.-Gen. Arthur E. Percival (the General Officer Commanding Malaya) met Lt.-Gen. Sir Lewis Heath (commanding the 3rd Indian Corps) to discuss the news that suggested the Japanese invasion had begun. That morning an Australian pilot, J.C. Ramshaw, had spotted a Japanese flotilla of cruisers, destroyers and troop-carrying ships heading west from southern Vietnam. On hearing this, Percival issued the codeword 'Raffles', signifying the first stage of an agreed plan to deal with a Japanese invasion. The second stage, codenamed 'Matador', had been worked out months earlier and could have stopped the Japanese at a decisively early stage of their campaign. The Matador plan called for troops to cross the northern border with Siam (Thailand) and wait for the Japanese on the beaches of Singora (now Songkhla) and Pattani— the two places where the plan had (accurately) predicted the invaders would arrive. But the Matador codeword was never issued because Percival and Air Chief Marshal Sir Robert Brooke-Popham, the Commander-in-Chief Far East, decided the time was not right. It was the wrong decision.

Under Japanese occupation the three main races in Malaya were treated very differently. The Chinese were persecuted and murdered in large numbers and the Indians were sent to labour camps in Burma and else-where. The Malays, however, were spared most of the customary brutality and inveigled into complaisance—collusion at worst—with a promise of independent control over their country.

In September 1945 the British returned. However, the Malays were deter-mined to achieve independence and after gaining this in 1957 attention began to be focused on the fact that economic power remained largely with Chinese owned companies. The word *bumiputra* (meaning 'sons of the soil') was coined in the context of government-decreed positive discrimination on behalf of Malays. In 1969 this led to race riots in Kuala Lumpur which left a number of fatalities. The fabric of a multi-racial Malaysia seemed to be in danger of implosion, but it was saved by a gradual economic awakening that promised dividends to all three cultural groups. Kuala Lumpur continues to be the standard bearer for the country's new prosperity.

Kuala Lumpur is not an easy city to orientate oneself in, partly because the older, colonial part of the city is geographically distinct from the main accommodation and shopping areas. The distances between different parts of the city are often too great to walk, but it is easy to fall back on inexpensive taxi rides and the new light railway system (STAR-LRT) is a great help.

The prestigious accommodation and shopping area is to the east of the city, bordered by Jalan Ampang to the north, Jalan Imbi to the south and linked by Jalan Sultan Ismail (The Golden Mile), Jalan Raja Chulan and Jalan Bukit Bintang. It is sometimes referred to as The Golden Triangle because part of the area forms a triangular shape on a map.

Merdeka Square marks the western edge of the city centre and within walking distance are most of the important historical buildings. The railway station is due south of the square and Chinatown to the southeast. Jalan Tun Perak is a main road to the east of the square. It leads eastwards to the Puduraya bus and taxi station. Jalan Tuanku Abdul Rahman heads north from the square and has cheaper accommodation and shops.

■ Practical information

Getting to and from Kuala Lumpur
By air. Subang International Airport is 30km west of the city centre. There is a taxi coupon system in operation at the airport. Purchase a coupon for your destination at the taxi counter, which is on your right as you leave the departure hall, and present this to the taxi driver. It costs just under RM30 to the city centre. There is also a bus service—No. 47—that operates every half hour between 06.00 and 21.00 and leaves from outside the departure hall. Tickets cost RM2 and are purchased on the bus. In town, the terminal for this bus is on Jalan Sultan Mohammed, opposite the Klang bus station.

For flight enquiries call ☎ 03-7461833 (Terminal 1, international flights), ☎ 03-7472168 (Terminal 2, Singapore flights) or ☎ 03-7472169 (Terminal 3, domestic flights).

As well as international connections (see p 17) there are domestic flights (single fares given) to Alor Setar (RM113), Ipoh (RM66), Johor Bahru (RM104), Kota Bharu (RM104), Kota Kinabalu (RM437), Kuala Terengganu (RM104), Kuantan (RM74), Kuching (RM262), Langkawi (RM135), Miri (RM422), Penang (RM104) and Sibu (RM320).

Airlines

Aeroflot: Ground Floor, Wisma Tong Ah, 1 Jalan Tun Perak (☎ 03-2613231)

Air India: Angkasa Raya Building, Jalan Ampang (☎ 03-2420166)

American Airlines: Angkasa Raya Building, 123 Jalan Ampang (☎ 03-2480644)

British Airways: Wisma Merlin, Jalan Sultan Ismail (☎ 03-2426177)

Cathay Pacific: UBN Tower, Jalan P. Ramlee (☎ 03-2383377)

China Airlines: Floor 3, Amoda Building, 22 Jalan Imbi (☎ 03-2422383)

Delta Airlines: UBN Tower, Jalan P. Ramlee (☎ 03-2324700)

Garuda Airlines: Floor 1, Angkasa Raya Building, Jalan Ampang (☎ 03-2482524)

Japan Airlines: Floor 1, Pernas International Building, Jalan Sultan Ismail (☎ 03-2611733)

KLM: Ground Floor, Pernas International Building, Jalan Sultan Ismail (☎ 03-2427011)

MAS: MAS Building, Jalan Sultan Ismail (☎ 03-2610555)

Pelangi Air: Wisma On Tai (☎ 03-2624448)

Philippine Airlines: Wisma Stephens, Jalan Raja Chulan (☎ 03-2429040)

Qantas: UBN Tower, Jalan P. Ramlee (☎ 03-2389133)

Royal Brunei: Floor 1, Wisma Merlin, Jalan Sultan Ismail (☎ 03-2426511)

Singapore Airlines: Wisma SIA, Jalan Dang Wangi (☎ 03-2987033)

Thai International: Kuwasa Building, Jalan Raja Laut (☎ 03-2937100)

United Airlines: MAS Building, Jalan Sultan Ismail (☎ 03-2611433)

Kuala Lumpur will have a new international airport in the near future, located at Sepang some 60km to the south of the capital. It was planned to open for the Commonwealth Games, to be held in Kuala Lumpur in 1998, but 1999 now seems a more likely date. When it does open, it should be accessible by the new light railway system (STAR-LRT). The present airport at Subang will then serve domestic flights, including those to Sarawak and Sabah,

By train. The entrance to the city's railway station (☎ 03-2747435, 2738000 or 2747442 from 6.30 to 22.30) is on Jalan Sultan Hishamuddin but taxis cannot be hailed from here. They leave from the back of the station, outside platform 4, and there is a taxi office here, where coupons can be purchased for the journey to your hotel. It is advisable to book as far ahead as possible for sleeper accommodation on trains south to Singapore and north to Butterworth and Thailand. During holiday times, especially around Chinese New Year, sleeper accommodation can be fully booked for weeks ahead. Timetables can also be obtained from the information desk in the railway station in Kuala Lumpur and from Tourism Malaysia offices abroad.

By bus. The main station for long-distance buses is the Puduraya bus station (☎ 03-2300145) on Jalan Pudu, to the east of Merdeka Square and Chinatown. It can seem a chaotic place but really is well organised, with the different routes, times and fares clearly shown above the various ticket windows. It is best to buy a ticket the day before departure. Most buses leave early in the morning, or at night for the longer journeys. Outside the station there are smaller companies plying most of the main routes. Inside the station there is a left-luggage office open until 22.00.

Buses for Jerantut (for Taman Negara) and some east coast destinations use the Pekeliling bus station (☎ 03-4421256), off Jalan Tun Razak. Other east coast buses use the Putra bus station (☎ 03-4429530) next to the Putra World Trade Centre. Buses to locations west of the city in Selangor state use the Klang bus station (☎ 03-2307694) on Jalan Sultan Mohammed.

Bus tickets can be bought at the large Tourist Information Complex on Jalan Ampang (see below).

Nice express buses operate between Kuala Lumpur and Penang (RM40), Johor Bahru (RM38), Ipoh (RM19) and Singapore (RM43). Their office (☎ 09-444 3911) and departure point is at 14 Jalan Raya Laut, opposite the Legend Cinema.

By taxi. The long-distance taxi station is located at the Puduraya bus station, on the upper floor. Taxis depart fairly regularly, especially in the morning, for nearly all the main towns. As a general rule, expect to pay about twice as much as the bus fare.

Getting around Kuala Lumpur

A word of warning: almost complete gridlock can set in during morning and evening rush hours and walking—while not always practicable—is often quicker than any bus or taxi.

Taxis are the most convenient way to travel around the city. Fares are inexpensive, starting at RM1.50 and increasing by 10 *sen* for every 200m (with a 50 per cent surcharge between midnight and 06.00). All taxis have meters and if the driver is unwilling to turn his on then the passenger is almost certainly going to be overcharged. Unless you know what the fare should be, insist the meter is used. Taxis can be hailed on the street but most of the larger shopping complexes and main shopping streets have designated waiting areas. A taxi can be booked by telephone (☎ 03-7330507, 03-7815352, 03-4420848) for an extra RM1.

Trains. The first phase of the city's light railway system, STAR-LRT, became operational in 1996. Its 13 stations stretch from the Golden Triangle area in the east to the junction of Jalan Sultan Ismail and Jalan Raya Laut in the north of the city. The second phase of the system should be working before the end of

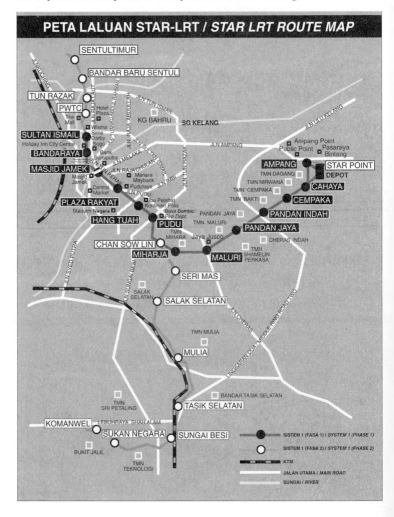

1998 and will stretch south of the city and connect with the main, national railway station on Jalan Sultan Hishamuddin and the new international airport at Sepang. Another, elevated section will be added to the northern line in 1999. Single trip tickets and stored value tickets are obtainable from ticket offices in the stations.

Buses are inexpensive and regular but not usually air-conditioned and the myriad routes are difficult to master. It is easier to use the inexpensive taxis, though a bus will save money on trips to places like Shah Alam and Petaling Jaya (see p 88). There are two types of bus: regular city buses, run by a host of competing private companies, and pink mini-buses. Regular buses charge 20 *sen* for the first kilometre and then 5 sen for each additional kilometre. The mini-buses charge a flat fare of 70 sen.

The Klang bus station on Jalan Sultan Mohammed serves buses for Petaling Jaya, Shah Alam and Port Klang.

Car hire. There is little to be gained by driving in Kuala Lumpur, other than the ease of excursion trips to places around the city. Apart from the complicated road system, there are interminable traffic jams and during the morning and evening rush hours the main roads in and out of the city are invariably clogged with traffic which reduces everything to a crawl.

All the major car rental companies have offices at Subang International Airport as well as in the city:

Avis: 40 Jalan Sultan Ismail
(☎ 03-2423500)
Budget: 163 Jalan Ampang
(☎ 03-2611122)

Hertz: Floor 2, Antara Bangsa Complex (☎ 03-2433433)
National: 70 Jalan Ampang
(☎ 03-6264613)

Helicopter tours of Kuala Lumpur provide a bird's-eye view of the city from 457m (1500ft) and may surprise you by showing just how small the nation's capital is. A 15-minute trip costs RM120 per person, with a minimum of four passengers, from Guthrie Aviation (☎ 03-6264613).

Tourist information
The biggest tourist office in town is the **Malaysian Tourist Information Centre** (☎ 03-2643929), MATIC, at 109 Jalan Ampang, open daily from 09.00 to 21.00. Accommodation information is available here for Kuala Lumpur and the rest of the country, and bookings can be made. There is a separate desk for the booking of accommodation at Nusa Camp in Taman Negara (National Park) and a desk for the booking of long-distance bus tickets. Performances of cultural dances are held each afternoon at 15.30 on Tuesday, Thursday, Saturday and Sunday (RM2) (see also Entertainment, below).

There is also the **KL Visitors Centre** (☎ 03-2746063) on Jalan Sultan Hishamuddin, just outside the main entrance to the railway station, open from 09.00 to 21.00. The **Malaysian Tourist Development Corporation** (☎ 03-4411295) has its headquarters and an office for the public on the second floor of the Putra World Trade Centre, close to the Pan Pacific hotel and The Mall shopping centre. It is open from 09.00 to 16.30 Monday to Friday.

There is another tourist office, the **KL Tourist Information Centre** (☎ 03-2936664), not far from Merdeka Square, on Jalan Parlimen near the junction of Jalan Tun Perak and Jalan Raja Laut, open from 09.00 to 21.00.

Finally, at the airport there is a tourist office (☎ 03-7465707) in the arrivals hall of Terminal 1.

Currency exchange can be transacted at a number of the big banks around the city centre during their normal opening hours, Monday to Friday between 10.00 and 16.00, Saturday 09.00 to 12.30. All the city centre branches of the United Malayan Banking Corporation (UMBC) will change money. Their main bank is in the UMBC Building on Jalan Sultan Sulaiman. Bank Bumiputra is on Jalan Melaka, Chase Manhattan is in the Pernas International Building on Jalan Sultan Ismail, and Standard Chartered Bank at 2 Jalan Ampang.

Outside banking hours, and usually with slightly better rates, licensed money-changers can be found in most of the shopping centres. They stay open until the shops close at around 21.00. The American Express office (☎ 03-2613000) is in the MAS Building on Jalan Sultan Ismail.

The least attractive rates of exchange are available at most of the big hotels.

Postal, telephone and fax services. The GPO is on Jalan Sultan Hishamuddin next to the Dayabumi Complex, between the railway station and Merdeka Square, and is open from 08.00 to 17.00 Monday to Friday, 08.00 to midday Saturday. There is a poste restante and a fax sending service here.

A good place for making international telephone calls is the **Malaysia Tourist Information Centre** on Jalan Ampang where there is a Telekom office open until 17.00, Monday to Friday. The main **Telekom office** is on Jalan Raja Chulan, and this is open daily until 21.00.

Emergencies and hospitals

Dial 999 for police, ambulance or fire. The tourist police can also be called on ☎ 03-2496593. The police station on Jalan Tun H.S. Lee (☎ 03-2325044) is the most centrally located. Twenty-four hour emergency hospital treatment is available at Pudu Specialist Centre (☎ 03-2429146) on Jalan Pudu.

Tour operators

Day tours around Kuala Lumpur can usually be arranged from your hotel. The standard **city tour** lasts about three hours and takes in Chinatown, the National Mosque, Railway Station, National Museum, Padang and Masjid Jame. The countryside tours usually include a visit to the pewter factory, batik workshop and the Batu caves. There are also a number of larger companies which can organise tours to other parts of peninsular Malaysia as well as to Sarawak and Sabah. Try to compare prices with at least a couple of companies before making a decision. **Asian Overland Services** (☎ 03-2925637), at 35 Jalan Dewan Sultan Sulaiman, is a reliable and experienced company for eco-tourist trips. Two other companies that have an ecological bias are **Kingfisher Tours**, Suite 1107, 11th Floor, Bangunan Yayasan Selangor, Jalan Bukit Bintang (☎ 03-2421454; fax 03-2429827) and **Wilderness Experience**, 6-B, Jalan SS21/39, Taman Damansara Utama, Petaling Jaya, Selangor (☎ 03-7178221; fax 03-7172298). Also worth consulting are **Borneo Travel** (☎ 03-

2612130), based in the Equatorial hotel on Jalan Sultan Ismail, and **Insight Travel** (☎ 03-2612488) on Floor 9 of MBF Plaza on Jalan Ampang.

Embassies and immigration

For a visa extension contact the **Immigration Office** (☎ 03-7578155) which is on Jalan Pantai Bahru, off Jalan Damansara.

Countries with embassies and consulates in Kuala Lumpur include:

Australia: 6 Jalan Yap Kwan Seng (☎ 03-2423122)

Brunei: 113 Jalan U. Thant (☎ 03-2612860)

Canada: Floor 7, MBF Plaza, Jalan Ampang (☎ 03-2612000)

China: 229 Jalan Ampang (☎ 03-2428495)

Denmark: Angkasa Raya Building, Jalan Ampang (☎ 03-2416088)

France: 192 Jalan Ampang (☎ 03-2484235)

Germany: 29 Jalan Ampang (☎ 03-2429666)

India: Floor 20, Wisma Selangor Dredging, Jalan Ampang (☎ 03-2617095)

Indonesia: 233 Jalan Tun Razak (☎ 03-9842011)

Japan: 11 Pertiaran Stonor (☎ 03-2427044)

Netherlands: 4 Jalan Mesra (☎ 03-2431141)

New Zealand: 193 Jalan Tun Razak (☎ 03-2486422)

Philippines: 1 Changkat Kia Peng (☎ 03-2484233)

Singapore: 209 Jalan Tun Razak (☎ 03-2616277)

Sweden: Floor 6, Angkasa Raya Building, Jalan Ampang (☎ 03-2485433)

Switzerland: 16 Persiaran Madge (☎ 03-2480622)

Thailand: 206 Jalan Ampang (☎ 03-2488222)

UK and Republic of Ireland: Floor 13, Wisma Damanara, Jalan Semantan (☎ 03-2487122) Passport Office, 186 Jalan Ampang (☎ 03-2487122)

USA: 376 Jalan Tun Razak (☎ 03-2489011)

Accommodation

Top range hotels are not in short supply and many of the rates quoted here can be discounted by at least 25 per cent if booked through an agent or simply by asking for a business traveller reduction. Two of the very best are the **Regent** (☎ 03-2418000; fax 03-2421441) on Jalan Bukit Bintang and the **Shangri-La** (☎ 03-2322388; fax 03-2301514) at 11 Jalan Sultan Ismail. Both charge over RM500 for a room, boast impeccable service and superb facilities and restaurants.

One of the newest is **Hotel Istana** (☎ 03-2441998; fax 03-2495500), an imposing edifice at 73 Jalan Raja Chulan where doubles begin at RM460. **The Legend** (☎ 03-4429888; fax 03-4430700) is a fortress of a building at the top of Jalan Putra; inside the hotel everything has an ostentatiously expensive style. Doubles start at RM360. More expensive, but with real class, is the **Carcosa Seri Negara** on Taman Tasik Perdagna (☎ 03-2821888; fax 03-2827888), on the site where Sir Frank Swettenham, the first Resident, began the construction of his official home. Until 1941 when the Japanese moved in, it was the home of the highest British representative.

Concorde Hotel (☎ 03-2442200; fax 03-2441628), 2 Jalan Sultan Ismail, charges RM220 for a standard double, which is less than many of its neighbours. The **Park Royal** (☎ 03-2425588; fax 03-2415524) is also on Jalan Sultan Ismail, close to the Lot 10 shopping centre, with rooms for RM400. The **Ming Court** (☎ 03-2618888; fax 03-2612393) is on Jalan Ampang with rooms from RM218. The **Federal Hotel** (☎ 03-2489166; fax 03-2482877), at 35 Jalan Bukit Bintang, is less expensive at RM201.

There are two Holiday Inn hotels: **Holiday Inn City Centre** (☎ 03-2939233; fax 03-2939634) deserves its name, being located on Jalan Raja Laut (but the swimming pool is minute), while **Holiday Inn on the Park** (☎ 03-2481066; fax 03-2481930) is on Jalan Pinang. Rates are the same at RM370.

Middle range hotels include the **Kowloon** (☎ 03-2934246, fax 03-2926548), centrally located at 142 Jalan Tuanku Abdul Rahman with clean, modern singles/doubles at RM92/109. The **Asia Hotel** (☎ 03-2926077; fax 03-2927734) is at the other end of the same road, at 69 Jalan Haji Hussein, with equally good rooms: doubles only at RM110 and RM141. **Hotel Malaya** (☎ 03-2327722; fax 03-2300980), on Jalan Hang Lekir in Chinatown, is a well-established place with singles/doubles for RM165/190. The **Hotel City Inn** (☎ 03-2389190; fax 03-4419864), at 11 Jalan Sultan, has a useful location and the RM80 rooms are modern and clean.

Very good value is **Hotel Puduraya** (☎ 03-2321000; fax 03-2305567), on the fourth floor of the Puduraya bus station in Jalan Pudu near Chinatown. It is a far better—and quieter—hotel than the location might suggest with large singles/doubles for RM103/115, lots of facilities, including sauna and gym, and ideal if leaving by bus or taxi.

The **Agora** (☎ 03-2428133; fax 03-2427815), at 106 Jalan Bukit Bintang on the east side of the city, has decent singles/doubles for RM130/150 and a small café which does a good Western breakfast. Not far away, on Jalan Sultan Ismail, **The Lodge** (☎ 03-2420122; fax 03-2416819) is a comfortable and hospitable place with singles/doubles for RM115/230 and boasts a small swimming pool and an upmarket address.

The **Heritage Station Hotel** (☎ 03-2735588; fax 03-2735566) on Jalan Sultan Hishamuddin is very convenient if travelling by train and its location and architecture lends is some charm. Rooms start at RM130.

Budget range hotels include a number of hostels that are worth considering. The **Chinatown Guest House** (☎ 03-2320417), at 103 Jalan Petaling, is not going to be the quietest place in town at night but the RM10 dormitory beds include breakfast and there are singles/doubles for RM15/22. Popular and often full is the **Backpackers' Travellers' Inn** (☎ 03-2382473), 60 Jalan Sultan, with dormitory beds and private rooms with/without air-conditioning for RM40–50 and 22–30. The **Kuala Lumpur International Youth Hostel** (☎ 03-2736871), at 21 Jalan Kampung Attap, just south of Chinatown, has beds for RM15 the first night and then RM12 (RM5 extra for non-members) and good facilities. .

There is a certain inverted snobbery about staying at the famous old **Coliseum Hotel** (☎ 03-2926270), at 98 Jalan Tuanku Abdul Rahman. Rooms are RM28 and RM40, with a shared bathroom, but they are large and clean, the whole establishment is full of character, and there is a good bar and restaurant downstairs. Travellers turn up around 10.00 to secure a room.

Restaurants

Expensive. Most of Kuala Lumpur's best restaurants are to be found in the hotels. The set lunches are moderately priced while à la carte dinner will cost around RM150–200 for two diners.

The **Lai Ching Yuen** (☎ 03-2494250) at the Regent offers award-winning Cantonese dishes—dim sum at lunchtime and with traditional Chinese music played live on the wooden *zheng* and *kim* in the evening. The **Shang Palace** (☎ 03-2322388) at the Shangri-La is also famous for its Cantonese food, prepared by Hong Kong chefs. The **Ming Palace** (☎ 03-2618888) at the Ming Court hotel is best for Sezuan dishes, and **Museum** (☎ 03-4429888) at the Legend serves Teo Chew and Cantonese food (amidst purchasable artefacts, paintings and sculptures). The **Melaka Grill** (☎ 03-2482322) at the Hilton mixes Eastern cuisine with Western dishes in an ancient Chinese courtyard setting.

For Japanese food there is the **Edo Kirin** at the Regent hotel and the set lunch here is particularly good value. Equally renowned is **The Keyaki** (☎ 03-4425555) at the Pan Pacific hotel with its three *teppanyaki* counters, a sushi bar and a *robatayaki* counter. The RM38 *keyaki zen* set dinner—an assortment of tempura, raw fish, rice and miso soup—is recommended.

For top-class Western food, **Restaurant Lafite** (☎ 03-2322388) at the Shangri-La hotel re-creates a classical European elegance to serve French food: a buffet at lunchtime Monday to Friday, candlelit à la carte intimacy at night. The wine list is one of the best in Malaysia. **The Grill** (☎ 03-2425588) at the Park Royal hotel is a carnivore's delight, specialising in roasted American beef. **Chalet Restaurant** (☎ 03-2617777) at the Hotel Equatorial specialises in Swiss and continental haute cuisine, while the **Bologna** at the Istana Hotel (☎ 03-2419988) offers a good-value Italian set dinner for around RM100.

The **Kapitan's Club** (☎ 03-2010242) at 35 Jalan Ampang has a colonial Malaya style and offers a number of Nonya dishes as well as its speciality—curried chicken.

Recommended for high tea is the **Carcosa Seri Negara** in Lake Gardens—a very smart hotel (see above)—where the colonial atmosphere makes the cucumber sandwiches seem simply divine. Lunch and dinner are considerably more expensive.

Middle range. The food at **Le Coq d'Or** (☎ 03-2619732) is not the main attraction compared to the fading elegance of a colonial-style restaurant that was once home to a tin millionaire. Reservations are advisable for the inexpensive lunch, and a drink on the verandah is always a pleasant experience. The location is 121 Jalan Ampang (ask the taxi driver for the Angkasa Raya Building which is next door).

Also resonant with a sense of the past is **The Coliseum** (☎ 03-2926270), 98 Jalan Tuanku Abdul Rahman, next to the cinema of the same name and close to the Masjid Jame. The first steaks were served here in 1921 and, except for a brief interruption during the Japanese Occupation, it has remained open for business since then. Original cartoons by Lat, the famous contemporary Malaysian artist, adorn the walls, and the ancient ceiling fans are merely decorative for the place is air-conditioned. Open from 10.00 to 22.00, give yourself time for a drink in the bar area while perusing the menu of steaks, chicken and fish.

Reasonably priced seafood and grills are served at **Eden** (☎ 03-2414027) on

Jalan Raja Chulan, not far from the Hilton hotel. Open for lunch and dinner, the restaurant can be relied on for its fresh fish and steaks. Specialities include lobster with garlic and giant tiger prawns with a spicy touch. Recommended for authentic Italian cuisine is **Ciao** (☎ 03-9854827) at 428 Jalan Tun Razak.

The Mall (at the top of Jalan Putra) is one of those shopping plazas that play loud music continually, but on the second level the **Cili Padi Thai Restaurant** (☎ 03-4429543) is insulated from the noise. A set dinner is RM22, more for à la carte. At weekends the dinner buffet is good value at RM24.

The Ship (☎ 03-2418805), on Jalan Sultan Ismail, is famous for its steaks but seafood is also served in the dark interior of this restaurant by waiters wearing naval officers' attire.

Inexpensive. Off the bottom end of Jalan Tuanku Abdul Rahman there are two recommended Indian restaurants. At 5 Jalan Medan Tunku, the **Omar Khayam** (☎ 03-2988744) serves generous portions of north Indian dishes at around RM35 for two; while close by, at 60 Jalan Tuanku Abdul Rahman, **Bangles** (☎ 03-2983780) is a little dearer. For excellent vegetarian Indian food, try **Annalakshmi** (☎ 2823799) at 44 Jalan Maarof, Bangsar, a short taxi ride from town. The price will be around RM40 for two; no alcohol is served.

Gandhi's Corner, near the junction of Jalan Thambypillay and Jalan Berhala in Brickfields, east of the railway station, is famous with locals for its vegan kebab and other dishes cooked by a chef born on the day Mahatma Gandhi was assassinated (30 January 1948). It is open from the evening until the early hours of the next morning. The **Bilal** restaurants at 33 Jalan Ampang (☎ 03-2380804) and 37 Jalan Tuanku Abdul Rahman (☎ 03-2928948) are well known to locals for their chicken curries and tasty *naans*.

For Chinese vegetarian food, try the aptly named **Cameleon Vegetarian Restaurant** (☎ 03-4423526) on the corner of Jalan Putra and Jalan Thamboosamy, just down the road from the Pan Pacific hotel. The mock meat dishes are excellent.

The **Heritage** restaurant (☎ 03-2735588) in the railway hotel of the same name, reached by turning right when leaving the railway station by its main entrance, has a faded elegance which helps compensate for an uninspring menu of standard Malay and British dishes (including beans on toast!).

Hawker food can be enjoyed with the benefit of air-conditioning on the top floor of The Mall shopping complex on Jalan Putra. It is called **Medan Hang Tuah** and replicates the pre-war eating stalls of Penang and Melaka. The food is mainly local Malay favourites such as *bak kut teh* (pork ribs soup).

All the familiar Western fast-food chains have outlets dotted around town: opposite Central Market, the bottom of Jalan Tuanku Abdul Rahman, around the bus station and in the shopping malls at the junction of Jalan Sultan Ismail and Jalan Bukit Bintang.

Entertainment

There is very little in the way of traditional theatre and dance other than what is offered at the restaurants with cultural shows. The **Yazmin** restaurant (see above) is the best in this respect. There is also an afternoon cultural show at the Malaysian Tourist Information Complex (see above) on Jalan Ampang.

There is no shortage of cinemas (see the *New Straits Times* for details) showing the latest Western films in English with Malay subtitles.

Good pubs include **The Coliseum** (see above), where it is not necessary to have a meal, and **The Pub** at the Shangri-La hotel. The **Hard Rock Café** is in the Concorde hotel on Jalan Sultan Ismail and has loud rock music every night except Sunday. The **Bull's Head** at Central Market is popular with tourists and expatriates.

There are lots of discos in Kuala Lumpur, most of which are situated in the Golden Triangle area and don't come alive until after midnight. **Betelnut**, at the corner of Jalan Pinang and Jalan P. Ramlee, has long been a favourite place—especially the outdoor bar—despite a number of other discos and clubs in the vicinity.

Sports

Badminton and squash courts can be booked at the Bangsar Sports Complex, Jalan Terasek Tiga, Bangsar Baru.

Bowling is quite popular and can be played at Federal Bowl, in the Federal Hotel, Jalan Bukit Bintang or the Miramar Bowling Centre, Wisma Miramar, in Jalan Wisma Putra.

Golf clubs abound. There is an 18-hole golf course at the Royal Selangor Golf Club in Jalan Kelab Golf off Jalan Tun Razak. The Saujana Golf and Country Club is at Subang with an 18-hole course.

Watersports are on offer at Water World, Sugei Besi Tin Mine, a converted open cast mine where power boats, waterskis, and canoes can be hired. No phone number or address at the moment.

Shopping

The **Karayeneka Centre**, on Jalan Raja Chulan, has a good cross-section of Malaysian craftware for sale and is open 09.00 to 18.00. **Wisma Batik**, on **Jalan Tun Perak**, has a good selection of clothes for sale. **Jalan Masjid India** is worth wandering along for Indian fabrics, as is **Lebuh Ampang** off Jalan Gereja.

Jalan Sultan Ismail is home to two of the biggest shopping malls, **Lot 10** and **Sungai Wang Plaza**, connected by a pedestrian bridge across the road. Each is anchored by a Japanese department store with a wide range of souvenirs, handicrafts and consumer goods in general. The Isetan department store in Lot 10 is probably the best in this regard. Both plazas also have numerous small outlets selling optical goods, clothes, shoes and so on. The top floor of Lot 10 is devoted to designer clothes. Around the corner in Jalan Imbi, **Imbi Plaza** is a small centre for computer hardware and pirated software.

Within walking distance, at the corner of Jalan Ampang and Jalan Tun Razak, there are three more shopping centres: **City Square**, **Yow Chuan Plaza** and **Ampang Park**. They contain a variety of boutiques, tailors, handicraft and carpet shops. City Square has the Metro department store, the best-priced place for quality clothes.

The Mall is another self-contained shopping area at the top of Jalan Putra opposite the Pan Pacific Hotel (near the Putra Bus Station). It has five levels and includes a Yaohan—a middle-range Japanese department store. There is a good bookshop here.

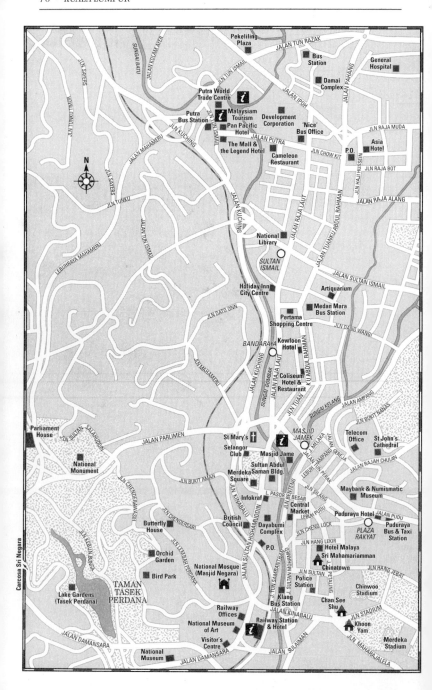

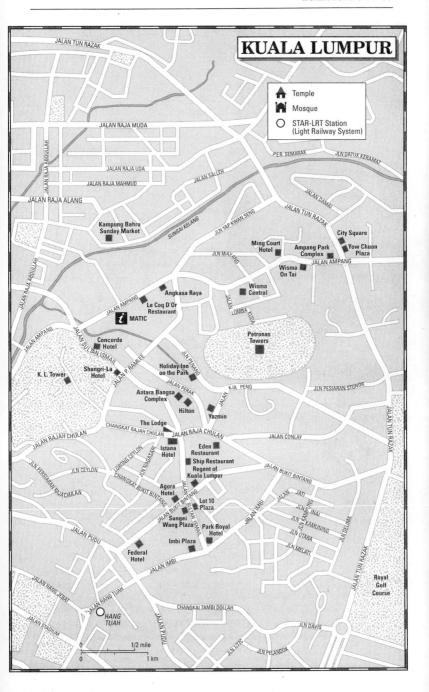

The Petronas Towers, constructed in 1996 as the tallest buildings in the world

The Hilton, Shangri-La, Park Royal and Concorde hotels each have half a dozen upmarket outlets for designer names such as Gucci, Armani and Hugo Boss. They also have a smaller number of quality arts and crafts shops selling porcelain, cloisonné, lacquerware and the like. The widest selection and best prices are to be found at Lim Arts & Crafts on the second floor of the Hilton shopping arcade.

A place to browse for souvenirs and handicrafts is the **Central Market** at Jalan Hang Kasturi. Batik, pewter, rattan, wickerwork and souvenirs are generally available here. The **Infokraf** near Merdeka Square is also worth a visit for traditional craft items at fixed prices (open from 09.00 to 17.00 seven days a week except public holidays). The batik, cane and pottery are reasonably priced, but while there is some interesting furniture for sale the shop does not arrange a shipping service.

Genuine art and antiques are sold at **Artiquarium** (☎ 03-2982406) at 237 Jalan Medan Tuanku. The building is also known as Loke House, after the multi-millionaire Loke Ye—he was so rich he had his own bank notes printed—who built the place as his mansion in 1904. It was the first house in the city to have electricity installed and, after being left empty for years, was used by the Japanese during the Occupation. It has now been carefully restored and the whole place is more like a museum than a shop. Everything is for sale, though, ranging from affordable craft items to authentic Melakan furniture. A shipping service is available.

Royal Selangor (☎ 03-4221000) is a pewter factory, located some 4km northeast of town on Jalan Usahawan Enam, Setapak Jaya. Visitors are invited to join a complimentary tour of the factory to see the pewter (97 per cent tin and 3 per cent copper and antimony) being designed. There is a large shop selling the full range of products at prices that are often better than those found in the city shops. The factory and shop are open from 8.00–17.00 Monday to Friday, 08.30–16.45 Saturday, and 09.00 to 16.00 Sunday. If you take one of the countryside tours that operate from all the main hotels there is usually a stopover at the factory. Or take a taxi or bus W12.

A good place for imitation designer clothes, imitation designer watches, T-shirts, jewellery, belts, bags and pirated computer software is the part of **Jalan Petaling** just southeast of the Central Market. At night it is closed to traffic and stalls spring up on both sides of the road. Bargaining is essential; aim to pay between 40 and 60 per cent of the asking price. At weekends, the pavements along **Jalan Tuanku Abdul Rahman** transform themselves into a busy street market but it is never as much fun as Jalan Petaling where occasionally a stall pops up selling something unusual, such as crafts from Tibet or Nepal.

A market that can compete with Jalan Petaling for atmosphere is **Chow Kit Market**. It is in the north of the city, on the opposite side of Jalan Tuanku Abdul Rahman to where Jalan Chow Kit actually is, occupying the block between Jalan Haja Alang and Jalan Raja Bot. The best time to visit is in the morning because by late afternoon the pulse has slowed down and most of the stalls will be closing up. You may not actually buy anything here but Chow Kit Market is still well worth a visit: on sale is a bizarre mix of fruit, vegetables, clothes and sundry items, and the general clamour should not put one off enjoying a cup of coffee and *roti canai* at one of the food stalls.

Colonial-Era Walk

This could also be called the Hubbock and Norman Walk because many of the interesting buildings encountered along the way were designed by one or other of two architects: A.B. Hubbock and A.C. Norman. They both spent time in India before coming to Kuala Lumpur and there is no doubting the impact that Moghul architecture made upon them. More generally, though, this walk takes in a self-conscious and imaginative range of styles, dating back to the turn of this century, that competes favourably with the complacent materialism of contemporary Asian architecture.

This walk lasts from one to three hours and it is advisable to bring a bottle of mineral water with you because refreshments are not readily available along the way.

The walk begins at the magnificent **railway station** on Jalan Sultan Hishamuddin which was completed in 1911 following the designs of a British architect, A.B. Hubbock. His only experience prior to this had been alterations to site plans. The interior of the station is not dissimilar to that of any large Victorian railway station in England but the astonishing exterior is truly unique. The Oriental treat of spires, turrets and seven minarets that blend in around Arabian arches would be visually satisfying in itself, but this mix of the Moghul, Moorish and Islamic is only one half of the architectural equation. There is a Gothic imagination at work—or is this just an accidental result?—in the sheer multitude of arches and crevices, and there is no mistaking the Edwardian feel to the overall solidity of the masonry.

It is said that the completion of the roof was delayed because its design failed to meet the British specification that a station roof should be capable of holding one metre of snow. What is finally most impressive about the railway station, built by convict labour, is that the eclectic combination of styles—described by an unknown writer as belonging to the 'Late Marzipan' period—succeeds in a wholly unforced and whimsical manner. A good place to view and photograph the station is from across the road in the similarly styled **Railway Administration Building** which was designed by the same architect and completed in 1917.

Just a short walk from the Railway Administration Building, on Jalan Sultan

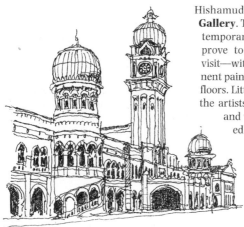

The Sultan Abdul Samad Building, now the Supreme Court, Kuala Lumpur

Hishamuddin, is the **National Art Gallery**. The ground floor is devoted to temporary exhibitions—which may prove to be the highlight of your visit—with the collection of permanent paintings on the second and third floors. Little information is provided on the artists whose work is represented, and while the paintings undoubtedly provide the visitor with interesting images of traditional Malaysian country life, there is very little that challenges or engages the viewer. The gallery is open from 10.00 to 18.00 daily, except Friday when it closes from 12.15 to 14.45; admission is free. The art gallery building itself was once the Majestic Hotel, top of its class during the years of colonial Malaya, and used by the Japanese during the Second World War as their headquarters. The gallery's ground floor exhibition area was the Majestic's dining room and ballroom and the paintings upstairs hang in what were once the bedrooms.

Walk north from the art gallery back past the railway station on Jalan Sultan Hishamuddin, passing the **Masjid Negara** (National Mosque) on your left. This huge construction—it holds well over 8000 devotees and the minaret is some 70m high—was one of the first (1965) of a new breed of modernistic mosques that while undoubtedly achieving a visual splendour lost some of the spiritual form evident in their smaller predecessors. The 18-point star that forms the main dome of Masjid Negara represents the five pillars of Islam and the 13 states of Malaysia. The most interesting feature is the abstract geometry of the external grillwork. Visitors can enter between 09.00 and 18.00, except Friday when the hours are 14.00 to 18.00. Shoes must be left outside and women should not wear shorts.

Continue north along Jalan Sultan Hishamuddin until you see a sign on the left for the British Council. On the other side of the road it is impossible to miss the 35-floor **Dayabumi Complex**. This type of Islamic-influenced architecture—the Islamic detail is most obvious in the open fretwork—is no longer original, but when the Malaysian architect Nik Mohammed designed and built the skyscraper in the 1970s it was very unusual. For many years it was home to the national oil company, Petronas, which has now deserted this edifice for its own Petronas Towers (see above).

On the same side of the road, one block north, the stone building that comes into view was once the General Post Office but is now the **Infokraf**—a craft centre selling traditional items from all parts of peninsular Malaysia (see Shopping above). The architect A.C. Norman designed both this building and the one further along with the 40m-high clock tower flanked by two lacquered copper domes, the **Sultan Abdul Samad Building**. Both were completed in 1897 and it would seem that Hubbock was striving to surpass Norman in the use of Moorish themes when he set about designing the railway station shortly after. The Sultan Abdul Samad Building was built to house the colonial bureaucracy and is now home to the country's Supreme Court.

On the other side of the road is **Merdeka Square**, resonant with both colonial and nationalist sentiment. The Tudor-style building at the rear is the **Royal Selangor Club** which was first constructed in 1884 on swamp land drained for the purpose. The architect was again A.C. Norman. The ground in front was then drained to provide a police training ground and this later became the *padang* where colonialists enjoyed a pleasant afternoon's cricket. It is much foreshortened now, having made way for the square itself.

> The club was the favourite meeting place of expatriate tin and rubber merchants, a place where the colonial masters threw back their *stengahs* at the long bar and exchanged polite gossip; the archetypal setting for a scene in a Somerset Maugham story. The building still functions as an exclusive club for the country's élite—Malaysian now instead of British—and unfortunately it is not possible to gain admittance to view the long bar and the notable collection of old photographs that adorn the walls. During colonial times, planters and their wives could sit on the verandah and chat or play bridge to a background of batting and fielding on the *padang*. During the Japanese occupation, the green was used to grow bananas and tapioca before it was returned to its sporting function after 1945. It was quite fitting that this stretch of green should provide the location for Malaysia's proclamation of independence—*merdeka* being Malay for freedom—on 31 August 1957.

On the eastern side of the square there is a 100m-high flag-pole, with the fairly meaningless distinction of being the tallest in the world.

On the northern side of the square is the Anglican **St Mary's Church**, reached by turning left down Jalan Raja Laut. It dates back to 1894, and was designed by A.C. Norman for British families to pray and sing to the accompaniment of a pipe organ built by the famous 19C British organ maker, Henry Willis.

Walk back to the Sultan Abdul Samad Building and turn into Leboh Pasor Besar. You will soon reach a small girdered bridge from where, looking to your left, there is a view of **Masjid Jame** (the main entrance is on Jalan Tun Perak). This elegant little mosque (built in the first decade of this century) marks the spot where, at the confluence of the two rivers, the pioneering tin-miners established their trading post in the 1850s. Notwithstanding the significance of its location, sandwiched between the Kelang and Gombak rivers, the mosque has an intrinsic and disciplined aesthetic based on small-scale harmonies that evoke an air of intimacy; surprising when one considers that the same architect (A.B. Hubbock) was responsible for the 'Late Marzipan' extravaganza of the railway station.

Hubbock based his design on that of a north Indian Moghul mosque. The surrounding palm trees shelter the mosque from the urban surroundings and add to the atmosphere of calm produced by the pastel coloured brickwork, domed minarets, arched colonnades and cool marble surfaces. Until the Masjid Negara was opened in 1965, this was the central place of worship for Muslims in the capital.

The mosque is open to visitors from 09.00 to 12.45 and from 14.30 to 16.15, except Friday, when the hours are 08.00 to 10.30 and 14.45 to 16.15. Even though it is closed at sunrise and sunset, these are often the best times for appreciating the play of light on the mosque. The black and white drawings that are sold for around RM25 outside the mosque are worth considering.

A short walk south down Jalan Benteng concludes this walk in the vicinity of the **Central Market** where refreshments and taxis are available.

The Central Market was built in 1928 as a wet market; it was converted to a modern shopping mall in the early 1980s but has retained many of its original features. The slabs where butchers and fishmongers cut and displayed their meat and fish are now used to display tourist souvenirs and inexpensive craft items. The upper floors are home to various hawker stalls serving inexpensive local food. The overall art deco style of the edifice has been preserved and the high ceilings have been repainted in light blues and pinks.

The Central Market is open from 09.00 to 22.00. In the evening, an open space at one side of the building is available for local street artists to entertain the public.

Chinatown Walk

The area immediately southeast of the Central Market is Chinatown—bordered roughly by the Central Market and Jalan Sultan to the north and south respectively, Jalan Tun H.S. Lee (still also known by its old name of Jalan Bandar) to the west and Jalan Petaling to the east. The main interest in walking this area, apart from viewing the Indian and Chinese temples, is the encounter along the way with aspects of Chinese daily life in the coffee houses, shops and restaurants that seem to litter the streets and often the pavements as well.

Look for the apothecary whose shop will have a mix of familiar brand-name Western medicines alongside glass and ceramic bottles containing the base ingredients for alternative remedies: shark's fin, dried herbs and roots and powders from crushed plants and roots that await translation. Depending on the nature and severity of the illness, the apothecary weighs out the precise amounts required and wraps them in paper. Other shops you will pass include jewellers and goldsmiths, coffin makers, cobblers, Chinese sign makers and dry goods' shops with sackfuls of rice, beans and myriad dried fish out on the pavement.

The walk starts at the top of Lebuh Pudu—there is a McDonald's on the corner-opposite the Central Market. Walk down Lebuh Pudu a short distance and look for Lorong Bandar on your right; it is basically an alleyway with food stalls down one side. Half-way down this alleyway on the left is the entrance to the small **Sze Yah Temple** (sometimes spelt as **Szu Yeh**). The temple's exact date is unknown but it may well be the oldest in Kuala Lumpur because Yap Ah Loy, who was Kapitan China of Kuala Lumpur between 1868 and 1885 and whose fading photograph can be found inside the temple, provided the land and helped finance its establishment. Sze Yah Temple reveals its age: smoke has been rising from burning joss sticks from some time in the 1880s and most of the interior is consequently blackened and gloomy.

From the Central Market it is a short walk one block east to Jalan Tun H.S. Lee and then south down the same road to the colourful Hindu **Sri Mahamariamman Temple**. This temple was founded in 1873 by Tamils who had emigrated to Malaya to find work on the railways and roads and in the rubber plantations. The temple was rebuilt on its present site in 1885; in the 1960s craftsmen and sculptors from India set about a major refurbishment of the *gopuram* (gateway) which was again renovated in the 1980s. The final result is what you see today: a plethora of gods and idols enacting scenes from the *Ramayana* (one of the great Sanskrit epics of ancient India) in a frenzy of colour and frozen movements, extravagantly embellished with gold, precious stones, and vivid tiles imported from Spain and Italy. During the Thaipusam festival a large chariot, dedicated to Lord Murgan (Subramaniam), leaves the temple each year to head the procession to the Batu Caves (see p 91). Early evening and Friday lunchtime are usually good times to visit the temple; music is played inside, while outside small crowds of Hindus mingle with the garland sellers and small stalls serve south Indian sweet cakes. The crumbling houses opposite the temple are mostly still inhabited by tradespeople and you may well see a tailor or seamstress at work behind an upstairs window.

Continue down Jalan Tun H.S. Lee and turn left into Jalan Sultan at the corner with the 7-Eleven store. At the junction with Jalan Petaling, turn right and stay on this side of the street passing the coffin makers before reaching the round-about where the **Chan See Shu Yuen Temple** comes into view on the left. This ornately decorated temple marks the southern boundary of Chinatown. It was built in 1906 and is dedicated to Chong Wah, a Sung dynasty emperor. The gaily coloured exterior is typical of Chinese Taoist temples and the projecting roof façade is a particularly good example of its kind; the human figures at the edge carrying poles and lanterns guard the temple.

Immediately across the roundabout, reached by crossing Jalan Stadium, is another temple—the **Khoon Yam Temple**. It was built around the same time as the Chan See Shu Yuen Temple by the city's Hokkien Chinese but is not as colourful or as carefully crafted.

This walk concludes by turning and walking back up Jalan Petaling all the way to Lebuh Pudu where a left turn will return you to the Central Market. There are shops along Jalan Petaling to tempt the traveller. However, it is worth waiting until nightfall to return here when the top half of the street is closed to traffic and Kuala Lumpur's liveliest *pasar malam* (night market) comes to life (see Shopping, p 75).

Parliament Area Walk

This walk is more spread out than the others and entails a shadeless walk of nearly half an hour between the first two places of interest. In the tropical heat this can be a hot trek and an alternative is to treat the National Museum as a separate visit and begin this walk at the National Gardens. In this case, take a taxi to the main entrance to the gardens, which is west of Merdeka Square along Jalan Parlimen, or bus No. 22 or 38 from Lebuh Pasar Besar. Alternatively, visit the museum in the mid afternoon so that you reach the Lake Gardens in the late afternoon when the temperature is less punishing.

The **Muzium Negara** (National Museum) is on Jalan Damansara, a 15-minute walk from the railway station. The museum is open daily from 09.00 to 18.00 and admission costs RM1.

The building, characterised by the broad sweeping roof of Minangkabau architecture (see p 52), occupies the site of the old Selangor Museum that was badly damaged by an air raid in 1945 when the east wing was accidentally hit by bombs intended for the nearby railway marshalling yards. The new museum, opened in 1963, is the best in peninsular Malaysia. If you are hesitating over whether to pay it a visit, just look in to see what kind of special exhibition happens to be on show at the time (☎ 03-2826255). These are often quite spectacular and justify a visit in their own right. Some of the most interesting sections of the permanent exhibition are the ethnographic ones, covering aspects of Malay culture such as the traditional circumcision ceremony. These are on the ground floor. The upper floor has a predictable display of natural history with stuffed specimens and dioramas depicting mammals and birds in their typical habitats. There is also a collection of entomological specimens. The second floor has a more rewarding display of traditional musical instruments and the weapons and traps of the Orang Asli.

From the museum it is a short walk along Jalan Damansara to a tunnel that crosses the road to reach the southern entrance to the **Lake Gardens** (Taman Tasek Perdana). This 100-hectare spread of greenery owes its origin to Alfred Venning, a British treasury administrator in Malaya during the last two decades of the 19C; since then it has been extensively developed. From the southern entrance it is a short walk to the lake where there are boats for hire. The **Tun Abdul Razak Memorial** is close by but is hardly worth a visit. Tun Abdul Razak was a highly revered figure in the country's post-independence era; he was Malaysia's second prime minister from 1970 to 1976 with a family lineage that went back to Sultan Abdullah who ceded Penang to the British. His official residence, **Seri Taman**, on the south east edge of the park is now open to the public. There is no admission charge to view the collection of memorabilia made up of records, documents, gifts and awards. The most exciting exhibit is his personal collection of walking sticks. The residence is open 09.00 to 18.00 Tuesday to Sunday, closed 12.00 to 15.00 on Fridays.

From the lake head towards the northern and main entrance to the gardens, on Jalan Parliamen. Along the way there are a number of places open to the public. The **Butterfly House**, open from 09.00 to 17.00 and RM5 for admission, has a large collection of butterflies—some alive, others dead. More varied and diverting is the **Bird Park** which is open from 09.00 to 18.00 and also charges RM5 for admission. It is set in a natural valley and covered by netting so that most of the birds exist in a state of relative freedom. There are around 4000 birds there and about 120 different species, including the enormous beaked hornbills. Very close by are the **Orchid** and **Hibiscus Gardens** (admission free) where some of the plants are also for sale, although before you buy, you should remember that many countries restrict the import of plants.

Just before reaching the main entrance, the massive **National Monument** commands attention. Felix de Weldon, famous for his Iwo Jima monument in Washington DC, completed this in 1966. It is a memorial to those who fought and died during the Communist Emergency (1948–60). As late as 1975 an attempt was made to blow up the memorial by the outlawed Communist Party.

More sculptures can be found in the nearby **sculpture garden** which is home to a mixed collection of art from neighbouring ASEAN (Association of Southeast Asian Nations) countries.

From the main entrance to the Lake Gardens it is a short walk to **Parliament House** which overlooks the gardens. There are two buildings—an 18-storey House of Representatives and the smaller Senate—which can be visited when parliament is sitting providing you have obtained prior permission from the City Hall.

The **Thean Hou Temple** is close to the Muzium Negara on Jalan Klang Lama, off Jalan Tun Sambathan. It is dedicated to the Goddess of Heaven and protector of seafarers. Temples dedicated to this deity were often the first that the thankful immigrants set up. It is set on a hill with wonderful views over the city. A Buddhist shrine is close by.

Other museums in Kuala Lumpur

The **Maybank Numismatic Museum** is on the first floor of the Maybank Building on Jalan Tun Perak, at the Pudu Raya roundabout. Opened in 1988, the museum has an impressive collection of numismatic items—from cowrie shells and blocks of silver through Portuguese and East India currency to British and finally Malaysian coins and notes. It is open daily from 10.00 to 18.00, with free admission.

The **Asian Art Museum** was established in 1973 in the University of Malaya and also houses the Malay Ethnographic Museum with a small collection of artefacts relating to Malay culture. The Asian Art Museum contains sculptures, ceramics, weaponry, basketry, brassware and musical instruments. The museum is open Monday to Friday from 09.00 to 17.00 and from 09.00 to midday on Saturday. Admission is free. The university is 6km from the city centre and can be reached by taxi or bus No. 40 or 238 from the Klang bus terminal.

The **Royal Malaysian Police Museum** is primarily part of the Police Training Centre (☎ 03-2980133, ext. 1128) at Jalan Semarak, about 5km from the city centre, but visits by the public are possible if planned in advance. Strictly speaking, visitors need to write to the Commandant of the Police Training Centre for permission but a telephone call in advance will sometimes suffice. Items on display relate to various aspects of crime, including gaming and secret societies. There is also a forbidding collection of lethal weapons captured from criminals and insurgents. The museum is open from 08.00 to 16.00, Monday to Friday, and Saturday morning until midday. A taxi to the museum from the city centre costs about RM5 or you can take bus No. 19, 237B or 255 from Jalan Chow Kit.

The **Natural Rubber Museum** is in the village of Sungai Buloh, about 15km from the city centre. The museum (☎ 03-6561121) is open Monday to Saturday from 08.00 to 16.15, closed from 12.15 to 14.45 on Friday, and admission is free.

The museum opened in 1992 in a former bungalow of a rubber estate's assistant manager, now in the grounds of the Rubber Research Institute of Malaysia. It is a pity that this museum's location discourages visitors because it is a fascinating place. Exhibits include planting equipment and the variety of tools used to tap and process the latex.

There is a graphic history of the natural rubber industry, from the decisive theft of rubber seeds from Brazil by the Englishman Henry Wickham in 1877 through to contemporary examples of furniture made from the wood of rubber trees, showing the continual progress in the technology of rubber production. Attention is also paid to the social history of the rubber industry. Models of workers' houses illustrate the lives of the many thousands of Indians and Chinese labourers who, by leaving their own countries in the hope of a better life in British Malaya, formed the basis of peninsular Malaysia's multi-ethnic society.

The **Malaysian Armed Forces Museum** is on Jalan Gurney. Exhibits include weapons confiscated during the Emergency and pictures and paintings. It is open from 10.00 to 18.00 Monday to Thursday and Saturday. Admission is RM0.60.

Excursions from Kuala Lumpur ~ west

Places of interest west of Kuala Lumpur are spread out from one another; although they can all be reached by bus and taxi, a good case could be made for renting a car.

History

Historically, Kuala Lumpur is a part of the state of Selangor; indeed, it was only in 1974 that the city was formally ceded by the Sultan of Selangor and became the **Federal Territory**. A hundred years earlier, when Kuala Lumpur was still only a raw, remote and lawless settlement where only the hardiest of Chinese miners and merchants survived, the heart of Selangor state lay to its west in the valley of the **River Klang** (now spelt Kelang).

What created Kuala Lumpur—deposits of tin—is what made the Klang valley worth fighting over for centuries by just about every power group in this part of the Malay world. In the 15C, the revenue accruing from the tin trade went into the coffers of the sultan of Melaka who controlled the region. When the **Portuguese** destroyed Melaka's hegemony, they were unable simply to slot into the complex political and commercial networking that included the Klang valley. Other interested parties included the **Minangkabau** from Sumatra (Port Klang still has a ferry link to Belawan in Sumatra) who eventually lost out to **Bugis groups** from Celebes (Sulawesi), notwithstanding a failed attempt by the Dutch to cash in on the tin trade. The Dutch built a fort at the coastal settlement of Kuala Selangor, which was where the Buginese installed a sultanate around 1750. Over the next hundred years, Chinese entrepreneurs brought in their own labourers to dig for tin. It was a business partnership between Chinese merchants and Selangor chiefs that financed the 1857 trip up the Klang river that led to the foundation of **Kuala Lumpur**. By then the sultanate of Selangor was based in the town of Klang, where the river came into the sea.

Once the potential wealth of the tin-mining around Kuala Lumpur began to be realised, the Selangor chiefs squabbled over the dividends and when this descended into violence the Chinese miners became embroiled. The various **Chinese secret societies** also fought among themselves and the resulting power struggle became known as the **Selangor Civil War**. In 1871 Kuala Lumpur was almost burnt to the ground and two years later the civil war came to an end. By then the tin trade was in a shambles and

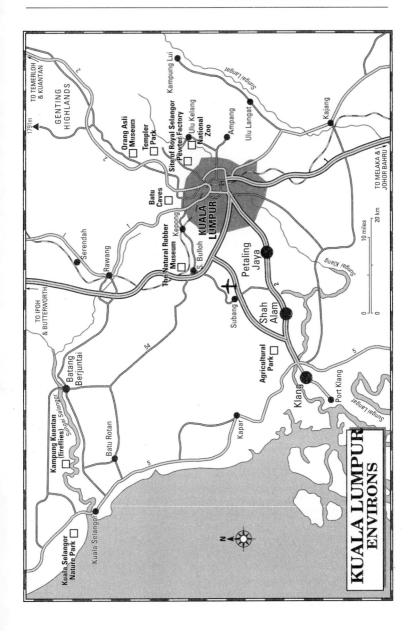

the British decided it was time to become involved. Frank Swettenham was installed in Klang as British Resident in 1874 and two years later Selangor became part of the Federated Malay States. In 1880 the headquarters of the British Residency were shifted to Kuala Lumpur itself.

In the first half of the 20C the Klang valley lost its economic and historical importance. During the past 20 years, however, the old ground has been reclaimed and today the highway connecting Kuala Lumpur with Port Klang (some 4km southwest of Klang) is clogged with traffic, testimony to the growing economic importance of the area. The satellite towns of **Shah Alam** and **Petaling Jaya** continue to grow and prosper but, despite all the hurried development, the western half of Selangor still has places of interest worth exploring as excursions from Kuala Lumpur.

Petaling Jaya

Situated 12km southwest of Kuala Lumpur, Petaling Jaya—referred to as PJ by almost everyone—started life as a small satellite town over 20 years ago. It has grown rapidly into a thriving middle-class mini-city and has a number of good restaurants and nightclubs. **Holiday Villa** (☎ 03-7338788), Jalan SS 12/1, is the largest hotel, with excellent sport and recreation facilities, and a good French restaurant. Further up the same road from Holiday Villa is **Remmes**, an inexpensive Indian restaurant that serves both south Indian and Moghul dishes. The main cluster of restaurants, however, are located together in a part of PJ where the streets are anonymously numbered after the Section 2 (SS2) to which they belong. The central block of shops, restaurants and nightclubs is called Damansara Utama. There is also a popular hawker stall area in SS2 which comes alive at night with stalls cooking Malay, Chinese and Western food.

Mini-buses Nos 28, 30, 33 and 35 run regularly from Kelang bus station to an area of PJ called State and from here it is best to take a taxi to Damansara Utama.

Shah Alam

Some 2km further west of the city than Petaling Jaya is Shah Alam, established as the capital of Selangor in 1982. The centre of attraction, visually at least, is the **Sultan Abdul Aziz Shah Mosque**. It was designed to command attention (often visible from the air when using Subang Airport), which it successfully manages to do mainly because of the sparkling blue colour of its 92m-high dome. With a prayer hall that accommodates over 12,000 worshippers, this mosque claims to be the largest in Southeast Asia. It can also claim to be a state-of-the-art mosque, with a porous dome that enables the rainwater to be collected, channelled off and distributed to the devotees taking their ablutions, who automatically release the water when they break a photo-electric beam.

Visitors to the mosque need to be appropriately attired: a headscarf for women and a shirt for men and no shorts for either sex. This dress code applies to all mosques in Malaysia.

The **Sultan Alam Shah Museum**, close to the mosque, was opened in 1989 to house artefacts relating to the history of the state of Selangor. Apart from tribal and folk arts and crafts, there is a particularly good collection of porcelain and terracotta jewellery. The museum (☎ 03-5597604) is open daily, except Monday, from 09.30 to 17.30 and on Friday from 09.30 to 12.30 and 14.45 to

18.00. Admission is free. A taxi from the city centre costs about RM12 or red bus No. 222 or 206 from Klang bus terminal.

A whole day excursion to Shah Alam could combine a morning visit to the mosque and museum, lunch in the **Holiday Inn** hotel (☎ 03-5503696) which is right next door, and the afternoon at the **Agricultural Park**. The most interesting feature in the park is the paddy field exhibition which has six separate plots simultaneously showing each stage in the cultivation of rice. To complete the process there is also a working rice mill. At the park headquarters, pick up a map that shows the locations of the various other agricultural exhibitions and the network of paths that wind their way through the 1214 hectares of the park.

Bicycles can be hired at the park and, if you are staying overnight, an early morning climb to the top of Sapu Tangan Hill (788m) can be undertaken. Accommodation (☎ 03-5506922) is available in the park's chalets from RM30–120 a night. There is no restaurant and you will need to bring your own food to make use of the cooking facilities. Avoid visiting the park at weekends and school holidays, when large noisy groups invade the place.

To reach the park from Kuala Lumpur take the Klang bus No. 222 from the Kelang bus station. The journey takes about 45 minutes.

Klang (Kelang)

It is only in Klang, 32km southwest of Kuala Lumpur, that the visitor can seek out some reminders of Selangor's historic past. Until 1880 this town was the capital of the state. It was from here, in 1857, that the 87 miners set off up the Klang river to search out new tin deposits (see p 64)—the success of the expedition spelling the demise of Klang which for the previous 300 years had been the political centre of Selangor.

In the old southern part of town, on the southern banks of the river, is Gedung Raja Abdullah on Jalan Raja Abdullah, in the vicinity of the Klang police station. **Gedung Raja Abdullah** is a museum devoted to the history of Klang. It occupies a building that belonged to Raja Abdullah bin Raja Jaafar, the son of the Sultan of Selangor. He was one of the prime motivating forces behind the 1857 expedition—the same year that he erected this building as his home and tin warehouse. The main attraction in the museum is the unrivalled collection of photographs pertaining to the history of tin, supplemented by miscellaneous items like currency made from tin. The museum (☎ 03-3327383) is open Monday to Thursday from 10.00 to 18.00, free admission.

Klang is easily reached by bus from the Klang (Kelang) bus station in Kuala Lumpur; from the bus station in Klang it is a 15-minute walk to the museum. A taxi will only cost a few *ringgit*.

Some 8km further west is **Port Klang** (Kelang), formerly known as Port Swettenham after the British Resident Frank Swettenham. Today, the town is known for its seafood and as the ferry port for travel to Belawan in Sumatra. The one-way fare is RM120; this includes the bus ride from Belawan to Medan, the nearest town and the obvious destination.

Kuala Selangor

Located on the coast some 60km north of Kelang (65km from Kuala Lumpur), Kuala Selangor was the original place of residence for the Sultan of Selangor and hence the state's first capital. Two fortresses were built here but only the remains of **Fort Altingberg**, established in the 18C and the larger of the two, remind the visitor of the town's historic importance. The fort was originally built under the local Malay nobility and called Fort Melawati, but was captured by the Dutch in the 1780s as part of their attempt to take over part of the tin trade. During the 1867–73 Selangor Civil War, the fort was badly damaged by the British who bombarded it from their gunboats, signalling their intervention in the war over the tin-rich Klang valley. The intact remains now house a small museum, the chief exhibit of which is an execution block. The museum is open daily from 09.00 to 16.30 and admission is free.

However, the only—though eminently sufficient—reason for travelling to this historic coastal corner is to visit the **Kuala Selangor Nature Park**. The 250 hectares of mudflats and neighbouring forest attract a fascinating variety of birdlife, and the trails that begin from the main entrance facilitate the chances of spotting the characteristic mangrove birds: the ashy tailorbird, mangrove blue flycatcher and the mangrove whistler are all readily seen. The Egrets Trail is the shortest walk, taking only ten minutes to reach a bird hide looking out across a lake. From this and other hides you should see kingfishers and bee-eaters as well as kites. Three other longer trails—the Brahminy Trail, the Macaque Trail and the Langur Trail—are named after the species that visitors are most likely to see. The longest walk is that to the Boardwalk, through secondary forest and mangrove, from where mud skippers are a common sight.

The park lies along the East Palaeartic migratory route and therefore migratory birds from Siberia, China and Russia stop over here before flying south towards Australia. To view many of the migratory wading birds—including rarities such as the spoon-billed sandpiper and Nordmann's greenshank—it is worth travelling 6km north, across the river, to Tanjung Karang. If you have your own transport you can drive to Tanjung Karang along the main road heading north.

Within the main park area the mammal to try and identify is the silver leaf monkey. It has a long tail, like the far more common macaque monkey which also lives in the park, but is easily distinguished by its silvery fur and small crest. From the hides it is also possible to watch the smooth otter and the small-clawed otter.

A rare attraction near the park is the opportunity to view the **luminous fireflies** that glow each evening along the banks of the river.

> Of all the fireflies (*Lampyridae*) in southeast Asia, the luminous fireflies are the most unusual because of their synchronised flashing. It is only the male of the *Pteroptyx malaccae* beetle that emits the flash—roughly one per second—in perfect time with thousands of others and it is quite an incredible sight. A satisfactory explanation for this behaviour has yet to be found though it seems to be part of a mating ritual. The female beetles, which emit a dimmer and unsynchronised light, land in the trees first and are later joined by the males. Local villagers used to collect and bottle the fireflies as a ready-made torchlight. The best time to watch them is around 19.30; a moonless night adds to the sense of theatricality.

From the village of Kampung Kuantan, about 8km inland from Kuala Selangor, **boat rides** (RM24 per ride for about 40 minutes) are organised to view the phenomenon further up the river. Without your own transport a taxi is needed to reach Kampung Kuantan from Kuala Selangor. It will cost about RM50 to charter a taxi, which will take you there and also wait to transport you back to town or to the park chalets.

Accommodation is booked through the Malayan Nature Society (☎ 03-8892294 before 17.00); they can also arrange for transport to Kampung Kuantan. Two- and four-bedroomed chalets cost RM25 per person; a three-bedroomed chalet is RM45. There is also a communal kitchen area so bring your own food and drink. Remember to pack some mosquito repellent. Binoculars are very useful, though some are available for hire at the park. The park centre is open daily from 09.00 to 17.00. Accommodation is also available at the government resthouse (☎ 03-8891010) from RM30. There are not many rooms, so book ahead.

Transport from Kuala Lumpur is by bus No. 141 from the Puduraya bus station to Kuala Selangor. From here take a taxi for the 10-minute ride to the Nature Park.

Excursions from Kuala Lumpur ~ north

Orang Asli Museum

This museum (☎ 03-6892122) is 24km north of Kuala Lumpur, just off Jalan Gombak, and is really a day's excursion from town. The trip is worthwhile if you want to find out more about the country's Orang Asli ('first people'), or aborigines as they are officially called. Despite the rapid modernisation that is engulfing Malaysia, there are still numerous pockets of Orang Asli communities in the more remote rural and jungle areas. This small museum, opened in 1987, has over 800 artefacts relating to the culture of the various tribes. Apart from the usual tableaux and dioramas depicting hunting scenes, there are more interesting collections of the real tools used to hunt and prepare food—blowpipes, traps and fishing equipment. There are also historic photographs of Orang Asli groups that were more or less coerced into helping the British fight the Chinese Communists during the Emergency.

The museum is open Saturday to Thursday from 09.00 to 17.30, and admission is free. There is a small souvenir shop but no cafeteria so pack some refreshments. To reach the museum take a taxi, or bus No. 174 from Lebuh Ampang which takes almost an hour. A couple of stops before the museum is the Mimaland Amusement Park (see below).

Batu Caves

Situated 13km north of Kuala Lumpur, these caves are sacred to Hindus and contain a number of shrines. During the Thaipusam festival (see p 36) some half a million devotees arrive here in the space of two days but for the rest of the year they are relatively empty and visitors are free to wander around. The caves, part of a huge limestone formation, are millions of years old but only became known to the public after their discovery in 1881 by the American adventurer and naturalist William Hornaby. A decade later, after a small Hindu shrine was constructed in the cave, the place gradually became more and more popular. The original dedication to Lord Subramaniam was added to by a shrine to Ganesh, the elephant-headed god, and today the caves function as a general place of worship for all Hindus. Hopefully, in the near future, some serious renovation work will commence; the paintwork on the statues is peeling off, soot from camphor burning is everywhere and maintenance is generally poor.

A relatively easy climb of 272 steps leads to the large cave which contains the temple to Lord Subramaniam. There is a smaller inner temple guarded by two figures at the entrance. Back at the bottom of the steps, on the left side, there is an entrance path to a smaller cave, which is a museum of sorts which displays a variety of statues of Hindu gods against a background of colourfully painted walls.

Getting there. To reach the caves from Kuala Lumpur, take the mini-bus No. 11 from Central Market or the Pertama Shopping Centre on Jalan Semerang, off Jalan Raja Laut. The journey takes almost 45 minutes. Most of the countryside tours that can be booked through your hotel include a visit to Batu Caves; these tours usually include a stopover at **Pak Ali's House**, which is also on the bus route. The house, built in 1917, is a fine example of traditional Malay domestic architecture and the family who live there today charge RM3 for a short tour of the place.

During the time of the **Thaipusam festival** there are extra buses, as well as a special train service, to the caves. Be sure to get there as early as possible and bring food and drink for the day. You will see the penitents skewering their flesh with hooks without apparently suffering any pain. See p 344 of the chapter on Singapore for more information on this festival.

Templer Park

Named after the last British High Commissioner, Sir Gerald Templer (1898–1979), this is a tract of jungle and park land which covers an area of about 12 square kilometres. It is a pleasant day's excursion from Kuala Lumpur, and although it is very popular with city folk at weekends and holiday times, only a few complete the jungle treks that are clearly marked for visitors. Most visitors congregate at the natural swimming pool areas along the fall of the river. The main trail follows the river for about an hour to a waterfall; here the main trek continues to work its way through the jungle for about another hour before you need to turn about and return by the same path. From the waterfall there is another path that heads off to the left which meets a surfaced road near the main entrance after about an hour. The park contains several large limestone outcrops and networks of underground caves.

There are some food-stalls near the main entrance but it is better to bring your own provisions for a picnic. The park is 23km north of Kuala Lumpur and may be reached by taxi or bus No. 66 or 72 from the Puduraya bus station. By car, the park is reached by a signposted right turning off the North–South Highway some 2km after joining the road. A visit to Templer Park could be combined with a trip to the Batu Caves, 10km south of Templer Park, from where the No. 11 mini-bus will access the main road north and from where the No. 66 bus can be picked up.

Mimaland Amusement Park

Situated some 16km from Kuala Lumpur, this provides an entertaining day out for children. It is best avoided at weekends when the place can become crowded. The fun facilities include a long water slide, a very large swimming pool, a boating lake and a small zoo. Bus No. 174 from Lebuh Ampang stops at the bottom of a hill from where it is about a 1km walk uphill to the park entrance. Ask the bus driver to make a stop for the Amusement Park.

National Zoo and Aquarium

This is 13km east of the city centre and includes a forest and a lake. There are 1000 species of Malaysian plants and animals as well as some from other parts of the world. There are elephant rides and other things to interest children. The zoo is open from 09.00 to 17.00 Monday to Sunday. Entrance is M$4. Bus No. 170 or minibus No. 17 from Lebuh Ampang to Len Seng goes past the zoo.

Genting Highlands

Nowhere near as bucolic as the name might suggest, this is a noisy gambling resort with an 18-hole golf course and a theme park. The location, on top of a hill 50km north of the capital, is the only attractive natural feature, but the resort is well organised for those who want to gamble. This is the only place in Malaysia where gambling is legal. Accommodation is at the **Genting Highlands Resort** (☎ 03-2111118), **The Pelangi** (☎ 03-2112812) or **The Highlands** (☎ 03-2112812).

It takes one hour to reach Genting from Kuala Lumpur and there is an express bus from the Puduraya bus terminal (☎ 03-2326863). Taxis also leave fairly regularly from the bus terminal.

The West Coast: Kuala Lumpur to Perlis

The first part of this chapter covers the route north from Kuala Lumpur to Butterworth (510km), a town of little interest except as a departure point for Penang. The journey is mostly through the state of Perak; also included, however, are two hill stations (Fraser's Hill and Cameron Highlands) in the state of Pahang which are best reached from the main road between the capital and Butterworth. The chapter ends with a visit to the island of Penang and the little-visited states of Kedah and Perlis.

■ **Perak Tourist Information Centre**, Jalan Tun Sambanthan, 30000 Ipoh, Perak (☎ 05-2412957, fax 05-2412958).

Fraser's Hill

Fraser's Hill is a popular spot, 99km north of Kuala Lumpur. At over 1500m above sea level, it is considerably cooler here than in the city. Besides golf and tennis, there are some interesting leisurely walks in the forests. Fraser's Hill is a very popular weekend destination for people who live in the city, so it is a good idea to make your trip during the week and outside Malaysian and Singaporean school holidays.

History

On maps this hill station appears as **Bukit Fraser** but it is still commonly referred to as Fraser's Hill. **Louis James Fraser** was an English adventurer who arrived in the area in the 1890s. He had travelled first to Australia hoping to discover gold, and it is probable that he came to Malaya for the same reason. He discovered deposits of tin in a group of seven hills that until then had been simply known as Ulu Tras; after the solitary Englishman had built a camp at the top of one of them, the group was renamed Fraser's Hill. Chinese miners were brought in and stories circulated that Fraser was also running an opium den and gambling house. These were staple elements of any mining camp but at that time it was unusual for a non-Chinese to be involved; this may well be part of the explanation for Fraser's mysterious disappearance. In November 1917 a search party under **Bishop Ferguson-Davie** from Singapore found the camp deserted and Fraser was never seen again (he is known to have died sometime before 1904). Ferguson-Davie, however, had discovered a site for a cool mountain retreat, at 1524m above sea level.

The hill station never became as popular as the Cameron Highlands, possibly due to the surrounding dense jungle and relative difficulty of access—factors which appealed to Communist guerrillas during the **Emergency** (see p 44). In 1951 they ambushed the British High Commissioner, **Sir Henry Gurney**, who was travelling to the summit. The

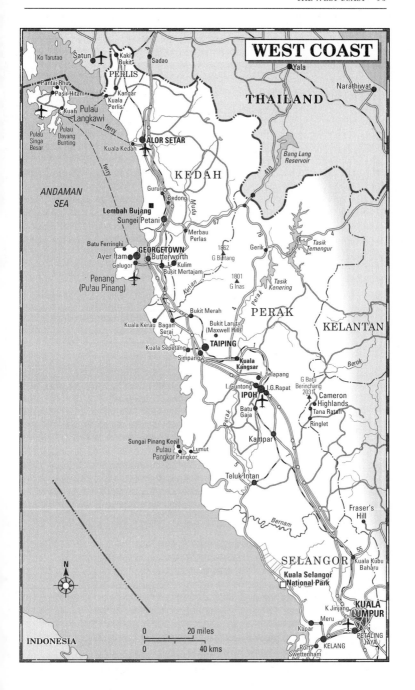

guerrillas were after guns and food and had no idea of the identity of the man whom they had killed.

Practical information

Getting to and from Fraser's Hill
By bus. Take an early bus from Kuala Lumpur's Puduraya bus station to Kuala Kubu Bharu; from here a bus leaves at noon for Fraser's Hill. It departs from Fraser's Hill at 10.00 and 14.00.

By taxi. A taxi could be taken from Kuala Lumpur all the way to Fraser's Hill or just from Kuala Kubu Bharu.

By car. On the main road north of Kuala Lumpur, one hour's drive away, turn off at **Kuala Kubu Bharu** for the beginning of the Gap road northeast to Fraser's Hill. It is 8km up this narrow, winding road, which only carries one-way traffic between 06.30 and 19.00 (outside those hours, make sure your car headlights and hooter are functioning). Traffic is permitted up or down the road in half-hour segments so a short wait may be necessary. There is no petrol station at Fraser's Hill.

Tourist information
There is a **tourist information office** (☎ 09-3622201) next to the clock tower on the right side of the road shortly after entering Fraser's Hill at the top of Jalan Gap. A map of the walking trails is available here, bicycles can be hired, and accommodation booked. There is a **post office** next to the tourist information office and **moneychanging** can be conducted at the Hotel Merlin.

There is a **9-hole golf course** which costs RM30 during the week; golf clubs can be rented for an additional charge. **Tennis courts** can be rented at RM6 an hour through the tourist information office and there is a **sports complex** in the town centre with saunas, squash courts and a **swimming pool**.

The equatorial **climate** is moderated by the altitude. The average temperature during the day is 24°C, dropping to around 13°C at night. There is often a heavy mist in the early morning.

Accommodation and restaurants
At weekends and during public and school holidays many of the hotels and restaurants will be busy with visitors from Kuala Lumpur.

The most luxurious place to stay is **Ye Olde Smokehouse Hotel** (☎ 09-3622226) which, as the name might suggest, has a mock-Tudor appearance, four-poster beds and busts of Henry VIII. **Fraser's Pine Resort** (☎ 09-3622122), at the top of Jalan Quarry, has one- and three-bedroom apartments with kitchens. The **Guest Resort** (☎ 09-3622300), overlooks the golf course. The rates are from RM125 to RM450. There are various affordable but run-down chalets and huts managed by the Fraser's Hill Development Corporation (☎ 09-3622044, 093622194, 09-3622195); their **Temerloh Bungalows** have good views and are more peaceful than many of the places in the town itself.

Afternoon tea with strawberries at Ye Olde Smokehouse Hotel is popular with Malaysians and Singaporeans who may harbour the illusion that this is still typical of English life. Despite the kitsch, the colourful flower arrangements contribute to a congenial atmosphere. The **Temerloh Steak House** is a 20-minute walk north of town at the Temerloh Bungalows and the Guest Resort has a restaurant and coffee shop serving meals. At the bottom of the hill the **Gap Rest House** has a restaurant that has more character than anywhere on Fraser's Hill itself.

Jungle trails
The attraction of Fraser's Hill lies in the undemanding walking trails that are easily covered in less than two hours. The walk to the **High Pines Lodge** is recommended for bird-watching and a circular route begins just past the tourist information office by turning right into Jalan Lady Guillemard. Another pleasant stroll (5km) is along the road past the Ye Olde Smokehouse Hotel to the **Jeriau Waterfall**. You can swim in the cool waters of the pool below the waterfall.

Cameron Highlands

This is the best known of Malaysia's hill stations, some 214km north of Kuala Lumpur, 1524m above sea level, in the central chain of fold mountains that stretch down from southern Thailand. The Highlands are a series of valleys with the river Bertam and its tributaries running through them.

> The Highlands are named after **William Cameron**, a British surveyor who was mapping in the region in 1885 when he accidentally 'discovered' them. However, it is likely that Cameron never stepped foot on these Highlands, since it is thought that the place he actually found was the Blue Valley, further west. The Highlands themselves were first mapped by a Malay, Kulop Riau. It was not until the 1920s that government bungalows began to be built for foreign residents needing to escape the heat and humidity. Tea planters from India and Chinese vegetable farmers also moved in once they realised the climate was ideal and in the years before the Second World War wealthy individuals built second homes here. In the last 20 years luxury hotels and condominiums have sprung up to accommodate the growing number of visitors. However, the place is large enough to retain its unique combination of an English-country look with rolling jungles in the background.

There are now three areas constituting the Cameron Highlands: 46km up the mountain road from Tapah there is **Ringlet**, a centre for flower nurseries and not the best place to stay; **Tanah Rata**, 13km further up the road, is the main tourist centre although the best accommodation is a little further along the road; **Brinchang** is 3km further, past the golf course, and here there are more places to stay and eat.

▪ Practical information

Getting to and from the Cameron Highlands
By bus. An express bus leaves the Puduraya bus station in Kuala Lumpur for Tanah Rata early in the morning (08.30). There are also regular buses from the same bus station to Tapah from where there is an hourly bus to Tanah Ratah and Brinchang.

By taxi. Either from Kuala Lumpur to Tanah Rata or just from Tapah.

By car. Look for the turn-off on the main Kuala Lumpur-Ipoh road is at Tapah (158km north of Kuala Lumpur, 60km south of Ipoh). It takes about one hour to drive the 59km northeast from Tapah to Tanah Rata. Petrol is available at Tanah Rata.

Tourist information

All the places listed here are in Tanah Rata. A **tourist office** (☎ 05-4911200) is at the western end of the main street in Tanah Rata, on your right when travelling from Ringlet. Call in here to collect maps and to enquire about tours of the principal sights, if you are short of time. The tourist office is open daily from around 08.00 to 19.00. There are banks that change money and a post office along the same road. A police station (☎ 05-901222) is opposite the Garden Inn and there is a hospital (☎ 05-901966) also on the main road, near the clock tower that is in the park.

The **18-hole golf course** was originally completed in 1935 as a 5-hole course for the British who are said to have ignored the presence of tiger tracks across the green and sand bunkers when playing. The daily charge is RM40, half that for an afternoon game; shoes, clubs and balls can be hired.

The **climate** can produce surprisingly cool evenings and regular showers of rain. Try to avoid the monsoon months between November and February, although it is more important to avoid holiday times such as Hari Raya when busloads of daytrippers invade the place.

Accommodation and restaurants

There is a wide range of accommodation. **Ye Olde Smokehouse** (☎ and fax 05-4911215; fax 05-4911214), near the golf course in Tanah Rata, was built in the 1930s as a resthouse for planters. There are 21 rooms, each carefully crafted in olde English kitsch, and this is the most exclusive place to stay. The man who built the place, Colonel Stanley Foster, eventually sold it only to construct a similar kind of establishment at Ringlet. Called **The Lakehouse** (☎ 05-4956152; fax 05-4956213), it is less expensive than the Smokehouse but without your own car there is little point in staying in Ringlet. **Strawberry Park** (☎ 05-4911166; fax 05-4911949), back at Tanah Rata, is an international-class resort with good recreational facilities.

At the top end of the middle-range places is the **Sheraton Cameron Highland** (☎ 05-4911211; fax 05-4911178), overlooking the golf course. Also in Tanah Rata is the **Garden Inn** (☎ 05-4911911; fax 05-4915165) which boasts its own cinema and snooker tables.

Good value for budget travellers is the **Cameronian Holiday Inn** (☎ 05-901327), at 16 Jalan Mentigi, a short walk from the centre of Tanah Rata. It has a quiet location and the rooms are comfortably furnished.

Afternoon tea at the Ye Olde Smokehouse is a suitably sedate affair and in the evenings a log fire adds to the atmosphere. The restaurant serves Western food only and there will not be much change out of RM100 for a roast meat dinner. The **Rajah Brooke** restaurant at the Guest Resort serves Western and Chinese food. Inexpensive banana-leaf places serving *murtabaks* and *roti canai* and curries can be found along the main road in Tanah Rata, and there is a good food centre next to the bus station.

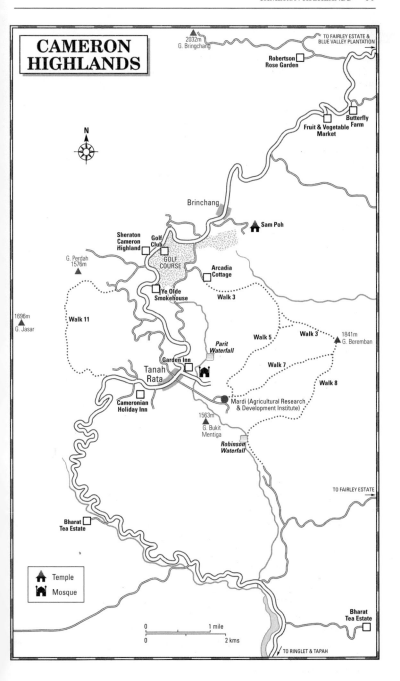

CAMERON HIGHLANDS

2032m
G. Bringchang

TO FAIRLEY ESTATE &
BLUE VALLEY PLANTATION

Robertson
Rose Garden

Butterfly
Farm

Fruit & Vegetable
Market

Brinchang

Sam Poh

Sheraton
Cameron
Highland

Golf
Club

GOLF
COURSE

Arcadia
Cottage

G. Perdah
1576m

Ye Olde
Smokehouse

Walk 3

1696m
G. Jasar

Walk 11

Walk 5

Walk 3

1841m
G. Beremban

Parit
Waterfall

Walk 7

Garden Inn

Tanah
Rata

Walk 8

Cameronian
Holiday Inn

Mardi (Agricultural Research
& Development Institute)

1563m
G. Bukit
Mentiga

Robinson
Waterfall

TO FAIRLEY ESTATE

Bharat
Tea Estate

Temple

Mosque

Bharat
Tea Estate

N

0   1 mile
0   2 kms

TO RINGLET & TAPAH

Places to see

A visit to one of the **tea plantations** is recommended. There are several plantations, many providing free guided tours. While the **Fairley Estate** (☎ 05-996032) below Tanah Rata packs the tea as well as drying and fermenting it, the **Blue Valley** plantation above Brinchang is bigger and has more to offer: tours are normally conducted mid-morning but telephone ahead (☎ 05-996032) to make sure.

Tea-picking in the Cameron Highlands

The process of picking and drying the tea has changed little over the last hundred years; this is dramatically obvious when you see the gatherers carrying their baskets of shoots on their heads. The shoots are now picked using modern shears about every ten days, but handpicking is still required for the less accessible parts of the bush. The drying process is handled by machines that simply blow air underneath the leaves; other machines roll and grind the leaves to break up their cell structure and thereby initiate the fermentation. The process of grading the leaves is explained during the tour. Nearly all the technology is simple but effective—no microchips or computers to be seen.

Some 10km beyond Brinchang there is a **Butterfly Farm**, open from 08.00 to 18.00 (RM3), where hundreds of varieties of butterfly dart around the flowers. More interesting for many visitors is the **Robertson Rose Garden**, also north of Brinchang, open from 10.00 to 18.00 with free admission. A wide range of roses is on display, and the views of the surrounding countryside are impressive; there are dried flowers and honey for sale.

The **Sam Poh Temple**, just below Brinchang, is reached down a signposted small road. It takes about half an hour to walk there from Brinchang. While there is nothing architecturally interesting about the temple or attached monastery, built in 1965, it makes for a pleasant stroll.

Above Brinchang there are a number of **vegetable farms** where cabbage, cress, cauliflowers and leeks are grown on precarious ledges cut out of the hillside. A cable system is used to transport the vegetables up to the road from where they are collected and transported to places such as Hong Kong and Singapore.

Walks

The good news is that there are plenty of walking trails to suit all ages and levels of fitness; while there is little chance of seeing much in the way of wildlife or spectacular views, there are rich rewards for anyone with an interest in flowers and plants and the climate is never debilitating. The bad news is that the numbered walks are poorly maintained and signposted and the maps available from the tourist office are barely adequate. This should never become a hazard but follow the routes carefully.

Walk 11 is one of the easiest walks, beginning at the weather station which is off the road midway between Tanah Rata and Brinchang, and heading for Gunung Jasar (1696m) but bypassing this strenuous climb and heading south and then east to end up in Tanah Rata. It takes less than two hours.

Walk 3 takes over two hours and is a little more demanding. It begins at the Arcadia Cottage, southeast of the golf course, and is capable of increasing the heartbeat on the ascent of Gunung Beremban (1841m). **Walk 5** branches off Walk 3 before the climb up to Gunung Beremban and heads south to the Malaysian Agriculture Research and Development Institute (MARDI) from where the road north to Tanah Rata can be picked up. Walk 5 takes about an hour and avoids the more strenuous part of Walk 3.

A fairly tough climb is **Walk 8** from the Robinson Waterfall to Gunung Beremban which takes about three hours. **Walk 7** from MARDI to the peak is equally arduous, but exhilarating views may be enjoyed at the top.

Perak

Perak is the second-largest state in Malaysia, stretching up the west coast from 70km north of Kuala Lumpur to just below the island of Penang, increasing in width as it turns inland and forms the border with Thailand for some 90km. The largest town in this state of 21,000 square kilometres is **Ipoh**, conveniently located on the Singapore–Thailand railway line and the main North–South Highway. The next largest town is **Taiping**, about 50km to the north. Between Ipoh and Taiping is the small town of **Kuala Kangsar**, the royal town of the state, and home to the Sultan of Perak.

Perak is the Malay word for silver; it actually refers to the shining tin which was extensively exploited in the 19C, making the state famously rich as well as attracting a large number of Chinese immigrants. The ethnic mix of Chinese and Malays is one of the state's most attractive features. The towns of historical interest complement the appeal of sand and sun on the easily reached island of **Pangkor**.

Despite the many places of interest and the ease of travelling within the state, many visitors still only see Perak through a train or bus window as they travel to or from Penang in the northwest of the country. The relatively small number of tourists helps to make a visit here even more enjoyable.

The earliest period of Malaysia's **colonial history** is closely linked with Perak and many of the places of interest are associated with the first arrival of the British. There are splendid examples of Straits Chinese and Edwardian architecture in Ipoh, including the aptly named Majestic Station Hotel which can boast more colonial atmosphere than the revamped Raffles in Singapore. Bukit Larut (Maxwell Hill), just outside Taiping, was the first hill station built by the British, and it continues to offer refuge from the tropical heat. The story of rubber, the other great natural resource that turned the peninsula into a colony, has its origins in the small town of Kuala Kangsar. A tree still stands here which was grown from the first seeds brought from the Brazilian jungle (see p 42). The most popular location in Perak is undoubtedly the lush island of Pangkor, offering sand, sun, water sports and with a range of accommodation to suit all budgets.

History

The history of Perak is a turbulent one: the state was constantly preyed on by neighbouring and foreign powers all wishing to cash in on its valuable tin deposits.

In the 16C, Perak was known for its deposits of tin; this attracted the attention of **Ayudhya** (or Ayutthaya; a kingdom of Siam in 1350–1767), but because Perak's royalty was related to Melaka's prestigious rulers the territory was readily brought into the Malay fold and Siam was kept at bay. However, after the fall of Melaka to the Portuguese, Perak was conquered by the **kingdom of Aceh** (north Sumatra); this then led to a quarrel between Aceh and the Portuguese over the tin trade. In the early 17C, open warfare erupted and peace was only established after Aceh's defeat by the Portuguese. Later in the century, Perak's nobility turned to the Dutch for protection against the renewed interest of Siam in the state. Once this threat subsided, however, the latent hostility between the Dutch and the Perak court rose to the surface. Relations were strained and disagreements over how to share the revenue produced by taxing the tin brought down the rivers simmered for decades.

In 1826, a British officer, **Captain James Low** of Penang, negotiated a treaty whereby the **East India Company** promised aid if needed to protect Perak's independence. The treaty was never formally ratified by the British government but it gave it a foot in the door. In the decades that followed, immigrant miners arrived from various parts of China and the rival secret societies they brought with them inevitably led to conflict and violence. While this provided the British with an excuse to intervene, the crucial factor was a dispute over the Perak sultanate. By agreeing to recognise one of the claimants, **Raja Abdullah**, as the rightful heir to the throne, the British secured in return a 'suitable residence for a British officer to be called Resident who shall be accredited to his Court and whose advice must be asked and acted upon on all questions other than those touching Malay religion and custom'. This was the important clause in the 1874 Treaty of Pangkor and it formalised the British desire to take economic and political control.

This decision did not meet with unanimous support from all the Malay chiefs and there was a minor insurrection that began with the assassination of the first British Resident, **James Wheeler Birch**. He had been appointed in November 1874 and was murdered the following year by men acting under a local chief who refused to accept the British presence. The murder happened at **Pasir Salak**, a small village and home of the local chief, when Birch was washing by the water's edge and his interpreter was putting up a proclamation announcing the Resident's powers. The rebels were easily crushed by an army brought in by the British and executions followed. The complicity of Raja Abdullah was proved and he was exiled to the Seychelles; the rival claimant, **Raja Yusuf**, was promoted in his place.

Raja Yusuf had his home at a *kampung* called Kuala Kangsar; this was chosen as the place of residence for the new Resident of Perak, **Sir Hugh Low** (1824–1905) (see also p 42).

During the 12 years of Low's tenure of office (1877–89), secure foundations for British rule were laid down. Low was an enlightened man who ruled with tremendous tact and respect for Malay culture, qualities that had been lacking in the abrasive and less diplomatic Birch. Low, like many of these early colonial rulers, was also an eccentric individual. Isabella Bird, an intrepid Victorian traveller, visited Kuala Kangsar in 1879; when she sat down for dinner she was surprised to see places had been laid for two other diners. Low happened to be away at the time and she was not expecting any company for dinner. Surprise turned to astonishment when the servant led two apes to the table where they took their seats and proceeded to partake of the same curry and pineapple meal. Low's two pet apes had their dinner like this every evening.

Low was a keen naturalist and encouraged planters to come and work in Perak. He planted the first rubber tree seeds, and the first rubber trees to blossom and bear fruit in the East did so in Kuala Kangsar.

It was under Low's successor, **Frank Swettenham** (1850–1946), that Taiping developed as the administrative centre for British rule. Swettenham had a cricket ground built in Taiping—Low had already started a museum there—and a rest house was opened in the mid 1880s 'for the convenience of gentlemen who came to the country with a view to investing in it'. In 1896 Perak became part of the Federated Malay States and remained so until 1948 when the Federation of Malaya was created.

Getting around Perak

Transport is never a problem in Perak. Malaysia's main railway line, and major roads, connect the towns of Ipoh, Kuala Kangsar and Taiping with Penang in the north and Kuala Lumpur to the south. There are also frequent bus connections, including ones to the coastal town of Lumut (RM3.50 from Ipoh) where boats regularly ply to and from the tropical island of Pangkor (RM2). In addition, Pelangi Air makes speedy connections between Ipoh and Kuala Lumpur (RM165), Langkawi (RM267) and Melaka (RM300); there are also flights between Pangkor and Singapore (RM500)

A **tour** of Ipoh, Kuala Kangsar and Taiping would take at least two days, skipping quickly by bus between the three towns; or four days or more with a stopover in the hill station of Bukit Larut for a more leisurely pace. From either Taiping or Ipoh it is easy to reach the island of Pangkor. A couple of days lazing around on the beaches would round off a trip of four to seven days.

Ipoh

Ipoh, 205km northwest of Kuala Lumpur, is one of Malaysia's largest cities, with a population of around half a million. Its growth started around 1880 following the discovery of a major deposit of tin. Perak had long been renowned for its tin—since at least the 16C; Ipoh had for centuries been a small *kampung* dwarfed by massive outcrops of limestone that dominate the surrounding landscape. Arriving in Ipoh by air offers panoramic views of the surrounding jungle-topped limestone hills and karsts, and the aftermath of the vast tin mining industry is evidenced by the number of water-filled pits that are scattered across the countryside. The town is said to get its name from the ipoh (upah) tree, whose poisonous sap was used by the orang asli to coat the darts of their blowpipes.

Today, Ipoh continues its prosperous growth although the importance of tin has diminished tremendously since the fall in world prices in the 1980s. A number of small industries are developing apace but fortunately the old part of town, on the western side of the sluggish Sungai Kinta, remains intact as the focus of visitors' interest. There are a number of short excursions worth considering, so at least one night's stay is recommended.

◾ Practical information

Getting to and from Ipoh

By air. Pelangi Air in Ipoh (☎ 05-3124770) flies daily to Singapore (☎ 7357155) and Melaka (☎ 06-351175), on Monday, Wednesday and Friday to Kuala Lumpur (☎ 03-2624446), and on Monday, Wednesday, Friday and Sunday to Langkawi (☎ 04-9552261). There is a regulated taxi fare, RM10, from Ipoh airport to any of the town hotels.

By train. Check with the railway station (☎ 05-2510072) for ticket availability and times of trains to Kuala Lumpur and Singapore, and Kuala Kangsar, Taiping and Butterworth.

By bus. Ipoh is on the main North–South Highway and there are frequent buses to Kuala Lumpur, Melaka, Singapore, Butterworth and Kota Bharu. The long-distance bus station that serves these destinations, on Jalan Tun Abdul Razak, also handles buses to Lumut. On the other side of the road is the local bus station with buses to Kuala Kangsar and Taiping. *Nice* express buses (☎ 05-241 6809) also run a fast and comfortable service to and from Kuala Lumpur, four times a day, for RM19. Their office is at Medan Kidds.

Car hire. There is an Avis car hire at Sultan Azlan Shah Airport (☎ 05-3122459/3120569) and a Hertz at the Royal Casuarina Hotel at 18 Jalan Gopeng (☎ 05-2555555).

Tourist information

The **tourist office** (☎ 05-2412957) is on Jalan Tun Sambanthan, near the railway station.

Money exchange can be conducted at most of the big banks along Jalan Dato' Maharaja Lela. The Syuen and Casuarina hotels also have exchange facilities and there's a money exchange shop at 74 Persiaran Greenhill (☎ 05-2543686).

The **General Post Office** is next to the railway station and the big hotels will sell also stamps and post letters.

Taxis are needed to visit most of the attractions in and around Ipoh. The standard unmetered fare for any journey within town—say from the railway station to the Casuarina Hotel—should not be more than RM5 (always agree on the price beforehand).

The **railway station**, **bus stations** and **taxi stand** are grouped close to one another at the western end of town.

There is a **shop** on level 4 of the Syuen Hotel selling Chinese arts and handicrafts. For general shopping there is a large Parkson Grand department store, across the road from the Syuen Hotel, with a supermarket in the basement and a bookstore on the third level. Out of town on Jalan Kuala Kangsar, not far from the Perak Tong Temple, Oriental Pewter has a factory shop—tours of the factory are not available—selling pewter items from RM30 pendants upwards.

Accommodation

Comfortable rooms around RM100 are available at the **Ritz Garden Hotel** (☎ 05-2547777; fax 05-2545222) at 79 Jalan C.M. Yusuf and there are a number of other less expensive hotels in this area, some of which can be noisy from the street traffic. **Hotel Mikado** (☎ 05-2555855; fax 05-2557855) at 86–88 Jalan Yang Kalsom is good value with clean rooms and en-suite bathrooms.

The **Majestic Station Hotel** (☎ 05-2555605; fax 05-2553393 and in Kuala Lumpur at ☎ 03-2732841; fax 03-2732842) has boxy rooms downstairs for over RM120 but the de luxe rooms on the third level, costing over RM150, have more space and open onto the grand balcony.

The pleasant **Casuarina Hotel** (☎ 05-2555555; fax 05-2558177), 18 Jalan Gopeng, has long been popular with tourists, despite being a taxi ride away from the town. Rooms cost around RM200 and there's a swimming pool.

The plush **Syuen Hotel** (☎ 05-2538889; fax 05-2533335), 88 Jalan Sultan Abdul Jalil, is the eponymous creation of a local millionaire and could probably gain an entry in the *Guinness Book of Records* for the number of panes of glass in its eccentric edifice. Rooms with a view are around RM200; although the rooftop pool is small the health and fitness facilities are first class. In the same part of town the pool-less **Hotel Excelsior** (☎ 05-2536666; fax 05-2536908), 43 Jalan Sultan Abdul Jalil, costs about RM150 with breakfast included.

Restaurants

Ipoh is justifiably renowned for its food, and *char kway teow* (rice noodle fried with seafood in black bean sauce) and *nga choi kai* (bean sprout chicken) are recommended Chinese dishes. There are good restaurants providing Indian, Italian and Japanese food—and the ubiquitous franchises of McDonald's and Kentucky Fried Chicken have infiltrated Ipoh.

The hotels offer the most comfortable and more expensive restaurants. At the Casuarina Hotel, **Il Ritrovo** is a cosy Italian place where a three-course meal with wine would cost little short of RM200 for two. The hotel's **Garden Terrace** has European and Asian dishes for around RM30, and a buffet lunch. The Excelsior Hotel has the **D'Bombay** Indian restaurant, open from 11.00 to 15.00 and from 18.00 to 23.00, where a chosen chilli-rating determines the spiciness of the food. The hotel's **Palace** restaurant serves Cantonese cuisine, and the 24-hour **Dulang Coffee House** serves moderately priced Asian and Western meals.

Smarter are the outlets of the Syuen Hotel: Chinese at the **Syuen Palace**, expensive European at **The Mines**, and a Japanese chef master-minding the **Japanese Corner**. The buffet at the hotel's **Bougainvillea Coffee House**, open 24 hours, is the best value for money.

A recommended restaurant for an evening meal is the **Restoran Cowan St** on Jalan Raja Musa Aziz, where a good Chinese meal for two should be around RM25. Equally unpretentious and similarly priced is the north Indian **Restoran Pakeeza** off Persiaran Greenhill (☎ 05-2501057).

For inexpensive Chinese and Malay meals there is the excellent **Wooley Centre**, located outside the town centre but worth the taxi ride. A more convenient cluster of **food-stalls** can be found outside the railway station. Along Jalan Raja Ekram there are a number of inexpensive but none-too-wonderful Chinese and Malay eating places; however, just off this street, at 63 Jalan Mustapha Al-Bakri, there is a classic Chinese-style **coffee shop** that is shared by both a Malay stall and a Chinese one. The food is reasonable and you can even listen to 'Rhinestone Cowboy' on the juke-box! Also, at night, the **Restoran Wah Pan**, at the corner of Jalan Raja Ekram and Jalan Leong Sin Nam, is fine for fresh fruit juice or beer.

At any time of day, the entire top level of **Parkson Grand** on Jalan Abdul Jalil is home to an array of food outlets serving everything from fish and chips and apple pie to *yong tau foo* and *gensing* chicken soup, all for around RM7 a dish. The **Majestic Restaurant** at the railway hotel of the same name serves reasonably priced Asian and Western dishes and the setting compensates for the mediocre cuisine. Enjoy a breakfast here for around RM10.

Old Town Walk

The old town, which dates back to the 1890–1930 period, is remarkably well preserved. It is best seen as part of an evening stroll, beginning at the hotel bar and restaurant which is part of the splendid **railway station** and **Majestic Station Hotel**, built in 1917. Its architecture successfully combines Moorish features—its dome and patterned stonework—with 19C Gothic style columns and arches and, most impressive of all, a grand balcony on the third floor which should not be missed. The balcony runs the entire length of the building, complete with marble floor and huge fans that help to conjure up a picture of expatriate planters and civil servants relieving their ennui by sinking a few *stengahs* each evening.

Looking across the palm-topped garden and the main road from the balcony of the hotel there are views of the **High Court** and **Town Hall**, both built in the Edwardian period and still evocative of a long-gone era.

From the station, walk down Jalan Dato' Maharaja Lela, between the High Court and Town Hall (in Malay, the Dewan Bandaran). On your left is an example of the many solid Edwardian structures built by the British in their heyday—the **Hong Kong and Shanghai Bank**. It was built in a commanding position on a corner of the street, with ornate Corinthian columns on the second floor, more offices on the third level, and all topped by an elegant tower supported by smaller columns.

At the junction with Jalan Sultan Yussuf turn right and then right again into Jalan Dato' Sagor. This block, and many of the nearby streets, contain what are probably the best-preserved examples of **Chinese town architecture** in Malaysia. They were built as shops with accommodation above. The bedrooms upstairs have louvred wooden shutters on the windows—notice that the more affluent shop owners had designs sculptured above the windows.

The **Birch Memorial**, a clock tower just off Jalan Dato' Sagor, is a reminder of more tumultuous times when Malay consent to foreign rule was not a matter of course. The memorial is a square tower with four panels depicting the growth of civilisation. There is a portrait bust of James Wheeler Birch, the first British Resident of Perak, whose lack of diplomacy in pushing forward British influence cost him his life in 1875 (see p 102). Also on Jalan Dato' Sagor is the State Mosque.

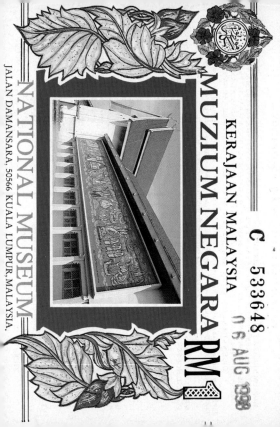

KERAJAAN MALAYSIA

C 533648

0 6 AUG 1998

MUZIUM NEGARA

RM1

NATIONAL MUSEUM

JALAN DAMANSARA, 50566 KUALA LUMPUR, MALAYSIA.

PENERANGAN UMUM/GENERAL INFORMATION

MUZIUM NEGARA YANG DILETAK DI BAWAH JABATAN MUZIUM DAN ANTIKUITI BERADA DI BAWAH PORTFOLIO KEMENTERIAN KEBUDAYAAN, KESENIAN DAN PELANCONGAN MALAYSIA, TELAH DIBUKA DENGAN RASMINYA PADA 31 OGOS 1963, DENGAN OBJEKTIFNYA SEBAGAI TEMPAT MENYIMPAN KOLEKSI KHAZANAH WARISAN BUDAYA MALAYSIA YANG BERHARGA DAN BOLEH DIGUNA DAN DIMANAFAATKAN UNTUK MENYAMPAIKAN ILMU PENGETAHUAN

The National Museum which is under the Museums Department and Antiquity is in the portfolio of the Ministry of Culture, Arts and Tourism Malaysia, was officially opened on 31 August 1963, with an objective, to be a repository of Malaysia's rich cultural heritage and utilise the collections for imparting knowledge

WAKTU MELAWAT *VISITING HOURS*	DIBUKA TIAP-TIAP HARI DARI PUKUL 9.00 PAGI—6.00 PETANG. DITUTUP 2 HARI SETIAP TAHUN PADA HARI RAYA PUASA DAN HARI RAYA HAJI.
	Open Daily 9.00 a.m.—6.00 p.m. Closed for 2 days in a year on Muslim Festive Seasons—Aidiladha and Aidilfitri celebration.
BAYARAN MASUK *ADMISSION FEES*	RM1.00 UNTUK ORANG DEWASA DAN KANAK-KANAK BERUMUR 12 TAHUN KE ATAS. KANAK-KANAK BERUMUR 12 TAHUN KE BAWAH DAN KANAK-KANAK YANG BERPAKAIAN SERAGAM SEKOLAH MASUK DENGAN PERCUMA.
	RM1.00 for adults and children above 12 years old. Children under 12 years and students with school uniforms are free.
TIKET *TICKET*	SAH DIGUNAKAN PADA HARI DIKELUARKAN SAHAJA.
	Valid on day of issue only.
PERATURAN MUZIUM *MUSEUMS REGULATIONS*	SEBARANG JENIS MINUMAN, MAKANAN, MEROKOK, MEMBAWA BINATANG PELIHARAAN, RADIO, SENJATA-SENJATA MERBAHAYA, DAN MEMEGANG BARANG-BARANG PAMERAN DILARANG KERAS DI DALAM BALAI-BALAI PAMERAN.
	Beverage, food, smoking, pets, radios, offensive weapons, and touching of exhibits are strictly prohibited in the galleries.

SILA SIMPAN TIKET INI UNTUK PEMERIKSAAN
Please keep the ticket for checking purposes.

Dengan Perintah
By Order

KETUA PENGARAH
DIRECTOR GENERAL
JABATAN MUZIUM DAN
ANTIKUITI,
JALAN DAMANSARA,
50566 KUALA LUMPUR,
MALAYSIA

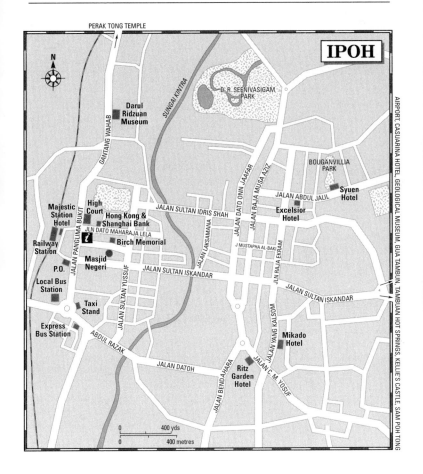

Museums

Ipoh became legendary for the number of 'tin millionaires' it spawned in the early decades of this century; convincing proof of the wealth generated by the metal can be seen by a visit to the **Darul Ridzuan Museum** on Jalan Panglima, Bukit Gantang Wahab. The entire edifice was built in 1926 as a suburban residence by Foo Choong Yiy, a successful tin entrepreneur. Inside, the museum houses an interesting collection of old photographs of the town as well as images of the tin-mining process and the Japanese occupation. The less interesting second floor is devoted to exhibits on the logging industry and the indigenous wildlife. Take a taxi to the museum as it is a longish walk along the road that runs north past the railway station. It is open from 09.30 to 17.00 (seven days a week) and admission is free.

Only worth considering if you have a keen interest in the subject, is the **Geological Museum** on Jalan Harimau, away at the east side of town, and definitely requiring a taxi. There are hundreds of examples of minerals, including cassiterite (the ore from which tin is extracted), as well as precious stones and rocks. The museum is open 08.00 to 16.15 Monday to Friday and until 12.45 on Saturday; there is no entrance charge.

Excursions from Ipoh

There are a number of cave temples built into the limestone outcrops around Ipoh: the two main ones are easy to reach as they are situated by the side of the main roads heading north and south out of town. To reach one of them, the **Perak Tong Temple**, which is 6.5km north of Ipoh and open from 09.00 to 16.00, take a town bus for Kuala Kangsar and ask for the temple, or take a taxi for around five ringitt.

The Perak Tong temple was built in 1926 and contains some 40 statues of Buddha. The wall paintings seen just inside the main entrance at ground level have been painted, over a period of years, by pilgrim artists from different regions of Southeast Asia. The huge bell is ceremoniously sounded if and when you make a contribution to the temple. The massive 12m golden Buddha is flanked on either side by a number of forbidding figures. Just before the interior steps begin, there is a more genial and colourful Buddha that lightens the mood somewhat. Winding steps lead to an opening about 100m above ground where there is a painting of Kuan Yin, the Goddess of Mercy, seated on an elephant. There is a good view of the surrounding countryside from here.

To reach the other cave temple, the **Sam Poh Tong Temple**, 5km south of town and open from 09.00 to 16.00, take a town bus for Kampar and ask for the temple, or take a taxi for around five *ringitt*. This cave temple attracts a larger number of visitors and worshippers. Although the exterior façade dates only to the 1950s, the temple itself dates back to the late 19C. The story goes that a monk from China found the caves while travelling through the area and decided to stay here and meditate for the rest of his life. Inside there is a remarkably squashed-looking reclining Buddha. The pathway through the cavern leads to an open area surrounded by towering limestone walls. A small, dirty-green pond here has become the repository for an inordinately large collection of tortoises, looking very much like the symbols of longevity they are supposed to be. These creatures have been known to bite at unsuspecting visitors who think they like to be stroked when really they are just queuing up for food.

A more worthwhile attraction is the cavernous vegetarian restaurant situated just to the right of the main entrance.

The most bizarre site in the area, **Kellie's Castle**, is 14km south of Ipoh off the road to Batu Gajah; unfortunately no bus goes very close and it takes half an hour by taxi. William Kellie Smith was a Scottish rubber tycoon

Kellie's Castle, near Ipoh

who made his fortune in the first decades of this century and commissioned a Victorian-style extravaganza to be built here as his second home. Work started in the early 1920s but an outbreak of flu decimated the Tamil workforce and the sympathetic Smith financed the construction of a **Hindu temple** at the site. Among the Indian deities on the roof of the temple is a suited man wearing a *topi* (hat) who presumably represents Smith. When work resumed on the 'castle' Smith left for a trip back to Scotland, but he died in Europe and the building was left in its present uncompleted state. The substantial remains suggest that Smith had hoped to re-create in the tropics a nostalgic reminder of a Scottish castle.

Gua Tambun (Tambun cave) is 3km from Ipoh, close to **Tambun Hot Springs**, developed by the Japanese during the Occupation. The hot springs have two naturally heated pools while the cave above contains 10,000 year old paintings. The pools are open 09.00 to 18.00 Monday to Sunday. Entrance is RM5.

Kuala Kangsar

Situated on a tributary of the Perak river, 255km northwest of Kuala Lumpur and 50km north of Ipoh, half-way between Ipoh and Taiping, Kuala Kangsar has been home to the Sultans of Perak for over 500 years. The royal palace (*istana*) where the present sultan lives is closed to visitors; the real attractions lie elsewhere—in the town's history and the architecture of some of its buildings, plus the opportunity to visit a sleepy Malaysian town that has not been tarnished by tourism.

Given that the Sultan of Perak had his palace in Kuala Kangsar it was the logical base for James Wheeler Birch, the first British Resident, to take up his duties as agreed in the 1874 Treaty of Pangkor (see p 42). Hugh Low arrived here in 1877, after Birch's assassination, learnt to speak fluent Malay and stayed for 12 years, during which time he became a model for enlightened and diplomatic rule that was not always followed by his successors.

■ Practical information

Getting to and from Kuala Kangsar
The town can be taken in on a journey between Ipoh and Taiping or by way of a day's excursion from either town. Inexpensive accommodation is available in Kuala Kangsar but if you are visiting the town in transit it is possible to leave luggage at the bus station.

The town is linked by rail and road to Taiping and Butterworth in the north and Ipoh and Kuala Lumpur in the south. The local buses from Taiping and Ipoh are slower and less comfortable than the express buses which also stop in Kuala Kangsar. A taxi from Taiping or Ipoh will cost about RM40.

Tourist information
There is no tourist office but a useful map of the town is available from the Ipoh tourist office (see p 104).

Adventure tours are organised by a local company, Perak River Safari Tours (☎ 05-7769717), No. 04A, MDKK, Jalan Tambang, Bandar Diraja, Kuala Kangsar, Perak 33000. River trips, canoe hire and nature and adventure trips are all available but contact the company in advance.

The **railway station** is a 25-minute walk from the clock tower that marks the centre of town.

The **bus station** is at the bottom of Jalan Raja Bendahara, a ten-minute walk to the southwest of the clock tower.

Accommodation and restaurants

The best place to spend a night is at the **Rest House** (☎ 05-77863872) on Bukit Chandan. The facilities are poor but the location and river views are superb. An alternative is the **Mei Lai Hotel** (☎ 05-77861729) on Jalan Raja Chulan in town. Both places have rooms for around RM50.

There are a number of food-stalls and small restaurants around the bus station. At 53 Jalan Kangsar, the main street that runs through town, **Muslim Restoran** serves a tasty lunch of *murtabak* and lime juice. A few doors down at No. 33, **Restoran Rahmaniah** has a larger menu.

Places to see

In 1877 rubber seeds were brought to Kuala Kangsar by Hugh Low (see pp 42 and 102) and the first nine rubber trees took root and grew in Malaysia. One of **Malaysia's first rubber trees** can still be seen on the pavement corner next to the District Office, with a commemorative plaque in front. To find the rubber tree from the central clock tower roundabout, continue five minutes down Jalan Kangsar from the bus station, turn into the road with the police headquarters and the rubber tree is on the left just after the District Office.

In 1820, when the only rubber plants were those growing wild in South America, the total world demand was a tiny 100 tonnes a year. By the end of the century, the use of pneumatic tyres for bicycles and carriages—foreshadowing the accelerating demand that would be generated by the arrival of the motor car—had enormously increased interest in the latex secretion of *Hevea brasiliensis*, the Brazilian rubber tree. Seeds from the tree had been brought to England and germinated in Kew Gardens in London (Brazilian law forbade their export and the seeds were surreptitiously transported to England). From London some of the seeds went to Singapore and although the first batch died, there was sufficient scientific and commercial interest to ensure continued experimentation.

In 1878 H.N. Ridley was appointed as Director of the Botanical Gardens in Singapore, and he championed research into rubber farming; his enthusiasm—he carried seeds about in his pocket and distributed them to any farmer who would listen to him—led to his being nicknamed 'Rubber Ridley' and 'Mad Ridley'. However, his persistence was eventually rewarded: Low brought the first seeds to Kuala Kangsar, and while Ridley was patiently improving farming techniques back in Singapore, world demand for rubber was steadily increasing. Ten years before the first rubber boom in 1905, a successful plantation had got underway in the Malay peninsula and within three years every state in Malaya had rubber plantations. By 1918 rubber had already become Malaya's chief export and today 90 per cent of the world's rubber still comes from Asia with over half originating in Malaysia and Indonesia. All the rubber trees in Asia are direct descendants of those first seeds that were smuggled out of Brazil.

The other attractions in Kuala Kangsar are reached by the road that follows the river out of town and up a small hill, Bukit Chandan. It can be a hot walk during the day and a taxi ride will cost only a few *ringitt*. The first site is the photogenic **Ubadiah Mosque** on the left which looks quite beautiful with its minarets and golden domes shimmering

Istana Kenangan, the Royal Museum, Kuala Kangsar

in the heat. It took a long time to build: construction was finally completed in 1917 after being interrupted by the First World War and, on another occasion, by two rogue elephants who ran over the costly Italian marble tiles imported for surfacing the floor.

Further up the hill, the imposing **Istana Iskandariah**, the official residence of the Sultan of Perak, comes into view. White walls seem to be the dominant and monotonous theme; infinitely more interesting architecturally is the neighbouring **Royal Museum** which was the sultan's residence before the Istana Iskandariah was completed in 1930. The exhibition of royal regalia inside the museum is of little interest, partly because the explanations are only in Malay, but the building itself is a wonderful testimony to crafted woodwork. It was built, apparently, by a family of craftsmen from Penang without the aid of any drawings or plans. The overall effect is one of grace and harmony, and the intricate lattice work on the exterior is superbly finished. The museum is open from 09.30 to 17.00, but closed between 12.15 and 14.45 on Friday.

Back in town, if time allows, it is worth stopping to gaze at the **Malay College** on Jalan Tun Razak, half way between the railway station and the clock tower. It was founded in 1905 by the British after a group of sultans petitioned for their own élite school. It is still a prestigious school, hence the maintenance of the original neo-classical architecture, including the stately columns and decorated pediments.

Taiping

Taiping is 88km south of Butterworth and 304km north of Kuala Lumpur. Known as Larut to the 19C British colonisers, this town had a reputation as a wild and lawless place. In the 1860s and 1870s, ferocious feuds erupted between rival groups of Hakka and Hokkien Chinese secret societies over the control of the rights to the rich tin deposits in the area. The fighting led to British intervention in 1874; afterwards, they confidently renamed the town Thai-Peng ('everlasting peace'). The peace remained intact until the Second World War when the Japanese took over the town. They built a prison which, still standing and functioning, is now the oldest in the country. In the 1950s it was used by the British to detain Communist guerillas captured during the Emergency; today the inmates include prisoners arrested under Malaysia's own Internal Security Act as well as 'death row' detainees charged under the draconian drug laws.

On a more cheerful note, Taiping is a pleasant, laid-back town where remnants of the colonial-Malay architecture are being restored and where the visitor can enjoy good local food and accommodation, stroll through languid **Lake Gardens** (Taman Tasik), and make an exhilarating 1019m ascent to **Bukit Larut**. There is no tourist office but it is not difficult to find your way about and foreign visitors can still enjoy being regarded as more of a novelty than a nuisance.

▓ Practical information

Getting to and from Taiping
By train. The main train route between Butterworth and Singapore stops at Taiping and a connection with Ipoh is also possible.

By bus. Buses to Kuala Lumpur and Ipoh run regularly; there are also buses to Lumut and Kuala Kangsar. There is a private express office opposite the Jaya supermarket, close to the local bus station, from where coaches depart about every two hours to Lumut from 07.00 to 19.45 (RM4.70) and every hour to Ipoh from 6.30 to 20.30 (RM3.50).

Tourist information
There is no tourist information office. The **railway station** is about 1km west of the town centre where hotels, amenities and the **bus station** are located. There are branches of the **banks** Bumiputra and UMBC on Jalan Kota.

Accommodation
Rooms with air-conditioning and baths at the **Meridien** (☎ 05-8071133), a short walk from the railway station at 2 Jalan Simpang, are in the region of RM55. Similar rooms, but costing less, at RM37, are at the **Government Rest House** (☎ 05-8072044) in Taman Tasik (Lake Gardens). This is the best value for a room and you cannot complain at a breakfast of eggs on toast for RM3. The centrally located **Panorama Hotel** (☎ 05-8074192), at 61 Jalan Kota, used to be the smartest place with rooms around RM100 but the new **Legend Inn** (☎ 05-810000; fax 05-816666) now offers the best facilities with rooms starting at around RM150.

Restaurants
Inexpensive Malay and Chinese food is best enjoyed in the streets close to the bus station. The **Cashier Food Centre**, two blocks up from the Jaya supermarket (with an adjoining McDonald's) on Theatre Road, is home to a wide variety of food-stalls and its popularity with locals stands as a sound recommendation. Behind this food centre can be found the town's indoor market and on one of the corners outside, at 37 Market Square, the **Perak Muslim Restoran** serves a decent light lunch of *prata* and lime juice. Opposite the Jaya supermarket the **Restoran Al-Patani** serves a hot Thai *tom yam* as well as Malay dishes.

The setting of the **Government Rest House Restaurant** at Lake Gardens is a lot more appealing than the actual menu which consists of bland Western and Chinese dishes for around RM20. For a better meal, plus air-conditioned comfort, try the **Coffee House** in the Legend Inn hotel (see Accommodation above), where steak and chips costs about RM30.

Places to see

Many of the places to visit are in the vicinity of the **Lake Gardens** (**Taman Tasik**), built out of an exhausted tin mine northeast of the town centre, where a small zoo as well as boats for hire increase its recreational value for locals. Bukit Larut—formerly Maxwell Hill—is one of the hills that loom over the lush greenery of the Lake Gardens that is nourished by regular downpours of rain; between September and December you are likely to receive a drenching of warm rain. Beside the Lake Gardens there is an **Allied War Cemetery** that bears witness to the many soldiers who died in a vain effort to halt the relentless Japanese advance in December 1941.

> On 18 December 1941 General Percival, in charge of the Malaya Command, flew to Ipoh for an important strategy meeting. The Japanese advance was so swift that the futility of trying to halt their movement anywhere north of Ipoh was accepted. Nevertheless, the next day a battalion of the Argyll and Sutherland Highlanders had orders to confront the invaders, which they did to the west of Taiping, 54km north of Kuala Kangsar. They managed to delay the enemy until nightfall when they were forced to retreat. Percival's new strategy was to try to delay the Japanese until Churchill's promised reinforcements could reach Singapore. For the next week Allied troops, especially Indians, suffered dreadful losses as they tried to dent the enemy's progress, but by 26 December the Japanese commander, General Yamashita, had established himself in a Chinese high school in Taiping to oversee the occupation of Ipoh.
>
> The strongest Allied defence then shifted to the area around Kampar, south of Ipoh on the road to Kuala Lumpur; by 2 January so successful was their resistance that—just as the Allied troops were ordered to retreat—the Japanese commanders for the first time ever were thinking of retreating. The last attempt to slow down the Japanese before they could reach Kuala Lumpur was now focused on the Slim River; by 7 January that attempt had failed after terrible losses sustained by mostly Indian and Scottish troops.

From town a walk to the **Perak Museum**, at the north side of the Lake Gardens, on Butterworth Road, will take in the innocuously sited **prison**, which is directly opposite the museum; non-alcoholic refreshments en route are available at the Government Rest House which provides a pleasing view over the Lake Gardens. The Perak Museum, built in 1883, is the oldest museum in Malaysia. The Victorian building, with whitewashed walls and green roof tiles, is the most interesting exhibit. Inside there is an unimaginative display of archaeological finds and aboriginal implements. Not far from the museum is the Anglican **All Saints' Church**, erected out of wood in 1889. The graveyard includes victims of the Japanese Occupation who were imprisoned nearby.

Back in town, there are two temples located in Station Street: the Chinese

Ling Nam Temple and an Indian **Hindu Temple**. The brightly painted Chinese temple has a boat figure dedicated to the Chinese emperor who constructed the first canal in China. The Indian temple has an attractive *gopuram* with a modest collection of colourfully painted Hindu figures. Both temples are worth a visit and there are no entrance charges.

Bukit Larut (Maxwell Hill)

The oldest and smallest hill resort in Malaysia is 12km east of Taiping at an altitude of 1035m above sea level. Official tourist literature goes somewhat over the top when speaking of its 'striking resemblance' to summer in Switzerland but, yes, the air is refreshingly cool and the roses, dahlias and lupins do bestow a non-tropical grace to the well-kept gardens. One night's stay, or two at the most, will suffice because the number of walks are limited and the food available in the resort's restaurants is none too enticing. However, except for holiday weekends you are likely to have the place to yourself and the isolation and coolness can be a real treat. A little initiative is needed for forest walks because there are no sign-posted trails and it is a matter of heading off the surfaced road and making your own way. A walk to the summit is signposted—follow the markers for the Cottage from the accommodation areas—from where it is possible to view the sweep of coastline from Penang to Pangkor.

■ Practical information

Getting to Bukit Larut
It was only after the Second World War that work on a road to the top of the hill got underway, with the labour provided by Japanese prisoners of war, and it was 1948 before the road was completed. Private cars are not allowed on the hill and the jeep service—RM2 per person—which runs every hour between 09.00 and 19.00 is best booked in advance; be sure to book your return trip too (☎ 05-8077243). The 40-minute journey by jeep to the top can be a dizzying experience as the driver speeds through 72 hairpin bends safe in the knowledge that there's no traffic coming the other way. From Taiping it is best to get a RM4 taxi-ride to the point where the jeeps depart. It is possible to make your way on foot but allow about three hours for the journey up.

Accommodation and restaurants
There are two resthouses which can be booked (☎ 05-8077241): **Bukit Larut** and, a little nearer the top, **Gunung Hijau**, both at RM15 for a room which sleeps two. The rooms are very basic and in need of renovation but at this price you can hardly complain. **Beringin** is one of several bungalows which sleeps up to 8 and costs RM150.

If you are staying at one of the resthouses, as opposed to the bungalows, meals can be ordered from the kitchen. The food is basically rice with chicken and/or vegetables, with toast and eggs for breakfast, so it helps to bring a few snacks with you. No alcohol is available so bring your own if necessary. The bungalows have kitchens with crockery and cutlery but bring all your food with you.

Teluk Intan

If you have the time and transport, the small town of Teluk Intan is worth the detour while travelling to or from Lumut and Palau Pangkor. The town is situated by the side of Perak river and it receives very few visitors. It does, however, have one claim to fame: a **leaning clock tower** which, if the tower at Pisa finally keels over, will be the largest in the world. It was built in 1885 by a Chinese merchant, Leong Choon Chong, as a memorial to his parents. Built in the form of a pagoda, it began to lean after 1889 but remained solid enough for the Japanese to use it as an observation tower during the Second World War. The roof tiles at the top had been removed by the Japanese but were replaced by the British after the war.

The tower has eight tiers and the clock is on the seventh level. The colonial influence shows in the choice of Roman numerals for the clock and they blend uneasily with the Oriental pagoda-style of the rest of the tower. Every Wednesday afternoon a man arrives with a crank to wind up the clock, thus ensuring that for the rest of the week it chimes twice every 15 minutes, four times every half hour and six times every 45 minutes. Every 60 minutes it chimes eight times before striking the hour.

Meals are available at food-stalls that are liberally scattered around the town's square and food as well as accommodation is available at the **Government Rest House** (☎ 05-614505) for RM40.

Pulau Pangkor (Pangkor Island)

Situated 83km southwest of Ipoh, the island is 12km in length and 4km at its widest. The palm-fringed beaches and the opportunities for water activities and jungle walks make Pangkor a most attractive destination. There is plenty of accommodation and restaurants and a stay of two or three days could easily slip past. Despite the presence of two international-style hotels, one of which owns the small offshore island of **Pangkor Laut**, Pangkor has a quiet and serene atmosphere. Most of the island's inhabitants, who make their living from fishing, live on the east coast, while the sandy beaches and tourist amenities are all on the west coast. The interior is mostly mountain and jungle and the trails connecting the two coastlines are a short but vigorous trek.

Unlike many of Malaysia's islands, Pangkor can be easily reached throughout the year. This makes it popular with Malaysians during weekends and school holidays, but even then it is possible to find an isolated spot of beach. Off the coast of this island the historic Treaty of Pangkor was signed in 1874, whereby the British were first allowed a foothold in the Malay states.

■ Practical information

Getting to and from Pangkor
By air. Pelangi Air flies between Kuala Lumpur (☎ 03-9821688; fax 03-9828303) and Pangkor (☎ 05-6852673) every day of the week (RM300). There is also a service to and from Singapore's Seletar airport (☎ 7357155; fax 7359692) on Tuesday, Wednesday, Friday and Sunday (RM500).

By boat. Ferries leave from Lumut, a small river port 101km southwest of Ipoh, every 20 minutes between 06.45 and 21.00 for RM2. The first stop is Sungai Pinang Kecil, then Pangkor village. The service from Palau Pangkor back to Lumut has the same frequency; it starts at 06.30 and ends at 20.00. There is a separate ferry for the Pan-Pacific and Pangkor Laut resorts that leaves every two hours.

By bus. There is a bus service between Pangkor village and Pasir Bogak that is supposed to run at regular intervals. The fixed taxi fare to Pasir Bogak is RM4 but this jumps to RM18 for a trip to the Pan-Pacific resort.

Tourist information

There is no tourist information office on the island but there is one in Lumut, on the mainland, across the road from the jetty (☎ 05-6834057); it is open from 09.00 to 17.00 seven days a week except Saturday when it closes at 13.45. Money can be changed at banks in Pangkor village.

Accommodation

There are rooms to suit all budgets but location is also a factor worth considering; Pasir Bogak can be busy while a little further north at Teluk Nipah the beach is quieter and more beautiful. The deals that include meals are of debatable value—all the restaurants welcome non-residents and if you are staying for a while this does not tie you down to one menu.

Pasir Bogak. Furthest south on this beach strip is the **Sea View Hotel** (☎ 05-6851605; fax 05-6851970), with standard doubles for RM115, family rooms for RM161 and chalets for RM207, all including breakfast. The rates are negotiable if demand is low. On the other side of the junction where the road from Pangkor village crosses the island, the **Beach Huts Hotel** (☎ and fax 05-6851159) has air-conditioned doubles for RM115 (fan only for RM95) and chalets with refrigerator for RM170, but no breakfast included. Further up, and inconveniently located away from the beach on the other side of the road, is the **Pangkor Standard Camp** (☎ 05-6851878) with small chalets for RM42 and even smaller A-frame huts at RM31 for up to three people. The next place up the road is the **Pangkor Anchor** with more A-frame huts for RM23. The last two places face each other across the road. **Khoo's Holiday Resort** (☎ and fax 05-6851164) has rooms with air-conditioning for RM78 and with fans for RM52, including breakfast. The **Pangkor Village Beach** has chalets with air-conditioning at RM140 for two including breakfast and dinner as well as some tents for RM14 per person.

Teluk Nipah. Travelling north from Pasir Bogak the first place in this cluster is **The Hornbill** (☎ 05-6852005; fax 05-6852006); it is smarter than the others with air-conditioned rooms overlooking the road and the sea for RM75–85, including continental breakfast. Next door, **Sukasuka** (☎ 05-6852494) has rooms without air-conditioning for RM50. The **Coral Beach Camp** (☎ 05-6852711; fax 05-6852006) has A-frame huts without a fan at RM25 for two, dormitories at RM10 a bed, and chalets with shower, toilet and fan at RM50. Right next door is **Joe Fisherman's Village** (☎ 05-6852389) with basically the same range of rooms at similar prices. Also here is the **Pangkor Indah Beach Resort** (☎ and fax 05-6852107), quite good value, with air-conditioned bungalow rooms, plus 'TV, video and soothing toilets for tourist usage', at RM95 for two. The next one up is the **Nipah Bay Villa** (☎ 05-6852198) with air-conditioned cottages that include meals for RM160. Further off the road is **Nazri Nipah Camp** (☎ 05-6852014) with huts and fan for RM38 and chalets and fan for RM70.

Resorts. The best for general access to the island is the **Sri Bayu Beach Resort** (☎ 05-6851929; fax 05-6851050, or through Kuala Lumpur at ☎ 03-2444430; fax 03-2444366) at Pasir Bogak. Wooden chalets set in landscaped gardens, with a small swimming pool, are RM370 and this includes breakfast and buffet dinner for two.

Tucked away in the north of the island at Teluk Belanga, the **Pan-Pacific Resort** (☎ 05-6851091; fax 05-6852390, or in Kuala Lumpur at ☎ 03-4413757; fax 03-4415559) has rooms around RM350, and the usual host of water sports are available plus a 9-hole golf course.

Beach resorts do not come any more exclusive than at **Pangkor Laut Resort** (☎ 05-6991100; fax 05-6991200, or in Kuala Lumpur at ☎ 03-2416564; fax 03-2418562) where the entire 122-hectare island is inhabited only by residents and staff of the resort. The least expensive rooms, the Royal Hill Villas (RM632), are sited on a hillside looking down on the sea. For RM862 there are Sea Villas picturesquely set on stilts in the water and connected by walkways. All the expected amenities and recreational facilities are available—tennis, squash, sailing, scuba diving courses, etc.—and the beaches are idyllic.

Both the Pan-Pacific and the Pangkor Laut are perfect for self-contained holidays; food, drink and recreation are as accessible as your plastic card will allow but guests are inclined to restrict themselves to the resorts' restaurants, bars and beaches. The easiest place to break out from is the Pan-Pacific: half an hour's walk leads to Teluk Nipah and a little beyond the resort's checkpoint, just before the right turn that leads to the airport, look for the Malay general store on the water's side. Sacks of rice and coconuts around the doorway conceal a small restaurant tucked away inside where authentic light Malay dishes can be enjoyed for a the price of a tip at the resort.

Restaurants

The best restaurants are at the **Pan-Pacific Resort** and the **Pangkor Laut Resort**, especially the latter. Both restaurants can be visited by non-residents but there's an entry fee of RM40 to each resort. In Pangkor village there are a number of small Chinese restaurants, look for ones serving local seafood.

Pasir Bogak. Inexpensive food is served at most of the places offering accommodation; meals are around RM12. There are Malay stalls on the beach side of the road and the **Pangkor Restaurant** is an inexpensive restaurant off the road. The **Sea View Hotel** restaurant has a pleasant setting down near the beach.

Teluk Nipah. The places with accommodation are again the best places for cheap meals. The **Bayview Café** is on the main road just past The Hornbill which also owns this restaurant. The Malay stalls on the other side of the road serve tastier though less varied dishes. The restaurant at **The Hornbill** itself offers mainly Western food, and has a wine list; better value for money is the **No. 1 Seafood Restaurant**, just before the Sri Bayu Resort, which is part of a little complex with a souvenir and T-shirt shop. Dishes average about RM8 and there is a menu for children.

Activities

The **beaches** are a prime reason for coming to Pangkor; while the one at **Pasir Bogak** is pleasant enough, it is well worth moving up towards the beautiful **Coral Bay** and/or stopping off at any point along this sandy coastal strip. The **Golden Sands** (Teluk Belanga) beach is also lovely but the **Pan-Pacific** collects RM40 from non-residents and the same tariff applies to the even more idyllic **Emerald Bay** on Pulau Pangkor Laut. It was at Emerald Bay that the Englishman Spencer Chapman waited for his submarine pick-up after his three years (1942–45) in the jungle fighting the Japanese; his book, *The Jungle is Neutral*, appropriate reading while on the island.

Snorkelling equipment can be hired at most of the hotels but the best bargains are from local Malays on the beach at Teluk Nipah; they charge about RM10 for a day's use of snorkel and flippers and RM20 for a canoe that will take you to the small islands in the bay where the coral can be observed (but not removed!). Boats will also take you out and return for an arranged pick-up. Emerald Bay has the best coral. Other water activities—catamarans, wind surfers, wave skis and fishing trips—are available at the two resorts.

Cycling is a good way to travel around the island, and bikes can be hired by the hour (RM3) or the day (RM15) from most of the accommodation places along the beach strips. Choose your bike with care because there are some short but steep gradients and not all of them are well maintained. **Motorbikes** can also be hired.

The island can be explored on foot and there is a 3-hour **forest trail** across the island that begins at Pasir Bogak near the Standard Camp. The highlight of any walk is spotting a pied hornbill—early evening is a good time to see them squatting on the branch of a tree.

Places to see

The east coast, between Sungai Pinang Kecil and Pangkor village, constitutes a **Chinese fishing village** that makes an interesting stroll at any time of the day. Look for *ikan bilis* (anchovy) drying in the sun, busy boatyards, and the **Foo Lin Kong Temple** signposted from the main road. The temple was built in the 1950s and has a miniature replica of the Great Wall of China dedicated to the temple deities. Just north of Sungai Pinang Kecil there is the **Sri Pathirakaliaman** Hindu temple which serves the thousand or so Indians who live on Pangkor.

At the southern end of the east coast, at Teluk Gedong, there are the reconstructed remains of **Kota Belanda**, a Dutch fort that was first erected in wood in 1670 when the Dutch were attempting to extract duties on boats exporting Perak's tin. Malay interests put up a spirited resistance and in 1690, despite the fort being fortified in stone, the contingent of Dutch soldiers was forced to abandon it. Notwithstanding a brief period of reoccupation by the Dutch, the fort was finally abandoned in 1743 and it succumbed to the jungle until the early 1970s when the present reconstruction was completed.

A short way beyond the fort there is a 300 year old stone bearing the logo of the Dutch East India Company with a carved memorial to a Dutch child who supposedly provided a hungry tiger with a meal. The other version of this event, that he was kidnapped and killed by anti-Dutch Malays and Bugis, is probably closer to the truth. The inscription dates back to the middle of the 18C.

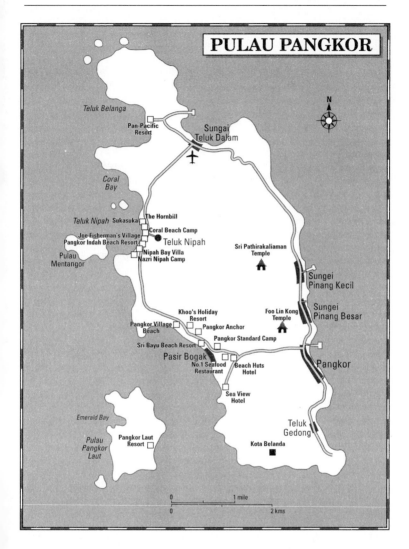

PULAU PANGKOR

Teluk Belanga

Pan-Pacific Resort

Sungai Teluk Dalam

Coral Bay

Teluk Nipah Sukasuka

The Hornbill

Coral Beach Camp

Joe Fisherman's Village
Pangkor Indah Beach Resort

Teluk Nipah

Nipah Bay Villa
Nazri Nipah Camp

Pulau Mentangor

Sri Pathirakaliaman Temple

Sungei Pinang Kecil

Khoo's Holiday Resort

Foo Lin Kong Temple

Sungei Pinang Besar

Pangkor Village Beach

Pangkor Anchor

Sri Bayu Beach Resort

Pangkor Standard Camp

Pangkor

Pasir Bogak

No.1 Seafood Restaurant

Beach Huts Hotel

Sea View Hotel

Emerald Bay

Teluk Gedong

Pulau Pangkor Laut

Pangkor Laut Resort

Kota Belanda

| 0 | | 1 mile |
| 0 | | 2 kms |

Upper Perak

The mighty Perak river, the second largest river in peninsular Malaysia, flows southwards from Upper Perak. This region, which stretches as far as the border with Thailand, is mostly jungle and mountain and you really need your own transport to get around. There is only one road between Kuala Kangsar and **Gerik**, where the East–West Highway can be joined to reach either Penang to the west or Kota Bharu to the east.

In the 19C, Upper Perak was under Siamese suzerainty and it was not until

1909 that the territory became part of Perak. It is said that the British district officer at that time, Hubert Berkeley, took a group of men out at night and shifted the boundary stones further north so as to increase Perak's size. The eccentric Berkeley was very much left to his own devices and acquired a reputation as the 'uncrowned king of Upper Perak'. Anecdotes about Berkeley became part of the folklore of Perak:

> 'One day he was going out on an elephant ride, which he used to do very regularly. As he got up on his elephant and was about to go, the Court Clerk came running to him and said, "Sir, you've got cases in court today." Berkeley turned round and said, "Blast it," and then asked how many cases there were. The Court Clerk said, "Twenty-five sir." "What are they?" said Berkeley. "Minor offences, sir." "Have you read the charges?" "Yes sir. They all plead guilty." "All right. Odd numbers discharged, even numbers fined five dollars." Then he turned round and rode away. (*Tales from the South China Seas*, edited by Charles Allen, London 1983.)

Accommodation by way of a **Government Rest House** (☎ 05-891066) is available in **Gerik** for RM50; the town has a number of small nondescript restaurants serving staple dishes such as chicken and rice.

Some 35km west of Gerik the road descends to **Lake Temengur**. This was once the catchment area of River Temengur which was flooded by the construction of a dam in 1974, said to have been built in order to flush out Communist guerrillas who had infiltrated this region and posed a security threat. Banding, one of the highest peaks in the Temengur basin, became an island and a resthouse was built here to house people working on the building of the East–West Highway. The resthouse is now the **Banding Island Resort** (☎ 05-7912273, fax 05-7912288) with rooms from RM70–150. Activities include nature treks, river trips and rafting. The island is connected to the shore by way of the highway.

Penang

Penang is the name both of a state and an island but the name Penang usually refers to the island (more correctly called Pulau Pinang) of nearly 300 square kilometres that lies off the northwest coast. The small mainland part of Penang state, Seberang Prai (known once as Province Wellesley, and named after Colonel Arthur Wellesley, later the Duke of Wellington), is of little interest to visitors, although its commercial centre—the town of Butterworth—is where the ferry to the island is boarded. Butterworth is 369km northeast of Kuala Lumpur, and 90km northeast of Taiping.

The capital of the island is **Georgetown**. It was named after George IV, then the Prince of Wales, as the land was acquired on his birthday. Sometimes confusingly also called Penang, it is a bustling and colourful place that is hardly characteristic of Malaysia as a whole but none the less exciting because of this. The second largest city in Malaysia, it has the finest Chinese architecture in the country as well as equally important examples of colonial architecture. It is a place to walk and wander in and soak up a unique atmosphere; not the least of its attractions is its superb food.

Time should also be allowed for a visit to **Batu Ferringhi**, the beach strip, along the north coast. It was once famous as a stopover meeting place on the hippy trail across Southeast Asia and while 5-star hotels are where most people stay today, it is still a vibrant place at night.

Allow at least three or four days for a visit to Penang and try to arrange an itinerary that takes in both Georgetown and Batu Ferringhi.

History

The Malay name for the areca nut palm, more commonly known as the betel nut palm, is *pokok pinang*. In the 16C, the Portuguese named the island Pinang, after the tree which they found growing there (as it still does), and this became 'penang' in English. The British named the island **Prince of Wales Island** (after the future George IV) but this was dropped after independence in 1957.

Before the British arrived, the island was home to a number of Malay families whose livelihood was fishing. Pirates had invaded the island for years but had been expelled by Penang's ruler, the Sultan of Kedah, in 1750. By the 1770s the **Sultan of Kedah**, Muhammad Jawa Mu'Azzam Shah II, was in difficulties caused by civil war as well as by the constant threat of invasion by Siam. The sultan was anxious to find an ally to help him resist the Siamese, so when he was approached by an Englishman seeking a lease on the island he struck a deal in return for a promise that the British would help him defend Kedah against the Siamese. The Englishman was **Captain Francis Light**.

Light had been searching for a base of operations for his employers the East India Company, and in 1771 made an agreement with the sultan whereby he personally had control over the Kedah coasts as far south as Penang. Light's part of the bargain was to protect the sultan from his enemies. The deal lasted for a year before it collapsed, whereupon Light left the region for modern-day Phuket where he continued his work for the East India Company. Eleven years and a new sultan later, a new deal was struck: in return for protection from Siamese invasions, Light, on behalf of the East India Company and the British government, was given possession of Penang, then virtually uninhabited and covered in jungle.

The East India Company had no intention of offering the sultan military support, although the degree to which Light was party to this duplicity has been argued over by historians. In 1790 the new sultan tried to put pressure on the British by demanding the return of the island but Light attacked his fort on the mainland and defeated the sultan's forces.

Settlers flocked to the island from all over Asia because the company was only taxing the island's produce and grants of land were freely available to merchants. Georgetown began to grow around the harbour. A stockade was built and Prince of Wales Island was declared a free trade port, attracting many traders away from the Dutch settlement at Melaka. By 1800 the population had grown to 10,000.

Light died in 1794 from malaria. After his death, and despite an increasingly cosmopolitan population, the island remained essentially British, adopting the British judicial system in 1801. In 1800, his successor negotiated another treaty with the sultan in which Kedah ceded a strip of land opposite the island, 5km wide and 48km long, in return for $10,000 a year. This strip of land became Province Wellesley and it gave the British control over the stretch of water surrounding Georgetown Harbour. In 1805 Penang became a Residency with a Governor, and Stamford Raffles came to the island as a clerical officer.

In the closing decades of the 19C, Chinese immigration reached its peak and by 1900 the Chinese made up half of the total population. They brought with them their clan system and sometimes clan rivalries: 1867 saw the outbreak of the **Great Penang Riot** when gang warfare broke out between the Hokkien-dominated Red Flag Society and the Cantonese White Flags. Barricades went up, business went down, and batteries of heavy cannon were used to restore the peace. Periodic bouts of disorder were also occasioned by the arrival of big ships in the harbour; at such times, the police helpfully rang a loud bell to warn respectable folk off the streets.

Penang, Melaka and Singapore formed the **Straits Settlements** after the 1826 treaty with the Dutch clearly demarcated British and Dutch spheres of influence. Penang was the administrative centre of the Straits Settlements until 1832 when Singapore took over. Throughout the 19C, the growing tin trade in Perak benefited Penang because the island offered the most convenient port. When steam navigation used the new Suez Canal (1869) to reach the Far East, Penang and Singapore became important coaling stations along the route. In time Singapore eclipsed Penang both as a trading centre and port of call.

During the Second World War, the island was occupied by the Japanese, after one of the more shameful episodes in British rule. The Governor of the Straits Settlements issued secret orders for every British national to evacuate the island without informing the other inhabitants. Three days later, the Japanese arrived. Penang was occupied by the Japanese from 1941 to July 1945. It was regularly bombed by the Allies but most of its buildings were undamaged.

Penang bridge was opened in September 1985 and at 13.5km is the longest bridge in Asia.

▓ Practical information

Telephone numbers in Penang are gradually being changed to nine digits by adding the prefix 2.

Getting to and from Penang
By air. The international airport is at Bayan Lepas (☎ 04-6430811/6430691) in the southeast of the island. There are international connections from Singapore as well as from Thailand (Bangkok and Phuket) and Indonesia (Medan) but most planes arrive via Kuala Lumpur. Within Malaysia there are direct flights from Kuala Lumpur (RM104 single), Kota Bharu (RM87 single) and Langkawi (RM51 single).

Airline offices in Georgetown. The MAS office (☎ 04 2620011) is on the third floor of Komplex Tun Abdul Razak (KOMTAR) on Jalan Penang. Cathay Pacific (☎ 04-2620411) is at 28 Lorong Penang, Singapore Airlines (☎ 04-2263201) at Wisma Penang Gardens, Jalan Sultan Ahmad Shah and Thai

International (☎ 04-2266000) at Wisma Central, Jalan Macalister.

Most other means of reaching Penang depend on travelling first to Butterworth on the mainland and then taking a ferry or taxi to Georgetown.

By train. The railway station is next to the ferry terminal at Butterworth and reservations can be made either at the station (☎ 04-3312796) or at the Railway Booking Station at the ferry terminal in Georgetown (☎ 04-2610290). The first train to Kuala Lumpur departs daily at 08.00, costing RM67 first class and RM34 second class (both classes have air-conditioning). The nightly service departs at 22.00 and costs RM79–89 (upper and lower bunks) first class and RM37–40 second class.

By bus. The bus terminal is next to the ferry terminal in Butterworth. There are also a number of private long-distance bus companies that operate from Georgetown and this saves the trouble of making your own way by ferry or taxi across to Butterworth. There are buses to all the main towns in Malaysia, as well as to Singapore and Hat Yai, Phuket and Bangkok in Thailand.

On Lebuh Chulia there are a number of agents offering competitive rates for bus travel: Hock Ban Trading (☎ 04-2619197) at No. 382, or Syarinor (☎ 04-2623830) at No. 63. More agents can be found in the Komtar Building; Komtar Tours (☎ 04-2624222) is on the ground floor next to the Ban Hin Lee bank. *Nice* express buses run a comfortable and efficient service between Penang and Kuala Lumpur and on to Singapore. Their office and terminus is at the Garden Inn Hotel at 41 Jalan Anson (☎ 04-2298504).

By ferry. There is a 24-hour passenger ferry service (☎ 04-2633211) between Butterworth and Georgetown which takes 15 minutes. Between 06.00 and midnight a ferry leaves every 20 minutes; at other times it is an hourly service. The fare of 60 sen is only charged when travelling from Butterworth. There is also a car ferry (RM7) that runs slightly less frequently until 22.00 (or 01.30 at weekends).

There is a ferry service between Georgetown and Langkawi, and between Georgetown and Medan in Sumatra, Indonesia. The ferry for Langkawi departs at 08.00 and costs RM45 for a first-class single (RM80 return) and RM35 for economy class (RM60 return).

The ferry service to and from Medan in Sumatra departs from Georgetown at 10.00 (Tuesday, Thursday and Saturday) for RM110 for a first-class single (RM200 return) and RM90 for economy class (RM160 return). The service from Medan to Penang departs at 13.00 (Wednesday and Sunday) and 11.00m (Friday). The same office handles a ferry service from Medan to Lumut in Perak with ticket prices the same as the Medan to Penang service.

The ferry office (☎ 04-2625630) is next to the tourist offices near Fort Cornwallis, open from 07.00 to 20.30 (Monday to Saturday) and 07.00 to 13.30 (Sunday). There is another ferry office next door (☎ 04-2631943), Ekspres Bahagia, that also has a Penang–Medan service for the same prices but with a different timetable: departing Penang at 10.00 (Wednesday and Friday) and at noon (Monday).

Ferry tickets for Langkawi and Medan can be booked at the Penang Tourist Guides Association office (☎ 04-2614461) on the 3rd floor of the Komtar building on Jalan Penang in Georgetown.

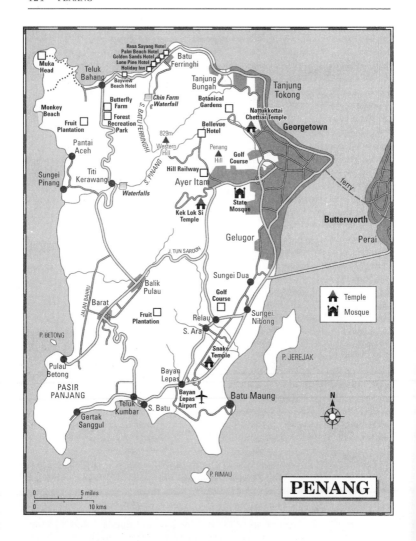

By taxi or car. There is a regular taxi service between Butterworth and Georgetown (RM19), using the 13km Penang Bridge, for which there is a RM7 toll. A taxi from the airport to Ferringhi beach is RM28.

Getting around Penang

To and from the airport. The Bayan Lepas airport is 18km south of Georgetown and taxi coupons are purchased from a desk in the airport and then presented to the taxi driver: RM19 into Georgetown and RM28 to Batu Ferringhi. A Yellow Bus No. 83 only costs RM1 to or from Georgetown (Lebuh Chulia) but takes twice as long (1 hour).

Buses, belonging to five different companies, operate from two main departure points. City buses (MPPP Buses) operate from outside the ferry terminal at Lebuh Victoria and most of them can be picked up at the bus stops along Lebuh Chulia.

The other bus companies operate from Pengkalan Weld, next to the ferry terminal: Yellow Bus, Lim Seng Bus Co., Hin Bus and Sri Negara Transport and go to various destinations on the island.

Taxis do not use meters; you are tempting fate if you wait until the end of your journey to enquire about the price. If possible, ask your hotel for the likely fare for your planned journey.

Self-drive/car rental is worth considering because places of interest are spread out between Georgetown, Batu Ferringhi in the north, and some secluded beaches in the south of the island. Car rental companies can be found at the airport—Avis, (☎ 04-6439633), Hertz (☎ 04-6430208), National (☎ 04-6434205). In Georgetown, Hertz has an office at the Casuarina hotel (☎ 04-811711) on the road to Teluk Bahang

Trishaws, three-wheeled vehicles propelled by pedal power, are a common form of transport around Georgetown. Agree on the price before your journey and be philosophical about paying a little more than the locals do. As a rough guide, expect to pay RM2 per kilometre or RM14 per hour.

Georgetown

What makes Georgetown so vibrant and fascinating is its earthy and authentic Chinese atmosphere; it does not suffer from the sad sobriety that sometimes seems to inhibit Singapore. More than anywhere else in peninsular Malaysia, Georgetown is a place where you need to allow time for random walks and unscheduled pauses; otherwise you will not catch the casual sights and sounds that are such a unique feature of the town.

■ Practical information

Getting to and from Georgetown
See the Getting to and from Penang section (above) for details of the ferry, taxi and road links between Butterworth and Georgetown, as well as information on how to reach and leave Butterworth.

Car and bicycle hire
The airport has a number of car hire offices: Avis (☎ 04-2631685/6439633), Hertz (☎ 04-6430208, National (☎ 04-6434205); Hertz at Casuarina (☎ 04-8811711). Trishaws can be hired at RM14 per hour. The Swiss Hotel at 431 Lebuh Chulia has bicycles for hire at RM10 a day. Bicycles and motorbikes can be hired from several places along Lebuh Chuliah as well as many of the budget hotels. You should have a licence with you if you want to use a motorbike.

Street names
If you are finding your own way around Georgetown, you should be aware of the various spellings of street names. The Malay word for road is *jalan* so that Penang Road may be called Jalan Penang or even Jalan Pinang. In addition, the

Malay word for street is *lebuh* so that Penang Street (altogether a different place from Penang Road) may be called Leboh or Lebuh Pinang or Penang.

Tourist information

There are two tourist offices on Jalan Tun Syed Sheh Barakbah, near Fort Cornwallis. The most helpful for country-wide information is **Tourism Malaysia** (☎ 04-2620066/2619067), open from 08.00 to 12.45 and 14.00 to 16.15 (Monday to Thursday), with a longer lunch break from 12.15 to 14.45 (Friday), and from 08.00 to 12.45 (Saturday). The **Penang Tourist Centre** is just around the corner in the same building and is open from 08.30 to 16.30 (Monday to Friday), closing for lunch 13.00–14.00 (Monday to Thursday) and 12.30–14.30 (Friday). Open from 08.30 to 13.00 (Saturday).

Tourism Malaysia also has an information counter at the airport (☎ 04-6430501), open from 09.00 to 17.00.

The best place for accurate and helpful information about Penang is the **Penang Tourist Guides Association** (☎ 04-2614461) on the third floor of the Komtar building on Jalan Penang, open from 10.00 to 18.00 (Monday to Saturday) and 11.00 to 19.00 (Sunday).

The best **tours** of the island are conducted by the Penang Tourist Guides Association; they can be booked direct from their office in the Komtar Building or through most hotels and travel agents. The basic charge is RM20 and if you are pressed for time the **City Tour** usefully packs in all the sights. There is also a **Hill and Temple Tour** for RM24 that takes in Penang Hill and a number of different temples.

Currency

Money exchange can be handled at a number of large banks along Lebuh Pantai. Similar rates, but with far longer opening hours, are available at numerous moneychangers whose small shops can be found where Lebuh Chulia meets Jalan Penang. American Express have an agent at Mayflower Acme Tours, Tan Chong Building, Pengkalan Weld (☎ 04-2623724).

Postal and telephone services

These are available from the General Post Office on Lebuh Downing, not far from the tourist offices, open from 08.30 to 16.30 (Monday to Saturday). There are also post offices on Lebuh Buckingham, near Khoo Kongsi, and on the ground floor of the Komtar Building.

On Jalan Burma, a 15-minute walk from the 65-storey Komtar Building, is the Telekom office which is open 24 hours a day and from where international calls can easily be made.

Consulates

UK—contact one of the tourist offices for details of the UK consulate which, at the time of writing, was being relocated.

France (☎ 04-2629707) Wisma Rajah, 82, Lebuh Bishop.

Germany (☎ 04-832011) OE Design, Byan Lepas Free Industrial Zone 3.

Thailand (☎ 04-379484) 1 Jalan Tunku Abdul Rahman.

Emergencies and hospitals

In an emergency you should ☎ 999 for an ambulance. Outpatient care is available to tourists at the General Hospital on Jalan Residensi (☎ 04-2273333) or the Penang Adventist Hospital at 465 Jalan Burma (☎ 04-2261133).

Accommodation

Top range hotels. For colonial nostalgia, the **Eastern & Oriental** (E&O) on Lebuh Farquhar (☎ 04-2630630; fax 04-2634833) wins hands down. It is being renovated and will reopen early 1998. Double rooms will cost around MR300, depending on the views. Close by, at the top of Jalan Penang, the **City Bayview** (☎ 04-2633161) at 25A Lebuh Farquhar lacks atmosphere but has lots of amenities, including a revolving restaurant at the top of its tower. Rooms from RM210–240 (but promotional rates can bring this down to below RM150). The **Sheraton** (☎ 04-2276166; fax 04-2276615), off Jalan Burmah at 3 Jalan Larut, has the best town views and good restaurants. Singles/doubles are RM295–330.

Middle range hotels. The **Oriental** (☎ 04-2634211; fax 04-2635395) is centrally located at 105 Jalan Penang and offers decent rooms for RM115. The **Cathay** (☎ 04-2626271), at 15 Lebuh Leith, is a clean and well-kept establishment with large rooms from RM58–69. In the same class is the **New Pathe** (☎ 04-2620196), at 23 Lebuh Light, with rooms from RM44–66. The **Peking Hotel** (☎ 04-2636191) is centrally located at 50A Jalan Penang and has rooms from RM63–92.

Budget hotels are either on Lebuh Chulia or very close to it. The **Broadway Hostel** (☎ 04-2628550), 35F Jalan Masjid Kapitan Keling, is near the Kuan Yin Teng Temple and has a family room with air-conditioning for RM40 and rooms with a fan for RM30. There is a laundry, lockers, and bus tickets can be arranged here. The **Swiss Hotel** (☎ 04-2620133), at No. 431, is popular with back-packers, charging RM41 for a double with a fan and no advance booking allowed. It is a matter of turning up early in the morning and waiting for an empty room. There is a small restaurant serving Western food.

Restaurants

The Emperor at the Sheraton hotel (☎ 04-2276166) has a Hong Kong chef who prepares Cantonese dishes; the dim sum lunch is popular. The **E&O Hotel** (☎ 04-2630630) serves lunch inside and on the terrace overlooking the sea. The **Eliza** (☎ 04-2633161) in the City Bayview hotel is the only place where a good Malay meal can be enjoyed in comfortable surroundings. In the basement of the Oriental hotel the north Indian **Kashmir** (☎ 04-2634211) is the smartest Indian restaurant in town. The **Kurumaya** (☎ 04-2283222) is a good Japanese restaurant at 269 Jalan Burmah, open daily from 11.00 to 14.30 and 17.30 to 10.30. Set lunches are RM25–58 and set dinners RM35–58—throw-away prices for the Japanese customers who patronise the place.

Poshni, on the corner of Lebuh Light and Lebuh Penang, is a Thai restaurant with good-value dishes around RM7. On Lebuh Chulia, the **Coco Island Bar** is a gregarious place that attracts budget travellers with its large menu of inexpensive Asian and Western dishes. The **Dawood**, at 63 Lebuh Queen opposite the Sri Mariamman Temple, is a well-established, strictly no frills Indian restaurant serving cheap curries. The Komtar Shopping Centre has the ubiquitous fast-food chains.

Penang is famous for the quality of its **hawker food**, dished up from pavement stalls in a number of popular locations: Lebuh Carnarvon, Gurney Drive, the Esplanade and Jalan Macalister. Specialities worth trying include *laksa assam*, a piquant fish soup with noodles, and *laksa lemak* which is similiar but enriched with coconut milk.

Shopping

The **Komtar Shopping Centre**, at the western end of Jalan Penang and the only high-rise building in Georgetown, is difficult to miss. It contains a typical array of Malaysian shops, including a Japanese department store, Yaohan, and a Popular Bookshop which is as good a bookshop as you are likely to find outside Kuala Lumpur. The fourth floor has a couple of shops dedicated to computer software. Other bookshops include the United Book Ltd on Jalan Penang and a useful secondhand shop opposite the Swiss Hotel on Lebuh Chulia. The small English bookshop in the E&O hotel is also worth a look.

Jalan Penang is famous for its pavement stalls specialising in fabrics, inexpensive watches and fake designer perfume. It is open until late at night. The shops along **Lebuh Chulia** are always worth looking at for rattan wares and general bits and pieces. **Lorong Kulit** and **Lebuh Bishop** have a varied selection of general goods, antiques and plain junk.

Entertainment and Sport

Most of the big hotels have discos, especially at Batu Ferringhi. There are cultural shows at Eden Seafood Village and Penang Cultural Centre which are both out at Batu Ferringhi. The Mutiara has its own jetty with several yachts for hire to the public. Penang Bowl is Jalan Sultan Ahmad Shah and also at Sunshine Square. The **Vor** (☎ 04-2270300), 33 Jalan Anson, Georgetown, is a new venue offering a dinner and dance show each evening at 19.30.

Festivals

The date of the Chinese New Year varies from late January to late February and it is always a lively and loud occasion in Penang. (Unlike Singapore, there is no prohibition on fireworks.) Look out for the dragon dances and the *wayang* (traditional Chinese opera).

The most astonishing festival in Penang is the Hindu **Thaipusam** (see p 62), held every year on one day in the month of Thai in the Hindu calendar (between 15 January and 15 February). During the festival Jalan Utama is closed to traffic and this is a good place to watch the procession pass by as it makes its way to the Hilltop Temple at Penang Botanical Gardens.

Colonial Walk

As this walk progresses, the opportunities to pause for refreshments diminish. The E&O Hotel is the best place for a drink or a meal but most of the walk is still ahead of you. The last part of the walk, along Lebuh Pantai, is in the busy business centre of town and there are a few small cafés here.

The walk begins at the **Protestant Cemetery** (1789–1892) on Jalan Sultan Ahmad Shah where, shaded by the frangipani trees, the **grave of Captain**

GEORGETOWN

N

0   200 yds
0   200 metres

Tourism Malaysia Penang Tourist Centre
Tourist Office
S S S BARAKBAH
JLN TUN SYED BARAKAH
Clock Tower
JEBUH DOWNING
Fort Cornwallis
Immigration Office
P.O.
Padang Kota Lama
Dewan Bandaran
Dewan Undangan Negeri
Standard Chartered Bank
Bus Station
Town Hall
LEBUH LIGHT
Hong Kong & Shanghai Bank
Ferry Terminal
Penang Library
LEBUH BISHOP
PENGKALAN WELD
French Consulate
Supreme Court
LEBUH CHINA
St. George's Church
Broadway Hostel
LEBUH PASAR
LEBUH FARQUHAR
Penang Museum and Art Gallery
LEBUH QUEEN
Sri Mariamman Temple
MPPP Bus Station
LEBUH CHULA
Cathedral of the Assumption
Kuan Yin Teng Temple
LEBUH PITT
LEBUH VICTORIA
Chinese Water Village
Eastern & Oriental Hotel
LORONG CINTA
Masjid Kapitan Kling Mosque
JLN PANTAI
Khoo Kongsi
LEBUH ACHEH
City Bayview Hotel
Cathay Hotel
LEBUH MUNTRI
JLN BUCKINGHAM
PENGKALAN WELD
LEBUH FARQUHAR
Cheong Fatt Tze Mansion
LEBUH LEITH
Oriental Hotel
LEBUH CHULIA
Swiss Hotel
LEBUH CANNON
Grave of Captain Light
Protestant Cemetery
LEBUH CAMPBELL
LEBUH CINTRA
Police Station
LEBUH FARQUHAR
JALAN PENANG
LEBUH CARNARVON
Wisma Penang Garden
JLN SULTAN AHMED SHAH
JALAN TRANSFER
Market
JLN KUALA KANGSAR
LEBUH KIMBERLEY
PRANGIN
LEBUH TEK SOON
Cathay Cinema
Penang Tourist Guides Association
JALAN MAGAZINE
LORONG HUTTON
Police Headquarters
Komtar Shopping Centre
J BRICK KILN
JALAN ARGYLL
JALAN BURMA
Telekom Office
Ong Kongsi
Wisma Central Dept Store
JLN MACALISTER
JALAN DATO KERAMAT
JALAN CLOVE HALL
WAT CHAYAMANGKALARAM
Sheraton Hotel
The Var
Garden Inn
JALAN ANSON
LORONG ABU SITI
JLN NANNING
JLN SELANGOR

PENANG HILL   PENANG BUDDHIST ASSOCIATION TEMPLE, MASJID MELAYU   BATU FERRINGHI, DHARMMIKARAMA TEMPLE

Francis Light (see p 121) can be found. Under British rule an annual ceremony was conducted in the cemetery on 21 October to mark the anniversary of Light's death. His gravestone is one of the most modest in a cemetery where a number of extravagant mock-classical monuments betray their High Victorian origins.

There is a map of the various tombs at the entrance to the cemetery and the earliest gravestone is that of H.D.D. Cunningham who died in 1789. Some of the inscriptions provide poignant reminders of Penang's early history: 'Christopher Henry Lloyd...murdered by a gang of Chinese robbers in the night of the 25 Oct 1878'. The graves of 12 Chinese Christians who fled China during the Boxer rebellion are also here.

The E&O Hotel, Georgetown

From the cemetery gates facing the sea, cross the road and, keeping the Toyota car showroom on your right and the Penang Bowl on your left, walk down Lebuh Farquhar to the **E&O Hotel**. The Eastern and Oriental Hotel was established in 1885 by the Sarkies brothers, three Armenians who also created the Raffles Hotel in Singapore and the Strand in Rangoon. Apparently, Arshak Sarkies, the youngest of the brothers, was sometimes to be seen waltzing round his hotel ballroom in Penang with a whisky and soda balanced on his head.

At the time of writing, the hotel was being renovated. It is to be hoped that the original style and atmosphere of the place will be retained as much as possible.

Original advertisements, framed in the lobby, proclaim its status as the 'premier hotel East of Suez' and boast how the annex added in 1922 provided the 'longest sea front of any hotel in the world'. Walk through the lobby to the lawns facing the sea where drinks can be enjoyed. Two famous guests, Rudyard Kipling and Somerset Maugham, had their tiffin out on this terrace, but so too did most of the Europeans who passed through Penang during the heyday of colonialism.

'We bathed at the swimming club, motored round the island, drank stengahs on the verandah of the sea-fringed E&O Hotel where we were staying, and one morning we climbed up the great 2,500-feet high Penang Hill named the Crag. I say "climbed", though we went up in bamboo stretchers carried by perspiring Chinese coolies as became the lords and masters of creation.' (From Reginald Campbell's Teak-Wallah, Oxford, 1986, first published 1935, an account of a young Englishman who was a teak inspector in northern Thailand in the 1920s.)

George Bilainkin, a newspaper editor who was working in Penang in the late 1920s, had the temerity to entertain a Chinese guest on the hotel's veranda: he was immediately snubbed by the other Europeans for his breaking of protocol.

Continue along Lebuh Farquhar, passing the double spired **Cathedral of the Assumption**, a Catholic cathedral, and stop at the **Penang Museum and Art Gallery**. It is open from 09.00 to 17.00 (Monday to Sunday) but closes between 12.15 and 14.45 on Friday. Admission is free but as the museum is presently undergoing renovation this may change (it is due to reopen early 1998).

The building was formerly part of the Penang Free School which was founded in 1816 and was the first English language school in southeast Asia. Outside the museum there stands a statue of Francis Light, cast to mark the 150th anniversary of the founding of Penang, and removed by the Japanese during their period of occupation but replaced by the British in 1945, minus its sword. Inside the museum there is a catholic collection recalling Penang's history: Straits Chinese furniture, Malay weaponry, paintings and etchings, old photos.

A little way past the museum, at the corner of Lebuh Farquhar and Jalan Masjid Kapitan Kling (also called Lebuh Pitt), stands the elegant **St George's Church** with a circular columned edifice in front dedicated to Francis Light. The church was built between 1817 and 1819 by the East India Company using convict labour. It was designed by Captain Robert Smith, a military engineer and amateur painter (some of his paintings can be seen in the museum) who is said to have based his plan on an Anglican church in Madras. The church has the distinction of being the first Anglican church to be built in Southeast Asia.

St George's Church was rendered roofless during a Japanese air raid in December 1941 and was not reopened until 1948. It is a superb example of neo-Georgian architecture—enhanced by its Asian setting—with fine coupled stone columns forming a portico at the west end. The interior is best visited on a Sunday morning when the louvred doors on either side are open wide and the fans swirl above a mixed congregation of Asians and Westerners. It was not always so—until 1870 non-white Christians were barred.

Cross the road outside the church—unless you want to include a visit to the Chinese Kuan Yin Teng Temple (see below) which is just down Jalan Masjid Kapitan Kling—and head north one block to reach Lebuh Light. Turn right here to view the **Town Hall** directly across the road. The other side of this building, built during the last quarter of the 19C, faces the *padang*, hence the town hall's balcony that was built to accommodate élite audiences whenever a procession or event was taking place below on the green. The fountain next to the town hall was built as a donation by Kok Seang Tat, a Chinese merchant who had his grand mansion behind the town hall. After entertaining the Duke of Edinburgh in 1869 his house became known as Edinburgh House.

Head east along Lebuh Light towards the **Clock Tower**, a memorial to Queen Victoria's diamond jubilee; hence its height of 60 feet (18m), one foot for each year of her reign between 1837 and 1897. The building of the monument was financed by a self-made Chinese tin millionaire, Cheah Chin Gok.

Between the clock tower and the sea is **Fort Cornwallis**, marking the spot where Captain Light arrived on 17 July 1786. Accommodation and a defensive wall were quickly constructed out of wood and the stockade was named after

Charles, Marquis Cornwallis, who was then the Governor-General of the East India Company. In 1808 work commenced using convict labour on the stone structure, the outer walls of which are the only remains still to be seen. It took some persuasion by Light to convince the East India Company that money should be spent rebuilding the fort in stone; in fact the fort was never involved in any conflict and the cannons you see dotted around the place were never fired in defence of Penang.

As if in keeping with its pacific past, the interior has been turned into a small park. The biggest cannon, facing the sea to the north, is known as **Seri Rambai**—named after the ship that the British used when transporting this cannon to Penang—and it dates back to the early 17C. It was originally Dutch (as are most of the other cannons in Fort Cornwallis) before being presented to the Sultan of Johor. It was then captured by the Achenese who kept it for nearly 200 years before taking it to Kuala Selangor where it was eventually captured by the British. They hauled it away to Penang in 1871 and threw it overboard from the *Seri Rambai* into the sea facing the fort (an alternative but less reliable account has pirates throwing it overboard).

A small museum is housed in one of the underground powder magazines and contains old photographs and documents relating to the fort and Penang. The displays are informative, though not especially reader-friendly, and they go some way towards compensating for the distinct lack of history evoked by the remains of Fort Cornwallis.

Back at the clock tower, walk down Lebuh Pantai to look at some fine Anglo-Victorian buildings. Both the **Standard Chartered Bank** and the **Hong Kong and Shanghai Bank** would not look out of place in the City of London or in most other European capitals but here in Lebuh Pantai their grandeur seems incongruous and unnecessary. They represent capitalist self-confidence on an imperial scale, but the human scene that surrounds them is more small-scale and fragile: Indian moneylenders with unimpressive profit margins, Chinese shops waiting to be swamped by a supermarket, and the noisy traffic of mopeds and old cars.

At the end of Lebuh Chulia at Pengkalan Weld is the **Chinese Water Village**, some stilt houses arranged along the jetties which reach out into the sea. About 2000 Chinese people live here, each jetty being named after the clan which lives beside it. Most of the families have lived here for generations. Among the houses are shops and temples, and below are mangroves and the sea, while alongside the jetties are the junks owned by the inhabitants. None of the families pay any tax since they do not technically live on Penang soil.

Chinatown Walk

There is no problem finding places to rest for a drink or a meal along this walk and time should definitely be allowed for a local coffee in one of the coffee shops along Lebuh Chulia.

The main street in Chinatown is **Lebuh Chulia** and a walk down this busy thoroughfare can commence at its busy junction with Jalan Penang. The name of the street (*chulia* is Malay for a merchant from South India) points to the fact that this area was also used by Indian immigrants—a mosque (see below) is not far away—but the predominant character is unmistakably Chinese. A number of

Chinese-owned inexpensive hotels are located in this area, hence the number of budget travellers and small restaurants.

The typical Chinese house here has shuttered windows and decorated tiles on the walls; some of the finest examples of domestic architecture are to be found in **Lebuh Muntri**, which runs parallel with Lebuh Chulia and can be reached by turning left into **Love Lane** (Lebuh Cinta in Malay) and walking around the block. Along Lebuh Muntri it is not uncommon to find furniture spilling out of homes onto the pavement. Bright red embroidery often hangs above doorways and some houses have a small altar nailed to the main supporting column on the pavement.

Continue up Lebuh Muntri until it meets Jalan Penang and turn left so that you walk back to the junction with Lebuh Chulia where the walk began. Do not turn into Lebuh Chulia but carry on for two blocks until a left turn brings you into **Lebuh Campbell**. This is the commercial heart of Chinatown and along this street, and the ones that follow, look out for varied aspects of Chinese culture: betting shops running a tote, antique barber shops and exotic medicine stores, pavement stalls with baskets piled full of salted duck eggs, small mirrors outside houses to ward off evil spirits, and the ubiquitous goldsmith's shop which invariably has far more shop assistants than customers. There is plenty to observe at any time of the day, although early morning is a particularly interesting time.

The first turning on the right, **Jalan Kuala Kangsar**, is full of small fruit and vegetable stalls where local people do their shopping. Go through Jalan Kuala Kangsar and turn left into Lebuh Kimberley and walk down to the T-junction and turn left again into **Lebuh Carnarvon**. Along this street there is a market on the left—look for the bamboo cages full of squawking chickens waiting to be dispatched—and just past it on the other side of the road make a right turn into **Lebuh Buckingham**. At the bottom of this short road there is the **Masjid Kapitan Kling**, a mosque originally built in the first half of the 19C by the Indian Muslim community. The mosque is named after the headman ('Kapitan'), Caudeer Mohudeen, of the Indian community which arrived in Penang as sepoys under Francis Light. Until the 1930s, *klings* was a generic term for Indians in the Malay peninsula, based on an old name for a coastal region of southeast India called Kalinga. The building you see today was largely rebuilt in 1916 after British architects were commissioned by the Muslim and Hindu Endowments Board. Mogul domes rise above walls painted white and ochre yellow, and a small garden separates the mosque from its minaret (built in 1916), which rises from a square base with each corner topped by a miniature Moorish dome.

Turn right at the junction with the mosque and head west along Lebuh Pitt (Jalan Masjid Kapitan Kling) which runs into Lebuh Cannon, so-called because of the holes made in the ground here by cannon balls fired during the Great Penang Riot of 1867 (see p 122).

Look for the sign that points the way left under an archway and through a lane to the magnificent **Khoo Kongsi**. Before reaching the *kongsi* (clan house), pause along the lane to examine the well-preserved Chinese townhouses on your right that date back to the mid 19C. Above the teak swing-doors a small board carries the family name in gold calligraphy. On the left side of the lane there are other terrace houses from the late 1930s. At the end of the lane enter the *porte-cochère* of Khoo Kongsi.

There are a number of clan houses in Penang but none is as splendid as the one belonging to the house of Khoo. The Khoos were wealthy traders who first made their money in Melaka, before moving to Penang where a complex clan organisation was established. It provided educational help, social welfare and financial services to clan members. Building work for a grand temple started in 1894 and when it was finally completed eight years later the roof caught fire. The second roof was designed to be less ostentatious—there was speculation that the fire had been started deliberately by another clan jealous of the Khoos—but it is difficult to imagine how it could have been more ornate than the present one.

The whole structure was designed and built by master craftsmen from China, and it has a host of architectural features worth admiring for their detail and execution: the upturned roof with the ridges covered in mythological beasts, painted ceilings, a superb black and white fresco on one of the walls, gilded panels and beams carved and shaped out of wood, and stone pillars carved in detail by unknown artists. The Chinese builders also cannily incorporated Malay building techniques that suited the local environment. Like the typical Malay *kampung* dwelling, Khoo Kongsi is built on piers to protect it from flooding and dampness.

Inside there is a main chamber which contains an image of the clan's patron, Tua Sai Yeah, who was a renowned general of the Ch'in dynasty (221–207 BC). On either side of the main hall there are two smaller chambers: the one on the left is a shrine to Tua Peh Kong, the god of prosperity, while the other one contains gilded ancestral tablets that date back to 1840. There is a balcony above with scenes in bas-relief from Chinese mythology.

Outside, at the top of the steps, there are two small dragons—one male and one female—each with a ball inside the mouth which visitors touch for good luck. Khoo Kongsi is open daily from 09.00 to 17.00 and admission is free.

Cheong Fatt Tze Mansion. This rather crumbling state monument on Lebuh Leith was built c 1860 by Thio Thaw Siat. You cannot go inside because it is still privately owned but it is worth walking past to have a look. It is one of only three surviving buildings of its kind, the other two being in Medan and Manila.

Temples

The **Kuan Yin Teng Temple**, also called the Goddess of Mercy Temple, is the busiest Chinese temple in Penang; it is situated on Lebuh Pitt (Jalan Masjid Kapitan Kling) around the corner from St George's Church. While it has little architectural significance beyond its sweeping roof with richly decorated ridges and two protective dragons, it is the best place to observe the pragmatic Taoist synthesis between materialism and spiritualism. Worshippers come here daily to pay homage to their ancestors—hence the burning of paper money and joss sticks—but there is also a desire to create good fortune by placating the spirits through homage, prayer and token gifts of fruit and flowers. The goddess Kuan Yin is particularly associated with fertility rituals and general benevolent forces and this is one reason for the temple's popularity. The temple was built in the 1880s by the first generation of Chinese immigrants to settle in Penang.

The **Sri Mariamman Temple**, built in 1883, is the earliest Hindu temple in Penang. It is situated in the heart of Chinatown, at the corner of Lebuh Queen and Lebuh Chulia, and in the immediate vicinity a variety of Indian shops and restaurants helps cement this lively little enclave of Indian culture. The temple's *gopuram* (covered gate) is vividly decorated with a collection of 38 gods and four swans. Inside there are a number of statues of deities but it is not too difficult to recognise the one of Lord Subramaniam because it is the most lavishly decorated. Subramaniam, the son of

Kuan Yin Teng Temple, Georgetown

Shiva and destroyer of evil, is the focus of worship during the Thaipusam festival (see above).

Wat Chayamangkalaram is a Thai temple situated on Lorong Burma, a turning off Jalan Sultan Ahmad Shah, the main road out to Batu Ferringhi. It is known as the 'Temple of the Reclining Buddha' because of its famous 32m-long Buddha, spuriously claimed to be the third longest in the world but none the less very impressive. The site for the temple was given to the community by Queen Victoria in 1845.

At the entrance to the main hall, huge *naga* serpents form the balustrades; the real giants, however, are the twin bodyguards outside, with their hands clasping gigantic multi-coloured weapons which look like a cross between truncheons and swords, and their faces wrapped in forbidding grimaces. These legendary monsters are the *kinnara*, with the upper body of a human and the legs and wings of a mythical Himalayan bird.

Just across the road there is the Burmese **Dharmmikarama Temple** which can also be visited free of charge. Two sedate elephants made of stone stand guard either side of the gates.

The **Penang Buddhist Association Temple**, on Jalan Anson, was built in the 1920s and highlights the difference between the more pragmatic Taoist temples where there are often several deities as well as Buddha represented and the more ascetic Buddhism seen here. The muted colours, Italian marble Buddhas and glass chandeliers create an atmosphere of silent meditation.

The **Shiva Temple** in Jalan Dato Keramat is not very visible, being behind high walls, but is worth having a peek inside. The **Nattukotai Chettiar Temple** on Waterfall Road, dedicated to Lord Subramaniam, is the largest Hindu temple in Penang. The Thaipusam festival (see p 62) is celebrated here. Bus No. 7 from Lebuh Victoria goes along Waterfall Road to the temple, which is close to the Botanic Gardens.

The **Malay Mosque** or **Masjid Melayu**, in Lebuh Aceh not far from Khoo Kongsi, has an unusual Egyptian style minaret—Moorish style minarets are much more typical in Malaysia. There is a hole halfway up the minaret, said to have been made by cannon fire from the Khoo Khongsi during the riots of 1867, when a group of Malays who sided with the Hokkien Chinese used the mosque as their base and were subsequently attacked here.

The **Penang State mosque** in Jalan Ayer Itam is large and new and accomodates 5000 people. Bus No. 1 from Lebuh Victoria goes to the mosque.

Excursions from Georgetown

Penang Hill

At 830m above Georgetown, the top of Penang Hill is popular as one of the few places offering a respite from the humidity and heat of the street level.

> Early colonialists were convinced that the Eastern climate shortened the life of Europeans; the enervating heat was seen to sap the Western lifeblood, and before malaria was identified, the 'fever' was seen in this light—a fatal aspect of the white man's burden. Penang Hill developed a reputation as a sanatorium and a bungalow for convalescence was built by the government early in the 19C. A dispensary was added to the bungalow and a medical attendant was on hand to assist British army officers and their families. An article in the *Singapore Chronicle* and *Commercial Register* (1833) by a Dr Ward offered general advice to those coming to work in Penang: 'Take regular exercise; light a fire; use mosquito curtains; take sometimes a dose of sulphate of quinine, powdered ginger or cayenne pepper at bedtime; smoke a cigar or hookah and preserve confidence and equanimity.'

The alleged recuperative powers of Penang Hill made it famous throughout the Straits Settlements and to mark Queen Victoria's Diamond Jubilee a **cable railway** was planned to run to the top of the hill. This first attempt at a railway was a dismal failure: dignitaries gathered at the station in 1899 for the opening ceremony—including Arshak Sarkies who planned to turn the hotel on the summit into another E&O—and the train did not move a centimetre. New technology was applied, but it was 1923 before a funicular railway system was operating successfully. The system still works but the half hour it takes to reach the summit is sometimes less than time spent queuing up for a seat. Try to avoid weekends and holidays and turn up as early as possible.

Apart from being about 5°C cooler than the town, the summit also offers panoramic views of the island and the hills of Kedah. Refreshments can be enjoyed in a small café or at the **Hotel Bellevue**. There is also a small Hindu temple and a Muslim mosque.

To reach the funicular station, take the MPPP city bus No. 1 from Lebuh Chulia or Pengkalan Weld to Ayer Itam and then the green-coloured No. 8 to the station. Bus Nos 1, 101, and 85 may also be boarded from the Komtar bus station for Ayer Itam. The cable-pulled cars run from 06.30 to 21.30. It takes a good three hours to climb the 8km to the top, starting from the Moon Gate at the Botanical Gardens.

Kek Lok Si Temple

This is the largest Buddhist temple in Malaysia, the origins of which date to 1885 when a travelling monk was passing through the area and experienced a spiritual vision that led to the establishment of the temple. Building work started in 1890 but it was 1910 before the construction was completed. The centrepiece is the Ban Po Thar ('Ten Thousand Buddhas') Pagoda, made up of seven tiers and 30m high, and dedicated to Tsi Tsuang Wang who magnanimously declined to enter Nirvana in order to help others on the path to enlightenment. A spiral staircase winds its way to the top of the tower which is adorned everywhere with Buddhas.

Before reaching the entrance there are countless shops and stalls lining the way, offering a miscellany of uninteresting souvenirs.

To reach the temple take a city bus No. 1, or a Lim Seng bus No. 91 from along Lebuh Chulia to the Ayer Itam terminal.

Botanical Gardens

The Gardens were laid out in 1844 by Charles Curtis, the first superintendent, and over the years a fine display of tropical plants and flowers has been created. The very nosey *kera* (leaf monkey) are likely to be encountered, as they roam around freely looking for food. The gardens are also known as the Waterfall Gardens because of a stream that runs down from Penang Hill through the 30-hectare park.

To reach the gardens, take a city bus No. 7 from Lebuh Chulia for the 7km journey to the end of Jalan Kebun Bunga.

Island tour

A 70km tour around the island by car or motorbike takes in a number of sights and could easily be made to occupy a whole day. If you plan to include one of the walking trails west of Teluk Bahang, definitely allow a full day and consider an overnight stop. There is no accommodation in the south or west of the island but an overnight stay is possible at **Teluk Bahang**. An alternative to driving is a tour bus (see above) that takes in most of the main sites. The public bus system could be used but there is no one bus route that completes a circuit of the island; details of the different buses available are given below for each sight.

The route followed here is in a clockwise direction from Georgetown, heading south along the main road to the airport.

15km south of Georgetown is the 'Temple of the Azure Cloud', or **Snake Temple**. The temple was built in 1850 as a dedication to a Chinese monk, Chor Soo Kong, who gained fame in the area for his healing powers. A figure of him, draped in red and yellow, sits in the main square. The temple is famous for its collection of Wagler's pit vipers. Normally highly venomous, they lounge about in the dimly lit and smoky interior, hanging from twigs laid about the altar. If you wish, one will be draped over your shoulders for a photograph—the incense smoke from the temple is said to render them innocuous but they have probably been doctored. When not benign, tubular fangs which contain the venom are rotated from their horizontal position inside the mouth to a vertical position so that they are ready to strike when the snake's jaws open.

To reach Snake Temple by bus, take a Yellow Bus No. 66 or 78 from Lebuh Chulia.

Continuing south for a short while brings you to a turn-off for the coastal village of **Batu Maung**. There is a good but fairly expensive seafood restaurant built over the water on stilts here but not much else, apart from the scenic views. Back on the main road and past the airport, there is the village of **Teluk Kumbar** where the main road heads north.

Further west, the road winds scenically to a dead end at **Gertak Sanggul** where there is an attractive beach and, apart from weekends and holidays, few people to disturb the beauty and calm of the place.

Back on the main road heading north, the village of **Barat** offers the choice of a road southwest to **Pulau Betong** or one northeast to **Balik Pulau**. There are no amenities at Pulau Betong and the road ends here anyway so it is best to head for Balik Pulau where a number of restaurants and cafés make it the obvious place to have lunch. The quick route back to Georgetown heads east via Ayer Itam, where you can stop off to see **Bat Temple**, erected about 60 years ago by Madam Lim Chooi Yuen. But to complete the island tour, head north.

Sungei Pinang and **Pantai Aceh** are two small Chinese villages reached by turning west off the main road. Few tourists come here because there is little to see other than villagers getting on with the business of repairing their boats and nets. At the signpost to Pantai Aceh, the main road climbs north to the disappointing **Titi Kerawang Waterfalls** before levelling off to reach the **Forest Recreation Park**. There is a small natural history museum and a number of signposted, moderately interesting forest trails that lead through the 100 hectares of the park.

The **Butterfly Farm** is the next stop, where there are thousands of live butterflies—fluttering about for their brief two-week sojourn—in every colour and size imaginable. There is also an ecologically incorrect mounted insect display, and a large souvenir shop. Open from 09.00 to 17.00 (18.00 at weekends), entrance is RM5.

There is a **batik factory** about 1km further along the road, waiting patiently for another tour bus to deposit a crowd of potential customers. Give it a miss and head north where smaller batik workshops can be found at Teluk Bahang.

Teluk Bahang on the north coast marks the western extremity of the northern beach strip (see below). The village itself is a typical *kampung*, earning its living from fishing, and there are a few restaurants dotted along the main road. The **End of the World** restaurant is easily the best for fresh seafood. From a point near to the pier at Teluk Bahang, there is a worthwhile 2-hour trek that heads west following the coastline to a lighthouse at **Muka Head**. There are good beaches around this headland but the best beach of all is to the south, **Monkey Beach**. To reach this spot head west from the pier towards Muka Head but take the first trail that heads off into the interior on the left. It takes a good two hours to reach Monkey Beach, also called Coconut Beach, but it is well worth the trek: a beautiful large beach, no crowds, wildlife (but no monkeys) and wonderful scenery.

Budget accommodation at Teluk Bahang is available at **Rama's Guest House** (☎ 04-8811179); **Miss Loh's**, off the main road that heads south back to the butterfly farm, has doubles for RM35. Top of the scale is the nearby **Penang Mutiara** (see below).

The Hin Bus No. 93 runs between Telik Bahang and Georgetown.

Batik

As you travel around Malaysia you will see many examples of batik. You can see it manufactured and even make your own designs. Several forms of batik are made in Malaysia. The most common involves a pattern blocked onto a sarong length piece of cotton using a copper block covered in wax. The cloth is then dyed, all the material taking up the dye except the waxed areas. Then the cloth is boiled to remove the wax and another pattern drawn, and so on until a complex pattern of various colours is made. Two types of wax are used: the first is a lighter wax which comes off in the initial hot wash; the second is a longer-lasting substance, designed to last through several hot washes. The latter type of wax produces a marbled effect on the cloth. Originally an error, this kind of pattern has developed as a distinctive style of batik.

Another method is to use little pots of wax to hand draw quite fine designs. Further patterns are added via small pots of dye which are poured on to the cloth. Shades of colour are obtained as the dye spreads unevenly across the fabric. Batik factories are more common along the east coast of Malaysia and at several budget hostels along the east coast you can try your hand at making a T-shirt design using these techniques. Batik printing is done on cotton, silk and linen. At Mukim 2, Teluk Bahang, at the very end of the luxury hotel strip, there are several factories which sell batik and give demonstrations of its manufacture.

Batu Ferringhi

The official tourist literature is a tiny bit misleading when it describes Batu Ferringhi as having 'expansive stretches of glittering sand interspersed with secluded coves' because, despite a reasonably successful effort to combat the pollution and litter largely created by tourism, the sea is not quite as clear as one might expect. For this reason, it might be a good idea to keep to the hotel swimming pools. The coral that once grew around the shoreline at Batu Ferringhi is gone due to sedimentation caused by the construction of the bridge. Notwithstanding these drawbacks, the place does have its own character, especially at night when the main road is alive with neon-illuminated restaurants, shops and stalls, all helping to fill the air with a buzz of hedonism.

■ Practical information

Getting to and from Batu Ferringhi
A taxi from Georgetown costs around RM20 while the 202 bus, which stops outside the ferry terminal, is RM1.40.

Tourist information
There are no tourist offices but your hotel should be able to help with local information. Hotels will also change money and travellers' cheques and there is an **exchange bureau** (☎ 04-8812776) opposite the Golden Sands hotel. Jeep and car hire can also be arranged here.

MAS (☎ 04-6482144) have an office on the ground floor of the Park Royal hotel.

Accommodation
The top-range hotels are all beach resorts and, apart from the Mutiara, the postal address is just Batu Ferringhi. They all have swimming pools and water activities and nearly all have access to the beach behind them. The quoted room rates are for the least expensive doubles.

Top range hotels. The **Penang Mutiara** (☎ 04-8852828; fax 04-8852351), 1 Jalan Telok Bahang, is the ultimate in luxury, tastefully situated away to the west of the main hotel strip, and with all rooms overlooking the sea. Rooms are priced from RM385 to RM600. The nearest hotel to the east of the Mutiara is the **Bayview Beach Hotel** (☎ 04-8812061) which benefits from a good beach area close by. Rooms start at RM250.

The **Park Royal** (☎ 04-8811133) is the most westerly of the main hotel cluster and the closest to the restaurants and shops. Rooms from RM295. Next door, the family-oriented and newly renovated **Holiday Inn** (☎ 04-8811601) has rooms from RM220. The **Golden Sands** (☎ 04-8811911), rooms from RM285, is by a small river and is one of the hotels belonging to the Shangri-La group. It is popular with families. Another is the **Rasa Sayang** (☎ 04-8811811), which disguises its hotel status by cleverly incorporating Malay architecture into its design. Rooms are from RM310 and it is the quietest of the three hotels. Further east, the **Ferringhi Beach** (☎ 04-8905999) is the last of this cluster; it has great views and rooms from RM225.

Tanjung Bungah is the first stretch of beach you will see if arriving from Georgetown. The beach is not that good and you will need a bus or taxi to reach the shops and restaurants. The **Crown Prince** (☎ 04-8904111) charges from RM230, but the **Novotel Penang** (☎ 04-8903333) costs less, from RM200, and has access to a private section of beach. The **Beach Chomber Paradise Resort** (☎ 04-8908808) has similar rates.

Middle range hotels. The **Lone Pine Hotel** (☎ 04-8811511) has rooms from RM130, no swimming pool, but is close to the other hotels and shops of Batu Ferringhi. At Tanjung Bungah, the **Motel Sri Pantai** (☎ 04-8909727) has basic rooms from RM70.

Restaurants

A variety of restaurants are spread out on either side of the main road from Teluk Bahang in the west to Tanjung Bungah in the east, with a concentration between the Bayview Beach and the Golden Sands hotels. They are mostly, but not only, seafood restaurants and some of the finest are located in the hotels. The Penang Mutiara has the Italian **La Farfalla** (☎ 04-8852828), as well as Japanese and Chinese restaurants. The Shangri-La hotels all have good Chinese and European restaurants, including a 24-hour coffee house.

Restoran Hollywood (☎ 04-8907269) is a little out of the way, between Tanjung Bungah and the Golden Sands hotel, but it has a vast menu of seafood and Chinese dishes and tables facing the sea. Main dishes are about RM30. Opposite the Golden Sands hotel there are two big restaurants, brightly lit at night: **The New Last Drop**, serving Western and Asian dishes around RM20, and **Pearl of the Orient** which is a little more expensive. Close by and difficult to miss is the **Eden** restaurant (☎ 04-8811236). Just wander in to gaze at the aquaria of seafood sold by weight. They also have a tourist shop, a dance show at 20.30 and a menu with a reasonable wine list. Expect to pay around RM120 for two people for an à la carte meal. The speciality is lobster thermidor. Next door to the Eden is **The Ship** restaurant (☎ 04-8812142) which looks like a ship from the outside (it isn't), while inside the speciality is steak and seafood.

Opposite the Park Royal hotel, next to the police station, the **Moghul Arch** (☎

04-8812891) is the only north Indian restaurant in Batu Ferringhi; its set meals are around RM30.

Activities

A range of **water activities** can be arranged through your hotel—water-skiing, canoeing, windsurfing, etc.—but independent operators working on the beaches usually offer better rates for some sports. As evening draws in, a meal at one of the many restaurants and a stroll past the pavement stalls is a popular activity. Next to the Restoran Hollywood at Tanjung Bungah there is a large pottery shop. A **cultural dance** takes place daily at 20.45 at the Penang Mutiara's The Catch restaurant (see also the Eden under Restaurants above). There is no admission charge and a meal is not obligatory; buying a drink will suffice.

The **Pinang Cultural Centre** (☎ 04-8851175) is near the Penang Mutiara hotel at Teluk Bahang. There is an exhibition gallery, a restaurant, a stage and, across a small bridge, a number of dwellings built in traditional Malay style. Check in advance to find out what the daily programme consists of; usually it is a mixture of craft and sport demonstrations, including *gasing* (top spinning) or *silat* (martial arts), plus music and dance.

Kedah and Perlis

Kedah and Perlis are the least visited states in Malaysia, with the significant exception of the island of Langkawi. This is partly because the rest of the country has been more successful in promoting its attractions but also because there are fewer places to visit in these two northwest states. But it is also due to the geographical location: unless you are travelling through to Thailand there is little option but to turn about and retrace your route due south.

Both states are predominantly agricultural, and in peninsular Malaysia this means unbroken vistas of rice paddies stretching away on either side of the road. The only town of interest is **Alor Setar**, the capital of Kedah state; the other place worth visiting is **Lembah Bujang**, where there are archaeological finds. Apart from these two locations, most visitors find themselves travelling to the region to board a ferry to the island of Langkawi for a spot of rest and recreation.

History

Until 1842, when Siam divided the state, Perlis was a part of Kedah so, not surprisingly, they share a common history. Before the 15C this history is the subject of debate due to the problems raised by the archaeological discoveries at **Lembah Bujang** (see below). However, an unambiguous thread running through any historical narrative from around the 10C to the 19C is the influence of Siam immediately to the north.

The first serious interruption to the Siamese hegemony came with the rise of **Islamic Melaka** in the 15C. The new religion spread northwards and contributed enormously to the developing sense of difference between Kedah and the Siamese. In the first half of the 19C, suffused with Islamic zeal after the **Wahabi sect** took Mecca (see Religion, p 51), a holy war erupted. This *jihad* lasted nearly 20 years, simmering as a source of cultural discontent and sporadically breaking into open warfare. In 1842 Siam divided the state and created Perlis.

From 1850 a *modus operandi* was achieved with Malay chiefs recognising Siamese control but expecting and receiving no political pressure. This worked quite well until the region came under the influence of the **Straits Settlements** whose investments in Kedah and Perlis came from Chinese merchants in Penang. Under the terms of the 1909 agreement Kedah and Perlis came under British influence.

■ Practical information

Getting to and from Kedah and Perlis
By air. Sultan Abdul Halim airport (☎ 04-7144021) is 11km from Alor Setar. There are at least four daily flights to Kuala Lumpur (RM113 single) and one daily flight to Kota Bharu (RM71 single). The local MAS office is in Alor Setar (☎ 04-7311106).

By train. The Butterworth to Bangkok train stops at Alor Setar and Arau (in Perlis) but, inexplicably, the Bangkok train south to Malaysia does not make a stop at Alor Setar. From either Alor Setar or Arau, a bus or taxi connects with Kuala Kedah or Kuala Perlis for the ferry to Langkawi.

By bus. Alor Setar is the centre for buses north to Hat Yai in Thailand and south and east to Malaysian towns, and to Singapore.

By car. The main road from Kuala Lumpur to Butterworth continues north along the coast to Alor Setar and on to Kuala Perlis where the passenger ferry to Langkawi can be boarded. The road continues north into Thailand. It takes about five hours to drive from Kuala Lumpur to Alor Setar.

Tourist information
The Alor Setar **tourist office** (☎ 04-7301957) is in Wisma Darul Aman. Money can be changed at the **banks** along Jalan Raja in Alor Setar.

Lembah Bujang

Sungei Petani, the unremarkable town 35km north of Butterworth on the main road, is only important as a marker for Lembah Bujang which is 10km north-west of the town.

The **archaeological museum** (open daily 09.00 to 17.00, free admission) is the best place for information on the excavations in the Bujang area. Bujang is thought to come from a Sanskrit word meaning serpent and the area may have been the site of the capital of a 5C Hindu kingdom called Langkasuka which features in many traditional Malay stories. One theory suggests that this is the earliest Hindu state, dating back 200 years before Ankor Wat in Cambodia. The city may have been used by Indian traders as an entrepôt with China. To avoid the pirate infested Melaka Strait goods were taken ashore at Kuala Merbok and carried overland. Later it may have been used by the Srivijaya Empire from Sumatra.

A large number of 10C *candis* (temples) have been excavated in the area—the work is still continuing—and photographs and artefacts relating to the project are exhibited in the museum. Eight of the temples have been reconstructed, using the original materials, outside the museum building.

Unfortunately it is not a particularly informative exhibition and it fails to draw attention to the unique nature of the Buddhist temples that are to be found in the Bujang valley. When they were first found in the early 19C, it was commonly assumed they were influenced by Hinduism because this was thought to be the religion that Islam replaced in the Malay world. The discovery that some of the temples are more Buddhist than anything else has upset the conventional history and there is still uncertainty about the implications of these finds. One theory is that Bhuddist and Hindu influenced temples are from different periods, the Bhuddist ones predating the Hindu temples by several hundred years.

Getting to Lembah Bujang
By car, take the road from Sungei Petani to the village of Bedong, 8km away, and then follow the signs for the museum. Without a car it is advisable to take a taxi to the museum from Bedong. Local buses run regularly from Sungei Petani to Bedong.

Gunung Jerai

The town of Gurun is 20km north of Sungei Petani and 33km south of Alor Setar. Gurun is unremarkable, but the town serves as an access point for the massive limestone outcrop, **Gunung Jerai**, 1200m above sea level.

Gunung Jerai (Kedah Peak) is the highest point in Kedah and offers panoramic views of the state's rolling rice fields, Perlis to the north, Penang to the southwest and the Langkawi islands to the northwest. Half-way up the mountain is the **Sungai Teroi Forest Recreation Park**, home to a variety of plants including pitcher plants and orchids. There are picnic sites and short walking trails. There is a far less interesting **Museum of Forestry** at the peak which detains most visitors for only a short time.

Getting to Gunung Jerai
From Gurun there is a regular jeep service (RM5) to the peak, at least once an hour between 08.00 and 17.00. It takes about two hours to walk up. If you don't have your own transport to Gurun, there is a local bus from Sungei Petani to close by the jeep departure point.

Accommodation
The only accommodation is at the **Gunung Jerai Resort** (☎ 04-4234345), just below the peak. It was originally built in the 1920s as a resthouse but there are now seven two-bedroomed chalets with attached kitchens.

Alor Setar

Some 33km north of Gunung Jerai is the state capital of Kedah, Alor Setar (pronounced 'alorstar'), and for most visitors this is the furthest north they travel in Malaysia. Despite the geographical proximity and historical links to Thailand, evidenced by a sizeable number of Thais working and living in the town, Alor Setar is very recognisably Malaysian.

Most of the places of interest are to be found around the centrally located **Padang**, close to the train and bus stations. It is difficult to miss the large Moorish mosque, **Masjid Zahir**, built in 1912—especially at night when it is lit up like a Christmas tree. Opposite is the **Istana Balai Besar**, first built in 1898, with an attractive exterior due to its carefully proportioned columns and detailed wooden fretwork. Inside is the Royal Throne, still in use on ceremonial occasions. The **Balai Nobat** on Jalan Raja is a small yellow and white octagonal tower with an onion dome which is not open to the public. Inside are the sacred instruments of the royal orchestra which are only seen and used when a sultan is crowned, married or buried.

There is a small **royal museum** behind the Istana Balai Besar but a little more interesting is the **Muzium Negeri** on Lebuhraya Darul Aman, less than 2km north of the Padang. It has some useful information on the archaeology of the Bujang valley and a valuable collection of Chinese porcelain; open daily from 10.00 to 18.00 except Friday when the hours are 10.00 to 12.00 and 14.30 to 18.00. Admission is free.

Accommodation and restaurants

There is plenty of accommodation, including the **Hotel Grand Continental Kedah** (☎ 04-7335917; fax 04-7335161) on Jalan Sultan Badlishah (RM110–170) and the **Regent Hotel** (☎ 04-7311900), RM50–75, on the same street. There is also 4-star **Holiday Villa** (☎ 04-7349999, fax 04-7341199).The **Samila Hotel** (☎ 04-7318888; fax 04-7339934) at 27 Jalan Kanchut is especially good value with rooms costing RM70–100. The inexpensive but spacious **Station Hotel** (☎ 04-7333786) is above the bus station; rooms are about RM50. Another budget hotel is the **Seri Malaysia** (☎ 04-4234060, fax 04-4234106).

The hotels all have reasonable restaurants, the Western food at the Samila is a cut above average. The best place for Thai-inspired dishes is the **Restoran Hajjah** one block south of the Grand Continental.

Langkawi

Langkawi is the name of a group of 104 islands—five of which disappear when the tide comes in—in the Andaman Sea close to Malaysia's border with Thailand. The group name is taken from **Pulau Langkawi**, the largest and most populated of the islands and the one that visitors come to for sun and sand without the brouhaha of Penang. The name Langkawi derives from the ancient kingdom of Langkasuka whose full title—Negari Alang Kah Suka—means 'the land of all one's wishes'. Its capital is thought to have been built at the base of Gunung Jerai on the mainland (see above) and its kings were known as *daprenta-hyangs*.

The beaches are superb, rivalled on the west coast only by those on the island of Pangkor some 300km to the south, and there are exciting opportunities for scuba diving, windsurfing, canoeing and sailing. It should be said, though, that there is very little else in the way of attractions. The few places of minor historical interest have been played to the hilt in an attempt to manufacture a tourist myth that Langkawi is steeped in legends concerning wronged maidens and lovesick princes.

History

Until recent times, Langkawi's only notable moment was the small part it played in the history of Siam's attempts to incorporate the state of Kedah (which includes Langkawi) into its territory. In 1821 a decisive episode in this history was the surprise invasion of Kedah by the Siamese with a force of 7000 men; the farmers of Langkawi put up a stout resistance, burning their own granaries and rice fields to deprive the enemy of loot. Before then the islands were merely infamous as a haunt of pirates, although **Admiral Cheng Ho** did chart the islands in his 1405 expedition to Melaka.

The years prior to Siam's invasion are associated with the story of Mahsuri who, if she did exist, was probably born in the reign of Abdullah, Sultan of Kedah from 1762 to 1800. Other versions of the story place her in the 10C and 13C. The lack of primary sources concerning Mahsuri has allowed a fanciful 'history' to be nourished in the interests of tourism.

Datuk Seri Kermaya Jaya (so one version of the story goes) was a local chief whose plans to make the beautiful young **Mahsuri** his second wife were thwarted by his wife. As a ruse he had the young maiden married to his son instead, hoping to take advantage of her when her young husband was away. Jaya's wife again thwarted his devious plan by falsely accusing Mahsuri of adultery. After an unfair trial she was found guilty and ordered to be punished by *sula* (in which the victim is buried in sand up to the waist and killed by plunging a *kris* between the shoulder blades). After this dastardly deed, white blood poured from her wound as proof of her innocence and purity and in her dying moments she cursed Langkawi for seven generations. Seri Kermaya Jaya, who started all this, is said to have died while fighting the Siamese at sea.

The best evidence for the legend of Mahsuri (see above) is to be found in the ill-luck that seemed to plague Langkawi until very recently. In the 1980s, one of Malaysia's most powerful construction companies poured millions of dollars into an ambitious tourist complex on the island which failed miserably and was never completed. Around the same time, Prime Minister Mahathir (who comes from Kedah) nurtured a plan to turn Langkawi into a tax-free haven that would draw in trade and fuel development. This too fell prey to a downturn in the country's economy and wise men pointed a finger to the curse of Mahsuri. Now the tourist trade is flourishing, fuelled by investors from Singapore and Hong Kong, and a second runway is being constructed to accommodate charter flights from Europe; the seven generations are said to have run their course.

■ Practical information

Getting to and from Langkawi

By air. Langkawi International Airport (☎ 04-9551322) is 18km from Kuah, the island's main town. MAS have a minimum of four daily flights from Kuala Lumpur (RM135 single), three from Penang (RM51 single), and four weekly from Singapore. Until the second runway becomes operational, all international flights involve changing planes at Kuala Lumpur. Pelangi Air (☎ 04-9552261) flies between Langkawi and Ipoh four times a week (RM107 single).

By boat to and from Kuala Perlis and Kuala Kedah. There is a regular hourly service between Kuala Perlis and Langkawi (☎ 04-9854406; RM12), from 08.00 to 18.00, taking under one hour. At the Kuah jetty the various companies will have their schedules posted up, and while tickets can be purchased in advance this is rarely necessary. There is also a regular service, almost as frequent as the Kuala Perlis route, between Langkawi and Kuala Kedah (☎ 04-7621201; RM15). This is more convenient for reaching Alor Setar.

By boat to and from Penang. There are two services between Penang and Langkawi, departing Georgetown at 08.00 and 08.30 and costing RM45 for a first-class single (RM80 return) and RM35 economy class (RM60 return). The ferry office (☎ 04-2625630) is next to the tourist offices near Fort Cornwallis, Georgetown, open from 07.00 to 20.30 (Monday to Saturday) and 07.00 to 13.30 (Sunday). The ferry from Langkawi to Penang departs at 18.00. There is also a direct service from Penang to Pulau Payar (see p 149), which operates on Sundays, departing at 09.00, and costing RM88.

By boat to and from Thailand. There is a twice-weekly ferry to Phuket (RM90 single) and a regular daily service to Satun on the Thai coast. There is nothing of tourist interest at Satun.

Getting around Langkawi
To and from the airport. A coupon system is employed for paying for a taxi from the airport into town. It costs at least RM20 to most of the resorts. There is no public transport to or from the airport.

By bus. The bus station is in the centre of Kuah, near the hospital; there is an hourly service to Pantai Cenang, a 2-hourly service to Pantai Kok and Burau Bay, and an hourly service to Padang Lalang and Teluk Ewa. The first bus usually departs around 07.00 and the last bus back to Kuah around 18.00.

Car hire. Companies hiring cars have desks at the airport and most of the bigger resorts can also arrange car hire.

Motorcycle hire. This is the most economical way to travel around the island, using easy-to-ride 70cc step-thru motorcycles. A quick lesson will be given to anyone using one for the first time. The roads around the island are nearly all new and under-used, making it a pleasure to tour by motorcycle. A circuit of the island could easily be done in one day.

Bicycle hire. Most of the places in Kuah, Pantai Cenang and Pantai Kok that hire motorcycles also rent out bicycles.

Tourist information
The **tourist office** (☎ 04-9667789) is located on Jalan Pesiaran Putra in Kuah.

The only banks that **change money** are to be found in Kuah. The resort hotels may also be used to change money and travellers' cheques but the rates will not be so good. Kuah is the only place on the island with a **post office**, **police station** or **hospital**.

Many of the resorts will arrange a coach tour of the island, taking in most of the main attractions, or contact Sala Tours (☎ 04-9667521). **Boat cruises** for fishing or pleasure are available through Langkawi Adventure (☎ 04-9551533) or Mofaz Marine (☎ 04-9557361).

Accommodation

New resorts have mushroomed over the last few years, responding to affluent Malaysians and Singaporeans as much as to Westerners. Between late November and the end of the Chinese New Year around February, many resorts will be nearly full but during other months visitors have more choice. A selection of resorts is given here according to location and price.

The widest choice is to be found at **Pantai Cenang**, including the top-notch **Pelangi Beach Resort** (☎ 04-9551001; fax 04-9551122). A good middle-range place is the 20-room **Beach Garden Resort** (☎ 04-9551363), with its own pool and less than half the price of the Pelangi. The **Semarak Langkawi Beach Resort** (☎ 04-9551377; fax 04-9551159), is another small place with a choice of air-conditioned rooms and ones with a fan.

Pantai Kok has a better beach and there is a choice of two upmarket resorts, each monopolising a little bay: the **Burau Bay Resort** (☎ 04-9591061; fax 04-9591172), with rooms for around RM250, and the **Sheraton Langkawi Resort** (☎ 04-9551901; fax 04-9551968) at Teluk Nibong with rooms around RM350. The best budget places are the **Country Beach Motel** (☎ 04-9551395) and **The Last Resort** (☎ 04-9551046).

In the southwestern tip of the island, south of Pantai Cenang, there are a couple of interesting places at **Pantai Tengah**: the inexpensive **Sunset Beach Resort** and the upmarket but not outrageously priced **Langkawi Holiday Villa Beach Resort** (☎ 04-9551701; fax 04-9551504). A standard double is RM230.

There is no beach at **Kuah** but if accommodation is required, the **Captain Resort** (☎ 04-9667100; fax 04-9666799) at Lot No. 82 Jalan Penarak is good value. Chalets with and without air-conditioning are available, between RM60 and RM100, and the place has a quiet location tucked away outside the town. A free pick-up from the jetty may be arranged on the phone.

Restaurants

At Kuah the best place for a meal with a view is the **Sheraton Perdana Resort** on Jalan Pantai Dato Syed Omar. Dotted around the town is a mixed array of hawker stalls, Indian cafés and seafood restaurants. The *pasar malam* (night market) in Kuah is usually held along Jalan Sungai Kuah every Tuesday and this is worth a visit for the inexpensive satay, fried chicken and *murtabaks*. The best choice of restaurants is to be found at Pantai Cenang, where nearly all the resorts have a restaurant, and part of the fun is eating at a different place each evening. The restaurant at the Semarak Langkawi Beach Resort is recommended. Different visitors have praised and criticised the two restaurants at the Pelangi Beach Resort. At Pantai Kok the **Last Resort** is recommended; the setting is relaxing and the food reliable and not too expensive.

Island tour

This is a 100km circuit of the island that begins at Kuah and takes in most of the places of interest and beaches. The circuit could be completed in one day using a car or motorcycle, two days or more with a bicycle.

The first leg of the tour is north from Kuah and after a couple of kilometres the **Kedah Marble** centre is passed on the right. There is a sales room but it is not possible to observe the marble being worked. After another 14km the **Air Hangat Village** (Telaga Air Hangat) is passed. This is a fairly hideous tourist attraction featuring a hot spring fountain and murals depicting a local legend. It costs RM4 to enter the village, from 09.00 to 16.00, which also has shows of traditional Malay dances. At **Kilim**, on the way to the Air Hangat Village, is the Galeria Perdana which is dedicated to items belonging to Prime Minister Mahathir.

Continue north through paddy fields and rubber plantations to Padang Lalang where a right-turn at the roundabout heads northeast to **Pantai Rhu**, 23km from Kuah. This is one of the best and least crowded beaches on the island and at low tide it is possible to walk across to the offshore island of **Pulau Pasir**. The nearby **Radisson Tanjung Rhu Resort** serves meals and there are Malay stalls on the beach. Boats and snorkelling gear can be rented on the beach or from the hotel.

On the other side of the promontory, and only reached by boat, is the **Gua Cerita** cave (Cave of Legends). It bears a mid-18C Jawi (Malay using an Arabic script) inscription recording the death of one Sheikh Baharuddin. The name may well refer to an Arab missionary as the sultan reigning at that time, Mohamed Jiwa II, was known to have encouraged Arab missionaries to Kedah. There is a wooden staircase up to the cave's entrance but once you have climbed to the top and peered in there is little to do but come down again. The lovely deserted beach invites a longer stay, so if a boat trip is made be sure to bring a picnic and plenty of water and suntan lotion.

Travel back to the Padang Lalang roundabout and head west for about 12km until a turning for **Teluk Datai** is reached. On the way to the turn-off do not bother to stop at **Pasir Hitam** and its black beach (caused by tourmaline, a black-coloured mineral). There is little here apart from some souvenir stalls and an ugly little narrow beach. Teluk Datai, which is 12km from the turn-off, is an optional diversion. The road passes a couple of inviting coves where you will be all alone, and a CITES-registered **crocodile farm** (09.00 to 17.00, RM5) where you will be in the company of about one thousand crocodiles and alligators. The ultra-expensive **Datai Resort**, with its private beach, serves meals and there is a golf course here.

Continuing on the main road west from the turn-off leads to **Pantai Kok**, unarguably the finest beach on the island and well worth considering as an accommodation base. There are resorts to suit most budgets, and a laid-back atmosphere to enjoy. Just before reaching the nearby Burau Bay Resort, a small track on the right leads up to **Telaga Tujuh**, a series of waterfalls connecting seven (*tujah*) rock pools (*telaga*), a local beauty spot which is good for swimming but often spoilt by uncollected litter. The steep 45-minute walk to the waterfalls is best enjoyed in the evening when the heat is less punishing.

The main road heads south from Pantai Kok and then east back to Kuah but at **Padang Matsirat** (claimed to be the village home of Datuk Kermaya Jaya, the pursuer of Mahsuri, see p 145) there is a turn-off for **Pantai Cenang** in the southwest of the island. This is the main accommodation area on the island and has a beach which is only noteworthy because it is safe for swimming. Back near Padang Matsirat, it is a short journey to the **field of burnt rice** where the island's rice granary was burnt in 1821 to frustrate the Siamese. Heavy rain is said sometimes to bring traces of the buried burnt rice to the surface. Mahsuri's glaring white tomb is passed on the road back to Kuah.

At Pantai Kuala Muda there is Langkawi Aquabeat, an indoor water theme park, while at Pantai Tengeh there is a large aquarium called Underwater World.

Other islands

There is no scheduled boat service to most of the other islands in the Langkawi archipelago but boat trips can be arranged through most of the larger resorts and the tourist office. The main reason for organising a trip would be for snorkelling or scuba diving, although **Pulau Singa Besar** is an exception. It takes about 40 minutes to reach this small island (640 hectares) from Pantai Tengah (at Pantai Tengah there is a large aquarium that you might want to visit). Its attraction is ecological; there is a small information centre and animal sanctuary, two jungle tracks and a superb beach on the south side of the island. There is neither accommodation nor restaurants so arrive early and bring a picnic.

Pulau Dayang Bunting (Island of the Pregnant Maiden) is the second-largest island after Pulau Langkawi and has the attraction of a cave, Gua Langsir (Cave of the Banshee), which is reputed to be haunted. There is also a freshwater lake which has collected a number of legends but, as with anywhere else on Langkawi, it is always difficult to separate tourist hype from genuine folk-lore.

The latest island to be developed for visitors is **Pulau Payar**, a 45-minute boat ride from Langkawi using the daily catamaran service from Kuah at 10.30. Langkawi Coral (☎ 04-9667318) on the jetty have a package trip for RM180 that includes transport, lunch and free use of snorkelling equipment and a ride in a glass-bottomed boat. Diving gear can also be hired. There is also now a direct service from Penang to Pulau Payar on Sunday at 09.00, RM88.

Perlis

The smallest of the Malaysian states, around 800 square kilometres, is usually just passed through on the way to Thailand or Langkawi. There is little reason to do otherwise. The state capital is **Kangar** but there is nothing here to detain the traveller. At the small port of **Kuala Perlis**, 10km away, a ferry can be boarded to Langkawi. The only place really worth visiting, if you have transport, is the tin mine at **Kaki Bukit**, just 14km from the border with Thailand. A wooden walkway can be used to view the tin-mining process.

Melaka Bandaraya Bersejara

Covering an area of only 1650 square kilometres, Melaka State is one of Malaysia's smallest states. The major reason to visit the state lies in the ancient city of the same name and the state's history is really the history of the trading port.

Melaka

Melaka city, the capital of Melaka state, is 144km to the southeast of Kuala Lumpur. The sleepy Malaysian town of 15 years ago can still be experienced here, in between the main traffic routes and the shopping malls. There are also the remnants of several hundred years when Melaka (formerly Malacca) was not a commercial backwater but the hub around which the trade of the Far East turned. All routes once led to Melaka, and control of the Straits of Melaka promised untold riches to those maritime nations strong enough to hold off rival powers.

The city itself is more than enough reason for undertaking the bus or plane journey, but there are other attractions outside the town which might make visitors glad that they came. There are pretty **beach resorts** unaffected by the winter monsoons, an island to explore and a whole gaggle of newly created sights at **Taman Mini Malaysia**, including a butterfly park, a zoo and model villages showing the various lifestyles of Malaysia's ethnic groups. All this can extend your stay in the ancient town for days.

History

The earliest history of Melaka, the *Sejarah Melaya* (Malay Annals), written sometime in the 15C or 16C, explains how the first settlement came to exist and how it got its name. It was supposedly founded around the 1390s by a refugee Sumatran prince called Parameswara (see p 38) who was inspired by the sight of a mousedeer, which had the courage to fight off his hunting dog, to build his city here. He named the place 'Melaka' after the tree that he had sat under. On the other hand, a more likely explanation of the origin of the name connects it with the Arabic word *malakat* or market.

A quick glance at a world map will show why Melaka grew rapidly from a fishing *kampung* to a great entrepôt. It sits in a commanding position in the Straits of Melaka, a sea sheltered from the monsoons by the island of Sumatra. Ships crossing from China to India would find it a natural resting and refuelling point. Later still, as Melaka's resources grew, it became a trading post where ships from India could come to do business with merchants who had crossed from China, thus halving their journeys and saving themselves the long wait for the right weather. The deepest and therefore safest part of the straits lay close to the Melakan coastline and whoever controlled the town controlled all the shipping in the area.

From the early 15C the Chinese offered the city protection from Siamese raiders in exchange for a cut of the profits. Legend has it that the Chinese admiral **Cheng Ho** arrived at Melaka bearing, among other things, a yellow silk parasol, now the emblem of the Malaysian sultans. Links with the Chinese court grew stronger, a whole language and etiquette based on the Imperial palace developed, and finally Parameswara himself visited the Emperor in China, beginning a tradition which his heirs maintained.

Chinese interest in Melaka began to wane in the 1430s. To obtain a powerful new ally, the third ruler of Melaka, Sri Maharajah, married into a Sumatran royal family. He embraced Islam and began the gradual conversion of the whole country.

By the late 15C, Melaka was more than just a trading post. The city controlled the mainland from Johor in the south to Perak in the north and inland to Pahang. Spices, silks, gold, tin, Chinese porcelain and Indian and Persian textiles all passed through the port of Melaka on their way to the cities of Europe and Asia. Religions and races intermarried leading to the emergence of the **Peranakans** (see p 164), a mixture of Chinese and Malays who worshipped the Chinese pantheon, and the **Chittys**, a mixture of Malays and Indians who were largely Hindu.

By the 16C, the imperialist powers of Europe—Spain, Britain and Portugal—had their eyes on the city and its dependent territories. Most Far Eastern trade with Europe passed through the hands of Arab merchants as well as the Melakan entrepreneurs, both of whom took a sizeable portion of the profits and put up prices. It occurred to the European powers that if they were to cut out these middle men their profits would be all the greater.

The first European power to try taking over Melaka was Portugal. The **Portuguese** landed in 1509 but were driven out. However, two years later they were back with a fleet and an army. The sultan fled to Johor and the Portuguese took over the city, building a fortress, some of which remains today, and St Paul's Church, also still partly in existence. During this time **St Francis Xavier** lived in the city which remained resolutely Muslim despite its Catholic overlords. Another new ethnic group—the Eurasians—was created, out of the marriages between the Portuguese and the local girls; their names can still be seen today above shops and especially in the Portuguese settlement outside the city centre.

The Portuguese empire gradually waned as things grew difficult at home and by the mid 17C the **Dutch** dominated trade in the area through their treaties with the Johor sultans. Trade shifted to Jakarta and to Johor and the slow decline of Melaka began. Eventually the Dutch, with the aid of troops from Johor, took the city, which they controlled for the next 150 years. Their legacy can be seen today in the staid Dutch architecture of the Stadthuys.

The Dutch held the town against encroachments from pirates from Sumatra until problems in Europe turned their attention away from the Malay peninsula. They never gave up the colony, but rather allowed a caretaker British administration to control the place until 1824 when Melaka officially joined the Empire. In 1826 Melaka became part of the British **Straits Settlements** which included Penang and Singapore. But by that time the harbour at Melaka had silted up and Singapore and Penang flourished while the once vital seaport gradually became a backwater. At the end of the 19C, rubber cultivation began in the area and Melaka revived a little.

The rest of Melaka's history is a quiet one. The British stayed (with a brief Japanese interlude) until 1957 when Malaya gained its independence.

■ Practical information

Getting to and from Melaka
By air. There are daily flights into and out of Melaka from Singapore and Ipoh by Pelangi Air (☎ 06-3174175). The same airline also operates a twice-weekly service to and from Pekan Baru in Sumatra. Tickets can be booked at the MAS office (☎ 06-2835722) on the first floor of the City Bayview Hotel on Jalan Bendahara. The airport is 10km out of town at Batu Berendam. Bus No. 65 from the local bus station goes there.

By train. Trains stop at Tampin, the nearest station, 38km north of the town with bus connections to Melaka. Book tickets in advance to be sure of a berth or seat. The Melaka office can be contacted on ☎ 06-2823091; for Tampin station ☎ 06-4411034.

By bus. There are any number of long-distance, air-conditioned buses which cruise along the new expressways. Buses are rarely fully booked and tickets can be bought in advance from the ticket booths at the Express bus terminal just off Jalan Tun Mamat.

By ferry. There is a ferry service to and from Dumai in Sumatra. The journey takes about four hours and ferries leave at regular intervals daily. Two companies run ferry services: Madai Shipping (☎ 06-2840671) at 321 Jalan Tun Ali and Tunas Rupat Utama (☎ 06-2832506) at 17A Jalan Taman Merdeka. A **visa** is needed to visit Sumatra.

Getting around Melaka
Within town, **trishaws** are ubiquitous although a ride from the smart hotels to the old part of the city can be perilous. **Taxis** are less obvious and more often used for long-distance journeys where their rates for a shared taxi compete well with the express buses. **Local buses**, **express buses** and taxis all begin their journey in the same area near Jalans Hang Tuah and Tun Mamat. There are two places that hire **bicycles** at RM5 per day, one on Jalan Hang Jebat and the other on Jalan Parameswara. Enquire at the tourist office for details. **Car rental** is available from Avis (☎ 06-2846710) at 27 Jalan Laksamana.

Tourist information
The local **tourist office** (☎ 06-2836538) is right in the centre of old Melaka, on Jalan Kota, opposite Christ Church). It is open from 08.45 to 18.00 Monday to Saturday (09.00 to 12.00 Sunday); closed for lunch on Friday. River tours can be booked from here.

There is a branch **post office** beside the Youth Museum in the centre of old Melaka.

Currency exchange
Moneychangers and banks offer very similar exchange rates; the moneychangers are the better option as they are open for longer hours. Major banks are Bank Bumiputra on Jalan Kota and the Hong Kong and Shanghai Bank at 1a Jalan Kota.

Emergencies

The **Southern Hospital** (☎ 06-2835888) is at 169 Jalan Bendahara. In an emergency ☎ 999. There is a **tourist police station** near to the tourist office on Jalan Kota.

Tour operators

The tourist office (see above) arranges trips along the river to Kampung Morten. **Stadhuys Tours and Travel Sdn Bhd** (☎ 06-2846373; fax 06-249022) at 151 Jalan Bendahara offers several local tours to a rubber plantation, a city tour, to Air Keroh, a night tour including the excellent Sound and Light Show, a trip to an aboriginal village and a tour taking in the ethnic mix of Melaka.

Accommodation

Top range hotels. The **Malacca Renaissance Hotel** (☎ 06-2848888; fax 06-2849269) is centrally located in Jalan Bendahara with all the amenities expected of it, including pool, disco, fitness centre and eight restaurants. The rooms are spacious and well appointed and offer stunning views over the town or the sea. A basic double room is RM308. On the same road is the **City Bayview Hotel** (☎ 06-2839888; fax 06-2836699) with a similar range of facilities but not the same views or style. Double rooms are RM172.

At the bottom end of the range of expensive hotels in town is the **Emperor Hotel** (☎ 06-2840777; fax 06-2838989) on Jalan Munshi Abdullah, with rather cramped and ageing rooms at RM113 from Sunday to Thursday and RM136 on Friday and Saturday. It has a pool, gym, coffee shop, Chinese restaurant and theatre lounge. The **Riviera Bay Resort** (☎ 06-3151111) at Tanjung Kling 9km northwest of town offers 5-star resort facilities.

West of town is the **Tanjung Bidara Beach Resort** (☎ 06-3842990; fax 06-3842995) with a similar range of prices and amenities. On Pulau Besar is the **Panda Nusa** (☎ 06-2818007) with rooms and chalets at around RM200.

Middle range hotels. In this range hotels tend to be clean and carpeted, with some facilities in the rooms. The **Palace Hotel** (☎ 06-2825115; fax 06-2848833) in Jalan Munshi Abdullah is typical with rooms at RM97. The **Metropole** (☎ 06-2810080; fax 06-2810233), centrally located on Jalan Munshi Abdullah, has a varying rate of RM73 on weekdays and double rate at weekends. It has many facilities, including a health centre. The **Heeren House** guesthouse (☎ 06-2814241; fax 06-2814239) at 1 Jalan Tun Tan Cheng Lock has been recommended as a place to stay, not least because of its central location.

Budget range hotels. The most expensive in this area is the **Majestic** (☎ 06-2822367) on Jalan Bunga Raya. It has crumbling rooms, ancient bathrooms but lots of atmosphere, and has fought for years to stave off the developers. Double rooms are RM52. The **Hotel Visma** (☎ 06-2838799), on Jalan Kampung Hulu, has tiny rooms at RM40. The **May Chiang Hotel** (☎ 06-2839535) is at 52 Jalan Munshi Abdullah, on the first floor. Its rooms are big, but spartan with cold water only but it is well kept and very clean. Rooms are RM40. Perhaps cheapest of all is the **Central Hotel** (☎ 06-2822984) at 31 Jalan Bendahara. Rooms with a fan are RM15.

Restaurants

Melaka is not a good place for eating out in the evening. Most restaurants in town close early and few serve any alcoholic drinks. The most interesting food in Melaka are the two indigenous cuisines—Portuguese and Peranakan; both are best sampled in the small local restaurants rather than in the big hotels which tend to offer blander versions. The café at Heeren House is a good place to start as it serves set lunches and dinners with a choice of Peranakan, Portuguese or Western food.

Portuguese. For Portuguese food there are three restaurants at Medan Portugis, to the east of the town—**de Lisbon**, the **Santiago** and the **Restoran D'Nolasco**. The food served at all three is good, authentic and inexpensive. On Saturdays these restaurants put on cultural shows, which display real energy. The de Lisbon has a little souvenir shop and its owner, George Alcantra, will be pleased to tell you all about the settlement.

Peranakan (see p 164). The oldest and most expensive Peranakan restaurant is **Jonkers** (☎ 06-2835578) at 17 Jalan Hang Jebat. The restaurant is in a Peranakan-style shophouse which includes an art gallery. It is open from 10.00 to 19.00 and has several vegetarian choices. If you are nervous about trying a new style of food there is a set menu. Another good place for Nyonya food is **My Baba's** at 164 Jalan Munshi Abdullah in a modern shophouse but with Peranakan-style decor. Similar is **Ole Sayang Restaurant** (☎ 06-2831966) at 198–199 Jalan Taman Melaka Raya. It is open from 11.30 to 14.30 and 16.00 to 21.30. The decor is Peranakan with a mixture of Malay and Peranakan styles. Prices are moderate.

Chinese. For Chinese food, the smartest place in town is the **Long Feng Chinese Restaurant** at the Melaka Renaissance where one dish will cost about the same as a whole meal in many other places. However, the ambience and the quality of the food are worth the cost. The style of cooking is a mixture of Cantonese and Sezuan which means that you can mix the more delicate sauce-based dishes with spicier stir-fried dishes.

Other restaurants are east along Jalan Taman Melaka Raya—at No. 542 is the **Mei Lin** which serves vegetarian food disguised as meat dishes. A meal for two should cost under RM20.

Indian. Melaka has some excellent Indian restaurants, especially of the *daun pisang* or banana-leaf variety. The best is at the junction of Jalan Bunga Raya and Jalan Bendahara where they meet Jalan Kampung Pantai. The place is clean but basic. It serves excellent *roti canai* and chicken *biriyani* and fresh lemon juice for a few dollars. It is best at breakfast. The **Banana Leaf** on Jalan Munshi Abdullah, just past the Bunga Raya junction, serves *roti canai* and a variety of meat and vegetable curries. It may look a little shabby but the food is excellent. The **Moti Mahal** (☎ 06-2837823) at 543 Jalan Taman Melaka Raya, is a north Indian restaurant and specialises in tandoor cooked food and breads. A meal for two should work out at about RM20.

Western. If you want safe Western or fast food, all the major hotels have coffee shops and restaurants serving pretty bland stuff. There is a **Delifrance** in Makhota Parade which serves lunches at around RM6. In the same plaza are **McDonald's** and **Kentucky Fried Chicken**. More fun is to try the **food centre** in the Makhota which serves the whole gamut of local dishes at very reasonable prices. There is a **Pizza Hut** at the junction of Jalans Bendehara and Munshi.

Malay. For Malay food the hawker areas are best. There is **Gluttons' Corner** down at the beach, or rather the fence, at Jalan Merdeka. Near the Bank Bumiputra at Bukit Baru is **Ngah Satay** which serves the Melakan speciality dish, *Melaka satay*. It is open from 19.00 to 24.00; closed on Thursday. A good restaurant to try for Malay food is **Sang Kancil Satay** (☎ 06-2822123), at 627 Taman Melaka Raya. It serves traditional Malay dishes such as *satay*, and its signature dish is *satay* noodles, fried *mee* with soy sauce, topped with *satay*, egg and salad. For dessert try the *chendol*, a coconut milk-based dessert filled with red beans and *pandan* jellies.

Shopping
Melaka's shopping possibilities have opened up a little in the last couple of years. The **Mahkota Parade**, a huge complex, has a Parkson's department store and lots of smaller places aimed at tourists, as well as some nice clothes shops. The 50 or so handicraft stalls along Jalan Taman sell all kinds of gewgaws made from shell and bamboo and pottery, bottles of spices, fans, toys, baskets and much more, but all of it pretty dull.

Jalan Hang Jebat, or Jonkers Street, is the real shopping heart of Melaka with many antique and arts and crafts shops. Most of them sell pretty much the same things—wooden puppets and masks from Indonesia, pottery from China, antique furniture, chests, brassware, jade and gold jewellery, lamps and so on. A pleasant hour or so can be spent browsing here. Probably the best and most authentic items are some of the restored pieces of furniture which call for some hard bargaining as well as creating shipping problems. The **Malacca Art Store** sells fine Chinese furniture as well as more portable painted carved panels from temples. The **Tribal Art Gallery** at the far end of the road retails crafts from Sarawak. The **Malacca Junk Store** at No. 55 has one of the best collections of antique and restored furniture as well as ceramics and many other items. If you find something that you want to buy, don't appear too pleased with it because bargaining is in order here. If it isn't an antique, the same thing will be in another shop further along the street and the dealer knows it. The curio shops have spread beyond Jonkers Street now into Jalan Tokong. You might also like to buy some of the tin items or an intricate bamboo bird cage in Jalan Hang Kasturi.

Jalan Tun Tan Cheng Lock has several antique shops and three art galleries, two of which are owned and operated by artists.

Around the Stadthuys are a few small handicraft shops and along Jalan Kota is a Karyaneka handicraft shop with some items for sale. Out at **Taman Mini Malaysia** (see below) are more handicraft stalls as well as a fine exhibition of craftwork from all over Malaysia, which, unfortunately, you cannot buy.

Entertainment

There is a cinema in Jalan Bunga Raya which often has English language movies. The Portuguese settlement has **cultural shows** on Saturdays at around 08.30. The Sound and Light Show on the *padang*, opposite St Paul's Church, is a very biased view of Melaka's history. It is on every day at 20.00 (Malay) and 21.30 (English). Admission is RM5.

Sport

For golfing enthusiasts there is the Ayer Keroh Golf and Country Club (☎ 06-2330822), 14km north of Melaka. Green fees are RM60.

Festivals

At Easter the Church of St Peter comes alive with processions on Good Friday and Easter Sunday. Later in June the same community celebrates the Festa San Pedro. The fishing boats at Portuguese Square are blessed and prayers are offered at the church for a good fishing season. A Malay festival called Mandi Safar is celebrated at Tanjung Kling in the Muslim month of Safar. It is a sea bathing festival.

Melaka on foot

The city of Melaka can be rather nicely divided up into two half day walks, one encompassing the Dutch part of the city while the other winds around the older Chinese and Malay areas. Both walks are bound up with the history of the city and include visits to the local museums as well as some opportunities for buying souvenirs of the city. Both walks can begin at the very noticeable tourist information centre on Jalan Kota, close to the Stadthuys.

Museum Tour

At the centre of the old Melaka is the **Stadthuys**, on Jalan Kota, and this is a good place to begin a tour of city. The museums are little havens of shade and cool on a sweltering Melakan day and many of them are fascinating repositories of information about the history and culture of the town. The Stadthuys itself is an important relic of the past. It was built around 1650 as the residence of the Dutch governor and his officers. The Dutch architecture with its characteristic wide stairwells and large windows has been adapted to suit the Malaysian climate with the addition of thick walls and broad verandahs.

The sophistication of the Dutch architects of the 17C can be seen in the foyer of the building where underground drainage pipes have been exposed during building works. In the back of the building the same works uncovered an old well which it is thought once provided a previous settlement with its water supply. In Dutch times the Stadthuys stood in the centre of a fortified settlement facing the gate to the river. The lurid red paint of the building is a modern attempt to re-create what was probably once a red brick façade. When this was found to leak, the bricks were cemented over and whitewashed.

The building remained in use as government offices until 1980 when it became the **Museum of Ethnography and History**. The downstairs exhibits are the most interesting, with old furniture and porcelain from Portugal, Holland and China and a display of wedding tableaux from the various ethnic groups. Not seen anywhere else in Malaysia is the exhibit covering the lifestyle

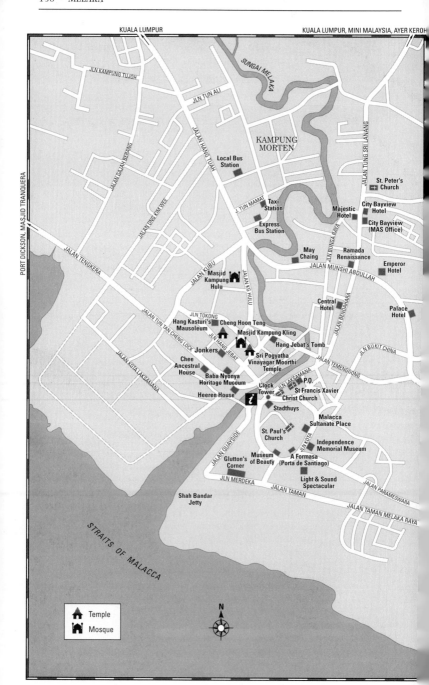

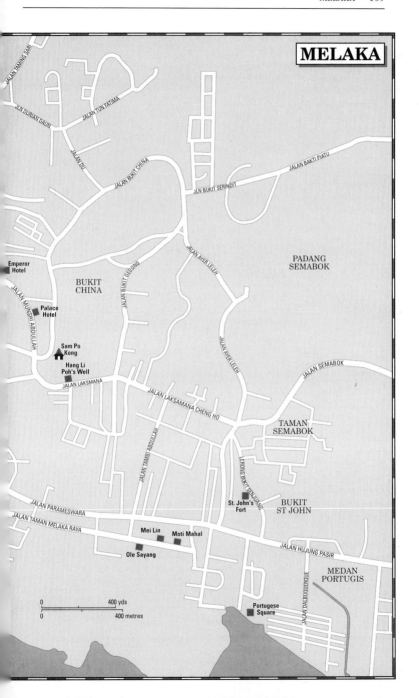

of the **Chittys**, the cultural mix of Malays and Indians. A 17C Dutch dining room is also represented including the hand-operated coolie fans. Upstairs is a series of paintings and dioramas depicting the history of Malaysia.

The Stadthuys is open from 09.00 to 18.00, Monday to Saturday, closed 12.15 to 14.45 Friday; entrance RM2.

In front of the Stadthuys and mimicking its style is the **clock tower**, erected in 1886 by the family of Tang Bee Sweng, a wealthy *baba*, as the Peranakan men were called (see p 164). The fountain beside it was built in 1904 to commemorate Queen Victoria's diamond jubilee. The kitsch stone mousedeer around the fountain are the tourist board's idea of culture: they remind us of the legend of Parameswara founding the city (see p 151).

Turning to the right in front of the Stadthuys brings you to **Christ Church**, another Dutch building, erected between 1741 and 1763 to commemorate the centenary of the Dutch occupation. This building was built of bricks brought from The Netherlands and faced with red laterite, an iron and aluminium-based rock which forms in tropical areas. The porch and vestry through which you enter the church are more recent additions, cosntructed by the British in the 19C. Inside, the church is simple in design with no chancel. The pews are still the originals while the roof beams can be seen to be single pieces each 15m in length. Plaques on the walls bear testimony to the many deaths from epidemics during the Dutch occupation. This is the oldest Protestant church in Malaysia. Christ Church is open to the public from 09.00 to 17.00, Sunday to Friday, and entrance is free.

Giving the **Muzium Belia Malaysia**, with its endless photos of smiling youths being congratulated by government ministers, a miss, the next point of interest is the Porta De Santiago around to the left of the Stadthuys, along Jalan Kota past the tourist police post. On the way you will pass the **Museum of Beauty** where images of beauty from all cultures have been collected, together with handicrafts from all over Malaysia, some of which are for sale.

The **Porta De Santiago** is all that remains of **A Famosa**, the 16C Portuguese fortifications that kept out invaders. The fortifications were built by Alfonso d'Albuquerque and the gate was once part of a four-walled fort which included four towers and walls 2.4m thick. One wall ran along the bank of the river so that supplies could be brought up into the garrison. The most distinctive feature of the fort would have been the keep in the northwestern corner which stood four storeys high. The walls were guarded by 120 big guns while inside the fort were two palaces, schools, hospitals, and several churches including St Paul's (see below). Local tombs and other buildings were destroyed for their stones, which were put into the walls, and hundreds of slaves laboured in the building work.

The position of the port meant that ships at anchor in the river mouth were protected by the big guns while attacks could be made against trading ships passing through the straits. These walls remained impervious until 1641 when they were finally broken by the Dutch and the city was taken.

The Dutch in their turn used the fortifications, adding a moat and drawbridge, until 1795, when they peaceably gave up Melaka to the British. The walls finally came down for economic reasons. In the early 19C, Melaka was foundering as a trading port under fierce competition from Penang to the north. Plans were put in motion to abandon Melaka as an unnecessary expense and rather than have another power make use of its fortifications it was decided to destroy the walls. This was no easy task as the walls were 4.5m thick and 18m high. At first they were taken down with picks and shovels but when this proved too difficult the British Governor, Mr Farquar, decided to blow the fort up. Huge pieces were blown high into the air and landed in the river, many of them still visible decades later. However, the demolition work was stopped by Sir Stamford Raffles; then a government secretary in Penang, he argued persuasively against abandoning the settlement. Raffles won his point and the British continued to occupy Melaka.

All that remains today is this gate, which once stood at the mouth of the river. The land you see in front of it has been reclaimed and was once the harbour mouth. The coat of arms above the gate is a Dutch addition—the crest of the Dutch East India Company and the date 1670.

Through the gate steps lead up Bukit St Paul to the remains of **St Paul's Church**. A small chapel was first built here in 1521 by a Portuguese sailor who had narrowly escaped death at sea. Before the Portuguese arrived, the sultan's palace had been situated here. The church was originally Catholic, and known as Nossa Senhora da Annunciada (Our Lady of the Annunciation). St Francis Xavier, co-founder of the Jesuit Society with St Ignatius Loyola, lived in Melaka for a time and preached in the church.

When the Dutch took over Melaka, they forbade Catholic worship. The church was renamed St Paul's and became a Protestant place of worship for 112 years. Once St Peter's was built though, the church was no longer used and during the British occupation became a military store. Today the ruins of the church make a pretty walk and the headstones of the Dutch and British settlers inside the church and in the graveyard below tell interesting stories about the lives of those who lived here. The empty tomb in the centre of the church once held the body of St Francis Xavier before it was removed to Goa.

> **St Francis Xavier** (1506–52) was a Spanish missionary, and one of the founders of the Jesuit order. He began his missionary work in the Portuguese settlement at Goa and then came to Melaka in 1545. He was critical of the way in which traders in Melaka accumulated wealth, and preached sermons in St Paul's Church on the subject. Melaka is full of reminders of his presence here. In the reclaimed land behind the stalls of the night market, a little rock is fenced off and people believe that it marks the spot where Francis Xavier first set foot in Melaka.
>
> Another story tells of the Pope's request for Xavier's right arm to be removed from his corpse so that it could become a holy relic and be kept in Rome. The story goes that when the body was exhumed it had not decomposed and when the arm was cut off blood flowed from the wound. In 1953 a statue of the saint was commissioned and erected on St Paul's Hill where it still stands today. But one night in a storm the statue was knocked down by a falling tree and when it was recovered the same right arm was broken off.

From the church go back down the hill to Jalan Kota and the Porta De Santiago. Within sight are the next two stops on the museum walk—the Malacca Sultanate Palace and the Malacca Club, now known as the Memorial of the Proclamation of Independence.

The Malacca Sultanate Palace houses the Muzium Budaya

The **Malacca Sultanate Palace**, or Istana Ke Sultanan, which holds the Muzium Budaya, is a little dull. It concentrates on Malay culture and the structure of the sultan's court. Downstairs the court is displayed as a series of bewigged dummies, sitting and standing, according to rank, around the sultan's throne. There are also displays of artefacts such as ceremonial knives, toys, headgear from various states, and costumes. Upstairs, is the sultan's bedroom. Another diorama tells the story of Hang Jebat and Hang Tuah, local legendary heroes who came to a bitter end (see below).

The building itself—a reconstruction of the original—is far more interesting in describing the Malay culture than any of the bits and pieces it contains. Built of beautiful dark wood, the interior is dark, cool and silent, and as you wander around it is difficult to think of the sultan's palace as being anything other than a serene place. The roof is typical of complex Malay building, with steep layers made entirely of wooden shingles. In fact the sultan did not spend much time in the palace; he lived outside Melaka in his country residence, coming into town for business. The museum is open 09.00 to 18.00 Saturday to Thursday, 09.00 to 12.00 on Friday.

Hang Jebat and Hang Tuah

It is not possible to get far around Melaka without encountering the famous characters of Hang Jebat, Hang Tuah and their companions. According to the Malay poem 'Hikayat Hang Tuah', the five friends were martial arts experts who saved the life of the Bendahara Paduka Raja, the prime minister of the Sultan Shah, in the 17C. As a reward they were given positions in the Malay court and pledged themselves to serve the sultan. Hang Tuah became a highly esteemed official in the court and was given a special Malay sword, called Taming Sari. This sword had magical powers. Other court members grew jealous of Hang Tuah and spread rumours that he had seduced one of the king's consorts. The sultan ordered his execution but instead the Bendahara hid Hang Tuah away.

The story continues that when Hang Jebat heard the news of his friend's execution he became enraged and ran amok, killing many people. No one could stop him until Hang Tuah came out of hiding in order to protect the sultan from Hang Jebat's fury. Hang Tuah wrestled with his conscience for some time, knowing that his friend was revenging himself for his supposed death, but finally he decided that loyalty to the sultan and justice for those Hang Jebat had killed were more important than his friendship. An epic battle took place between the two men which ended with Hang Jebat's death at the blade of his old friend.

Hang Jebat's mausoleum is in Jalan Kampung Kuli while one of the other companions, Hang Kasturi, is buried in Jalan Hang Jebat. Some 4km south east of Melaka on the road to Muar is Hang Tuah's well where the soul of Hang Tuah is said to live in the shape of a white crocodile that only the holy can see.

Next door to the palace is the **Memorial of the Proclamation of Independence**. Inside are videos, photographs and memorabilia associated with the handing over of independence in 1957. The building is as interesting as the displays inside. It was built in 1912 and was formerly the Malacca Club, a watering hole for jaded planters and their memsahibs. It is said that the story which became *Footprints in the Jungle*, a short story by Somerset Maugham, was told to the author in this club. The tale takes place partly in the club. The colonial style mansion, with its two onion domes rising above the more sedate Victorian structure, was once part of British colonial

The Memorial of the Proclamation of Independence, Melaka

life. To the east of the building, now the gardens of the Sultan's Palace, was the *padang* where ceremonies were held, cricket and football were played and people strolled from their bank to the club, the resthouse, to Christ Church or the government offices in the Stadthuys. The museum is open from 09.00 to 18.00 Saturday to Thursday and 09.00 to 12.00 Fridays. Entrance is free.

In front of the Malacca Club are some stalls selling locally made artefacts and paintings, and you can take a ride in a traditional ox cart.

If you have the energy for more museums, head down towards the sea, past the A&W restaurant and the handicraft stalls and across Jalan Taman Merdeka where you will see the exhibition hall showing the remains of the ship *The Diana*, a full-size reproduction of a Portuguese sailing ship which sank in the straits in the 16C. Other exhibits here include models of ships, samples of the spices that the ship carried and some objects which might have been found on such a ship. The museum is open 09.00–18.00 Saturday to Thursday, 09.00–12.00 Friday. Admission is RM2.

The Straits of Melaka might have been safe waters but over the centuries many ships still managed to sink in its deep waters. *The Diana* has recently been salvaged and its cargoes went on sale at Sotheby's in spring 1995.

A more interesting ship which has yet to be recovered is the *Flor Del Mar*. This is the ship in which the Portuguese Alfonso d'Albuquerque loaded a fortune in loot from the newly conquered Melaka and set sail for Goa. Unfortunately for d'Albuquerque the ship hit a reef and sank in 37m of water. D'Albuquerque was saved, along with a sword, a crown and some other items which are now in a museum in Lisbon, but the rest is probably still underwater. During the 1980s, many attempts were made to find the wreck and salvage the treasure, estimated by Sotheby's at about US$9 billion—the most valuable wreck in existence. Unfortunately it is probably lying in Indonesian waters, opening up all kinds of difficulties about who has the rights to the treasure. After much wrangling, Malaysia and Indonesia have made a joint venture to salvage the wreck but nothing has officially emerged from the sea bed yet, although there have been rumours of covert salvage operations. The current story is that the ship is buried under 10m of solidified mud.

Chinatown Walk

This walk, which winds around the west side of the river, concerns itself with some of the other groups which have made up the population of Melaka over the years. The walk begins at the tourist information office on Jalan Kota. Walking across the river from here, stop to peer over the bridge for a few moments. Very large monitor lizards can be seen splashing along the muddy banks and in the shallow water of the river. Walk down Jalan Tun Cheng Lock, avoiding the noisy traffic whirling past—the road was never built for motorised traffic and has no footpaths. The houses on both sides of the street are in the typical style of the **Straits Chinese** or **Peranakan family houses** with a narrow frontage, intricately carved doors and a narrow fenced-in courtyard.

On the right-hand side of the road at Nos 48–50 is the **Baba Nyonya Heritage Museum**, a privately run museum. The three houses were built in 1896 along traditional Peranakan lines and are still owned by the family that built them. Standing on the opposite side of the road, it is possible to discern the eclectic nature of Peranakan architecture. The tiled roof is Chinese in origin while the highly ornate shutters on the windows and the eaves display Malay carving styles. Red Chinese lanterns proclaim the family name and messages of good luck. The hand-painted tiles are just as likely to have come from Venice or England as China, while the columns supporting the overhead room are mock Ionic, copying a 19C English building style.

Inside, the houses hold a remarkable collection of furniture, ceremonial clothes and porcelain as well as fascinating photographs. What stands out again is the eclectic nature of the Peranakan living style. Planter's chairs and Venetian glass share space with specially designed pottery and Royal Doulton sinks. Tours are conducted around the house at regular intervals and are very informative. Particularly interesting is the security system which locked up the first storey at night, with a barrier over the staircase so that no one could leave once they were in bed; and also the tiny peep hole in the front upper room so that visitors could be inspected before they were allowed inside. In the family shrine, each wooden block containing the ancestor's name has the whereabouts of the grave written on the back to make sure that the family will always be able to find it.

The museum is open 10.00 to 12.30 and 14.00 to 16.30; admission RM7.

The Peranakans, or the Babas and Nyonya

The Peranakan came into existence in Melaka. During the Ming dynasty, the Chinese had large fleets of ships and dominated the region. Under Admiral Cheng Ho, a Chinese mission arrived in Melaka in 1405 and again in 1433, offering protection from piracy and invasion in exchange for tributes. Evidence suggests that some of these Chinese settled in Melaka. Early travellers describe the Chinese community here in the 15C while the *Malay Annals* says that the well in Bukit China was dug during this time by the Chinese.

Emigration from China began in earnest in the 17C, despite the fact that the Manchu dynasty banned it. Political exiles fled to places such as Melaka, Java, Borneo, the Philippines—anywhere where there were foreign communities and trade and a chance of a peaceful settlement. The first to arrive in Melaka in large numbers were the Hokkien speakers, followed later by Cantonese, Hakkas and Teochew. The various dialect groups kept apart and often waged small wars against each other just as they were to do later in Singapore.

Under the Portuguese, the Chinese were allowed to do business but could not own land in Melaka and they were taxed more heavily than other races. However, the Dutch, who took over in the late 17C, encouraged Chinese settlers. During the period of Dutch rule the Chinese flourished, coming to dominate trade, crafts and even farming. In a census of 1678, there were 852 Chinese living within Melaka, owning 81 brick houses and 51 attap (roofed with palm leaves) houses. In 1750 the Chinese population had increased to 2161 and by 1827, when the town was under British rule, there were 4000. By 1931 this figure had increased to 85,000 and the Chinese made up 40 per cent of the population.

At the end of the 19C, Chinese were farming, selling opium, and working in tin mines and on tapioca plantations. The first rubber plantation in Melaka was laid out by a Chinese, Tan Chay Yan. Heeren Street became known as Millionaires Row because many of the wealthiest Chinese built town houses here in the style of the houses which make up the Baba Nyonya Heritage Museum. The houses were built narrow-fronted, to avoid window tax, while light was let into the house by means of a central light well open to the sky. In through this space came water as well as light and beneath it a small courtyard and pool would be surrounded by the family's main living area. Most of these very wealthy people lived part of the time in much larger bungalows out of town.

It is within this community that the Peranakan culture developed. The first of the Chinese settlers took Malay wives and adopted certain Malay customs. The women wore Malay-style clothes and cooked in a traditional Malay way, making coconut and lemon grass based stews rather than quickly fried meats and noodles as the more traditional Chinese cuisine dictated. In the second generation the Chinese-Malay families intermarried, choosing other Peranakans for husbands or wives or new Chinese settlers rather than Malays. The religion was Chinese and the customs surrounding marriage and death were largely Chinese while the language was Malay, many families having lost the use of their mother tongue altogether.

The word Peranakan means 'locally born'. They were also known as Straits Chinese. The men were called 'Babas' while the women were 'Neonís' (often spelt Nyonyas). In other aspects the Peranakan adopted Western habits, enjoying billiards and bowls and sending their children to English schools. In the museum can be seen many artefacts that were specially imported by the Babas from Europe. They particularly avoided contact with non-Peranakan Chinese, barring them from their social clubs. All the houses in this area of town reflect the Chinese influence. They are small and uniform in design with a covered walkway linking each house.

An interesting aspect of the culture is the slightly different interpretation put on the origins of the culture by the Singaporean Straits Chinese. They are often at pains to make clear that there was no intermarriage between Chinese and local women and that the families absorbed the culture through lifestyle and the influence of their servants rather than through marriage.

After visiting the museum continue away from the centre of town, noting No. 117 Jalan Tun Tan Cheng Lock which is the **Chee Ancestral House**, an imperious white building with a silver dome. This was the town home of another of Melaka's Chinese millionaires who made their fortunes as planters. Turn right into Jalan Lekir where there are shops making coffins for Chinese funerals. The coffins are very ornate and expensive items carved from solid teak. In Melaka the tradition is to cover the coffins with an embroidered cloth, some of which you will have seen in the Baba Nyonya Heritage Museum.

This road brings you to **Jalan Hang Jebat**, formerly Jonkers Street. There is much to see in this street, which is full of antique and curio shops as well as some of the oldest buildings in Melaka. Opposite the coffee shop with a very low roof is the oldest building in Melaka—a Dutch trading house built in 1610. Walking to the far end of Jonkers Street where it joins Jalan Tokong, you will come to the **mausoleum of Hang Kasturi**, one of the five musketeers and friends of Hang Tuah (see p 162).

Turning sharp right back into Jalan Tokong, or Temple Street, you will find yourself in the 'Street of Harmony' so called because in this road the temples of three different religions have stood almost side by side for three centuries. The first you will come to is the **Cheng Hoon Teng**, or Merciful Cloud Temple. This is said to be the oldest Chinese temple in Malaysia. It is dedicated to Kuan Yin, the goddess of mercy, and was built in 1646 by 'Kapitan China' Lee Wei King, a fugitive from China, who fled the chaos at the fall of the Ming dynasty. The temple is very large, covering an area of 4600 square metres.

The main statue in the temple is Kuan Yin while beside her is Tin Hau, the Queen of Heaven and protector of all who travel at sea. All the materials to build the temple were brought from China, except the bronze for the statue of Kuan Yin which was forged in India. Huge incinerators burn up all the remains of offerings brought to the temple, while in the main room supplicants discover their future by shaking *chim* from bamboo pots as they pray. In the rooms behind the temple are thousands of wooden tablets carrying the name, and in some cases photographs, of the ancestors. Many of the older ones are blackened from the soot of incense sticks. The temple recognises the three faiths of the Chinese—Buddhism, Taoism and Confucianism.

Opposite this ancient temple is a much newer one dedicated to Buddhist beliefs and surrounding both are shops selling the necessary items for worship—paper 'hell money', paper dolls, furniture, etc, which are burnt and so sent up to the ancestors. The shiny plastic windmills you may see here are prayer wheels. Once the wheel is blessed it can be taken home and as the wind moves the sails the prayer will be repeated over and over, bringing good fortune to the house.

Heading back towards town along Jalan Tokong, past Jalan Leiku, you come to the **Masjid Kampung Kling**. You may not enter the mosque itself unless you are a Muslim, but you are permitted to stand in the courtyard. The mosque was built in 1748 in a style more typical of Sumatran mosques. The roof, usually in the shape of an onion dome, is here tiered and made of green tiles which are rather more Chinese in style, matching the pagoda style of the minaret from where the faithful are called to prayer at dawn and dusk. The tiles around the water baths where the faithful carry out the ritual washing are English and Portuguese, while an English chandelier hangs over the prayer hall.

Virtually next door is an early 19C Hindu temple, the **Sri Pogyatha Vinayagar Moorthi Temple**, dedicated to the elephant-headed god Ganesh or Vinayagar. It is small and has little of the gaudy carvings of other *gopurams* on its roof.

From the temple turn left into Jalan Hang Kasturi. Along this road are tinsmiths making small temples and lanterns, and birdcage-makers using split bamboo as their material. From Jalan Hang Kasturi turn right onto Jalan Kampong Pantai where on the corner you will see the **mausoleum of Hang Jebat**, killed unjustly in a duel of honour with his friend Hang Tuah (see p 162).

Walking away from town again, Jalan Kampung Pantai brings you to the **Masjid Kampung Hulu**, built in 1728 and the oldest mosque in Malaysia. It has the same style of roof as the Kampung Kling mosque, a tiered, Chinese-looking structure, and a minaret in a pagoda style.

St Peter's Church

This quiet little church, the oldest Roman Catholic church in Malaysia, was built in 1710 during the Dutch occupation by Portuguese settlers: prior to this time Catholicism was proscribed. It has some interesting stained glass and a barrel-vaulted ceiling. The church gets little use except during Easter when the Portuguese community and many other Malakans come to the church for the service. The church is on Jalan Tun Sri Lanang.

St Francis Xavier's Church

This rather dull neo-Gothic church in Jalan Gereja was built in the 19C by a Frenchman, the Revd Farve.

Kampung Morten

This is a traditional Malay-style village surviving in the heart of a city. A foot-path just beyond the Majestic Hotel, leading off Jalan Bunga Raya, brings you to a very unstable looking footbridge over the river. The houses here are in a traditional style, built up on stilts to protect them from animals and floods, and to provide storage space and ventilation. They are fronted by ornate tiled steps leading up to a long, narrow verandah covered by the low roof.

Here, at **Villa Sentosa**, built in the 1920s, you can gain an insight into the lives of the Malay inhabitants. It is an unofficial museum and the family will show you their heirlooms. The museum is open from 09.00 to 17.00 and a voluntary donation is much appreciated.

Masjid Tranquera

This mosque, 2km of town on the road to Port Dickson, is interesting because of its pagoda-like minaret and Chinese-style structure. The grounds contain the tomb of Sultan Hussein (see p 311), the man who Raffles made a deal with in 1819 in order to secure the island of Singapore.

Medan Portugis

This settlement for the Eurasian community of Melaka was created in 1933 in the face of the increasing poverty and declining numbers of the city's Portuguese inhabitants. (The community numbered about 2000 in 1871, the year of the first census.) Melaka's Portuguese are the descendants of the Portuguese sailors and settlers who came to the area in the 16C. They inter-married far more readily than did the Dutch, and from their families emerged a hybrid Portuguese/Malay culture and language. The language they speak is a patois of the two parent languages. They have their own dances, cooking style and traditional dress. About 500 people live here now, many of them indistinguishable from Malays except in their language and surnames. They are Catholic and have their own school and church.

Portuguese Square, built in 1985, is a great tourist attraction and every night there are cultural shows where Portuguese and Malay dances are performed. There are several good **restaurants** in the area and a pleasant evening can be made of the short trip out here. The most authentic Portuguese-style food in Melaka can be found here.

The Medan Portugis can be reached via No. 17 or 25 bus from Jalan Paremaswara.

> Melakan Portuguese food is characterised by strong spices and the flavourings of chilli and lemon grass. Candlenuts and coconut milk are used to thicken sauces, anise to give it aniseed flavour and vinegar to bring out the other flavours. Onion and ginger intensify the spiciness and remove some unpleasant flavours. Saffron colours it and gives it a pungent taste, while coriander, tamarind and cinnamon add flavours and textures of their own. Typical of this style of cooking is curry devil where the spices are ground together and fried before the meat is added and cooked in the spicy sauce. A drier curry is *curry seku* cooked with a slightly different set of spices. The various curries are served with rice or bread.

Near to the square is **St John's Fort**, an ancient site hardly worth the trip, but providing excellent views over the town and the straits. The fort was built by the Dutch in the 17C. The turning for the fort is about 500m before that for the Portuguese settlement. A right turn at the next roundabout and then up a track brings you to the base of the hill.

Bukit China

This is an interesting site outside the main city.

> Bukit China was first given to the Chinese in 1459 when a Chinese princess, Hang Li Po, became the wife of the first Sultan of Melaka. She and her 500 handmaidens settled on the hill. Today the hill and the two adjacent hills

form an enormous and rather untidy Chinese graveyard. This is the largest **Chinese cemetery** outside China; it contains 12,000 graves, some dating back to the Ming dynasty. The Chinese like to bury their dead on hills for several reasons. The hill protects them from bad *chi*—the evil life force which may disturb their rest, and the vantage point also allows the ancestors to keep a watch over their living relatives. A sea view is often chosen so that the dead can benefit from the good *chi* brought in by the sea. The kind of elaborate graves seen here are now very rare—in modern Hong Kong each set of remains is allowed only five years in its burial place before it is turned out to make way for another's. At Bukit China pressure is on the administrators of the hills to make them available for redevelopment but so far the developers have been unsuccessful.

The Portuguese, not recognising the Chinese ownership of the hill, built a monastery on the hill which was destroyed by the Chinese in 1629.

At the foot of the hill is a **well** named after the princess Hang Li Po who used it daily. It is said to be very pure and to bring good luck to those who drink from it. In the time of the Dutch, it provided much of the town's water supply. It is now a wishing well and if you want to come back to Melaka you must throw a coin into it.

Next to it is the **Sam Po Kong Temple**, dedicated to Admiral Cheng Ho when he visited Melaka in 1409. The story goes that on one of his trips from China to Melaka, the admiral's ship was struck and a hole was made in its keel. The ship was prevented from sinking by a kind fish which jammed itself into the hole, thus saving the admiral and all his crew. The fish is known as 'Sam Po'—which gave the temple its name.

Excursions from Melaka

Ayer Keroh

About 12km north of town, this area has been developed into a series of attractions for locals and tourists alike. The **Recreational Forest** includes well-signposted walks, and cabins can be rented for an overnight stay. Next door is the **Crocodile Farm**, reputed to be the biggest in the country, where various breeds of crocodiles are reared.

Across the road is **Taman Mini Malaysia** where complete houses in the various styles of the 13 states have been built and furnished. Next door and along the same lines is another set of houses, this time representing the various domestic building styles of the other countries of ASEAN (Association of Southeast Asian Nations). In the same area is a zoo, a recreational lake, a butterfly park and an aquarium. The zoo has some of the very rare Sumatran rhinoceros and is open from 10.00 to 18.00. All these attractions are situated along the same stretch of road, accessible by No. 19 bus.

Pulau Besar

This small island, 4km off the coast, is accessible by a boat which sails irregularly from **Jeti Umbai**, near Merlimau. The Panda Nusa Resort (see p 154), with a 5-star hotel, has been built here, but it is possible to do a day trip with a little advance planning. The island has good beaches and is excellent for snorkelling and swimming. At some stage in the future a regular air-conditioned ferry should make the trip to the island from Melaka town. Enquire at the tourist office for details.

Tanjung Bidara

This is a long strip of sandy beach about 35km northwest of Melaka. The **Tanjung Bidara Beach Resort** has lots of amenities, if you enjoy spending a day at the beach. Buses 51, 42 and 18 leave from Jalan Tengkera. A taxi there will cost about RM3.

The East Coast: Kota Bharu to Johor Bahru

This chapter covers the east coast of peninsular Malaysia from Kota Bharu, capital of the state of Kelantan, just south of the border with Thailand, to Johor Bahru in the south from where a causeway connects with Singapore. Although this route follows a north to south coastal route it could just as easily be followed in the other direction. Distances both south and north are given below in the different sections.

Kelantan

The state stretches along the coast from Malaysia's border with Thailand to the state border with Terengganu to the south. The main town in Kelantan is Kota Bharu, 30km from the Thai border crossing at Rantau Panjang.

Although Kelantan occupies nearly 15,000 square kilometres, the visitor is most likely to travel only along the 80km coastal strip. However, this narrow area of land reveals much of Kelantan's special character, in particular various aspects of traditional Malay culture. Activities such as top spinning, kite-flying, shadow puppet shows, basket and batik making are not practised here solely to serve tourists. The people of Kelantan are conservative, friendly and relaxed. The state has acquired a certain notoriety because it records the highest percentage of votes for an ultra-conservative Islamic party and this can be used to label Kelantan as a pro-fundamentalist state, with the implication that its people are in the grip of extremism. This is very misleading because the people of Kelantan are really very tolerant and open and the visitor is likely to be struck by the friendly and easy-going pace of life.

History

Archaeological and cultural evidence shows that around 2000 years ago Kelantan was under the influence of the kingdom of Funan which was based to the east in what is now southern Cambodia and Vietnam. The *wayang kulit* shadow play, for example, is traced back to Funan culture. A more pervasive influence came from the always powerful kingdom of Siam (Thailand) to the north, and until the spread of the Melaka sultanate in the 15C, Kelantan was annexed by the Siamese. There was a period in the 14C, however, when Kelantan fell under the influence of the Javanese Majapahit empire. After the fall of Melaka in 1641, the state fell under the suzerainty of Johor in the 17C—converting to Islam in the process—and then Terengganu in the 18C. By the 19C, Thai control was asserted once more, helped by the bickering between the various chiefs within the Malay state over the right of succession. During this period, emissaries from European companies were not welcomed and the state was able to retain its traditional Malay character. Siam helped to keep out the British throughout most of the 19C while the rest of peninsular Malaysia was gradually being amalgamated into a colony. There was never any need to attract immigrants from China or India and the lack of ethnic diversity helped to create a sense of difference between Kelantan's mono-culture and the cosmopolitan mix of the west coast.

It was not until 1900 that the first concession of land, for mining purposes, was granted to a British company—with the wary approval of Siam. As in other parts of Malaya, it was rivalry between European states that came to play a significant role in developments. In Kelantan, in the early 20C, Britain and France agreed to support Siam as a buffer state against the threat of German imperialism. A deal was made in 1909 whereby Siam conceded its interest in the states of Kelantan and Terengganu in return for a British guarantee of Siam's independence, plus investments of money in the country.

The treaty in 1909 was never welcomed by the people of Kelantan and there was a short revolt in 1912. As it happened, the British stayed for only three decades: in 1941 they were defeated by the Japanese.

It was 03.25 on 8 December 1941, Tokyo time, when Pearl Harbor was attacked, but the inaugural act in the Pacific war had occurred just over an hour earlier when more than 5000 Japanese troops landed on beaches 13km northwest of Kota Bharu (00.15 local time). The Indian defenders cut down one in three of the invaders but in less than 48 hours the airfield was captured. Australian and British pilots flew Hudsons from the airport at Kota Bharu and two Japanese troopships were hit from the air and sunk—the first Japanese naval losses in the war—but late on 12 December orders came for the Indian 8th Brigade troops to withdraw. Before this could happen it was necessary to withdraw supplies and equipment that could be of use to the Japanese. By 16 December troops began their escape down the railway line from Kuala Krai. Successful rearguard action ensured that by 22 December the troops had withdrawn.

By the 1950s Kelantan politics were bound up with the Persatuan Islam Sa-Tanah Melayu (PAS) and the consistent election of PAS politicians to both state and national assemblies continues to subvert prime minister Mahathir's hegemonising political and social order. The PAS has set about creating an Islamic state and has passed state laws embodying *Syariat* law—as laid down in the Koran—including the mandatory severing of limbs for crimes such as robbery, and lashes of the cane for fornication and intoxication. Using the constitution, the federal government in Kuala Lumpur has blocked these draconian measures and relations between national and state government remain frosty. In 1996 the PAS introduced a law segregating the sexes whilst queuing in supermarkets in Kelantan.

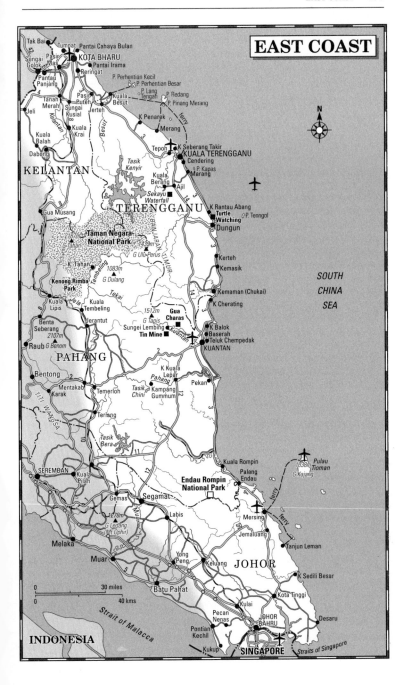

EAST COAST

N

Tak Bai
Tumpat Pantai Cahaya Bulan
Sungai Pasir
Golok Mas
KOTA BHARU
Pantai Irama
Pantau Reringat
Panjang
P. Perhentian Kecil
P. Perhentian Besar
Tanah Pasir Kuala P. Lang
Merah Puteh Besut Tengah P. Redang
Jeli Sungai Jerteh P. Pinang Merang
Kusial
Kuala K Penarek
Kuala Krai
Balah Merang
Dabong Tepoh K Seberang Takir
KUALA TERENGGANU
KELANTAN Cendering
Tasik Kuala P. Kapas
Kenyir Berang Marang
Gua Musang Ajil
Sekayu
Waterfall
TERENGGANU K Rantau Abang
Turtle P. Tenggol
1439m Watching
Taman Negara Dungun
National Park
G Uli-Perus
K. Tahan G Ulu-Perus
1083m Kerteh
G Dulang Kemasik
Kenong Rimba
Park
Tekai Kemaman (Chukai)
Kuala Kuala
Lipis Tembeling K Cherating
Benta Jerantut 1512m Gua
Seberang G Tapis Charas K Balok
2107m Sungei Lembing Baserah
Raub G Benom Tin Mine Teluk Chempedak
KUANTAN
PAHANG
K Kuala
Bentong Lepar
Mentakab Pahang Pekan
Karak Temerloh Tasik Kampang
Chini Gummum
Teriang
Tasik
Bera
Kuala Rompin
SEREMBAN Kuala Palang
Pilah Endau Pulau
1038m Tioman
Endau Rompin G Kajang
Gemas National Park
Segamat
1278m Labis Mersing
G Ledang
(Mt Ophir) Jemaluang
Melaka Tanjun Leman
Muar Yong
Peng Keluang JOHOR
K Sedili Besar
Batu Pahat
Kota Tinggi
Kulai Desaru
Pecan
Nenas JOHOR
Pontian BAHRU
Kechil
Kukup SINGAPORE Straits of Singapore

SOUTH
CHINA
SEA

Strait of Malacca

INDONESIA

0 30 miles
0 40 kms

Kota Bharu

Settled along the mouth of the Kelantan river, in the northwest corner of the peninsula—30km from the border with Thailand—is Kota Bharu, the state capital. Like Kuala Terangganu, 168km to the south, it is unusual in being a large town with a predominantly Malay population. The Islamic influence is readily apparent in the way virtually all women keep their heads covered but, given the colourful choice of their headscarves and sarongs there is little sense of dull conformity or female subjugation.

There are a number of attractions in the town centre which is conveniently compact.

■ Practical information

Getting to and from Kota Bharu

By air. The airport (☎ 09-7737000) is 8km from town and a taxi costs RM15. The MAS office (☎ 09-7447000) is in Kompleks Yakin. There are flights (all prices stated are for single fares) to Alor Setar (RM71), Johor Bharu (RM194), Kuala Lumpur (RM104) and Penang (RM87). The MAS office in town is on the ground floor of Komplek Yakin on Jalan Gajah Mati (☎ 09-7447000), opposite the clock tower.

By train. There are two railway stations serving Kota Bharu—Tumpat and Wakaf Bharu—but the nearest to town (7km) is Wakaf Bharu (☎ 09-7496986). Use a taxi or bus Nos 19 or 27 to get to or from the station. The express train service to Gemas, from where connections for Singapore and Kuala Lumpur are made, departs at 15.00 and reaches Gemas at 12.20. The Timuran Express, on Wednesday, Friday and Sunday only, departs Wakaf Bharu at 19.40 direct for Singapore where it arrives the next morning at 08.00. The second-class berth fare is RM51.

By bus. The state bus company, SKMK (☎ 09-7440114), operates its long-distance routes from the Langgar bus station on Jalan Pasir Puteh and another bus station on Jalan Hamzah. There are regular daily services to Kuala Terengganu (RM7.50, three hours), Kuantan (RM16, six hours), Singapore (RM35, 12 hours) and most other towns. Other bus companies also operate from both bus stations. Tickets can be bought in advance.

Local buses, to the airport and beaches, depart from the central bus station on Jalan Padong Garong.

By taxi. The taxi station (☎ 09-7447104) is close by the central bus station on Jalan Padong Garong and as soon as four passengers fill a taxi there are connections to Kuala Terengganu (RM12), Kuantan (RM25), Kuala Lumpur (RM45), Penang (RM45), Ipoh (RM30) and other towns.

To Thailand. The Thai border is at Rantau Panjang, 30km southwest of Kota Bharu. It takes about 1.5 hours by bus No. 29 from the central bus station. From where the bus stops it is a short walk across the border to Sungai Golok where trains and buses run to Bangkok. Trains leave Sungai Golok (☎ 073-611162) at 10.00 and 11.20 and arrive in Bangkok early the next morning. The bus to Bangkok takes 10 hours.

Getting around Kota Bharu

Trishaws are the cheapest and most pleasant way to travel around town. A short journey should cost about RM3. **Buses** around the city or to some local villages leave from the central bus station in Jalan Hilir Pasar. Local taxis are not easily come by. **Car hire** can be arranged through the tourist office at a good rate of around RM100 a day. Hedaco Travel & Tours (see below) rent cars and there is also Avis (☎ 09-7484457) and South China Sea (☎ 09-7736288).

Tourist information

The **tourist office** (☎ 09-7845534; fax 09-7486652) is on Jalan Sultan Ibrahim, near the clock tower. It is open from 09.00 to 17.00 Saturday to Wednesday. Thursday is a half day and on Friday it is closed. During Ramadan the hours are 09.00 to 15.00.

Organised tours are available through the tourist office. A river cruise costs RM60 and there are also tours that take in visits to local craft workshops where it is possible to purchase some of the crafts. There is also a three-day 'kampung experience' tour, staying in a local village (*kampung*), for RM160–200. Sightseeing tours of Kota Bharu and the countryside are organised by **Hedaco Travel & Tours** (☎ 09-7462178), based at the Hotel Perdana on Jalan Mahmood. The three-hour cultural town tour is RM30, the night market tour is RM20 and a countryside tour, visiting Thai villages, Buddhist temples and the market at Tumpat, is RM50. Similar tours are run by **Ria Holidays** (☎ 09-7470737) in Rum Amal Tg Muhd Faris.

Banks and government offices generally are closed Thursday afternoons and all day Friday but are open all day Saturday and Sunday. Banks hours are 09.30 to 15.00 Saturday to Wednesday and 09.30 to 11.30 on Thursday. Bank Bumiputra is on Jalan Doktor, the Hong Kong and Shanghai Bank on Jalan Padang Garong, Jalan Sultan and Jalan Mahmood.

The **General Post Office** is on Jalan Sultan Ibrahim; it is open Monday to Thursday, and on Sunday, from 08.00 to 14.30. The **Telekom** office on Jalan Doktor is open daily from 08.00 to 17.00.

Embassies and immigration

The **Royal Thai Consulate** (☎ 09-7482545) is on Jalan Pengkalan Chepa and visas for travel to Thailand are issued here, Sunday to Thursday from 09.00 to 16.00. The **Immigration Department** is on the 2nd floor, Wisman Persekutuan, Jalan Sultan Zainab (☎ 09-7482120), and is open 08.30 to 17.30, Thursday 08.30 to 13.15 only, closed Friday.

Emergencies and hospitals

The **police headquarters** is on Jalan Sultan Ibrahim (☎ 09-7485522). The **General Hospital** (☎ 09-7485533) is on Jalan Hospital.

Accommodation

The **Hotel Perdana** (☎ 09-7485000; fax 09-7447621) on Jalan Mahmood is the top hotel, though overpriced, despite the swimming pool and good sports facilities. Rooms start at RM230. The **Dynasty Inn** (☎ 09-7473000; fax 09-7473111) on Jalan Sultanah Zainab charges RM100, including breakfast. **Kencana Inn** (☎ 09-7447944; fax 09-7440181), on Jalan Padang Garong, has decent doubles from RM70 with facilities such as refrigerators in the rooms. Under the same management is the slightly cheaper **Kencana Inn City Centre** (☎ 09-7440944; fax 09-7440181) in Wisma Suara Muda on nearby Jalan Doktor. Rooms here start at RM49 and both hotels are close to the bus and taxi station.

The **Hotel Murni** (☎ 09-7482399; fax 09-7447255) on Jalan Datok Pati is a reliable place with rooms from RM85–150. **Hotel Ansar** (☎ 09-7474000; fax 09-7461150) is a newish hotel on Jalan Maju with rooms from RM105. The **Tokyo Baru** (☎ 09-7444511) on Jalan Tok Hakim is good value for money: large rooms for around RM60, comfortable and clean. The best budget accommodation is the **Ideal Travellers' Guest House** (☎ 09-7442246) down a small side street off Jalan Pintu Pong. Rooms are RM15, and RM25 with an en suite bathroom. The **Friendly Guest House** is nearby, just off Jalan Kebun Sultan, under the same management, where there are rooms with en-suite bathroom for RM15.

Restaurants
The **nightmarket**, by the SKMK bus station on Jalan Tok Hakim, is undoubtedly one of the most interesting places for a meal. Look for a stall with *nasi kerabu* on the menu—a Kelantanese dish consisting of rice, ground coconut sauce mixed with fish, fish crackers, and local herbs and spices. It comes in three forms, depending on the colour of the rice: *putih* (plain), *kuning* (yellow) and *hitam* (blue). The *nasi kerabu* goes very well with a plate of *ayam percik*—another Kelantanese speciality—chicken marinated in spices and coconut milk and then roasted over a charcoal fire. As a dessert or a takeaway, consider some of the local sweets such as akok, duck and chicken eggs cooked in brown sugar and flour or *pisang murtabak* (banana pancake).

For excellent curries, vegetarian and non-vegetarian, there is nowhere better than the **Meena Curry House** on Jalan Gajah Mati. For a meal in air-conditioned comfort, the best place is the Hotel Perdana. Try the *siakap* (Malay fish) at the hotel's Chinese halal restaurant or the reasonably priced coffee house.

Alcohol is not easy to find in Kota Bharu and even the small bar in the Hotel Perdana serves only fruit cocktails. Chinese *kedai kopis* are the only places with a licence. Try **Golden City Restoran** on Jalan Padang Garong.

Shopping
Shopping for handicrafts in Kota Bharu could begin with a stroll down two streets, Jalan Sultan and Jalan Sultanah Zainab, which have shops selling silverware, kites, puppets and other handicrafts. The road from town to Pantai Cahaya Bulan (see below) passes a number of local workshops that demonstrate their craftskills and sell their produce. Two villages, **Kampung Penambang** and **Kampung Kijang**, are worth visiting for their batik and kite-making workshops.

Entertainment
There are regular cultural shows at the **Gelanggan Seni** (cultural centre) in Jalan Mahmood, near the Perdana Hotel. Shows are at 15.00 and 21.00. There are no performances during Ramadan.

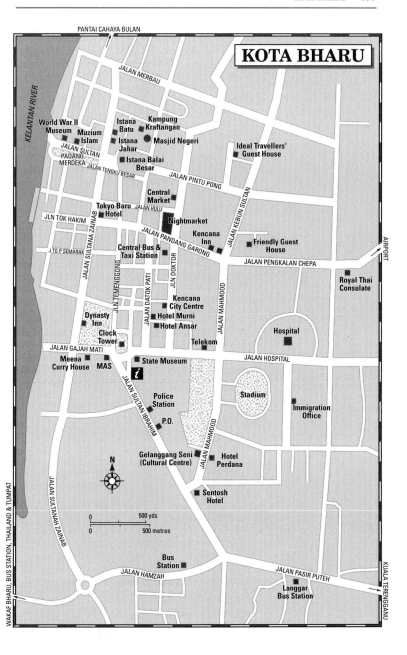

PANTAI CAHAYA BULAN

KOTA BHARU

JALAN MERBAU

KELANTAN RIVER

World War II
Museum

Muzium
Islam

Istana
Batu

Kampung
Kraftangan

Istana
Jahar

Masjid Negeri

Ideal Travellers'
Guest House

JALAN SULTAN
PADANG
MERDEKA

Istana Balai
Besar

JALAN TENGKU BESAR

JALAN PINTU PONG

Central
Market

Tokyo Baru
Hotel

JALAN HULU

JLN TOK HAKIM

Nightmarket

JALAN PANDANG GARONG

Kencana
Inn

JALAN KEBUN SULTAN

Friendly Guest
House

JALAN SULTANA ZAINAB

J TG P SEMARAK

Central Bus &
Taxi Station

JLN DOKTOR

JALAN PENGKALAN CHEPA

JLN TEMENGGONG

Royal Thai
Consulate

Dynasty
Inn

JALAN DATOK PATI

Kencana
City Centre

Hotel Murni

Hotel Ansar

JALAN MAHMOOD

Clock
Tower

Telekom

Hospital

JALAN GAJAH MATI

Meena
Curry House

MAS

State Museum

JALAN HOSPITAL

i

JALAN SULTAN IBRAHIM

Police
Station

Stadium

P.O.

Immigration
Office

N

Gelanggang Seni
(Cultural Centre)

JALAN MAHMOOD

Hotel
Perdana

JALAN SULTANAH ZAINAB

Sentosh
Hotel

0   500 yds

0   500 metres

AIRPORT

KUALA TERENGGANU

WAKAF BHARU, BUS STATION, THAILAND & TUMPAT

Bus
Station

JALAN HAMZAH

JALAN PASIR PUTEH

Langgar
Bus Station

Sport

Golf is available at **Royal Kelantan Golf Club**, in Jalan Hospital. Fees are RM50.00.

Festivals and events

The sultan's birthday, 30 March, is the occasion for a **bird-singing contest**. Throughout the year there are smaller bird-singing contests on a weekly basis. The location tends to change each week but the tourist office will have details. Also check with the tourist office for the dates and times of the annual **kite-flying festival**, usually held in May, the **drum festival** in July and the **top-spinning contest**, usually in October.

Around Padang Merdeka

The small **Padang Merdeka** (Independence Square) was originally the town's marketplace, built as a memorial following the First World War. In 1915 the body of the Malay patriot, Tok Janggut, was displayed here after he had been executed by the British for leading a rebellion of 2000 Malays against the system of land taxes. In the immediate vicinity of Padang Merdeka there are a number of small museums as well as the **Masjid Negeri** (State Mosque, 1926) and the **State Religious Council Building** (1914).

At the western end of the square, at the corner of Jalan Sultan and Jalan Pantai Cinta Berahi, the **World War Two Museum** (**Bank Kerapu**) is appropriately housed in a building that was used by the Japanese army as their headquarters. It is the oldest brick building in town (1912); it was first the Mercantile Bank and later the Hong Kong and Shanghai Bank. The museum has a good display of photographs relating to the Japanese Occupation and a collection of Japanese weapons. It is open Saturday to Thursday from 10.30 to 17.45; admission is RM2.

Next door is **Muzium Islam**, dedicated to showing why Kelantan has been regarded by her neighbours as *serambi Mekah* ('verandah of Mecca'). It has a collection of Islamic art and handicrafts. Admission is free and the museum is open daily, Saturday to Thursday, from 10.30 to 17.45.

Turning left outside the museum and continuing along the road, the **Istana Jahar** comes into view. Building on this palace started in 1887 during the reign of Sultan Ahmad (1886–89). It was a wedding gift from the sultan to his son Long Kundur who succeeded him as Muhammad III (1889–90). It has a traditional wooden portico, intricately carved panels and iron grilles. Sultan Muhammad IV added the Italian marble floor and the spiral staircase in 1911. Inside, there is a rich collection of brassware, textiles and royal jewellery. It is open Sunday to Thursday from 10.30 to 18.00, Saturday from 10.30 to 22.00, and Friday from 10.30 to midday and 14.30 to 22.00; admission is RM2.

Next door is **Istana Batu**, the Royal Museum, built as an extension of the Istana Jahar in 1939 as a wedding gift from Sultan Ismail (1920–44) to his nephew, the future Sultan Yahya Petra (1961–79) who lived here until 1961. It functioned as the official residence for the heir to the throne until 1991 when it became the Royal Museum. It contains an array of royal possessions, including the dining room lavishly laid for a meal with crockery from England. Other rooms are crowded with antique furniture and laden with silver and brassware

Istana Jahar, Kota Bharu

and countless bits and pieces of decorative art. Open every day except Friday from 10.00 to 16.45, admission RM2.

Directly opposite the Istana Batu is **Balai Getam Guri**, the Handicraft Museum, in an attractive timber building. Inside, there are examples of Kelantan handicraft: embroidery, woven *songets*, batik, silverwork and matting. The museum is part of the **Kampung Kraftangan**, the Handicraft Village, surrounded by palm trees planted to evoke a traditional *kampung* atmosphere. Demonstrations and workshops in the various handicrafts are organised here and it is a matter of turning up to see what happens to be in progress. There is no admission charge.

To the south of Balai Getam Guri is **Istana Balai Besar** (Palace with the Big Audience Hall). It was built in 1844 under Sultan Mohammad II and is now only opened for ceremonial occasions, although the external wooden decorative panels can be appreciated. The interior contains royal furniture, the throne room and a barge that was built for the sultanate but only ever used once, in 1900, when the reigning sultan indulged in a river cruise.

Central Market

To the southeast of the complex of museums and palaces, off Jalan Doktor, the Central Market is well worth a visit. It is open from 09.00 to 17.00, and during the morning hours especially it is a thriving and colourful place. The octagonal building has three floors: vegetables, fruit and meat on the ground level and kitchenware, basketware and assorted goods on the floors above. It is always an interesting place to wander around with a camera—the human scene made up mostly of women traders is as fascinating as the variety of foodstuffs for sale.

Gelanggang Seni

This is Kota Bharu's Cultural Centre, on Jalad Mahmood opposite the Hotel Perdana, open from February/March to October, except during Ramadan. There are free displays of traditional activities such as *rebana* (giant drums), *wau ubi* (kite-flying), *wayung kulit* (shadow puppets) and *gasing* (top spinning). Other possible shows include demonstrations of *silat* (self defence) and a performance of the royal Mak Yong dance drama and the *Menora*, both based on local folk narratives and highly influenced by Thai art forms. *Mak Yong* characters are played by women and three men, backed by a traditional orchestra, while the *Menora* uses only male performers and employs grotesque masks.

Usually, performances are held during the afternoon and evenings on Monday, Wednesday, Saturday and Sunday. Check with the tourist office for the exact times. Admission is free.

Top spinning, *gasing*, is an adult sport. Participants practice assiduously to perfect their techniques. There are two types of competition: the 'spinning contest' and the 'striking game'. In the former, the winner is the player who launches a top that maintains its spin for the longest period of time. The current record is around two hours, using tops that weigh up to 5kg. In the striking game players attempt to use their top to unbalance their competitors'. The skill in both types of game lies primarily in the ability and strength to launch a powerful spin, using a 5m rope wound tightly around the top and tied to a tree. Skill is also needed for the next step, which is to scoop up the spinning top from the ground and place it on a post where it is timed until the spinning stops. The tops themselves are crafted and carved from roots of Merbau and Afzelia trees.

Kite-flying, *wau ubi*, has been a traditional Kelantanese sport for centuries and is known to have been popular among the Malay nobility in the 15C. (The logo of the national airline, MAS, features a traditional kite design.) The object is to maintain one's kite as high in the sky as possible—500m is not uncommon—although in the past participants endeavoured as forcefully as possible to upset their opponents' attempts to do the same. Competitors at kite-flying competitions are judged for the height and duration of their kite-flights and the skill with which they manoeuvre them. The characteristic Kelantan kite (*wau bulan*) is crescent-shaped.

Drumming has its origins as a means of communication between neighbouring *kampungs* but is now a highly colourful and noisy spectacle at festivals and special events. The drums (*rebana*), about 60cm in diameter, are cut from logs, covered with buffalo hide and brightly decorated. At the annual Festival of Drums, usually held in July, teams compete before judges who award points for consistency of rhythm and tone. The drummers use both their fingers and padded drumsticks to beat out the rhythm. A different kind of drum is the *kertok*, fashioned from large coconuts and with a piece of *nibong* wood (taken from the sago palm) fastened across the mouth to form a sounding board.

Shadow puppets, *wayang kulit*, performances use puppets crafted from buffalo hide and mounted on sticks of rattan. The *Tok Dalang*, puppeteer and narrator, is backed by a traditional orchestra providing a rhythm and melody for the enactment of romantic tales adapted from the *Ramayana* and *Mahabrata*. The Indian connection goes back to the 14C when the Javanese Majapahits are thought to have introduced the Hindu epics to Kelantan.

State Museum. The museum is on Jalan Sultan Ibrahim, close to the tourist office, and has a disappointing collection of art and artefacts relating to the history of Kelantan. The *krises* and musical instruments are the main interest. The museum is open daily, except Friday, from 10.30 to 17.45, admission is RM2.

Excursions from Kota Bharu

See the chapter on 'Into the Interior' for information on inland Kelantan, Terengganu and Pahang—easily accessible from Kota Bharu using the jungle railway line that starts at Tumpat and meets the main Singapore–Kuala Lumpur line at Gemas.

Beaches

Pantai Cahaya Bulan (PCB), 10km north of Kota Bharu, is the most promoted of all beaches in the vicinity. It was formerly called Pantai Cinta Berahi, its English name, the 'Beach of Passionate Love', guaranteeing its appeal. But under Syariat Islamic law Malays risked prosecution for the crime of *khalwat* ('close proximity') if tempted by the semantics, so even the name has been changed to Pantai Cahaya Bulan ('Moonlight Beach')—but because the initials remain the same everyone refers to it as simply PCB. Being the closest beach to town there are always crowds at weekends and school holidays. It is a broad sandy beach but the sea can be rough. Bus No. 10 from outside the Central Market or along Jalan Padang Garong goes to the beach, and the route is well signposted for travel by car.

There are a number of **accommodation** possibilities at the beach. One of the best is the **Perdana Resort** (☎ 09-7733000; fax 09-7739980), complete with swimming pool and tennis court, which can be booked through its sister hotel in Kota Bharu. The Perdana Resort is also a good place for a meal. Further south along the beach, the **Pantai Cinta Berahi Resort** (☎ 09-7742020; fax 09-7741466) has good rooms and a swimming pool. The restaurant is very affordable. The **H.B. Village** (☎ 09-7734993) is on the other side of the Perdana Resort, heading away from Kota Bharu, but is recommended for inexpensive accommodation and meals. Rates are RM60 for a room with bath and air-conditioning.

Pantai Irama ('Beach of Melody') is situated about 25km south of Kota Bharu at Bachok. Local tourist literature claims it as possibly the most beautiful beach along the east coast. This is definitely an exaggeration but it is the best beach for a day trip from Kota Bharu and is safe for swimming. Take bus No. 2a or 2b from the local bus station in town. Inexpensive chalet accommodation is available at **Pantai Irama Chalets**, just north of the bus station.

Other beaches include the historically important **Pantai Dasar Sabak**, 13km from town and 3km beyond the airport. Here, just after midnight (Tokyo time) on 8 December 1941, three Japanese troopships appeared off the coast. The first strike force of over 5000 men landed at Sabak and the nearby Badang beaches. The remains of a bunker can be found on the beach but there is little else of interest and the rough sea does not invite swimming. Bus No. 8 or 9 from town will take you there.

Pantai Bisikan Bayu ('Beach of the Whispering Breeze'), also known as Pantai Dalam Rhu, is 50km from town. Bus No. 3 goes to Pasir Puteh from where it is 19km to the beach on bus No. 96. It is a pleasant, often empty, beach where shade for a picnic is provided by casuarinas.

Masjid Kampung Laut

This mosque can claim to be one of the oldest in the country. Constructed of cengal, a highly regarded hardwood, it was built at the end of the 17C by Muslims from Java as an offering of thanks for being saved from pirates. It originally stood just across the river from Kota Bharu at Kampung Laut but, having suffered repeated damage from monsoon floods, it was taken apart and moved inland to its present location at Kampung Nilam Puri, 10km south of Kota Bharu. To get there, take a taxi, bus No. 44 or Express bus No. 5.

Tumpat area

The area around the small town of Tumpat covers the countryside northwest of Kota Bharu as far as the Thai border. It is characterised by Thai-style buildings, the occasional Thai temple, and bucolic scenes of green rice paddies being tended by their farmers.

Wat Phothivian at Kampung Berok, 12km south of Kota Bharu, boasts a 41m reclining Buddha statue that was built in 1973 by chief abbot Phra Krupraspia Chakorn. To get there take bus No. 27 or 19 to Cabang Empat from where it is just over 3km away. The walk there provides an ideal opportunity to appreciate rural Kelantan at close quarters. On the bus or car journey from Kota Bharu, look for the **Wat Pracacinaram** on the right side of the road just after leaving Wakaf Bharu. It is not worth stopping for, but it is a good example of a shiny new Thai temple. The best time to visit any Thai temple in the region is during the Wesak Festival, usually held in August.

Tokong Mek Chinese Temple

This colourful little Chinese temple is 1km north of town on the PCB road. If you like temples, a good time to visit is between 09.00 and 10.00 when it is particularly busy. The No. 10 bus to Pantai Cahaya Bulan goes nearby. Get off at a sharp right bend, turn left at a vegetable market along a dirt track and go through the Chinese gate.

River trips

One hour by bus from Kota Bharu is Kuala Krai from where several boat trips are possible. Boats go upriver to **Kuala Balah**, a 2 hour journey. At Kuala Balah there is a resthouse where it is possible to stay overnight; or you can get a ride to Jeli near the Thai border, and from there a bus goes to back to Kota Bharu. A boat returns to Kota Bharu from Kuala Balah early in the morning. Alternatively, you can get off the boat at Dabong, a small *kampung* before Kuala Balah, and catch a train back to Kota Bharu, a slow 5 hour journey; or it is possible to get to Kuala Krai, a 3 hour trip, and make the rest of the return journey by taxi. A train goes through Dabong at about 13.45. Dabong also has a resthouse.

Terengganu

The coastline of Terengganu stretches 250km, from the state border with Kelantan to the north to the state border with Pahang to the south. It contains the vast 370 square kilometre man-made lake Tasik Kenyir. The main town is Kuala Terengganu, 168km south of Kota Bharu and 209km north of Kuantan in Pahang.

The state of Terengganu has a lot in common with its neighbour Kelantan. They are both predominantly agricultural with a relaxed pace of life and a largely Islamic population. Apart from Kuala Terengganu, there are no large towns and the appeal of the area lies in the lovely beaches and the leatherback turtles that come ashore at Rantau Abang between May and September. The best beaches of all are found in Pulau Perhentian (Perhentian Islands) which lie off the coast in the South China Sea. They are reached from the small village of Kuala Besut in the north of the state, just before Kelantan state.

History
Terengganu was under Siamese influence for centuries until the Melaka sultanate established its power in this part of the peninsula in the 15C. After Melaka fell to the Portuguese in 1511, the ascendancy passed to Johor, but Terengganu achieved a significant degree of autonomy. Relations were peaceful, however: the state formally came into existence in 1724 and the first sultan was related to the Johor court. For the rest of the 18C, the state developed its textile industry and traded extensively with Siam, China and Cambodia. Also during this century, the Terengganu sultanate took control—through marriage—of Kelantan. This paved the way for the resumption of Siamese influence which lasted throughout the 19C.

In 1909 the state passed into British hands (see the history of Kelantan above) and it remained a sleepy colonial outpost until the Japanese seized control during the Second World War. After the war there was little to change the character of the state, until the 1980s when the discovery of offshore oil and gas brought a sudden and unexpected prosperity to sections of the community. Despite the evident modernisation that can be seen in towns like Kuala Terengganu, the state continues to share with Kelantan a traditional image as an Islamic stronghold.

Kuala Besut

There is little reason to visit this small fishing village other than to wait for a connection to or from Pulau Perhentian (see below). It is also possible to catch a boat from here to Pulau Redang (see below). The best place for a meal or an overnight stay is the **Primula Beach Resort** (☎ 09-6956311/03-2425588), about 1km south of the village and over the bridge at Pantai Air Tawar. Rooms here are RM138. Less expensive accommodation, which is also closer to the bus and taxi station, is available at the **Nan Hotel** (☎ 09-6910892) on Jalan Hj. Mohammad, Depan Bazar Mara. A double room with air-conditioning costs RM55.

Pulau Perhentian

There are two islands: the small **Perhentian Kecil** and the larger **Perhentian Besar**, which at their closest point are separated by a few hundred metres. They are located 20km off the coast and reached by boat from the coastal village of Kuala Besut (78km south of Kota Bharu, see above). They remain the least developed and disturbed of all the idyllic islands lying off the coast of Malaysia, offering a perfect retreat for anyone wanting sand and surf but without resort hotels dominating the scene. (Inevitably, there are plans to develop the islands' tourist potential and build resort hotels.) Between November and the end of the monsoon period around April and May there is no regular boat service and it is inadvisable to think of going there. Travellers have found themselves stranded waiting for the sea to calm sufficiently to allow safe passage by boat.

There are no facilities for changing money on either island or in Kuala Besut.

■ Practical information

Getting to Pulau Perhentian
Boats for the 75-minute journey from Kuala Besut leave each morning around 10.00 (earlier if demand is high) and continue throughout the day until late afternoon, on an approximately two-hourly basis. The quayside is conveniently located just behind the bus station. The fare is RM30 return (RM50 for a fast 20-minute boat) and it impossible to miss the agents' shops selling tickets. **Bonaza Express** (☎ 09-6910290) and **Yaudin Holidays** (☎ 09-6410887) are two of the half dozen or more companies offering passage by boat. They all offer a boat and accommodation package and these are always worth considering for the sake of convenience. The larger island has two jetties.

From Kota Bharu take bus No. 3 from the bus station in Jalan Hamzah for the 36km south to Pasir Puteh from where it is a half-hour bus trip on No. 36, or a shorter taxi ride, to Kuala Besut.

From Kuala Terengganu take any bus bound for Kota Bharu as far as Jerteh from where local buses and taxis run to Kuala Besut.

Accommodation on Perhentian Besar
The larger of the two islands is the more developed, with most of the accommodation scattered along the western and southern sides. The beautiful 2km-long southern beach, Telok Dalam, is where in 1944 the Allies dispatched a reconnaissance Malay team across to the mainland prior to an invasion. Unfortunately, the noise of the Catalina flying boat alerted the Japanese and the Malays were captured.

The **Perhentian Island Resort** (☎ 03-2448531) has a superb location with chalets and bungalows overlooking the gorgeous Telok Pauh ('wild mango bay'). Rooms with a fan are RM120, with air-conditioning RM190–240. The hotel restaurant is a little disappointing and many residents simply eat elsewhere on the island. **Flora Bay** (☎ 011-6977266), on the south side, is considered by many to be the best value for rooms with air-conditioning (RM120).

Back on the west side, below the **Perhentian Island Resort, Coral View** (☎ 03-2488011) has a slightly crowded set of chalets with en suite bathrooms for

RM30–90. Immediately south is **Paradise**, with chalets for RM40–70, and then **Mama's Place** with budget accommodation for RM25 and a primitive shower. Further to the south, **Cozy Chalets** (☎ 09-9879818) has a range of chalets for RM20–90, as do most of the other places nearby—**ABC**, **Ibi's** and **Abdul's**. The latter is the least expensive and the quietest of all at RM18.

Also on the south side, on either side of the Flora Bay Resort, **Pelangi** and **Fuina** and **D'Lagoona** are all budget places charging around RM30.

Camping is not restricted anywhere on the island but there is an official campsite at the Perhentian Island resort.

Accommodation on Perhentian Kecil

The island has one jetty at the solitary village of Kampung Pasir Hantu in the southeast. The best accommodation is **Pasir Petani**, just to the west of the village, with pleasant chalets for RM50. Around on the western side **Mira's Place** has its own little bay and is often full, partly because the restaurant here serves better food than most of the others. Further up this western side of the island, **Coral Bay** and **Rajawali** (☎ 09-979818 and 011-971615), under the same management, are often quieter.

Long Beach, on the eastern side of the island, has lovely sand, and new places to stay are opening up all the time. **Mata Hari** has been around for a while and charges the same rate, around RM20, as do nearly all the other places dotted to the south and north—**Long Beach** and **Moonlight** being only two of them. **D'Lagoon** is different; tucked away in the northeast of the island, it offers a retreat for those who want isolation. **Cempaka** has been recommended for its friendliness and atmosphere. Nearly all the accommodation places have their own restaurants which are all open to non-residents.

Activities

Not surprisingly, water-based activities come first to mind. The white sandy beaches are superb for sunbathing and the crystal clear waters and coral beaches are ideal for snorkelling and scuba diving. Bring your own equipment or hire it on the island: it costs about RM10 to hire a snorkel, mask and flippers. The **Perhentian Island Resort** (see above) offers PADI courses for around RM1000 for the four or five days of the course. Qualified divers can hire a boat and equipment for the day. On Perhentian Kecil, contact **Turtle Bay Divers**. As well as multi-coloured tropical fish and fresh coral, there are opportunities to see turtles and the occasional stingray and reef shark.

There is deep sea fishing, between July and October; expect to pay about RM200–250 to hire a boat. Fairly undemanding jungle treks are possible and there is plenty of good exercise to be had by walking around Perhentian Besar trying the different restaurants. Between May and September the larger island is also good for turtle watching; **Three Coves Bay** in the north of the island is especially rewarding in this respect. The bay cannot be reached on foot; you should expect to pay around RM100 for a motor boat for the day.

There are a number of pleasant walks to be enjoyed. On Perhentian Besar it takes about 45 minutes to walk from Telok Pauh to Telok Dalam along a route signposted 'Jungle Tracking'. On the smaller island there is a trail from Pasir Panjang to Telok Aur which takes about half an hour, and a longer hour and a half walk from there to the fishing village.

Merang

Not to be confused with Marang, which is almost 60km to the south, Merang is a fishing village about to suffer the mixed blessings of modernisation and increased tourism. It is sited 38km north of Kuala Terengganu and 130km south of Kota Bharu. When small groups of travellers first discovered this sleepy *kampung* about 20 years ago, the local community responded by offering accommodation and meals in their homes, and visitors were able to experience rural Malaysia while sunbathing on the gorgeous beach and reading a book under a coconut tree as the sun went down. It is still a friendly place but the idyll is being threatened by the development of offshore **Pulau Redang** as a major upmarket resort island. Merang is the departure point for Pulau Redang and a new jetty is being built and there are plans to pull down many of the original dwellings and install a modern shopping area.

■ Practical information

Getting to Merang
From Kuala Terengganu. The main road between Kota Bharu and Kuala Terengganu runs inland via Jerteh; as Merang is located on the quiet coastal road that runs between Kuala Terengganu and Penarek, public transport is limited. There are daily buses covering the 38km between Kuala Terengganu and Merang (RM2.40), some of which continue north to Penarek.

From Kota Bharu. Ask the bus driver to stop at Permaisuri on the main route south; from there take a bus to Penarek and then a taxi to Merang.

Accommodation
The best place to stay and eat at is the **Merang Inn Beach Resort** (☎ 09-6243435). The budget accommodation centre, **Naughty Dragon's Green Planet** (no ☎), has a reputation for being a very friendly place. Twin rooms without air-conditioning are RM26 and the price includes meals. All the accommodation places have restaurants open to non-residents.

Pulau Redang

27km off the coast from Merang, this island is 8km long and 6km wide with a shoreline characterised by rocky outcrops interrupting pure white beaches. The interior supports primary rainforest. The 200 or so families who live on the island nearly all make their living from fishing, supplemented by tourism.

Off the southern tip of the island, the smaller **Pulau Pinang** has a turtle hatchery which is open to the public. The water around the island has been declared a **Marine Park**, but the scale of the tourist developments on such a small island make a mockery of any attempt to protect the environment. Already, a number of families have been relocated as part of the development plans.

In the early 1990s the coral in the Marine Park was seriously threatened by an invasion of crown-of-thorns starfish (*Acanthaster planci*). The starfish is infamous for its ability to eat its way through coral, and the Fisheries Department had to remove the predators one by one and bury them on land to ensure the safety of the coral.

■ Practical information

Getting to Pulau Redang
Pulau Redang can be reached from either Kuala Terengganu, Merang or Kuala Besut. As most visitors visit the island as part of a package, transport is included.

Accommodation
There are a number of resorts, chief among which are the **Berjaya Beach Resort** (☎ 09-6973988) and the **Berjaya Inn** (☎ 03-2429611; fax 03-2442527), the **Redang Beach Resort** (☎ 09-6224612), the **Coral Redang Island Resort** (☎ 09-6676923) and the **Redang Pelangi Resort** (☎ 09-6223158; fax 09-6235202). The **Berjaya Redang Beach Resort** (☎ 09-6971111; fax 09-6973811) has an 18-hole golf course. Chalets are RM350–430. Most of these resorts like to offer packages combining a chalet with meals; a typical example is the Berjaya Resort's three day/two night package, which includes breakfast and transport for RM335–365 per person. The bigger resorts have their offices next to each other on Jalan Bandar in Kuala Terengganu (see below). Coral Redang Island Resort's offices are on the first floor of Wisma Awang Chik on Jalan Sultan Mahmud. All the accommodation places have restaurants open to non-residents.

Activities
The coral reef here used to be exemplary but parts of it have now been severely damaged by the fishing boats anchoring on the island and the construction work involved in the tourist developments. Pulau Redang is still arguably one of the best locations for snorkelling and scuba diving along the east coast as the coastal waters are incredibly clear. The prime sites for snorkelling are on the Pulau Redang side of the small Pulau Lima, which is reached from Pasir Panjang on the south of Redang, and the west side of Pulau Redang where there is little coral but good snorkelling at Pasir Mak Kepit. Most of the resorts hire out equipment.

Kuala Terengganu

Kuala Terengganu, the capital of Terengganu state, 168km south of Kota Bharu, is located on a headland formed by the Terengganu river and the South China Sea. Up to 20 years ago it was the archetypal sleepy Malay fishing village until the discovery of offshore oil suddenly injected a spurt of prosperity. However, despite the few high-rise commercial buildings and general air of economic well-being, the town retains its appeal and vies with Kota Bharu as the most interesting town on the east coast. There is a vibrant little Chinatown, a couple of places to visit, opportunities for shopping, and it is the ideal place to enjoy the unhurried pace of life while considering the options for further travel in the region.

The main street in town is Jalan Sultan Ismail where the banks are to be found. The old part of town stretches along Jalan Bandar.

■ Practical information

Getting to and from Kuala Terengganu

By air. The airport (☎ 09-6664204) is 13km northeast of town, RM15 by taxi. The MAS office (☎ 09-6221415) is at 13 Jalan Sultan Omar.

By bus. There are two bus stations. The long-distance bus station is the blue-roofed building on Jalan Sultan Zainal Abidin and the new local bus station is off Jalan Masjid. There are regular buses south to Marang (RM1.20), Rantau Abang (RM3.30), Kuantan (RM9), Mersing (RM16) and Singapore (RM25). Buses to Kota Bharu (RM8) leave about every two hours. There are also buses to Kuala Lumpur, Butterworth and Melaka. In practice, buses leave for many destinations from both stations.

By taxi. The taxi station is on Jalan Masjid near the local bus station. Taxis leave when full, or the whole taxi may be hired for the following rates: Marang (RM10), Rantau Abang (RM24), Besut (RM40), Kota Bharu (RM50), Penang (RM200) and Kuala Lumpur (RM140). There is another long distance taxi station beside the jetty on Jalan Bandar.

Tourist information

The **state tourist office** (☎ 09-6221553) is close by the post office on Jalan Sultan Zainal Abidin. Hours are 09.00 to 16.00 on Monday to Wednesday and Saturday, closed between 12.45 and 14.00, and from 09.00 to 12.45 on Thursday. Closed on Friday. **Tourism Malaysia** (☎ 09-6221433) has its own office a long walk away at the eastern end of the same street.

Currency exchange is only possible at banks, and Standard Chartered, UMBC and Malayan Banking are all located along Jalan Sultan Ismail.

The **General Post Office** on Jalan Sultan Zainal Ibrahim offers a poste restante service. The **Telekom** office on Jalan Tok Lam is open 08.30 to 16.15.

Car hire from Kabras Car Rental (☎ 09-6235915) is around RM140 daily, RM850 weekly for a Proton Saga.

There are **left luggage offices** at both bus stations (see above).

Immigration

The Wisma Persekutuan office is on Jalan Pejabat; it is open Saturday to Wednesday 08.30 to 18.00, Thursday 08.30 to 13.00, and is closed on Friday.

Emergencies and hospitals

The main **police station** (☎ 09-622222) is on Jalan Sultan Ismail. The **state hospital** (☎ 09-6222866) is about 1km southeast of town, on Jalan Peranginan off Jalan Sultan Mahmud.

Tour operators

These include **Ping Anchorage Travel & Tours** (☎ 09-6220851; fax 09-6228093) at 77A Jalan Dato' Isaac who offer the most competitive rates for a wide range of tours. For example, a three day/two night trip (rooms with air-conditioning) on Kapas is RM385, Pulau Perhentian (RM340–380), Lake (Tasik) Kenyir (RM320). Local river trips are RM40 (in a group of four persons). **Ria Holidays** (☎ and fax 09-6220998), in Wisma MCIS on Jalan Sultan Zainal Abidin, do town and night market tours, river cruises on the Terengganu and

Marang rivers and trips further afield to various islands, Lake Kenyir and Gunung Tebu. The latter is a four-day jungle eco-tour to the 1037m mountain, Gunung Tebu, near the border of Kelantan and Terengganu. The state tourist office can also arrange a number of local tours.

Accommodation

For a short stay, the **Seri Malaysia** (☎ 09-6236454; fax 09-6238344) is centrally located on Jalan Hiliran, close to the river and Chinatown, with modern, smart rooms for RM100. The riverside rooms have the best views in town. The **Primula Beach Resort** (☎ 09-6222100; fax 09-6233360) is a little out of town at Jalan Persinggahan, offers more than the concrete exterior might suggest, with rooms for RM218, plus a swimming pool and a choice of restaurants.

Functional but economical, the **K.T. Travellers Inn** (☎ 09-6223666; fax 09-6232692) on Jalan Sultan Zainal Abidin has doubles for RM69 and larger rooms for families around RM100. The **Hotel Seri Hoover** (☎ 09-6233833; fax 09-6233863), at 49 Jalan Sultan Ismail, has similarly priced doubles, but they are not as good. **Perpel Lodge** (☎ 09-6239115) on Jalan Kamaruddin is a new place with a range of rooms from RM10 (dormitories), RM36 (rooms with bathroom and fan) and RM56 (rooms with air-conditioning).

The best place for budget rooms is **Ping Anchorage** (☎ 09-6220851) at 77A Jalan Dato' Isaac. Rooms with a fan are RM18, with an en suite bathroom for RM20. A dormitory bed is RM6. There is an attractive rooftop restaurant, laundry facilities, tour agency, and the noticeboard functions as a good source of tourist information. There is also the **Triple A** (☎ 09-6227372) on Jalan Sultan Zainal Abidin, opposite the Central Market, with rooms for RM12–30. If you are just staying overnight, **Seri Pantai** (☎ 09-6232141), at 35A Jalan Sultan Zainal Abidin, has rooms for RM17 and dormitory beds. It is close to the express bus station.

Awi's Yellow House is recommended as a place to go native for a couple of days. A room is RM14 (RM5 for a dormitory bed) and there is a self-catering kitchen. It is situated on Pulau Duyong (see below), a short boat ride from behind the Seri Malaysia hotel or accessible by road using the modern bridge.

Restaurants

The novelty at **Restoran Cheng Cheng**, 224 Jalan Bandar, is the collecting of price-coded colour pegs as you choose dishes from the buffet. The Chinese food is tasty and inexpensive enough for you not to worry about the colour of the pegs you collect. For Western and Asian food in air-conditioned comfort, try the Primula Beach Resort or the less expensive Seri Malaysia hotel. For Indian dishes visit **Taufiq** at 18-C Jalan Masjid Abidin or, for a better range of vegetarian and non-vegetarian dishes, **Shalimar Tandoori** at the southern end of Jalan Masjid. It is probably the only restaurant in Malaysia that has a ban on smoking.

Food-stalls are located on Jalan Tok Lam and at Pantai Batu Buruk, the town beach, south of the Primula Beach Resort. The food-stalls at the beach are good for seafood and satay at night. There are also a couple of speciality seafood restaurants. **Nil**, on Jalan Pantai Batu Buruk near the Pantai Primula Hotel, is famous for its crabs.

KUALA TERENGGANU

SOUTH CHINA SEA

N

TERENGGANU RIVER

PANTAI BATU BURUK

PANTAI BATU BURUK

Hospital

Primula Beach Resort

JLN PERSINGGAHAN

JALAN SULTAN MAHMUD

Temple

Mosque

JALAN MUDA

JLN SULTAN ZAINAL ABIDIN

KT Travellers' Inn

Tourism Malaysia

JALAN SULTAN SULAIMAN

JALAN PUSARA

Express Bus Station

Seri Pantai Hotel

Wisma Persekutuan

JLN SULTAN ISMAIL

MAS

JALAN SULTAN OMAR

J SULTAN ZAINAL ABIDIN

Taufiq

Istana Maziah

Triple A Hotel

Ping Anchorage Travellers' Homestay

Food-Stalls

Telekom

JLN PEJABAT

Police Station

JALAN BATAS BHARU

JALAN CHERONG LANJUT

J DATO ISAAC

Local & Express Bus Station

JLN TOK LAM

JALAN SULTAN ISMAIL

P.O.

Bukit Puteri

Masjid Zainal Abidin

BUKIT KECIL

Central Market

Restoran Cheng Cheng

JLN BANDAR

Taxi Station

JLN MASJID ABIDIN

Seri Hoover Hotel

Seri Malaysia Hotel

JALAN HILIRAN

Ferries to Pulau Duyung

Awi's Yellow House

SULTAN MAHMUD BRIDGE

State Museum

TO AIRPORT

200 yds

200 metres

0
0

A Terangganu speciality is *nasi dagang*, made with glutinous rice cooked in coconut milk and served with *gulai ikan tongkol* (tuna fish and tamarind).

Shopping

The second floor of the Central Market, **Pasar Besar Kedai Payang**, on Jalan Bandar, is crowded with small shops selling *batik*, *songket* (textile wrap woven with gold or silver thread), brassware and woven items. **Desacraft**, located in Wisma Maju, Jalan Sultan Ismail, sells silk, batik, silvercraft, brassware, handicraft products and souvenirs. **Batik Gallery**, at 194 Jalan Bandar, has a range of batik products such as sarongs, shirts, dresses, bed-sheets, tablecloths, etc. Batik and some handicrafts are also available at **Aked Mara** in Jalan Sultan Zainal Abidin. **Kalek Antique**, at 118A Tinkat Bawah on Jalan Sultan Ismail, has a selection of pottery and odds and ends.

Quality handicrafts, for which Terengganu is famous, are best sought out at some of the workshops located south of the city along the coastal road that leads to Marang. The traditional method of casting, known as the 'lost wax' process, involves coating a wax replica of the object with clay which is then baked until the wax melts. The mould is then filled with molten metal and baked until hard. The **Sutera Semai Centre** at Cendering, 6km south of town along the coastal road, is a silk-weaving centre. There are other handicraft workshops and showrooms in this area. Any Marang-bound bus passes the workshops and showrooms.

Places to see

Located along the city beach at Pantai Batu Buruk, the **Cultural Centre** (**Pengkalan Budaya**) is the venue for displays of traditional Malay dances and other cultural shows. Performances are usually held on a Friday from 17.00 and Saturday from 21.00, between the first weekend in April and end of October (but it is worth checking with the tourist office). The Cultural Centre building itself is a fine example of traditional Malay domestic architecture—it was originally in the town but was dismantled and rebuilt here.

The new **State Museum**, sited just beyond the Sultan Mahmad Bridge, consists of several buildings—the main museum is built on stilts, following traditional architecture in Terengganu. There are ten galleries in all, ranging from Textiles, Craft and Ethnology to Islamic Art and Natural History. There is also a maritime museum focusing on the evolution of fishing technology in Terengganu.

Town Walk

This walk begins near the state tourist office where steps lead up to the 200m-high **Bukit Puteri** (09.00 to 17.45, 50 sen admission). On top there is a fort, constructed of bricks and lime mortar, that was used in a local civil war in the early 19C when two sultans were fighting over the throne of Terengganu ('defending the state from enemy attacks' reads the local tourist literature). Also on top is an 18m flagpole, now only used when a new sultan takes the throne, and a disused lighthouse that used to guide fishermen into the river Terengganu. There are also aerial views of **Istana Maziah**, the sultan's palace that is not open to the public (built 1897), and the **Masjid Zainal Abidin**. The mosque was originally built of timber by Sultan Zainal Abidin between 1793 and 1808.

It was rebuilt in stone in 1852 and renovated in 1972, so that it now holds 2500 people.

After descending the steps, turn to your left and walk down Chinatown's Jalan Bandar. This is the most interesting street in Kuala Terengganu, with its Chinese temple and original shophouses that will, no doubt, soon disappear to be replaced by concrete and glass. On the right by the riverside, the **Central Market** (Pasar Besar Kedai Payang) is located in a modern building; it is a crowded and colourful place with a wet market downstairs, textiles and souvenirs upstairs, and a wonderful array of fruits and vegetables spilling across the pavements outside. Look for *keropok lekor*, a local delicacy made from a mixture of sago and fish.

Continue west along Jalan Bandar until reaching the Seri Malaysia hotel. The narrow lane on the right, just before the hotel, leads to the jetty for **Pulau Duyong**. Small boats ply the river regularly and the 50 sen trip is worth making to observe the traditional **boat-building** that Terengganu was once famous for and is now only practised on this island. The builders work entirely from memory and experience and many of the workshops along the island seafront have been in the same family for generations. The only restaurant on the island is the one at Awi's Yellow House (see Accommodation above). The last boat back to town is around 19.00.

Excursions from Kuala Terengganu

Lake (Tasik) Kenyir

This lake of 360 square kilometres, the largest in Asia, was created by the flooding of a tropical valley for the construction of the country's largest hydro-electric dam which was completed in 1985. The area is being heavily promoted as a tourist attraction, mainly to the domestic market at the moment; but it will become more widely known if plans to use the area as a gateway to Taman Negara are imple-

Boat on Tasik Kenyir

mented. Present attractions are water activities such as jet skiing and windsurfing as well as fishing and canoeing; best of all, there are opportunities for jungle trekking in the surrounding countryside.

Getting to Lake Kenyir. The lake is 55km southwest of Kuala Terengganu. A bus or taxi takes you to Kuala Berang from where a local taxi completes the journey. Package trips will include transport.

Accommodation includes the **Primula Lake Resort** (☎ 09-622100; fax 09-633360) with chalets from RM100. There is also **Uncle John's Resort** (☎ 09-6971563), which has its office on the second floor of the Hoover hotel at 166 Jalan Tuan Hitam in Kuala Terengganu. A three day/two night package, including transport and meals, is RM225. **Ping Anchorage** (see p 188) also offers various packages which include treks in the jungle. Other companies offering packages include Kenyir Woods (☎ 09-2638188) and **Traveller Houseboat** (☎ 09-2671191).

Sekayu Waterfall

Located 15km from Kuala Berang, the chief attraction is the natural swimming pools. Nearly all the travel agents in Kuala Terengganu offer day trips and overnight stays. There are inexpensive chalets and a resthouse, which need to be booked in advance through the District Office in Kuala Berang.

Marang

18km south of Kuala Terengganu, Marang was a small Malay fishing village until gold was discovered in the area in 1989. Then, in 1995, the government lifted its freeze on the issuing of licences to landowners to carry out mining on plots of land less than 20 hectares. The result has been a home-grown gold rush. This development, allied to the growth of more sophisticated tourist amenities and a complete rebuilding of the main street, is gradually changing the character of the place. Nevertheless, Marang remains an attractive location with its photogenic fishing boats, empty palm-shaded beaches and access to the offshore island of Pulau Kapas. The people are friendly but conservative and, like the state of Kelantan, regularly vote for the Islamic PAS party instead of for Prime Minister Mahathir.

Getting to Marang

Local buses, taking about 40 minutes, run regularly between Marang and Kuala Terengganu. Some of the express buses travelling between Kuantan, Kuala Terengganu and Kota Bharu will stop close to Marang.

Accommodation and restaurants

The smartest hotel is the **Seri Malaysia** (☎ 09-6182889), on the main road in the village, with rooms for RM90. The **Marang Inn** (☎ 09-6182132), 190A Bandar Marang, is also on the main street near the bus station. Rooms with a fan are RM12 and there is a decent restaurant and laundry. The hotel is under the same management as Ping Anchorage in Kuala Terengganu, and also doubles as a competitively priced tour agent for virtually every location in the state. Another pleasant place is **Angullia Beach House Resort** (☎ 09-6181322), a couple of kilometres south of the village, with a beautiful beach on its doorstep. Chalets are between RM20 and RM120. Nearby is the **Bell Kiss Beach Resort** (☎ 09-6181579) with decent rooms with bathrooms for RM60. Half a kilometre south again is the **Rhu Muda Motel** (☎ 09-6182328) with air-conditioned rooms for RM80. All of the above have restaurants open to non-residents.

The **Marang Resort & Safaris** (☎ 09-6182588; fax 09-6182334), nestling by the sea, is 8km south of Marang but offers enough activities to make an enjoyable stay of two or three days. It is easily reached by taxi from Kuala Terengganu and the buses between Kuantan and Kuala Terengganu will stop outside on request. Chalets range from RM140–280 and various trips are organised: a day-long jungle trek (RM150), day trips to Pulau Kapas (RM50), gold-mining up the river (RM50). A swimming pool and adventure park make it ideal for families.

Pulau Kapas

Situated 6km offshore, a 30 minute journey by boat, Pulau Kapas is less than 2km in length and 1km at its widest. It has superb beaches that attract daytrippers at weekends but are mostly empty the rest of the time. The idyllic beaches are on the western side of the island and an adventurous clamber over rocks will discover a number of secret little coves with their own private beaches.

There are more secluded coves at the northern tip of the island from where, across a channel of a few hundred metres, lies **Pulau Gemia** (see below). This tiny island, about 200m long, has small beaches, and caves for swimming or snorkelling. The eastern side of Pulau Kapas is mostly rocky.

While the coral around Pulau Kapas is not as good as that around Pulau Redang, it is still an exciting environment to explore by snorkelling or scuba diving. Turtles, stingrays, sharks, grouper and barracuda can all be readily seen. The larger resorts hire out equipment; a five-day certificated scuba diving course at the Kapas Garden Resort is RM1200. An introductory half-day dive is RM150.

Walking trails cover the island from north to south and west to east, though care is needed when approaching the cliff tops on the eastern side.

Getting to Pulau Kapas
Boats depart regularly from Marang for RM30 return. The 30-minute trip is cut in half by a hovercraft that costs about twice as much. There is no schedule because the boats leave as soon as they are full. Abdul's Boat Service (☎ 09-6182513) is one of the more established companies.

Accommodation and restaurants
All the accommodation possibilities are located on the west side of the island. The **Primula Kapas Island Resort** (☎ and fax 09-6236110) has a restaurant and swimming pool, plus equipment for snorkelling, windsurfing and scuba diving. Night fishing trips for squid are also possible. Chalets with air-conditioning cost RM120–150. The **Kapas Garden Resort** (☎ 011-971306; fax 09-6181276) has chalets with en suite bathrooms and fan from RM50–70. The beachside restaurant here is recommended for its location.

Less expensive places include **Sri Kapas Lodge** (☎ 09-6181529) with rooms with a fan for RM45, and the similarly priced **Mak Cik Gemuk Beach Resort** (☎ 09-6181221). Neither place is particularly comfortable and the Kapas Garden Resort is far better value.

Pulau Gemia

This tiny island (also spelt Gumia), under 3.5 hectares, takes 15 minutes to reach from Marang. It is owned by the **Gem Isles Resort** (☎ 03-2824884; fax 03-2821579) so there is no choice of where to stay. There are 44 chalets hugging the coastline and fish from the surrounding waters supply many of the meals. There is a small turtle hatchery on the beach for the hawksbill turtles. Scuba divers rate the waters off Pulau Gemia as excellent—and indeed they are wonderfully clear. The cost is RM170 including meals; transport to and from the island is RM25.

Rantau Abang

Continuing south along the coastal road from Marang brings you to Rantau Abang, long famous for its turtle watching opportunities and now increasingly important as one of the few places where the giant leatherback turtle is guaranteed to be seen between early May and September. The best time is during June and July and, especially, August. Unfortunately, August also coincides with the school summer holidays, which bring in more families and groups than turtles.

There is a **Turtle Information Centre** (☎ 09-8441533), open all year from 08.00 to 23.00. During the months of June, July and August, interesting films about turtles are shown between 18.00 and 20.00 (RM3).

Leatherback turtles

Sea turtles share with sea snakes the distinction of an unbroken heritage stretching back some 150 million years to the age of the dinosaurs. Of the seven species swimming around the world, four visit the coasts of Malaysia —the leatherback, hawksbill, green turtle and the olive ridley—but it is the annual visit of the leatherback (*Dermochelys coriacea*) that has made Rantau Abang popular. The deep water approach combined with a heavy surf and a steep slope make the beach an attractive proposition for the leatherbacks.

The leatherback is the largest of all the sea turtles. They grow up to 3m in length and weigh an average of 350kg (the world record belongs to a 900kg male leatherback). They are reputed to live for hundreds of years.

Current estimates suggest there are about 60,000 female leatherback turtles left in the world's oceans. The total male population remains a mystery because the male leatherbacks never return to land after emerging from the egg and crawling into the sea. That the number of leatherbacks in the world is declining can be deduced from the fact that the number of females nesting on Rantau Abang is now about 5.5 per cent of the number arriving 40 years ago.

Leatherbacks live mainly off a diet of jellyfish which they manage to consume without the benefit of teeth or a tongue. As jellyfish are mostly water, a leatherback needs to consume at least its own weight in jellyfish every day. A source of nutrition for the turtles is found in the plankton that often clings to the tentacles of the jellyfish.

Turtles roam the oceans searching for their source of food. The females are believed to return to the island they were born on to lay their own eggs, so they clearly migrate large distances. Leatherbacks tagged in Malaysia have turned up in the waters of China and Japan. They do not usually swim in large groups and are most likely to be seen swimming alone in the sea. How they navigate remains uncertain; one of the more recent theories is based on the discovery of magnetite in the brains of turtles. It may be that this highly magnetic substance, also found in bees, is part of the turtles' navigational equipment whereby they tune in to the Earth's magnetic fields.

The female lays between 50 and 150 eggs in one night, and over the course of one nesting season will rest for up to two weeks between each of

Leatherback turtle hatchlings

her half-a-dozen nesting sessions. A hole is dug in the sand, 50–80cm deep, and after the eggs have been laid the hole is covered up. It takes about two months for the eggs to incubate and usually three-quarters of the eggs successfully produce hatchlings. It takes a couple of days at least for the hatchlings to reach the surface of their sand nest and once they emerge out of the sand they hurry with all their might down to the sea. It seems they are attracted by the brightness of the horizon because they are easily distracted and confused by artificial sources of light.

Once the baby turtles reach the sea, they face the first of many threats to their survival. Fish and gulls feed on the defenceless creatures, while those that survive and grow to adulthood face far greater dangers from humans. Sea pollution—plastic bags and oil slicks—takes its toll and the use of trawl nets causes thousands to drown as turtles must surface periodically to replenish their stock of oxygen. Turtles are also hunted for their shells, which can be fashioned into ornaments, and turtle meat is eaten by non-Muslims across Southeast Asia. Their eggs are also collected and sold in markets for consumption.

Getting to Rantau Abang

Coming from the north, buses run every half hour from Kuala Terengganu and Marang and they will stop right outside the Turtle Information Centre. If you are coming from the south, you need to catch a local bus which departs regularly from Dungun (20km from Rantau Abang). From Dungun there are bus connections to Kuantan, Mersing and Singapore.

Accommodation and restaurants

The most comfortable accommodation close to the turtles is at the **Rantau Abang Visitor Centre** (☎ 09-8441801; fax 09-8442653), 1km north of the Turtle Information Centre. During the peak season, June to August, chalets with air-conditioning are RM150, with a fan RM120. During April, May and September the rates are RM140 and RM110, and the rest of the year RM100 and RM70. Each chalet has two double and two single beds, making them ideal for families and groups. The **Tanjong Jara Beach Hotel** (same ☎ number as above or through Kuala Lumpur, ☎ 03-2542188), 8km to the south, is under the same management. It is superbly located, constructed over a lagoon overlooking one of the best stretches of beach on the entire east coast, and built in the style of an 18C Malay palace. Double rooms are RM290. Tours to Pulau Kapas and Kuala Terengganu are arranged by the hotel.

Right by the Turtle Information Centre, **Awang's** (☎ 09-8443500) has rooms with air-conditioning for RM70 and rooms with a fan and bath for RM15–20. It is not a particularly attractive place but better than some of the other budget hotels.

The **Merantau Inn** (☎ 09-8441131) is at Kuala Abang, about half-way between Rantau Abang and Dungun. Chalets with air-conditioning are RM120; half that for ones with a fan. Turtles also come ashore along this stretch of beach.

The **Danau Restaurant** at the Tanjong Jara Beach Hotel is the best place for a meal. A set Malaysian or Western lunch is RM23 and RM28 respectively, dinner RM27 and RM33. The restaurant at Awang's is also quite good.

Turtle watching

The beach is divided into three sections during the turtle season: a prohibited area, a supervised public section and an open stretch of beach where visitors can wander and wait at will. At the supervised section, visitors can pay a couple of *ringgit* to be woken at night when a turtle is spotted.

> One cause for the decline in the number of leatherbacks visiting Rantau Abang can be directly attributed to tourism. The 1987 Turtles (Amendment) Enactment Act imposed 'a fine not exceeding one thousand ringgit or imprisonment not exceeding six months or both' for disturbing or injuring the turtles. This was the culmination of growing evidence that unsupervised tourism was driving the turtles away. Beach parties with bonfires were held by locals while they waited for the turtles to arrive; when they did, the poor animals were tortured with flashlights and poking and prodding. People even took turtle rides and pulled their flippers. It is now illegal to use flash photography or torches, and visitors should keep at least 5m away from the turtles.

Dungun to Cherating

The journey from Dungun, just south of Rantau Abang, to Kuantan is 131km. The chief place of interest, Cherating, is 50km north of Kuantan.

The beach area where the leatherbacks come ashore ends at **Dungun**. The town itself has nothing of interest and visitors only pass through when changing buses to Rantau Abang. Between Dungun and Cherating there are a couple of towns, Kerteh and Kemaman, that are equally uninviting. Kerteh's development is tied up with Esso and Petronas, which have their oil refineries here, and many of the ugly buildings along this stretch of coast are residential blocks for oil workers. The beaches are still beautiful, however, though the absence of accommodation gives little reason to interrupt a journey south or north.

Cherating

Just across the state border into Pahang, Cherating (sometimes spelt Ceraring), by comparison, is picturesque. The local tourist literature talks of how the 'village maidens nimbly weave the pandanus leaves into mats' and while this hyperbole needs to be taken with a large pinch of salt, it is true that Cherating is a place where you can unwind and enjoy sand and sun in a relaxed setting.

Just to the north, at **Chendor Beach**, it is sometimes possible to watch green turtles toiling ashore to lay their eggs. Cherating is now well established as a budget traveller's base along the east coast with sarong-clad Europeans becoming part of the human landscape. Upmarket resorts are not in short supply either, chief among which is Asia's first Club Med. There are also several bars which complement the growing number of small restaurants.

Getting to Cherating

From the north, any bus travelling to Kuantan will stop on the main road close to Cherating. From Kuantan there are regular local buses, taking about one hour.

Accommodation and restaurants

The best resorts are a little south of Cherating. The **Cherating Holiday Villa** (☎ 09-5819500; fax 09-5819178) is 4km south at Mukim Sungei Karang. It is close to a lovely beach and has its own pool and there is a range of air-conditioned rooms from RM181. There is a tour agency within the hotel and equipment for water activities and sports can also be rented. Close by is the **Palm Grove Beach Resort** (☎ 09-439439/03-2614599) which is more expensive, although the style of the chalets cannot compare with the Cherating Holiday Villa. A small problem with both these resorts is that, unless you have your own transport, walking north to the main Cherating village means crossing the Cherating river. At low tide wading across is not a problem but high tide presents a barrier.

The **Ombak Beach Resort** (☎ 09-5819166; fax 09-5819433) is part of the Berjaya group and has 30 rooms for RM140, good value if the rates do not escalate because the rooms are well equipped and there is a good range of recreational facilities. The other main resort is **Club Med** (☎ 09-5819131/2614599), north of Cherating village, with its own private beach.

Around the village of Cherating itself, there is an untold number of budget accommodation places with rooms from RM12–20. Many do not have telephones and it is a matter of wandering around and checking out a few until something satisfactory is found. On the main road, the popular **Mak Long Teh** (☎ 09-5819290) has been around for a number of years but faces competition from numerous newer establishments that have quieter locations and more modern bathroom arrangements. **Matahari Chalets**, between the main road and the beach, offers large rooms with balcony and refrigrator and a kitchen for communal use. Other places that have been recommended by travellers include **Ranting Holdiay Resort** and the **Duyong Beach Resort**.

Balok Beach, 15km north of Kuantan, is excellent for windsurfing; equipment can be hired from the **Coral Beach Resort** (☎ 09-5367544).

All the above chalet operators and resorts have their own restaurants offering a mixture of Malaysian and Western cuisine. In the village of Cherating the best places are the **Blue Lagoon** for Chinese food, the **Sayang** for Indian tandoori dishes and the **Restoran Cherating Steakhouse** for grills and the like. Bars are easy to find and the **Beach House Beach Bar**, just south of the Blue Lagoon, is currently the best of them all.

Pahang

The largest state in peninsular Malaysia, Pahang stretches down the east coast from Cherating to Kuala Rompin, including Pulau Tioman, and deep inland almost to Kuala Lumpur, taking in a large part of Taman Negara as well as other national parks and the Cameron Highlands. Only the coastal section is covered in this chapter; see the 'Into the Interior' chapter for the inland attractions of a state that is mostly tropical forest.

History

According to Malay folklore, the name Pahang comes from a giant Mahang (softwood) tree that grew near Pekan and was worshipped by the Orang Asli as a sacred guardian. In the Malay adoption of the word it became Pahang. A more prosaic explanation is that it came from the Khmer word for tin, *pahang*, which fits in with the legends surrounding Tasik (Lake) Chini and the ancient tin mine at Sungei Lembing.

From the 8C to the 14C Pahang was part of the Sumatran **Srivijaya Empire**. Independence of a kind was gained in the following century when Melakan forces attacked the Siamese who had quickly taken over Pahang after the collapse of Srivijaya. For most of the 16C, Pahang was fought over by rival kingdoms in **Johor** and **Acheh** and the Dutch and Portuguese were equally keen to control a state that was fabled to contain great mineral wealth. From around 1650 to the middle of the 19C, Johor ruled Pahang without any serious threat.

In 1858 a **civil war** broke out between two sons of the chief minister and this dragged on until the youngest son, **Wan Ahmad**, felt secure enough to declare himself the first sultan in 1863. Wan Ahmad's unpopularity as a ruler, however, gave the British an excuse to declare the state a **protectorate** in 1887. The British were keen to ensure that Pahang's sultan did not carelessly hand out mining concessions to non-British companies. In 1896 the state became part of the **Federated Malay States**. The British were disappointed to discover that the putative wealth of Pahang could not be as easily tapped as the tin of Selangor. The state remained an outpost of the empire, a place where aspiring colonial civil servants were sent before obtaining more prestigious posts, or a sinecure for those who lacked ambition. Until a road from Kuala Lumpur was built in 1901, the state was completely cut off from the west coast states.

During the Second World War, the ferry crossing at Kuantan was heavily targeted by the Japanese airforce in an attempt to cut off the Allied forces who were fleeing to Singapore. The remnants of the ferry ramp used by the soldiers can still be seen by the banks of the river next to the bridge that was constructed in 1963.

On the morning of 10 December 1941, the British Prime Minister, Winston Churchill, received a telephone call in bed informing him that the battleship HMS *Prince of Wales* and the battle cruiser HMS *Repulse* had been sunk off the coast of Kuantan by the Japanese. In his memoirs Churchill recorded: 'So I put the telephone down. I was thankful to be alone. In all the war I never received a more direct shock. As I turned and twisted in bed, the full horror of the news sank in upon me.'

The ships, two of the most powerful in the British navy, had arrived in Singapore on 2 December with four escort destroyers. On the evening of 8 December they left Singapore and moved north up the Malayan coast with the intention of intercepting and preventing further Japanese landings. In less than 24 hours they were spotted by a Japanese submarine and when Japanese scout planes were seen overhead the commander of the squadron realised that, lacking air cover, they were an easy target. He ordered the squadron's return to Singapore.

Just before midnight on 9 December, however, the commander received a message that the Japanese were landing troops at Kuantan and he ordered his ships to intercept. The next morning, when the message was discovered to be mistaken, the ships once again turned around for the journey home— but it was too late. A Japanese force had located them in calm waters and moved in to attack. The *Repulse* was the first to go down; the attacking Japanese pilots allowed the accompanying destroyers to pick up survivors. The same mercy was shown to the men on board the *Prince of Wales* when she began to sink. From a total crew of 2921 survivors numbering 2081 were brought back to a numbed Singapore aboard the escort destroyers.

Kuantan

The modern capital of Pahang state at the mouth of the Kuantan river marks the end—or the beginning, if travelling up the coast—of the 300km of beach. If travelling down the coast from Kota Bharu, an area largely Malay in atmosphere and population, the visitor is likely to be struck by the Chinese character of this bustling and busy centre of commerce. The town itself has few attractions—it is a noisy and polluted place—but, due to the transport network that converges on Kuantan, many visitors find themselves staying overnight. The recently built Sultan Ahmad Shah mosque in the centre of town is worth a quick look, especially in the morning. The main reason for staying longer is **Teluk Chempedak Beach**, 4km outside the town.

Getting to and from Kuantan
By air. The Sultan Ahmad Shah airport (☎ 09-5381291) is 13km from town. The MAS office (☎ 09-5157055) is in Wisma Bolasepak Pahang, Jalan Gambut. There are direct MAS flights to Kuala Lumpur (RM74) and Singapore (RM158). Pelangi Air (☎ 09-5381177) flies a daily service to and from Tioman (RM72 single).

By bus. The long-distance bus station is on Jalan Besar, close to the river. There are regular buses to Kuala Lumpur (RM12), Kota Bharu (RM16), Johor Bahru (RM17, Melaka (RM10), Butterworth (RM25) and most other towns.

By taxi. The long-distance taxi station is off Jalan Markota next to the long-distance bus station; expect to pay about twice the bus fare for a taxi seat.

Tourist information
The **tourist office** (☎ 09-5135566) is at the end of Jalan Markota, opposite the 22-storey Kompleks Terantum which is the main shopping centre in town.

Money exchange is available at most of the big banks clustered along Jalan Besar and Jalan Markota. In this small area are also found the **post office** and the **Telekom** office.

Car hire is available through Avis at 102 Jalan Telok Sisek (☎ 09-523666), National (☎ 09-527303) at 48 Jalan Telok Sisek or Orix (☎ 09-5383894) who have offices at the airport.

Accommodation and restaurants

The best hotels are northeast of the town near the beach, or 10km north at Beserah (see below); there is little choice of decent accommodation in Kuantan itself. The best-located hotel is the **Samudra Riverview** (☎ 09-555333) on Jalan Besar. The **Suraya Hotel** (☎ 09-554266), 57 Jalan Haji Abdul Aziz, is busy but efficient and the **Hotel Pacific** (☎ 09-5141980), 62 Jalan Bukit Ubi, is in the same price and comfort bracket. Expect to pay around RM80–100 at any of these places.

The **Hotel New Meriah** (☎ 09-525433), 142 Jalan Teluk Sisek, has carpeted rooms with en suite bathroom and air-conditioning for around RM50 and is good value for a short stay. Similarly priced is the **Hotel Makmur** (☎ 09-5141363) on Jalan Pasar Baru.

The hotels all have their own fairly characterless restaurants but for somewhere more interesting try **Tiki's Restoran** at the end of Jalan Markota. It does not open at night but for breakfast or brunch it serves up reassuring eggs and toast. Lunch, Western or Malay, is equally tasty. Recommended. In the same street **Min Heng Steakhouse** has good value grills. Indian places can be found on Jalan Bukit Ubi and there are plenty of food-stalls around the central market and bus stations.

Teluk Chempedak

If travelling northwards, this is the first of the big beaches (4km northeast of Kuantan) and, while it is by no means the best of what is on offer along the east coast, it is pleasant enough. In many ways Teluk Chempedak is not typical of the east coast beach strip. The foreshore is paved and lined with tourist amenities and Europeans and Singaporeans outnumber the locals. The beach is not really suitable for swimming as the waves are fairly strong. There are a few jungle walks that can be enjoyed here, the easiest being a 45-minute walk which goes behind the Merlin Inn Resort to a mini zoo on the hillside. The resorts also organise various day trips into the surrounding countryside.

Getting to Teluk Chempedak

Teluk Chempedak is 4km northeast of Kuantan and can be reached from town by taxi or bus No. 39 from the local bus station or the bus stop on Jalan Teluk Sisek.

Accommodation and restaurants

The **Hyatt** (☎ 09-5661234; fax 09-5677577) has a lot to recommend it: low rise, pool, suitably styled to suggest a virgin jungle setting, good water sports facilities, fine views and good restaurants. The **Hotel Kuantan** (☎ 09-5130026), opposite the Hyatt, has rooms with air-conditioning for around

RM70, with just a fan for RM50. It is a clean and well-run place. Similarly priced, the **Samudra Beach Resort** (☎ 09-555333) is on the other side of the headland and thus a little out of the mainstream, but it is another good-value middle-range place. The best budget accommodation is available at the **Sri Pantai Resort** (☎ 09-5685250), which has a range of rooms with fan or air-conditioning for under RM50.

The restaurants at the Hyatt are very good and not particularly expensive. Outside on the beach, the hotel has a converted Vietnamese refugee boat where drinks are served. On the beachfront, **Pattaya** offers good seafood and **Nisha's Curry House** serves north Indian cuisine. Also on the beachfront is a food centre serving local and Western dishes.

Excursions from Teluk Chempedak or Kuantan

Beserah

This small fishing village is 10km north of Kuantan; notwithstanding its inflated reputation as a handicraft centre, it is still an interesting place to visit for its scenery and souvenir shops. Most of the fishing is for anchovies (*ikan bilis*), and water buffaloes can sometimes be seen on the beach pulling cartloads of fish from the boats to the village. There is a good beach immediately to the north at Batu Hitam.

Getting to Beserah. The easiest way to get there is by joining one of the tours that the hotels and tour agents run from Teluk Chempedak. Bus Nos 27, 28 and 30 run regularly from the local bus station in Kuantan.

Accommodation and restaurants. For those seeking a quiet, rural setting Besearh is becoming a good alternative to Chempedak. The **Gloria Maris Resort** (☎ 09-5447788) has rooms with air-conditioning and equipment for water sports. The **Beserah Beach Rest House** (☎ 09-587492) has ten rather basic rooms for around RM30. More comfortable is **Jaafar's Guest House** which has been around for a long time and is well used to accommodating travellers. The best restaurant is the one at the Gloria Manis.

Gua Charas (Chara Caves)

These limestone caves (sometimes spelt Carah Caves), dramatically situated amongst the surrounding palms, have an interesting history. In 1954 the sultan granted a Thai Buddhist monk permission to build a temple inside one of the caves here, known as the 'yawning skull' cave. It is a stiff climb up 200 steps to reach the cave entrance (admission RM2) and inside there is a 9m-long reclining Buddha carved from the rock. Bring a torch or hope to hire one at the cave in order to find your way through the gloomy darkness.

Getting to Gua Charas. The caves are 25km northwest of Kuantan. Take the No. 48 Sungei Lembing bus from the local bus station in Kuantan to the village of Pancing. From the village there is a sign pointing the way down a track through plantations for 4km. Bring lots of water and hope for a lift. By car take the Pancing and Sungei Lembing road from Kuantan and look for a right turn at the 24km mark.

Sungei Lembing and Gunung Tapis

If travelling by car, continue along the main road from the caves (Gua Charas) for another 24km to Sungei Lembing, an old tin-mining town. The underground lode mine existed before the British arrived but it was expanded and developed under the British-owned Pahang Consolidated Company in 1883 and a small town grew up as a result. A few of these colonial buildings and old Chinese shop-houses can still be seen and the mine can be visited.

About 15km north of Sungei Lembing is Gunung Tapis, a new state park that is hardly ever visited because of the difficulty of getting there. The 'road' from Sungei Lembing requires a four-wheel drive vehicle. Enquire at the tourist office in Kuantan about possible trips there and the camping facilities that are available.

Tasik Chini (Lake Chini)

Not one lake but 12 connecting lakes cover an area of around 20 square kilometres. In the summer months lotuses cover the water and, while it helps if you have your own transport, a trip here is well worthwhile. The **Jakun Orang Asli** live in the area and their oral tradition attributes an aura of magic to Tasik Chini.

> The **Orang Asli** tradition goes back to a time when the lake did not exist. One day a group of hunters came across a mysterious old woman who claimed the territory was hers. To establish this fact, she lodged a stick deep in the ground and then she disappeared. There are different accounts of how the stick was removed from the ground. One version places the event years later when, during the monsoon period, the stick was accidentally pulled out and the hole began to flood with water and spread in size until the lake was formed. Another version places the creation of the lake immediately after the old woman had disappeared. One of the group's hunting dogs alerted them to the presence nearby of a large log. When a spear was stuck in it blood began to pour forth, the sky grew dark and lightning flashed. In the confusion that followed, the stick was uprooted and water poured forth to create the lake.
>
> Other stories that won't go away talk of an ancient city that lies at the bottom of the lake. Fanciful accounts relate how the inhabitants of the lost city built a series of aqueducts to flood their homes in the event of an attack with the intention of draining the water away once the enemy had departed. It is possible that the ruins of a Khmer settlement do lie beneath the lake's surface, although there have been unsuccessful attempts by scientists and others to add substance to the legends.

Getting to and from Tasik Chini

Take a non-express Kuantan–Kuala Lumpur bus and ask the driver to stop at the Chini turn-off on the left, 56km from Kuantan, from where the Maran–Belimbing bus (every three hours from Maran from 06.00 to 15.00) can be picked up. Alternatively, stay on the bus until you reach Maran where the time of the bus to Kampung Belimbing (12km) can be confirmed. At Belimbing a boat may be hired (RM50) to cross the Pahang river and through to the lake. An alternative route is to take a bus from Kuantan to Kampung Chini, which is

8km east of the lake. From here a motorbike taxi will take passengers to the lake.

Without your own transport it is worth considering taking a taxi or one of the tours to Tasik Chini. Enquire at the tourist office in Kuantan.

Accommodation and restaurants

The **Lake Chini Resort** (☎ 03-4086308), on the southern side of the lake, is the only place offering regular accommodation. There are inexpensive dormitory beds and chalets, and camping equipment—tents, stoves and sleeping bags —may be hired. There are also a café and a restaurant, both serving fairly basic meals.

The only alternative accommodation is to be found in **Kampung Gummum**, which is only five minutes by boat from the Chini Resort or 30 minutes on foot. Kampung Gummum is a spread-out Orang Asli village where a shop sells authentic and interesting local handicrafts. **Rajan Jones** is a guest house and small restaurant. A bed for the night with dinner and breakfast is RM20. There is no electricity or running water, but it is a real adventure. Rajan Jones also organises treks into the jungle, overnight if you wish, and fishing trips.

Activities

Boat trips are the obvious activity and there is a small office by the jetty where a boat can be booked. Expect to pay around RM50 for a two-hour tour of the lake which should include **Laut Melai**, carpeted in lotus flowers. A short boat trip may also be taken to the Orang Asli display village, not Kampung Gummum where most of the locals actually live, where blowpipes and carvings are on sale.

There is a walking trail of about 2km from the Lake Chini Resort to Kampung Gummum. Longer walks can also be made. Consult the map at the resort or arrange for a guide.

Tasik Bera

The second largest lake in Malaysia is difficult to reach but worth the effort because a number of Orang Asli settlements may be found around its banks. Large areas of the lake have choked with *rasau*, a fast-growing plant, and navigation on the lake is by means of narrow channels of water just wide enough for a canoe.

Getting to Tasik Bera

First obtain a permit from the government district office in Temerloh, which can be reached by bus from Kuantan or Kuala Lumpur or Jerantut. From Temerloh, take a local bus or taxi to Triang (Teriang) and then a taxi to Tasik Berah.

The nearest village is Kota Iskandar where there is a government resthouse. The real difficulty is getting back to Triang and unless a taxi has been arranged there is no alternative but to hitch hike. At Tasik Bera a boat trip on the lake can be arranged through the Sudin family (to find them enquire at the resthouse) and accommodation is available in rather primitive huts on stilts that overlook the lake. Bring your own food and drink although fish meals are available from the Sudin family.

Kuantan to Mersing

The distance between Kuantan and Mersing is 191km. There are only two places worth visiting along this section of the east coast: the town of Pekan, the royal capital of Pahang state, and Endau for access to the Endau Rompin Nature Park. Travelling south, many visitors will not stop in their keenness to reach Mersing and the beautiful offshore islands. Travelling north, many visitors will be equally keen to reach Kuantan, as it marks the beginning of the glorious 300km stretch of beach up to Kota Bharu and the Thai border.

Pekan

Until 1898 Pekan was the state capital and as it remains the home of the Sultan of Pahang it is still the state's royal capital.

Getting to Pekan
Pekan is easy to reach from Kuantan, 44km away, by the regular local bus service, No. 31, which takes about 45 minutes. If travelling south from Kuantan to Mersing without your own transport, it is better to return to Kuantan after visiting Pekan; alternatively take a taxi to Kuala Rompin or Mersing. The taxi station is by the bus station near the waterfront.

Tourist information
The post office and Telekom office are both close to the bus station, and there is a bank (Bumiputra) at 117 Jalan Engku Muda Mansur.

On 24 October the sultan holds a birthday celebration with dances, a procession and a polo match on the polo ground at the Istana.

Accommodation and restaurants
There is nowhere comfortable to stay. The **Pekan Hotel** (☎ 09-421378) has very basic rooms from RM10–20; the **Government Resthouse** (☎ 09-421240) is a better bet if an overnight stay is necessary. The food scene is equally dismal; the hotel and resthouse have unexciting restaurants and on Jalan Tengku Arrif Bendahara a couple of Indian cafés can be found.

Places to see
There are a number of undistinguished former palaces around the town, all closed to the public, and the palace where the current sultan lives—the Istana **Abu Bakar**. To reach this palace—passing on the way a number of older ones that are now empty—turn right outside the bus station and walk along Jalan Sultan Abu Bakar for half a kilometre and turn left into Jalan Istana Abu Bakar. Continue down this road for another half a kilometre where a left turn leads to the palace. It is difficult to miss this ostentatious edifice, with its modernistic roof design, because it seems so inappropriate and charmless compared to most of the other buildings.

The **Museum Sultan Abu Bakar**, on the other hand, is an engaging colonial building. It was built by the British as their administrative headquarters and Japanese officers used it as their headquarters during the Second World War.

The museum displays a miscellaneous collection of historical items—glassware, ceramics, royal regalia—which includes a superb set of porcelain treasures recovered from a wrecked Chinese junk in the South China Sea. The museum is between Jalan Sultan Abu Bakar and the riverfront, a short walk from the bus station. It is open from 09.30 to 17.00 except Monday; on Friday it closes from 12.15 to 14.45; free admission.

Just beyond the museum there are two contrasting mosques. The **Masjid Abdullah** is the mosque with the blue domes and elements of Art Deco in its design. It no longer functions as a place of worship as next door is the more modern **Masjid Abu Bakar**.

On the road to Tasik Chini, 5km out of town, is a **silk weaving centre** in the village of Pulau Keladi. The silk-making process can be observed and scarves and sarongs are for sale.

Endau Rompin National Park

Covering an area of 870 square kilometres (bigger than Singapore), the Park straddles the borders of Pahang and Johor states. It was declared a National Park in the late 1980s following concerted campaigns by environmental groups who were becoming increasingly alarmed at the destruction being wrought by logging companies on one of the biggest areas of virgin rainforest on the peninsula. It has the same appeal as Taman Negara (see 'Into the Interior') but with none of the tourist infrastructur, so a visit here is a real eco-adventure.

At the moment there is no accommodation nor any facilities within the Park and a visit here is best planned through one of the tour agents who specialise in the area and can arrange permits. After the accidental drowning of a Singaporean visitor here in 1992, the authorities now insist that a permit is obtained by anyone visiting the Park (see below).

> With open access is denied, there are substantial rewards to be gained from a visit to the park. There are crystal-clear mountain streams to swim in, spectacular waterfalls with natural bathing holes, treks through the jungle and up hills, and overnight camps deep in the jungle to be shared with a host of nocturnal creatures followed by early morning calls by gibbons. The rare Sumatran Rhinoceros is not likely to be seen because it inhabits the western side of the park which is largely off-limits to visitors, but it is good to know that the park is one of its few remaining homes. Sightings of tigers and leopards are not so rare, and elephant and tapir tracks can be spotted along the river banks. Easily found is the spectacular *Livistona endauensis*, a tall fan palm with a remarkably slender trunk. A rich variety of pitcher plants (some with the recently discovered crab, *Geosesarma malayanum* living inside) and outstanding orchids (including *Bromheadia* and *Spathoglottis*) can be seen on a trip through the park to **Gunung Keriong**. Hornbills, the Malayan rail-babbler, the lesser fishing-eagles and argus pheasants are just some of the more memorable of the 200 species of bird that inhabit the forest.

Getting to Endau Rompin National Park

Travelling by yourself involves hiring passage on a motorboat at Endau, which is 130km south of Kuantan and 37km north of Mersing. The boat will cost at least RM200 and once you reach the Visitor's Centre at **Kuala Jasin** there will be various entrance charges. You will need to show your permit (obtainable from Perbadanan Taman Negeri Johor, JKR 475, Bukit Timbalan, 82503 Johor Bahru; ☎ 07-2237344; fax 07-2235253). Then, having collected a map, you are on your own and will need to have with you all your own food and camping equipment. Not surprisingly, most visitors work through a specialist tour agency. For details of availability and prices, contact **Wilderness Experience** (☎ 03-7178221), 6B Jalan SS 21/29, Damansara Utama, 4700 Petaling Jaya, or **Giamso Safari** (☎ 07-792263), 27 Jalan Abu Bakar, Mersing. Expect to pay about RM300 for a three night/four day package.

Johor

Johor state is a largely rural area where fishing is still a major pastime. However, as Johor Bahru, its frenetic capital city, expands into the surrounding area more and more small villages are being swallowed up by it.

History

In 1511, when the Portuguese drove the Melakan sultans out of Melaka, they decamped first of all to the Riau Archipelago (the group of islands south of Singapore, the largest of which is Pulau Bintan) and then in the 1530s to Johor. At first it was an unstable kingdom which endured attacks by the **Acehnese** from northern Sumatra and by the Portuguese themselves. In 1623 the Acehnese destroyed the capital of the sultans on Pulau Linnga in the Johor river and the court was forced to resettle. Then when the Dutch began to take an interest in Melaka, Johor's prospects took a turn for the better. A treaty was signed with the Dutch, and in return for support for the Dutch attack on Melaka in 1641, the Johor rulers were promised protection and freedom from trading restrictions with that state. Subsequently Johor became politically stable and its economy devleoped quickly. By the end of the 17C, Johor was one of the leading powers in the region.

The 18C was characterised by factionalism within the court and attacks from the other local kingdoms, the **Bugis** and the **Minangkabau**. The sultan was overthrown in 1719 and replaced by **Raja Kecil of Siak** who in turn was deposed by the Bugis. The Bugis reinstalled the Johor sultans and they remained more or less in power until the 20C. The Bugis' influence was driven out when the **Dutch East India Company** took control of the Riau islands in 1784. The sultanate was still broken up by factional fighting and when **Sir Stamford Raffles** arrived in 1819, he was able to make use of the disputed succession to the throne to negotiate a treaty to create a **British Settlement** in Singapore. After the **Anglo-Dutch treaty** of 1824, which divided the region into British and Dutch spheres of influence, the sultanate finally found its role, dominating the region of Johor and amassing enormous wealth in taxes on the many rubber plantations which sprang up. At the same time the sultans managed to avoid political control from London, Johor finally becoming part of the **Malay Federation** in 1948.

Mersing

This small fishing town is unremarkable but because it serves as the departure point for the offshore islands, primarily Tioman, visitors often find themselves spending some time here. It is not difficult to while away a few hours although there are no specific sights worth mentioning. A stroll along the beach up to the Government Rest House is pleasant enough and there is a good beach at **Ayer Papan** (also spelt Air Papan), 9km north of town, which is signposted off the main road. About 6km south of town there is another good beach, **Sri Pantai**, which does not attract as many people. At night the **Masjid Jamek** in Mersing shines out invitingly from its hilltop location but its dome and minaret look best from a distance and an actual visit to the mosque is unrewarding.

Getting to and from Mersing
Mersing is 189km south of Kuantan, 133km from Johor Bahru and 353km from Kuala Lumpur. Long-distance buses from Johor Bahru, Kuantan and Kuala Lumpur stop outside the Restoran Malaysia by the roundabout and tickets can be purchased in the restaurant. Buses to Singapore depart from the R&R Plaza near the jetty. Tickets for Singapore, Johor Bahru, Kuantan, Kuala Terengganu, Kota Bharu and Kuala Lumpur can also be purchased at most of the travel and tour agents dotted around the town. The taxi station is near the bus station.

Tourist information
The **post office** is on Jalan Abu Bakar; the **Telekom** office is off Jalan Ismail; for money exchange, see below.

Accommodation and restaurants
It is very possible that an overnight stay at Mersing will be necessary when travelling to or from the islands. The most pleasant place to stay is the delightfully shabby **Government Rest House** (☎ 07-7992102) at the top of Jalan Ismail. The rooms are large and slightly dilapidated but those with seaviews are excellent value for under RM50. The place is very popular so try to book ahead. A **Seri Malaysia** hotel (☎ 07-7991876; fax 07-7991886) has recently opened in the town; its comfortable modern rooms cost RM100. By comparison with the Seri, the similarly priced **Mersing Merlin Inn** (☎ 07-7991313) seem poor value, although it does have a pool: it is 2km north of town on the main road to Endau.

The **Country Hotel** (☎ 07-7991799; fax 07-7993787), next to the bus station, is comfortable and clean with rooms around RM60. The **Mersing Resort** (☎ 07-7991004), on Jalan Dato' Mohammed Ali, is the best of the inexpensive places with air-conditioned rooms, and ones with a fan, all with en suite bathroom.

Good food is readily available in Mersing despite the lacklustre appearance of most places. The **Golden Dragon** restaurant in the Embassy Hotel on Jalan Ismail has the best Chinese and seafood menu in town, although the **Mersing Seafood Restaurant** on the same road runs a close second. There are a couple of good Muslim restaurants serving *murtabak* and curries; try **Zam Zam** on Jalan Abu Bakar or the one opposite the Parkson Ria supermarket.

Preparing for the islands

Before departing for Tioman or any of the other islands ensure that you have sufficient currency. **Money exchange** is possible at either of the two banks on Jalan Ismail or the licensed moneychanger, part of a goldsmith shop, on Jalan Abu Bakar. The R&R Plaza also has a moneychanger.

Bottled water, suntan lotion, insect repellent and snorkels and the like can be purchased at the Parkson Ria supermarket on Jalan Ismail which stays open until 21.00.

What is called the **Tourist Information Centre** (☎ 07-791222), near the ferry jetty, is a collection of agents for the various boats and island resorts. It is useful to shop around here and compare prices. In the R&R Plaza there is a display showing the various times of departures.

Pulau Tioman

Despite its high profile, Tioman—38km in length and 19km at its widest—remains one of the most attractive islands off the coast of Malaysia. The ease of access (it is 56km off the coast from Mersing), the range of accommodation and a modest but adequate tourist infrastructure, combine to make it very visitor-friendly, and the growing numbers of tourists have not yet spoilt its appeal as an idyllic island retreat.

Much of Tioman's interior is heavily forested and while there are a few small *kampungs* along the coast it is the white coral-sand beaches that attract visitors, especially Singaporeans who arrive every weekend when the weather permits.

The sea around Tioman is clear to a depth of 30m, and snorkelling is a major attraction of any visit. Multi-coloured cardinal, parrot, damsel and butterfly fish abound in the waters.

The highest points on the island are the twin granite peaks of Nenek Semukut and Batu Sirau at 1000m. These peaks and a number of smaller but equally jagged ones have their origins in a local legend that a female dragon, journeying from China to Singapore, was so struck by the sea that she landed and transformed herself into an island. Another version tells how the dragon got her feet stuck in the coral. Either way the jagged peaks are the back of the dragon.

History

The island's location on the sea route between China and India gave Tioman a navigational and logistical significance to Chinese and Middle East traders. The earliest written reference, over 1000 years ago, is from an Arabic account of trading with India which mentions Tioman as a useful source of drinking water. Ceramic finds, Chinese and Malay in origin, dating from the 11C to the 14C, have been found at Nipah in the south and Juara in the east of the island. Many are pieces of large storage jars, supporting the idea that Tioman was a vital watering stop for traders. Later finds of Vietnamese origin from the 16C and 17C centuries suggest that Tioman developed into a well-established stopover point. A Chinese navigational chart of 1620 marks the island and an early 18C Chinese account

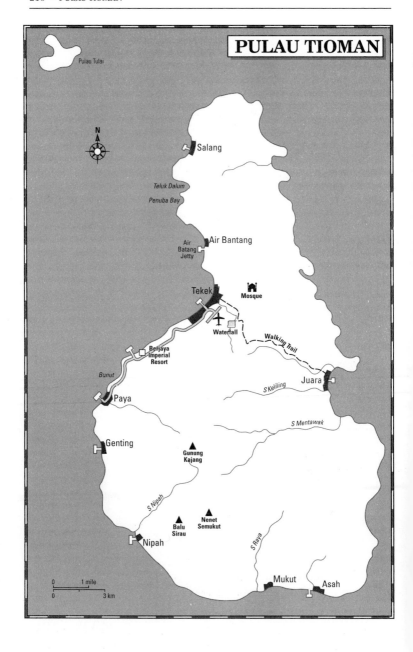

singles out Tioman as the marker for turning west to reach the Malay world.

In the 19C, the inhabitants fell prey to the rampant piracy in the region. At one time the island was uninhabited after the survivors of pirate raids fled to the mainland for a more secure existence. In the 1920s, an outbreak of malaria wiped out large numbers of islanders and whole villages died. During the Second World War, a small number of Japanese soldiers were based on the island but no fighting occurred. After the war the island remained anonymous until the *South Pacific* film unit arrived in 1958; this, presumably, helped *Time* magazine include it in their 1970 list of the ten best desert islands in the world.

■ Practical information

Getting to and from Tioman
By air. There are flights to Kuala Lumpur (RM120 single), Kuantan (RM72 single) and Singapore (RM112 single) by Pelangi Air (☎ 03-7463000) and Tradewinds (☎ 02-2254480). Bookings and confirmations for the return flight can be made at the Berjaya Imperial Resort (☎ 09-4145445).

By boat from Mersing. There are a number of boat companies operating from Mersing but they all charge the same (RM25 one way) and take roughly the same time (1.5–2 hours). There is a secure car park for motorists.

By catamaran from Singapore. Between March and October the catamaran service takes 4.5 hours. It departs from the World Trade Centre early in the morning and costs S$143 return. The agents are Resort Cruises (☎ 2784677), 02-03, 337 Telok Blangah Road in Singapore and the Berjaya Imperial Resort on Tioman.

Tourist information and orientation
Between November and February, during the monsoon period, it is difficult for boats to make the crossing; during July and August many, but never all, of the accommodation places will be full.

There is a small **tourist information centre** (☎ 03-7995212) at the Air Batang jetty and boat schedules can be checked here.

Travellers' cheques can be changed at the Berjaya Imperial Resort and there are a few **moneychangers** at Air Batang, but the rates will be better at Mersing.

The only stretch of road is along part of the west coast (although there are plans to build a road on the east side), connecting **Paya** with **Tekek** and the airport with the Berjaya Imperial Resort. Most of the budget accommodation is strung out to the north of the road around Air Batang. Further north is **Salang**, a beautiful bay and a good diving centre, while south of Paya is **Genting**. The more barren south coast, only accessible by boat, has **Nipah** and **Mukut** and a short way east of Mukut is **Asah**. Cineastes are generally disappointed after seeing the waterfall here, a 20-minute walk north of the jetty at Asah, that was the setting (or so everyone says) for a scene in the 1958 film *South Pacific*. The only settlement on the east coast is **Juara**.

Transport around the island is provided by a **sea bus** that skips from one jetty to another. The trip between Tekek and the Berjaya Imperial Resort is the most popular route and there are half-a-dozen journeys daily. Each morning around 09.00 there is also a **round-the-island cruise** from Air Batang.

Accommodation

The sprawling 400-room **Berjaya Imperial Resort** (☎ 09-4191000; fax 09-4191718; 1 800-5281234 in the USA and 0181-541 0033 in the UK) is the only real resort on the island, complete with restaurants, pool, 18-hole golf course, tennis courts and all water sports. Chalets with air-conditioning range from RM340 to RM430, and all the rooms under RM400 can be full in July and August.

There are a few other places with air-conditioning but the bulk of the accommodation is in the form of wooden chalets with their own bathroom (that is, shower and sink). Expect to pay up to RM120 for air-conditioning; chalets with fan and bathroom will cost between RM30 and RM90, while a mattress on the floor can be had for RM15 or less. What follows is just a selection of the better establishments; new ones with better facilities are being planned.

Tekek. The better places are south of the jetty and at the far northern end. **Swiss Cottage** (☎ 07-2248728) has the best chalets, including some with air-conditioning, and is often full. **Ramli's** (☎ 07-7993767) has basic but pleasant chalets and **Sri Tioman Chalets** (no ☎) is also a decent place.

Air Batang. This is the main place for budget accommodation and it has its own jetty in the middle of the beach. **ABC** (☎ 011-349868), at the northern end, includes two chalets worth enquiring about, without air-conditioning but beautifully located over rocks, for RM40. **Nazri's Beach Cabanas** (☎ 07-4993244) has large chalets with and without air-conditioning. **Mokhtar Place** and **Johan's** lack phones but are the best of the budget places.

Salang. Rapid development here is in danger of spoiling what is probably the loveliest beach on the island. The **Indah Salang** (☎ 011-730230) has the best range of rooms from basic to family chalets with air-conditioning. The **Salang Beach Resort** is a little overpriced but comfortable and **Zaid's** is the most popular of the budget places.

Juara. The most isolated of the accommodation centres, Juara is still a quiet and conservative community of Malays. **Mutiara** (☎ 07-7992309) has the widest choice of rooms and **Paradise Point** is also worth considering.

Paya and **Genting**. The best places at Paya are the **Paya Tioman Resort** (☎ 011-324121) and the **Paya Beach Resort** (☎ 07-7991432) which has some chalets with air-conditioning. Genting is not the prettiest location to stay overnight and tour groups from Singapore often take over the place. The best place to stay is probably the **Genting Damai Resort** (☎ 07-7994355) or the **Sun Beach** (☎ 011-713866).

Nipah and **Mukut** are the places to head for if you want some Robinson Crusoe ambience. The ferries from Mersing do not usually stop at Nipah (though there is a jetty so enquire anyway), so it will probably be necessary to hire a taxi-boat from Genting. The only place to stay at the moment is the **Nipah Village Beach Resort** (☎ 011-328134). The beach is lovely but apart from snorkelling and canoeing there is not much else you can do here. Mukut is equally difficult to reach but there is more choice of chalets and a bit more life. **Chalets Park and Sri Tanjung Chalets** (neither has a ☎) both have picturesque settings.

Restaurants
Most of the accommodation places have their own restaurants and, as they are all open to non-residents, part of the afternoon can be spent checking out their menus. Some of the better places are mentioned below.

Not surprisingly, the best restaurants are at the Berjaya Island Resort, especially the Chinese **Fortune Court** and the European **Bali Hai**. At Tekek, **Liza** has an interesting menu of Western and seafood dishes and there are good views from the **Norhidayah Café**. At Air Batang, the **ABC** restaurant is always popular because of its good food and reasonable prices—two people could enjoy a three-course meal for around RM25. Also worth looking in at is **Nazri's Beach Cabanas.**

At Juara there are good meals at Paradise Point and Ali Putra. Mukut and Nipah are both a little disappointing by comparison, while at Genting and Paya there is more choice but nowhere stands out.

Activities
Walking. The most popular trek is across the island from Tekek to Juara. The easy-to-follow shaded trail starts about 1km north of the jetty at Tekek and begins a fairly steep ascent shortly after passing the mosque. The descent to Juara meanders through a rubber plantation and then coconut palms. The walk takes anywhere between two and three hours, depending on your pace and how long is spent paddling at the waterfall about half way there. The Sea Bus leaves Juara at 14.30 for Air Batang and Tekek.

Another walk can be made from Tekek south to the Berjaya Imperial Resort by clambering over rocks and then across the golf course to the beginning of a trail to Bunut beach and Paya and then on to Genting. From Tekek it is also possible to walk north over the headland to Penuba Bay and Salang: this will take about three hours. A climb could be made to the top of the 1000m-high **Gunung Kajang**, centrally located in the south of the island, but it would be advisable to hire a guide from the Berjaya Imperial Resort. It takes about four hours to reach the top from Paya.

Snorkelling and scuba diving. Snorkelling is one of the pleasures of Tioman and nearly all the accommodation places will hire out equipment. Tioman is also a good place to gain a PADI scuba diving certificate with a five-day open water course costing around RM800. Contact Ben's Diving Centre (☎ 011-730230) at Salang or the Berjaya Imperial Resort. There is a Coral Island boat trip (book at the Berjaya Imperial Resort) to the small island of Tulai for snorkelling and the round-the-island tour also allows time for snorkelling at Teluk Dalum in the north east of the island.

Pulau Rawa

This beautiful little island, 16km from Mersing, has an unforgettable beach and excellent snorkelling. There is only one place to stay, the **Rawa Safaris Island Resort** (☎ 07-7991204), which is operated by members of the Johor royal family. It is perfectly situated on the west side with a white beach in front of the chalets shaded by casuarinas and palms. The price is around RM100 per night. Look out for pied pigeons flying overhead—mostly white with black wing tips—called *rawa* in Malay and hence the island's name. A short way north of the resort over the rocks lies a small secluded beach and another one lies to the south. On a calm day canoes can be hired to encircle the island.

Getting to Pulau Rawa from Mersing is by a boat belonging to the Rawa Safaris Island Resort. It takes just over an hour to reach the island so a return day trip is feasible. The Resort discourages daytrippers from bringing picnics but there is a good restaurant so this is not a problem.

Pulau Babi Besar

This island is 5km long and 2km at its widest point. Most of the islanders live on the western side, where all the resorts are, and there is an easy-to-follow footpath running the stretch of this side of the island. There are a couple of beaches on the eastern side which can be reached easily but the beaches on the western side are the best. **Radin Island Resort** (☎ 07-7994954; fax 07-7991413) has the best set-up for accommodation, although the **Perfect Life Resort** has the finest beach in front of its chalets. Another large resort is **Sun Dancer Island Resort** (☎ 07-7994995; fax 07-7995279).

Getting to Pulau Babi Besar. Regular boat journeys from Mersing take one hour.

Pulau Tinggi

The island is 7km long, 4km at its widest point, and distinguished by a cone-shaped, 2000m-high volcanic mountain. Like Pulau Babi Besar, all the accommodation is on the western side while the eastern side is dominated by cliffs and a few secluded beaches. There are a couple of comfortable places to stay and the **Tinggi Island Resort** (☎ 011-762217) is recommended for anyone coming to the island for water sports because equipment for snorkelling, windsurfing and canoeing can be hired. Also worth considering for a holiday package is **Nadir's Inn** (☎ 07-7995582; fax 07-7995797)

Getting to Pulau Tinggi. There are regular boats from Mersing.

Pulau Sibu

This island has many of the attractions of Tioman, though on a smaller scale. Sibu is only 6km long and less than 1km wide, with a narrow middle point that almost divides the island into two. Most of the safest beaches are to be found on the northeast coast where accommodation is easy to find. There is little coral here but the snorkelling is still rewarding.

Getting to Pulau Sibu. Most of the accommodation places arrange their own transport from **Tanjung Leman**, which is 30km south of Mersing and unhelpfully located if you do not have your own transport. Contact O&H Kampung

Huts for details of their boat service from Mersing (☎ 011-717109) and see the Johor Bahru section (p 216) for agents who handle trips from Mersing and Tanjung Leman.

Accommodation and restaurants. The closest to luxury accommodation is available at the **Sea Gypsy Village Resort** which offers packages of room and meals. Equally comfortable chalets are found at the **Rimba Resort** (☎ 011-231493) on the northern coast. Middle-range chalets belong to **Sibu Island Cabanas** (☎ 07-317216). The best budget place belongs to **O&H Kampung Huts** (☎ 07-793125) with chalets for RM30. All of these have restaurants with Malay and Western dishes at economical prices.

Johor Bahru

If you are arriving in Johor Bahru—or JB as it is known locally—from Singapore then your system is in for a major shock. Arriving from Kuala Lumpur or anywhere else in Malaysia it will appear busy and crowded; but coming from well regulated and tidy Singapore JB will seem to be all noise and chaos. Burnt out Singaporeans come here in droves at weekends to revel in the licence of it all, eat cheap seafood, fill up with groceries, shop at the malls, and go to a sleazy karaoke joint or worse. The causeway is blocked with traffic from mid afternoon on Fridays and Singaporeans officials are busy checking the petrol gauges of Singaporean cars to ensure that they are at least three-quarters full. The rate of exchange between the ringgit and the Singaporean dollar was encouraging drivers to visit Johor Bahru for cheap petrol until Singapore passed a law prohibiting this. But Johor Bahru is an experience not to be missed. It has history, interesting shopping, great food and some resorts and countryside to enjoy.

History

Johor Bahru came into being in 1866. Until then it had been a small village called Tanjung Putri. It was renamed by the Singapore *temenggong* (heredi-tary chief), Abddul Rahman's grandson. Abdul Rahman is famous for making the concessions to Raffles which brought about the birth of colonial Singapore (see p 310). His grandson, Abu Bakar, became known as the Maharajah of Johor and was officially recognised as Sultan by Queen Victoria in 1885. Johor was the last state to join the Malay Federation in 1914. A sorry episode in the history of Johor Bahru, for the British at least, was the collaboration of the sultan of Johor with the Japanese in exchange for protection for Malays. General Yamashita directed the invasion of Singapore from a tower overlooking the island and the tower still stands today and is used as a government building. It is just south of Plaza Kotaraya and is easy to recognise due to its faded appearance which contrasts sharply with the modern shopping centre. Known as the **State Secretariat Building**, it was built in 1940 on a small hill called Bukit Timbalan.

The Causeway which links Johor Bahru with Singapore, and over which Japanese forces marched in 1942, was built in 1924. The British army demolished part of it in January 1942 in order to frustrate the Japanese advance but it was quickly repaired. There is a pedestrian walkway which can often prove to be a quicker way of crossing between countries than travel by bus or taxi. The large pipes which can be seen next to the walkway carry essential supplies of water from Malaysia to Singapore.

Getting to and from Johor Bahru

By air. Johor Bahru is served by Senai Airport (☎ 07-5994500), which is 25km north of the city. It can be reached by a regular bus service from the main bus station in Jalan Gertak Merah. A shuttle bus also goes out to the airport from the Tropical Inn. Internal MAS flights from Johor Bahru are deliberately set at a lower price than flights into Malaysia from Singapore in order to attract Singaporean customers; check fares with the MAS office on the first floor of the Menara Pelangi Building in Jalan Kuning Taman Pelangi (☎ 07-3341003). There are daily flights to Kota Kinabalu, Kuala Lumpur, Kuching, Langkawi and Penang.

By train. There are several trains a day passing through Johor Bahru to Kuala Lumpur and the north. For Melaka the nearest stop is Tampin. There are also stops at Seremban, Tapah Road (for the Cameron Highlands), Ipoh, Taiping and Butterworth (for Penang). The train journey south continues on into Singapore. Trains are often fully booked, especially the sleeper train. The railway station is off Jalan Tun Abdul Razak.

By bus. The bus station is on Jalan Gertak Merah. Express buses leave throughout the day for the major towns. There are several bus companies with ticket booths at the bus station and tickets can be bought just before departure—unless it is a public holiday when you should book in advance.

To get to Singapore by bus, the No. 170 leaves every 15 minutes from the same bus station to Queen Street in Singapore. Tickets cannot be booked in advance and there may be crowds at peak times. A taxi is often more reliable. An air-conditioned bus, the Singapore-JB Express, also leaves from the bus station but it too can be very crowded. Both buses disgorge passengers at the causeway causing long delays. Another possibility is to walk across the causeway to Woodlands (the Singaporean town at the other end of the causeway) and get a local bus or cab into Singapore.

Nice express buses run regular daily services between Singapore and Johor Bahru and Kuala Lumpur in Malaysia. In Johor Bahru their buses arrive at and depart from the building on Jalan Ayer Molek where the tourist office is located.

By taxi. You can get long-distance shared taxis to most destinations in Malaysia if you are prepared to wait long enough for the taxi to fill. The taxis charge a standard fare regardless of the number of passengers and are likely to refill as passengers disembark. The long-distance taxi station is close by the Express bus station in Jalan Wong Ah Fook. A taxi to Singapore will cost almost RM30 but shared taxis are available for RM8 per person.

Getting around Johor Bahru

Taxis are by far the easiest way of travelling around JB. Taxis are metered and inexpensive. Flagfall is RM1.50 and increases by 10 sen every 200m. There is a 50 per cent surcharge after midnight. Taxis can be stopped almost anywhere. If by any chance your taxi's meter isn't working, find another taxi unless you know what the fare should be or you instinctively trust your driver. Any local journey will cost a maximum of RM5.

Car hire. There are branches of all the main rental agencies in JB: Budget (☎ 07-2230373); Orix (☎ 07-2241215); and Hertz (☎ 07-2237520).

Tourist information

The **Johor Tourist information Centre** (JOTIC; ☎ 07-2234935) is on the fifth floor of a shopping plaza on Jalan Ayer Malek. It is open 08.00 to 16.15 Monday to Friday and 08.00 to 12.45 on Saturday. **Tourism Malaysia** (☎ 07-2240288) also has an office on the same floor. Enquire at JOTIC about performances of cultural shows which are scheduled on a regular basis. It is open from 08.00 to 16.15 Monday to Friday and 08.00 to 12.00 on Saturday.

The **main post office** is on Jalan Tun Dr Ismail. Opening hours are 08.00 to 17.00 Monday to Friday, and 08.00 to 13.00 Saturday.

The **Sultanah Aminah General Hospital** is on Jalan Sekudai.

A number of resort agencies handling package trips to the offshore island of **Pulau Sibu** have offices in Johor Bahru. They include Sibu Island Cabanas (☎ 07-3317216), Turin Beach Resort (☎ 07-332 1493) and Sea Gypsy Village (☎ 07-223 1493).

Currency exchange

JB is littered with **moneychangers**, all of them offering exchanges at very competitive prices and open long hours. There are branches of the Bumiputra, Hong Kong and Shanghai, and United Asia **banks** on Jalan Bukit Timbalan. Avoid changing money at your hotel where you will get a poorer rate than on the street.

Accommodation

Top of the range is the **Puteri Pan Pacific** (☎ 07-2233333; fax 07-2236622) on Jalan Salim. This very plush hotel offers great views of the city and also peace and quiet in the heart of frantic JB; it also has lots of facilities and is priced at around RM310 for a double room (try asking for a discount). The **Holiday Inn** is on Jalan Dato' Sulaiman (☎ 07-3323800) close to the Holiday Inn Plaza. The **Tropical Inn** (☎ 07-2247888) is at 15 Jalan Gereja and has pleasant rooms at around RM155, including breakfast. No swimming pool.

Medium range hotels. At around RM70 there are several centrally located, clean places. The **Top Hotel** (☎ 07-2244755) is at 12 Jalan Meldrum. Rooms have air-conditioning and en suite bathroom. The **City View Hotel** (☎ 07-2249291; fax 07-2248868) at 16 Jalan Station has air-conditioned rooms, en-suite bathrooms, TV, etc., and a pleasant coffee shop. Rooms are RM60 for a basic double.

Budget range hotels. At this range you might want to ask yourself if you really want to stay in JB. For RM26 you can rent the double room at the **Footloose Homestay** (☎ 07-2242881) at 14 H. Jalan Ismail or take a dormitory bed for RM12. Other than that, you will find partitioned cubicles rather than rooms at the **Chuan Seng Hotel** at 35 Jalan Meldrum, or at the **Fortuna**

Hotel (☎ 07-2233210) at 29A in the same street. Rooms here are around the RM20 mark.

Restaurants

For Singaporeans, JB's speciality is its seafood restaurants. The best of these are located a little awkwardly out of town along Jalan Skudai. The **Marina View** (☎ 07-2241400) at the Straits View Hotel, 1D Jalan Skudai, is enormous and filled with the aroma of cooking seafood but well worth the experience. It is open from 11.30 to 14.30 and 17.30 to 22.30. The **Ani Ani Seafood** (☎ 07-2244654) restaurant is close by and provides some excellent seafood dishes.

Back in town, the smartest place to eat is the **Selasih restaurant** at the Puteri Pan Pacific Hotel. It has traditional Malay food, with specialities from the various regions of Malaysia. Most evenings your meal is accompanied by live Malay music played on traditional instruments. Special dishes to try are *nasi ulam*, a northern dish consisting of rice cooked with tapioca shoots and ginger flower; try it with *ikan bakan* (grilled fish). Another local delicacy is *mee rebus* (noodles, beansprouts, sweet potato and beef). *Johor laksa* is cooked in coconut gravy with fish, *otak otak* (don't ask what it is, just eat it) and prawns. The ambience here and the service are well worth the cost: the best value is the buffet lunch. The restaurant is closed on Friday. Opening hours are 11.30 to 15.00 and 18.30 to 23.00. The **Paulo Seafood Mediterranean Restaurant** in the same hotel specialises in oysters air-freighted from New Zealand, but also serves other fish dishes, meat (including steak), pasta and pizza (try the Pizza Johor Bahru); a three-course meal averages around RM70.

Going downmarket, JB has several excellent *daun pisang* (banana-leaf) places. The **Muthu Restoran** is at 54 Jalan Tan Hiok Nee and serves good *roti canai*, chicken *biriyani* served out a vast vat, *masala dosa* and lots of curry dishes chosen from the hotplates. Another similar place is at 32 Jalan Segget. On Jalan Wong Ah Fook near to the Komtar Building is the **Zam Zam Restoran** which serves *murtabaks*, a spicy pancake mixed with egg and meat or vegetables and served with Malay-style curry sauce. If you want to try real hawker food, there is a **Nightmarket** on Jalan Wong Ah Fook close to the railway station; it sells lots of local dishes such as *mee rebus*, chicken rice, *laksa* and much more at very cheap prices. Malay hawker food is available with the comfort of air-conditioning on the third floor of Plaza Kotaraya.

If you don't want to risk a night out in town, the other large hotels have good restaurants serving Western and local food, while the **Puteri Pan Pacific** also has Italian and Chinese restaurants.

Shopping

Most Singaporeans go to JB for the shopping: everything is cheaper here than in Singapore and many people come for their week's groceries. There are good computer software shops, plus leather shoes, cheap T-shirts and videos. The following are some of the major shopping complexes: **Plaza Kotaraya** is in the centre of town near the Pan Pacific hotel and has a department store, supermarket, bookshops and some smaller boutiques. The **Komtar Building** has one or two pretty craft shops selling local pottery.

A little way out of town is **Holiday Inn Plaza** which is very popular with Singaporeans. There used to be a train service directly to the shopping centre

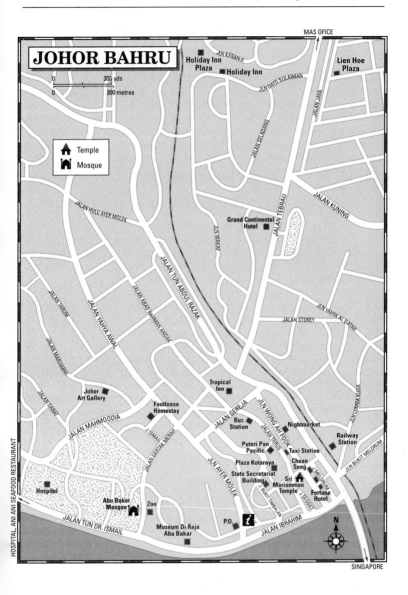

JOHOR BAHRU

MAS OFICE

Holiday Inn Plaza

Holiday Inn

JLN KERANJI

Lien Hoe Plaza

JLN DATO SULAIMAN

JALAN JAYA

0   300 yds
0   300 metres

JALAN SELADANG

Temple

Mosque

JALAN KUNING

JALAN HULU AYER MOLEK

JALAN TEBRAU

Grand Continental Hotel

JLN WAKAF

JALAN TUN ABDUL RAZAK

JALAN TARUM

JALAN YAHYA AWAL

JALAN ABAD RAHMAN ANDAK

JLN YAHYA AL DATAR

JALAN STOREY

JALAN MARIAMAH

JLN LUMBA KUDA

Johor Art Gallery

Tropical Inn

Footloose Homestay

JALAN GEREJA

JLN WONG AH FOOK

Nightmarket

Railway Station

JALAN DARAT

JALAN MAHMOODIA

J. ISMAIL

JALAN GERTAK MERAH

Bus Station

JALAN TERUS

Taxi Station

JLN BUKIT MELDRUM

Puteri Pan Pacific

JLN AYER MOLEK

Plaza Kotaraya

Chuan Seng

Hospital

State Secretariat Building

BUKIT TIMBALAN

Sri Mariamman Temple

J. MELDRUM

Fortuna Hotel

J. SENGI

Abu Bakar Mosque

Zoo

P.O.

i

Museum Di Raja Abu Bakar

JALAN TUN DR. ISMAIL

JALAN IBRAHIM

N

SINGAPORE

HOSPITAL, ANI ANI SEAFOOD RESTAURANT

until the Singaporean authorities began to get annoyed at their loss of income to JB. The plaza has lots of little boutiques, some nice touristy shops, especially those selling pewter, excellent leather shoe shops, and lots of stalls selling all manner of things, depending on whether there has been a police raid lately. Belts and handbags are good value, while there are handblocked T-shirts, ethnic jewellery, badges, jeans and lots more. Nearby is the **Lien Hoe Plaza** with more budget clothes shops, department stores, handicrafts, etc. Both shopping centres have fast-food outlets as well as good cheap food-stalls.

Sport

Like all the other sultan's Johor's has his own **golf club** at Jalan Larkin. Green fees are RM150. There is a **bowling alley**, the Holiday Bowl at Holiday Plaza, Jalan Dato Sulamein.

Places to see

The most fascinating place, well worth half a day's visit, is the **Museum Di Raja Abu Bakar** (☎ 07-2230555), unmissable along Jalan Tun Dr Ismail. The museum is open 10.00 to 18.00 every day except Friday. The ticket office closes at 16.00. For foreigners there is a special admission charge which is levied in US dollars. The charge of US$7 is roughly RM20 but will vary according to the exchange rate.

The palace was commissioned by His Royal Highness Sultan Abu Bakar and built between 1864 and 1866. It is one of the oldest buildings in JB and was built as the royal palace, a function which it still in part fulfils. The current sultan lives to the west of the city in Istana Bukit Serene. The museum has a definite English influence in its architecture: the sultan was interested in all things British, the building was designed by a British architect, and much of the furniture came from Europe. Wandering about the place you witness a remarkable combination of wealth and everyday living. The state rooms are open to the public and reveal surprisingly mundane items belonging to this enormously wealthy family—hairbrushes, towel rails, a lumpy looking bed. The sultan's bed is still used as the final resting place of the sultans. When a sultan dies, the bed is dismantled and taken to the huge banqueting room where the sultan lies in state before being interred.

> Abu Bakar, the sultan who commissioned the building, was the great-grandson of the sultan who sold Singapore to Raffles in 1819. He was an Anglophile and, as far as the times allowed, an international jet-setter. He was married three times, once to a Balinese/Danish woman, once to a Peranakan Chinese and once to a Turkish woman. His son, Ibrahim (1873–1959), son of the Danish/Balinese liaison, was born in the reign of Victoria, lived through the Japanese occupation into the reign of Elizabeth II, and saw the end of the British Empire. He, too, married a number of foreign women—a Scot, a Romanian and finally two Malays. It was he who cut the deal with the Japanese, the official record of which is on display in the museum alongside all his awards from various other royal families. The Japanese gave him the First Class Order of the Rising Sun which is also on display in the history section of the museum.

In the Treasury are countless gifts of silver and gold objects presented to the sultans at various times and which still do duty on state occasions. There is an amazing collection of silver *kris* knives showing the various curves and finishes awarded to each member of the royal family and the court. Sultans' *kris* knives had nine curves while ministers got five. There is also a special woman's kris, designed for self-immolation in the face of attack. Swords used for execution are also on display here. For the crimes of murder and adultery, the criminal is buried from the waist down and the sword thrust down through the collarbone into the heart. The animals suffered greater indignities—there are antelope feet ashtrays and elephant feet stools on display.

On Jalan Abu Bakar is the **Abu Bakar Mosque**, also commissioned by the 19C sultan and built between 1892 and 1900, although he never lived to see its completion. It is a glorious edifice and regularly accommodates 2000 people.

The **Johor Art Gallery**, off Jalan Mariamah, is of minor interest, with displays of weapons, manuscripts, currency and fine art.

Excursions from Johor Bahru

Kota Tinggi

The town itself has little to offer, the main reason for a visit here are the water-falls—a series of pools and rapids—on Gunung Muntahak (624m), at **Lumbong**, 15km northwest of the town (entrance fee to visit the falls RM1, (RM2 for a car). This is a pleasant country spot about 42km northeast of Johor Bahru on the road to Mersing. It is a little bit over-developed and gets extremely crowded at weekends and public holidays, but in the evening it is almost deserted except for the chalet residents, and it is then that the wildlife appears.

From Johor Bahru there is a 45-minute bus ride from the Express bus station; from Kota Tinggi bus No. 43 goes to the falls. The chalets (☎ 07-831146; book-ings essential) are good fun if you can put up with the animal noises during the night. There is also a camp site at the falls for hardy folk; and back in town there are several low-priced hotels with facilities to match the prices. There is a snack bar at the falls which seems only to operate when the crowds are there, while in town are some good cheap seafood restaurants plus Malaysian-style fast-food places. There are also a couple of good coffee shops and a supermarket if you plan to stay at the waterfalls.

Desaru

This is a seriously overrated sandy beach with strong waves and high winds most of the time. It is 100km from Johor Bahru and has three ugly beach resorts with expensive restaurants and lots of Singaporeans hitting the nearest bit of real beach to Singapore. But don't let me put you off. Nicer but utterly deserted is **Jason's Bay** or Teluk Makhota. It stretches for mile after deserted mile of strange black sand and there are few food-stalls to interrupt the view of coconut palms and jungle. Monkeys can often be seen swinging across the road. The turn off for Jason's Bay is 13km north of Kota Tinggi on the road to Mersing. From the turnoff there is a 24km drive to the beach. Accommodation here is limited to the **Jason's Bay Beach Resort** (☎ 07-818077).

Mount Ophir

On the road to Melaka is Mount Ophir, or Gunung Ledang (1278m), the highest mountain in Johor state, and closer to Melaka than Johor Bahru. It is a popular walking spot, with a series of waterfalls and pools for swimming, much nicer and more natural than the falls at Kota Tinggi (see above). From the waterfalls a trail goes to the top of the hill. Care should be taken not to wander away from the marked trails; people have got seriously lost on Mount Ophir.

From Johor you should take a bus to Muar, then continue on the bus to Segamat, getting off at the 40km marker. The waterfalls are signposted Air Terjun. From the road a 1km walk through oil palm plantations brings you to the first waterfall. The series of falls and pools is well visited (and littered). At the falls are lots of food-stalls and craft stalls while beyond it the litter and mess gradually gives way to real countryside. A major resort is planned for the area so all the natural beauty may soon disappear. There is no accommodation at the moment although many people camp here.

Kukup

This is a tiny fishing village which has become very popular with Singaporeans for its seafood restaurants which are built up on stilts over the water. It is about 40km southwest of Johor Bahru and is visited at weekends by hordes of hungry people on day trips.

Into the Interior

This chapter covers **Taman Negara**, Malaysia's magnificent National Park, and the inland route between Kuala Lumpur and the northeast of the country. Taman Negara is very much a destination in itself but it could be combined with a drive to the northeast from Kuala Lumpur by leaving your transport at Kuala Tembeling, 18km north of Jerantut, before you set off for Taman Negara. The other way to travel the inland route is by taking the train on what is called the **jungle railway** line. Road and rail details are given below.

Taman Negara

Over 4000 square kilometres of primeval rainforest in an area covered by jungle for some 130 million years, and untouched by the loggers that have wrought such destruction in East Malaysia, Taman Negara is as well-protected by statute as is possible in Malaysia. It is the National Park of Malaysia, and one of the great natural wonders of the world. As the world's remaining rainforests are being systematically plundered it becomes more precious as every year passes. It may be overdramatic to say 'see it while it lasts', but peninsular Malaysia alone pulls down over 200,000 hectares of jungle every year and there have been 'development plans' which would involve serious incursions into Taman Negara.

The origins of the nature park lay, ironically, with those who wanted to hunt its wild animals. In 1925, over 1300 square kilometres of tropical jungle was designated as a game reserve. In 1938, it became the **King George V National Park**; after independence it was named simply Taman Negara (National Park) and enlarged in size. A new and controversial chapter in its history began in 1991 with the decision to privatise the accommodation sector. Since then there have been substantial changes and today's visitor could be forgiven for thinking that the private company runs the entire National Park. Taman Negara Resort, part of the international SMI hotel chain, has aggressively promoted its ability to offer creature comforts in the depths of the jungle and the result is a mixed blessing, to say the least. Within a very short space of time, the environmental impact of attracting thousands of tourists to one resort has begun to be noticed. Erosion is taking place on some of the more popular trails, and the nature of Taman Negara is also in danger of being affected.

For the time being, Taman Negara remains the premier attraction of West Malaysia. A visit is highly recommended for the memorable experience of being in a tropical rainforest. Do not come in the expectation of seeing exotic or endangered species of animals—Taman Negara is not like the nature parks of India or Nepal. On the other hand, you will not be disappointed by what the rainforest has to offer. The sheer authenticity of the jungle, its size, natural sights and sounds, is something that you are unlikely to forget.

■ Practical information

When to go and what to bring

The best time to visit the park is between March and October, although the park is now open all year round. Between November and February the high water level means that some of the boat trips and trails are impractical.

Bring with you a good pair of walking shoes or comfortable gym shoes and plenty of insect repellent. Long trousers are best tucked into climbing socks; if wearing shorts spray footwear and socks with insect repellent to keep away the leeches. You will sweat a great deal in the jungle—temperatures rise to 35°C during the day and are about 20°C at night—so bring enough loose-fitting and lightweight cotton clothes for at least one change each day of your stay. Your camera will need a fast film, 400 if possible, and a flash will be useful. Binoculars are worth bringing, as is a small first-aid kit.

There are no kitchen facilities in the park but it is advisable to bring food with you. There are restaurants and a small shop at the park headquarters but the range in both places can be limited. A day out in the jungle is more enjoyable with a decent picnic and it is worth bringing a small Gaz burner and some plastic crockery. Packed lunches are available from the restaurants but these tend to be fairly monotonous in content. Bring your tea and coffee bags—your flask will be filled with hot water at the cafeteria.

If you are planning to spend a night or two in a jungle hide, there are other items worth bringing: a powerful torch, candles and matches, mosquito coils, and perhaps something to read. If you are planning one of the longer treks that involve camping, you will need a lightweight tent, a compass and water-purifying tablets. In theory, most of this equipment is available for hire at park headquarters but it is best to bring your own. If you are staying in a hide overnight, all food needs to be secure because rats will rummage around for anything they can find.

Tourist information

The park is spread across the states of Pahang, Terengganu and Kelantan. The **park headquarters** are at the Taman Negara Resort at Kuala Tahan in Pahang, where the rivers Tahan and Tembeling meet, and this is where visitors first arrive after entering the park. The park headquarters are part of a complex of small buildings: restaurant, cafeteria, library, hostel, chalets and shops selling a limited range of tinned food and some equipment such as batteries, toiletries and camping equipment for hire. Directly opposite the Resort, on the other side of the Tembeling river, there is a small village where there are a couple of small shops, cafés and two lodges with limited accommodation. Apart from campsites, there is accommodation at **Nusa Camp**, which is about 15 minutes up the river, a more expensive lodge at **Kuala Trenggan**, which is another 15 minutes up the same river, and further up the river again there is **Keniam Lodge**. If you plan to stay in a hide, make sure that you book one as soon as you arrive. There is a charge of around RM7 per night.

A fishing licence costs RM10, a camera licence RM5 and the park permit is RM1 per person. These charges are paid at park headquarters in Kuala Tahan.

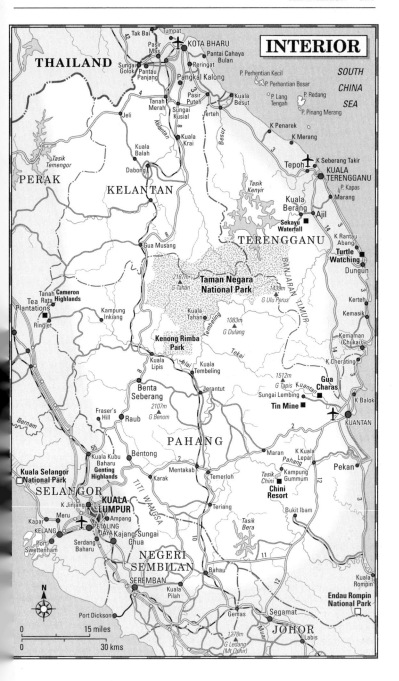

INTERIOR

THAILAND

Tak Bai
Tumpat
KOTA BHARU
Pasir
Mas
Pantai Cahaya
Bulan
Sungai
Golok
Pantau
Panjang
Reringat
Pangkal Kalong
P. Perhentian Kecil
P. Perhentian Besar

SOUTH

CHINA

SEA

Pasir
Puteh
Kuala
Besut
P. Lang
Tengah
P. Redang
Tanah
Merah
Sungai
Kusial
Jerteh
P. Pinang Merang
Jeli
K Penarek
K Merang
Kuala
Krai
Besut
Kuala
Balah
3
Tepoh
K Seberang Takir
KUALA
TERENGGANU
Dabong
P. Kapas
PERAK
Tasik
Temengor
KELANTAN
Tasik
Kenyir
Kuala
Berang
Marang
Ajil
Sekayu
Waterfall
Gua Musang
TERENGGANU
K Rantau
Abang
2187m
G Tahan
Taman Negara
National Park
1439m
G Ulu Perus
BANJARAN TIMUR
Turtle
Watching
Dungun
Tanah
Rata
Cameron
Highlands
Tea
Plantations
Kampung
Inkiang
Kuala
Tahan
1083m
G Dulang
Kerteh
Kemasik
Ringlet
Kenong Rimba
Park
Tekai
Kemaman
(Chukai)
Kuala
Lipis
Kuala
Tembeling
K Cherating
1512m
G Tapis
Kuantan
Gua
Charas
Benta
Seberang
Jerantut
Sungai Lembing
Tin Mine
K Balok
Bernam
Fraser's
Hill
Raub
2107m
G Benom
KUANTAN
PAHANG
Bentong
Maran
K Kuala
Lepar
Pahang
Pekan
Kuala Selangor
National Park
Kuala Kubu
Baharu
Genting
Highlands
Karak
Mentakab
Temerloh
Tasik
Chini
Kampung
Gummum
Chini
Resort
SELANGOR
KUALA
LUMPUR
K Jinjang
Kapar
Meru
Ampang
Teriang
Bukit Ibam
KELANG
PETALING
JAYA Kajang
Sungai
Chua
Tasik
Bera
Port
Swettenham
Serdang
Baharu
NEGERI
SEMBILAN
SEREMBAN
Bahau
Kuala
Rompin
Kuala
Pilah
Endau Rompin
National Park
N
Port Dickson
Gemas
Segamat
JOHOR
0   15 miles
0   30 kms
1379m
G Ledang
(Mt Ophir)
Labis

TITI
WANGSA

Getting to Taman Negara

Tour operators. See the Kuala Lumpur chapter (p 70) for details of tour operators who offer various packages to Taman Negara. If travelling on the east coast, Ping Anchorage (see p 188) in Kuala Terengganu offer two-night camping and chalet trips for RM330 and RM410 respectively, and a six-night trek for RM700.

There are no roads in Taman Negara so the choice is between a short flight by Pelangi Air, or a boat journey from the jetty at Kuala Tembeling. When arriving at the jetty at Kuala Tembeling, report to the park office before boarding the boat. From the jetty it is about a 3-hour journey (more or less according to the time of year) up 60km of the Sungai Tembeling in an eight-seater *perahu* (a wooden boat with an outboard motor). There are usually two departures a day, around 09.00 and 14.00. Accommodation should be booked in advance (see below) but the boat journey can be booked at Kuala Tembeling.

By air. There are three Pelangi Air (☎ 03-7463000) flights a week (Wednesday, Friday and Sunday) from Kuala Lumpur to an airstrip near the park headquarters. Boats will be waiting at the airstrip for the 30-minute journey to Kuala Tahan.

By train to Kuala Tembeling. From Singapore, the night train, which departs at 22.00, reaches Tembeling Halt very early the following day. From Tembeling Halt it takes half an hour to reach Kuala Tembeling, in time to catch the morning boat departure. From Kota Bharu, southbound trains depart from Wakaf Bharu at 08.10 on Wednesday, Friday and Saturday and reach Kuala Tembeling at 13.00. There is also an afternoon train that reaches Jerantut around 21.00. From Kuala Lumpur, trains leave at 08.00 and 14.45 for Gemas where there is then a long wait until 02.20 for the train coming up from Singapore. The inconvenient times make it easier to take a bus and/or taxi from Kuala Lumpur.

By bus/taxi to Kuala Tembeling. Taxis leave the Puduraya bus station in Kuala Lumpur for Temerloh or direct to Jerantut. Buses to Temerloh leave from Kuala Lumpur—be sure to leave no later than 08.00 in order to reach Kuala Tembeling in time for the afternoon boat. From Temerloh to Jerantut there are both buses and taxis. The 16km from Jerantut to Kuala Tembeling is best travelled in a taxi although a bus service is also available.

By car to Kuala Tembeling. It takes about three to four hours to drive to Jerantut from Kuala Lumpur. Take the Kuala Lumpur–Karak Highway, driving east to Mentakab and 3km after Mentakab turn left to Kuala Krau at the signposted junction. This leads to Jerantut. It is another 16km from Jerantut to Kuala Tembeling where vehicles can be left in the jetty car park.

Jerantut

Jerantut is a small town where you are likely to find yourself spending a few hours or a night en route to or from Taman Negara. There is one main street, Jalan Besar, which is five minutes away from both the bus and railway stations. The best place to stay is the comfortable **Jerantut Rest House** (☎ 09-2664488) on Jalan Benta, a 10-minute walk west of the railway station on the road to Kuala Lipis. Rooms with en suite bathrooms are RM20–49. The next best hotel is **Hotel Sri Emas** (☎ 09-2664499) on Jalan Besar, with rooms from RM20–64. Third choice would be **Hotel Jerantut** (☎ 09-2665568), also on

Jalan Besar. There is a good hawker centre with an array of food-stalls opposite the bus station, inexpensive Chinese cafés along Jalan Besar and a restaurant at the Rest House.

Getting from Taman Negara

Leaving the park involves a boat ride back down the river in the morning or after lunch. Book your place on the boat at the Resort a day or two before departure.

Catching the night train from Tembeling Halt south to Singapore can be quite an experience. The station is made up of one dilapidated shed and a concrete platform and it will be pitch black before the train arrives. As you wait, probably alone, on the platform it is difficult to believe that an international express train will really stop. I felt obliged to put my hand out as if flagging down a bus and was astonished when the train did indeed grind to a halt—a guard stepped off and politely enquired whether my destination was Singapore or not! It would be more sensible to take a bus or taxi to Jerantut and pass the evening there waiting for the train at a real station.

Accommodation

Kuala Tahan. **Taman Negara Resort** offers a range of accommodation. Top of the range are two-bedroomed bungalows with air-conditioning and kitchenettes (RM598); there are also one-room chalets with air-conditioning (RM143–200). Dormitory accommodation is available in double-deck bunkers in a hostel but without any kitchen facilities (RM35). Tents and camping equipment can be hired, or bring your own equipment for use in the campsite.

Accommodation should be booked in advance through **Taman Negara Resort** (☎ 09-2663500/2662200; fax 09-2661500), Kuala Tahan, 27000 Jerantut, Pahang. In Kuala Lumpur contact the sales office in the Istana Hotel, Lot 6, 2nd Floor, Jalan Raja Chulan (☎ 03-2455585; fax 03-2455430). The Resort is part of the international SMI Hotels & Resorts so information and reservations can also be arranged through their European office (Suite 43, Ludgate House, 107/111 Fleet Street, London EC4A 2AB; ☎ 0171-583 5212; fax 0171-936 2164) or their North American office (Suite 2100, Citicorp Center, 1 Sansome Street, San Francisco, CA 94104; ☎ 415-951-1086; fax 415-951-1087).

Nusa Camp. Accommodation at Nusa Camp cannot be booked through the Resort. Bookings are handled by MATIC (☎ 03-2423929), 109 Jalan Ampang, in Kuala Lumpur. Advance booking can also be made in Jerantut at 16 LKNP Building, New Town (☎ 09-2662369; fax 09-2664369).

Nusa Camp is a couple of kilometres further up Sungai Tembeling, a 15-minute boat trip. The accommodation is more like that offered in Kuala Tahan before privatisation. There are twin-bed chalets with en suite bathrooms that range from RM80 (Malay House), RM60 (Malay Cottage) and RM40 (Malay Chalet). These prices are all per chalet. Dormitory accommodation is RM9 per person. There is a regular boat service between Kuala Tahan and Nusa Camp.

Trenggan Lodge. At Kuala Trenggan, reached by travelling upstream on Sungai Tembeling for about an hour from Kuala Tahan, there are wooden chalets surrounded by the forest. The chalets are similar to those at Kuala Tahan, with en suite bathrooms.

Keniam Lodge. Located further up from Kuala Trenggan, two hours from

Kuala Tahan, there are more wooden chalets of the same type. Both Trenggan and Keniam lodges have their own restaurants and there is also a camping site at Keniam. The lodges should be booked in advance through the Kuala Tahan Resort, although you could also make a booking at Kuala Tahan when you arrive.

Perkai Lodge is the most remote of the lodges, in the northeast of the park. It has no facilities and no booking is required.

Restaurants

The best place to eat is the **Tahan Restaurant** at the Resort in Kuala Tahan; expect to pay about RM30 a head. Less expensive and with a less varied menu is the **Teresek Cafeteria**. The **KT Restoran**–built on a raft by the jetty—offers inexpensive and surprisingly tasty local food. Packed lunches can also be ordered here. On the other side of the river there are a number of food-stalls around the small village.

The two upriver lodges at Trenggan and Keniam both have small restaurants.

What to see and do

A minimum period of stay would be two or three nights. This would allow for an invigorating and rewarding climb up Bukit Teresek on day two. A third day could be spent enjoying a boat trip to Lata Berkoh or spending a night in one of the hides or lodges. Ideally, you should stay for at least a week. This would allow you to undertake one of the longer treks where you stay overnight in the forest. Details of the available trips and trails, as well as other activities, are given below.

The **boat journey** from Kuala Tembeling is where the adventure begins. At first there is evidence of local *kampung* life to be seen: children washing, mothers doing the laundry, working buffaloes having a day off and resting in the water up to their necks. Such scenes soon recede into the background and there is little to see except the majesty of the river and the occasional flash of colour as one of the three types of kingfisher dart across the water fleeing the sound of the boat's engine. Keep an eye on the banks for the 2m-long monitor lizard (*Varanus salvator*) which may be seen basking in the heat or stretched out along a log.

At **park headquarters**, Kuala Tahan, visitors book in when they first arrive. Be sure to collect the free map and make an advance booking for one of the river trips as soon as possible. If you are planning to stay overnight in the jungle, book accommodation in one of the jungle hides or lodges. If staying in a hide one night, you will need to have sufficient food and fuel and the necessary bed linen, and lanterns will need to be collected from park headquarters. There is a useful park guide that is worth buying. A 16mm film about Taman Negara is shown most nights around 20.00. Do not miss this and try to see it on your first or second night. It is very good and draws to a close with a rallying call to desert the park headquarters and sweat it out in the jungle—just what is needed to create the right frame of mind.

The **Park Canopy** is an elevated walkway that sways very gently some 25m above the forest floor and stretches for about 400m. It is a short walk from the Resort.

Jungle trails range from a 15-minute walk from park headquarters to a *bumbun* (a hide; see below) to the nine-day round-trip to Gunung Tahan, the highest mountain in peninsular Malaysia. Choose a trail that suits your age and

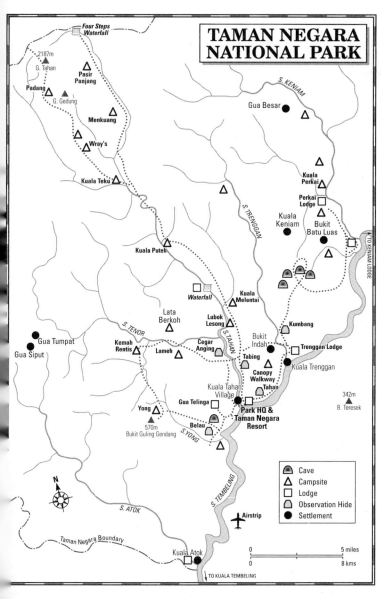

TAMAN NEGARA NATIONAL PARK

Four Steps Waterfall

2187m
G. Tahan

Pasir Panjang

Padang

G. Gedung

Menkuang

Wray's

Kuala Teku

S. KENIAM

Gua Besar

Kuala Perkai

Perkai Lodge

Kuala Keniam

Bukit Batu Luas

S. TRENGGAN

Kuala Puteh

Waterfall

Kuala Melentai

TO KENIAM LODGE

Lata Berkoh

Lubok Lesong

S. TENOR

Gua Tumpat

Gua Siput

Kemah Rentis

Lameh

Cegar Anging

S. TAHAN

Bukit Indah

Tabing

Canopy Walkway

Tahan

Kumbang

Trenggan Lodge

Kuala Trenggan

342m
B. Teresek

Yong

Gua Telinga

570m
Bukit Guling Gendang

Belau

S. YONG

Kuala Tahan Village

Park HQ & Taman Negara Resort

	Cave
	Campsite
	Lodge
	Observation Hide
	Settlement

N

S. ATOK

Taman Negara Boundary

Kuala Atok

S. TEMBELING

Airstrip

0   5 miles
0   8 kms

↓ TO KUALA TEMBELING

stamina and always set off with as much water as you can comfortably carry, plus food of course.

There are some **guided walks** organised by park officials and these can be signed up for at the main desk. They usually feature a trek to Bukit Teresek, a visit to an Orang Asli village, and a night walk through the jungle.

The **Bukit Teresek Trail** is a popular and manageable path that takes about three hours for the return journey. This can be lengthened considerably by stopping for rests and observations of wildlife, although it makes sense to head for the top of Bukit Teresek (342m) without too many breaks because it gets much hotter as the day goes on. Head off as early in the morning as possible.

The trail begins just east of park headquarters, the path is well-trodden and easy to follow and before half an hour's walking a junction is reached: left to Bukit Teresek, right to Bukit Indah. From the top of Bukit Teresek there are sweeping views of the countryside.

The **Bukit Indah Trail** takes longer than the Bukit Teresek Trail but does not involve such a steep climb. It is easy to follow and starts from the park headquarters, following the path along the riverside before heading off to the north.

Gua Telinga is a small limestone cave which is navigated by rope. Even if you decide not to enter the cave, the journey there makes for a short but enjoyable trek. From the jetty at park headquarters, take a *sampan* across the Tahan river; from this side it takes about two hours to reach the cave along a signposted route. The cave entrance looks ridiculously small and uninviting and once inside it becomes forbiddingly dark and claustrophobic. Children with a sense of adventure will enjoy crawling through the 80m cave but large adults will need to contort their bodies to negotiate the twists and turns. It is definitely not a trip for anyone who fears confined spaces or who feels squeamish about being uncomfortably close to bat guano. Inside, there are thousands of roundleaf bats, large toads, black-striped frogs and harmless whip spiders.

The **Rentis Tenor Trail** is the most manageable of the longer treks. It will take three or four days but a guide is not necessary. What is needed is an early start, a sense of adventure, plenty of stamina and careful planning in terms of food and equipment. The first day's journey involves crossing the Tahan river, following the route to Gua Telinga, and continuing for most of the day to the Yong campsite. The first day's journey is 10km. The second day could be spent making the optional ascent of Bukit Guling Gendang (570m) but this would only take about four hours and a second night would have to be spent at the same Yong campsite. Staying on the main trail, on the other hand, involves a full day's walking, either to Lameh campsite or, another 4km on, to Kemah Rentis where camping is by the side of the Tenor river. From Kemah Rentis it is a stiff 15km walk back to park headquarters, although the day's journey could be broken into two by spending a night at the Lubok Lesong campsite which is about half way.

The **Gunung Tahan Trail** is the trail for the hardy with nine days to spare for the entire trek. No special skills are required but a guide is compulsory and trekkers need to be in good physical shape. It is a hard slog, up and down countless hills, crossing rivers up to waist height, and generally pushing yourself for six to eight hours every day. The final day's climb to the top of Gunung Tahan at 2187m is definitely no mean feat. A lightweight sleeping bag—a tracksuit at a pinch—is needed for the two nights spent at an altitude where the nights are uncomfortably cold. Needless to say, by the time you return triumphantly to park headquarters, you are feeling utterly exhausted but on top of the world and justifiably proud. A number of attempted ascents ended in fatal accidents until 1905 when four Malays reached the summit as part of a British expedition.

If you are determined to complete this walk, make the necessary arrangements for a guide, plus any equipment you wish to hire, from the park headquarters before you arrive. A guide will cost RM500 for the nine days. Individuals or couples may telephone a few days before arrival to enquire about organised trips. If space is available it is obviously cheaper to join a group and share the cost of a guide.

Boat trips are terrific fun and cut down considerably on the physical demands of a long trek through the jungle. **Lata Berkoh**, for instance, a natural swimming area formed by huge rocks in the water, would take around four hours to reach on foot but only one hour by boat. Whatever the mode of travel, and you could walk there and arrange for a boat trip back, Lata Berkoh makes a delightful destination for a day's excursion. Once there, you can swim safely, fish (rods can be hired at park headquarters), or just relax by the water watching the butterflies and spotting birds.

Another recommended journey by boat is the 45-minute trip upstream on the Sungai Tembeling to Kuala Trenggan. From here it takes about 90 minutes on foot to reach a **visitor's hide**, from where you can rest and watch birds or stay the night and return the next morning. If the river is not too shallow, the return boat ride is especially good fun due to the numerous rapids.

Boats and accompanying boatmen are booked at the Resort office. Sometimes the popular routes are over-subscribed so make a booking as soon as possible after your arrival. There is nothing to prevent visitors negotiating directly with the boatmen at the jetty. Expect to pay about RM100 for a boat for two people for the whole day.

A **night out in the jungle** is highly recommended if time or stamina cuts out the possibility of one of the longer treks that involve overnight stays. Book a four-seater boat that will take you close to one of the lodges or hides and return you to park headquarters the next morning. The boatmen will probably stay the night somewhere nearby. Take food, matches, candles and a torch; as dark settles in, light a small camp fire and settle down to watch the dancing fireflies and listen to the jungle's amazing symphony of sounds. It is quite an experience to sit in the middle of the oldest primary rainforest in the world, surrounded by the blackness of night and feeling utterly insignificant. Try to wake up early the next morning: you will be amazed by the cacophony of noise that signals another day in the jungle.

Hides (bumbuns) have been built in a number of locations, overlooking a salt lick with the surrounding ground cleared away to facilitate the viewing of wildlife. Animals visit these sites to obtain essential body salts by licking up the water. If you are staying overnight you will need to bring a sleeping bag or tracksuit, or just sheets, which are available from park headquarters, and food and drinks. A strong torch is essential. Book your place in a hide at the park headquarters. The general idea is that those staying in a hide work out a rota for keeping watch through the night (or part of it), scanning the area with a torch every ten minutes or so. Do not come to a hide expecting to see a herd of wild elephants drop by. A group of monkeys is the best you are likely to see, a tapir or wild boar if really lucky, but anything you do observe becomes fascinating—infinitely more so than seeing them in a zoo. There are six hides to choose from:

Bumbun Tahan is the nearest to the park headquarters and can be walked there and back in 15 minutes. **Bumbun Tabing** takes about one hour to reach and has eight beds and a toilet. **Bumbun Cegar Anging** is a little to the south of Bumbun Tabing but on the other side of the river and takes about two hours to reach from Kuala Tahan. Usually the river can be waded across but if the water level is high due to rain the only way to reach the hide is by boat. **Bumbun Belau** and **Bumbun Yong** are southwest of Kuala Tahan and the first one, requiring a walk of about 1.5 hours, takes in Gua Telinga (see above). Bumbun Yong is another hour's walk from Bumbun Belau.

Trenggan and **Keniam Lodges** are the perfect bases for those who want to be away from most other visitors and explore the less-travelled parts of the forest. Trenggan Lodge is 12km from the park headquarters and Keniam Lodge another 8km up the Tembeling River. Keniam Lodge is a particularly good base because from it you could trek for a couple of hours to Peraki Lodge (no facilities or food here) for the bird- and monkey-spotting along the way. You could also undertake a 13km trek from Keniam Lodge down to Trenggan Lodge, either returning to park headquarters by boat or taking another day to trek there on foot.

Flora and fauna

The characteristic feature of the lowland forest, through which most of the trails lead, are the big, solid hardwood trees. The most common species are meranti (*Shorea spp*) and keruing (*Dipterocarpus spp*). They can be recognised by their size, the thick lianas (climbing plants) which curl around their trunks and the epiphytes (a plant that grows on another but which is not parasitic) they provide a home for. The tallest tree in Southeast Asia, the tualang (*Koompassia excelsa*), can also be found sharing the same territory. To help identify them in the forest, look at the two that are used to support the Resort's canopy. At higher altitudes in the park, clearly observed when ascending Gunung Tahan, oak and indigenous conifers are more common.

Taman Negara supports over 150 elephants, tigers, leopards, tapirs and sun bears—although these are rarely seen by visitors. More common is the barking deer, and the small groups of sambar which often come to the restaurant area. Flying foxes are frequently seen when walking, monitor lizards regularly raid the rubbish pits, macaques travel around noisily in bands and cobras and pythons are a regular sight.

Bird-watching can be rewarding even in the vicinity of park headquarters, while along the rivers kingfishers and the lesser fish eagle may be seen. Bulbuls, pittas and trogons are well represented. Between September and March there are large numbers of migrant species. Unmissable when they fly overhead honking are the huge hornbills.

From Kuala Lumpur to the northeast

Information on the road and rail routes between Kuala Lumpur and the northeast are given below. There are few places of conventional tourist interest along the way; the main appeal of travelling this route, whatever the mode of transport, is simply that of passing through areas of peninsular Malaysia which relatively few tourists see. If time is at a premium there are more efficient ways to travel between the west and east coasts, but if you want to observe rural Malaysia at a leisurely pace, there is no better way.

Travelling to and from the northeast
By train. The railway line runs from Gemas (168km southeast of Kuala Lumpur) to Kota Bharu. But it makes little sense to travel south from Kuala Lumpur to Gemas in order to catch another train going north. Instead, take one of the regular early morning buses from the Puduraya station in Kuala Lumpur to Mentakab, where the jungle railway crosses the Kuala Lumpur–Kuantan road. The train from Gemas to the northeast reaches Mentakab around 14.00.

By car. There are two routes from Kuala Lumpur: one via Fraser's Hill and the other via the Genting Highlands. For the first route, take the highway north from Kuala Lumpur, turning off at Kuala Kubu Bharu for Fraser's Hill and continuing past Raub to Kuala Lipis. The second route follows Route 2 to the Genting Highlands, then north at Bentong on Route 8 to Raub and on to Kuala Lipis. The journey from Kuala Lumpur to Kuala Lipis is 171km.

From Kuala Lipis Route 8 heads north to Gua Musang, following the railway most of the way, to Kota Bharu. This is a journey of 303km.

Kuala Lipis

Kuala Lipis is a sleepy little town of 5000 souls, slumbering on a bend of the Jelai river and surrounded on all sides by hills, forests and plantations. Its main purpose as a tourist destination is its proximity to the **Kenong Rimba Park**, but the evocative colonial buildings—most of which have maintained their original functions in one way or another—are a good reason for paying a visit to the town. It also has an interesting museum cum resthouse, and the Friday night markets at the bus station can be pretty lively.

History
In the late 19C, when the lure of tin brought the British and the Chinese to Perak and Kuala Lumpur, the unknown state of Pahang was rumoured to be an El Dorado, with even greater deposits of tin and gold. Before the British moved in, the small settlement of Kuala Lipis was only of interest to a few local Chinese merchants who traded with Orang Asli groups from the jungle interior. There was no road and the river was the only mode of transport.

After the successful establishment of Kuala Lumpur, the British thought Pahang would bring them even greater riches, and as Kuala Lipis was the only known trading centre in the region it was chosen as the logical centre for colonial rule. Since 1887, the sultan had been Wan Ahmad; as he had already given mining concessions to other foreign powers, the British did not waste any more time. They brought their customary pressure to bear and forced him to sign a treaty whereby, in 1896, Pahang became one of the four **Federated Malay States**. The British already had a presence in Kuala Lipis but it now became the state capital. It was not until the late 1920s, after geological research, that the El Dorado myth finally evaporated.

Tourist information

The **railway station** and **bus station** face the river with most of the places of interest directly behind them. The small **tourist office** (☎ 09-3121341) is at the roundabout 200m from the railway station. To get there, turn right outside the station onto Jalan Besar, past the post office, and bear right at the clock tower. It is open daily from 09.00 to noon and from 14.00 to 19.00.

Accommodation and restaurants

The obvious choice for accommodation should be the **Government Rest House** (☎ 09-3121562), on Jalan Bukit Resident, with 14 rooms from RM35–50. It takes over 20 minutes to walk there from the railway or bus station. Jalan Resident begins at the roundabout where the tourist office is. **Hotel Jerai** (☎ 09-3121562) is on Jalan Jelai, the riverfront road directly north of the railway station, with rooms from RM20–36. The rooms are basic but clean.

There is little choice when it comes to a meal. Try the **Rest House** or the **Pahang Club** (see below) or, at a pinch, the restaurant at the **Gin Loke** hotel at 64 Jalan Besar (between the bus station and railway station).

Colonial buildings

The **Government Rest House**, on Jalan Bukit Resident, was built by Hugh Clifford, the first Resident in the state, as his official residence. It is still a place of residence for government officials, and although they have priority in booking accommodation, other visitors are unlikely to find the place full. The place also functions as a useful little **museum** with a miscellaneous collection of odds and ends relating to the town's history.

Most of the other colonial buildings are also connected with Hugh Clifford. The **Pahang Club**, up the road from the hospital which is close to the tourist information centre, was built as a social club for the British. It still is a club, albeit less exclusive, with a restaurant and bar that are well worth visiting. The billiard room has its original Edwardian billiard table.

It is difficult to miss the **Clifford School**, which is immediately south of the Pahang Club. Look for a large grey roof over buildings painted deep red and fronted by a magnificent verandah. It remains the kind of institution it was originally built for in 1913: a multi-racial private school for the élite.

Kenong Rimba Park

The park covers an area of 128 square kilometres and is located to the south and west of Taman Negara. It has many of the natural attractions of Taman Negara but the visitor infrastructure is not so well developed; if travelling there independently, the dearth of places to eat is a disadvantage. There is only one café at the park headquarters, which serves basic meals. Independent visitors also need to obtain a permit and book accommodation through the park head-quarters or from the Government Office (☎ 09-3121273/3124106) in Kuala Lipis. On arrival visitors must report to the park ranger, and may only enter the park when accompanied by a local registered guide.

Getting to the park can also be a problem because the 20-minute boat ride from Kuala Lipis only runs regularly on a Saturday at 14.00; on other days, the *sampan* will need to be chartered. For all these reasons it is advisable to take one of the three-day tours which are available through the tourist office, the Gin Loke hotel (☎ 09-311654) in Kuala Lipis, or KTM (☎ 03-2747435).

The principal activities in the park are jungle walks and a short walk to the **Gua Batu Tinggi**, a limestone cave which is interesting because of the orchids that grow inside. There are other larger caves which can also be visited.

Sabah

Sabah, formerly known as British North Borneo, occupies the northeast corner of the island of Borneo, between 4° and 7° north of the equator. It acquired its title of 'The Land Below the Wind' because it manages to escape the typhoons that strike to the north and south.

Sabah is about the size of Ireland and boasts some tremendous natural environments. Its centrepiece is **Mount Kinabalu**, at 4100m the highest mountain in Southeast Asia but accessible to any reasonably fit person. Near the town of **Sandakan** there is an orang-utan settlement and offshore, close to the Philippines, a tiny island where endangered turtles come to lay their eggs— guarded by Malaysian soldiers with M-16 machine-guns. To the south of Sandakan, along the **Kinabatangan river**, the rare proboscis monkey can be seen down by the water's edge most evenings. The capital, **Kota Kinabalu**, where most visitors first arrive, is little more than a mess of concrete but has the benefit of nearby islands that make up **Tunku Abdul Rahman Park**.

The air fares mentioned in this section are all single fares.

History

There is archaeological evidence that **prehistoric cave-dwellers** (20,000 BC) inhabited what is now eastern Sabah, but the first historical records date from the 8C and are Chinese accounts of trading for swiftlets' nests, a rare delicacy believed to have a medicinal value and used in bird's nest soup, as well as camphor wood, pepper and timber. The following centuries, when the region was part of Brunei's domain, are largely lost to time: in 1521 **Magellan** sailed along the northern coast of Sabah. By the early 18C Brunei's control was beginning to wane, and the sultan had to call in help from his neighbours to put down a rebellion against increased taxes in the area; in 1763 a trading post was established on behalf of the British East India Company but failed to develop and closed down quickly.

In 1846 the British made a deal with the **Sultan of Brunei** whereby they acquired the island of Labuan. They were motivated partly by concern over the growing influence in the region of James Brooke, Raja of Sarawak (see also p 267), and partly to counter the potential threat to British aspirations in the region posed by the trade agreement made the previous year between the US Navy and the Sultan of Brunei. British fears about America's intentions proved unfounded.

In 1860 **Claude Lee Moses** became American Consul-General in Brunei. He was less interested in American influence in the area and more interested in making a personal fortune. He persuaded the Sultan of Brunei to cede him land which he then sold to Hong Kong-based American businessmen who wanted to set up trading links. They formed the American Trading Company of Borneo and established grand houses around Kimanis. The venture collapsed six years after it had begun.

The American cession was taken up in 1878 by a joint venture organised by **Baron Gustav von Overbeck**, the Austrian consul to Hong Kong, and **Alfred Dent**, a wealthy English businessman based in Hong Kong. They arranged a deal with the Sultan of Brunei in which they would take over the

American venture with additional land, extending the cession to include most of modern Sabah, in exchange for 15,000 Straits dollars. However, the Sultan of Sulu (a province of the Philippines) also claimed the region. He was bought out for an annuity of 500 Straits dollars. Dent later bought out von Overbeck, and in 1880 the British North Borneo Chartered Company was formed.

The company made money from rubber and tobacco before moving into timber and making its capital in Sandakan (the head office was in London). It also made money by raising taxes and this caused one of the very few revolts against the British in this part of the world.

The administration of the region, roughly equivalent to modern-day Sabah was carried out by a very small number of largely inexperienced, young men. By their own admission they treated local people like children. That treatment included the levying of taxes on nearly all forms of trade on the island—on fishing, rice cultivation, sales of birds' nests, local alcohol production and land ownership—as well as a poll tax.

In opposition to the loss of their lands and the taxes imposed on them a local rebellion emerged, led by the legendary figure of **Mat Salleh**. He was the son of a Sulu chief who led a successful guerrilla campaign against the British administration for six years. His first major assault came in 1897, when his followers attacked and burnt the British headquarters on Pulau Gaya, close to modern-day Kota Kinabalu. Mat Salleh was declared an outlaw and a bounty of 700 Straits dollars was put on his head. His reputation as a guerrilla leader grew as he evaded the best efforts of the Governor to track him down until he was believed to have magical powers, seeming to be able to call down lightning and speak in flames. Eventually the managing director of the North Borneo Chartered Company struck a deal with Mat Salleh. He was to settle his people in Tambunan and would not be bothered by the British. The deal was immediately reneged on by the British authorities and Mat Salleh's fort in Tambunan was attacked by British forces who were driven back, unable to penetrate the fort's defences.

At the end of 1899, the British government joined forces to launch a more sustained attack; after nearly two weeks of shelling in January 1900 the end was only a matter of time. On the last day of January, Mat Salleh was killed by a stray bullet. The company recovered from the revolt (and a subsequent one which reached its zenith in 1915) and made tidy profits for the next half century. For almost 30 years British North Borneo quietly went about its business administered by 50 or so British men, producing rubber, tobacco and timber.

On the first day of 1942, the Japanese army landed on Labuan and before the end of the month Sandakan had been taken. By the end of the war both Sandakan and Jesselton (see p 240) had been virtually destroyed and thousands of Allied soldiers (many sent there as prisoners from Singapore) had died at the hands of the Japanese. The worst of many atrocities was the 1944 Death March when 2400 prisoners of war were forced to march from Sandakan, where they had built an airstrip, to Ranau: only six Australians survived the ordeal. No other single event claimed so many Australian lives during the Second World War.

Fierce resistance to the Japanese in Sabah came from the Chinese and others, under the leadership of Albert Kwok Hing Nam. In October 1943, he led a successful attack on Jesselton and neighbouring towns. The Japanese retaliated from the air before retaking the towns. As a warning to others there followed a public mass execution when 175 prisoners were decapitated.

In June 1945, under the command of General MacArthur, Australian troops captured Labuan in June 1945. There followed a heavy bombardment of Jesselton and Sandakan before the Japanese surrendered in September. Many thousands of Japanese were killed in retaliation for their atrocities.

After the war the British took over Sabah from the North Borneo Chartered Company and in 1961, following Malaysian independence, Sabah was invited by Malaysia to join the Federation (see p 44). Elections took place in 1962 and for a period of 16 days Sabah became an independent state before joining the Federation. Both the Philippines and Indonesia had justifiable claims on the territory—far more so than Malaysia in the eyes of many observers—but Sabah and the government in Kuala Lumpur have had a mutual interest in preserving the alliance. In recent years Sabah's anomalous position has come to the surface again. In 1985 a Christian party (Parti Bersatu Sabah) won local political power. This strained relations with the Muslim government in Kuala Lumpur and in the mid-1990s the PBS was forced out of office.

The Peoples of Sabah

There is such an incredible array of different peoples in Sabah that, when you go there, it is quite difficult to accept that Sabah is part of Malaysia. Three main ethnic groups predominate: Kadazans, Bajaus and Muruts,

Kadazans account for one in three of Sabah's population. ('Kadazan' is a generic term for a variety of people descending from a score or more tribes, each possessing its own dialect.) Although many have now migrated to the towns, traditionally they lived on the land. Originally animists, they have mostly converted to Catholicism as a result of some serious evangelising work in the 1930s.

The various tribes of the Kadazan, living mostly around the west coast of Sabah, are called after their tribal place names. Like most Sabahans, they once lived in longhouses—long wooden buildings built on stilts, housing a hundred or more families—but such communities are now rare, most Kadazan living in *kampung*-type settlements. In the 19C the Kadazans were fierce warriors, head hunting and armed with blow pipes, but in recent years they have become pastoralists, selling their produce at local markets or wayside stalls.

Many Kadazan still take part in the annual Harvest Festival where priestesses, speaking the ancient language of the Kadazan, perform rites to ward off the evil spirits and make up an offering to the spirit of the rice. The festival also involves buffalo races, and wrestling matches, as well as a beauty pageant whose participants wear the traditional black velvet skirt and top with headgear and belts made of silver coins.

Bajaus came originally from the Philippines during the 18C and 19C. They are Muslims, live along the northern coastal regions, and constitute the second largest ethnic and cultural group in Sabah. They originate from the Philippines

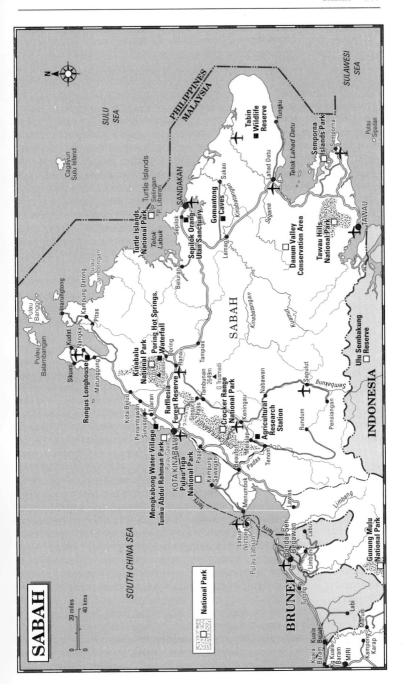

and were traditionally pirates and are still considered excellent horsemen. It was from this fierce tribe that Mat Salleh (see p 237), the leader of the rebel forces at the turn of the century, emerged. They build *attap* houses on mangrove trunk stilts over the water, connected by rough walkways. Today, fibreglass speedboats with outboard motors are moored alongside their houses.

Muruts, like the Kadazans, are an agricultural people with possible ethnic connections to groups in Sarawak, Indonesia and the Philippines. There are various sub-groups, each with its own dialect, and different religions—Christianity and Islam—cut across these tribal divisions.

Many rural Murut still live in longhouses; those that live in lowland areas are wet rice farmers, while those in the higher regions pursue a slash and burn type of farming. Rice and tapioca form an important part of the Muruts' diet, the tapioca being harvested from the wild. The huge-trunked cassava trees, from which the tapioca is obtained, take several days to fell and harvest. The Muruts were the last tribe in Sabah to abandon head hunting.

Some 20 per cent of the population is **Chinese**. They first came to Sabah towards the end of the 19C, in response to the North Borneo Chartered Company's need for additional labour. The early immigrants were mostly Hakka; they were joined in the 20C by a Cantonese community from Hong Kong and some other smaller dialect groups.

The number of **Filipinos** legally residing in Sabah is very small and bears no relation to the number of illegal immigrants. There could be as many as one million, no one knows for sure. They began to arrive in the 1950s when the timber industry needed their labour; their numbers swelled in the 1970s after the eruption of fighting in Mindanao in the Philippines. Today, they live mostly along the east coast and there is also a sizeable community around Kota Kinabalu, especially on the offshore islands. Many Filipinos were born in Sabah and it now seems politically unrealistic that they will ever be forced to leave.

Kota Kinabalu

KK, as it affectionately known by those who live here, is a pretty but bland modern city, due no doubt to the fact that it was razed during the Second World War. But it is worth spending a day or two here—and a visit is essential if you intend to climb Mount Kinabalu. A most interesting couple of days can be spent in the Tunku Abdul Rahman Park, a brief but dizzying boat ride from the city, while the State Museum and Art Gallery and State Mosque are close together and well worth a visit.

History

The North Borneo Chartered Company chose the offshore island of Pulau Gaya as the site of their first headquarters, but these were burned down in 1897 during the revolt led by Mat Salleh (see p 237). New headquarters were built on the mainland close to the island, near a *kampung* called Api Api (Fire Fire). The name referred to the frequency with which the *kampung* was set ablaze by roaming pirates, but it was hardly a suitable name for the company after what had happened on Pulau Gaya. In the early years of the 20C it was renamed **Jesselton**, after Sir Charles Jessel, the then vice-chairman of the company, but although it prospered the capital remained

at Sandakan. At the outbreak of the First World War, there were 11
European company officers residing in the town.

As a result of the Japanese Occupation (1942–45), the Allies were keen
to destroy the town's harbour and sustained bombing from the air resulted
in the town's destruction. The present tourist office is one of only three
buildings that survived the bombardment. In 1967 the rebuilt town was
named Kota Kinabalu (Kinabalu City), usually shortened to KK, and more
recently massive land reclamation projects have resulted in modern
commercial buildings fronting the sea.

Practical information

Getting to and from Kota Kinabalu
By air. The airport (☎ 088-203301) is 8km out of town. To take a taxi from the
airport, purchase a RM12 coupon from the taxi desk on the concourse outside
the airport.

There are non-stop flights to Kuala Lumpur (RM437) and Johor Bahru
(RM347) in peninsular Malaysia; to Kuching (RM228), Miri (RM104) and Sibu
(RM180) in Sarawak; Sandakan (RM83), Labuan, Tawau and Lahad Datu
within Sabah; and international flights to Manila, Hong Kong, Singapore, Taipei
and Tokyo-Narita.

The **MAS** office (☎ 088-213555) is in the Karamunsing Complex, a little way
out of town past the Hotel Shangri-La and near the Berjaya Palace. **Discovery
Tours** (see below, under Tour operators) can reissue tickets for a small charge.

By train. The railway station (☎ 088-262536/254611) is near the airport,
5km south of town at Tanjung Aru. A daily service to Beaufort and Tenom
departs at 10.00, with a faster train leaving at 16.05 only on Sunday (Railcar).
Parts of the route offer spectacular views but the buses are faster.

By bus. The long-distance bus station, for places such as Kinabalu Park and
Sandakan, is east of Jalan Padang along the side of the road. Destinations are
clearly marked on the mini-buses but check the time of departure as they do not
leave until full. Most leave before 11.00 and tickets cannot be bought in
advance. The single bus fare to Sandakan is RM25 and this route passes
Kinabalu Park. Buses to closer locations, such as Penampang, leave from behind
the post office, on Jalan Tun Fuad Stephens.

By taxi. Expect to pay about RM120, one way, for a taxi to Kinabalu Park,
RM160 to Poring Hot Springs, RM100 to the Rafflesia Centre.

Getting around Kota Kinabalu
By taxi. Unmetered taxis are inexpensive. Expect to pay around RM7 to the
museum or any other location around town (RM5 to locals), RM10 to Tanjung
Aru. There are always taxis outside the Hyatt, the Hotel Capital and Centre
Point.

Car hire is available at the airport, through the larger hotels, or **Adaras** (☎
088-216671) on the ground floor of Wisma Sabah. A saloon car is around
RM190 a day but a Toyota four-wheel land cruiser at RM450 a day is more
useful for Sabah's roads.

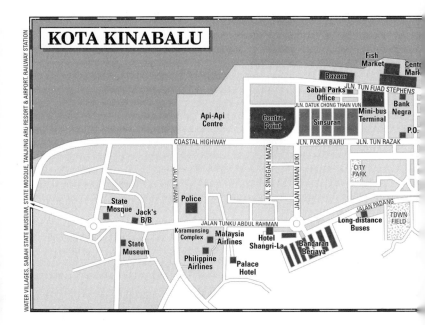

Tourist information

There is a **tourist office** at the airport (☎ 088-223767), open from 09.00 to 17.00 Monday to Friday, 09.00 to 14.00 on Saturday and Sunday. **Sabah Tourism** (☎ 088-218620) has an office at 51 Jalan Gaya in an historic building. (It started life in 1916 as a printing office, became a post office in 1936 and in 1945 (see History, above) was one of only three buildings in the town left standing.) **Tourism Malaysia** (☎ 088-211732) has an office in the Wing On Life Building on Jalan Sagunting, open 08.00–12.45 and 14.00–16.15 Monday to Friday, Saturday morning only, 08.30–12.45.

Banks are open from 09.30 to 15.30 Monday to Friday, 09.30 to noon on Saturday. There is a bank next to the Sabah Parks Office, though a slightly better rate can be obtained from moneychangers on the ground floor of Centre Point and Wisma Merdeka. The main **post office** is in the centre of town on Jalan Tun Razak. Most phone boxes use Uniphone cards but some require Telekom cards.

The **Sabah Parks Office** (☎ 088-211881/212719; fax 088-211585/221001) is in Block K of the Sinsuran Shopping Complex on Jalan Tun Fuad Stephens. This is where accommodation is reserved for Kinabalu Park and Tunku Abdul Rahman Park. It is open Monday to Thursday 08.30 to 12.00 and 14.00 to 16.00, Friday 08.30 to 11.30 and 14.00 to 16.00, and Saturday 08.30 to 12.00.

Immigration

The Immigration Office (☎ 088-216711) is on the 4th Floor, Wisma Dang Bandang, Jalan Hj Yaakob. It is open from 08.00 to 12.30 and 14.00 to 16.15 Monday to Friday, and from 08.00 to 12.45 on Saturday.

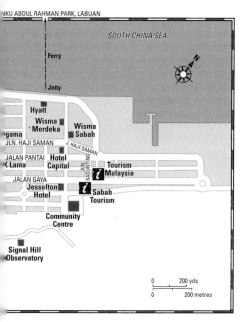

NKU ABDUL RAHMAN PARK, LABUAN

SOUTH CHINA SEA

Ferry

Jetty

Hyatt

Wisma
Merdeka

gama

Wisma
Sabah

JLN. HAJI SAMAN

J. HAJI SAMAN

JALAN PANTAI
Lama

Hotel
Capital

Tourism
Malaysia

JALAN GAYA

Jesselton
Hotel

i Sabah
Tourism

Community
Centre

Signal Hill
Observatory

JLN SAGUNTING

| 0 | 200 yds |
| 0 | 200 metres |

Emergencies

In an emergency, ☎ 999. The Queen Elizabeth Hospital (☎ 088-218166) is outside town, beyond the Sabah State Museum, on Jalan Penampang.

Tour operators

There are a number of tour operators and it is worth comparing their prices. **Transborneo** (☎ 088-247876) does city tours and Kinabalu Park. **Discovery Tours** (☎ 088-221244) in Wisma Sabah is a reliable company covering Kinabalu Park and the Sandakan area. **Borneo Eco** (☎ 234009), 2nd floor, Shoplot 12A, Lorong Bernam 3, Taman Soon Khiong Luyang, covers nearly every wildlife location in Sabah—islands, jungles, mountains, rivers. (A two-day/one-night package to Kinabatangan river will cost RM245.) **Borneo Wildlife Adventure** (☎ 088-213668), at Lot 4 Block L Sinsuran Complex, also specialises in ecological trips, including bird-watching and nature walks. **Coral Island Cruises** (☎ 088-223490),10th floor, Wisma Merdeka, organises trips to the offshore islands.

Accommodation

The **Hyatt** (☎ 088-221234; fax 088-218909), on Jalan Datuk Salleh Sulong, has the best location in town, with rooms from RM230. The elegant **Jesselton** (☎ 088-223333; fax 088-240401), 69 Jalan Gaya, looks very colonial and is the oldest hotel in town (1954). A standard double is RM196, a superior RM280. The **Berjaya Palace** (☎ 088-211911; fax 088-211600) is a 20-minute walk from the town centre but there is a free shuttle bus. Rooms are around RM200 and include breakfast. The other top-class hotel is the **Tanjung Aru Resort** (☎ 088-225800; fax 088-216585) on the beach near the airport, with doubles starting at around RM400.

A good middle-range place is **Hotel Capital** (☎ 088-231999) at 23 Jalan Haji Saman. Doubles are RM110 and large de luxe rooms are RM143. **Hotel Shangri-La** (☎ 088-212800; fax 088-212078), at 75 Bandara Berjaya, has doubles from RM200. The **Mandarin** (☎ 088-225222), 138 Jalan Gaya, is fine for a short stay with doubles for around RM100 and conveniently close to the long-distance bus station.

Budget rooms are available at **Jack's B&B** (☎ 088-232367) for RM18, including breakfast, but it is a 20-minute walk from the town centre at No. 17, Block B, Jalan Karamunsing.

Restaurants

At the Hotel Shangri-La a buffet breakfast is RM17, lunch RM25 and dinner RM25. The evening buffets at the **Tivoli House** here (RM25) have a different food theme each night. At the Hyatt the **Tangoing Ira** coffee house is open 24 hours for Asian and Western meals. Also here is the **Phoenix Court** Chinese restaurant and the **Semporna Grill** for steaks. The best Malay food in town, and reasonably priced, is at the **Sri Capital Restaurant** in the Hotel Capital on Jalan Haji Saman. The **Gardenia** at the Jesselton has a Western set lunch for RM20 and the afternoon tea makes a pleasant escape from the heat. The **Yesterday Café** at the Berjaya Palace has a buffet lunch for RM15 and Western and local dinners for RM20.

In the basement of Centre Point there are fast food places and Islamic cafés serving inexpensive Malay/Indian meals. The **Sri Latha Curry House**, at the end of Jalan Berjaya 4, tucked away behind the Hotel Shangri-La, is a good place for inexpensive vegetarian and non-vegetarian curries around RM45.

Tapai, or rice wine

Tapai, an extremely potent wine made from fermented rice, was the traditional drink of the tribes of Sabah. The Murut and Kadazan in particular were well known for their tendency to use the stuff, that is until their respective conversions to Islam and Christianity put a stop to the practice. Rice wine was made by putting down layers of boiled glutinous rice and yeast in a huge storage pot and allowing the mixture to ferment for a year or so.

When the mixture was ready the surface of the brew was covered with broad leaves and the pot filled to the top with water. Straws were put through the leaves and the mixture was drunk communally, custom dictating that drinking did not stop till all the water had filtered down into the brew. It was then refilled and the drinking started again. An even more potent brew was made by distilling the mixture.

Shopping

In Wisma Merdeka, **Borneo Crafts** is a typical place for shopping for ethnic gifts and souvenirs. There is a Yaohan department store in Centre Point for general shopping, and on the first floor of Centre Point the **Borneo Handicraft & Ceramic Shop** has a good selection of merchandise with fixed prices. Avoid the shop selling arts and crafts on the corner adjacent to the Hyatt; there are no fixed prices and they will charge what they think you might pay.

Every Sunday morning there is a flourishing **street market** that fills Jalan Gaya from about 08.00 onwards. There is a **Filipino market** near the local bus station on Jalan Tun Fuad Stephens where the occasional stall will have something interesting for sale. For **books** try the Yaohan department store in Centre Point or the one in the lobby of the Hyatt. The upstairs office of the Sabah Parks Office (see above) sells a general guide to the national parks, a specific one to Kinabalu Park (both RM8) and a book on the birds of Mount Kinabalu (RM56).

Places to see

Sabah State Museum and Art Gallery

Sabah State Museum and Art Gallery is a little out of town, on Jalan Tunku Abdul Rahmann, and it is advisable to take a taxi there. Admission is free and there is a very unappetising canteen that is best avoided. Opening hours are from 10.00 to 18.00 Monday to Thursday, and 09.00 to 18.00 on Saturday, Sunday and public holidays.

The museum is built in the style of a longhouse. The highlight of the interesting archaeology section, on the second floor, is a carved wooden coffin, found in a cave on the east coast, and richly decorated with spiral motifs. On the other side of this floor of the museum there is a collection of musical instruments: gongs, drums, *tongkungon* (a large bamboo tube with thin strips cut from its surface to form strings), *sundatang* (long-necked strummed lute), *turali* (bamboo nose flute), and *gabang* (a xylophone-like instrument). There is also a collection of rice-farming equipment. Also on this floor are *sininggazanaks*, which look a little like totem poles and are erected on the land of a man who dies without heirs.

The State Museum, Kota Kinabalu

The third floor has the usual dull collection of fading stuffed animals. The collection of ceramics—Chinese jars called *pusaka*—is far more satisfying. *Pusaka* are tribal heirlooms, traded with China in the distant past for forest products such as honey, beeswax or camphor wood. A family's status was reflected in the quality and size of its jars, which were used for storage and wine brewing, and were also associated with death rituals.

Next door is the **Art Gallery**, with a collection of works of varying quality by local artists. The attempts at modern art are not as successful as the scenes of rural and cultural life by artists such as Dickson Chin Kee Seng and Kelvin Chap Kok Leong.

In the same building as the Art Gallery there is a Geology Museum that may well have been sponsored by Shell because it is largely devoted to that company's exhibits on oil exploration.

Masjid Sabah (State Mosque)

If you are visiting the museum, it is worth taking a look at the State Mosque which is nearby and difficult not to identify. It was built in 1975 and is one of the best examples of modern Islamic architecture anywhere in Malaysia. It is the exterior that claims attention. The main structure is supported by a dozen broad columns, each topped with a small golden dome. The mosque's central dome is decorated with a hexagonal grey and golden design and the minaret is topped in gold. Visitors are allowed inside, after removing their footwear.

Water villages

One or two other places of interest in town are the water villages around the shoreline south of the city, the largest of which is **Kampung Ayer**. These villages are gradually disappearing as the shoreline is reclaimed. For an interesting view over town you might want to visit either **Signal Hill**, on the eastern edge of the city centre, or the **Sabah Foundation Building**, which at 31 storeys also has some good views. The building looks very surreal in its surroundings of open countryside, 4km out of town at Likas Bay.

The Sabah Foundation is an organisation set up in 1966 by the Federal Government to improve the quality of life of native Sabahans. It has logging rights to an area of forest and uses the funds to provide educational grants to students and various other social benefits.

Tunku Abdul Rahman Park

The Park is located on offshore islands, a short boat ride northwest of Kota Kinabalu. It is made up of five islands—Gaya, Mamutik, Manukan, Sapi and Sulug—all a short distance from the jetty behind the Hyatt. **Pulau Gaya** is the largest and has a number of walking trails that criss-cross the island. The beaches are safe for swimming, and snorkelling quite close to the shore can be rewarding.

Pulau Sapi (Cow Island) is smaller, only 10ha in size, but with equally stunning beaches for swimming and snorkelling. **Pulau Manukan** has the park headquarters and tourist facilities and is best avoided at weekends and public holidays. **Pulau Mamutik** is nearby and has perfect beaches. **Pulau Sulung** is the least accessible and the quietest of the islands.

Undisturbed forest

Pulau Gaya is one of the few places in Sabah still to retain its coastal dipterocarp forest. Look for the distinguishing orange bark of the *Tristania* tree and the tall *Dipterocarpus grandiflorus*, crowned with large stiff leaves, that can be seen close to the beach near the jetty. The coral life around all of the islands is superb. Brain corals, lettuce and cauliflower corals with crinkly formations that give rise to their names, and staghorn corals are common. Parrot fish and razor fish, heads pointing downwards, may also be spotted. Spotting a lion fish is exciting, with its alarming white and red fins and red body with white stripes. Sea urchins are found near the edges of the reef and should not be handled.

Coral Island Cruises run a daily boat service that departs at 10.00 for all five islands for RM16 return. The return pick-up time is 15.30. From the same jetty behind the Hyatt, there is a regular daily service for the same price to Pulau Manukan, departing at 08.30, 10.00, 12.00 and 16.00, returning at 07.30, 11.00 and 15.00.

Accommodation on Pulau Manukan can be booked through the Sabah Parks Office (see above, under Tourist information) for RM140. For accommodation on Pulau Mamutik (RM170) contact Borneo Divers (☎ 088-222226). There is a **restaurant** on Pulau Manukan but it is better to bring your own food and plenty to drink.

Excursions from Kota Kinabalu ~ south

If time is limited, the best way to travel south from Kota Kinabalu is through an organised tour from any of the main tour companies in town (see p 243). The ideal way to travel south from Kota Kinabalu is in a hired four-wheel vehicle but this will be expensive. Using buses and trains is a viable alternative but more time is required.

Rafflesia Centre

The centre, located in the **Crocker Range**, is dedicated to the world's largest flower. It may be worth telephoning the Tambunan Forest Office in advance (☎ 087-774691) to find out whether a rafflesia will be in bloom when you are there—you may be lucky because there are a number of different sites. From the main entrance it will take 30–60 minutes to reach one of the flowers; the information desk will draw you a rough sketch of the route if you ask for guidance. Bring a good supply of water and perhaps a picnic as well because there is a scenic stop along the main path through the centre.

There are 14 species of **rafflesia**, three of which are found in Sabah. At the Centre, the most commonly found is *Rafflesia pricei* which grows to a maximum of 30cm in width. A smaller *Rafflesia tengku-adlinii* has recently been found in the interior of Sabah which grows to a maximum width of 20cm. The *Rafflesia kethii*, which grows up to 80cm wide, is found, though not very often, on the slopes of Mount Kinabalu up to 400m. The real giant, though, is *Rafflesia arnoldii* (over 100cm in diameter), discovered by Sir Stamford Raffles and Joseph Arnold in 1818 in Sumatra.

The rafflesia is a leafless parasite that feeds off *Tetrastigma* vines on which it also grows. The buds emerge from inside the roots of the vine after a growing period of between nine and 18 months and the flower opens during the night only to fade and die within a couple of days. When fading, it gives off a smell of rotting meat and this attracts carrion flies which carry the pollen from the male flower to a female one. After pollination the female flower produces a

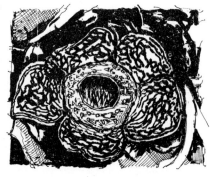

Rafflesia pricei

fruit packed with seeds; these are distributed by rodents who eat the fruit, and, with luck, some of them come to rest on a potential host vine.

Getting to the Rafflesia Centre. Any mini-bus to Tambunan or Keningau from the long distance bus station will stop outside the centre. Returning to Kota Kinabalu requires waiting on the main road for a bus coming back to town, but if you try hitching (see p 30) a friendly driver is very likely to stop. A number of the tour operators in town include tours to the centre.

The nearest **accommodation** to the Rafflesia Centre is at the **Gunung Emas Highlands Resort** (☎ 011-811562), 7km from the Centre along the main road to Kota Kinabalu. A double room is RM80 and there is a restaurant serving Western and Chinese meals. It is worth noting that nights are quite cold, with an average temperature of 15°C.

Tambunan and Keningau

The journey by road from Kota Kinabalu to Tambunan and Keningau (respectively 50km and 100km southeast of Kota Kinabalu) is more exciting than either destination. Before reaching the Rafflesia Centre, the road winds up a steep ascent to the **Sinsuran Pass** at 1649m, and later, 17km before Tambunan, the rice paddies of the **Tambunan Plain** are spread out before you like a tapestry. It was here that Mat Salleh withdrew to build his fort that was besieged by the British North Borneo Chartered Company in 1900 (see p 237). At **Kampung Shabbier**, a few kilometres before Tambunan, a memorial stone marks the site of the ill-fated fort. Both Tambunan and Keningau can be reached by minibus from KK.

Tambunan itself is usually devoid of interest, but there are two places offering decent accommodation and meals: the **Government Rest House** (☎ 087-774339), close to the mosque and a five-minute walk from the central shopping centre, where the price is about RM45 per person, and the **Tambunan Village Resort Centre**, 1km north of town towards Ranau, where rooms cost around RM100 (☎ 087-774076),

Between Tambunan and Keningau is **Gunung Trusmadi**, the second highest mountain in Malaysia at 2649m. There are two routes to the top: the northern route is a round trip of seven days while the southern one takes four. Climbing the mountain is a major expedition and requires considerable advance planning and climbing skills. Guides are essential: they can be contacted via the District Officer in Tambunan.

It is 50km from Tambunan to **Keningau**, a boom town spawned by the timber trade; it is only worth stopping here for a meal and a stroll around the **Chinese temple** next to the bus station. Many of the small hotels are brothels; the **Hotel Tai Wah** (☎ 087-332092) and **Hotel Hiap Soon** (☎ 087-331541) are honourable exceptions. If you have a four-wheel drive, you can follow the rough road from Keningau via Kampung Nabawan that leads south to **Sapulut** where some of the few remaining Murut longhouses can still be seen. The road stops at Sapulut so you will have to go back to Keningau by the same road. Both Tambunan and Keningau are accessible by bus from Kota Kinabalu.

Tenom and Beaufort

The town of **Tenom** (45km southwest of Keningau) has a pleasant rural character but the only place of interest—the **Agricultural Research Station**—lies 15km to the northeast, at Lagud Sebrang. The station conducts experiments into cocoa, coffee and other crops as well as bee culture and has an orchid centre, open from 08.00 to 13.00 Monday to Friday. Buses for the station leave from beside the sports field in Tenom at hourly intervals.

Along the Padas river south towards Sarawak are several longhouse settlements at *kampungs* **Marais** and **Kalibatang**. Here you may see blowpipes being made. Buses travel to these villages or you might be able to charter a boat.

The town of **Beaufort** (40km northwest of Tenom by train) gets its name from Leicester P. Beaufort who was one of the early governors of the British North Borneo Chartered Company. That a town should be named after him is surprising since historians agree that Leicester P. Beaufort was monumentally inconsequential. The town's main appeal—strictly from a tourist's point of view—is when you leave it, because the train journey between Beaufort and Tenom offers a spectacular ride through tropical jungle. For the best views sit on the right-hand side of the train (left-hand side if coming from Tenom).

Pulau Labuan

This small island (120km by ferry southwest of Kota Kinabalu. 10km west of Menumbok) is an important transit point between Brunei and Sabah and, despite there being few places of interest to visit, it has important historic connections.

In 1846 Captain G.R. Mundy claimed it for Britain after the Sultan of Brunei agreed to cede it, and James Brooke became the first governor. Its coal deposits, coupled with a deep-water harbour, made it for a time a valuable anchorage for steamships plying to and from China. In 1942 the Japanese used the island to launch their invasion of north Borneo, and after the accidental death of the local Commander-in-Chief of the Japanese forces, General Maida, they renamed it Maida Island. It reverted to its original name after its successful capture in June 1945 by the Australian 9th Division, under the command of General MacArthur. Shortly after, the island witnessed the trial of the Japanese officers held responsible for the POW Death March from Sandakan.

One of the few places worth visiting is the **Labuan War Cemetery**, 2km east of town along Jalan Tanjung Purun. On the other side of town there is a **Peace Park** at Layang Layangan which marks the spot where the Japanese surrender took place.

Getting to Pulau Labuan. There are boats from Kota Kinabalu run by three different companies: the first boat is at around 07.30 and the second at 10.00 or 13.30; return boats leave Labuan in the morning and afternoon. The boats leave Kota Kinabalu from the jetties behind the Hyatt. The booking offices are also here. The first-class fare is RM33. Boats to the island also go from Penumbang and Memumbuk as well as Limbang in Sarawak.

Accommodation and Restaurants. The best place to stay and eat on Labuan is the **Sheraton Manikar** (☎ 087-418700; fax 087-418740). Double rooms are RM300 (with an ocean view) or RM240; a weekend two-night package, that includes breakfast and one dinner, is RM400. The hotel restaurant serves Western and Asian dishes. A cheaper alternative is the **Federal Inn** (☎ 087

417811) at Jalan Dewan which is new and well appointed; doubles here are RM100. Cheaper still is the **Pertama Hotel** (☎ 087-413311) at Jalan OKK Awang Besar next to the fish market.

For an international menu there is the **Labuan Beach Restaurant** (☎ 087-415611) at Jalan Tanjong Batu. The **Restoran Zainab**, at Jalan Merdeka opposite the Duty Free shop, serves good Malay food. There are foodstalls at the wet market next to the Island Club, and some hawker stalls behind the Hotel Labuan.

Sports
There are several **scuba diving** organisations in Labuan which organise trips to various diving sites. The best is Ocean Sports (☎ 087-415389) at 134 Jalan OKK Awang Besar. They organise scuba diving courses and reef dives around local wrecks as well as a trip to Terumba Layang Layang close to the disputed Spratly Islands where diving is said to be excellent. For **golfers** there is the Kelab Golf at Jalan Tanjong Batu, which also has tennis courts and a swimming pool.

Excursions from Kota Kinabalu ~ north
The easiest way to travel north is with a tour group, although it is possible to make your way with your own transport. The trips north provide interesting insights into local Baju and Rungus culture.

Tuaran, 33km from Kota Kinabalu, is popular with tour operators. The town itself is uninteresting but nearby there are two Bajau villages, **Mengkabong** and **Penambawan**, which provide an opportunity to observe rural life in Sabah.

The small town of **Kota Belud**, 75km northeast of Kota Kinabalu, is only worth visiting on a Sunday when it comes to life as one of the most colourful *tamus* (open-air markets) in Sabah. It provides a good opportunity to view exotic fruits and vegetables and, while traditional dress is rarely seen, Bajau, Kadazan, Rungus, Chinese, Indian and Malay folk from outlying rural areas do congregate here on a Sunday morning and add atmosphere to the commercial wheeling and dealing. As well as the fresh produce on sale there is a water buffalo auction; sellers of patent medicines come to hawk their cures and horse dealers trade animals, but there are few crafts for sale. The *tamu* is underway by 08.00, and to get there in time you should leave Kota Kinabalu by 07.00 at the latest. Nearly every tour operator in town runs a Sunday trip to the market.

With your own transport it is possible to travel 90km further north to **Kudat**, where the East India Company established a short-lived trading station that fell prey to frequent attacks by pirates. Here there are still traditional Rungus (a Kadazan sub-group) longhouses to be seen. The most interesting of these longhouses is at **Matunggung** on the main road south of Kudat. It is often visited by tour groups and you will be allowed to inspect the premises. It is considered polite to bring a gift.

Near to Kudat are some good beaches, such as **Bak Bak**, 11km to the north, which has clear water, fine sand and good facilities. A taxi from Kudat to Bak Bak would cost at least RM12. Further north again are more good beaches backed by small fishing villages; you would need your own transport to explore these.

About 23km southwest of Kudat, and accessible by mini-bus, is **Sikuati**, with a pleasant beach and a good Sunday *tamu* where it is possible to buy Rungus craftwork.

Kinabalu Park

What makes Kinabalu Park the highlight of any trip to Sabah is the magnificent **Mount Kinabalu** that dominates the landscape at 4101m. The park itself, established in 1964, covers an area of 754 square kilometres. Mount Kinabalu is half the size of Everest and the climb is worth considering.

> Mount Kinabalu is only about nine million years old, created when a massive granite lump forced its way up and through the sandstone rocks of the Crocker Range. Time and the elements have worn away the softer sedimentary rocks and the Ice Age carved out the dramatic jagged peaks that are so unforgettable a sight on the final stage of the climb to the summit. The summit itself is divided into two arms by the chasm known as Low's Gully. The mountain is still growing at the rate of about 5cm a year.

There are a number of trails radiating out from the park headquarters and there is usually a free guided walk each morning at around 11.00. There is an **Exhibit Centre** that focuses on the unique flora and fauna of the area and a slide show at 19.30 each Friday, Saturday and Monday. The park headquarters is also where accommodation and restaurants are located. There is also a **Mountain Garden** where labelled plants can be appreciated, including some beautiful orchids like the *Paphiopedilum rothschildianum* and the bright red *Reanthera bella*.

▪ Practical information

Getting to Kinabalu Park
The park is 113km from Kota Kinabalu, 270km from Sandakan. Mini-buses (RM10) take about two hours from the long-distance bus station in Kota Kinabalu to the park headquarters. A taxi could also be hired from town or direct from the airport. All the tour companies have a package deal to the park.

Accommodation
Accommodation at the park needs to be booked through the **Sabah Parks Office** in Kota Kinabalu (Sabah Parks, First Floor, lot1-3, Block K, Sinsuran Shopping Complex, PO Box No. 10626, 88806 Kota Kinabalu, Sabah; ☎ 088-211881/ 212719; fax 088-211585/221001). Demand is heavy during school holiday periods: at the end of January and early February, the first week in March, 20 May–11 June, 19–26 August, 28 October–30 November. Book as far in advance as possible. The first rate below is for weekdays, the second for school holidays and weekends.

At the park: cabins are RM150 and RM200; Nepenthes Villa is RM180 and RM250; Kinabalu Lodge is RM270 and RM360; annex suites are RM100 and RM160; two-bed cabins RM50 and RM80; and a hostel bed RM10.

Accommodation for climbers at **Laban Rata Resthouse** is RM200 for a suite with en suite bathroom; RM100 for a two-person room and RM25 for a dormitory bed. Other huts on the mountain, but without the benefit of a restaurant, cost RM10 per night.

Restaurants

There are two restaurants at the park headquarters: the canteen-like **Liwagu Restaurant** and the smarter **Kinabalu Balsam**, both open until 22.00. For climbers the only restaurant is at the **Laban Rata Resthouse** (at 3300m) and after climbing this far up the mountain a meal here seems like the ultimate luxury. Bring your own drinks and picnic food for the ascent to the resthouse and the second day's climb and then descent. On the first day's climb there are tanks along the trail where water bottles can be refilled.

How the mountain got its name

Accounts differ as to how the mountain acquired its name; one version points to the Kadazan phrase Aki Nabalu ('holy place of the dead') which fits in with the fact that the Kadazan have long considered the mountain peak to be the final resting place of the departed. When Sir Hugh Low made his first attempt to climb the mountain in 1851 (see below) he was warned off by local Kadazans—only after various magical rites had been performed to appease the resident ghosts were some of them reluctantly persuaded to accompany him.

The Chinese have a more mercantile explanation for its name. In this story, a prince succeeded in taking a priceless pearl from a dragon who guarded it on the mountain's summit. The rich prince then married a local Kadazan girl, only to desert her later when he returned to China. The woman pined away after fruitlessly climbing the mountain hoping to see her husband's boat returning across the sea. Eventually she died from grief—the widow (*balu*) of the Chinese (*kina*).

Climbing Mount Kinabalu

Climbing the highest mountain in Southeast Asia may well sound more daunting than it actually is. The failure of the first attempts to conquer the mountain in the 19C were due not to its being a difficult climb but to the problems in reaching the starting point. The point where climbers today begin their ascent at that time could only be reached after days cutting a trail through thick jungle. Any reasonably fit person will make the summit; children under ten and people in their sixties are among those who proudly claim their certificate of a successful climb. Sound advice is to climb the mountain at your own pace. You can take all day to reach the Laban Rata Resthouse—just make sure that you are there before darkness falls. Do not be put off by other climbers who might well walk faster (Gurkhas hold the record for going up and down the mountain in under three hours).

In 1851 Hugh Low, at the time an untitled government officer in Labuan, made the first recorded non-Kadazan assault on the mountain. He stopped short of the summit, comforting himself with the thought that only 'winged animals' could make it to the top. He made two further attempts— one in 1858 with Spencer St John, then Brunei's British Consul—but only the South Peak was reached. This now bears Low's name, as does the gully that cuts down through the top of the mountain. Finally, in 1888, a scientist named John Whitehead made it to the highest peak.

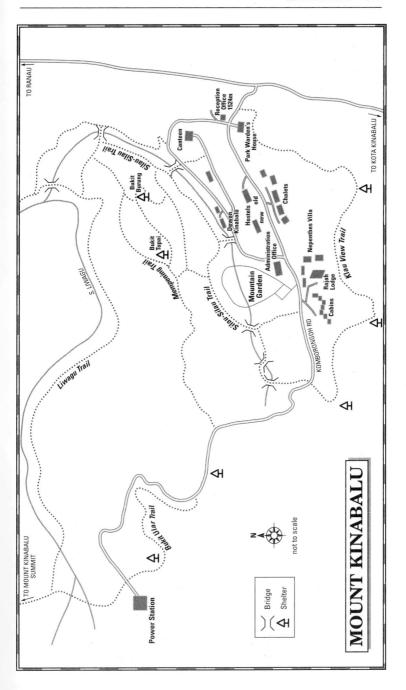

MOUNT KINABALU

TO RANAU

TO KOTA KINABALU

Reception Office 1524m

Canteen

Park Warden's House

Chalets

Hostels old new

Dewan Kinabalu

Administration Office

Nepenthes Villa

Mountain Garden

Rajah Lodge

Cabins

Bukit Burung

Bukit Tupai

Silau-Silau Trail

Mempening Trail

Silau-Silau Trail

S. LIWAGU

Kiau View Trail

KOMBORONGOH RD

Liwagu Trail

Bukit Ular Trail

TO MOUNT KINABALU SUMMIT

Power Station

N

not to scale

Bridge

Shelter

A minimum of two days is required to reach the summit. Useful equipment includes a torch, suntan lotion, a change of clothes and at least one layer of warm clothing for the very cold start on day two; plus a waterproof rucksack to keep everything dry in case of rain. Climbing boots are not necessary; a sturdy pair of training shoes will suffice. Sleeping bags can be hired.

A **guide**, costing RM25 for up to three people (RM28 for 4–6 people; RM30 for 7–8 people), is obligatory and there is also a RM10 **permit** charge. Arrange all this the night before your climb and confirm the time you need to be outside the park headquarters' reception area the next morning, usually around 07.00.

The 8km trail to the summit begins at 1830m and there is a bus laid on for the journey from park headquarters to this point. There are resting places along the way, including huts with beds at 3300m and 3800m. An overnight stay is usually made at the first of these huts, **Laban Rata**, where hot water and a restaurant can be found.

On the second day a pre-dawn start gets underway around 03.00 for the final stretch to the top before the clouds set in. The second day's climb takes a minimum of three hours—it may take you longer if you are not fit. There is a more demanding section where a rockface needs to be crossed with the help of ropes. When Hugh Low reached the summit he celebrated with a bottle of Madeira. Even though thousands of people now make it to the top each year one still feels a tremendous sense of achievement on getting there.

The vegetation changes as the altitude increases, from montane oak forest through to stunted trees surviving in pockets of soil, and finally to where there is no soil at all, just bare granite and noticeably thinner oxygen. It is the lack of soil and not the presence of snow that determines the treeline, which is not far above the Laban Rata Resthouse.

Flora

Little fauna will be seen while climbing the mountain but the flora is exceptional. Bring with you the free booklet, *Guide to the Summit Trail* (available at the Sabah Parks Office in Kota Kinabalu and at the park headquarters which also sells some books on the park's plant life); it contains colour photographs of the more common plants that may be identified along the way. Orchids, pitcher plants and rhododendrons are the botanical treats to look out for, but there are over 1000 species of plants in the park.

During your climb you will notice the change in plant life as the habitat changes. At the start of the walk is tropical rainforest, with large trees with buttressed roots forming a canopy while underneath thousands of different plants fight for the remaining sunlight. After 1300m is the montane zone where oak and chestnut dominate, gradually becoming more dwarfed and stunted as the soil becomes thinner. The highest reaches of the mountain is cloud forest, where plants which take their nourishment from the air survive. Above 3300m all that survives are lichens, sedges and club mosses.

Pitcher plants

The largest of the pitcher plants is the *Nepenthes rajah*, 30cm in diameter and holding two litres of liquid. During his 1858 ascent Spencer St John saw one with a dead rat floating inside and since his time others have found examples with frogs trapped inside. Unfortunately, the *Nepenthes rajah* is not seen close to the park headquarters or along the mountain trail. But there are another eight species.

Pitcher plants usually grow in areas of little soil and compensate for this by catching insects in a digestive fluid that fills the characteristic cup of the plant. Pitcher plants also have a lid to their cup and the lid opens when the cup's glands have produced sufficient digestive fluids. The inside surface of the cup is often smooth and slippery to facilitate the insect's entry to its fatal bath. This grisly image of a plant that eats insects alive is a little misleading because botanists now think that most of the insects collect nectar safely from inside the cup and under the lid and, therefore, in a nectar-deficient environment, the relationship between the pitcher plants and the insects is more mutual than predatory.

Between the park headquarters and about an hour before Laban Rata the small mountain pitcher plant, *Nepenthes tentaculata*, may be seen along the edges and sides of the main trail. More common is the *Nepenthes villosa*, always found on the ground or at the base of trees, and distinguished by a flange-like peristome that points down into its cup. Low's pitcher plant (*Nepenthes lowii*) may be seen at around the 2000m level, while above 2438m another plant bearing his name, Low's rhododendron, is difficult to miss due to the yellow-peach coloured blooms up to 30cm across. On the higher reaches of the mountain it is easy to miss the small but easily identified heath rhododendron with bright scarlet tubular flowers. This plant is one of many which are unique to Mount Kinabalu.

Nepenthes rajah, *a pitcher plant*

The last leg of your journey will begin in darkness. Climbing as the sun rises you will find ropes to guide your way up the rock face towards the summit. The views at the top are breathtaking, but looking into the black depths of Low's Gully, 1000m down, should persuade you to turn about and begin the descent. You should be back at the park headquarters by the afternoon; be prepared for some stiff leg muscles the next morning.

A post-climb visit to the Porings hot springs (see below), some 40km away, for a warm bathe in the sulphurous waters is an attractive idea but there is no public transport there. However, package trips from Kota Kinabalu will often include the springs as an optional extra.

Ranau and Poring hot springs

Mini-buses travelling between Kota Kinabalu and Sandakan usually stop at **Ranau** but visitors will only disembark in order to change buses for a visit to Poring Hot Springs. Ranau is 20km from Kinabalu National Park and it is another 19km to Poring so an overnight stay is sometimes convenient. On the journey between Kinabalu Park and Ranau there is a **war memorial** at Kundasang to the Death March of 1944 when the Japanese force-marched 2400 POWs and consequently killed nearly all of them (see below).

Soaking in a sulphurous bath at **Poring**, in an outdoor tub, is especially appreciated by anyone who has climbed Mount Kinabalu (see above). The tubs have hot and cold water taps so the temperature of the bath can be regulated.

A good place to stay in Ranau is the **Kinabalu Hotel** (☎ 088-876028) near the town square. Rooms are RM30 to RM65. The **Hotel Perkasa** (☎ 088-889511; fax 088-889101) is suitable for a longer stay, with a package trip to Kinabalu Park (RM440 for two people, with two nights and breakfast at the hotel, a guide for climbing Kinabalu and a night at Laban Rata), and transport to Poring and the War memorial. It has a restaurant, the **Tinompok**, serving Malaysian, Chinese and Western food. Rooms are RM155 on weekdays, RM190 at weekends. Accommodation at **Poring Hot Springs** can be booked through the Sabah Parks Office: cabins are RM60 and RM80, weekdays/weekends and school holidays respectively; chalets RM180 and RM250; and hostel beds RM10, all plus 5 per cent service tax.

Sandakan

Virtually destroyed during the Second World War, Sandakan is a dull little town laid out in a grid system of simple concrete buildings. Nevertheless it is Sabah's biggest fishing port, and is the gateway to some of Sabah's most interesting sights: **Sepilok Orang-Utan Rehabilitation Centre**, the **Turtle Islands National Park** and the **Kinabatangan Basin**.

History
The town of Sandakan started life as a tiny trading settlement where 18C and 19C merchants from Sulu came to buy beeswax. In 1879 an Englishman, William Pryer, came here as part of Baron von Overbeck's team with a brief to establish an outpost of the Chartered Company that Overbeck had founded. Ada Pryer remembered their resources: 'He had with him a West Indian black named Anderson, a half-cast Hindoo named Abdul, a couple of China boys. For food they had a barrel of flour and 17 fowls and the artillery was half a dozen sinder rifles.'

Pryer succeeded in establishing a small town that grew rich and became the capital of British North Borneo in 1885. The source of wealth came initially from trade in birds' nests from the caves at Gomantong and then from the export of timber. In 1942 the Japanese occupied the town and set up a prisoner of war camp from where the infamous Death March to Ranau began in September 1944 after the inmates had been forced to build an airport (the site of the present airport). Allied bombardment virtually destroyed the town and after the war the capital shifted to Jesselton (Kota Kinabalu) while Sandakan rebuilt itself.

In the late 1950s the new town of Sandakan began to prosper from a renewed trade in timber. Many of the timber tycoons were Chinese and the wood for the Temple of Heaven in Beijing came from Sabah through

Sandakan. The virgin forest was systematically logged until there were no more trees to fell and the wasteland has now been given over to oil palm and cocoa plantations. At the height of the timber boom in the 1970s, Sandakan was reputed to have a higher concentration of millionaires than anywhere else in the world. Today, the town has a large number of Filipinos and, on occasions, an atmosphere of frontier town lawlessness.

■ Practical Information

Getting to and from Sandakan
By air. The airport (☎ 089-660525) is 13km outside of town and the MAS office (☎ 089-273966) is on the ground floor of the Sabah Building in Block 31 of Second Avenue. There are five daily flights to and from Kota Kinabalu (RM83) and two daily flights to and from Tawau. Taxis from the airport to town (RM15) operate under a coupon system.

By bus. The long-distance bus station is at the western end of town. Most buses to Kota Kinabalu leave early in the morning and will stop at Kinabalu Park on the way. The local bus station is in Labuk Road.

Tourist information
Banks are located in the centre of town on Third Avenue and Jalan Pelabuhan. The **post office**, west of town on Jalan Leila, is open from 08.00 to 17.00 Monday to Friday, and from 10.00 to 13.00 on Saturday. The **Telekom** office, 6th Floor, Wisma Khoo, is open daily from 08.30 to 16.45. The main **police station** (☎ 089-211222) is on Jalan Sim Sim.

The **Sabah Parks Office** (☎ 089-273453) is on the 9th floor of Wisma Khoo Siak Chiew at the end of Jalan Tiga. Unless travelling in a tour group, this office is where reservations for Turtle Islands National Park are made. Arrangements for transport to the island may also be made here. The **Wildlife Department** (☎ 089-666550), where permits for the Gomantong Caves are arranged, is on the 6th floor of the Urusetia Building, Mile 7, Labuk Road.

A number of **tour companies** are either based in Sandakan or have an office here. **Borneo Eco** (☎ 089-220210) is located in the lobby of the Hotel Hsiang Garden. **Coral Island Cruises** (☎ 089-669912) has an office at the airport. **SI Tours** (☎ 089-213502: fax 089-271513), on the third floor of the Yeng Yo Hong Building, is an experienced local company. **Wildlife Expeditions** (☎ 089-219616) has an office on the 9th floor of Wisma Khoo Siak Chiew and in the Renaissance hotel. **Discovery Tours** (☎ 089-274106) is on the 10th floor of Wisma Khoo Siak Chiew. The least expensive tours are available through **Uncle Tan** (☎ 089-531639) at Mile 17.5 Labuk Road.

Accommodation and restaurants
The **Renaissance Hotel** (☎ 089-213299; fax 089-271271), outside of town on Jalan Utara, is a smart resort hotel, complete with swimming pool and recreation centre. Rooms start at RM335. **Hotel Hsiang Garden** (☎ 089-273122) on Jalan Leila is the next-best hotel in town. **Hotel Nak** (☎ 089-272988), on Jalan Edinburgh, is a good middle-range hotel with clean, largish rooms for RM94. The best budget accommodation is at **Uncle Tan's** (☎ 089-531917) on Labuk Road. Buses from Kota Kinabalu know the place and will stop outside.

From Sandakan take bus No. 19. A room and three meals is RM20.

The Renaissance hotel has a buffet dinner for RM23 and a lunch buffet for RM21. A meal at the hotel's Chinese **Ming Restaurant** costs about RM60 for two. The **XO Steak House**, opposite the Hotel Hsiang Garden, is the best place for a steak and the seafood is also good here. The **Supreme Garden Vegetarian Restaurant**, in Block 30, Bandar Ramai Ramai on Jalan Leila, is recommended for its Chinese vegetarian food; no alcohol is served.

Sports and Entertainment

There is a cinema which shows some English language movies in Jalan Buli Sim Sim near the town mosque. For golf fans there is Sandakan Golf Club.

Places to see

All the tour companies offer a Sandakan town tour and it will often be part of the standard package that includes the Turtle Islands National Park and the Sepilok Orang-Utan Rehabilitation Centre.

The liveliest spot in town is definitely the **fish market**—probably the biggest and best in Sabah—on Jalan Pryer where illegal turtle eggs, imported from the Philippines, are openly on sale.

Utterly different in character is the very English-looking **St Michael's and All Angels' Church**, at the top of Jalan Puncak, which managed to survive the bombing of the Second World War. It was built of stone (very unusual for Sabah) in 1893.

The Chinese temple usually included in the town tour is the **Puu Jih Shih Temple**, 4km west of town at the top of a hill. It is an architecturally undistinguished building, with a lurid and lavish appearance that suits its provenance; it was completed in 1987 after millions of dollars were donated by Chinese merchants who had made fortunes out of timber. Inside, the teakwood pillars

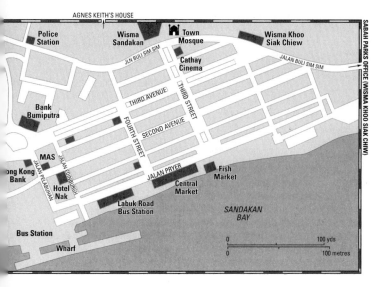

AGNES KEITH'S HOUSE

Police Station

Wisma Sandakan

Town Mosque

Wisma Khoo Siak Chiew

JLN BULI SIM SIM

Cathay Cinema

JALAN BULI SIM SIM

SABAH PARKS OFFICE (WISMA KHOO SIAK CHIW)

THIRD AVENUE

THIRD STREET

Bank Bumiputra

FOURTH STREET

SECOND AVENUE

MAS

Hong Kong Bank

JALAN EDINBURGH

JALAN PELABUHAN

Hotel Nak

JALAN PRYER

Fish Market

Central Market

Labuk Road Bus Station

SANDAKAN BAY

Bus Station

Wharf

0   100 yds
0   100 metres

from Macau are the only interesting feature. There are good views of Sandakan from outside the temple but unless you take a taxi it is a long walk here and hardly worth the effort.

There are two other Chinese temples: the **Goddess of Mercy Temple** is on Jalan Singapura and is the oldest Chinese temple in town; it was built in the 1880s. The other is the **Three Saints Temple**, which, like thousands of other coastal Chinese temples, is dedicated to Tin Hau, the goddess of the sea who saved her family from drowning. Wherever the Chinese go, temples dedicated to this goddess are among the first to be constructed. It is at the end of the Padang at the junction of Jalan Singapura and Jalan Tokong.

Some of the town tours include a visit to **Agnes Keith's House**, situated near the Renaissance Hotel in Jalan Utara. Agnes Keith was an American writer who lived with her English husband, the Conservator of Forests, in this house from 1934 to 1952. She wrote three books about her life in Sabah, one of which, *Three Came Home* (made into a film), dealt with her time as a prisoner of war on the nearby island, Pulau Berhala. The house was destroyed during the war but when, in 1946, her husband returned to his post it was faithfully reconstructed. Close by is the Observation Pavilion with good views across the bay and the town.

At Mile 8 Labuk Road is a **crocodile farm**, which is a commercial enterprise producing skins and meat from the couple of hundred sad residents. It is open to the public and visitors can see concrete pits overcrowded with animals. Admission is RM2. It is open 08.00–17.00.

The **Sandakan Mosque**, a very futuristic building, was erected in 1988. It is on Jalan Buli Sim Sim, 1km east of town. Close by is *kampung* **Buli Sim Sim** an interesting stilt village built over the sea.

Excursions from Sandakan

Sepilok Orang-Utan Rehabilitation Centre

The centre was established in 1964 as a retraining home for orang-utans released from illegal captivity, although most of the animals here now are refugees from the jungle logging that has robbed them of their homes.

The centre is open from 09.00 to 11.00 and 14.00 to 15.30, but make sure that your visit coincides with one of the feeding sessions which are at 10.00 and 15.00. Bring some insect repellent. It is advisable to be there before 09.00 to sign up for an optional walk, after the 10.00 feeding session, to a second feeding place which involves an enjoyable 40-minute trek through the jungle. There is an entrance charge of RM10. A cafeteria serves rice, chicken and noodles.

The idea of a rehabilitation centre was inspired by Barbara Harrisson, wife of Tom Harrisson (see p 306), who first began rescuing young orang-utans after the Second World War. In 1962 she highlighted the possible extinction of orang-utans and in 1963 a law was passed that prohibited their keeping. Somewhere was needed to keep the liberated animals and Sepilok, formerly a timber reserve area belonging to the Chartered Company, was chosen as a site for rehabilita-tion. The increasing popularity of Sepilok is now in danger of turning the place into an open air zoo. In 1997, Malaysia's *Star* newspaper reported incidents of theft from the Sepilok centre of baby orang-utans by childless couples wanting to bring them up as if their own children. Sadly, the animals are sometimes mistreated by their captors when they do not behave as required.

Orang-utans

Orang-utan (*Pongo pygmaeus*) is Malay for 'jungle man' and the ape's gentle human-like behaviour is what endears it to the daily contingent of tour buses that visit the centre. An adult male reaches a height of over 1.5m while their armspan is 2.4m. They are not aggressive animals, which is just as well because they have the strength of half-a-dozen men—which you will quickly appreciate if one of them takes you by the hand for a compul-sory stroll!

Orang-utans sleep alone in a nest of twigs in the fork of a tree. Their diet is basically vegetarian, with a smattering of termites and bark, and an adult will share an area of about 2 square kilometres with others of its kind. They are not territorial, and only come together when sharing a source of food. Young orang-utans stay with their mother—who forms a temporary mating relationship with a male—until four or five years old. Most orang-utans spend most of their day leisurely wandering through the forest looking for trees in fruit. Around dusk they begin constructing their nest for the night.

It is estimated that there are between 10,000 and 20,000 orang-utans in Sabah, mostly inhabiting swampy forest areas, and while they seem to have survived the logging of forests, the ongoing clearance of land for agricul-ture poses a real threat to their future survival.

Getting to Sepilok Orang-Utan Rehabiliation Centre. Buses leave for the centre from the bus station in Labuk Road and the mini-bus marked 'Batu 14 from the long-distance station will also take you here. A taxi should charge RM60 for taking you there and back, with a wait of two hours.

Turtle Islands National Park

The three turtle islands are 40km north of Sandakan and very close to Philippine waters. Pulau Selingan, Pulau Bakkungan Kecil and Pulau Gulisaan are part of 1700 hectares of sea, coral reefs and land that form the nature reserve. The only island where visitors are allowed to stay and observe the turtles nesting and hatching is **Pulau Selingan**. On Bakkungan Kecil there is a small mud volcano, and the island is patrolled by automatic weapon-carrying guards on the lookout for Philippine invasions or egg stealers.

The most common turtle that comes ashore is the green turtle (*Chelonia mydas*) The male turtle waits out at sea while the female comes ashore at night to nest above the high water mark, returning to the water after two hours of hard work digging a metre-deep hole in the sand with the aid of her front and rear flippers. Hawksbill turtles (*Eretmochelys imbricata*) are less common, preferring to nest on Pulau Gulisaan.

What is special about Pulau Selingan is that after watching the eggs being laid it is then possible to visit the hatchery. Here, eggs that were collected months earlier and buried by the rangers will be ready to hatch out. This happens almost every night and it is a delightful sight, especially for children, to watch the little turtles emerge from under the sand and scuttle bravely down the beach to face an uncertain future in the sea.

Getting to Turtle Islands National Park. Most visitors travel to an island as part of a tour because otherwise it is necessary to book accommodation at the Sabah Parks Office in Sandakan and then arrange transport. If there are empty places on a group visit, the Sabah Parks Office will arrange a seat for you. **Uncle Tan's** (☎ 089-531639) has the best package deal at RM150 for accommodation and transport. Expect to pay twice as much through the other tour companies. There are only 20 beds on the island so try to book ahead if you are travelling between July and October. Bring your own drinks and snacks although **Rose's Café** on the island serves meals. Most package deals will include dinner and breakfast the next morning.

Kinabatangan Basin

If time is limited and choices have to be made about where to go in Sabah for wildlife, a visit to the Kinabatangan Basin merits serious consideration as the first choice. Besides the more widespread hornbills, monitor lizards, macaques, and orang-utans it is one of the few places where the proboscis monkey can be seen (Bako National Park in Sarawak is the next best place to see them but the population there is a lot smaller). It is also possible to see rare sightings of rhinoceros and elephants.

Proboscis monkeys

The proboscis monkey (*Nasalis larvatus*), endemic to Borneo, is a strange-looking animal and seeing them in the wild is likely to prove an unforgettable experience. Their Malay name—*kera belanda*—translates as 'Dutchmen monkeys'; the sunburnt early Europeans from the Dutch East

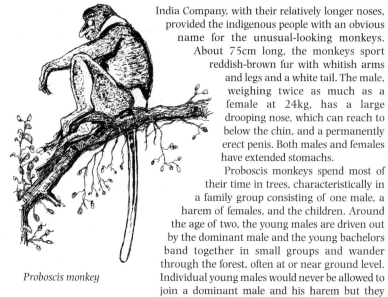

India Company, with their relatively longer noses, provided the indigenous people with an obvious name for the unusual-looking monkeys. About 75cm long, the monkeys sport reddish-brown fur with whitish arms and legs and a white tail. The male, weighing twice as much as a female at 24kg, has a large drooping nose, which can reach to below the chin, and a permanently erect penis. Both males and females have extended stomachs.

Proboscis monkeys spend most of their time in trees, characteristically in a family group consisting of one male, a harem of females, and the children. Around the age of two, the young males are driven out by the dominant male and the young bachelors band together in small groups and wander through the forest, often at or near ground level. Individual young males would never be allowed to join a dominant male and his harem but they always hope to attract a female into leaving the harem.

Proboscis monkey

Around 16.00 proboscis monkeys come to the river but they are still most likely to be seen high up on the branches of trees. They spend the day deep in the forest but evenings and nights near the river. The reason for this behaviour is not certain. It may be for protection from predators as the monkeys are excellent swimmers—their back feet are partly webbed—and they even swim underwater. Gathering near the river also provides an opportunity for socialising and networking: studies have shown that they like to cross the river to mix and mate.

Proboscis monkeys feed almost exclusively on the leaves of one tree, the *Sonneratia*. For survival they need a large area to roam in freely and the constant clearing of land in Sabah is reducing their numbers. It is likely that they will soon become an endangered species.

There are also excellent opportunities for **bird-watching** and one of the most beautiful birds to be seen is the Asian paradise flycatcher (*Terpsiphone pardisi borneensis*), easy to identify because of the two white tail feathers up to 45cm long. Even more dramatic are the hornbills which are frequently seen in the area of the Kinabatangan river.

Hornbills

The visually splendid hornbills have every right to proclaim themselves the aerial lords of the Bornean jungle. The male's whooping hoot is unmistakable; and this magnificent bird can reach a metre or more in length—showing off its eponymous upcurved horn and magnificent streaks of colour. The huge bills of the hornbills are often topped with a casque—a 'horny excrescence' as writer Bertram Smythies (see below) calls it—which is usually hollow. One species, the **helmeted hornbill**, has a solid casque, hence the highly valued 'hornbill ivory' which the bird is killed for.

Three species of hornbill can be seen along the Kinabatangan river. The black hornbill, up to 84cm long, is all black except for white tips to the outer tail feathers and sometimes a white stripe over the eye. The male bill is pale yellow, blackish in the female. The **pied hornbill** is about the same size, with a pied belly, and white outer tail feathers and wing tips. The **rhinoceros hornbill** is the largest of the three, up to 107cm long, with a black bar across a white tail and a black body. It is easily recognised by its size and the red colour on its yellow bill, and its upturned casque. It is characteristically seen on the top of the taller trees. In Sarawak, the Ibans are fond of collecting their feathers.

Hornbills

There are five other types of hornbill, two of which—the wreathed hornbill and the wrinkled hornbill—can be seen in the forest around the Kinabatangan river.

The hornbill's dedication to protecting its young is spectacular and bizarre. A nest site is found in the hollow of a tree and here the female bird incarcerates herself—literally—by blocking up the only entrance, using her gluey droppings as cement. Meanwhile, on the outside, the male is busy applying mud to secure the fortress. Finally there remains a narrow slit for the female's protruding beak to receive food or drop waste. When the first of the chicks hatches out the mother chips her own way free, quickly repairing the hole to ensure the continued protection of the chicks from predators. As each chick is ready to leave the nest the wall is breached and repaired again until all the chicks have finally flown the nest.

▦ Practical information

Kinabatangan Basin is 80km southwest of Sandakan. A tarred road from Sandakan is being constructed and this will reduce the driving to a little over an hour. The journey from Sandakan is dominated by the sight of huge palm oil plantations. The sludge from these plantations is deposited directly into the river, which helps to account for the dead fish often seen floating on the surface. The people living in the area of the Kinabatangan river are mostly Malays—unusual in Sabah—and it may seem incongruous to hear prayers being recited from the mosque's loudspeakers and echoing down the Conradian landscape.

Most of the Sabah tour companies have their own lodges spread out along the banks of the river; in the late afternoon a boat ride is taken along the river to look for the proboscis monkeys. Along the way hornbills are often spotted and there are also bird-watching tours that can be arranged through the lodges.

All the tour companies in Sandakan and Kota Kinabalu arrange tours that include **accommodation**. **Wildlife Expeditions** (☎ 089-219616; fax 089-214570) is perhaps the most ecologically sound of the companies offering tours and accommodation along the river. The company is building its own walk-in hostel and already has its own lodge for tour groups. Around the lodge there are forest trails. **Uncle Tan** (☎ 089-531639) has the least expensive deal at around RM130 and RM15 for each day's accommodation. All the lodges have a small library of books on the area's bird-life, but it is a good idea to bring your own guide book. The best of all is *The Birds of Borneo* by Bertram E. Smythies (see Further Reading).

Gomantong Caves

Most of the tour trips to the Kinabatangan river include a visit to the Gomantong Caves in the 3600 hectare Gomontong Forest Reserve, 32km south of Sandakan Bay—a short detour off the main road near Sukau. If you have been to the Niah Caves in Sarawak, there is nothing new to see here. The best time to go is between February and March or between July and September when the swiftlet nests are being collected. There are two main caves and the one most often visited is **Simud Hitam** (the Black Cave), home to the black-nest swiftlet whose nests are presently commanding a price of over US$50 a kilogram. This explains the barrier across the entrance road where entry to the caves is monitored.

Getting to the caves is difficult unless you go with a tour company. Lahad Datu mini-buses make the two-hour journey. Get off at the Sukau turnoff. From there infrequent buses make the 20km journey to the turn off for the forest reserve. From there it is 4.5km walk to the reserve headquarters.

Danum Valley Conservation Area

The conservation area covers an area of 438 square kilometres, mostly lowland rainforest and the **Borneo Rainforest Lodge**, where all visitors are based, is designed to show that eco-tourism plus comfortable accommodation has a future in Sabah. Guided walks and jungle treks are the main attraction; there are also visits to the Danum Valley Field Centre which attempts to show how forests can be logged with due regard for the environment.

Because Danum Valley is surrounded by logging areas there is a high concentration of wildlife close to the field centre which means that you have a very good chance of seeing interesting creatures; there are some rare species to be spotted if you are lucky, including Sumatran rhino, clouded leopards and banteng. More common are orang-utan, elephants, gibbons and hornbills.

The lodge is 85km west of Lahad Datu. Visitors will be met at Lahad Datu airport, which has two daily flights to and from Kota Kinabalu (RM106). Expect to pay around RM300 a night, including full meals and activities. Bookings and enquiries can be made through Kota Kinabalu on the 3rd floor of Block D, Lot 10, Sadong Jaya Complex, PO Box No. 11622 (☎ 088-243245; fax 088-243244).

Semporna and Pulau Sipadan

Between Lahad Datu and Tawau is **Semporna**, an interesting Bajau town with a lively market. It has a large and thriving stilt village close by as well as a cultured pearl farm off the coast. Its main interest, though, is the fact that it is the departure point for Pulau Sipadan. Mini-buses leave Lahad Datu regularly for this town. The journey is 160km and takes about 2.5 hours.

Pulau Sipadan, three hours from Semporna by boat, is Malaysia's only oceanic island because it is not on the Sunda Shelf. It is believed to have the largest variety of soft corals anywhere in the world and ever since the French marine biologist, Jacques Cousteau, gave it the full mark of approval in 1989 ('an untouched piece of art'), it has become an obligatory destination for dedicated and professional scuba-divers. This has tended to create the impression that the place is not suitable for amateur snorkellers but the beaches and coral can be appreciated by everyone and no special expertise is required.

The island itself is also of interest to wildlife enthusiasts who can expect tropical rainforest, monitor lizards and flying foxes. It is part of a marine reserve and was declared a wildlife sanctuary in the 1930s. Another highlight of the trip may be the sight of warships since the island is disputed territory between Malaysia and Indonesia.

The number of visitors to the small island is restricted and it is necessary to book through a company. In Kota Kinabalu, contact **Borneo Divers** (☎ 088-222226; fax 088-221550) on the 4th floor of Wisma Sabah, or **Coral Island Cruises** (☎ 088-223490; fax 088-223404) on the 10th floor of Wisma Merdeka. Typical packages for two days (one night) cost RM675 per person, which covers air, road and sea travel from Kota Kinabalu, accommodation and meals and four dives; the diving equipment can be hired. There should be no hidden extras. In Semporna another company, **Pulau Sipadan Resort** (☎ 089-784937), has an office but their main postal address is Block P, Bandar Sabindo, Tawau (☎ 089-765200). Accommodation is quite basic with A-frame huts or chalets, in some cases with en suite bathrooms.

Non-divers should make a day trip from Semporna to the island and hire snorkelling equipment from the boatman. This is easily arranged by the jetty in Semporna but expect to pay at least RM450 for a one-day package.

Tawau

This small, ugly commercial town is 150km southwest of Lahad Datu and is as far south as you can get in Sabah. It is being heavily logged but there are several reaforestation projects in the area. Its chief interest is the **Tawau Hills Park**, which has volcanic hills surrounded by rainforest, and a waterfall which is a popular picnic spot. There are no other places of interest in or around the town but it does provide access to **Kalimantan** (Indonesia) which can be seen across the bay—boats leave from the jetty which is west of the bus station in Jalan Wing Lock. You will need a visa for entry into Indonesia by this route, and these can be obtained from the Indonesian Consulate in Jalan Kuharsa. There is also a twice-weekly MAS flight to Cebu in the Philippines. It is possible to travel by land-cruiser from Tawau back to Kota Kinabalu via Merotai and Keningau.

Sarawak

The state of Sarawak may be part of Malaysia (indeed it is the country's largest state, covering an area of 124,967 square kilometres) but most visitors experience it as another country. The fact that your passport will receive a separate stamp upon arrival in Sarawak might suggest that the state authorities also think this. Culturally, Sarawak has little in common with peninsular Malaysia—see the section on cultural groups below—and the physical geography is also very different. One small part of the island of Borneo, it is characterised by mighty rivers, jungle and forest, and while there are relatively few historical places of interest, museums or sandy beaches to attract visitors, there are other excellent reasons for visiting the state.

A major part of the appeal of the place lies in the **indigenous cultures** of the inhabitants. Chinese and Malays do make up a sizeable proportion of the total population but if you escape the few large towns and travel upriver for a few days it is easy to forget that you are still in Malaysia. Equally exciting is the unique opportunity that Sarawak provides to experience **nature** and its **wildlife**: orang-utans, proboscis monkeys and hornbills being three of the best reasons for visiting Sarawak. There are also a number of superb **national parks**: the Bako National Park outside Kuching, easily accessible and requiring no strenuous physical activity yet home to pitcher plants, proboscis monkeys and hornbills; Gunung Mulu National Park near Miri, boasting the world's largest caves; and Niah National Park, also near Miri, famous for its prehistoric rock paintings.

Transport within Sarawak usually involves a combination of internal MAS flights and turbo-charged boats that travel up and down the rivers. Some overland routes are possible but the journey times are inordinately long; internal MAS flights are short and relatively inexpensive. The key to a successful time in Sarawak is planning your itinerary and getting to where you want as quickly as possible.

Accommodation is plentiful in all the towns and areas of interest. Spending at least one or two nights in an upriver longhouse is a major attraction. It provides an opportunity to experience the local culture at first hand and is invariably a thoroughly enjoyable event.

Getting to and from Sarawak is usually accomplished by air to **Kuching**, the capital of Sarawak, from either peninsular Malaysia, Singapore or Kota Kinabalu in Sabah. See p 273 for details.

There are some very experienced **tour operators** which handle guided tours to the National Parks, short or extended stays at longhouses and treks in the jungle. The best companies are based in Kuching and Miri; see pp 274 and 298.

History
The Niah Caves were inhabited some 40,000 years ago and archaeological discoveries shows evidence of a Neolithic settlement. The relationship, if any, between these inhabitants and the various tribes of Sarawak is unknown. China was trading along Sarawak's coast as early as the 7C. Malays from Kalimantan began moving north sometime in the 16C.

In the 14C, Sarawak became part of the Sultan of Brunei's domain but at the beginning of the 18C there were signs of Malay discontent as the Brunei sultanate weakened. In 1827 Pangiran Mahkota, one of the sultan's 14 brothers, was sent from Brunei to reassert control over the valuable mining and export of antimony. The name 'Sarawak' comes from the Malay word for antimony, *serawak*. In 1836, however, a number of Malay chiefs openly rebelled against Mahkota and Raja Muda Hashim, an uncle of the Sultan of Brunei, was dispatched to deal with the matter. Into this state of flux sailed **James Brooke** in 1839.

James Brooke was born in 1803 in India where he joined the army, only to have his career curtailed by injuries received on the battlefield. After recovering in England he sailed for the East in the early 1830s and fell under the spell of Raffles' achievement in Singapore. Back in England he purchased a schooner and sailed to the East again, looking for adventure.

In Singapore in 1839 he was asked by the governor to deliver a letter to Raja Muda Hashim and in doing so he found the adventure he was looking for. Hashim rashly offered Brooke the title of Raja of Sarawak if he would help him deal with the Malay rebels. This Brooke duly did and in 1842 he claimed his title. Pangiran Mahkota became a bitter rival and joined forces with Iban pirates to try and depose Brooke. Dealing with the pirates became Brooke's priority for various reasons: to eliminate Mahkota, to extend his control, and to establish safe waters as a prerequisite for trade.

So began Brooke's notorious war—'pacifying' was the euphemism he preferred—against the Ibans. It was naked aggression and in the process thousands of Ibans were slaughtered, but Brooke successfully extended his territory with the blessing of the Sultan of Brunei. By 1861 he had gained even more territory by similar methods and at his death in 1867 more than half of what is now the state of Sarawak was under his personal control. In spite of the slaughter, Brooke governed in an informal, paternal style based on consultation with the local chiefs. The Brookes came to be known as the 'White Rajahs'.

Towards the end of his life James Brooke quarrelled with his eldest son and disinherited him. The second Raja of Sarawak was another son, **Charles Brooke**, who took his title in 1863. He was less of an adventurer than his father but managed nevertheless to expand his domain in 1884, 1890 and 1905. By the time the First World War began Charles Brooke, aged 84, was running a country larger in size than England. Before he died, in 1916, he passed the throne on to his son, **Charles Vyner Brooke**, who ruled until the Japanese invaded at the end of 1941. Vyner Brooke had no children and his heir was a nephew, Anthony Brooke, who took umbrage when Vyner introduced a constitution and a council of Malays. For a second time there was a dispute over the succession but the Japanese solved the problem with their invasion. After the war there was disagreement between the British government and Anthony Brooke about who should rule Sarawak: no one thought of asking the people who lived in Sarawak. The drama was not over though—the elderly Vyner, realising the absurdity of the family's claim to rule the country, issued a public statement advising the people of Sarawak to renounce the Brookes and accept rule by the British government.

A British commission of inquiry came to the conclusion that the people of Sarawak did want to be ruled by Westminster, notwithstanding violent scenes of disagreement from local groups and the assassination of the British governor, Mr Duncan Stewart, in 1949.

After Malaya's independence in 1957, Sarawak remained under British control until 1963 when it became part of the Federation of Malaysia, weathering the storm caused by Indonesian opposition and a consequent guerrilla war waged by communist opposition in Sarawak to the federation, supported with finance and training from Kalimantan. Long after Indonesia had ceased to support the communist guerrillas, the civil war continued until 1973 when most of the forces surrendered, having been offered amnesties. The very last few opponents of the Federation surrendered in 1990.

Meanwhile Sarawak was finding its feet within the larger body of the Federation of Malaysia. As part of its agreement to become part of the Federation, Sarawak, along with Sabah, was given a degree of autonomy over state finances, agriculture and forestry. But gradually things began to turn a little sour as Malay was introduced as the language of education and Malays were brought into the civil service in Sarawak. In 1966 the dominant political group, the Sarawak National Party (SNP), lost power and a Muslim dominated coalition took power. Since then local issues have given way to national needs as Sarawak has become a major gas timber and oil producer. Today, only a tiny percentage of Sarawak's income from its natural resources goes into state funds while local politicians become wealthy from their logging interests.

Peoples of Sarawak

About half the population of Sarawak is neither Malay nor Chinese and it is the cultures of the various indigenous groups that helps to make Sarawak such a fascinating place to visit.

Before shotguns became available, **blowpipes** were used to hunt game in the forest. The Penans are regarded as the most skilful hunters and most proficient users of the blowpipe. The darts for blowpipes are made from splinters shaved off the stem of the sago palm (*nibong*) to fit the bore of the blowpipe. The poison is extracted from the ipoh tree (*Antiaris toxicaria*) by collecting sap from the bark and heating it until it forms a treacle-like substance which can be wrapped in a large leaf and thus carried around.

Ibans, the fierce headhunters of days long gone, make up about 30 per cent of Sarawak's population. Today many live in towns, such as Kuching and Sibu, where they are distinguishable by their liking for tattoos on the hands and throat. The best account of traditional Iban culture is to be found in Tom Harrisson's *World Within*. He traces the fearsome reputation of Iban warriors to their traditional practice of attacking in an open, frontal assault and the importance they attach to open displays of bravery.

Ibans moved north from Kalimantan in the 16C and in their relentless search for new land evolved a warrior ethos that included the taking of enemies' heads. More attractively, they also developed a non-hierarchical society with no need for chiefs or slaves. Their involvement with piracy gave them the title of 'Sea Dyaks' (*Dyak* being a Malay word for the tribespeople of Borneo), which is misleading because their traditional homes are in longhouses built above the banks of Sarawak's many inland rivers. One part of most visitors' itinerary is an overnight stay in an Iban longhouse. Despite the overt commercialisation of most such visits, it remains a memorable experience. The Ibans are traditionally a very friendly and fun-loving people, as described in Redmond O'Hanlon's *Into the Heart of Borneo*, and this is very evident during an evening's entertainment in a longhouse.

> Any visit to a longhouse will invariably produce the local toddy, a rice wine called **tuak**. It comes in two forms: a distilled clear version and a cloudy and sweet one. In both cases the rice is boiled and mixed with a local yeast (*ragi*) before being left to ferment for a couple of months. It can then be bottled for the cloudy *tuak* version. Most visitors prefer the drink after it has been further distilled, then the sweet taste has more bite and the alcohol level is considerably stronger.

In modern times the Iban work at logging, in the oil industry and many have moved into towns and taken up a contemporary lifestyle. Many more still live the life of traditional farmers, using a slash and burn type of farming—cultivating one area for growing dry rice and then leaving it to regain fertility while moving on to another patch of land. But even in these settlements the longhouses are equipped with televisions, refrigerators, and four-wheel drive trucks. The longhouses remain essentially the same as they always were—a kind of terrace built on stilts with each door opening to an individual family unit of living- and sleeping-rooms, kitchen and loft. Many Iban have converted to Christianity but retain their traditional easy-going attitudes to sex. The Iban celebrate the harvest in May–June with great parties where *tuak* makes an inevitable appearance.

The **Bidayuh**, it is claimed, were saved by the Brooke dynasty from extinction by the more aggressive Ibans. Now the majority of Bidayuh live to the west of Kuching, spreading south into Kalimantan. They make up less than 10 per cent of the state's population, with only about 50,000 still living in longhouses, but their cultural contribution to Sarawak is significant. Their bamboo-work and carpentry is regarded as exemplary, and Bidayuh wine is very drinkable— related, no doubt, to their traditional occupation as rice farmers.

The people who live in the upper regions of Sarawak's rivers are collectively known in Malay as **Orang Ulu**. These tribes include the Kenyah and Kayan and various smaller sub-groups such as the Kejamans, Skapans and Berawans.

Kenyahs and **Kayans** live in longhouses but not along rivers. They are inland people, once as warrior-like as the Ibans, their traditional enemies, and put up stout resistance to the Brookes family (see p 267). Like most of the other tribal peoples in Sarawak, much of their traditional pagan culture has been erased by evangelising Christians.

The **Melanaus** live between the Baram and the Rejang rivers, mostly along the coast. Their traditional dwellings were built on wooden stilts, very high off the ground, as a defensive measure against marauders from the sea. Today, their homes are indistinguishable from Malay dwellings and culturally they are also merging with Malays by adopting Islam and intermarrying more than the other tribal peoples.

The **Kelabits** live on a plateau, known as the Kelabit Highlands, southeast of Miri and stretching to the border with Kalimantan. Their main settlement is Bario, only accessible by air, and the region is famous for the quality of the rice that the Kelabits cultivate. The Kelabits are also renowned hunters and, like the Penans, their traditional hunting ground is being destroyed by logging companies. Today, there are about 8000 Kelabits and they are mostly Christians, converted by the Borneo Evangelical Mission after the Second World War.

> According to the British naturalist, Sir David Attenborough, the Kelabit people have named farming months after particular migrant birds that arrive in the Kelabit Highlands at the end of summer when the cold is creeping in to their native homelands in the Asian interior. When the yellow wagtail appears in August, the farmers know it is time to start planting the rice paddies; come October, when the brown shrike is seen, it is time to be finishing the sowing.

The **Penans** are in danger of being extinguished as a cultural people . They are nomadic hunter-gatherers who, until made to do so by the government, rarely came out of the forest; hence their light pigmentation. They still use blowpipes and their prowess in the art of jungle survival is unmatched by any other tribal people. Until recently, they had stoutly resisted the government's attempts to encourage them out of the forest and into longhouse accommodation where they are cut off from their traditional way of life. The timber companies, encroaching on their land, are proving equally destructive and before the end of this century it is almost certain that they will be no more Penans in the forest.

> The plight of the Penans was brought to the attention of the rest of the world with the help of Bruno Manser, a Swiss national who first came to Sarawak in 1984 as a member of a geological expedition to explore the Mulu caves. Protests against logging were getting underway at the time and Bruno became involved with the campaign to save the forests. His visa expired but he stayed and became closely involved with the Penans, learning their language and living with them in the jungle. A dramatic escape from police custody helped to create his Robin Hood image and publicised the Penans' fight to protect their way of life. Manser finally left Sarawak in 1990 and continues to agitate on behalf of the Penans in Europe.

Logging and the future of the Penans

It is hard, having visited the Penans, to be objective about the logging taking place in Sarawak. Everywhere you go, there is evidence of the industry, from huge timber carrying trucks, to logs floating down the river, to the sight from your plane window of the logging operations, to the ugly boom towns where the loggers are based.

Sarawak depends on the logging for its wealth since most of the revenue from the lucrative gas and oil fields goes to the federal government. The

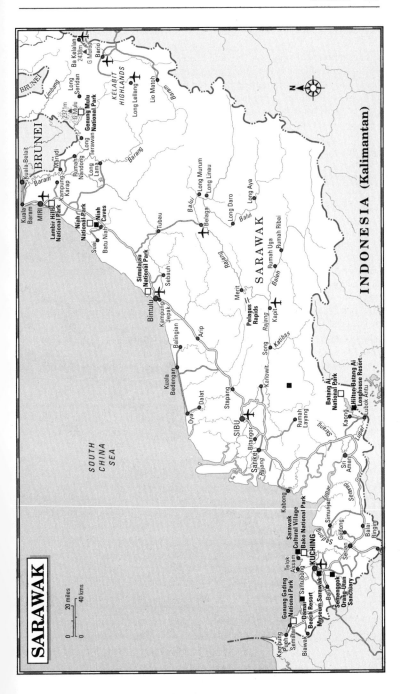

government also claims that it has cut back logging and is practising sustainable forestry—taking out valuable timber while leaving saplings to regenerate. It says that the indigenous forest peoples need to be given the benefits of civilisation which it can only do if they live settled lives out of the rainforest. Furthermore, Britain, the USA, and Canada have exploited their forests to the full, without any foreigners taking the high moral standpoint. So, why is there so much passion connected with the logging of the Sarawak rainforests?

First of all, the sustainable forest idea sounds good but it ignores the enormous damage done to the environment by the use of the huge logging machinery. The delicate forest soil is churned up, potholes are created where mosquitoes can breed, and soil is washed down to the rivers, silting up the main arteries of the country, fouling drinking water and killing fish. It takes 25 years for the forest to regenerate, but some areas are officially logged three times in that period. Illegal, unsustainable logging goes on unchecked. There is little recognition of the rights of the people who have always inhabited the forest. Forest people like the Penans have made it obvious that they wish to be left alone. Just one visit to the sad plywood government-built Penan longhouse at Batu Bungan proves that they are better off left to themselves. At the current rate of logging the forests will be gone within a decade and the rare plant and animal life that depends on it will be gone from the planet forever. The Penans' fate is already sealed: the food they depended on is too scarce to support them, they are catching diseases hitherto unknown to them and soon they will all be living in shabby government-built longhouses, selling baskets to tourists.

There are well over 300,000 **Malays** in Sarawak, mostly concentrated around Kuching and the Limbang District close to Brunei, and occasionally small Malay communities are found upriver. Under the Brookes (see p 267, Malays were employed in the lower ranks of the dynasty's civil service. There is some intermarriage between Malays and the Melanaus (see above). The Islamic influence is generally less keenly felt amongst the Malays of Sarawak, which is not to say that they are any less devout, only that the political force that pushes Islam in peninsular Malaysia is not a factor that comes into play here. For example, Malay women in Sarawak are not under any pressure to dress according to the Islamic code and there is no talk of introducing Islamic law.

The **Chinese** were in Sarawak long before James Brooke, as gold-miners in Bau near Kuching and as the first merchants who acted as middlemen between the people of the interior of Borneo and the outside world. There was always an underlying animosity between the Brookes and the Chinese, but in the 1880s a sizeable contingent of Foochows were encouraged to settle near Sibu where they gradually emerged as the local capitalists. Now the Chinese make up about one-third of Sarawak's total population and in nearly every town they have a commercial presence as shopkeepers.

Kuching

The glory of Kuching is that parts of it seem to have changed very little. One side of the river remains completely undeveloped and affords the visitor the most evocative vista to be found in any town in Malaysia: the small *sampans* that provide the only transport across the water contribute their own nostalgic touch—only close up do their wooden roofs reveal advertisements for fast-food restaurants.

The town centre is strung along the other side of the river and, mainly because no bombs were dropped on the town during the Second World War, much of its 19C character has been retained. The few high-rise buildings and shopping centres that do exist are clustered together at the other end of town.

History

It was tin that created Kuala Lumpur and antimony that created Kuching. In 1829 a small settlement was begun here on the banks of the Sungei Sarawak by overlords from Brunei who wanted to keep an eye over the anti-mony-mining in the neighbourhood. It also became the base for Chinese traders involved in the export of the metalloid to Singapore. James Brooke first arrived here in 1839 and when he became Raja two years later decided to make it his capital. In Malay, Kuching means 'cat', and there are several theories which attempt to account for the name. It may have been named after local wild cats, or after a local fruit tree *buah matah kucing*. One theory suggests that Rajah Brooke asked someone what the name of the town was and the other person thought he was asking the name of the animal that was walking past!

■ Practical information

Getting to and from Kuching

By air. Kuching International Airport (☎ 082-454255) is 11km from town. The MAS office (☎ 082-246622) is at Lot 215, Jalan Song Thian Cheok. There are non-stop routes to Kuala Lumpur (RM262) and Johor Bahru on peninsular Malaysia. Within Sarawak there are non-stop routes to Miri, Sibu and Bintulu. There are also direct flights to Singapore, Brunei, Hong Kong, Manila, Pontianak and Tokyo-Narita.

The taxi fare between the airport and town is RM15. Bus No. 12A operates between the airport and town and can be boarded from outside the GPO (on Jalan Tun Abang Haji Openg) or the bus station in Lebuh Jawa. For the timetable, contact the Sarawak Tourist Association (STA); see Tourist information, below.

By bus. The long-distance buses leave from Jalan Penrissen which is 5km outside town and best reached by taxi. P.B. Express (☎ 082-461277) runs a direct express service between Kuching and Sibu (RM32) and Miri (RM70) at 06.30 and 09.00. Borneo Highway Express (☎ 082-427035) and Biaramas Express (☎ 082-452139) run similar services.

By boat. Boat companies run similar services between Kuching and Sibu (RM35) from Pending, about 6km east of town and reached by taxi or bus Nos

17 or 19 from outside the market on Main Bazaar. For times of departure contact Hoover Marine Express (☎ 082-335516) or their booking agent, Wingka Rubberstamp Co, 77 Jalan Padungan (☎ 082-429252). Another company is Ekspres Bahagia (☎ 082-421948) at 50 Jalan Padungan.

Getting around Kuching
Car hire can be arranged at the airport, through some of the hotels, or from Petra Jaya Car Rental (☎ 082-416733). Expect to pay around RM148 a day, RM838 a week.

Tourist information
The **Sarawak Tourist Association** (STA) has an office (☎ 082-240620) on Main Bazaar. It is open from 08.00 to 12.45 and 14.00 to 16.15 Monday to Thursday; 08.00 to 11.30 and 14.30 to 16.45 on Friday; 08.00 to 12.45 on Saturday. There is also an STA office at the airport (☎ 082-240620) but the waterfront office has more local travel information and sound advice on transport to other parts of Sarawak.

Tourism Malaysia (☎ 082-246575) has an office on Floor 2 of the Rugayah Building on Jalan Song Thian Cheok. There is also the Sarawak Tourist Information Centre (☎ 082-410944) on Jalan Barrack where bookings for Bako National Park are made.

The best bank for **changing money** is the Hong Kong & Shanghai Bank on Jalan Tun Abang Haji Openg, not far from the STA office. Opening hours are 09.30 to 15.00, Monday to Friday, and 09.30 to 11.00 on Saturday. The Mohamed Yahia bookshop in the basement of the Sarawak Plaza also changes money and stays open daily until 21.00.

The **General Post Office**, on Jalan Tun Abang Haji Openg, opens from 08.00 to 16.00 Monday to Friday; 08.00 to 18.30 on Saturday; 09.00 to 16.00 on Sunday. The **Telekom** office is on Jalan Batu Lintang, and opens from 08.00 to 18.00 Monday to Friday, and from 08.00 to 12.00 on Saturday.

Embassy and immigration
The **Indonesian Consulate** (☎ 082-241734), 5a Jalan Pisang, is open from 08.30 to 12.00 and 14.00 to 16.00 Monday to Thursday.

Immigration (☎ 082-240301), First Floor, Bangunan Sultan Iskander, Jalan Simpang Tiga, Petra Jaya, is open from 08.00 to 12.00 and 14.00 to 16.30 Monday to Friday.

Emergencies
The main **police station** (☎ 082-245522) is off Jalan Courthouse. Contact the hospital, **Kuching General** (☎ 082-257555), on Jalan Ong Kie Hui, for all medical emergencies.

Tour operators
Regular city tours, overnight visits to local longhouses, trips to the Semenggoh Wildlife Rehabilitation Centre and to Bako National Park are all available. Many of the companies have desks in the main hotels or may be contacted direct. Established companies include **Saga Travel** (☎ 082-418705), which also does a more demanding tour of caves near the old mining town of Bau, and **Journey**

Travel Agencies (☎ 082-421603), Lobby Floor, Hilton, Jalan Borneo. More specialised longhouse tours are available through **Asian Overland** (☎ 082-251163), 286-A First Floor, Westwood Park, Jalan Tabuan, and **Tour Exotica** (☎ 082-254607), on the first floor at Nos 1–3 Jalan Temple. Well worth checking out as well is **Tropical Adventure** (☎ 082-413088/413104) on the first floor at No. 17 Main Bazaar.

Accommodation

Top range hotels are the **Riverside Majestic** (☎ 082-247777; fax 082-425858), the **Hilton** (☎ 082-248200; fax 082-238546) and the **Holiday Inn** (☎ 082-423111; fax 082-426169), all on Jalan Tunku Abdul Rahman. Rooms are from about RM290. The most relaxing of the three is the Hilton. If you have little time in Sarawak and want to see the interior, the Hilton also runs the **Batang Ai Longhouse Resort**, a 4-hour, 275km journey inland from Kuching, which costs over RM400 for a double room.

Middle range hotels include the **Borneo Hotel** (☎ 082-244121-4) at 30 Jalan Tabuan. A double is RM86 and there is a good restaurant attached. **Longhouse Hotel** (☎ 082-249333), at 101 Jalan Abell, has decent rooms from RM65–90. The **Fata Hotel** (☎ 082-248111-4), on Jalan Tabuan facing the roundabout, has well kept rooms atRM40–85.

Budget places include the **Anglican Rest House** (☎ 082-240188) on Jalan McDougall, with en-suite rooms as well as twin-bed rooms with shared bathrooms. The **Mandarin** (☎ 082-418269), at 6 Jalan Green Hill, has small rooms but with the benefit of air-conditioning.

Restaurants

Kuching has the best range of restaurants in Sarawak and prices are affordable: even in a smart hotel like the Hilton, the **Riverside Café** serves pizzas and local dishes for RM10–20. The Hilton also has the more expensive **Steakhouse**, as well as the best takeaway pastry counter in Kuching. The **River Palace** at the Riverside Majestic serves Cantonese and Szechuan dishes and the hotel's **Sri Sarawak** has a Malay and seafood menu. The **Meisan Restoran** at the Holiday Inn is good for *dim sum* at lunchtime. Check the daily *Sarawak Tribune* for current details of the various food promotions by particular hotels.

The **Steamship Restaurant** in the Sarawak Steamship Company Building on the waterfront has a pleasant Chinese and Thai menu, with meals around RM15. At 21 Jalan Bishopgate, not far from the tourist office, **Min Joo** is a good Chinese vegetarian cafe, serving soup and *kueh tiaw* for a couple of ringitt. The **Cosy Corner Café** attached to the Borneo Hotel on Jalan Tabuan is fine for a Western breakfast or meals around RM15.

Shopping

For general shopping there is a **Parksons** department store next to the Riverside Majestic, and the **Sarawak Plaza**, next to the Holiday Inn, is crammed with shops of every description. There is a supermarket in the basement and a Times bookshop on the first floor. A wider selection of **books** on Sarawak's culture can be found in the Mohamed Yahia bookshop in the basement of the Sarawak Plaza and also in the lobby of the Holiday Inn.

For **ethnic gifts and souvenirs** there is a general selection at the shop in the

Sarawak Museum and along the Main Bazaar between the STA office and the Hilton. **Siam Company** at No. 28 and **Elegance** at No. 38 Main Bazaar both have selections of reasonably priced sculptures of head-hunters and the like. **Native Arts** at No. 94 has the best selection of wood-carvings. Most of these shops close around 18.00 on Sunday, otherwise they open until around 21.00.

The Sarawak Steamship Company Building on the waterfront near the STA office has half-a-dozen shops catering to tourists. For genuine antique artefacts visit **Dynasty** in the basement of the Sarawak Plaza, next to the Holiday Inn. The **Batik Art Shop**, opposite the temple on Jalan Temple, has original batik paintings by local artist Pang Ling from RM150 to RM1000. A number of pottery shops are along Jalan Penrissen, the airport road.

There are several interesting **markets** in Kuching. The Sunday market, on Jalan Satok, just outside of town, is the most unusual. *Dyaks* from the surrounding countryside come into town with things to sell ranging from wild boar to bats as well as fruits gathered from the farms and forest. There are vegetable and wet markets in Jalan Gambier and a market at the Ban Hock wharf where cheap clothes and fake designer gear can be found.

Entertainment

There are daily cultural shows of a very inauthentic nature at the Damai Beach Cultural Village (see p 285). More interesting to visitors might be the football matches held in the Stadium Negari Sarawak in Petra Jaya. There is also horse racing at the Turf Club on Jalan Serian. Check local newspapers for events at these places.

Sport

There is a profusion of golf courses around Kuching, from the prestigious Damai Beach Resort 18-hole course to the 9 and 18 hole courses at the Sarawak Golf and Country Club at Petra Jaya.

Colonial Walk

This walk consists of a stroll down and back up Jalan Tun Abang Haji Openg before crossing the river to visit what was once the Brooke residence.

The walk begins outside the **Square Tower** on the waterfront, near the tourist office. The tower was built in 1879 as a prison, though it was later used as a ballroom. Inside, on the first floor, a video of the town's history is shown between 10.00 and 14.00 and 16.00–21.30 daily, except Friday when the hours are 10.00–11.30 only. There is also a small but interesting collection of photographs of the colonial era.

From outside the Square Tower, cross the main road to where the **Courthouse**, built in 1874, faces you. It is difficult to miss the broad verandah supported by large tapering pillars, with steps leading up to the square portico with four sets of twin columns at each end and a single column in between on each side. It was designed to create a large area of shade—ideal for a public building in the tropics. Charles Brooke built it as his regime's administrative centre. It included a law court, which still functions as the state's central law court. The clock tower was added in 1883.

Outside the courthouse, the **Charles Brooke Memorial** was built in 1924. The bronze panels in each corner of the base commemorate the four

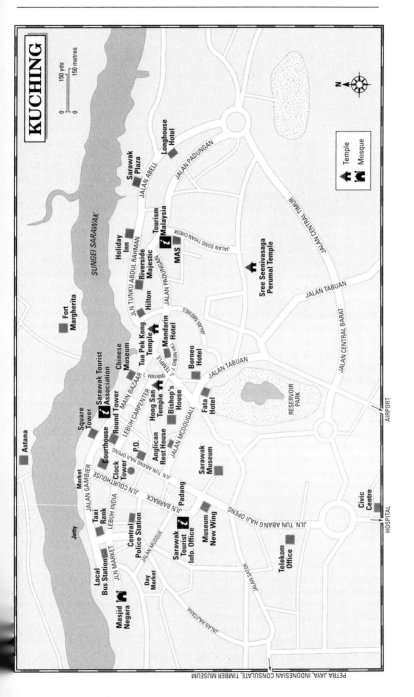

KUCHING

0 ____ 150 yds
0 ____ 150 metres

Temple
Mosque

SUNGEI SARAWAK

Astana

Fort Margherita

Square Tower

Sarawak Tourist Association

Chinese Museum

Tua Pek Kong Temple

Holiday Inn

Riverside Majestic

Hilton

Tourism Malaysia

MAS

Sarawak Plaza

Longhouse Hotel

JALAN ABELL

JALAN PADUNGAN

JLN TUNKU ABDUL RAHMAN

JALAN PADUNGAN

JALAN SONG THIAN CHEOK

Sree Seenivasaga Perumal Temple

JALAN TABUAN

JLN CENTRAL TIMUR

Round Tower

Courthouse

Clock Tower

P.O.

Market

Taxi Rank

Jetty

Local Bus Station

Masjid Negara

Day Market

JALAN GAMBIER

LEBUH INDIA

JLN MARKET

JLN COURTHOUSE

LEBUH CARPENTER

MAIN BAZAAR

L WAYANG

Hong San Temple

Bishop's House

Anglican Rest House

JALAN MCDOUGALL

JLN TUN ABANG HAJI OPENG

Central Police Station

JALAN MUSQUE

Sarawak Tourist Info. Office

Museum New Wing

JLN BARRACK

Padang

Sarawak Museum

Mandarin Hotel

JALAN MATHIES

J. TEMPLE

J. GREENHILL

Borneo Hotel

Fata Hotel

JALAN TABUAN

RESERVOIR PARK

JALAN CENTRAL BARAT

Civic Centre

Telekom Office

JLN. TUN G HAJI OPENG

JALAN HAJI TAHA

JALAN SATOK

HOSPITAL

AIRPORT

PETRA JAYA, INDONESIAN CONSULATE, TIMBER MUSEUM

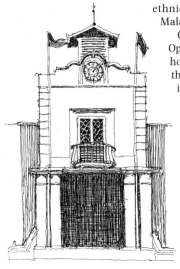

The Courthouse at Kuching

ethnic groups of Sarawak: Ibans, Chinese, Malays and Orang Ulu.

On the other side of Jalan Tun Abang Haji Openg, the **Round Tower** was designed to house a dispensary but when it was built in the 1880s the troubled times deemed it fit to incorporate defensive features; hence its military style of architecture. It is currently used as a government building.

Walk down Jalan Tun Abang Haji Openg to the stately **General Post Office** on the left-hand side of the road. One wonders if its neo-classical design seemed any more appropriate in 1931, when it was built by the last Rajah, Vyner Brooke, than it does now. The massive Corinthian columns front a façade with semi-circular arches and ornamented capitals and decorative friezes. The parapet walls hide a pitch roof.

On the other side of the road the Pavilion, currently being renovated, was built in 1909 and was known until recently as the Education Department Building because that was the department's headquarters. Inspired by this, perhaps, the Japanese used it as an 'information bureau' during their Occupation. It was originally built as a hospital with a nursing home on the first floor.

Retrace the route back to the Square Tower and enquire at the nearby tourist office if the jetty for boats across to **Fort Margherita** is now in front of the Square Tower (it may have moved). From the jetty point on the other side of Sungei Sarawak, it is a short walk to the strategic spot where James Brooke built a fort in 1841 to command a view of Kuching and any approaching enemy using the river. In 1857 the original fort was burned down during a rebellion by Chinese miners; Charles Brooke built a new fort in 1879 and named it after his wife Margaret. It is the best of all the Brooke fortifications—there are a number of them dotted across Sarawak—and the only one open to the public.

Inside, there is an interesting **Police Museum**, open Tuesday to Sunday from 10.00 to 18.00 with free admission (bring your passport), with material on the Japanese Occupation, the communist insurgency of the 1960s and various other illicit activities.

Charles Brooke also built on this side of the river a new residence for his wife which was completed in 1869. Known as the **Astana** (a version of Istana, the Malay word for palace), it was originally a complex of three bungalows, with a crenellated tower added in the 1880s. Unfortunately, it is now only open to the public on Hari Raya Puasa at the end of Ramadan.

Multi-cultural Walk

The walk—best begun early in the morning—starts at the junction of Main Bazaar and Jalan Courthouse, the next block west from the beginning of the colonial walk above. Walk down Jalan Courthouse and take the turning on the right into **Jalan India**. This is a colourful pedestrianised street full of small shops and Indian coffee shops that hark back to the days when Indian immigrants settled here to be close to their employment at the neighbouring docks.

At the end of Jalan India, cross the road onto **Jalan Market** and look for the **Nam Sen** coffee shop at No. 17 on the right-hand side of the street. This is a classic Chinese coffee shop: large swirling fans, marble-topped round wooden tables and noodles being prepared at the entrance using giant chopsticks. To add to the ambience there are cabinet shelves crowded with bottles of liquor and Chinese wines. Drop in and enjoy a cup of coffee.

The coffee shop is on the corner of **Lorong Dock**, a narrow alleyway crowded with stalls selling clothes, locks, watches and toiletries. A stroll to the end of Lorong Dock brings you to a small vegetable stall with plates of ginger, lime and peppers for sale and opposite there is a small Malay café.

Back on Jalan Market, walk to the end of this busy commercial section of the street to where there is a **mosque** on the right with an old cemetery in the grounds. This is a Malay quarter of town and there are some well-preserved houses from the turn of the century to be found in the side streets.

Retrace your route back to the junction of Jalan Market and Jalan India and turn to the left, past the ranks of taxis, up to Jalan Gambier facing the river. Do not cross the street, where there is a busy poultry market, but turn to the right along **Jalan Gambier**. This side of the street is crowded with noise and colour emanating from the shops of Indian and Chinese merchants whose produce— sackfuls of dried fish, rice, flour, spices of every type—spills out onto the pavement. Merchants established themselves here to be close to the river where boats arrived and departed with their stock.

Continue along Jalan Gambier as far as the Square Tower and turn right into Jalan Tun Abang Haji Openg and then left into **Jalan Carpenter**. Most of the street was accidentally burned down in 1884 and the *godowns* you see here were built after the fire. The shopowners and their families live behind their shops, just as they did a century ago. Despite the **National Islamic Café** on the right, this is predominantly a Chinese street and just past the café there is a brightly coloured Taoist temple. Continue past the temple, however, to the end of the street where there is a more important Taoist temple, the **Hong San Temple**, at the junction of Jalan Carpenter and Jalan Wayang. It was built in 1897 to honour Kuek Seng On, a Hokkien Chinese who was deified at the end of the 19C. Looking to the south from outside the temple, it is possible to see the **Bishop's House** on high ground. This is the oldest surviving building in Kuching (1894) but it is not open to the public.

Turn right into Jalan Wayang, go down to the Rex cinema and turn left back up **Jalan Temple**. The street takes its name from the **Tua Pek Kong Temple** at the top of the street facing the river. It was built in 1876 and is the most popular temple for the Chinese community in Kuching.

Sarawak Museum

The Sarawak Museum, the finest in Malaysia, overlooks the Padang and is easily reached on foot from the town centre. It is open daily from 09.00 to 18.00, except Friday; admission is free. The new wing contains a **shop** on the ground floor with a wide selection of souvenirs and small gifts and some more expensive

modern wood-carvings. There is a canteen outside the new wing which serves
drinks and basic meals.

> The museum was built under Charles Brooke in 1891 but was inspired by
> Alfred Russel Wallace (1823–1913), whose travelling in the Malay world
> helped him to develop a theory of evolution by natural selection indepen-
> dently of Darwin. Apparently the museum was designed by Brooke's French
> valet along the lines of a town hall from his home in Normandy. It is in two
> parts—the main building and a new block connected by a footbridge across
> Jalan Tun Abang Haji Openg. For most people there is too much to see in
> one visit and each part is best seen on a separate day.

The **main building** is the original museum building and its **ground floor**
contains a fairly uninteresting collection of stuffed animals and birds that has
aged less gracefully than the building itself. The dusty skeletons of an orang-
utan and proboscis monkey, if seen and pondered upon by Wallace, may have
given him an idea or two.

The **second floor** has two rooms: one is largely taken up with a re-created
longhouse complete with authentic shrunken skulls; the other is packed with
ethnographic originals. There is a fine collection of *kris*: most of them have a
wavy or serpentine blade, said to be associated with the Hindu serpent god Naga.
The collection of masks is impressive: Kenyah, Kayan and Iban ones used in
harvest and fertility festivals and soul-catching ceremonies. The Melanau sickness images—*blum*—are fascinating: an expert carves an image of the particular spirit thought to be responsible for the sickness and a spell is pronounced
which culminates in the spitting of a mixture of betel-nut, chewed lime and
sireh leaves at the image. Not surprisingly, the spirit hastily departs.

On this floor are displayed what are perhaps the most magnificent artefacts in
the whole museum. Before they were converted to Christianity, the native
peoples in the Belaga and Baram areas used to carve ceremonial poles from a
single tree trunk and erect them in front of their longhouses for use in head-
hunting, farming and rite of passage ceremonies. Up to 5.5m high, they are
superb. Equally eye-catching are the examples of original wood-carvings from
the different cultural groups.

The **new block** has two floors with two rooms on each. The **ground floor** is
largely devoted to the history of Kuching and the room on the left as you enter
is the more engaging of the two. The early years of antimony-mining through to
the Japanese Occupation are well covered, with photographs and artists' impres-
sions of early tin mining and the town. The room on the right has too many
glass cases stuffed with uniforms and photographs of forgettable council leaders
to detain most visitors.

The **first floor** is the real attraction. In the room on the left there are ceramics
and Chinese furniture, a fascinating illustrated description of sago processing,
and an ethnographic section that will whet the appetite of most visitors for a trip
to Sarawak's interior. There are displays of Iban cotton-weaving, a Bidayuh
longhouse, and authentic examples of ethnic wood-carvings, masks and basketwork. The section on the Penans includes the innocuous-sounding announce-
ment: 'It is the policy of the government to persuade the nomadic Penan to lead
a settled life. Schools and longhouses have been built for them.' To back this up

there are colour photographs purporting to show how they have 'adjusted' to longhouse life: the expressions on the Penans' faces show just what this amounts to.

The other room on the first floor includes a mock cave to display the art of birds' nest collecting and some interesting archaeological finds from the country's early history. Look for the *batu lesong*, a phallus on a base that was found in 1848 and was an object of veneration to the Hindu Pallavas who came to the Malay peninsula from south of Madras sometime in the 12C. Outside the museum annexe is a garden and aquarium.

Kuching, a view from the river

The Chinese Museum

The building itself is part of the celebration of Chinese life in Kuching. It was built in 1912 as the Chinese Court, consisting of a main hall and two side rooms. A pair of scales can still be seen over the two 2.5m doors that form the main entrance. The Court was dissolved in 1921 and the building housed a government office until 1930 when it became the Chinese Chamber of Commerce Building.

The museum covers Chinese involvement in the development of Kuching from the early pre-Brooke days of bartering with tribal peoples for forest products right up to contemporary events, represented by a colourful dragon model used in the dragon dance festivities during the Chinese New Year. The main contents of the museum are a series of panels, supported primarily by old photographs, on the various cultural groups of Chinese that found their way to Kuching: the Hakka, Cantonese, Hokkien, Chao Ann, Teochew, Hainan, Luichew and Foochew.

The Timber Museum

The Timber Museum is on Jalan Wisma Sumbar Alam, next to the stadium in Petra Jaya, and best reached by taxi or bus from outside the GPO. It was opened in the mid 1980s, at the height of the controversy over logging, to offer a defence of the timber industry in Sarawak. As well as presenting factual information on the technology of logging, the museum purports to show that ethnic groups have benefited economically and socially from the industry. The crux of the problem, however, is how one defines economic and social progress, and the museum is predicated on only one definition, which excludes consideration of the intrinsic worth of cultures that hold quite different values.

The Islamic Museum

This was the first museum of its kind in Southeast Asia, with examples of architecture, coins, costumes, jewellery, weapons, pottery and textiles. The museum is close to the Sarawak Museum. Admission is free. It is open Monday to Thursday 09.15–17.30, Saturday and Sunday 09.15–18.00.

The Civic Centre

This distinctive building is on the south side of the river on Jalan Tun Abang Haji Openg. From its viewing platform you can see panoramic views of Kuching. It can be reached by bus from Lebuh market. It houses an art gallery, open 09.00–17.30 Monday to Saturday. It also houses the Sultan Iskander Shah Planetarium. Opened in 1989, this interesting exhibition has seating for 170 and a 15 metre dome. Shows are daily at 15.00 with an extra show at 19.30 on Tuesday and Thursday.

Excursions from Kuching

Bako National Park

For the visitor who enjoys nature walks, this is a highly recommended excursion to the mouth of the river Bako; at least one night's stay at the park is necessary to make the journey there worthwhile. The walking trails, 16 of them covering a total of 30km, are clearly marked and range from a 1-hour return trip to a 7-hour trek.

The park was established in 1957 and, although small by Malaysian standards at 2728 hectares, displays an amazing variety of habitats. Particularly stunning are the shorelines with eroded sandstone cliffs behind isolated sandy beaches and strangely shaped sea stacks. In the park itself is an interesting information centre which explains the geology and wildlife in the park. The information centre is open daily from 08.00–22.00.

The unique proboscis monkey (see p 261) can sometimes be spotted in the Telok Assam and Telok Delima areas. They can also be seen at Telok Paku around dusk, less than an hour's walk from the park headquarters. Unless travelling on to Sabah, it is well worth making the effort to try and see these extraordinary creatures.

Other animals that might be seen are the bearded pig and, at night with the help of a torch, the lesser mousedeer and flying lemur. Some 153 species of bird have been identified in the park and around the chalets at Telok Assam the mangrove blue flycatcher is a regular visitor. Telok Assam is also a good place to see mangrove forest.

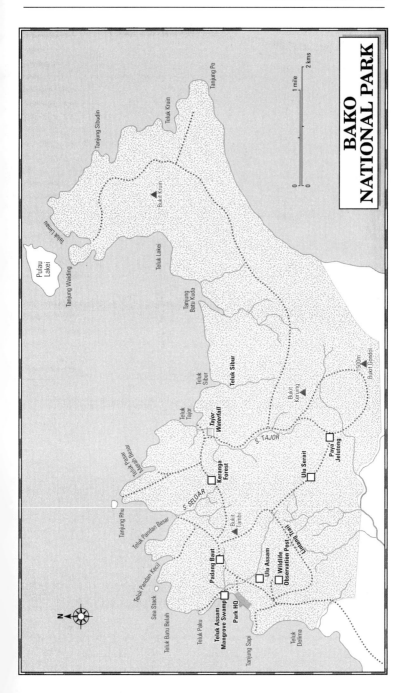

Mangroves and mudskippers

Growing on the muddy coastline, mangroves are a unique family of tropical trees, able to survive in a salt-water environment that would cause terminal shock to any other tree. They can be recognised by their alien-looking root structure which, when exposed at low tide, can be seen to radiate out from the main trunk in an arched cluster of wiry roots that disappear into the mud, thus buttressing the tree against the shifting tide of mud and water. The trees have evolved ways of desalinating the water in order to minimise the amount of salt in their sap. Some species have a filtering system that excludes it from the roots; others collect the salt before excreting it from the twigs or leaves. One species, the *Rhizophora*, is unique in that its fruit grows an early root and leaf before it drops from the tree. The seedlings, with the attached root, grow up to 60cm in length before dropping off. The sharp-pointed root then embeds itself in the mud and quickly grows into a new tree.

The amphibious **mudskippers** are unusual, not because they are amphibious but because they are fish. They are easy to spot because of their sudden darts across the mud. They are best appreciated through binoculars if you cannot get close to them. You will recognise them by their eyes which are located on the top of their head. Their enlarged gills contain water and air, allowing them to filter oxygen from the air, but they need to return regularly to the mud in order to refill their gills with a fresh supply of water. Their pectoral fins have evolved into a kind of crutch that allows them to lever their way across the mud—in soft mud they skip along, hence the name—and their pelvic fins are joined to act as a sucker, enabling them to cling to the roots of the exposed mangroves when the tide is out. The blue-spotted *Boleophthalmus boddaerti* is most commonly found in the mangroves while the orange-spotted *Periophthalmus chrysospilos* dwells more inland.

Getting there is by way of bus No. 6 to Kampung Bako from Jalan Market in Kuching (37km). It takes about two hours and involves a short ferry crossing. From Kampung Bako it is a 30-minute journey by longboat into the park headquarters at **Telok Assam**. Most of the tour operators in Kuching run trips to the park, although it is not difficult to make your own travel and accommodation arrangements.

Accommodation, and the longboat journey, needs to be pre-booked through the Sarawak Tourist Information Centre in Kuching (☎ 082-410944; ☎ 084-246477), on the corner of Jalan Barrack. The resthouses are adequate, and include linen, kitchen facilities and a refrigerator. There is a choice of accommodation, ranging from hostels and camping through to standard resthouses and a more expensive lodge. A double room is M\$30 plus, while a whole simple lodge is M\$60 plus. There is a canteen but it is better to bring your own provisions.

The **Lintang Trail** is recommended for anyone who wants to feast their eyes on **pitcher plants**; after a moderately steep climb to an open and barren plateau, the plants are easy to find among the shrubs. Look for *Nepenthes graclic* which hangs from trees, *Nepenthes ampullaria*, recognised by its pot shape, and *Nepenthese rafflesiana*, with red and white stripes around its bowl. The plateau is also home to the bulbous ant-plants which cling to the trees and are easy to spot because of their shape and the tubers which grow out from them. The walk takes from one hour to a whole afternoon depending on how far you choose to walk and how long you spend searching for plants.

One popular walk is to the **Tajor Waterfall**; it takes somewhere between two and three hours depending on how often you pause to rest and examine the plant life. It is also possible to branch off this walk to reach **sandy beaches**—a rare sight anywhere in East Malaysia—which are usually utterly deserted.

Semenggok Wildlife Rehabilitation Centre

This centre, 32km southeast of Kuching on the Serian road, was established in the mid 1970s, from a forest reserve set up by Vyner Brooke in 1920 to provide a temporary home for animals that had been kept illegally or found injured in the forest. The main attraction is the opportunity to see orang-utans at feeding times, including the resident 'Bullet' who first came here after being shot in the head by a hunter and is now too institutionalised to leave. The centre is not as famous as the sanctuary at Sepilok in Sabah, but neither is it so much of an exhibition, and a visit here is worthwhile.

Tour companies run trips from Kuching or you can take bus No. 6 from Jalan Market which stops at the centre's main entrance. Buses leave at 08.30, 10.30, 12.00 and 13.30. Be sure to arrive to catch the feeding times: 08.30–09.00 and 14.30–15.00. Visitors need a permit to visit the centre. These can be obtained, free of charge, from the Tourist Information Centre in Kuching on Main Bazaar, open 08.30–15.45 daily.

Damai Beach and Sarawak Cultural Village

The **Holiday Inn Resort** (☎ 082-411777) is the main destination for visitors to **Damai Beach** (the beach is not open to non-residents). Accommodation is in traditional-style chalets and a full range of water activities are available. The nearby fishing village of **Santubong** makes for a pleasant evening's stroll and there are a couple of seafood restaurants here. Fresh prawns may be purchased at roadside stalls and taken to one of the seafood stalls for cooking.

Located next to the Holiday Inn Resort, the **Sarawak Cultural Village** consists of a number of outdoor displays relating to the lifestyles of the various peoples in Sarawak. Longhouses have been reconstructed, showing the ethnic differences in architecture, and there is an authentic example of a traditional Melinau longhouse which is now rarely seen anywhere in Sarawak. Various characteristic arts and crafts are also on display. A theatre has daily programmes of ethnic dances, very touristy and inauthentic. Allow a full morning or afternoon to visit the place; admission is RM40.

Both the resort and the village are easily reached by taxi or bus No. 2B from Kuching, although a trip to the village can be arranged through a tour operator. Looming over the resort is **Gunung Santubong** at 810m. It is possible to climb the east side of the mountain. The trail begins by the Palm Beach Seafood Restaurant and Resort, about 2.5km before the Holiday Inn.

Visiting a longhouse

The tribal cultures of Sarawak are unique and a short stay of one or two nights in a longhouse is usually a part of most visitors' itineraries. A visit to a longhouse offers a window onto another world and a good tour company will have guides who are happy to act as interpreters between you and the inhabitants of the longhouse you are visiting. However, there are some points worth bearing in mind. As most of the longhouses are situated along the major rivers, a trip up the Skrang from Kuching or the Rejang from Sibu is likely to be the first stage of the trip. If the journey time on the river is only a few hours, it is likely to be an Iban community that is being visited. They are traditionally regarded as the most outgoing of the ethnic peoples and all the tour companies in Kuching or Sibu will have an arrangement with Iban longhouses to receive and entertain visitors. The downside to this is that some of the longhouses that are conveniently reached from Kuching are tourist ghettos. Ask the tour company plenty of questions about the types of longhouse trip they offer. If they have their own guesthouses built alongside the longhouses you will indeed have the benefit of modern conveniences, but little else: a day spent at the Sarawak Cultural Village would provide more insight into the indigenous cultures of Sarawak.

Even the Kayan and Kenyah who live further upriver in more remotely located longhouses are no strangers to the late 20C. Their tribal dances will be authentic but the dancers will be equally proud of the Reebok trainers they perform the dances in. At the same time, though, it is hardly befitting to expect total authenticity, i.e. that so-called primitive people should lack some basic amenities that visitors take for granted. However, as a general rule, the longer it takes to reach the longhouse—measured in days rather than hours—the more authentic it is likely to be.

The days when visitors could turn up unannounced at any longhouse bearing small gifts and expecting a warm welcome are the stuff of out-of-date travel books. The only reliable alternative to working through a travel company is to receive an invitation from someone who has a connection with a longhouse. There will be a charge for accommodation and meals; visitors should bring small gifts for the family. For a list of tour guides see p 274. As a general rule, remember to remove footwear at the door of a longhouse and to ask permission before taking photographs.

Serian

65km southeast of Kuching, Serian is popular with local people who visit the park built around a lake at Taman Danu. There are also some small waterfalls 5km out of town at Taman Rekreasi Ranchan. An express bus goes to Serian from Kuching, about an hour's journey. To stay overnight there is the **Kota Semarahan Serian Hotel** (☎ 082 874118) which has rooms at about RM20–30.

Sri Aman

Situated on the river Lupar, 200km east of Kuching, Sri Aman is the starting point for visits to a number of Iban longhouses on the tributaries of the river. The town itself suffers occasionally from a tidal bore. This is caused by a small island in the river whose position creates a bottleneck. In 1929 Somerset Maugham was almost drowned in one of these tidal waves; it later featured in his short story 'Yellow Streak'.

It is worth taking a look at **Fort Alice**, built by Charles Brooke in 1864 and constructed of *belian* (ironwood), with a small tower at each corner enclosing an open courtyard. Unusually, a type of drawbridge, which could be hauled up to close in times of trouble, was incorporated into its construction. The fort was built to prevent *dyaks* on the Skrang river from passing downriver to the sea from where they could launch pirate attacks on coastal shipping.

A number of the Kuching tour operators (see p 274) have trips to Iban long-houses based on the tributaries of the Lupar, and as a general rule they prove more interesting than the short trips up the Skrang river. All the longhouses have small gardens at the back for growing vegetables and a conversation on farming methods is a good way to learn something about the Ibans' daily life. (See also on p 268.)

Getting to and from Sri Aman is by bus. There is a regular bus service from Kuching and Sibu. **Accommodation**. The **Hoover Hotel** at 139 Club Road has rooms from RM29–72 (☎ 083-321985)

Sibu

Sibu is the second largest town in Sarawak, 60km from the sea and situated on the 563km-long Rejang, the longest river in Malaysia. The town has a stronger Chinese character than anywhere else in Sarawak, evidenced by narrow streets crowded with small shops and an atmosphere of buzzing commercialism that is not typical of the state.

The town is the commercial hub for the hinterland of the Rejang and most visitors find themselves here because it is the stepping-off point for travel up and down the Rejang and the settlements of **Song**, **Kapit** and **Belaga**. There are numerous **Iban longhouses** along the tributaries of the river and from Kapit and Belaga more adventurous visits into the interior may be arranged. The town itself has little of interest but there is enough to occupy a morning or afternoon while waiting for a boat connection upriver. You will hardly fail to spot the wharf with its moored boats and all manner of items being loaded and unloaded. Behind it is the market, open daily and selling all kinds of domestic parapher-nalia and a few bits and pieces of interest to tourists.

History

In the 15C **Ibans** began moving into this part of Sarawak from Kalimantan but the resident Malays who lived close to the coast, under the rule of the **Brunei sultanate**, had no wish to share their land with them. The Ibans moved upriver to what is now Sibu and found themselves in conflict with the **Kayans** who had lived here undisturbed for centuries. The Ibans warred against the Malays, though occasionally forming brief alliances when confronted with threats from other groups, or when they came together in piracy against passing ships. In 1853 Brunei sold the section of river from the coast to Kapit to **James Brooke** who immediately set about establishing his authority over the Ibans and Kayans. The evidence of this can be seen today in the colonial forts upriver.

At the turn of this century **Wong Nai Siong**, from China's Fukien province, explored the Rejang basin to find land suitable for development.

An agreement was reached with Charles Brooke to bring in settlers and about 70 farmers came to Sibu from the Fukien province. When the first farmers arrived they were provided with temporary dwellings and sufficient rice to last until the first harvest was collected. Cultivating rubber proved more profitable than rice and in the years that followed more immigrants arrived. Intrepid merchants expanded the trade that had always existed between the coast and the interior.

The town thrived, in spite of a fire in 1928 that destroyed most of its buildings. The shops along Jalan Channel are examples of the first new buildings constructed after the fire. Japanese forces occupied Sibu between 1942 and 1945 and the Chinese population was singled out for harsh treatment, with thousands forced into slave labour. In the 1950s a number of Chinese with the necessary capital began moving into the timber trade and fortunes were made. Timber is still the mainstay of the Sibu economy, as will be readily seen when travelling up the Rejang river.

■ Practical information

Getting to and from Sibu
By air. The airport (☎ 084-307199) is a 15-minute taxi ride from town (RM20). The MAS office (☎ 084-326166) is at 61 Jalan Tunku Osman. There are non-stop flights between Sibu and Kuching (RM72), Miri (RM112) and Bintulu (RM64). There are also local flights to Belaga (RM76), Kapit (RM48) and Marudi (RM100).

By boat. The river quayside has separate sections, clearly marked, for the various boat companies that travel up and down the Rejang and to Kuching via Sarikei. Times of departure are marked on clock faces at the front of the ekspres launches and tickets are purchased from the individual boats. Luggage can be safely deposited on your seat if you have a couple of hours to wait until departure time. Most boats leave from early in the morning until mid afternoon.

By bus and taxi. By road, Sibu is 240km northeast of Kuching. The combined bus and taxi station is on Jalan Khoo Peng Loong, facing the river, and a short walk from where the boats arrive and depart. There are buses to Bintulu and Miri, respectively 220km and 360km southwest of Sibu.

Tourist information
The **tourist office** (☎ 084-307072) is at the airport, open from 08.30 to 16.30, Monday to Friday, and on Saturday morning until 12.45. There are **banks** along Jalan Kampung Nyabor and Jalan Tunku Osman. The **main post office** and the **police station** (☎ 084-322222) are nearly opposite each other on Jalan Kampung Nyabor. The **hospital** (Lau King Hoe; ☎ 084-313333) is on Jalan Pulau.

Accommodation and restaurants
The **Tanahmas Hotel** (☎ 084-333188; fax 084-333288) on Jalan Kampung Nyabor is a good hotel and boasts an outdoor swimming pool. A double room is around RM150 if you produce a business card or convince the desk you are on business. The other decent hotel is the **Premier** (☎ 084-323222), on the same street, and is less expensive than the Tanahmas. The best middle range hotel is

the **Sarawak Hotel** (☎ 084-333455) at 34 Jalan Cross. The rooms are spacious and clean. The **Li Hua Hotel** (☎ 084-324000) is at the Longbridge Commercial Centre, along the river from the bus and taxi station. The best budget place is **Hoover House** (☎ 084-332973) next to a church on Jalan Pulau.

The best place for a meal is at the Tanahmas or Premier hotels. Closer to the boat quay is the Li Hua Hotel which has an inexpensive coffee shop serving breakfast and Western, Malay and Chinese food throughout the day. There are fast-food places on Jalan Kampung Nyabor.

Places to see

The Tua Pek Kong Temple is situated near Sarikei Boat Jetty, on Jalan Khoo Peng Loong. A Brooke government report in 1871 mentions a small wooden temple in Sibu, the site of the temple that was built in 1897. It is a typical Taoist temple, with a tiled roof, stone block floor, two concrete lions guarding the main entrance and lots of red paint everywhere. The statue of the chief deity, Tua Peh Kong, was imported from Amoy (a city on the coast of southern Fukien province) and is still in the main hall. The temple survived the 1928 fire but was destroyed in the Japanese bombardment in 1942. The present temple was constructed in 1957 and renovated in 1987 when the timber roof was replaced, and the decorative friezes and the seven-storey pagoda were added. The pagoda is dedicated to the Goddess of Mercy and there is also a Buddhist altar on the first floor.

Ceremonial bowl at the entrance to Tua Pek Kong Temple, Sibu

A key to climb the steps of the pagoda can be collected at the main entrance. Tan Teck Chaing is in charge of the temple and he will gladly entertain visitors with information on the temple and Chinese culture.

The **Mini Museum** is in the Civic Centre, 2km southeast of town on Jalan Tun Haji Openg, reached by taxi or bus from the bus and taxi terminal. Opening hours are 10.30 to 17.30, Tuesday to Sunday.

The museum is dedicated to the various races that live in Sibu and there are five galleries, each devoted to a different ethnic group and displaying aspects of their religion, customs and way of life. Compared to the Sarawak Cultural Village, these are fairly tame displays. What is more worthwhile is the collection of photographs covering the history of Sibu from the late 19Conwards.

Travelling up the Batang Rejang

The main reason for a visit to the Batang Rejang are the boat trips which can be made along it—and the towns along its banks, namely Kapit and Belaga; at the latter are the Pelagus Rapids. Along the river are many fully functional longhouses to which you can try to obtain an introduction.

Expres boats charge up the Rejang river from Sibu, stopping at Kanowit, Song and then Kapit. The fastest non-stop journey to Kapit takes 2.5 hours, 3 if stopping at Kanowit and Song. The steel-bottomed boats are fast; although you will soon adapt to their enclosed environment, the journey may prove initially shocking. Be sure to bring a book to read or suffer the nightmare of hideously tasteless videos that are shown throughout the journey at full volume. Whatever you do, try not to think of the risk to life these boats pose: passengers have little means of escaping if the boat capsizes and floating logs are a constant danger to the skilful pilots. Accidents do happen but are mercifully rare. The only alternative is to fly from Sibu.

The first half-hour travelling upriver from Sibu should leave little doubt that wholesale deforestation is still taking place in Sarawak. Wood processing yards are common sights on the banks of the river, fed by long rafts of logs brought downriver by tug boats.

Kanowit is the first stop and the only reason to alight here is to look at Fort Emma, built in 1859 to deter Iban raiding parties, and named after the sister of James Brooke. The fort is perched on high ground to the left of the jetty.

Song is the next stop and the only reason for stopping here would be to visit Iban longhouses along the **Katibas** river. There are no good restaurants or hotels but there are local guides and tour operators who will arrange longhouse visits if arrangements have not already been made.

Kapit

Until recently, Kapit was a fairly obscure outpost on the Rejang but it is now developing into a thriving small town. Nevertheless, when you arrive here after a journey of over three hours there is a sense of being close to the heart of Borneo and well away from modern civilisation. The town is growing but evokes the semi-permanence of a frontier town in the American Wild West. The presence of the jungle is pervasive, for Kapit is literally a clearing in its midst: do not be deceived by the number of cars travelling up and down the mere 20km of surfaced road—a short walk in any direction will soon lead to rainforest. To travel any further up the Rejang a permit is required, a mere formality nowadays and easily arranged in Kapit (see below, tourist information).

Redmond O'Hanlon's book, *Into the Heart of Borneo*, describes his adventure up the Batang Balleh, one of the tributaries of the Rejang reached from Kapit.

▨ Practical information

Getting to Kapit
This is by way of plane or boat from Sibu. The airfare is RM48 single in a Twin-Otter that only flies on Thursday and Saturday. The express non-stop boat is RM20 first class (distinguished as such because second-class passengers do not receive a complimentary bottle of mineral water). The last boat back to Sibu departs at 14.45.

Tourist information
The **airport** is 4km south of town and the MAS office (☎ 084-796344) is at 6 Jalan Temenggong Koh. To obtain a **travel permit**, which is needed for Belaga and beyond, visit the Resident's Office on the first floor of the State Government Complex, a short walk from the jetty (everywhere in Kapit is a short walk from the jetty). The hours are 08.00 to 12.30 and 14.15 to 16.15, Monday to Friday

There is no charge but your passport is required. There is a **post office** on Jalan Teo Chow Beng, the road that leads to the clock tower at the western end of town. There are no money-changing facilities.

A local **tour operator** is Tan Teck Chuan (☎ 084-796352; fax 084-796655) at 11 Jalan Sit Leong in Kapit Square. Regular trips include a two-day/one-night excursion on the Batang Balleh or a more adventurous week further up the same river at a Kenyah longhouse, hunting animals for food and spending some nights in the jungle in self-made shelters. For either of these tours, advance notice is required.

Accommodation and restaurants

The **Greenland Inn** (☎ 084-796388; fax 084-796708) is a modern place on Jalan Teo Chow Beng with rooms from RM65–100. The **Orchard Inn** (☎ 084-796325), at 64 Jalan Airport, has rooms for RM50. **Hotel Mahligai** (☎ 084-796611) on the same street has large rooms for RM50–90 but no restaurant.

The **Dung Fang**, at the clock tower roundabout at the western end of town, serves palatable food: a tasty bowl of *laksa* or plate of *tau fu* is only a couple of ringgit and it is less crowded than many of the other places. The **Orchard Inn Restaurant**, at 64 Jalan Airport, has an air-conditioned restaurant with inexpensive Malay food as well as local specialities such as venison and frogs' legs for around RM10. The **Chuong Hin Café**, the first coffee shop on the corner up from the jetty, is a favourite meeting place and is always a good place for a drink. The **Kah Ping Restoran** on Jalan Teo Chow Beng at Kapit Square is one of the best places for standard Chinese dishes.

Places to see

To the left of the jetty, coming from the boats towards the town, lies **Fort Sylvia**. Constructed out of belian (ironwood) in 1880, the fort was built to deter the Ibans from attacking other tribes and was named Sylvia, after Vyner Brooke's wife, in 1925. On the outside timber wall, high-water marks record the highest levels reached by the river in flood. There is also a plaque outside dedicated to the peace treaty of November 1924, signed at Kapit between the Kayans, Kenyahs and Kajongs of the Balui river and the Ibans of the Rejang. The feud between the different groups went back to 1886 but matters reached a head in 1922 when 15 Ibans were killed. The Raja arrived in Kapit on 12 November and the treaty was signed four days later. There are photographs of the event in the museum. The fort is not open to the public but it is remarkably well preserved—on the outside at least.

Some of Kapit's history may also be gleaned from a visit to the **museum** in Jalan Hospital. There are artefacts and old photographs, and information on the local cultures, and some accounts of the early Hokkien traders who came here from Sibu to trade for forest products. Opening hours are 08.00 to 12.45 and 14.00 to 16.15 Monday to Thursday, closing at 11.30 on Friday and opening again between 14.30 and 16.45. On Saturday the hours are 08.00 to 12.45; admission is free.

Beyond Kapit

The area around Kapit has many longhouses where the local people, mostly Iban, still live fairly traditional lives. If you wish to visit one of them, you are likely to find people in town who, for a fee, will introduce you to one. Many local longhouse dwellers come into Kapit for supplies, and if you happen to meet one of them you may be invited to visit. Such invitations are often meant kindly are not overtly commercial; however, you should expect to pay for meals and accommodation. To visit a longhouse along the river beyond Kapit you must have a permit (see p 290).

The main destination point upriver from Kapit is **Belaga** and the highlight of any journey there are the **Pelagus Rapids**.

> The 640km Rejang river is not especially long when compared to the Amazon—it is only one-fifth of that river's length—but the volume of water carried by the Rejang is tremendous due to the annual 5m of rain that Sarawak experiences. Only coastal Columbia has a higher annual rainfall.
>
> The rapids just beyond Kapit, known as the Pelagus Rapids, have always proved a barrier to travel further upriver. Negotiating the submerged rocks when the water level is low is no mean feat and only recently have more powerful boats reduced some of the dangers. The rapids limited the number of Iban raids heading upstream and provided a natural protection for the Kayans of the upper Rejang. In the past, travellers had to disembark before the rapids and follow a trail by land and pick up another boat on the other side.

It takes 40 minutes to reach the Pelagus Rapids and the **Pelagus Resort** (☎ 084-796050) offers accommodation overlooking the swirling waters in longhouse-style, air-conditioned chalets. **Guided jungle treks** are organised for RM10 and local **Iban longhouses** can be visited for RM100. It is certainly a splendid location but a standard room is overpriced at RM145 plus RM50 for the boat transfer. There is a restaurant and breakfast is included in the room rate but bring your own drinks and snacks because the choice of food is limited and prices are high. There is a Pelagus Resort sales office in Kuching (☎ 082-238033; fax 082-238050). The best time to be here is in November and December when the trees are in fruit and the bird life is abundant.

Further up the river beyond the rapids is a **Punan Bah longhouse**, where the inhabitants were originally either aristocrats or slaves. They follow the Bungan religion, a hybrid of Christianity and pagan animism, and their compound contains five burial poles, known as *klirieng*, cut from single belian trunks and elaborately carved to include a chamber for storing the bones of ancestors. The last *klirieng* is said to have been carved in 1882; at the last count there were only 20 *klirieng* left in the whole of Sarawak.

Closer to Belaga are the **longhouses** of the **Kayan** and **Kenyah**, and subgroups such as the Sekapan, Lahanan, Kejaman and Tanjong, while beyond Belaga are found the Seping, Ukit, Sihan and a few remaining Penans. When Ranee Margaret Brooke made the journey from Kapit to Belaga in the 1880s (a trip she described as the most exciting in her life), it took six days. Today it takes less than five hours.

Belaga

Belaga may prove disappointing because, after travelling for hours up the Rejang into the heart of Borneo, nothing of even remote interest seems to take place here. It often seems as utterly dull as one of those sleepy Malay towns that feature in Joseph Conrad's novels. Be prepared to spend an hour in a coffee shop, as everyone else seems to be doing, and with patience and some luck interesting folk may be seen. Collectors of wild honey from Kalimantan come to Belaga to trade and inhabitants from remote longhouses will be here waiting for a boat to the 'big city' of Kapit.

> At the beginning of this century, a few adventurous Chinese traders made it as far as Belaga in their search for rare jungle products that could be bartered for cooking oil and shotgun cartridges. With luck they could return to Sibu with bezoar stones, the gall-stones found in certain monkeys, especially the silver leaf monkey, and prized for their alleged aphrodisiac qualities.

Accommodation in Belaga consists of three hotels, all equally clean and comfortable places. **Hotel Belaga** (☎ 086-461244) is on Main Bazaar and there is an attached café serving decent meals. The **Bee Lian Inn** (☎ 086-461416) is next door and has small rooms with air-conditioning. **Hotel Sing Soon Hing** (☎ 086-461307) is on Belaga Bazaar.

A chief reason for coming to Belaga is to travel along the **Sungei Balui**, which branches off the Rejang and travels eastwards for some 200km into the mountains which separate Sarawak from Kalimantan. Individual tours to neighbouring longhouses on the Balui can be arranged from Belaga, but if your time is limited it is better to plan ahead and have a tour already organised. Longer trips up the river are possible, but can be very expensive.

Boats from Belaga depart in the morning for **Long Murum** and **Long Linau**, which takes three hours. Here you are well and truly in the heart of Borneo and at Long Murum the longhouse will accept visitors who just turn up, charging RM15 a night. Other trips are possible from Long Murum to **Long Lahanan** and **Long Daro** but there is no guarantee that a longboat will be travelling on the day you require and chartering one will cost around RM100. The reward for travelling this far into the interior is the opportunity to visit longhouses that receive relatively few visitors and at **Long Aya** for instance, reached from Long Lahanan, there is the one remaining Ukit longhouse in Sarawak.

To travel beyond Belaga another **travel permit** is required, obtainable from the government office close by the jetty. It is open from 08.00 to noon and 14.00 to 16.15 Monday to Friday.

Bintulu

The name Bintulu is said to derive from *Menta Ulau*, Malay for 'place of the gathering of heads', and refers to the pre-Brooke era when this stretch of coast was the haunt of pirates who decapitated their enemies. Now it is a thriving commercial town, fuelled by the discovery of off-shore natural gas. However, Bintulu is remarkably characterless; the most notable feature is probably the location of the airport right in the town itself, making it possible for visitors to walk from their plane to a hotel room in about ten minutes.

Bintulu is usually visited en route to the Niah National Park although Miri makes a better access point. The recently established Simulajau National Park, 20km northeast of Bintulu, is a better reason for coming to Bintulu.

Getting to Bintulu. Bintulu is 100km northwest of Belaga, 300km northeast of Sibu. MAS has a number of daily flights between Bintulu and Kuching, Miri and Sibu. There is also one daily flight between Bintulu and Kota Kinabalu. Buses also run between Bintulu and Miri and Sibu. Each day there are several buses which go direct to Batu Niah.

The **Telekom** office and **banks** are on Jalan Keppel; on Jalan Tun Razak are the **post office**, **police station** (☎ 086-332044), and the **Parks and Wildlife Department** (☎ 086-36101) and the **Immigration Department** (☎ 086-31441). The **hospital** (☎ 086-331455) is on Jalan Abang Galau.

Accommodation and restaurants are found at the **Plaza Hotel** (☎ 086-35111) on Jalan Abang Galau. A steak in the hotel restaurant is RM20 and Malay dishes are half this price. Less expensive hotels are dotted around town and the **Sunlight Hotel** (☎ 086-332577), at 7 Jalan Pedada, is typical at RM50 for a small room with air-conditioning, bathroom and television. There is a department store and supermarket just before the clock tower at the western end of Main Bazaar, and there is also a fast-food restaurant here.

Simulajau National Park

This is a recent national park, 20km north of Bintulu, and is interesting primarily for its flora and fauna. There are areas of mangrove, pitcher plants and orchids, and a mixed dipterocarp forest. Unusually the park is only 1.5 km wide, being a coastal strip of land. It has some excellent beaches such as **Pasir Mas**, a 3.5km stretch of beach where green turtles lay their eggs. 20km from Bintulu, it can be reached by road and current information about transport is available from the Bintulu Development Authority (☎ 086-332011). This office will also arrange accommodation in chalets here. There is a small restaurant in the park but this is best supplemented by your own supplies.

Bintulu Wildlife Park

This is just outside the town on the road to Tanjung Batu. It is a small park designed for locals rather than tourists but it has a small zoo and a botanic garden. Admission is M$1. The park is open from 08.00–19.00.

Niah National Park

Although known chiefly for its cave systems the 3000 hectare Niah National Park is set in rainforest with a large area of swamp land. The area was declared a national park in 1974 in order to protect the caves from the encroachments of logging companies. A variety of wildlife can be seen here and there are several marked paths such as Jalan Madu which crosses the swamp forest. It is a full day's walk.

The famous **Niah Caves** are located in this national park. Speleologically, they fade into insignificance compared to the Mulu Caves (see p 300) but in 1958 unique red haematite rock paintings, dating back 1200 years, were discovered in one of the caves. Also found was a 37,000-year-old human skull of a 15-year-old boy, along with stone tools, shell ornaments and other artefacts providing tangible evidence of the earliest prehistoric inhabitants in Southeast Asia.

The Niah Caves were first professionally explored towards the end of the 19C and were declared to be of no archaeological significance. In 1958, however, Tom Harrisson—explorer, ethnologist, curator of the Sarawak Museum and war-time hero from the Kelabit Highlands—discovered that Homo sapiens had once lived in the caves. This caused quite a stir in an academic community that until then had focused exclusively on Africa for evidence of early mankind.

The inhabitants of the Niah Caves, however, were not only prehistoric. Some of Harrissons's other finds date to the 1C AD and it is possible that the caves were home to a community with trading links until as late as the 15C.

▓ Practical information

Getting to the Niah Caves
Tour operators in Miri (see p 298) offer trips to the Niah Caves but there is no need to have a guide; the only advantage they offer is ease of transport. If you travel independently, bring a torch. Due to the copious amounts of guano in the caves, appropriate footwear precludes sandals.

The park is between Bintulu and Miri and can be reached by road from either town. It takes about two hours by car, longer by bus, to reach the town from Miri, closer to three from Bintulu. There are regular daily buses from Miri and Bintulu to **Batu Niah**.

The Park Headquarters are at **Pangkalan Lubang** near the town of Batu Niah; if arriving by bus you need to take a boat along the Niah river from Batu Niah to Park Headquarters (RM15), or walk along a path that takes half an hour, or hire a taxi (RM15). A **permit** is required to enter Niah National Park but this can be obtained at the Park headquarters or in Miri. Once inside the park, there is a small river to cross by sampan before walking 4km along a plank walkway to the caves. The Painted Cave is a 30-minute walk into the caves from the main entrance at the end of the walkway.

Accommodation
A hostel and resthouses are situated on either side of the Niah river at Pangkalan Lubang. A room in the resthouse with four single beds is RM30, or RM60 for a whole resthouse, while a bed in the hostel is only RM3. Both the resthouses and hostel have showers, refrigerator and cooking facilities, and there is a shop selling some provisions and a small restaurant serving basic meals. There is a supermarket in Batu Niah. It is advisable to make an advance booking, especially at weekends, at the National Parks and Wildlife Office on Jalan Pujut in Miri (☎ 085-436637).

Bats and birds' nest soup

The caves are inhabited by hundreds of thousands of **bats** and **swiftlets** which gather their food outside the caves but nest inside where they collectively deposit about one tonne of guano each day. Most of the bats are insectivorous; naked bats and Cantor's roundleaf bats are the chief species found here. It is worth being outside the main entrance to the caves at dusk when the bats swarm out and the swiftlets return to their nests. Be sure to bring a torch for the return journey along the walkway in the dark.

The guano (called *tahi timbang* if it has already decomposed and *tahi sapu* if gathered fresh off the surface) forms a living carpet on the ground of the caves where countless cockroaches, crickets and scorpions scurry about. The guano is collected as fertiliser and you are likely to encounter men carrying sacks of the stuff along the walkway that leads from the river to the cave.

The swiftlets (*Collocalia fuciphaga*) in the caves are of two types: those near the entrance are white-bellied ones while another type, the black-nest swiftlet, lives deeper inside the caves; like the bats, they employ an echolocation system for finding their way about in the dark. The birds build their nests onto the cave walls with an adhesive—edible saliva produced from a special gland. The black-nest birds mix feathers in with the saliva while the white-bellied swiftlets use pure saliva, making their nests more valuable. These edible birds' nests are regarded as highly medicinal by the Chinese, especially for bronchial complaints, and they command a high price by the time they reach the tables of expensive restaurants in places such as Hong Kong and San Francisco. The nests will also be sold in Chinese medicine shops to families who prepare their birds' nest soup at home.

If your visit coincides with a nest-collecting session (between August to December and from January to March), the collectors can be seen climbing their precarious 60m wooden poles to the roof of the caves where they balance on bamboo crossbars and scrape off the nests with 10m poles (called *penyulok*), with torch lights attached to their ends. There are no safety nets and fatalities are not unknown. The collectors are only licensed to remove the nests at two safe periods during the year: before eggs are laid (prompting the birds to build new nests) and after hatching, when the young swiftlets have flown away. The economic incentive has resulted in constant flouting of the rules and the swiftlet population is said to be rapidly decreasing. The caves were closed off for a period to deter poachers but should now be open. Confirm this with the tourist office in Miri or with the Park Office when booking accommodation.

Painted Cave. Do not trudge your way through the guano expecting to behold a prehistoric version of the Sistine Chapel. In fact, upon entering the Painted Cave, it is not immediately obvious where the paintings are. When Tom Harrisson (see above) first visited these caves he discovered wooden coffins, in the shape of boats, about 1000 years old. One of these coffins is preserved in the cave and the paintings can be seen on the wall behind the coffin. It is difficult to make out exactly what is being represented but it is possible to discern the outlines of skirted dancing figures and coffin ships voyaging, presumably, into the next world.

Great cave. These are the first two caves that you come to as you approach the system. In the Great Cave finds of Paleolithic and Neolithic tools and pottery were found by Tom Harrisson as well as skull fragments believed to be 37,000 years old. In the mouth of the cave you can still see Harrisson's house and office. In all 166 burial sites have been excavated here.

Miri

This is now the largest town in Sarawak and while Kuching remains the state capital Miri is undoubtedly the economic one. This is mainly due to the presence of oil both on the land and offshore. Malaysia's first oil well was sunk here in 1910 and there are now over 500 wells in the area pumping out over 80 million barrels a year. Miri is a far more pleasant town than Sibu and is the obvious base for a number of excursions: Niah National Park, Mulu caves and the Kelabit Highlands.

At the moment Miri has a certain amount of charm—but it is destined to be swamped by 'progress'. There is a government plan, known as Miri Resort City, that is due to mature in 2005. It includes the Herculean task of redirecting the course of the Miri river to facilitate the reclamation and development of prime land which will metamorphose into a marina, yacht club, etc. An 18-hole golf course is already well under way and the resort hotels on Brighton beach are just a taste of what is to come.

▦ Practical information

Getting to and from Miri
By air. The airport (☎ 085-417906) is 5km outside of town (RM12 by taxi), from where there are direct flights to Kuala Lumpur (RM422), Kuching (RM164), Labuan (RM66), Sibu (RM112), Bintulu (RM69) and Kota Kinabalu (RM104). There are also local flights to Bario (RM82), Limbang (RM450), Long Lellang (RM66), Long Seridan (RM57), Marudi (RM29) and Mulu (RM69). The MAS office (☎ 085-414144) is in the Beautiful Jade Centre on Jalan Yu Seng Selatan.

By bus. Different companies (☎ 085-427035/250657/434317) run buses to Bintulu, which is 150km to the northeast (RM18, three a day) and Kuching, 800km northeast (RM70, at 06.30, 07.00 and 07.30). The journey to Kuching is a gruelling 15 hours. The bus station is on Jalan Padang.

Tourist information
There is no tourist office in Miri but there is an **information counter** at the airport. **Banks** can be found on Jalan Raja and Jalan Bendahara. **Teck Soon** is a moneychanger at Lot 355 Jalan Brooke, next to the petrol station, and is open until 19.30 for cash transactions only.

On Jalan Gartak are the **post office**, the **Telekom** office and the **Immigration Office**. The **police station** (☎ 085-433777) is on Jalan King, and the **General Hospital** (☎ 085-432222) is the other side of the river; ferries run across every 15 minutes from 06.30 to 20.00.

For **shopping**, the **Wisma Pelita** has a supermarket, department store and various small shops, including a few that sell handicrafts and souvenirs. The **Long House Handicrafts** shop on the third floor is good for pottery, baskets and wooden sculptures.

Accommodation

There is a good choice of accommodation. The recently built **Mega Hotel** (☎ 085-432432; fax 085-432433) on Jalan Merbau justifies its name with a quoted room rate of RM230, but this is instantly reduced by 40 per cent at the desk. Two of the more established good hotels are the **Park Hotel** (☎ 085-414555; fax 085-414488) on Jalan Malay, with rooms for RM75–100; and the **Gloria Hotel** (☎ 085-416699; fax 085-418866), at 27 Jalan Brooke, with rooms for RM65–90. The **Cosy Inn** (☎ 085-415522) on Jalan South Yu Seng Selatan is a typical middle-range place with small but smart rooms and good amenities for RM60–90.

A short distance outside town, five minutes by taxi, are two luxurious establishments, the more magnificent being the **Rhiga Royal Hotel** (☎ 085-421121; fax 085-425057) on Brighton Beach, facing the South China Sea. The other resort-like hotel is the **Holiday Inn** (☎ 085-420788; fax 085-419999).

Restaurants

The **Chatterbox** at the Mega Hotel has a buffet service for breakfast (RM18), lunch (RM20), 'Hi-Tea' (RM12), dinner (RM20) and supper from 22.30 to 03.00 (RM10). The hotel also has a Chinese restaurant and a bakery, and there is a McDonald's in the same building. On the other side of the road, the **Bilal Restaurant** is recommended for its naan and murtabak (including a vegetarian choice) with fresh lemon juice (around RM5). The **Park Hotel** has a Western set lunch for RM13. The **Cosy Inn** has a coffee shop serving Western and Malay food.

The **Rhiga Royal Hotel**, outside town, has Japanese and Cantonese restaurants, as well as an informal coffee house serving Malay and Western dishes. The **Holiday Inn** has a Chinese restaurant and an English-style pub.

Tour operators

One of the most experienced tour operators in Miri is **Tropical Adventure** (☎ 085-419337; fax 085-414504/3) on the ground floor of the Mega Hotel. It runs trips to the Mulu caves, Bario Highlands, Niah Caves, as well as treks into the jungle from a couple of days to a week or more. Another company is **Transhine Tours** (☎ 085-420253; fax 085-420714), at 15 Jalan China. The following prices, quoted by Transhine Tours, will give some idea of the rates. They include accommodation and meals and usually a minimum of two people need to make a booking: a two-day trip to the Mulu Caves, RM195; a four-day trip to the Mulu Caves and climbing of the Pinnacles, RM435. **Transworld Travel Services** (☎ 085-429545; fax 085-410057) has offices in Miri town, the Holiday Inn, the Rhiga Royal Hotel and Royal Mulu Resort. Its standard day trip to the Niah Caves and an Iban longhouse is RM160 per person and RM45 for a tour of Miri town.

Permits are required for visiting the Kelabit Highlands and the Mulu caves, obtainable through the Parks Office (☎ 085-436637) off Jalan Pujut. The

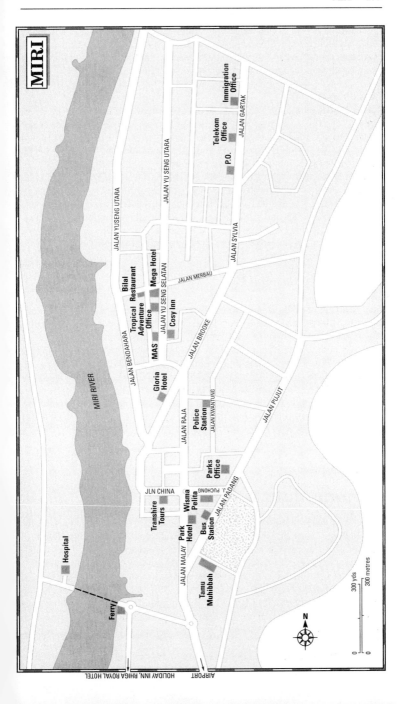

procedure is not as troublesome as it sounds: a form is collected in the Parks Office and taken to the Resident's Office (☎ 085-433203), two minutes' walk away, and then along to the police station which is another three minutes' walk away. Bring your passport and immigration departure card.

Places to see

Tamu Muhibbah is the best indoor **fruit and vegetable market** to be found anywhere in the state and a visit here is highly recommended. It is close to the Park Hotel off Jalan Padang. The main market building is a regular Chinese market but just past it is a smaller building with a red tin roof, where the Orang Ulu and other tribes come to sell their produce.

You will every strange fruit and vegetable that Sarawak produces: the *terap*, as big as a football but with protruding rubbery spikes, is difficult to miss, but there are lots of smaller ones which could be tasted by intrepid customers. Also on sale are snails, rice wines and various exotica that defy the normal nomenclature. Look for unidentifiable stems cut from jungle plants, heaps of jungle ferns (known collectively as *paku*), grubs that wriggle and squirm—all edible and probably highly nutritious.

Lambir Hills National Park

This 6952 hectare national park, 32km south of Miri, is an area of sandstone hills covered in rainforest and inhabited by gibbons, pangolins, and many other creatures. The park is good for short jungle walks or a picnic at the very popular waterfalls, about 15 minutes' walk from the park headquarters. It is less spectacular than some of the other parks in the area but now has some accommodation and so could make an interesting two-day, jungle and wildlife spotting trip.

Getting to and from Lambir Hills National Park. The park is on the main highway and can be reached via the Batu Niah bus or any non-express bus to Bintulu. Leaving the park the last bus back to Miri passes the main gate at about 16.30.

Accommodation can be booked at the park headquarters (☎ 085-?36637) where there is also a canteen and information centre.

Gunung Mulu National Park

Gunung Mulu National Park is most famous for its spectacular **cave system**, first explored between 1976 and 1984 when 26 caves comprising 159km of passages were mapped. It is thought that there are twice as many caves which remain unexplored, and some of these could be bigger than the enormous Clearwater Cave which is 50km in length. Apart from containing the biggest limestone cave system in the world, Gunung Mulu National Park also has the second highest mountain in Sarawak (Gunung Mulu, 2371m) and an astonishing ecology which has rewarded every scientific expedition by revealing previously unknown plant and animal species.

All of Sarawak's main inland vegetation types exist in Mulu, from peat swamp and mixed dipterocarp up through limestone and moss forests to the upper montane vegetation towards the summit of Gunung Mulu. The result is a staggering set of eco-statistics: 1500 species of flowering plants that include 170 species of orchid and 10 species of pitcher plant; 20,000 animal species; 8000 varieties of fungi; 262 species of bird; 50 species of reptile; and 280 species of butterfly.

It was a Royal Geographical Society expedition in 1976, under Robin Hanbury-Tenison, that presented a successful case for designating the area a national park.

■ Practical information

Getting to and from Gunung Mulu National Park
It is possible to travel independently to Mulu but most people join a pre-arranged tour because of the convenience. The authorities prefer travellers to be in groups and it is not always cheaper to travel independently. (See the relevant sections in the Kuala Lumpur, Kuching and Miri descriptions for details of tour operators, nearly all of whom run reliable trips to Mulu.)

By air. Twin-Otters fly daily to Mulu from Miri (RM69 single) and Marudi (RM40). The airport is 2km west of Park Headquarters and a longboat service transports passengers to their accommodation.

By boat. The first stop is Marudi, 15 minutes by air from Miri or reached by road (bus or taxi) as far as Kuala Baram and then by boat (they run hourly) to Marudi. From Marudi the next stage is a 3-hour boat journey to Kuala Apoh or Long Panai on the Tutoh river. If the water level is high enough, the boat will continue on to Long Terawan; if not, another change of boat is required. From Long Terawan, a journey by longboat is required for the final stage to Park Headquarters. It takes a whole long day from Miri to Mulu and it is essential to leave Marudi around 07.00 to make all the necessary connections.

Necessary **equipment** includes water bottles, walking shoes, mosquito repellent, torch, sun glasses or sun hat, basic first aid, light cotton clothing. Swimming is possible near Clearwater Cave so bring your gear.

If travelling on your own it is necessary to obtain a **permit**—from the Parks Office in Miri—but it is easier just to book accommodation through the Parks Office and pay for the permit at the Park Headquarters in Mulu when you arrive.

Accommodation and restaurants
Two people organising a trip through a tour company should expect to pay at least RM700 (RM480 single) for a two-day trip, including one night's accommodation and meals but excluding the airfare. A three-day/two-night trip will be at least RM1000 (RM700 single). Shorter trips include visits to the caves and a local Penan longhouse; longer trips cover a trek to the summit of Gunung Mulu, the Pinnacles, or adventure-caving.

All the tour companies have either their own accommodation centres or an arrangement with a private place and the cost will be included in the package price. Upmarket accommodation is offered at the **Royal Mulu Resort** (☎ 085-421122; fax 085-421088), a Japanese-owned 'luxury oasis in the jungle'.

Room rates average RM200 and the resort will be better value when incorporated into a tour. Park Headquarters have their own **chalets** at RM60 per room, sleeping four. There are five-bed **resthouses** for RM75 and a **hostel** bed for RM12. The accommodation needs to be booked ahead in Miri at the Parks Office.

There will be various charges, for entering the caves with a camera (RM5) and for the obligatory guide (RM18 per cave); these charges are payable in Mulu. Park Headquarters will also arrange adventure-caving (RM88 per cave) and jungle trekking (RM20 per day). All such extra charges should be covered in the cost of an organised tour.

If travelling with a tour company, meals at the private lodges will be included in the price of the package. Otherwise, there is a **canteen** at Park Headquarters serving basic meals; independent travellers should use the private lodges and pay more for substantially better meals.

The caves

Of the five caves open to the public, **Deer Cave** is the most astonishing visually, with its enormous entrance and cave passage—2km long and 220m at its highest point (big enough to hold St Paul's Cathedral, London). Your guide will point out unusual rock formations, including a silhouetted rock near the entrance that bears an uncanny resemblance to the profile of Abraham Lincoln. The pathway through the cave leads to a scenic spot where light floods in from a hole in the roof and jungle vegetation delights the surprised visitor. Deer Cave is home to countless thousands of horseshoe and wrinkle-lipped bats and it is worth being outside the cave—there is a special viewing area—around dusk when they swarm out to darken the sky. They fly off to the coast 80km away and return to deposit collectively some three tonnes of saline guano every day. Streams of saltwater running off the guano used to attract the eponymous deer.

Clearwater Cave, discovered in 1988, is only reached by longboat along the river from Park Headquarters. (Independent travellers must either charter their own longboat, which is expensive, or try to negotiate a place on a tour's longboat.) The name of the cave derives from the beautiful pool in the jungle from where an ascent leads to the entrance. At the entrance look out for two species of monophytes (single-leaved plants) that can be seen growing on the limestone. Inside there is a lighted footway. It explores only a small part of this giant cave which stretches for well over 60km (the longest in the world) and includes an underground river that is traversed in canoes, for a short distance, on most of the adventure tours.

A highlight of any visit to Clearwater Cave are the unusual photokarsts: miniature needles of rock that grow towards the light off horizontal layers of limestone. Algae eats away some of the softer rock and the harder rock left behind 'grows' about half a millimetre each year.

Cave of the Winds is linked through subterranean passages to Clearwater Cave but visitors make their entry up steps from another landing stage further along the river. This cave, like **Lang's Cave** which is reached further along the river again, has a stunning variety of stalactites, stalagmites, helictites (a twisted, branched stalactite) and myriad rock formations that make most other tourist caves in the world seem like pale imitations.

Sarawak Chamber, discovered in 1984 and recently opened to the public, is 600m long and 450m wide—big enough to hold 40 jumbo jets. It is claimed to be the biggest (as opposed to longest) cave in the world.

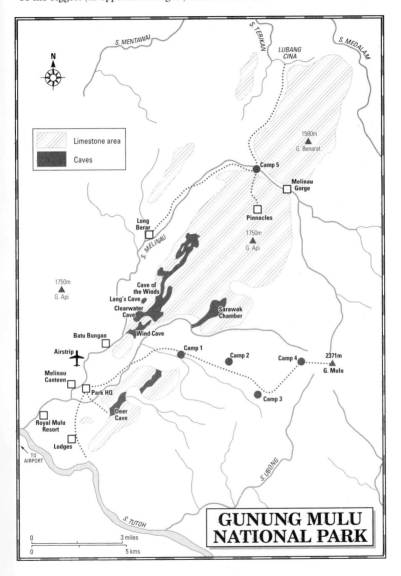

GUNUNG MULU
NATIONAL PARK

Gunung Mulu

The history of failed attempts to conquer Gunung Mulu should not deter non-mountaineers; climbing the mountain requires no special skills other than stamina and fitness.

The first known attempt to reach the 2376m summit of Gunung Mulu was the mid-19C expedition by Spencer St John, a British diplomat in Brunei. He turned back after concluding that pinnacles of rock made further ascent impossible. Equally unsuccessful was an attempt in 1893 by Charles Hose, a British officer serving under Charles Brooke. In the 1920s, however, a local hunter following the tracks of a rhinoceros managed to locate a manageable route from the southwest. In 1932, local hunter Tama Nilong successfully led an expedition under Lord Shackleton to the summit.

There are various numbered camps along the route and it takes a minimum of three days to reach the top. The first night is usually spent at **Camp 3** after a relatively easy day's walking. The camp is a very basic shelter. The second day is probably the most demanding, a long, hard 10-hour slog that ensures a good night's sleep at 1800m at **Camp 4**, again just a shelter which should have fresh water supplies. The third morning usually begins as early as possible in order to reach the summit as (or shortly after) the sun rises and before clouds obscure the magnificent views. The final leg of the climb is quite tough and there are ropes fixed on the rockface to aid the ascent. From the summit it is possible to make it back to your starting point on the same day—but be warned: unless your leg muscles are ready for it you may well wake up the next morning barely able to move! Consider spending another night on the mountain.

If you are part of an organised tour then all the necessary equipment will be ready. As an independent climber you will need to organise a guide through Park Headquarters and bring sufficient food, water and a sleeping bag.

Pinnacles

The Pinnacles is an astonishing stone forest more than half-way up the side of **Gunung Api**. The journey begins with a 3-hour boat trip from Park Headquarters to Long Berar from where it is an 8km trek to **Camp 5**, which is close to the Melinau Gorge and beside the Melinau river. The camp is very basic with a wooden shelter accommodating about 30 people and some sheltered outdoor cooking facilities. Water supplies come from the river and should of course be boiled.

The next morning involves at least six hours' climbing before the incredible Pinnacles are seen: limestone needles that rise up to 45m, towering over the treetops. It is not possible to continue on from here to the summit of Gunung Api—it was only finally conquered in 1978—and it will take four or five hours to get back down the mountain.

A word of advice: the climb up Gunung Api to view the Pinnacles is not easy. No special skills are required but anyone setting out on the trip should be fit and healthy and ready for a demanding climb. The final ascent to the viewing ridge that looks out on the Pinnacles is no mean feat. The sense of achievement for non-mountaineers is unparalleled, but unless you are fit and able you may be forced to turn back before getting there. In addition there is no water on the route and so it must be carried with you. You might also want to protect yourself from the limestone rocks with gloves and a long-sleeved shirt, particularly towards the end of the climb.

Penan Settlement

Nearly all the tour companies include a visit to the Penan settlement, **Batu Bungan**, on the Melinau river. It is about half-way between Park Headquarters and Clearwater Cave. A visit here is highly educational. It has always been argued that the Penans should leave the forest because their culture is a primitive one and they have the right, as Malaysians, to share in the developing progress of their country. When they are seen in this dismal longhouse the argument may not seem so convincing. Depressed-looking women sit around waiting for the next boatload of tourists who may buy some of their beautiful basketwork, while the men have no choice but to try and adapt to being the rice farmers they do not wish to become. They still leave the longhouse on hunting expeditions but this is becoming increasingly difficult as the logging companies extend further and further into the forest.

> Penan society is (though this may already require the past tense) one of the few functioning anarchist societies. There is no system of government and no history of violence and the only laws as such are offences against their sexual code. As far as is known there is no record of any Penan having slain another. Since at least the 1950s they have used shotguns to hunt, although the blowpipe is also used. Any game is shared equally between the different families in the nomadic group.
>
> The few detailed studies of Penan culture that have been made reveal a far more sophisticated society than that portrayed by those anxious to justify their forced removal from the forest. They possess a detailed ecological knowledge of the forest and move along trails that have been used and maintained for generations.
>
> Logging destroys the Penans by destroying their hunting grounds. It has also reduced the number of wild boar in this area—they feed from the fruits of certain species of Shorea tree which is being reduced by logging. (The fruits of the Shorea tree also produce an oil which is used for cooking.)

Kelabit Highlands

The Highlands are the highest inhabited part of Borneo at 1127m above sea level and a visit here is highly recommended, although the rainy season between October and March is best avoided as flights are often delayed due to the weather. The place is flat and cool with lush paddy fields, which produce undisputedly the highest quality rice in the country. Each morning, sackfuls of the rich rice along with fruit and vegetables are stacked up at the airport waiting for distribution through Marudi and Miri. The main settlement in the Highlands is **Bario** (sometimes spelled Bareo) and this is where you arrive from Miri or Marudi on a runway that was built by Tom Harrisson and his team. There are two other settlements, **Long Lellang** and **Ba Kelatan**, connected by a daily air service.

A visit to the Kelabit Highlands will be enriched by first reading *The World Within* by Tom Harrisson. Towards the end of the Second World War, Tom Harrisson and seven other men parachuted down to the Highlands (the only place where they could be sure of not being detected) with a plan to organise local resistance to the Japanese. Harrisson was deeply interested in the Kelabit culture and his book is a fascinating blend of anthropology and military memoir. He was able to observe the culture before Christian missionaries set about eradicating many of their traditional beliefs and practices, which included the building of megaliths and carving designs onto boulders of rocks. Their legendary feasts, where up to 500 people would gather for four or five days of merrymaking, are now tame Easter and Christmas festivals with no drinking or dancing.

Older Kelabits still have stories to tell about Harrisson and he remains a respected figure. In a longhouse near one of the salt springs, I spotted an old black-and-white photograph of Harrisson—next to a colour print of the Blessed Virgin.

The Malaysian army has a permanent base in Bario, on the other side of the airport. This goes back to the early 1960s when Indonesia was asserting its claim to Sarawak and Gurkha and British troops were stationed in the Highlands. Today, the threat is perceived to come from protesters against logging for not far away is the area where Bruno Manser (see p 270) lived with the Penans, and timber companies are busy at work in the region on one of the remaining areas of virgin rainforest.

▓ Practical information

Getting to and from Bario. 190km southeast of Miri. MAS flies Twin-Otters to Bario (no ☎) from Miri (RM70 single) via Marudi, daily. It is not uncommon for departures from Bario to be postponed due to weather conditions and this should be taken into account. Officially permits are needed to visit Bareo and these can be obtained from the Residents' offices in Miri or Marudi. No one seems to pay much attention to them though.

If part of an organised trip by a tour company, **accommodation** will be arranged in local homes or in small sheds in the jungle. **Tarawe's**, on the only street that runs through Bario, is an inexpensive lodging house run by a friendly couple; there are four rooms with three beds in each. **Meals** are available here, including wild boar and local vegetables. There are no banks in Bario.

The best **tour company** for organised trips to the Highlands is **Tropical Adventure** (see p 298). Most of the tours involve either local walks or longer treks in the jungle lasting a few days. Expect to pay at least RM200 for each day.

A viable alternative is just to turn up in Bario and make enquiries at the lodging house about **hiring a guide** for short or long walks. With luck, it may be possible to join an unforgettable night's hunting trip in the jungle. Guides are not expensive, from around RM50 a day, but you should bring your own food and drink. Stock up in Miri as the small shop in Bario sells only basic provisions.

Trekking from Bario

Bario is a place to unwind in, to enjoy short walks to local salt springs and observe the life of the community. It takes under two hours to reach a longhouse at **Pa Umor**: ask for directions at the lodging house which is where the pathway begins. From the longhouse a path continues over a small bridge to a **salt spring** and there are other longhouses along the main pathway at **Pa Ukat** and **Pa Lungan**. There is also a short walk, about an hour there and back, from Bareo to **Ulung Pallang**.

A longer walk, and best undertaken with a guide, is to trek from Pa Lungan to **Ba Kelalan**. This requires a night at Pa Lungan, where a longhouse accepts visitors for around RM15, and then a full day's walk to Ba Kelalan where an MAS flight could be picked up to Lawas and back to Miri (RM105). From Lawas it is possible to get a bus into Kota Kinabalu in Sabah.

Treks are also possible into **Kalimantan** (Indonesia) and out again and for some of these trails there is no need to worry about national boundaries or passport controls. A highly recommended four-day trip that stays within Sarawak is to **Pa Tik** and back. The highlight of the trip is the opportunity to see nomadic Penans who occasionally drop into Pa Tik to visit friends and relations.

This trip is fairly demanding but anyone who is reasonably fit will enjoy the challenge of trekking through deep forest, across rivers on log bridges, and sleeping nights in jungle-like huts. Guides for this trip can be arranged through the Tropical Adventure tour company in Miri, or direct in Bario. For the latter, enquire at the lodging house or ask for Peter Matu.

Trekking tips

If you have decided to make some treks around Bario and are not going with a tour group it is as well to make some preparations before you leave Miri or even before that. You should bring supplies for your trip unless you are good at wild boar hunting and can recognise edible fungus. Cooking pots are also necessary. Dried noodles and packet soups are good as well as lots of high calorie chocolate bars. These are also good for giving as gifts when you are invited to people's homes. A sarong is a good idea to act as a bedcover in jungle huts. You should have light clothes as well as a change of clothes and shoes rather than sandals to help protect against leeches. A torch is vital and mosquito coils are also useful as is a good first-aid kit.

For the longer treks a guide is essential. A good guide will collect food during the journey but they will expect to share any food you bring so make sure you have enough. Above all keep your pack as light as possible. The treks involve steep climbs and negotiating logs over rivers. Ask your guide to cut you a strong walking stick.

Singapore

Singapore is a strange country. Arriving at the clean, efficient airport and taking a taxi into town past manicured verges and block upon block of architecturally bland apartments, it is possible to imagine that you have entered one of those computer games where the perfect city state can be built. Ten years ago Singapore was a clean, well-run place but there were pockets of unaddressed messiness, just as there are in every other city—areas where litter swirled and vermin survived, and places with an interesting cultural identity. But as someone remarks to the eponymous hero of Paul Theroux's novel about Singapore, Saint Jack: 'Give them a few years and they'll pull this all down and build over it—apartment blocks, car parks, pizza joints, every lousy thing they can think of.' The prophecy has come true.

But having said that, there is much to see and experience in this tiny, cute and unnervingly safe place. There are gastronomic treats that outdo any other city in Southeast Asia, stunning shopping malls that will satisfy the most self-indulgent consumer, and little pockets of history and culture waiting to be discovered. There are also some fascinating ecological niches, such as the Bukit Timah Nature Reserve and some of the outlying islands, where pitcher plants, monitor lizards, macaques, racket-tailed drongos and coral snakes live out their lives, blissfully unaware of all the commercial activity around them.

History
Early history. The modern history of Singapore begins with the arrival of Sir Stamford Raffles in 1819, but the island was inhabited long before that time. According to 3C Chinese records it was known as Pu Luo Chung, 'the island at the end of the peninsula'; and Rajendra, ruler of the Indian Cola kingdom, attacked the island in 1025. in the 13C, during the dominance of the Sumatran **Srivijayan empire**, it is thought that there was a thriving town here. By the late 14C, the island was known as Temasek. It was a busy trading post ruled by **Parameswara**, a prince from Sumatra, who had fled to Temasek from Palembang. The Malay chieftain at the time offered Parmeswara asylum and was assassinated for his trouble. In 1398, warring Siamese and Javanese attacked Temasek, and Parameswara fled to Melaka where he set in motion the history of that city.

In the 15C, the island was for a time a vassal state of the Siamese empire, but later it was claimed by the Melakan sultanate. When the Portuguese attacked Melaka in 1511, the escaping Melakan leaders set up in Singapore, only to be wiped out by the Portuguese in the early 17C.

The name Singapore is a corruption of Singapura ('Lion City'). It is possible that it was named by Rajendra. The 15C or 16C Malay chronicle, *Sejarah Melayu*, relates the tale of a Shrivijayan (Sumatran empire) prince who on seeing a tiger on the island mistook it for a lion and thus named it Singapura.

Enter Raffles. For the next hundred years Singapore declined, becoming home to Orang Laut, a tribe of sea people, and pirates. Officially ruled by the

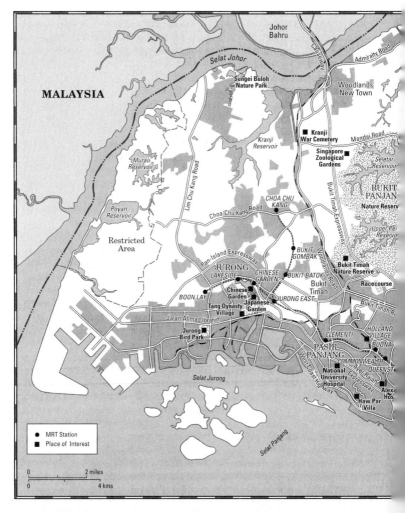

Sultan of Johor but effectively ruled by pirates, the island became an obscure and forgotten place. The British, however, were looking for another trading post on the east coast, preferably at the southern end of the peninsula. The Straits of Melaka and much of Indonesia were controlled by the Dutch and Britain's post at Penang was regarded as too far north. Stamford Raffles was sent to find a suitable alternative. He lighted on Singapore and sailed up the mouth of the Singapore river. A quick deal was struck with the local leader, **Abdul Rahman**, and then Raffles had to look to the official ruler of the state—the Sultan of Johor.

At that time there was disputed succession over the sultanate, with two rivals to the throne living on small islands in what is now the Riau archi-

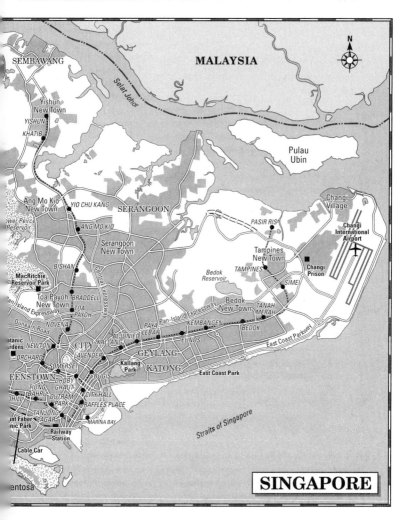

MALAYSIA

SINGAPORE

pelago: one sultan on Pulau Linggan and the other on Pulau Bintan. The Dutch had recognised the Bintan sultan so Raffles approached his rival, **Sultan Hussein Mohammed Shah**, with an offer he could not refuse— recognition of his status and 5000 Spanish dollars a year in rent in exchange for sole trading rights on the island. The British trading post was set up on 6 February 1819. (See also the earlier chapter on Singapore's history (p 42) for more information about Raffles and his pivotal role in the city-state's success.)

The Dutch were enraged by Raffles's action and serious diplomatic wrangling took place until 1824 when a deal was struck. Britain gave up Bencoolen, on the west coast of Sumatra, the Dutch ceded Melaka to Britain and agreed to tolerate the British presence in Singapore. Singapore became a part of the Straits Settlements, Penang in the north, Melaka in the middle and Singapore in the south. The imperial powers were happy.

Events conspired to make Singapore a boom town. The British East India Company, which had been running the Straits Settlements, began to decline and consequently lost its trade monopoly in the area. This opened up the town to trade with the many ships which passed by. In Sarawak, the Brooke sultanate (see p 267) was opening up new areas of trade which naturally came to Singapore. Trade with Siam increased. In 1867 Britain made Singapore a **Crown Colony**, improving its stability and prospects. In 1869 the Suez Canal was opened and trade through the Straits of Melaka was increased. Almost simultaneously, the development of steamships and massive investment in rubber plantations in Malaya made Singapore the world's leading centre for that commodity.

In 1874 Britain signed a protection treaty with the Malay sultanates which made Singapore the administrative centre of the Malay States as well as of the Straits Settlements and the protectorates of Sarawak, Brunei and North Borneo.

The racial mix. When Raffles first landed in Singapore, the majority of the population were **Malays**. Remarkably, within a year they were outnumbered by other racial groups—immigrants from China, India and over 40 other races. But the largest group by far came from China.

The **Chinese** had arrived in small numbers before Raffles came to Singapore, finding work on gambier (a plant used in tanning) and pepper plantations. Once the trading post was established they came in huge numbers, 400 to a junk, many of them dying of starvation on the journey. For the first year of their new life in Singapore they worked to pay for their passage. They found work on plantations, as coolies, servants, or peddlers, and were settled in modern Telok Ayer, around the waterfront and in the roads behind it.

Next in number were the **Indian immigrants**, the first arriving with Raffles as soldiers in the Bengal Native Infantry. Like the Chinese, they came to work on the plantations and, later, on cattle farms around the Serangoon Road area. They came from many different parts of India, spoke different languages—Tamil, Malayalam, Sindhi—and had different religions.

Another group which arrived in Singapore in significant numbers were **Arabs**. They came as merchants and tradesmen rather than as debentured workers. Armenians also arrived here, and their legacy to the island is in the beautiful old St Gregory's Church. **Jews** came too, chiefly from the Middle East, and built their own places of worship.

Perhaps the two most interesting groups to settle in Singapore were the **Peranakans** and the **Eurasians**, both groups being born out of the arrival of foreign settlers in Malaya. Most of the Peranakans came to Singapore from Melaka (see p 164). They were wealthy traders and took to English traditions willingly. The Eurasians too came chiefly from Melaka. They were the result of the intermarriage of European settlers with local peoples from Malaya, India and Ceylon. Many of them worked in the civil service and their lifestyle and dress was largely Western.

Other groups which can still be traced through street names in Singapore are the **Bugis**, who were traders, and of course the **Malays** who were also skilled sailors and boatmen. They mixed easily with the Arab, Bugis and Indian Muslim populations, often building mosques where all four groups worshipped together.

Each of the ethnic groups was given a specific area in which to settle, and for each area a 'kapitan' was nominated who took charge of law and orde among their own peoples.

The twentieth century. The 20C has been a time of massive change and political unrest. The Chinese immigrants had become the largest ethnic group on the island. Chinese Communist groups were organised among teachers' and student groups and there were anti-colonial riots in 1927 which led to the death of seven people after the police opened fire on demonstrators. The police leadership was British and had little understanding of the secret society wars that were carried on. Various clans held power in different parts of the Chinese community and ran brothels, sold opium, and collected protection payments from shop owners and small businessmen. Often disputes arose over jurisdiction and small but vicious wars broke out between the disputing clans. Singapore gained a reputation as the Chicago of the East.

The beginnings of mechanisation put the punkah-wallahs and rickshaw drivers out of business, and immigration controls were introduced to restrict the numbers of foreign male manual workers entering the country. Since this new legislation did not apply to the Indian immigrants, who were British citizens, the Chinese saw it as a racist policy.

Singapore suffered briefly during the Depression of 1929 and enjoyed the best of the boom period that followed. A massive public spending programme, aimed at clearing slums, and improving education, roads and public building, was brought to an abrupt end by the Second World War.

The Japanese invasion. Singapore tends to gloss over this period of its history, presumably out of deference to the sensibilities of a country with which it has important economic ties. The event gets three sentences in Singapore's official handbook, hardly doing justice to the suffering and death experienced by thousands of people during this time.

Legend has it that the British guns on Sentosa, the island to the south of Singapore, could only point south because the British believed invasion from the north to be impossible. In fact they could easily have been turned northwards but they were armour-piercing guns; their shells were useless against an army invading by land. The north coast of Singapore was bravely defended but, as the Allied troops fell back before the enemy's blistering advance down the Malay peninsula, the Japanese had the psychological advantage.

The Japanese may have had the psychological advantage but if the British commanders had known what the Japanese General Yamashita was later to admit, the outcome would have been quite different. 'My attack on Singapore was a bluff—a bluff that worked. I had 30,000 men and was outnumbered more than three to one. I knew if I had to fight long for Singapore

I would be beaten. This is why the surrender had to be at once. I was very frightened all the time that the British would discover our numerical weakness and lack of supplies and force me into disastrous street fighting.'

On 10 February 1942, the Japanese first moved across the Straits of Johor and engaged with the Australian 27th Brigade who were waiting for them with machine-guns and mortar fire. The Japanese panicked, only to discover, through a misunderstanding in orders, that the Australians were withdrawing.

By 11 February, the Japanese had repaired the Causeway across the Straits, which had been blown up by the British before their final withdrawal to Singapore, and were able to move troops and equipment across. Early on 13 February, Yamashita had established his headquarters at the Ford motor factory on Bukit Timah Road; there, two days later at 17.15, General Percival arrived to surrender.

The worst atrocity before surrender occurred on 14 February when Japanese troops arrived at the Alexandra Hospital and bayoneted to death all the medical staff, and a British corporal lying on an operating table. During the night 200 more patients were also bayoneted to death. As the Allies withdrew into the city, their instructions were to destroy anything that the Japanese could make use of, so cars were thrown into the sea, oil refineries destroyed, warehouses burned, liquor poured into the drains. A major department store gave a free outfit of clothing to every European child on the island.

The British and Australian troops and civilians were rounded up and detained in Changi jail, from where many would later be sent to their deaths in the Japanese work camps in Thailand. Chinese men aged over 18 were interrogated and if thought to be a threat were executed on Changi beach or on Sentosa; untold thousands of Chinese died in this manner. Malay collaboration was encouraged. Indian troops either collaborated or were considered to have forfeited their rights as prisoners of war and were executed.

After the Japanese surrendered in 1945, war crimes trials were held at what is now the Goodwood Park Hotel; some of the commanding officers were executed, either there or at Sentosa.

The post-war years. Singapore once more became a British Crown Colony, headed by a governor who was advised by a non-elected council. Unlike before the war, Singapore was separated from the other Malay states which had also been reclaimed by Britain. But things were no longer as simple as they had been. Many Chinese people who had fled from the Japanese had become communists; in Malaya, Britain had a serious problem for many years trying to put down communist attacks. Another complication was the race issue. Singapore was now predominantly Chinese and was therefore unwelcome as part of the Malay Federation. In both Singapore and Malaya, local political parties were forming to agitate for political reform. In Singapore, the Malayan Democratic Union wanted Singapore to be incorporated into a socialist Malaya. The Union was discredited and finally banned in Singapore because of its affiliations to the communist party of Malaya.

Two, more generally acceptable, parties were formed in Singapore: the

Labour Front, led by David Marshall, a lawyer of Iraqi-Jewish extraction, and the **People's Action Party** (PAP), led by **Lee Kuan Yew**. In the elections of 1955, David Marshall formed a minority government with a policy of self-government for Singapore. He failed to negotiate this and resigned in 1956.

The PAP meanwhile was rapidly undergoing changes, becoming communist-dominated as it gained in influence with trade unions and through Chinese language institutions. During this period Lee bode his time, and worked with communists to secure support. In 1959 Singapore was granted self-government and the PAP formed the first government under Lee's leadership. Communists and conservatives struggled for control of the party and the direction of Singapore's affairs. In 1963 the core of left-wing socialists, now in their own breakaway opposition party, were arrested and imprisoned, leaving the way clear for Lee to lead an anti-communist PAP.

Lee Kuan Yew wanted Singapore to merge with Malaya, hoping no doubt to alter the ethnic balance of the Malay states and dominate affairs. **Malaya** saw a Chinese party with plans to dominate the Federation of Malay States, and was reluctant to accept Singapore into the newly independent Malaya. The Federation formed with North Borneo, Sarawak, Malaya and Singapore did not last very long. There was dissent between Malaya and Singapore over each state's internal affairs and much opposition from Indonesia which began a bombing campaign in Singapore. The PAP fielded candidates in Malaya's election of 1964 and Lee tried to bring all the opposition parties together under the PAP. It was a bid for domination of the whole Federation—and it failed. Singapore was told to leave the Federation before it was thrown out and in 1965 Lee Kuan Yew wept as he announced Singapore's **independence**.

Singapore began to make its way alone—a state with a democratic government, committed to multiracialism, but with no natural resources. Singapore quickly became a one-party state, imprisoning communists and 'subversives', and muffling criticism through state ownership of the media and censorship of foreign publications. For most of the post independence period there has been little or no opposition to the PAP. The few men who have gained seats in Parliament and who do not support the PAP, such as J.B. Jeyaratnam, have had their lives made very difficult for them. Lee Kuan Yew retired in 1990, becoming Senior Minister. Until Lee's son, Brigadier General (or Baby God as he is affectionately known) Lee, is ready for the role, the genial Goh Chok Tong is in charge. In 1992, the news that Lee Hsien Loong (Lee Kuan Yew's son) had been suffering from cancer threw a shadow over his accession, but since his recovery it is still considered very likely that he will eventually succeed his father.

Repressive as it is in many ways, Singapore's regime is also paternalistic. There is little or no unemployment (and no unemployment assistance), and both employers and employees contribute to a compulsory savings scheme called the **Central Providence Fund** (CPF). Initially set up to provide a pension scheme for government employees, it now extends to other sectors of industry and can be drawn on for insurance schemes, mortgages, medical benefits, and education fees.

The Singapore of 1965 was largely a series of *kampungs*—small villages incorporating farmlands, the houses made of timber with very basic sanitation. Most people lived in these houses or in slums in the city. A massive building campaign has created huge satellite towns, such as the sprawling Clementi and more recently the outlying Tampines and Jurong. Unlike Hong Kong's deadly satellite towns which were built in the 1960s to house the thousands of Chinese fleeing over the border, these have a kind of monotonous village life atmosphere. Most Singaporeans now live in high rise, comfortable roomy flats with shopping units and recreation space at their base, while those wealthy enough buy their **HDB** (Housing Development Board) flats using their CPF funds or buy into private developments with swimming pools and tennis courts and a security guard at the gate.

If the **architecture** of the HDB is a little dull that of private industry is less so. Singapore may have little to offer in the way of ancient cathedrals or castles, having torn them all down in the 1960s, but its new wonders of architecture are its hotels and office blocks, each one reaching higher and outdoing its predecessors in glass and scale. More recently, the Urban Redevelopment Association has begun to renovate some of the older areas of town rather than destroying them but both these and some of the newer buildings in Orchard Road have an over cute appearance, looking more like buildings from a Disney movie with neat little arches and interesting turrets. In the conservation areas the original tenants have been moved out and rents have soared to the point where they could never move back. What tourists see now when they visit these areas is a rewritten version of the past tidied up and sanitised with the original inhabitants of the place languishing in Tampines, 25 storeys above the ground.

The basis for all this development has of course been Singapore's **booming economy**, growing at about 9 per cent per annum regularly since the 1960s. It has always had a stable economy and a compliant work force and both wages and rents are high by Asian standards. In modern times the per capita income of Singapore is around US$ 20,000, making it the ninth richest country in the world. The economy is based on shipping, banking, finance, light industry, especially electronics, oil refining and ship building. As in many other aspects of Singaporean life the government manages the economy in a way that belies its reputation as a free market state.

Singapore's government is loosely modelled on the Westminster system. It has a single body of 81 members elected by a complicated system of single member and group constituencies. Since there are usually less than four opposition members, the government can nominate election runners up from the other parties to at least give voice to opposition although they cannot vote on financial or constitutional law. In addition the government can choose non-aligned citizens to debate in parliament although these people cannot vote either.

The judiciary was also originally modelled on the British system with a High Court, Court of Appeal and Court of Criminal Appeal. Below this are the Magistrates courts and District Courts. Both the use of the British Court of Appeal as the final arbiter and the jury system were abandoned in the 1980s.

Conscription of adult males is compulsory, with a two-year period of national service followed by ten more years or so of membership in the reserves. Singapore is now a major investor abroad in projects such as the **New Singapore** in China where Singaporean businessmen are being given a virtually free hand to develop a mini-economy along Singaporean lines.

Singapore is a fairly simple place to orient oneself in. Most of the interesting areas—Orchard Road, Chinatown, Little India, Arab Street, the colonial heart and the business district are centrally located and easy to get to using the MRT. To the west is Jurong, the bird park, the Chinese and Japanese Gardens, which are all accessible by MRT, and Haw Par Villa; to the east is Changi, and the East Coast Park. To the north of the island are Bukit Timah Nature Reserve, the Central Catchment Area with its wildlife areas, the zoo and of course the causeway to Johor Bahru. These northern areas are best reached by bus or taxi.

■ Practical Information

Climate and When to Go
Singapore's temperatures are fairly constant throughout the year (see p 13) with a possible rainy season corresponding roughly to the wet season in Malaysia. The September to December period is often wetter than the during the rest of the year, although and there can be a second wet spell in April and May. But rain in Singapore is unlikely to spoil a holiday as it rarely rains all day and public transport is not affected. The rainy spells can provide some welcome cool weather.

Getting to and from Singapore

Airlines
British Airways: 01-56 United Square, 101 Thomson Road (☎ 65-253 8444)

MAS: 02-09 Singapore Shopping Centre, 109 Clemenceau Avenue (☎ 65-336 6777)

Northwest Airlines: 08-06 Odeon Towers, 331 North Bridge Road (☎ 65-336 3371)

Qantas Airlines: 04-02 The Promenade, 300 Orchard Road. (☎ 65-737 3744)

Singapore Airlines: SIA Building, 77 Robinson Road (☎ 65-223 8888)

United Airlines: 44-02 Hong Leong Building, 16 Raffles Quay (☎ 65-220 0711)

See p 17 for details on getting to and from Singapore.

Changi Airport (☎ 65-5418704) is at the eastern extremity of the island and the easiest way into town is by taxi. There is a S$3 surcharge for the taxi ride. There is a further additional charge after midnight. The basic fare into town will be about S$16.

There are also buses into town, running every ten minutes or so. Buses also go to Tampines Interchange from where you can get the MRT into town. Buses leave from the basement but only run until midnight after which your only option is a taxi. Remember that bus drivers do not give change so you should have some coins.

Travel between Singapore and Johor Bahru in Malaysia is possible by foot (by walking across the Causeway from Woodlands in Singapore to Johor Bahru), by bus from Queen Street station (No. 170) or by private coach from various companies. *Nice* express buses are efficient and comfortable and connect Singapore with Johor Bahru and Kuala Lumpur. They depart from the Royal Hotel in Newton Road and tickets can be booked through Damas Holidays (☎ 65-2915355). See the Johor Bahru (p 216) and Kuala Lumpur (p 66) sections for booking tickets within Malaysia. MAS run regular daily flights between Singapore and Malaysia.

Getting around Singapore

By MRT. Singapore has a cheap and efficient transport system: the **Mass Rapid Transport** (MRT), less than a decade old, is a well-oiled, efficient and air-conditioned way of getting about the island. Trains run from 06.00 to midnight at intervals of between three to eight minutes. Tickets can be bought through machines at any station and are single-journey fares. The two lines are colour-coded and each station has a name and number. Fares range from S$0.60 to S$1.50. A S$12 Transit-Link card can be used on the MRT and buses. Free MRT guide maps are available at stations in the city.

By bus. The bus service is inexpensive and extends throughout the island. Tourists can buy an explorer ticket which gives them one day (S$5) or three days (S$12) unlimited travel on the bus services. Bus stops are marked with the numbers of the buses. The Transitlink Guide costs S$1.50 and is well worth buying as it lists all bus routes and links all Singapore's street names with the relevant bus routes. Fares range from S$.60 to $1.90 depending on the length of your journey and you must have the exact fare—the driver can tell you what it will be. Few buses have bus conductors and most of them are not air-conditioned. For tourists there is special bus service called the Singapore Trolley. Tickets cost S$9 for a day's use. The bus travels through Orchard Road, the colonial area, the Central Business District and Chinatown.

Trishaws are still used in Singapore, but only for guided processions of tourists

By taxi. Taxis are plentiful, cheap, and metered, with clear indications of extra charges which should also register on the meter. Taxi rides can be educational and fun if your driver wants to chat; you can learn more about Singapore in five minutes in a cab than you will from any STPB leaflet. Taxi rides start at S$2.40 for the first 1.5km, after which 10 cents is added for each 250m. There are surcharges for calling a cab, transport from the airport, a ride after midnight, luggage, and various combinations of children and adults. Only four passengers are allowed in a taxi. If you want to go into the restricted zone (see below) during its hours of operation you must pay for a licence sticker or find a cab which has already bought one. They can be spotted on the front windscreen.

By car. Car hire is relatively cheap and can be arranged at the airport or through any of the big hotels. Only certain hire cars can be taken into Malaysia;

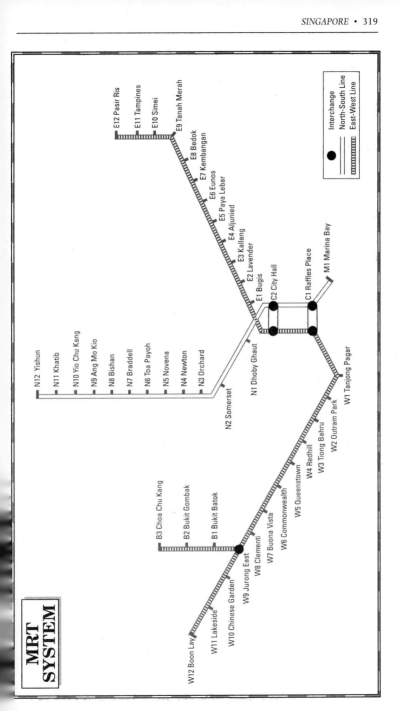

MRT SYSTEM

it would cost less to hire a car in Johor Bahru than to pay the extra fee for taking a Singaporean car into Malaysia. **Parking** usually involves a parking ticket on which you indicate time of arrival by punching holes. Tickets can be bought at 7-Eleven stores, supermarkets and any small general store. Driving is on the left hand side. There is a restricted zone in the city centre which encompasses the CBD, part of Chinatown, Orchard Road. The zone is in operation from 07.30–18.30 Monday to Friday, and 07.30–13.00 on Saturday. To drive into the area you must buy a daily licence from one of the booths stationed just outside the boundaries.

By Bicycle. Cycling can be very hazardous in car crazy Singapore. Bicycles can be hired in several places along the East Coast Park and at Pasir Ris and Sentosa Island. There are cycle tracks stretching along the coast at these places and the bikes are only really intended for use on these tracks. About a decade or so ago, bicycles could be seen all over the city but in more recent times only dedicated racing bikers are to be seen hurtling about the major roads on Sundays.

Tourist information

The Singapore Tourist Promotion Board (STPB) has two offices. One is on the ground floor of Tourism Court (☎ 1-800 7383778/4, toll-free in Singapore only), 1 Orange Spring Lane (off Cuscanden Road), open 08.30 to 18.00 Monday to Saturday. The other is at No. 02–34 Raffles Hotel Arcade, 328 North Bridge Road (☎ 1-800 3341335/6, toll-free in Singapore), which is open daily 08.30 to 19.00.

There is also a Touristline (☎ 1-800 8313311) which provides a 24-hour automated toll-free information system in English and German. General tourist information on Singapore is also available at STPB's website: http://www/newasia-singapore.com

Useful free publications in Singapore include the *Official Guide*, updated every month, with up-to-date prices and transport details. Various leaflets and booklets are available on shopping, food and wildlife areas.

Currency exchange. Money and travellers cheques can be changed at banks, open from 10.00 to 15.00 on weekdays and 1100 to 13.00 on Saturday, and at most hotels. Around the tourist areas are licensed **moneychangers** who have similar rates to the banks and thus better than the hotel rates. They are often found in the basement or ground levels of shopping malls.

There is an **American Express office** (☎ 65-299 8133) at No. 18-01/07 The Concourse, 300 Beach Road, and a **Visa Card Service Centre** (☎ 1 800 3451345) for lost or stolen cards.

Postal, telephone and fax services. The main post office is in Robinson Road and has a poste restante service for which you will need your passport in order to collect mail. You can also make long-distance phone calls here and make use of general services.

Long-distance phone calls and faxes can also be arranged at Comcentre, 71 Robinson Road. Long-distance phone calls from hotel rooms are often surcharged at around 25 per cent of the call, while local calls from hotels are either free or charged by the minute. Most phone boxes now operate using phone cards which can be bought at post offices, newsagents and supermarkets. With a high enough value phone card it is possible to make long-distance calls from phone boxes. There are also boxes which take the major credit cards.

Embassies and immigration

For visa extensions, contact the Immigration Department (☎ 65-532 2877), 08–26 Pidemco centre, 95 South Bridge Road.

Countries with embassies and consulates in Singapore include:

Australia: 25 Napier Road (☎ 65-737 9311)

Canada: IBM Towers, 80 Anson Road (☎ 65-325 3200)

France: 5 Gallop Road (☎ 65-466 4866)

Germany: 14-00 Far East Shopping Centre, Orchard Road (☎ 65-737 1355)

New Zealand: 391A Orchard Road 15-06 Ngee Ann City Tower A (☎ 65-235 9966)

Republic of Ireland: 298 Tiong Bahru Road 08-06, Tiong Bahru Plaza (☎ 65-276 8935)

Thailand: 370 Orchard Road (☎ 65-737 2644)

UK: 325 Tanglin Road (☎ 65-473 9333)

USA: 27 Napier Road (☎ 65-476 9100)

Emergencies and hospitals

☎ 999 for police, 995 for ambulance or Fire Brigade.

The larger hotels have a doctor on call. There are casualty departments at the Alexandra Hospital, Alexandra Road (☎ 65-473 5222), National University Hospital, Kent Ridge (☎ 65-779 5555) and Singapore General, Outram Road (☎ 65-222 3322).

Crimes must be reported to the police station in the area the crime was committed. The station for the Orchard Road area is Tanglin Police Station, 17 Napier Road (☎ 65-733 0000).

Tour operators

There are numerous tour operators in Singapore which offer good service and personalised tours, including **Holiday Tours** (☎ 65-738 2622), **Singapore Sightseeing Tours East** (☎ 65-332 3755), **RMG Tours** (☎ 65-220 1661) and **Singapore Explorer** (☎ 65-227 8218). They all arrange tours of the major sights and typical prices are S$43 for a night tour that includes dinner, and S$32 for the Tang Dynasty City tour. Most hotel lobbies will have at least one tour agent's desk to arrange tours. There is a free tour of Singapore for passengers with longer than a four-hour stopover at the airport.

Another good way to see some of the city is on one of the river tours or a harbour cruise. The river tours are organised by **Singapore River Cruise and Leisure** (☎ 65-336 6119) and the half-hour trip departs from Boat Quay or Clarke Quay at half-hourly intervals. Harbour cruises can involve a meal or just a trip around the harbour and southern islands. **Water Tours** (☎ 65-533 9811) does a series of trips in a Chinese junk, while **J&N**, (☎65-270-7100) operate *The Equator Dream*, a catamaran.

Most of the above companies also handle out-of-Singapore tours, especially to

Johor Bahru and Melaka in Malaysia, and Batam Island in Indonesia. Typical prices are S$25 for the tour to Johor Bahru, S$75 to Melaka and S$85 to Batam Island. **Grayline** (☎ 65-331 8244) cover Tioman Island and Desaru Beach in Johor.

Accommodation

Top range hotels in Singapore are of such high quality that it is almost impossible to choose between them. Prices are similar and each place has its own merits in location, amenities, views and ambience. Probably the nicest hotel in Singapore, although not by any means the most expensive, is the **Oriental** (☎ 65-338 0066; fax 65-3399537) at 3335 Raffles Avenue. Its rooms have excellent views and the atrium is one of the most spectacular in Singapore. Rooms are S$412 for a double. In the same complex is the **Marina Mandarin** (☎ 338 3388; fax 65-3394977) at 6, Raffles Boulevard, again beautifully designed with every amenity, located above an excellent shopping centre. The **Goodwood Park** (☎ 65-737 7411; fax 65-732 8558), on Scotts Road, is a listed building and has a long history and colonial atmosphere. The rooms are not as cosy as those at the Oriental but they are well appointed and pleasant. A double room here is S$405. The **Crown Prince** (☎ 65-7321111; fax 65-7327018) is usefully located around the mid-point of Orchard Road.

The **Beaufort Hotel** (☎ 65-275 0331; fax 65-2750228) on Sentosa is beautifully designed and very quiet with a large garden, swimming pool fronting the beach and huge trees with a varied wildlife. If you do not mind the daily trip back to Singapore, the Beaufort is a good choice and quite unlike the other hotels in atmosphere. A double room is S$350.

The **Amara** (☎ 65-224 4488; fax 65-2243910), on Tanjong Pagar Road, is a little way away from the main series of hotels, but has a pleasant atmosphere and larger than average rooms. A double room here is S$300.

The top flight hotels would not be complete without a mention of the **Raffles** (☎ 65-3371886; fax 65-3397650), 1 Beach Road. The rooms are individually designed and guests are kept well away from the casual visitors wandering the shopping arcades below. Room prices start at S$600.

Great fun if you have a head for heights is the **Westin Stamford** (☎ 3388585, fax 65-3371554), 2 Stamford Road, which soars above the city and has balconies even on its highest floors so you can peer out over the ant-like people walking below. It has a busy atmosphere and lots of tourists, good facilities and is centrally located. The **Concord** hotel (☎ 65-7330188; fax 65-7330989) on Outram Road has a breathtaking atrium and rooms from S$230.

Slightly out of town and with a very Chinese ambience is the **Furama** (☎ 65-5333888; fax 65-5341489) at 6, Eu Tong Sen Street, which has the distinctively shaped curved skyline. It has a particularly wacky Chinese restaurant which serves anything from deep fried bear's paw to snake or duck's tongue. Just out of the centre is the **New Otani**, (☎ 65-338-3333; fax 65-3392834) at 177 River Valley Road. It is vaguely Japanese in ambience, and is built above a good shopping centre close to Boat Quay, and has an excellent Japanese restaurant.

Way out of the tourist circuit but a nice quiet place to stay is **Le Meridien Changi** (☎ 65-542-7700; fax 65-5425295) AT 1, Netheravon Road. It has a pool, good restaurants, nicely appointed rooms, and offers great bargains at weekends. The regular rate is around S$300 for a double.

Middle range hotels. With land at a premium in Singapore anything that does not earn the maximum amount of money is torn down and rebuilt so medium range hotels are scarce. The best of them is the **YMCA** (☎ 65-3373444; fax 65-337 3140) at 1 Orchard Road. A double room is S\$118. You should book well in advance for a room here. The **Metropolitan YMCA** (☎ 65-737 7755; fax 65-235 5528), 60 Stevens Road, is a fair walk from the centre of Singapore but has a pool, a café and nice rooms. A double room is S\$64.

RELC (☎ 65-737 9044; fax 65-7339976) in Orange Grove Road is also a longish walk from Orchard Road but it is excellent value, with breakfast included and a reasonable Chinese restaurant. It is really an English Language Institute with hotel rooms for participants, but it lets rooms to tourists too. The rooms are huge, have balconies looking out over the city, and there are small kitchens where you can cook. There is also a launderette. A double room is S\$126.

The Strand (☎ 65-3381866; fax 65-3363149) at 25 Bencoolen Street is well situated in the colonial district and can be recommended. It costs around S\$100 for a double.

The **Metropole Hotel** (☎ 65-3363611; fax 65-3393610) at Seah Street is pleasantly appointed—close to the Raffles hotel, if you fancy a gin sling—and has air-conditioned rooms for around S\$100. The **Hotel VIP** (☎ 65-2354277), at 5 Balmoral Crescent, is again a good distance from the centre but is a pleasant, quiet place with a swimming pool which counts for a lot in Singapore's climate. Rooms are around S\$113.

At the very top end of the middle range is the **Equatorial** (☎ 65-7320431; fax 65-7379426) at 429 Bukit Timah Road. It is a little way out of town and in the low season offers good discounts on its room rates. It has a pool and a good Japanese restaurant. The rooms are around S\$160.

Budget range hotels are even rarer than medium range ones and tend to be homestays rather than hotels. The best of the hotels is the **Mitre Hotel** (☎65-737 3811), an ageing bungalow at 145 Killeny Road with a big garden and a shabby bar. Double, air-conditioned rooms are S\$36. At 10 Peck Seah Street in Chinatown is the **Air View** (☎ 65-2257788; fax 65-2256688). Air-conditioned rooms with a bathroom and TV are S\$60. In Jalan Besar, near Lavender Street at No. 407A, is the **Palace Hotel** (☎ 65-2983108) with big rooms with a balcony for S\$24. There are no air-conditioned rooms though. Lastly, the **Mayfair City Hotel** (☎ 65-3374542; fax 65-3371736) at 40–44 Armenian Street has a good location near the colonial area. Air-conditioned rooms with a TV cost S\$72.

Restaurants

For many visitors—and most Singaporeans—the most pleasurable activity in Singapore is eating. Singaporeans spend hours discussing the relative merits of hawker places, restaurants, buffets, coffee shops, and when a new place opens and gets a good review, everyone flocks there in droves.

The restaurants below are categorised by price range; the expensive and moderate places are also divided into cuisines: European, Chinese, and other Asian cuisines. This last group covers Indian, Malay, Japanese, Thai, Indonesian and Vietnamese. The less expensive places to eat usually offer a variety of European and Asian dishes.

Expensive

European. **Nutmegs** (☎ 65-7307112), at the Hyatt Regency in Scotts Road, serves an interesting Californian-style cuisine with the chefs working away in an open kitchen. As in many places in Singapore, the set lunches are the best value. Expect to pay well over S$100 for a meal. For fine dining on top of the world— well, the 39th floor of the Mandarin hotel in Orchard Road—the **Top of the 'M'** (☎ 65-7374411) offers a set lunch (around S$50) or set dinner (around S$100) as well as an à la carte menu. The restaurant revolves—it takes just over two hours to complete one revolution—and its high floor-to-ceiling windows provide views that stretch to the Causeway and Bantam Island in Indonesia. At night diners are serenaded by music. The 38th floor is an observation lounge where you can drink without dining.

Chinese. The **Cherry Garden** (☎ 65-3310538) at the Oriental serves an interesting mixture of Chinese cuisines in pleasant surroundings. The **Xin Cuisine** at the Concord hotel serves excellent Cantonese delicacies with style. In the most unusual surroundings you can imagine is the **Prima Tower Revolving Restaurant**, 201 Keppel Road (☎ 65-272 8822) which is built on the top of a fully operational grain silo. You take a lift up the side of the silo and get a glorious view over Singapore as you eat. The atmosphere is anything but muted, with children bouncing about. But the food is what everyone is here for: the speciality is Peking duck, or you can select your dinner from the cages and tanks littering the place. Dinner for two will cost well over S$100.

The **Pine Court Chinese Restaurant**, at the Mandarin in Orchard Road is decorated in style of imperial Beijing. Lunch is served from 12.00 to 15.00 and dinner from 19.00 to midnight. The food is expensive but in an exciting setting. Try the spicy and sour shark's fin soup or the scallops and snow peas. Beijing duck is a speciality.

Asian. For a Japanese evening out in Singapore, try the **Senbazuru** at the New Otani Hotel (☎ 65-4338693), on River Valley Road. It serves *sushi, sashimi* and *teppanyaki* (the last being the most fun as the chefs throw their utensils around in the ritual process of grilling food on an open hot plate), or you can mix and match your dishes. To finish, try the green tea ice cream.

Moderate

European. Cuppage Terrace and Cuppage Road, near Centrepoint on Orchard Road, have a number of moderately-priced restaurants serving a variety of cuisines. **Da Vinci's** (☎ 65-7354955), at 31 Cuppage Road, is located in a conserved chophouse where the old Peranakan floor tiles have been retained. The food is authentically Italian. A popular Western, Mediterranean-style restaurant, **Bastiani's** (☎ 65-4330156), is opposite the Merchant's Court hotel at Clarke's Quay. It serves an odd but interesting mix of European dishes in a bistro-style setting. A five-course meal will set you back around S$90. **Café Georges** at the Le Meridien hotel on Orchard Road is an informal, brasserie-style restaurant which serves Western and Asian dishes. Buffet and à la carte meals are available from around S$25 per person.

Chinese. The **Imperial Herbal Restaurant** (☎ 65-3370491), on the third floor of the Metropole in Seah Street, is a health restaurant with a difference— exotic ingredients are used for health-enhancing dishes according to traditional Chinese medicine. A set dinner is S$76; an à la carte meal will cost around S$38

Asian. There are too many restaurants at Boat Quay to list. They all cost around S$100 for two people to dine and they nearly all have tables set out along the riverside. Take your pick from Indian, Thai, Japanese and Sundanese cuisines. They are all popular with Singaporean yuppies.

The **Yukikawa** in Seah Street has set lunches for around S$12 and dinner dishes for about the same price. At 04-10/13 in the Tanglin Shopping Centre in Tanglin Road there is a **Tambuah Mas** Indonesian restaurant (☎ 65-733 2220); it is very popular and reservations are often needed. Classic Indonesian dishes such as *rendang lembu* (beef in coconut), *udang belado* (prawns with chilli), *gado gado* (vegetables in peanut sauce) are all reasonably priced. A branch of the same restaurant can also be found at 05-14/27 of the Shaw Centre (☎ 65-733 3333), at the junction of Scotts and Orchard Roads.

For Indian food try the **Aangan Restaurant** at 04-05 Funan Centre in High Street. The food is north Indian, there is a buffet lunch, and a music and dance show to accompany dinner. The **Tiffin Room** at the Raffles hotel serves a buffet dinner of Indian and Malay dishes for S$38.

Clarke Quay, like Boat Quay, is bursting with restaurants. Two that have been particularly recommended are **Thanying**, for Thai food, and **Want Jiang Fou Yunnan Kitchen** for Chinese. Indonesian and Indian restaurants are also popular here.

Inexpensive

The food court in the basement of the **Funan Centre** in High Street is recommended, but not at weekends when it can be crowded. All the dishes are around S$6 and include herbal soups, Indian, Malay and Chinese vegetarian cuisine.

One of the most pleasant **hawker centres** is the one opposite the main entrance to the Botanic Gardens. Try the *roti john* at stall No. 9 or the *roti prata* at No. 12. If spending any time at Changi village, the **Changi Hawker Centre** is worth eating at even though it does not look too smart. The stall numbered 01-59 does an excellent *yong tau foo* where you choose your own ingredients, mostly vegetables and fish, and 01-73 serves delicious Malay dishes on banana leaves. **Charlie's Corner**, opposite 01-73, serves a range of beers, and 01-13 is a sugar cane stall.

The **Chin Chin** restaurant at the end of North Bridge Street allows you to gaze at the Raffles while economising on Western meals for around S$5. The second floor of the MPH bookshop at the corner of Armenian Street and Stamford Road has a pleasant café serving light lunches for S$5–10. In the basement of the Tanglin Shopping Centre, in Tanglin Road, there are a couple of open-fronted pubs serving lunch specials for under S$10. **Clarke Quay** has a free seating area in the open air where you can eat whatever you have bought from the nearby fastfood stalls.

The **Shanghai Restaurant** at Changi Road is highly recommended. It can be reached by MRT Eunos and is worth the journey. More of a coffee shop than a restaurant, this type of once-archetypal Singapore eating place is fast disappearing. An excellent S$2 *mee rebus* is served for breakfast or lunch, a dinner of Malay dishes is around S$12. Further up this road there is a **House of Sundanese** restaurant and a Peranakan restaurant.

Serangoon Road (a continuation of Selegie Road) and its restaurants deserve a very special mention for providing some of the most interesting and exotic food in Singapore at reasonable prices. If you visit nowhere else, you should go to the **Madras New Woodlands** restaurant (☎ 65-279 1594) at 14 Upper Dickson Road. It serves only vegetarian food but you will not miss the meat. Try the VIP *thali* set dinner which is a whole series of little pots of curry, *lassi*, soup and dessert surrounding rice and a huge *bhatyura*, which is deep-fried bread which somehow explodes into a huge football. **Komala Vilas** is at No. 76 Serangoon Road, and serves a slightly different style of Indian food with the emphasis on *dosa*. **Racecourse Road** has many more inexpensive Indian places serving meat and vegetable dishes.

Shopping

Singapore can sometimes seem like one giant shopping mall. Although there is a great deal of protection for tourists against being cheated by unscrupulous merchants, it is as well to observe a few sensible rules. Look for the red merlion sign on the shop door or window, signifying approval by the Consumers' Association of Singapore. If you have a particular item in mind the most sensible thing to do is go to a department store and check the price. **Metro** and **Yaohans** are department stores with branches on Orchard Road and elsewhere. **Tangs** department store, at the corner of Orchard Road and Scotts Road, is a little more expensive than these last two stores. All these places have fixed prices.

After having established an idea of prices, you can try your hand at bargaining in malls such as the Far East Plaza on Scotts Road. With some shops, asking for a discount is enough to get you the real price while in others the proprietor starts off at a really silly figure just to see how much you know. Once you make an offer, which should be substantially below what you are actually hoping to pay, you are pretty much committed to serious bargaining, so if you are not really interested do not name a price.

It is claimed that **Orchard Road** (see map on pp 328–9) has the highest density of shops to space available in the world but this was not always the case. In the early days of Singapore's colonial life the top half of the road was a series of nutmeg plantations which gradually gave way to the huge bungalows of the wealthy settlers. The Dhoby Ghaut end was once a river where washermen plied their trade. Until the 1970s the main shopping area in Singapore was Raffles Place. The first store to take off in Orchard Road was CK Tang which was opened in 1942 as a curio shop. The long string of hotels and department stores which now make up the road came into being from the 1970s; the first big hotel to open was the Hilton, now quite low rise and modest by modern standards. As late as 1986 there were large areas of unused land where shopping fairs would be held periodically. The building boom continues today with new malls going up at an alarming rate despite the soaring rents and the fact that some of the stores are experiencing difficulties. For many Singaporeans, a good day out is to cruise the air-conditioned malls, looking but not buying—they do their real shopping in other places where they can negotiate a price.

The area is also home to the seriously wealthy residents of Singapore, many still living in the colonial style houses around Claymore Hill. Emerald Hill, at the western end of the road was Singapore's first real conservation area, the old Peranakan style houses rocketing in price as it became clear that they were not to go under the bulldozer like so many of Singapore's other older buildings.

Shopping centres. Which ones you choose to shop in depends on what you want to buy. For computers or software visit the **Funan Centre** at 109 North Bridge Road or **Sim Lim Square** at the corner of Bencoolen Street and Rochor Canal Road. Prices can be lower than in the West but if you want an international guarantee this will often rule out the cheaper, locally made machines.

For cameras, CD players and the like there are too many shops to begin compiling a list. It helps to have a good idea of prices and makes at home and then try Sim Lim Square or **Sim Lim Tower** on Jalan Besar or any of the shops in the shopping malls along Orchard Rd. A good place to check out is a tiny shop in Lorong Liput in Holland Village called **Paris Silk**; it has a long history of selling to expatriates and a no nonsense, fixed price, take it or leave it attitude.

Here follows a list of the major shopping centres and the important shops to be found in them.

From Tanglin Road near the Botanic Gardens to the Scotts Road junction on Orchard Road there are a number of plazas. **Tanglin Shopping Centre**, 19 Tanglin Road, has several shops on the second and third levels selling antiques and artefacts from around the region: the shop at 02-40 specialises in old maps and prints; 03-20 is a specialist art and history bookshop; 02-54 sells furniture and Buddhas. **Delfi Orchard** has European crystal and china, and a rattan shop. **Orchard Towers** is very tourist-oriented with tailors, silk shops, antiques and a supermarket. Some serious bargaining goes on here. **Forum Galleria** has a giant toyshop. The **Far East Shopping Centre** has more tourist goodies, clothes, tailors and porcelain stores. **Liat Towers** holds the upmarket Galleries Lafayette department store and designer boutiques. **Lane Crawford Place** contains the eponymous store, sprawling over five floors. In **Shaw House** is Isetan, probably the best-value Japanese department store.

Scotts Road has the huge **Far East Plaza**, dedicated to tourists and including a branch of **Metro**, the local, reasonably priced department store. The important shop in **Scotts Plaza** is **Cost Plus**, a shop selling electrical goods at fixed prices. There are also a whole range of clothes shops including China Silk House.

From the Orchard Road junction with Scotts Road to the Raffles Hotel is one long chain of buildings dedicated to consumers. **Tangs** is a large, locally owned department store which is especially good for clothes, jewellery and perfume. It also has a good selection of tourist paraphernalia. **Lucky Plaza** is one of the more aggressive bargaining places and there is nothing here that cannot be bought more pleasantly and for the same price elsewhere. It is full of clothes, leather goods, cameras and electrical goods, and tailors. In **Wisma Atria** is another Isetan department store, lots of good value opticians, shoe shops and small boutiques. **Ngee Ann City**, an ugly and sinister monstrosity of a building, is the newest of the shopping centres. It has a Takashimaya department store, supermarket and lots of restaurants and a sports centre.

In the **Specialists' Shopping Centre** is John Little, a very old established department store. Across the road in **Centrepoint** is Robinson's, a major department store, which has been trading in Singapore since 1858. In Centrepoint you can also find antiques, designer clothes, watches and much more. It is probably the most successful and popular shopping centre in Singapore. **Plaza Singapura** has an enormous branch of Yaohans department

Refc International
House Hotel

Goodwood Park
Hotel

Far East
Plaza

🏠 Temple

⊖ MRT Station

Shangri-La
Hotel

Royal
Holiday
Inn

Hyatt
Regency

ORANGE GROVE ROAD

Delphi
Orchard

Orchard
Towers

Thailand
Embassy

Shaw
House

Scotts
Tangs

Lucky
Plaza

Crown Prince
Hotel

Centrepoint

Peranakan
Place

Mer
Ho

Mer
Shop
Cer

Specialists'
Centre

Forum
Galleria

Hilton

Liat
Towers

ORCHARD ROAD

P.O.

Tanglin
Shopping
Centre

International

Far East
Shopping
Centre

Orchard

Wisma
Atria

Ngee Ann
City

The
Mandarin
Hotel

Somerset

SOMERSET ROAD

EXETER ROAD

Comcentre

0   200 yds

0   200 metres

ORCHARD ROAD
WALK

Mit
Hot

store with a wonderful collection of Japanese dinnerware. There are also music shops, vast shops selling Korean and Chinese furniture, antique shops and a supermarket in the basement. **Park Mall**, on Penang Road near to Dhoby Ghaut MRT station, is a bit out of the way but worth a trip over the road because it holds a lot of local designer shops as well as a clothing factory outlet called Stockmart.

Outside Orchard Road there are two major shopping malls. **Raffles City**, just in front of City Hall MRT station, has a Sogo department store with a good bookshop, and lots of jewellery and Chinese artefact shops. The other major location is **Marina Square**, on Raffles Boulevard, which can be reached from City Hall MRT station. Here there are a Metro department store, a good bookshop, and lots of shops selling leather goods, sports clothes and craftware. It also has a good hawker centre and lots of fast-food places.

Chinatown has some good shopping centres, particularly **Chinatown Point** where some bargaining is called for. There are any number of craft and curio shops, as well as unusual clothes, handbags and some paintings. Chinatown Point is at the junction of New Bridge Road and Upper Hokkien Street. The nearest MRT is Outram Park, from where you may walk back towards town along the shopping centres of New Bridge Street.

If you enjoy wandering around small open shops and bargaining, the **Arab Street** area, near Sultan Mosque, is a good place to visit. Here can be found a few remaining shops which have escaped 'conservation', retaining their five foot ways (see p 342) stacked out with beautiful crafts from the region and Malaysia in particular. Basketware is visible everywhere, ethnic-style handbags and beautiful sarongs fill the shops while other places sell prayer mats, skull caps, Malay-style dresses and wholesale cloth of all kinds. There are also perfume shops selling highly concentrated perfumes which can be mixed to order.

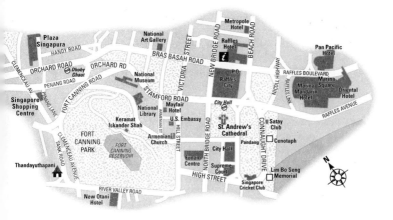

Holland Village, to the west of town, is an excellent shopping centre which caters for a large population of Western expatriates. It can be reached by bus 7 or 77 from Orchard Boulevard, or it is a short taxi ride. There is a superb arts and crafts shop called **Lim's**, several shops selling interesting fabrics, dress shops and, out on the street behind the shopping centre, **Lorong Liput**, more craft shops, a number of good small restaurants, and a shop called **Paris Silk**, which is recommended for cameras, CDs and the like.

A good place for arts and crafts is **Duxton Road** and the nearby **Tanjong Pagar Conservation Area**. There are countless shops here specialising in arts and antiques from every corner of Southeast Asia. Also recommended is the **National Museum shop**, next to the National Museum in Stamford Road, for paintings, books, sarongs, Burmese powder boxes and the like: the perfect place for souvenirs and gifts. It is closed on Sunday but, unlike the museum, not on Monday.

Bookshops do not come any larger than the MPH store at the corner of Armenian Street and Stamford Road. It has three floors and the largest stock of books in Southeast Asia. As well as books there is a floor devoted to CDs. The 7-Eleven store in the basement of Centrepoint on Orchard Road is good for foreign newspapers.

Sports

Boating is possible at the swimming lagoon at Sentosa Island where there are paddle boats and canoes for hire. Another boating lake is at the east Coast Park near the lagoon food centre at 1390 East Coast Parkway. It is open 10.00–18.00, closed on public holidays.

There are **sailing clubs** at Changi and the East Coast Park Sailing Centre (☎ 449 5118), 1210 East Coast Parkway. The Centre has windsurf boards and small boats for hire. They also do short courses in sailing for beginners.

Scuba diving courses and equipment hire can be found at the Sentosa Water Sports centre at the World Trade Centre. The Sentosa Sports centre on Sentosa Island rents out diving equipment.

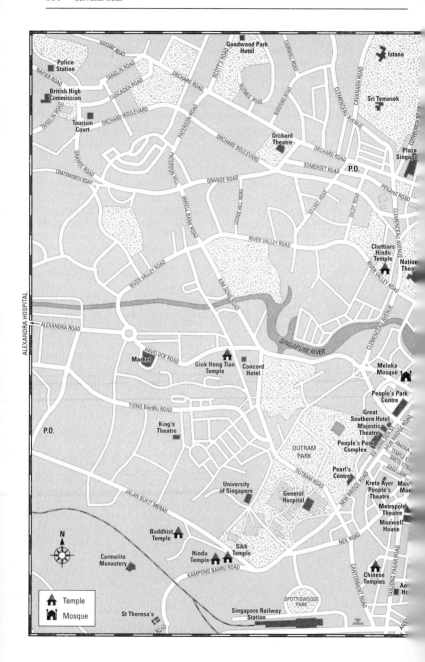

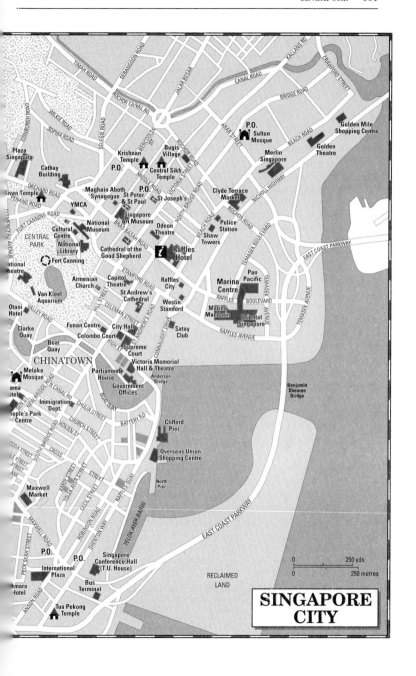

SINGAPORE CITY

There are public **swimming pools** throughout the island. Entrance is usually $2 or so. In addition, the Big Splash at East Coast Parkway has water slides, a wave pool and all the other paraphernalia. On Sentosa is Fantasy Island with slides, rubber boat rides, swings and lots of other fun water activities. CN West Leisure Park at 9 Japanese Gardens is a similar complex.

Golf fans will have great fun in Singapore. Most of the clubs are private but members of the public can play during weekdays. Changi Golf Club, 9 holes, is at Netheravon Road. The Raffles Country Club at Jalan Ahmad Ibrahim has two 18-hole courses. Sentosa Country Club has an 18-hole course and the Singapore island Golf Club has two 18-hole courses.

Bowling alleys charge around S$4 for a game. There are alleys at East Coast Road, number 542B, Kallang, at 5 Stadium Walk, Grange Road, and Marina Bay.

Roller skating can be found at Sentosa Island. It gets very crowded at weekends.

Entertainment and Nightlife

Before Singapore became clean and green it boasted a pretty sleazy but dynamic nightlife. In modern times the place is a little too well regulated and Johor Bahru is too close for those days ever to return but there are places to go and things to do at night. Singaporeans tend to go for karaoke or the cinema and there are plenty of these places to visit if you have a mind. Live music tends to be Phillipino and derivative but occasionally some big names pop up for one-off concerts.

Cinemas abound in Singapore and are very popular so you might want to call in earlier to buy tickets. Some of the multiplex cinemas are: the **Cathay** on the corner of Bras Basah and Handy Road, The **Jade** at the Shaw Centre in Beach Road and the **Capitol** on the corner of Hill Street and Stamford Road. Western movies predominate at cinemas in the centre of town, while Cantonese films can be found in the suburbs. You will find that films are censored drastically with conversations suddenly disappearing or sharp cuts to the story line. There is a new movie rating called 'R' which allows tasteful, artistically justified rude sections to be shown to those over 21 years of age.

Theatre. The most popular theatre events in Singapore are the Cantonese operas which area staged on street corners. Although incomprehensible to western eyes, they are well worth watching should you come across them. Several hotels often import entire London productions for a week and offer a dinner and theatre package; look out for these in the local press. **Substation** (☎ 337 7800) at 45 Armenian Street produces some good local theatre as well as poetry readings and exhibitions. The **Victoria Theatre** (☎ 336 2151) in Empress Place often has both imported and local amateur productions as does the **Drama Centre** (☎ 336 0005) in Canning Rise. The **Victoria Concert Hall** (☎ 338 1230) is home to the Singapore Philharmonic and often has visiting orchestras.

Music. Most hotels have several forms of **live music**, from a piano bar with some jazz music to full blown Phillipino bands. Places that have proved their popularity over the years include **Saxophone**, at 23 Cuppage Terrace, which hosts some famous jazz names who play from a tiny platform behind the bar while most of the customers eat and drink outside in the street. There is a wonderful atmosphere here and the music goes on well into the early hours. **Anywhere**, on the 4th Floor of Tanglin Shopping Centre, is still going strong after 15 years and is very popular with seasoned expatriot drinkers. The ubiquitous **Hard Rock Café** at 50 Cuscaden Road has live music after 22.00. Way out in Changi is the **Europa** bar where Phillipino bands play hard rock music. The very popular and ever-crowded **Brannigan's** at the Hyatt Regency, 10–12 Scott's Road, heaves the night away with jazz music till about 01.00.

Discos are popular with tourists and locals alike. Those that have weathered the ravages of time and police raids are: **Top Ten** on the 4th Floor of Orchard Towers which is primarily a disco but also has a live Philippino band; **Chinoiserie**, in the Hyatt Regency in Scott's Road, a very sophisticated place where local yuppies hang out; The **Library** in the Mandarin Hotel in Orchard Road has similar clientele; while the **New Warehouse** in Havelock Road is popular with the young.

Colonial Walk

Much of the glamour of Singapore rests in its colonial history and a walk around some of the areas where much of that history took place is probably the historical highlight of a trip to Singapore. Although many of the old buildings disappeared during the 1960s and 1970s what remains is now protected, and this walk will take you around what was once the social epicentre of late 19C island life—from the now gleaming Raffles Hotel, past the open space of the

padang and the Esplanade where carriages once brought their passengers to gossip, the city's cathedral, to the Victoria Theatre where the gentry went to watch their friends put on amateur theatricals, and to Fort Canning, where Raffles stood on the verandah of his bungalow and watched the ships come into the harbour.

You would be failing in your role as a visitor to Singapore if you did not to go to look at the $160 million revamp of the **Raffles Hotel**, so perhaps the best place to begin a visit to the colonial heart of Singapore is here. The hotel is difficult to miss as it occupies the best part of a block. Its front entrance, complete with traveller's palms and lackeys to open your limousine door, is in Beach Road, but the newly constructed part for the ordinary tourist is along Bras Basah Road. It is a shopping arcade full of designer goodies and bric-à-brac with the Raffles Hotel logo. There are also a number of restaurants and at least one bar where you can get the Singapore Sling cocktail. Some areas of the hotel are not open to non-residents.

The hotel site was originally occupied by a private residence, a beachfront bungalow owned by an Arab trader. It later saw service as a tiffin room owned by an Englishman, Captain Dare, before being bought up by the Sarkie brothers in 1886. These men eventually owned a chain of hotels all built in a similar style—the Eastern and Oriental Hotel in Penang and the Strand Hotel in Rangoon.

In its day, the Raffles had many famous and worthy visitors. Somerset Maugham wrote some of his short stories here, Rudyard Kipling and Joseph Conrad both stayed as guests in the early years of the century, although Kipling's advice was to stay at the Hotel de l'Europe (which no longer exists) and only eat at Raffles. Hermann Hesse, Noel Coward and Günter Grass also stayed here. Charlie Chaplin, Jean Harlow, Maurice Chevalier can also be added to the list of celebrity guests. More recently, and perhaps more in keeping with its current atmosphere, Michael Jackson lurked here for a while whilst avoiding bad publicity over his alleged misdemeanours.

Many famous events have taken place here. The last tiger to be shot in Singapore was found skulking beneath the bar in the billiard room in 1902 (not under the billiard table as some fanciful accounts have it). The Singapore Sling cocktail was invented here in 1910 by bartender Ngiam Tong Boon. It is a blend of gin, cherry brandy, sugar, lemon juice and angostura bitters. In 1942, many European families arrived here in flight from the Japanese. As the British surrendered on 15 February 1942, there was a dance and sing-song here among all those who were about to be interned and worse.

After the war, Raffles became a transit camp for Allied ex-prisoners of war and gradually fell into a kind of faded elegance. In its shabby days it opened its doors to one and all, unlike during its heyday when Chinese visitors were discouraged and never allowed to take to the dance floor. When the new Raffles was opened in 1991, a Chinese-American visitor to the hotel wrote to the *Straits Times* to say that she had been asked to leave because she was inappropriately dressed, despite the fact that many visibly 'Western' tourists were wearing similar outfits.

After your shopping and Singapore Sling in the newly reconstructed and relocated Long Bar, the **hotel museum** is an interesting place to visit. When the hotel was being renovated, an international search took place; past guests were asked to look in attics for mementoes and items that may have found their way into suitcases. The search turned up some fascinating stuff and it is only here in the museum, rather than in the over-reconstructed hotel, that any sense of history can be experienced. The museum is open daily from 10.00 to 19.00; admission is free.

From Raffles Hotel, turn left into North Bridge Road and then left again into Coleman Street, named after one of Singapore's early architects, an Irishman. At the junction of Coleman Street and St Andrew's Road, you are standing in the colonial heart of Singapore. In front stretches the **Padang**, once the social centre of colonial life, and still the site of some big sporting events. Genteel families would come here to take the air, followed by their servants carrying all the items necessary for their comfort. Cricket would be played here and on the site of the City Hall, to your right, was once a fives court where a game similar to tennis, but without rackets, was played. Once or twice a month the band of one of the troop companies would play and carriages would be drawn up around them to hear the music.

> In February 1915 the cricket match taking place on the Padang was interrupted by the news that the Fifth Light Infantry of the Indian army, then stationed in Singapore, had mutinied, after hearing a rumour that they were to be sent to Turkey to fight fellow Muslims. The soldiers ran riot through the streets, killing civilians and soldiers alike before being caught and publicly executed by a firing squad.
>
> Twenty-seven years later, almost to the day, the Padang saw the entire European population lined up here, men on one side, women on the other, before they were marched off to internment in Changi. For many of them it was their last journey.

On this same spot, on the steps of the City Hall (see below), Lord Louis Mountbatten accepted the surrender of the Japanese forces in 1945. Japanese prisoners-of-war were set to clearing the Padang of shell craters and once again the peaceful sound of leather on willow resounded around the green.

> On 12 September 1945, some of Japan's top-ranking commanders arrived at City Hall to surrender. General Seishiro Itagaki, commander of the 7th Area Army based in Singapore, represented the Japanese along with an air force chief and two admirals. Field Marshal Count Terauchi, Supreme Commander of Japanese forces in Southeast Asia, was not able to attend because he was recovering from a stroke. Suspecting duplicity, Mountbatten sent his own doctor to check that Terauchi really was ill. In front of the steps a Union Jack was raised—it had been kept hidden in Changi jail since 1942—before the dignitaries retired inside to sign eleven copies of the surrender document for the various Allied governments.

At one end of the Padang is the **Singapore Cricket Club**, a racially exclusive sports ground for many years. The original building went up in 1850 and was followed in 1884 by a two-storey edifice, the upper storey being used as a ladies viewing gallery. A matching building was constructed at the other end of the Padang for the Eurasian population.

Life in colonial Singapore

The British lifestyle, which became prevalent in Singapore shortly after the settlement was created, was already established in India. The typical house built by the settlers was the bungalow, a one-storey building with a central hall, a bedroom at each corner and verandahs running the length of the house covered by a low roof. In the heat of the sun, bamboo blinds were let down to provide the verandahs with shade. The whole building was raised on blocks about 60cm off the ground. This provided storage space, protection against floods and animals, and ventilation. Further ventilation of the house was achieved by open front and back entrances and by *punkahs*, which were a sort of fan: canvas sheets were suspended on frames across the ceiling of the room and these were hinged and joined to a series of pulleys, while outside stood a servant whose job it was to pull ropes which set the whole thing in motion.

The richer settlers built elaborate columns, porticoes and second storeys. They had a series of outhouses, including a garage, stables, kitchen and servants' quarters. Gardens were very important, both for growing vegetables and to help create the atmosphere of an English country home. A whole retinue of servants would have been employed—butlers, cooks, housemaids, nannies, chauffeurs, gardeners and, of course, *punkah-wallahs*.

Ladies sweated out an indolent existence, playing croquet and lawn tennis in the searing heat, and retiring for their afternoon bath and powdering ready for the formal dinner in the evening. Often, several families ate together and new arrivals were welcomed, both as a source of news about England and as potential wife or husband for the unmarried. Dinner was eaten early, at about four o'clock, and went on for many courses, culminating in the departure of the ladies from the room, leaving the men to savour their whisky and cigars. Even the most elaborate dinner was over by ten o'clock when the colony went to sleep.

The **City Hall**, on St Andrew's Road, was built in 1929, using Indian convict labour. Now it hosts the law courts, which can be visited by prior arrangement. The entrance is beyond the public galleries. Many wedding parties stop off here on Sundays for a photo call before moving on to the more picturesque Botanic Gardens.

Next to City Hall is the more architecturally interesting **Supreme Court Building**. On this spot, and demolished to make way for the current building, was the fabulous Hotel de l'Europe which rivalled Raffles in its heyday.

Turning west along St Andrew's Road brings you to another historically important building—**St Andrew's Cathedral**. It was built in the 1850s by convict labour to a neo-Gothic design by Colonel Ronald McPherson and consecrated in 1862 by the Bishop of Calcutta. A bell for the church was donated in 1843 by Maria Revere Balestier, the daughter of Paul Revere, who married Joseph Balestier, the first US Consul in Singapore. The bell is now in the National Museum.

The church seems to shine; this is due to the *chunam* plaster that has been used on the exterior walls. This is a mixture of egg white, coconut husks, lime and sugar which can be moulded into intricate patterns and polished to create the sheen that is so distinctive in the Singapore sunshine.

In the weeks leading up to the Japanese invasion of February 1942, the church became an emergency hospital. Pews were used as beds and operations were conducted in the vestry. Inside the church, nestling among the close circuit TV monitors,

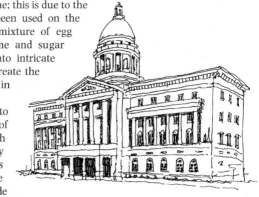

The Supreme Court, Singapore

is a plaque commemorating the victims of the Fifth Light Infantry mutiny, and a cross fashioned from nails taken from the ruins of Coventry Cathedral.

If you cross the Padang to Connaught Drive, some more modern Singaporean institutions lie before you. The **Satay Club**, a venerable hawker centre famous for its *satay* at S$0.30 a stick, is due to disappear after 25 years of business because the government wants to 'renovate' the area. Nearby is the **Cenotaph**, which commemorates the civilians who died in the two world wars.

Close to the Satay Club is a fountain dedicated to the memory of **Tan Kim Seng**, a late 19C philanthropist who contributed a large sum of money to the city council to introduce a clean water supply to the slum areas. But it took such a long time to raise the additional funds necessary for the project that by the time a decent water supply was provided Tan's contribution did little more than pay for the fountain.

Back up to the north of the Cenotaph is a park on reclaimed land, pleasant for a night-time stroll. At the start of the park is what looks like the remains of an electric can opener gone mad; called **Joyous Rivers** it is meant to represent Singaporeans in their cultural diversity straining forward with one common purpose to a better future. Head south beyond the Cenotaph where you will see a memorial plaque dedicated to **Lim Bo Seng**, a Hokkien Chinese who led the Chinese opposition to the Japanese invasion and was eventually caught and tortured to death.

A left turn by the bridge leads you to the beginning of Fullerton Road and the aesthetically dubious **Merlion** (half-lion, half-fish), whose eyes glow as it spits water at those entering the Singapore river. The handkerchief sized Merlion Park is open from 07.00 to 22.00 daily.

Over the river, past the Merlion is the **Fullerton Building**, now used as the tax office but which has had a long and chequered history. The first construction to occupy the site was Fort Fullerton, built in 1829 to protect the settlement from invasion by river. The current building was built as the General Post Office in 1928 but was also the Singapore Club and a hostel for female POWs. On Friday, 13 February 1942, Government House was bombed and the Governor,

Shenton Thomas, ran to this building for shelter. During the war the Japanese displayed the severed heads of looters here while inside, the official Union Jack lay hidden to be recovered and flown again after the war. The area beyond this, the Telok Ayer Basin, now the heart of the financial centre of Singapore, was a swamp when Raffles arrived and was reclaimed around the turn of this century.

Cross back to the east side of the river via the pedestrianised Cavanagh Bridge, built by more Indian convict labour in 1869 from parts manufactured in Glasgow. The bridge is named after Sir Orfeur Cavanagh, a former governor of the Straits Settlements. In front is **Empress Place**, undergoing its second major overhaul in a decade, the first having renovated the inside but not the foundations which are now crumbling. This was first completed in 1885 and in its later years became the Immigration Department, which I can remember as a grim bureaucratic place rather like the Circumlocution Office in Dickens's *Little Dorrit*. In the late 1980s it was boarded up and emerged as a pristine shopping mall and exhibition hall.

Beside Empress Place and closely resembling it in style is the **Victoria Concert Hall and Theatre**. It began life as the Town Hall in 1862 and became a concert hall in 1905. In 1922, when the great ballerina Anna Pavlova visited Singapore, the theatre, the biggest performance space in town, was closed to her because it was being used by the Amateur Dramatic Society for its rendition of Gilbert and Sullivan. Miss Pavlova danced instead in the Teutonia Club, the modern Goodwood Park hotel, and was showered with the contents of a litter bin by a waiter who had been told to produce snow.

Behind the concert hall is **Parliament House**, the oldest government building in Singapore, built originally to a design by George Drumgould Coleman in 1826. Somewhere among all the additions part of the original house still stands, but it is not visible. Entrance to the building is possible as far as the Strangers' Gallery; you cannot go beyond that point without a prior appointment (☎ 65-3308517). In front of the building is a bronze elephant donated by King Chulalongkorn of Siam in 1871 after the first visit by a Siamese monarch to the settlement.

Back upriver is the spot where Raffles disembarked in January 1819; it is marked by a modern marble statue of him which looks out over the central business district with a distinctively puzzled look on his face. He probably cannot believe what has happened.

Further upriver brings you to the North Boat Quay and further still to Clarke Quay. This part of the journey may best be done on the river itself in a bumboat **river tour** which, with a taped commentary, takes you briefly out into the harbour and then up the river. The boat ride—in a small wooden craft, once used for transporting goods from ship to shore—departs from Clarke Quay or Boat Quay, and is S$7 for adults, S$3 for children. Boats depart hourly and the cruise lasts about half an hour.

Clarke Quay, like Raffles Place and the Serangoon Road Conservation Area, has been renovated. The blocks of once-busy *godowns* or warehouses have been developed into chic restaurants, 'quaint' curio shops, fast-food places and electronic games rooms. At night Singaporeans come here in their hundreds, to look rather than to eat or buy, and restaurateurs, or their employees, lurk in the street encouraging people in.

The Boat Quay, Singapore

Opposite, in the **Boat Quay**, a slightly less stringent upgrade has gone on piecemeal and restaurants here are full to overflowing. Clarke Quay or Boat Quay might make good spots to pause for lunch and if you have children or enjoy such things, take a ride on the **Clarke Quay Adventure**, which is a boat ride through animatronic displays depicting the history of the Singapore river.

The next stage of the colonial walk takes us up Hill Street to the recently renovated Armenian **Church of St Gregory the Illuminator**. Designed by Coleman and built in 1835, this is the oldest church in Singapore. It was financed by contributions from various ethnic groups after the tiny Armenian community made an appeal for their own church. The government provided the site, all 6948 square metres, and a vicar was sent by the Archbishop of Persia to conduct services. For his work, Coleman received S$400, while the total cost of building was S$5058. The Armenians came from Indonesia and Calcutta and were involved in various trades in Singapore, including, of course, the hotel trade.

Coleman's design is said to be based on the 18C plan by James Gibbs for St Martin's in the Fields in London. Its internal structure is circular with four square porticoes outside. The original roof was octagonal with a bell tower supported by eight Ionic columns. That was replaced in 1847 by a square bell tower which was later removed. The present bell tower and the portico it rises above are later additions. The church itself holds a congregation of about 50 people. The grounds hold many old tombstones brought here from an earlier graveyard at Kampung Java. An interesting tombstone to look out for is that of Agnes Joaquim who discovered the natural hybrid orchid (the *Vanda Miss Joaquim*) which is now Singapore's national flower.

From Hill Street a brisk walk (left) up Canning Rise leads to **Fort Canning Park**. Its history goes back far beyond the advent of British colonialism. The Malays knew it as Bukit Larangan (Forbidden Hill), the ancient stronghold of the early rulers of Singapore and the place where Iskandar Shah, the last Malay ruler, is said to be buried. A shrine to Iskandar Shah is situated on the east side of the hill and is revered as a holy place or *keramat*.

Both Raffles and the first British Resident, Colonel Farquhar, built their homes here on the hill, hoping for a cooling evening breeze. The hill became known as Government Hill and Farquhar's house as Government House. Old Malay ruins were swept away as the British established themselves. In 1859 a fort replaced the bungalow, named after Viscount George Canning, a Governor General of India. Little of it remains except the gateway at the bottom of the hill and some of the wall. Prior to the Japanese invasion in 1942, Fort Canning was the headquarters of General Percival and the entrance to his underground bunker can still be seen.

> From the bunker General Percival made the decisions which led to the fall of Singapore. A crucial factor in the decision to surrender was the shortage of water supplies, an irony since the bunker was set beside the walls of the Fort Canning Reservoir and a well-aimed bomb could easily have drowned the whole of the British High Command. Fort Canning's bunker is now open to the public.

Little India Walk

Early 19C cattle dealers were the first Indians to come to the Serangoon Road area, hence some of the local street names—Buffalo Road and Lembu (cow) Road. Later the area became the centre of a brick kiln industry which brought many Tamils to the area. Indian merchants, mainly Chettiars (a south Indian group), settled in the shophouses and anything from garlands to wedding clothes to clay cooking pots could, and still can, be bought here. On Friday or Saturday evening, hundreds of Tamil workers gather on the open ground to chat with friends after visiting one of the temples in the area. Best of all is a visit during the Thaipusam festival when the road is crowded with followers of the event and a day-long parade of penitents takes place.

The walk begins at the top of Serangoon Road where the **Zhu Jiao** wet market buzzes with women getting their groceries or browsing around the clothing stalls upstairs. Various forms of tofu and the accompanying ingredients are sold, as well as dried sea products, all kinds of fresh animal parts, many of which you might be surprised to discover are edible, and Indian spices which are sold individually or mixed into various combinations. Upstairs are shops selling saris and general clothes and some interesting curio stalls.

Back out on the street the shophouses at the top of the road have been renovated very ornately. Further down on the right-hand side there are still many small Indian grocery shops and even an Indian mini-mart. A spice miller operates along this section of the road although for how much longer isn't clear. Inside, dusty men manhandle great sacks of spices which leave pastel rainbows around the floor, while strange ingredients get turned into the various flours for chapattis or dosas or naan. Along the five foot ways, garland-makers string together flowers, while outside the restaurants, men sell betel nut wrapped in leaves as a mouth refresher for satisfied customers.

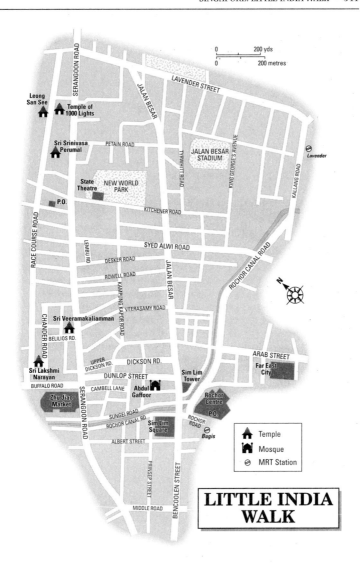

LITTLE INDIA WALK

The betel nut is obtained from the betel-palm (*Areca catechu*), daubed with lime for flavouring and wrapped in the betel-vine (*Daun sireh*), a different tree. The mixture of nut and leaf is chewed to keep gums healthy and breath fresh and the betel nut also features as a Malay cure for gonorrhoea and durian overdoses. The juice of the young nut is also used to heal the wounds of circumcision. The flowers of the betel-vine are used as ornaments in Malay weddings, and in Peranakan culture the betel nut is traditionally offered to guests as a symbol of hospitality.

Five Foot Ways

These pavements are probably one of the most interesting and civilised aspects of what is left of the old Singapore. Because of the daytime heat and the constant threat of deluge, the rows of shops were built with over-hanging upper storeys, creating a five foot-wide covered pavement so that trade could be carried out in relative comfort. Over the years, as shophouses were renovated or altered, these five foot ways have become a little like obstacle courses in some places with goods spilling out on to the footway and occasional steps making progress hazardous. In Arab Street in partic-ular the five foot ways have become glorious treasure caverns, with bamboo curtains hanging down to keep out the rain and sun, and cloth, basketware and goodies of all kinds strung up from the roof, almost forcing tourists and locals alike to inspect the produce as they make their way along the street.

Five Foot Ways: Tanjong Pagar Precinct, Singapore

Wandering around the side streets of this area—Campbell Lane, Dunlop Street and Upper Dickson Road—reveals more authentic and unrenovated Little India. Scrap merchants' shops are surrounded by all manner of partially decon-structed merchandise, barbers do a basic single-style haircut, glorious restaurants such as Woodlands do all-day meals while colourful saris dangle from the roofs of the five foot ways alongside prayer mats, plastic toys and other parapher-nalia.

Back on Serangoon Road, the first temple on the left side of the road is the **Sri Veeramakaliamman Temple**. Its origins date back to 1881 but the elaborate roof carvings are much later, being only about 30 years old. Looked at from the front, what dominate the view are the carvings on the roof or *gopuram* whose function is just that—to stand out and attract worshippers. Inside, the temple consists of a main hall for ceremonies, flanked by a series of shrines to the goddess and the other gods associated with her.

The temple is dedicated to the various manifestations of the goddess Kali, each one representing a different aspect of her powers. The main statue is dressed each day in a different sari, donated by her followers, and garlanded especially with lime flowers as those are her favourites. Each day's discarded sari is given to the needy or bought by a woman happy to wear one of Lakshmi's (a manifesta-tion of Kali) cast-offs. Beside her stand two blue-faced guards, the colour of their faces traditionally indicating their origins—dark-skinned south Indians.

The temple is enormously popular and anyone used to the hushed silences of European cathedrals will get a serious shock. Strident music plays, people walk around the temple, priests call out the names of devotees, incense burns, little piles of fruit and flowers are scattered around, people lounge about and eat, chil-dren play hide-and-seek, while at the back the kitchens are in constant use as people make food which is brought by devotees and laid at the goddess's feet or given out freely to all-comers. Above the amazing mix of the mystical and profane, a huge digital electric clock ticks away the minutes.

The statue at the rear of the temple shows the goddess in her fiercest form, eating her enemies and sparing no one, not even babies. In this form she is terrifying and is prayed to in order to keep her calm. New-born babies are brought to her for her blessing. In her other forms, women will ask her for fertility or for a good marriage or wealth or strength. Men also ask her blessing. The standard form of worship here is first to buy a coconut and a banana. The coconut is then broken in half as a way of asking forgiveness. The fruit represents desire and its offering symbolises the giving up of desire, the first step on the road to enlightenment. Then the worshipper walks around the temple nine times, stopping at each of the shrines for a prayer.

Another smaller shrine at the rear of the building shows Ganesh, the elephant-headed son of Parvadi, one of the goddess's milder incarnations. The child was born in normal human shape, the son of Parvadi and Shiva, the destroyer and life-giver. One day while Shiva was out hunting, Parvadi asked her son to guard the door and let no one in. When Shiva returned he grew angry at not being allowed in and struck off the boy's head. Instantly regretting his action, he gave the boy the life of the first creature that passed—an elephant.

The temple is open every day, and no one minds visitors entering as long as they are respectful. On Tuesdays and Fridays services take place and these can be exciting to watch. Devotees bring rice flour, rock sugar, almonds and raisins to the temple and the high priest makes these into offerings, praying as he does so.

Back on Serangoon Road, cross over the road to have a look in some of the sari and jewellery shops on the other side. There are several designs of dress for Indian women, reflecting area of origin, age and predilection. The dress most commonly worn by younger women tends to be the Punjabi suit, which is a loose-fitting pair of trousers covered by a calf-length shift with long sleeves. Another Punjabi suit less commonly worn is the *glara*; this has a shorter top and a flowing skirt. The sari is worn only by women who are past puberty. A girl who reaches 13 or so proudly puts on the *choli*—the short blouse worn under the sari which exposes a large section of midriff.

The jewellers' shops display the gold ornaments worn by women when they marry. The quantity of gold draped over a woman at her marriage is a mark of status and many women do not marry for lack of a dowry. Traditionally, the gold was the woman's dowry, but today the dowry is more likely to be a suite of furniture or a down-payment on an apartment, and the gold that is worn on the wedding day has been hired. Characteristic wedding ornaments include a kind of tiara, with round discs or coins which hang over the bride's forehead, and a broad choker around the neck, worn with many other chains.

Much further down the street on the left-hand side, past the Indian department stores which literally heave with people buying well-priced electrical stuff, clothes, crockery—in fact anything you can think of—is the **Sri Srinivasa Perumal Temple**. It is from this temple that the Thaipusam festival sets out. The temple is similar to the Veeramakaliamman temple and has a gaudily painted *gopuram*. It is was built in 1979, with money donated by a local Indian philanthropist. Inside, the large courtyard area provides room for the participants of the festival. At other times, this temple is less frequently used than the Veeramakaliamman temple. Its main deity is Murgan, with whom the Thai Pusam legend is associated.

> Legend tells that a man called Iduban chose to worship the god Murgan by climbing a mountain carrying offerings of milk and honey. To test the devotion of the man Murgan put many obstacles in his way, making his journey hazardous, but Iduban never gave up and on reaching the top of the mountain earned himself a place in heaven and also in Murgan's heart. The people who take part in the Thaipusam festival are following the example of Iduban. They may be asking for a cure for their illness or for help in their studies or work, or atonement for some misdeed. Most people take part for at least two years while others dedicate themselves to a lifetime as a devotee.

The **Thaipusam festival** usually begins on an evening in January, although sometimes it is in February. Those people who are going to take part in the event gather at the temple to pray and bathe and eat specially prepared food offered by the priest. They then spend the night praying in the temple. Early the next morning their families arrive and the preparation begins. Huge metal frames called *kavadis* are placed over the devotees' shoulders, the weight of the structure being borne in a series of metal spikes which are inserted through the skin of the chest and back of the devotee. More pins and hooks are added, weighted down with limes. Often the mouth and tongue are pierced with ornate spikes. The devotees apparently feel no pain and their wounds do not bleed. They then walk and dance from the temple to the **Thandayuthapani Temple** in Tank Road, a distance of about 5km. The participants are mostly men, although some women take part.

The metal frames are specially made by each devotee with rods brought in from India. Along the route they are offered milk and honey and are showered in water dyed with turmeric. If you are in Singapore during the festival it is an event not to be missed but Serangoon Road becomes very crowded especially around the temple itself. The people who take part are not undergoing punishment for a past sin but rather showing their devotion to their god.

An interesting contrast to these two temples is the **Sri Lakshmi Narayan Temple**, situated in Chander Road, close to the junction with Belilios Road. It is barely recognisable as a temple—it is smaller and has none of the gaudy colours or outlandish external decorations which characterise the other two temples. Inside it is carpeted, which suggests a very different use for this temple. It is a north Indian temple, and while it is dedicated to the same goddess as the Veeramakaliamman the atmosphere is quite unlike that of Perumal and Thandayuthapani. Above the carpeted prayer hall is a balcony where parties of celebrants eat food made by the priests or hold meetings.

There are two other temples to be visited while you are in Little India, neither of them associated with Indian culture. The **Temple of a Thousand Lights**, or the Sakayamuni Buddha Gaya Temple is situated in Race Course Road, just behind and to the north of the Sri Srinivasa Temple. The centrepiece of this temple is a gigantic statue of the Buddha surrounded by light bulbs—hence its name. The statue is 3m high and weighs 300 tonnes. It is also hollow and you can walk inside to see another (reclining) statue of the Buddha. There is also a replica of the Buddha's footprint as well as a reproduction of the branch of the bodhi tree under which the Buddha gained enlightenment. If you are in Singapore during May you might like to visit the temple on Vesak Day when there is a candlelit procession.

Opposite is another, much older, Chinese temple, **Leong San See Temple**, this one dedicated to the goddess Kuan Yin, the goddess of mercy. Like most Chinese temples this one shows the pragmatism of Chinese worshippers. The temple is a mixture of Buddhist and Taoist forms of worship.

Chinatown Walk

Chinatown is the area of Singapore which the early administrators of the new settlement allocated for the Chinese to settle in. Over the years it has expanded, and in turn been encroached on by the financial centre. Singapore's Chinatown has been undergoing urban renewal for several years now and while many buildings have been rescued from collapse, it has also meant that much of the area's cultural dynamism is now only a fond memory for many Singaporeans.

An interesting place to begin imbibing a sense of Chinese culture is along **Telok Ayer Street**. This was once the waterfront and would have been dotted with places catering to the needs of the transient population of merchant seamen and newly arrived debentured coolies. The streets behind it—China Street, Circular Road, South Bridge Road, Boat Quay, Upper Cross Street and the myriad smaller streets and alleys in the area—was the first place settled by the Chinese. The first thing the various clan associations did was to build a place of worship and a clan house.

The **Thian Hock Keng Temple** in Telok Ayer Street is the oldest surviving temple in this area. In 1821 the site was a joss house dedicated to the goddess of the sea. Construction began on a huge temple in 1839 with materials brought largely from China, including the shrine to the main deity, Tin Hau or Ma Zu Po, the celestial queen of heaven and protector of those at sea. The building was financed by a wealthy Hokkien of the Huay Kuan, a clan association. Donations also came from newly arrived seafarers, in thanks to the goddess for their safe arrival. The carved stone pillars are made of granite from China, some of the tiles are from Delft, and the cast-iron railings are from Glasgow. Like most Chinese temples, this has shrines to most of the important deities. Like all temples of its kind it holds hundreds of wooden tablets on which are inscribed the names and burial location of past worshippers. Door guardians are painted on the wooden doors to the building; two huge stone lions also stand guard.

At the back of the main temple there is a **courtyard** with an altar graced with a figure of Confucius. Students come here to request luck in their examinations; if they are successful, they will sometimes leave their books by the altar as a thanksgiving. There is also another, smaller temple in the courtyard. This has three altars: the central figure is Ma Zu Po, while on the left is a figure of a goddess of beauty (hence the boxes of face powder that are often left here as offerings), and on the right is a god of strength which attracts young men.

Two more temples, a block north of this one—the **Hakka Fuk Tak Chi**

Temple at 76 Telok Ayer Street and the **Wak Hai Cheng Bio Temple** on Philip Street—also date back to the 19C. At that time this whole area was settled by largely male Hokkien coolies, most of them living in stark bachelors' quarters in rooming houses.

While in Telok Ayer Street you might want to have a look at the **Al-Abrar Mosque**. A mosque was first built here in 1827 but the building you see now dates back to 1855. Both this and the Nagore Durgha Shrine (1829) further down the road were built by Indian Muslims.

From this area of temples marking the old waterfront you should make your way west, taking in **China Street**, with its old-style shophouses with the living quarters upstairs, high narrow windows providing ventilation, and a view over the life of the street. From these windows a selection of washing poles, drying chickens, and pots and pans too awkward to keep inside would have been hung. Until a few years ago, the shops below would have housed many different cottage industries, from tinsmiths to grocers to incense sellers, *popiah* (spring roll) skin makers and shops selling Chinese herbal medicines.

If the road is not yet renovated you will notice the amazing number of plants which grow straight out of the walls. They are mostly strangling figs which in the wild depend upon other plants for support but here have adapted to using cracks in walls. Their long roots are gradually feeling their way down to ground level where they expect to find soil rather than the tiled floors of the five foot ways.

From China Street cross Cross Street and head west along **Club Street**; this area has many craft workshops. Club Street houses several wood-carvers who make small statues of the deities for temples as well as door carvings and other temple ornaments. As the road meets Ann Siang Road, you may be able to see men making the intricate lion's head for the lion dancers as well as simpler smaller ones to sell to the tourists. This area was once a nutmeg plantation and the first buildings here were built by wealthy Chinese who put more decorative flourishes into their buildings. Occasionally the buildings are used as clan association meeting places.

The Lion Dance

It is difficult to miss this highly popular dance routine which takes place on a daily basis all over the island. You'll know when there are lion dancers near you because they drive around in open-backed trucks making the most awful clamour with drums and cymbals and shouting. Lions dancers are usually formed from the various clan association martial arts groups. A highly stylised lion suit is worn by two dancers who, at their best, perform highly complex acrobatic tricks as the drums and cymbals are played. The lion dance troupes are called out to special events such as a new shop opening and their dance, which in Malaysia is accompanied by firecrackers, is designed to drive out any unfriendly spirits which might be lurking about the place. They are particularly active around Chinese New Year when they go from shop to shop and even into people's houses to get rid of the old year's spirits.

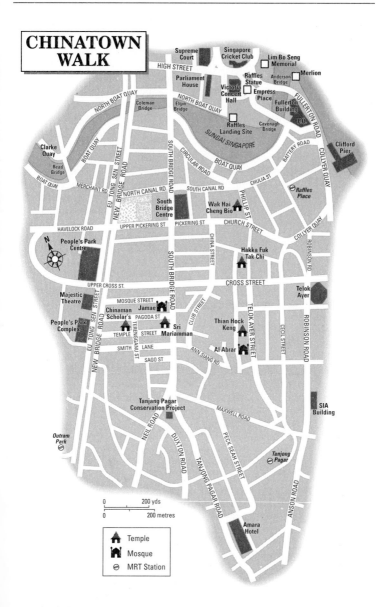

CHINATOWN WALK

Key to map:

🛕 Temple

🕌 Mosque

⊖ MRT Station

Going back down Ann Siang Road, cross South Bridge Road. This area was first laid out in 1836 while the smaller roads to the northwest—**Mosque, Pagoda, Temple, Sago Streets**—were laid out about 20 years later. The land here was owned by a wealthy Portuguese family, the d'Almeida, who leased it as smaller lots, no doubt making their fortune even bigger in the process. Most of these buildings are later ones put up in the early 1900s. These streets are wonderful to wander around. The five foot ways are crowded with piled up pots which once contained thousand-year-old eggs, snakes, temple paraphernalia and turtles waiting to be turned into soup.

In the more touristy areas, such as Smith and Temple Streets, many shops sell jade and ceramics, antique silver, ivory, kites, sandalwood fans. In Sago Street there are many medicine halls, selling stag horn, dried seahorses, Fa Chai (the black Chinaman's hair fungus), all kinds of bark, dried sea cucumber and sponges as well as the more familiar ginseng.

Life in Chinatown in the nineteenth century

Life in late 19C Chinatown was a hazardous affair. The annual life expectancy of the indentured worker was around 40 years. He could expect to die of many causes, including malaria, which in 1909 was responsible for one in nine of all deaths. Industrial accidents, food deficiency diseases, opium-related illnesses or street fights were the other common causes of premature death. Some aspects of life did improve though. In 1836 there were 15 men to every one woman but by 1891 the ratio was nearer four to one. Most people lived in bachelor quarters, tiny cramped rooms with only a wooden bunk for each man. In 1901, 12 of the 59 houses in Pagoda Street were such lodging houses. Opium dens abounded in this area, opium providing half of the colony's revenue. Most coolies were addicts and could only afford to smoke the used dregs of opium.

There was no fresh water supply nor any sewage system, night soil being carried away in carts. There was no state education, only a few schools for the children of the rich, set up by the Christian missions or philanthropic Chinese organisations. The only medicine available to the Chinese was also provided by philanthropic wealthy Chinese in the form of traditional Chinese medicine. This was dispensed from halls such as the Thong Chai Medical Institute; the building is still in existence in Eu Tong Sen Street although it is now occupied by a souvenir shop.

The narrow roads of this area would have been congested with bullock carts, private carriages, hackney carriages, and rickshaws which came to Singapore in 1880 from Shanghai. The drivers, who were mostly newly arrived and inexperienced immigrants, worked long hours and had no job security. The accident rate was very high.

Brothels were legal; prostitutes were either sold into the profession as young girls or came from China or Eastern Europe. In the 1870s 80 per cent of young girls arriving in Singapore had been brought in as prostitutes. Other girls from poor families were 'adopted' by richer families, often becoming unpaid servants or concubines.

The secret societies were everywhere in Chinatown. In 1876 the 'post office riots' broke out. Secret society leaders had offered a reward for the execution of anyone attempting to set up a post office service to China in competition with them. Until the end of the 19C, Chinese people went to their society head rather than to the state to settle their disputes. Most shops, gambling dens, opium houses, brothels and street hawkers paid the secret societies protection money.

Before continuing your wander around these old streets which make up the heart of old Chinatown, you should pop over New Bridge Road/Eu Tong Sen Street to the **People's Park Complex**, where much of Chinatown's activity has now shifted. Out on the street everything is being hawked while there are still people who will clean your ears, read your palm or write a letter for you. Inside is a collection of places dedicated to the more modern concerns of the people who live here. Shops blaring music sell Cantopop, watches, whirling battery operated toys, cheap clothes, and upstairs there are some truly gruesome medicine shops with 'before and after' photographs in the windows. Downstairs in the hawker stalls you can find some interesting things to try. The sugar cane juice stalls have huge bars of sugar cane waiting to be stripped and crushed to produce a very refreshing drink, or someone will hack off the top of a young coconut for you and stick a straw inside.

Back over in the network of streets between South Bridge Road and New Bridge Road, the next stop is the **Sri Mariamman Temple** in South Bridge Road. It is open from 06.00 to 12.30 and 16.00 to 21.30.

This was originally a wood and attap building which was rebuilt by convict labour in brick in 1843. It was founded by an Indian called Narian Pillai who accompanied Raffles on his second trip to Singapore in May 1819. He made his fortune with a brick kiln and as a building contractor. He later lost his fortune but was rescued by Raffles and provided some of the capital for the new temple. The temple has the distinctive *gopuram* designed to stand out and draw devotees to the temple. Some of the figures that can be identified include Krishna, at the bottom left under the umbrella, and Rama, also under an umbrella at the bottom right. The small gold figure at the bottom in the centre is Mariamman herself.

Inside, the main temple is dedicated to Mariamman and her ability to cure diseases. The temple has a similar structure to those in Serangoon Road with kitchens at the back manned by priests sent here from India, and a series of shrines around the temple. Penitents circumambulate the temple, stopping to say a prayer at each shrine. This temple becomes particularly busy during the Thimithi festival, in memory of Draupadi, the heroine of an epic poem, the *Mahabharata*. This temple is dedicated to the goddess Amman. The festival takes place around October. A bed of red hot coals is laid out inside the temple and hundreds of devotees walk briskly across it apparently without feeling a thing. If you are in Singapore when the festival takes place, the fire-walking usually begins at about 17.00 and the temple courtyard gets very crowded.

From the temple, walk around the streets to the southwest. In Trengganu Street, upstairs at No. 14B, is the **Chinaman Scholar's Gallery**, a private museum in a 120-year-old building. The single room re-creates the home of a Chinese scholar of the 1920s/1930s. The director of the museum takes the visitor around each piece, and offers tea or plays various musical instruments. admission is S$4 and the tiny museum is open from 09.00 to 16.00.

In Sago Street the chief industry used to be 'death houses', where those near death were brought by their families to see out their last hours. Now tourism brings in better profits and the streets are full of tourist-oriented goods, though in Sago and Temple Streets shops still make and sell paper goods for funerals. These can be anything from a paper cassette tape to a near full-size Cadillac with chauffeur inside. During the funeral the goods are collected together, blessed by a Taoist priest, and burnt: through burning they reach heaven and can be used by the newly departed relative.

Next make your way south along South Bridge Road to admire and browse around the **Tanjong Pagar conservation project**, which is located between Neil Road and Tanjong Pagar Road. This was once a nutmeg plantation but as the docks grew in importance it became the place where newly arrived Chinese immigrants would line up waiting for work. As the waterfront moved away it became the hub of the commercial sector and the Chinese men hanging around here were waiting with their rickshaws for customers. At 51 Neil Road is a small **exhibition of photographs** depicting life here in the early part of this century. It is open from 11.00 to 21.00; admission is free.

This area probably represents Singapore's conservation efforts at their best. The beautifully decorated old shophouses have been carefully restored and thoughtfully redeveloped into tourist-oriented businesses which re-create some of the crafts once practised in this area. There are kite shops, clog shops, calligraphers, herbal tea shops, and mask shops; one place especially worth visiting is the **Tea Chapter**, 9a Neil Road, where the old traditions of tea drinking are upheld and where after about 20 minutes of watching for fish eye bubbles and rinsing tiny mugs you finally get a sip of very nicely brewed tea.

National Museum and Art Museum

Sir Stamford Raffles first suggested that a national gallery should be set up in 1823. The building was erected in Stamford Road in 1887 and was called the Raffles Museum. It was left to decline into shabbiness until Singapore's awe-inspiring renovation machinery moved through it in 1991. Now, as the National Museum, it gleams.

The permanent collections are not particularly interesting but it is always worth enquiring to see what special temporary exhibitions are being shown: these are usually first-class international exhibitions. The museum, which is near the library on Stamford Road, is open Tuesday to Sunday from 09.00 to 17.30; admission is S$3.

The **History of Singapore Gallery** provides a useful introduction to the island's history from the time of Raffles onwards. The final model showcase shows the opening of Singapore's parliament; the side of the chamber traditionally filled with opposition members is empty! The **Legacy of Majaphit Room** also features the island's historical and cultural background, and a nationalistic audio-visual slide show is shown each day at 10.15, 12.15, 14.45 and 15.45.

On the second floor there is an eclectic collection of workaday objects from the three ethnic groups (Malay, Chinese, and Indian), including a betel nut-cutter, a wooden massager and a fine pair of women's fashionable shoes with stiletto heels from the 1960s.

The **Singapore Art Museum**, a short distance away on Bras Basah Road, is housed in what was once the island's premier secondary school. As with the National Museum, it is worth checking with the tourist office whether any temporary exhibitions are on display as these are often of high quality. The museum is open Tuesday, Thursday, Friday and Saturday, 09.00 to 17.30. Admission is about S$8 for a special exhibition.

Green Singapore

Surprisingly, there are pockets of land in Singapore which have not yet been commercially exploited, even with the rise in land prices. Singapore has small areas of mangrove swamp, some river estuaries where many migrant and local birds can be seen, small areas of primary rainforest, and some secondary forests surrounding reservoirs which provide habitats for an enormous variety of wildlife. Three per cent of Singapore's land mass is rainforest. Even in Singapore's small parks some exotic birds such as black-capped kingfishers or golden orioles can be seen. If you only visit one place it should be Bukit Timah Nature Reserve where you can encounter some strange and wonderful creatures. Other places of interest are Pasir Ris park with its mangrove area, MacRitchie Reservoir, Khatib Bongsu, Pulau Ubin, and Sungei Buloh. The zoo and the bird park are also worth a visit.

Singapore ~ West

Bukit Timah Nature Reserve

If you have no plans to spend any time in the forests of Malaysia then this visit is essential. With very little exertion it is possible to see some of the 800 species of plants and some of the exotic animal life. Bukit Timah represents one of the only two jungles within a city in the world. Some of the nature reserve is primary rainforest although most of it is secondary growth after the lower slopes were cut down to form gutta-percha plantations in the 19C.

The 71 hectare forest reserve is good for walking. Most people walk straight up the service road to the top of the hill but there are other routes around the forest. Bukit Timah is an excellent day out whether you just want to picnic at the top and watch the antics of the macaques, or orienteer your way through hilly forest terrain, or wander slowly with field glasses and wildlife books.

That such a large area has never been encroached on in this land-hungry state is down to Nathaniel Cantley, Superintendent of the Singapore Botanic Gardens. Even in the 19C, people were aware of the effect of deforestation on the local climate, and in 1882 Cantley was commissioned to establish a series of reserves. Of the several reserves created, all except Bukit Timah were selectively logged for the giant hardwood trees they contained. In 1937 most of the forest reserves were cut down to make way for building. Bukit Timah and two other areas survived under the protection of the National Parks Board.

The ecology of Bukit Timah Nature Reserve

Rainforest has a very delicately balanced ecosystem. The hills here are granite but this has little effect on the plant and animal life which depend entirely on a few centimetres of topsoil for their existence. The giant trees of the dipterocarp family have shallow roots which have developed a system of buttressing in order to support themselves. Around these trees the jungle survives. Lianas use their trunks for support as they climb upwards seeking light. The seeds of strangling fig trees lodge in cracks in the bark and send roots downwards and branches upwards, eventually killing the host tree and taking its place in the canopy. Epiphytes such as bird's nest fern or stag's horn fern use the branches of the trees for support, their wide, curling leaves trapping dead leaves and absorbing their nutrients. Rattan palms use the whorls of backward-pointing hooks along their stem to hook on to the trees in their search for light.

Occasionally a tree falls, crashing through the forest and creating a new opening. Then seeds germinate and new plants spring up fighting for the limited space. One plant often seen in these sunnier spots is the *Macaranga*; its hollow stem provides a home for the ants while the waste products of the ants' nest provide nutrients for the plant.

The space is soon filled by another young tree and the sun-loving plants which have sprung up will die off. If too big an opening is created in the forest, then sun-loving plants such as the fern *Resam* will dominate the other plants preventing that area of forest from regenerating.

On the forest floor, shade-loving ferns and ginger plants grow, as well as thousands of mushrooms and bracket fungi. Flowers are quite unusual on the forest floor but if you could get up into the canopy it would be a very different matter.

Birds are the most noticeable of the forest's animal life. Most in evidence are the white-bellied sea eagles which nest in the radio masts on the hill, and the racket-tailed drongos: big black birds trailing streamers behind them. The best time to see these birds is early morning when they are most active.

Other creatures of the forest are snakes. Spitting cobras are common as are pythons and pit vipers. Both cobras and vipers are poisonous but they will only attack if threatened, so a careful respect for where you put your feet is enough. If you are very lucky you might spot a tiny banded coral snake, which has a deadly bite. However, since it is so small that it could only inject venom into the folds of skin between your fingers or bare feet, coral snake bites are rare.

At the bottom of the hill a visitor's centre displays some useful photographs of the plant and animal life in the reserve. The area around the visitor's centre was once farmland and there are interesting planted trees to be seen. There is a group of six betel nut trees, tall and thin with nuts to be seen at the top, while the tallest tree of all here is the softwood *pulai*. Behind the pulai is a tamarind tree, dead straight trunk with buttress roots and small leaves.

Along the **South View Path** look for the sign on the right marking one of the reserve's few remaining gutta-percha trees. Also marked is the *Parishia insignis* tree with its remarkable buttress roots. The tree is related to the mango family and, unlike some trees here, the sap is quite safe. The *rangas* tree, on the other hand, has a black sap that can cause blistering for months afterwards if it gets on your skin. Rattan trees are common along this path but beware of its fish-hook thorns which it uses for climbing. You are in primary rainforest so look for the characteristic timber trees, which grow to a maximum of 50m; some are 200–300 years old. The *Shorea curtesia* (the Malay name is *Seraya*) is a fine example, with a reddish tinge to the trunk and deep grooves.

At the **top of the hill** the macaques hang out like a gang of bored hooligans; mostly happy to look cute and accept food from visitors, occasionally they become more aggressive, so try not to get too close. From the top of the hill it is possible to look over to the Central Water Catchment area and MacRitchie Reservoir. These three places form the last remaining areas of indigenous wildlife in Singapore, although Bukit Timah is the only area containing some primary rainforest.

Getting to Bukit Timah Nature Reserve. The nature reserve can be reached by bus from Scotts Road (Nos 171 or 182) or any of the buses which go along Bukit Timah Road from various parts of the island (5, 67, 75, 170, 171, 172, 173, 181, 852). Alight at Courts Furniture Store, notable for its subtle colour scheme, cross Bukit Timah Road and walk along Hindehead Road to the entrance of the reserve.

Subaraj Rajathurai (☎ and fax 65-787 7048 or through the tourist office) is recommended for guided tours of Bukit Timah and the other areas that are mentioned here as well as trips into some nature areas in Johor and beyond.

Haw Par Villa

A visit to Haw Par Villa is a must for anyone with children and is an entertaining afternoon for anyone who is young at heart.

Haw Par Villa, at 262 Pasir Panjang Road, is open from 09.00 to 18.00 daily. Admission is S$5 for adults and S$2.50 for children.

This was originally built in 1937 as the home of Aw Boon Haw, a Hakka Chinese born in Rangoon who made his fortune in Tiger Balm Ointment. Aw and his brother marketed the oil throughout Asia, the one settling in Singapore and setting up a Chinese newspaper, the other based in Hong Kong. Both built mansions. This one contained a large private zoo until a city by-law was passed making it illegal. Aw then proceeded to have statues modelled out of concrete depicting Chinese myths and legends. The park and its seven pagodas were largely destroyed by the Japanese during the Second World War and were rebuilt afterwards. Aw never returned after the war and the house fell into ruin.

For many years the park was open to the public who came to see the statues, some of them grisly in the extreme, depicting the various stages of hell entered into by the wicked. These statues are still around the park which has been turned into a mildly interesting cultural theme park. There are one or two good rides, one involving heart-stopping drops down water chutes. Besides the rides there are traditional games, street theatre, video shows of ancient myths, and of course the old statues.

Getting to Haw Par Villa. Can by reached from the centre by taking the MRT to Buona Vista and then bus No. 200 or bus No. 10 from Shenton Way or 143 from Orchard Road.

Jurong Bird Park

For many visitors, this is their favourite animal spectacle in Singapore, perhaps because many of the birds are not caged at all and can leave the park whenever they feel like it (and many do).

The bird park is well worth a day's visit. It is open from 09.00 to 18.00 although some of the exhibits close a little earlier. There are eight shows, feeding times and talks to attend throughout the day as well as breakfast surrounded by songbirds. Admission is S$10.30 for adults, S$4.12 for children; breakfast is S$9.50.

The walk-in aviary lets you come in close contact with the birds which are nesting and breeding quite happily inside. The cages of birds of prey are a little sad while the animal shows are excellent, particularly the hawk exhibition. The most spectacular creatures in the park are the hornbills and toucans. Hornbills are highly prized birds with vast bills and are still hunted in Malaysia by the Orang Asli who make jewellery from their bills. Some of the hornbills here fly free and they often turn up in people's gardens around the island where they make the most spectacular sight flying slow and low over houses in more rural areas, making a distinctive honking cry. A walk around the park can be a draining experience in the heat of the day but there is a shuttle service. Also of interest are the night birds' enclosure and the glassed-in Arctic section.

Getting to Jurong Bird Park. Take the MRT to Boon Jay station, then catch bus Nos 251 or 194 to Jalan Ahmad Ibrahim.

Chinese Garden and Japanese Garden

These support some interesting birdlife and should be of interest to gardeners. Each garden is 13.5 hectares but the Chinese Garden is by far the most popular. It is set on an island in Jurong Lake and has lots of traditional Chinese Sung Dynasty garden features such as the Penjing garden which is a huge landscaped area containing hundreds of bonsai. Each year at the lantern festival in September/October a huge display of lanterns is set up there and thousands of people crowd into the gardens. The Japanese gardens are more orderly, supposedly mirroring the natural order and layout of the land. The gardens are open 09.00 to 19.00 daily. Admission is S$4.50, S$2 for children.

Getting to the Chinese Garden and Japanese Garden. Both gardens are within a few minutes' walk of the Chinese Garden MRT stop.

Singapore Science Centre and Omnimax Theatre

The centre provides a good afternoon's play for adults and children. The Science Centre (☎ 65-5603316) has four main exhibition halls and some experimental gardens, all with lots of hands on equipment, especially in the children's room. Exhibitions change, so check the local press for details. At the same venue is the Omnimax Theatre where you strain your neck and eyes watching a huge screen. If you haven't experienced an Omnimax film you should do so. Check the local press in advance to find out what films are showing. The Omni Theatre also doubles as a planetarium. The Science Centre is open from 10.00 to 18.00 Tuesday to Sunday. Admission is S$1.50. The Omnimax shows films throughout the day from 12.00 to 20.00 Tuesday to Sunday. Admission is S$10, S$4 for children. The planetarium shows are at 10.00 and 11.00.

Getting to the Science Centre. Take the MRT to Jurong East. The centre is a brief walk from there.

Tang Dynasty Village

This 'village' is difficult to miss, being surrounded by a massive stone wall. It was built to be used partly as a film set for epic Chinese serials but has not really taken off in that area. The theme park is open from 09.30 to 18.30 (until 22.30 on Saturday). Admission is S$15.45 for adults, S$10.30 for children.

It is constructed like a 7C city, with blacksmiths, sweetmakers, model-makers all plying their trades, and animals, that may or may not have been a part of 7C city life, standing around waiting for photo opportunities. There are street theatre shows, video and live action theatre, an aerial fight, lifesize replicas of terracotta tomb figures and a sad wax museum with crumbling fingers and shabby-clothed replicas of Chinese historical figures. It is a long way to go unless you like folk parks with an emphasis on spending money, although you could make a day of it at Jurong and visit the bird park and the Chinese and Japanese gardens at the same time. It tends to be geared to tour bus groups with performances co-ordinated with arrival of large parties.

Getting to Tang Dynasty Village. Take the MRT to Lakeside and then bus Nos 154 or 240 along Jalan Ahmad Ibrahim to Yuan Ching Road.

Ming Village and Pewter Museum
This is a working factory making reproduction Qing and Ming Dynasty pottery which is available for sale. Tours are conducted around the factory where the whole production process is carried out including hand painting of the delicate blue and white designs. There is also an exhibition of Selangor pewter and of course a shop selling the pots. Admission is free and the factory is open from 09.00 to 17.30. To get to the factory take the MRT to Clementi and then bus No. 78 to 32 Pandan Road.

Singapore ~ North

Peranakan Palace
This was Singapore's first attempt at conservation and quite a good job it is too. The houses preserved in Emerald Hill Road are built in the style known as Chinese baroque. If you go up the hill a little way, past the café at the junction with Orchard Road, you can see the typical features of this architecture. The roof tiles are like those of a Chinese temple, shaped like bamboo and green or red in colour. The carved wooden fretwork below the roof is Malay in origin. Above the windows and doors are scrolls with Chinese characters while the columns supporting the front of the house are European-style, copies of Greek Doric or Corinthian columns. In the lozenge-shaped windows are representations of bats, considered a lucky animal because its name sounds like the Chinese word for good luck. These houses do not have the five foot ways (see p 342) of regular shophouses but instead have fences around a porch. Standing in one of the porches and looking up, it is still possible to see the old peep-hole through which visitors would have been observed before being allowed entry. Some of the front doors here still have their outer louvred swing-doors.

Half-way up the hill Hullet Road meets Emerald Hill Road at a 90° angle. In the Chinese art of geomancy, evil spirits are able to travel in straight lines so the house that stands opposite this junction stands in peril of very bad things happening to its occupants. Many houses have little hexagonal mirrors over the doors to deter such bad *chi* getting into the house but the bad influences here are much that a temple has been set up in direct line with the offending road. In this way the ancestors and the kitchen god can protect the house.

Back at the bottom of the hill is the **Peranakan Place Museum** in which traditional furniture, pottery and clothes have been collected. Not in the same league as the Peranakan Museum in Melaka, this still gives an excellent indication of the life of the *babas* and *nyonyas*. Those who settled in Singapore were third or fourth generation Straits Chinese. These people married either among their own kind or new emigrants from China so gradually the Malay influence declined, but still their cooking style, dress, language and lifestyle recalled their early influences. The Peranakans in Singapore were leaders among the Chinese but were deeply loyal to the British. Their lifestyle reflected this loyalty. Inside the museum, among the Peranakan pottery and beadwork, are planters' chairs from India, glassware from Europe, silver plate from Sheffield. The Straits Chinese were also known as 'The King's Chinese' because of their loyalty to the crown.

To visit the museum you will need to make a special group arrangement. The minumum number is 4–5 visitors; ☎ 65-732 6966 Mr Loh Han Tzen. Visiting hours are 10.30 to 15.30, Monday to Friday. The nearest MRT stop is Somerset. Admission is S$4.

Botanic Gardens

The Botanic Gardens cover 52 hectares including a tiny patch of primary rainforest. There is an orchid garden and a topiary garden and over 2000 specimens of plant life. The park is open from 05.00 to 23.00 weekdays, and until midnight at weekends; admission is free.

History

The origins of the Botanic Gardens date from the very early days of the colony. The settlers hoped to discover viable cash crops to boost the island's economy. The gardens were built on 19 hectares of the slopes of Fort Canning Hill. Convicts were sent to do the manual work and the hillside was terraced ready for planting. The first crops were nutmeg and clove which flourished for a time in the rich soil and climate of Singapore but which were abandoned in mid century after a series of diseases struck.

After these early experiments failed, little effort was put into the garden and so gradually the land was marked for other uses. Later attempts to produce enough coffee, vanilla, cotton and cinnamon for industry also failed. In 1836 a voluntary society made a fresh start on the gardens with only about 3ha of the original site. Again the gardens failed to thrive and the society which ran them was defunct by 1846. By this time the major crop in Singapore was gambier which was used as a tanning agent. But it was a poor investment—the land used was useless within 15 years of planting.

In 1859 interest grew again in the idea of experimental gardens and land was bought from a well-known wealthy Chinese merchant called Whampoa. This was the origin of the present site. The aim was to grow crops as well as to create attractive gardens. The hillside was terraced and set in flowerbeds and a bandstand was erected. The lake by the main gate was created at a later date. Most of the work was done by convict labour and financed by public subscription.

Major changes came about with the arrival of a new curator in the 1870s. He brought plants from South America, Ceylon, Australia and

Mauritius. Among these plants were the first rubber trees to be grown in the region. For a time the gardens also had their own zoo consisting of a tiger, two orang-utans, two leopards, several Australian animals and about 100 or so other creatures. The zoo did not last long, the animals dying off one by one as the cash to look after them ran out.

Nature is highly organised in these Botanic Gardens—even the rainforest keeps itself in order—but a pleasant few hours can be spent here and the park is home to a large variety of local birds. Most of the trees are labelled and you should look out for cannon-ball trees whose flowers and gigantic round fruit grow out of the trunk. The spot where the original rubber trees (see History, above) were planted is marked although the trees are now gone. There is an orchid garden and a topiary garden, ponds with turtles and fish and many interesting plants. Look out for the avenue of sealing wax palms so called because of the colour of their trunks. Early morning is the best time to visit: you will see much more birdlife as well as the balletic movements of folk doing their morning t'ai chi exercises. You can finish off your trip with a visit to the hawker centre opposite the main gate which is uncharacteristically laid back and serves wonderful *roti john*.

Getting to the Botanic Gardens. The nearest MRT station is Orchard and bus Nos 7, 106, 123 or 174 will take you from Orchard Road to the gardens.

Holland Village

This is an interesting shopping and eating place, heaving with expatriates and full of all kinds of shops. Here is the wonderful **Lims' Arts and Crafts**, cloth shops selling Indian material, sarongs, antique shops and too many good restaurants to visit even if you ate here every day of your trip to Singapore. A nice place to rest is **Bob's Tavern**. Opposite Bob's, you will find the best *roti prata* in Singapore.

Getting to Holland Village. The nearest MRT is Buona Vista from where you could get a cab to the bus 106 from orchard Road goes there.

Siong Lim Temple

This is a huge, modern working Chinese temple complex. Building began in 1908 but it has had many additions over the years. There is also a Chinese garden. The temple is dedicated to Buddha. It is at 184E Jalan Toa Payoh. The nearest MRT is Toh Payoh, from where you could get a taxi.

Kong Meng San Phor Kark See Temple

This temple complex is even bigger than Siong Lim and covers 12 hectares. It is very modern, built in 1981 in a mixture of Thai and Chinese styles. It includes a crematorium and old folks' home. The residents spend their time making paper models of the things they will need in the after life which are burned at their funeral and so sent up to their new home. A Chinese cemetery is conveniently located nearby. The Chinese believe that a death in the home brings bad luck and so in the past the elderly were often shipped off to death houses to die. This is a slightly more humane modern version. The temple is the typical eclectic Chinese with statues to several gods as well as Buddha. The biggest statue is dedicated to

Kuan Yin, the goddess of mercy. If you think you recognise some of the buildings it is because they are regularly used as the backdrop for kung fu movies.

The temple is at Bright Hill Drive. The nearest MRT station is Ang Mo Kio or Bishan, or the number 167 bus goes by.

MacRitchie Reservoir
Named after the chief engineer who planned the area, there are one-day trekking routes and excellent opportunities for wildlife spotting.

Singapore Zoological Gardens
This calls itself an 'open' zoo and to a certain extent it is; the animals are kept confined by a series of moats and ditches rather than by cages, although some of the big cats look pretty fed up with their quarters. But there is much to entertain you at the zoo. These animals work for their keep, taking part in animal shows, and petting and photo sessions. The orang-utan colony thrives, and orang-utans quite cheerfully give up their babies for endless photo sessions, dinner with the visitors, breakfast with the visitors and any time there is a special party to entertain. It is a child-friendly zoo, with petting farms and playgrounds, and the animal shows are genuinely entertaining.

The zoo is set in very natural surroundings in a rural area and the keepers have a hard time protecting some of the smaller animals from the depredations of local snakes.

Close by and of some interest are the Mandai Lake Orchid Gardens. This is a huge orchid producing business where you can wander around the vast displays of these exotic plants. The gardens are open daily 09.00 to 17.30. Admission is S$2.

Getting to the Singapore Zoological Gardens. The zoo (☎ 65-2693412) is in Mandai Lake Road. You can take the MRT to Ang Mo Kio and the No.138 bus to the zoo or bus No. 171 from Holiday Inn in Scotts Road and then No. 927 on Manchai Road. It is open from 08.00 to 18.00 daily. Admission is S$10.30 for adults, S$4.60 for children with a series of further costs for breakfast or tea with the orang-utans and bus rides; the animal shows are free.

The Night Safari
Not far from the Singapore Zoological Gardens, this is a night-time guided journey around the safari park by trolley. The safari is open from 19.30 to midnight; admission is S$15.45 for adults, S$10.30 for children.

The advantage of the live commentary is that the bus can pause by any interesting animals that show themselves. The less harmful animals are free to wander while the more dangerous are kept behind fences. The 40 hectares are divided up into eight regional zones. Within each zone, the various animals indigenous to the region are exhibited. One zone has animals from the Nepalese Valley, such as the rare one-horned rhinoceros, several species of deer, water buffalo, and many birds from the region. The animals from the Indian subcontinent include eight Asian lions, a sloth bear, several striped hyenas and a barasingha (a swamp-dwelling deer).

The ride in the electric tram around the park is quite eerie as most of it takes place in the dark the park is very quiet. Animals tend to loom up in the head lights or appear suddenly when a set of spotlights is turned on. The night safari is a truly Singaporean experience, with a buffet dinner as a possible start. After your ride you can wander at length around the pathways which are pretty much crowded with Homo Sapiens. In the entranceway, beside the stuffed dolphins and wooden parrot key-rings, are some quite stunning animals to stroke (if they don't get you first!).

Getting to and from the Night Safari. The Night Safari is next to the zoo and can be reached via the same MRT and bus routes. The half-hourly Bus Plus Zoo 1 stops at every bus stop on Orchard Road between 18.00 and 20.30 (last bus back as 23.00). For more details ☎ 65-4810166. The last train leaves Ang Mo Kio MRT station at 23.28 and the No. 138 bus from the zoo needs to be taken at 23.00 to catch this last train. The last bus leaves the Night Safari at 00.15.

Kranji War Memorial
Close to the Causeway off Woodlands Road this monument remembers the Allied troops that died during World War Two. There are thousands of graves and the names of many of them are inscribed on the walls. The memorial's design represents the three arms of the service, the army, navy and air force. SBS Bus 170 leaves from Rochor Road.

Sun Yat Sen Villa
Sun Yat Sen became president of the Chinese republic in 1912, following the overthrow of the Qing Dynasty. He lived for a time in Singapore in this old house which is still full of memorabilia of his life. Upstairs is a Chinese library. The villa is on Ah Hood Road. The nearest MRT is Toa Payoh while the bus 145 goes past Ah Hood Road from Balastier Road.

Sungei Buloh Nature Park
This 87 hectare area was once used largely for orchards and fish and prawn farming: in turning it into a nature park, in 1993, the government was making use of a habitat that already existed rather than creating a new one. The Park is open from 07.30 to 19.00 weekdays and opens half-an-hour earlier at weekends and public holidays; admission is S$1. The visitor's centre has video shows about the wetlands and guided tours are organised at 09.30 and 16.00, weather permitting. Tours must be booked in advance (☎ 65-793 7377).

The nature park consists of mangrove swamp, artificial ponds and natural stretches of water including estuaries and swamps. A long stretch of boardwalk extends out into the wetlands, and there are several hides overlooking strategic feeding and nesting sites. Footpaths also run through the park and although you never feel as engulfed in the habitat as you may do in Bukit Timah, the dedicated wildlife spotter will certainly see something of interest.

Getting to Sungei Buloh Nature Park. The park is located off Neo Tiew Road and Lim Chu Kang Road. To get there you can take bus No. 925 from Kranji MRT.

Khatib Bongsu

Khatib Bongsu is another very important breeding and feeding site for some endangered species such as the Chinese egret and Asian dowitcher. The area is still farmed, with prawn ponds and mangroves, but some of it is about to become part of Sembawang New Town. However, the thousands of birds which use the area should still have some sanctuary left, at least for a few more years. This area is not a national park and has no information centre but trips can be organised through Subaraj Rjathurai (☎ 65-787 7048). If you intend to visit you can get there on buses 801 or 804.

Singapore ~ East

The Arab Street Area

Unfortunately this area (see map on p 330–1) fell prey to the conservationists a few years ago and the same old pattern of removing the residents, and renovating and renting out to businesses has taken place. But the area still retains much of its original atmosphere and the mosque and shops are well worth a visit. The Sultan Mosque is on the corner of Arab Street and North Bridge Road. The modern building was completed in 1928 and designed by Swann and Maclaren in a eclectic mix of colonial, Turkish, Arab and Persian styles, but work first began here in 1819 using funds donated by Sir Stamford Raffles and the last sultan of Singapore, Iskandar Shah. The mosque has 14 entrances and is very busy on Fridays. If you wish to go in please observe modesty in dress. There are areas where women are not allowed.

Not far away in Sultan Gate is **Kampong Glam** which will soon fall down if the renovators fail to get their hands on it. It was the last home of the Sultan and is still occupied by some of his relatives. The house is not open to the public.

On the corner of Victoria Street and Jalan Sultan is another mosque—the **Jama-ath Mosque**—covered in blue tiles, and behind it is Kampong Glam cemetery where the Johor sultans are said to be buried. Further down Jalan Sultan to beach Road is the **Hajjah Fatimah Mosque**, built in 1845. This is the oldest mosque in Singapore and was built by a woman, Hajjah Fatima, out of love for a Bugis nobleman. Hajjah Fatima and some of her family are buried there. The mosque was restored in 1932 by a French company who added European touches to it, with Doric pilasters on the minaret. This is a national monument.

In this area is **Bugis Street**, right beside the Bugis MRT station. Many people have fond memories of Bugis Street when it was *the* place to go in Asia for a good rave up. It was closed down in the Eighties for being altogether un-Singaporean but has received the conservation treatment within the decade. Great care was taken to recreate the architectural style of the place but the filthy toilets and rats were left out and somehow the atmosphere has been left behind too. In the old Bugis Street transvestites were a major attraction and the company which oversaw the renovation did try to encourage them (properly registered and non-soliciting) back again, but they quite rightly felt that they were being exploited and now seem to prefer Changi Village and Cuppage Plaza as their local hangouts. But even if it doesn't rave on Bugis Street, it is good for a quiet drink or a seafood meal, although the rather desperate stall holders do get a little too enthusiastic in encouraging you into their establishments

Perhaps when the shine has rubbed off Boat Quay this will be the new trendy place to be seen.

Katong and Geylang Serai

While there is no particular attraction to draw you to this area it might make an interesting afternoon or evening's wander. It is a little enclave of Peranakan style architecture, house after house of ornate plaster work and shuttered windows, and although a lot of it has been renovated it is not as kitsch as Peranakan Place or Chinatown. There are still some traditional coffee shops in the area as well as junk shops in Joo Chiat Road. At one time, the waterfront here was where the middle classes had their weekend bungalows. Some of them are still here. Nearby is **Geylang Serai**, which has a distinctly Malay atmosphere to it. There is a Malay Cultural Village here but it is often closed, so check with the tourist office before setting off to look for it. If you are lucky, there might be exhibitions of Malay crafts, traditional dress and dancing. If not, try Geylang market instead.

Getting to Katong and Geylang Serai. The nearest MRT stop is Paya Lebar.

East Coast Park

This is a long stretch of parkland, beach and leisure activities stretching along the newly created east coast. The sand on the beaches is imported and the water is murky to say the least but it is a popular place at the weekend. Bicycles, canoes and sailboats can be hired; there are numerous fast food joints and hawker stalls, some of which are very good indeed; there is a tiny wildlife area, although the most you are likely to see are the ubiquitous minah birds; and there is long jogging/cycling/walking track, carefully delineated into its respective sections. The Big Splash (see p 332) is also here. The Crocodilarium, at 730 East Coast Parkway, and open from 09.00 to 17.30 daily, has a shop selling handbags and shoes made from the unfortunate inmates. (Do not go there if you do not wish to support the farming of wild animals.) Entrance is S$2. Also here is the East Coast Recreation Centre with crazy golf, bowling, rides and places to eat. Further east again is the East Coast Lagoon with the UDMC Seafood Centre and the East Coast Sailing Centre (see p 329). Bear in mind that this is one of the few cheap and easily accessible open spaces in Singapore, and thousands of Singaporeans make full use of it, especially at weekends when cycling (or walking) along the track is more of an obstacle course than a sporting activity.

Getting to the East Coast Park. The easiest, and laziest way to get there is by taxi but if you want to do it the hard way bus No. 401 goes along the park service road from Bedok MTR station on Sundays and public holidays. At other times bus 16 from Bras Basah Road goes to Marine Parade road from where you can walk to the park.

Pasir Ris

Pasir Ris is an extensive area of parkland, mostly reclaimed land with saplings and painted signs on the footpaths telling you which side you can walk or cycle on, but there is also a tiny piece of mangrove swamp and estuary with a boardwalk and observation post so that you can keep your feet dry. Entrance to the park is free.

Getting to Pasir Ris. MRT to Pasir Ris and then the No. 403 bus to its terminus.

Excursions from Singapore

Sentosa

Ten years ago Sentosa was a sad place, with decaying Second World War fortifications, some old aircraft from the same period that nobody really wanted, a few crumbling attractions, a closed down hotel, grubby beaches and a thriving wildlife (three native types of pitcher plant can still be spotted on the island's nature walk). Now, after millions of dollars' investment, it is a prime tourist attraction and part of it will soon be a highly bijou satellite town for the extremely rich.

> Sentosa first became important to the defence of Singapore in 1886 when, as Belakang Mati, it was fortified as part of the plans to defend the harbour against the developing naval power of Russia. Singapore saw little action during the First World War and, in the years that followed, a new naval base was built in the north of the country. Sentosa was a base for the southern defence of Singapore and the protection of the harbour. The invasion, when it came in 1942, was from the north; the naval base had no fleet to protect it and was scuttled by the retreating Allied troops. Sentosa's big guns were useless. During the war, Sentosa was occupied by the Japanese military and many prisoners-of-war were executed here.

Much of the island's history is remembered in the **Pioneers of Singapore** and the **Surrender Chambers** exhibition and the **Fort Siloso exhibition** which use archive film and animatronics to bring those times alive again.

In its new, more cheerful role Sentosa is a good day out, especially for visitors with children. The **Underwater World exhibition** is recommended: a moving walkway takes you below an enormous tank containing all kinds of sea creatures. Fantasy Island is fun for children as is the butterfly park. There is a lapidary museum and a maritime museum; the latest exhibitions re-create an Aztec civilisation and the inside of a volcano. Another, rather dull set of rides is called 'The Asian Village'.

A rather creaky monorail takes you around the island, or you can hire cycles, and the two hotels, a hawker centre and a selection of fast-food restaurants provide the necessary nourishment. A whole day could be spent here.

At the other end of the cable car ride is another pleasant spot to visit—Mount Faber park. It is the highest spot in the city area and has fine views over the city.

Getting to Sentosa. Ferries and the cable car for Sentosa leave from the World Trade Centre, off Telok Blangah Road (reached by bus Nos 65 and 143 from Orchard Road or 61, 84, 145, and 166 from Raffles City). The ferry ride is S$1.30 return; the cable car is S$6.90 return. Basic island admission is S$5 for adults or S$3 for children, but be prepared to pay extra for each exhibit or ask about the Sentosa Explorer and Merlion Explorer tickets. Prices range from S$16 for the Fantasy Island water park to S$1 for the smaller exhibits.

Pulau Ubin

One of the few places to escape 'conservation', Pulau Ubin is a little gem of messy, laid-back, natural Singapore. Even the journey here is gloriously unregulated: a bedraggled jetty at Changi where unrenovated bum boats wait in a haphazard gaggle for enough people to come along to make the 10-minute journey worthwhile. The outside boat is always the first to go so you must hop from boat to boat until you get to the right one. In the bare mud around the island's jetty are mangrove trees where primeval mudskippers flip around. A bare strip of wooden houses are nearby, mostly dedicated to bike hire (S$4–15 all day) and food-stalls.

The island has many different habitats for plant and animal life including mangrove swamps, fruit orchards, fish farms, open ponds, a river estuary and coastline. A booklet, 'Pulau Ubin', is available in the Singapore Environmental Heritage series which describes the many plants and animals you can see in a trip around the island. A taxi both ways will cost about S$25. If you have your own sleeping bag it may be possible to find budget accommodation in a private house for about S$5 a night.

St John's Island and Kusu Island

Apart from a cafeteria, **St John's Island** is quite undeveloped so you should take whatever food you might need. Bungalows are available for hire from the Sentosa Information Office in the World Trade Centre (☎ 65-270 7888). There are toilets and changing rooms and some good safe places to swim.

The nearby **Kusu Island** has a Taoist temple which is visited by hundreds of people in the ninth lunar month, sometime between October and November, but is deserted for most of the rest of the year. There is a tortoise sanctuary and good swimming lagoons and beaches as well as a varied birdlife. There is also a Muslim shrine on the island dedicated to Sahed Abdul Rahman, which is very popular despite the fact that the Islamic faith does not endorse worshipping at shrines.

Getting to St John's Island and Kusu Island. Ferries to St John's Island leave from Clifford Pier, near the Fullerton Building, and from the World Trade Centre, off Telok Blangah Road. Ferries to Kusu Island also leave from the World Trade Centre, and operate from 07.00 to 17.00 during the ninth lunar month, but only twice-daily on weekdays. It costs S$6 for adults.

Pulau Hantu, Pulau Seking and Sisters Island

Swimming and snorkelling are the chief attractions on these three islands. They are all accessible by boats which can be hired, along with their captain, from Jardine Steps or Clifford Pier. At Seking is a Malay village—the last one left in Singapore. None of the islands have any facilities so you should bring a picnic for the day.

Changi Village and Prison

Changi jail is a real working prison where capital punishment by hanging regularly takes place. However, there are positive reasons for visiting the area. Changi village has some good restaurants, a hawker centre, and a couple of good bars with live music. The Le Meridian hotel often has good weekend offers; it has a good coffee shop style restaurant. During the evening very young transvestites hang out on the small green opposite the hotel. Close by are the ferries to Pulau Ubin and several small villages in Johor, and there is a surreal beach at Changi, which is completely artificial and stretches underneath the flight path of the 747s which start letting down their undercarriage as they wobble over the hundreds of people having fun on the sand.

Changi Jail is on Upper Changi Road and contains a small **museum** dedicated to the memory of the people who suffered in the jail during the Second World War as well as a replica of the prison chapel built by the prisoners of war.

Both men and women, civilians and members of the Allied Forces, were imprisoned here in separate areas. The museum contains reproductions of the artwork of some of the people imprisoned here as well as photographs that were taken secretly by 17-year-old soldier, George Aspinall. The prison chapel is attap-roofed and services are held there on Sunday evenings at 17.30. The museum is open Monday to Saturday 09.30 to 16.30.

Getting to Changi. Take the MRT to Bedok or Tanah Merah and then bus No. 2. Singapore Sightseeing Tour East (☎ 65-3323755) run tours every day except Sunday. They also go to the Kranji War Memorial.

Index

Alor Setar 141, 143
Ayer Keroh 169

Ba Kelalan 307
Ba Kelatan 305
Bak Bak 250
Bako National Park 282
Bario 305
Batang Rejang 289
Batu Bungan 305
Batu Caves 91
Batu Ferringhi 139
Beaufort 249
Belaga 292
Beserah 202
Bintulu 293
Bintulu Wildlife Park 294
Bukit Indah Trail 230
Bukit Larut (Maxwell Hill) 114
Bukit Teresek Trail 230

Cameron Highlands 97
Chendor Beach 197
Cherating 197
Conrad, Joseph 334
Crocker Range 247

Damai Beach and Sarawak Cultural
    Village 285
Danum Valley Conservation Area
    264
Desaru 221
Dungun 197

Endau Rompin National Park 206

Genting Highlands 93
Gerik 119
Gomantong Caves 264
Gua Charas 202
Gua Tambun 109
Gua Telinga 230
Gunung Jerai 143
Gunung Mulu 304

Gunung Mulu National Park 300
Gunung Santubong 285
Gunung Tahan Trail 230
Gunung Tapis 203
Gunung Trusmadi 248

Hang Jebat 162
Hang Tuah 162

Ipoh 101

Jalan Kuala Kangsar 133
Jerantut 226
Johor Bahru 207, 215
Johor state 207

Kalibatang 249
Kalimantan (Indonesia) 307
Kampung Shabbier 248
Kangar 150
Kanowit 290
Kapit 290
Katibas river 290
Kedah 141
Kelabit Highlands 305
Kelantan State 171
Kellie's Castle 108
Keniam Lodge 224, 227
Keningau 248
Kenong Rimba Park 234
Kinabatangan Basin 261
Kipling, Rudyard 334
Klang 89
Kota Belud 250
Kota Bharu 174
Kota Kinabalu 236, 240
Kota Tinggi 221
Kuala Balah 182
Kuala Besut 183
Kuala Kangsar 101, 109
Kuala Lipis 233
Kuala Lumpur 63
    Accommodation 71
    Asian Art Museum 85

Kuala Lumpur cont'd
  Bird Park 84
  Butterfly House 84
  Central Market 82
  Chan See Shu Yuen Temple 83
  Chinatown 82
  Dayabumi Complex 80
  Entertainment 74
  Infokraf 80
  Jalan Parliame 84
  Khoon Yam Temple 83
  Kuala Lumpur: Jalan Damansara
    84
  Lake Gardens 84
  Malaysian Armer Forces Museum
    86
  Masjid Jame 81
  Masjid Negara 80
  Maybank Numismatic Museum
    85
  Merdeka Square 81
  Muzium Negara 84
  National Art Gallery 80
  National Monument 84
  National Zoo and Aquarium 93
  Natural Rubber Museum 85
  Orchid and Hibiscus Gardens
    84
  Parliament House 85
  Petronas Towers 63
  Railway station 79
  Restaurants 73
  Royal Malaysian Police Museum
    85
  Royal Selangor Club 81
  Seri Taman 84
  Shopping 75
  Sri Mahamariamman Temple 83
  St Mary's Church 81
  Sultan Abdul Samad Building
    81
  Sze Yah Temple 82
  Thean Hou Temple 85
  Tourist Information 69
  Transport 66
  Tun Abdul Razak Memorial 84
Kuala Selangor 90
Kuala Tahan 227
Kuala Terengganu 187

Kuala Trenggan 224
Kuantan 200
Kuching 273
Kudat 250
Kukup 222

Lake Bera 204
Lake Kenyir 192
Lake Temengur 120
Lambir Hills National Park 300
Langkawi 144
Lata Berkoh 231
Leatherback turtle 195
Lembah Bujang 141-142
Lintang Trail 284
Long Lellang 305

Marais 249
Marang 193
Matunggung 250
Maugham, Somerset 334
Melaka 151
  Baba Nyonya Heritage Museum
    164
  Bukit China 168
  Chee Ancestral House 166
  Cheng Hoon Teng 166
  Chinatown 164
  Christ Church 160
  Clock Tower 160
  Jalan Hang Jebat 166
  Kampung Morten 167
  Malacca Sultanate Palace 162
  Masjid Kampung Hulu 167
  Masjid Kampung Kling 167
  Mausoleum of Hang Jebat 167
  Mausoleum of Hang Kasturi
    166
  Medan Portugis 168
  Memorial of the Proclamation of
    Independence 163
  Museum of Beauty 160
  Museum of Ethnography and
    History 157
  Muzium Belia Malaysia 160
  Porta de Santiago 160
  Sri Pogyatha Vinayagar Moorthi
    Temple 167
  St Francis Xavier 152

St Francis Xavier's Church 167
St Paul's Church 161
St Peter's Church 167
Stadthuys 157
Taman Mini Malaysia 169
Villa Sentosa 167
Mengkabong 250
Merang 186
Mersing 208
Mimaland Amusement Park 93
Miri 297
Mount Kinabalu 236, 251
Mount Ophir 221

Niah National Park 294
Nusa Camp 224, 227

Orang Asli 203
Orang Asli Museum 91

Pa Tik 307
Pahang state 199
Pangkor, island of 101
Pantai Bisikan Bayu 181
Pantai Cahaya Bulan 181
Pantai Dasar Sabak 181
Pantai Irama 181
Pekan 205
Pelagus Rapids 292
Penambawan 250
Penan settlement 305
Penang 120
  Batu Ferringhi 139
  Penang Hill 136
  Penang Island (Pulau Pinang)
    120
  Balik Pulau 138
  Barat 138
  Batik Factory 138
  Batu Maung 137
  Botanical Gardens 137
  Butterfly Farm 138
  Cathedral of the Assumption
    131
  Cheong Fatt Tze Mansion 134
  Chinese Water Village 132
  Clock Tower 131
  Dharmmikarama Temple 135
  E&O Hotel 130

Penang cont'd
  Forest Recreation Park 138
  Fort Cornwallis 131
  Georgetown 120
  Kek Lok Si Temple 136
  Khoo Kongsi 133
  Kuan Yin Teng Temple 134
  Lebuh Campbell 133
  Lebuh Chulia 132
  Lebuh Muntri 133
  Malay Mosque (Masjid Melayu)
    135
  Masjid Kapitan Kling 133
  Monkey Beach 138
  Muka Head 138
  Nattukotai Chettiar Temple 135
  Pantai Aceh 138
  Penang Buddhist Association
    Temple 135
  Penang Museum and Art Gallery
    131
  Penang State Mosque 136
  Protestant Cemetery 128
  Seri Rambai 132
  Shiva Temple 135
  Snake Temple 137
  Sri Mariamman Temple 134
  St George's Church 131
  Sungei Pinang 138
  Teluk Bahang 137-138
  Teluk Kumbar 137
  Titi Kerawang Waterfalls 138
  Town Hall 131
  Wat Chayamangkalaram 135
Perak State 101
Perak Tong Temple 108
Perhentian Besar 184
Perhentian Kecil 184
Perkai Lodge 228
Perlis 141, 150
Petaling Jaya 88
Pinnacles, the 304
Poring 256
Port Klang 89
Pulau Babi Besar 214
Pulau Besar 169
Pulau Dayang Bunting 149
Pulau Gemia 194
Pulau Kapas 194

Pulau Labuan 249
Pulau Langkawi 144
Pulau Pangkor (Pangkor Island) 115
Pulau Payar 149
Pulau Perhentian 184
Pulau Rawa 213
Pulau Redang 186
Pulau Selingan 261
Pulau Sibu 214
Pulau Singa Besar 149
Pulau Sipadan 265
Pulau Tinggi 214
Pulau Tioman 209

Raffles, Sir Stamford 310
Rafflesia Centre 247
Ranau 255
Rantau Abang 195
Rentis Tenor Trail 230

Sabah 236
St Francis Xavier 161
Sam Poh Tong Temple 108
Sandakan 236, 256
Santubong 285
Sapulut 248
Sarawak 266
Sekayu Waterfall 193
Semenggok Wildlife Rehabilitation Centre 285
Semporna 265
Sepilok Orang-Utan Rehabilitation Centre 260
Serian 286
Shah Alam 88
Sibu 287
Sikuati 250
Simulajau National Park 294
Singapore 309
    Raffles Hotel 334
    Al-Abrar Mosque 346
    Arab Street 360
    At Andrew's Catehdral 336
    Boat Quay 339
    Botanic Gardens 356
    Bugis Street 360
    Bukit Timah Nature Reserve 351

Singapore cont'd
    Cenotaph 337
    Changi Village and Prison 363
    China Street 346
    Chinaman Scholar's Gallery 349
    Chinatown 345
    Chinese Garden 354
    City Hall 336
    Clarke Quay 338
    Club Street 346
    East Coast Park 361
    Empress Place 338
    Five Foot Ways 342
    For Canning Park 339
    Fountain to Tan Kim Seng 337
    Fullerton Building 337
    Geylang Serai 361
    Hakka Fuk Tak Chi Temple 346
    Haw Par Villa 353
    Holland Village 357
    Jama-ath Mosque 360
    Jurong Bird Park 353
    Katong 361
    Khatib Bongsu 360
    Kong Meng San Phor Kark See Temple 357
    Kranji War Memorial 359
    Lee Kuan Yew 315
    Leong San See Temple 345
    Lion Dance 346
    MacRitchie Reservoir 358
    National Museum and Art Gallery 350
    New Ming Village 355
    Night Safari 358
    Omnimax Theatre 354
    Padang 335
    Parliament House 338
    Pasir Ris 361
    People's Action 315
    People's Park Complex 349
    Peranakan Place 355
    Pewter Museum 355
    Pulau Hantu 363
    Pulau Seking 363
    Pulau Ubin 363
    Satay Club 337
    St Gregory the Illuminator, Church of 339

Singapore cont'd
  St John's Island 363
  Science Centre 354
  Sentosa 362
  Singapore Cricket Club 335
  Siong Lim Temple 357
  Sisters Island 363
  Smith Street 348
  Sri Mariamman Temple 349
  Sri Srinivasa Perumal Temple
    343
  Sri Veeramakaliaman Temple
    342
  Sungei Buloh Nature Park 359
  Supreme Court Building 336
  Tang Dynasty Village 354
  Tanjong Pagar project 350
  Telok Ayer Street 345
  Temple of a Thousand Lights 344
  Temple Street 348
  Thandayuthapani Temple 344
  Thian Hock Keng Temple 345
  Victoria Concert Hall and Theatre
    338
  Wak Hai Cheng Bio Temple 346
  Zhu Jiao 340
  Zoological Gardens 358

Sinsuran Pass 248
Song 290
Sri Aman 286
Sungei Lembing 203

Taiping 101, 111
Tajor Waterfall 285
Taman Negara 223
Tambunan 248
Tambunan Plain 248
Tanjung Bidara 170
Tasik Bera 204
Tasik Chini 203
Tasik Kenyir 192
Tawau 265
Teluk Chempedak 201
Teluk Intan 115
Templer Park 92
Tenom 248
Terengganu 183
Thaipusam festival 344
Trenggan Lodge 227
Tuaran 250
Tumpat 182
Turtle Islands National Park 261
Turtle watching 197

Upper Perak 119

If you would like to receive more information about Blue
Guides, please complete the form below and return it to

Blue Guides
A&C Black (Publishers) Ltd
Freepost
Cambridgeshire
PE19 3BR

or you can fax it to us on
0171-831 8478

or e-mail us at
travel@acblack.co.uk

Name...

Address..

....

....